Mark Glaister
Pete Oxley

A guidebook to the sport and traditional climbing on Portland, Lulworth and Swanage

Text and topos by Mark Glaister and Pete Oxley
Edited by Stephen Horne and Alan James
All uncredited photography by Mark Glaister
Other photography as credited
Printed in Europe on behalf of Latitude Press Ltd.
Distributed by Cordee (www.cordee.co.uk)

All maps by ROCKFAX
Some maps based on original
source data from openstreetmap.org

Published by ROCKFAX in February 2012
© ROCKFAX 2012, 2005, 2000, 1994

www.rockfax.com

All rights reserved. No part of this publication may be reproduced, stored in a retrieval system, or transmitted in any form or by any means, electronic, mechanical, photocopying or otherwise without prior written permission of the copyright owner. A CIP catalogue record is available from the British Library

ISBN 978 1 873341 47 6

Cover photo:
Bridget Collier on *Stalker's Zone* (6a+) - page 158
Wallsend crags on Portland.

This page:
Gaz Fry on the popular arete of *Monsoon Malabar* (6a) - page 76
at the extensive Blacknor Central cliff on Portland.

AWESOME WALLS
CLIMBING CENTRES

www.awesomewalls.co.uk

Stockport Liverpool Stoke-on-Trent

0161 494 9949 0151 298 2422 01782 341 919

AWESOME BY NAME, AWESOME BY NATURE!!!

Trev Ford topping out on the fantastic sport pitch *Nothing but the Groove* (6c+) - *page 170* - on the seaside Coastguard North cliff, Portland.

Foreward by Mick Ward

The first Dorset Rockfax, back in 1994, came as a revelation. Portland, 'a cheesy, unfashionable Gogarth that no-one ever went to', had seemingly been transformed into a sport climbing playground. Surely it was too good to be true? The stunning front cover shot of Pete Oxley on *Mark of the Beast* must have been shot with filters, mustn't it? The sea and sky couldn't possibly be those sublime hues of azure... could they?

Glasgow
Dublin
Manchester
London

After spending most of the intervening 18 years climbing in Dorset, I now realise that it was all perfectly true. Amazing colours of sky and sea. Superb coastline. More good routes than you'll manage in a lifetime. The 'Swanage experience' of committing trad perfectly complements Portland's bolt clipping. You've got lots of bouldering and Deep Water Soloing. There's something for everyone – from Diff to 8c. Although no single aspect of Dorset climbing is perhaps world-class, when viewed as a totality, the place is near enough a world-class venue. Given that much of the UK climbing population lives in the crag-starved areas of London and the Southeast, Dorset is of obvious strategic importance. Nowadays, of course, it also attracts increasing numbers of visitors from abroad, drawn by its neo-Mediterranean climate and the huge variety of climbing on offer.

Bournemouth
Poole
Dorchester
Wool
Wareham
Weymouth
Lulworth
p.246
Swanage
p.262
Portland
p.50

While many people have contributed to development, one person has attained legendary status. Pete Oxley's lonely orgy of labour has made Dorset the climbing paradise that it is today. Although he now lives far away, the cliffs will always be imbued with his restless spirit.

The best way that we can celebrate Pete's vision is to go out and enjoy ourselves. It doesn't matter whether it's chasing that elusive Portland redpoint or scaring ourselves witless in the Ruckle. It might be an exhilarating DWS. It might be our first, tentative forays onto rock outdoors. It doesn't matter. What matters is that we climb safely, we climb at least half as well as we'd like and we enjoy the craic with our mates. Dorset gives us the chance to do all this and more.

Mick Ward, January 2012

Marti Hallett enjoying a perfect afternoon on the steep lower arete of *Under the Sky, Inside the Sea* (7a)- *page 176* - at Coastguard South.

Bridget Collier bridging up the popular *Amen Corner* (5) - *page 236* - at The Cuttings, one of the east coast of Portland's most sheltered cliffs. Photo: Paul Cox

The Isle of Portland and its west coast crags are picked out in evening light. In the foreground is the arc of Chesil Beach, St. Catherine's Chapel and hundreds of swans from Abbotsbury paddling in the Fleet - the body of enclosed water behind Chesil Beach.

The Book

The pace of development and the continued rise of the popularity of climbing at both Portland and Swanage have meant that this latest Dorset Rockfax guidebook is on the shelves only a little over six years since the publication of the previous Rockfax in late 2005. The sport climbing at Portland and Swanage has been extended with many new routes being added across both areas. The trad climbing at Swanage has also seen a rise in popularity and, as a result, more routes and even a few new crags have been added this time. On Portland, most of the trad routes on the cliffs covered are mentioned in the text, but no lines are presented on the topos. For detailed descriptions refer to the Climbers' Club guidebook - Portland.

This edition of the Dorset Rockfax is presented in the latest award-winning format, with full-page colour topos and action photography along with many new and updated features such as GPS, a Top 50, new maps and clearer topo lines and annotation.

In order to make space for the larger topos and increased coverage, we have dropped most of the bouldering. The most popular area - **The Cuttings Boulderfield** - is available in a 2012 PDF MiniGuide by Ben Stokes. Devon sport climbing has also been omitted but does feature in the Rockfax book **West Country Climbs,** published in 2010. There is still reasonable coverage of the deep water soloing but for a full picture track down Mike Robertson's superb guidebook **Deep Water**.

All these books are available from www.rockfax.com

Previous Guides

Portland by Steve Taylor, Ben Stokes, Jim Kimber *(Climbers' Club - 2008)*

Deep Water by Mike Robertson *(ROCKFAX - 2007)*

Dorset (3rd Edition) by Mark Glaister, Pete Oxley *(ROCKFAX - 2005)*

Dorset (2nd Edition) by Pete Oxley *(ROCKFAX - 2000)*

Into the Blue (DWS) by Jonathan Cook, Mike Robertson, Steve Taylor and Damian Cook *(Climbers' Club - 1996)*

Swanage and Portland by Nigel Coe *(Climbers' Club - 1995)*

Dorset (1st Edition) by Pete Oxley *(ROCKFAX - 1994)*

Swanage by Gordon Jenkin *(Climbers' Club - 1986)*

Dorset by R.J. Crewe *(Climbers' Club - 1977)*

Dorset Climbs by R.C.White *(Climbers' Club - 1969)*

Limestone Climbs on the Dorset Coast by B.Annette *(Climbers' Club - 1961)*

2005

2000

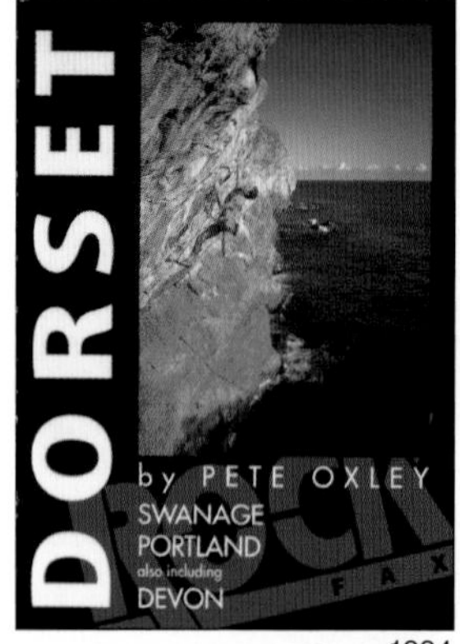

1994

Web Site www.rockfax.com

The Rockfax website is a mine of useful information about climbing all over Europe. It contains the Rockfax Route Database plus many PDF MiniGUIDES and updates both complementing the printed books produced by Rockfax and also covering new areas.

Rockfax Route Database - This database contains a listing of every route in the book (and most other Rockfax books as well). The Dorset section has been available for over a decade and has logged a huge number of comments and votes on the routes. All this information has been vital in putting together this book, getting the grades and stars right and keeping a check on developments. Thanks to all those who have contributed.

The current version of the database has been updated to reflect the routes as described in this edition of the book so you can start using it again to keep everyone informed about any changes or your own opinions on grades, stars and the routes in general.

Don't forget that it is possible to use the database to construct a personal and printable tick-list of routes by using the advanced search function to select a location, grade band and star range of routes and return a list with tick boxes, and page references in this guide.

Guidebook Footnote

The inclusion of a climbing area in this guidebook does not mean that you have a right of access or the right to climb upon it. The descriptions of routes within this guide are recorded for historical reasons only and no reliance should be placed on the accuracy of the description. The grades set in this guide are a fair assessment of the difficulty of the climbs. Climbers who attempt a route of a particular standard should use their own judgment as to whether they are proficient enough to tackle that route. This book is not a substitute for experience and proper judgment. The authors, publisher and distributors of this book do not recognise any liability for injury or damage caused to, or by, climbers, third parties, or property arising from such persons seeking reliance on this guidebook as an assurance for their own safety.

Cristiano Costa da Silva pulling though onto the upper section of *Tennessee* (7c) - *page 174* - Coastguard South on the west coast of Portland. Photo: Szymon Dziukiewicz

Many thanks to all who I have shared a rope with on the Dorset coast, and to those who have helped with this guide and the development of climbing and climbs in the area, especially the following: all the Cooks, Bruce Woodley, Beth Woodley, Brian Wilkinson, Mike Robertson, Barry Clarke, Steve Taylor, Mark Williams, Marti Hallett, Andy Long, Chegs Evans, Rich White, Rob Kennard, Dan Knight, Christine Forkin, Emma Medara, Gavin Symonds, Danie Rushmer, Ben Stokes, Nigel Tuckley, Bev Hull, Al Ashmore, Dave Pickford, Clare Dyson, Arran Deakin, Chris Gore, Rob Knight, Jonny Woods, Lee Proctor, Guy Blackwood, Steve Watt, Ken Palmer, Rob Sutton, Clarke Alston, Gaz Fry, Jude Summers, Bruce Walker, Julie Ashmore, Bob Hickish, Chris Weedon, Adam Perrett, Sarah Perrett, Mick Ward, John Leonard, Tom Beaumont, Anna Rayner, Paul Cox, Sarah Stirling, Dan Wicks, John Samways, John Warner, Mark Tomlinson, Dave Henderson, Carrie Hill, Ali Martindale, Phil Black, Bridget Collier, Neal Heanes, Helen Heanes, Si Rooms, Kimberley Waldron, Sarah Ahmed, Jason Ahmed, Sue Hazel, Daimon Beail.

Thank you also to those who have supplied the multitude of fantastic action photos - Keith Sharples, Szymon Dziukiewicz, Paul Cox, Oli Lyon, Marti Hallett, Tom Beaumont, Sarah Stirling, Dan Lane, Ben Fordesman, Mike Robertson, Mike Hutton, Daimon Beail, Dave Mason.

A huge amount of the information in this book has come from the Rockfax and UKC Route Database. I am very grateful to all those who have contributed, keep the feedback coming in.

The production of this guidebook has been a mammoth task. Thanks to Alan James and Stephen Horne for their skills and input in helping to produce this book - the 4th Rockfax to Dorset in 18 years.

Mark Glaister, January 2012

As I write this I am still recovering from a grade 6 two days before Xmas! Getting old is never easy for a sportsman, however I refer to another magnitude 6 after-shock that hit the quake-ravaged city of Christchurch in New Zealand where I now live. So to help bring to light this eagerly-anticipated fourth edition of the Dorset Rockfax has been a cathartic experience. It's been a pleasure that reinforces my original vision that Dorset is one of the best and most varied climbing spots in the world.

Mark Glaister, Stephen Horne and Alan James have done a great job again in updating the photos in to a new format and reworking many sections. The guide has fully matured and grown due to the sheer enthusiasm of new routers such as Mick Ward, Rob Kennard, Steve Taylor, Bob Hickish and many others. These people must also be thanked for the continued regearing of old sport climbs. All those who have contributed to the bolt fund over the years should receive a high five from the hordes that now drive to Dorset every weekend.

I personally wish to remember and thank the scores of great characters that I climbed alongside to help develop these cliffs in to what they are today. In particular the Cook Clan, Brian Tilley, Martin Crocker, Tim Dunsby, Nigel Coe, Steve Taylor, Mike Robertson, Mark Williams, Steve Williams, Jon Williams, Jon Biddle, Andy Bell, Chris Parker, Jimbo, Mike Morris, Rob Kennard, Richard White, Mick Ward, Barry Clarke and many others. I also wish to thank Dawn and Ivan at the Sugar Loaf for their warm support of climbers and the best cream teas available. Last but not least all my love again to Jan Rostron for 20 years together in 2012, out and about on the cliffs.

To quote the route – *Not Forgotten, No Fade Away* – I'll be back to visit soon and 'Old Painless' is still oiled and primed down under! Enjoy edition four.

Pete Oxley, January 2012

Sarah Stirling making the tricky finishing moves of *Return to Roissy* (6b+) - *page 84* - on the superb walls of Blacknor Central, Portland.

Portland
Lulworth
Swanage

Equipment Manufacturers

Black Diamond - *Outside back cover*
Tel: 01629 580484
www.blackdiamondequipment.com

Beta Climbing Designs - *Page 37*
Tel: 0114 255 8882
www.betaclimbingdesigns.com

Climbing Walls

Awesome Walls - *Page 2*
St. Alban's Church, Liverpool.
Tel: 01512 982422
The Engine House, Stockport.
Tel: 0161 494 9949
Sefton Road, Stoke-on-Trent.
Tel: 01782 341919
www.awesomewalls.co.uk

The Climbing Academy - *Page 25*
Charlton Street, Bristol. Tel: 0117 907 2956
www.theclimbingacademy.com

The Leeds Wall - *Page 19*
Gelderd Road, Leeds. Tel: 0113 234 1554
www.theleedswall.co.uk

Shops

Taunton Leisure - *Inside back cover*
East Reach, Taunton. Tel: 01823 275121
www.tauntonleisure.com

Rock On - *Page 291*
Mile End, London. Tel: 0208 981 5066
Craggy Island, Guildford. Tel: 01483 565635
Redpoint, Birmingham. Tel: 01213 598709
www.rockonclimbing.co.uk

V12 - *Back cover flap*
The Old Baptist Chapel, Llanberis.
Tel: 01286 871534
www.v12outdoor.com

Holidays / Guidance / Accommodation

Rock and Sun - *Inside front cover*
Mina Road, Bristol. Tel: 08456 864586
www.rockandsun.com

Swanage Auberge - *Page 21*
High Street, Swanage. Tel: 07711 117668
www.swanageauberge.co.uk

Tom's Field - *Page 21*
Langton Matravers. Tel: 01929 427110
www.tomsfieldcamping.co.uk

Weymouth Campsites - *Page 19*
Sea Barn Campsite. Tel: 01305 782218
www.seabarnfarm.co.uk
West Fleet Holiday Farm. Tel: 01305 782218
www.westfleetholidays.co.uk
Bagwell Farm Touring Park.
Tel: 01305 782575
www.bagwellfarm.co.uk

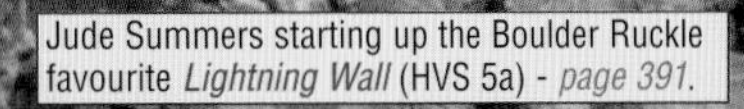

Jude Summers starting up the Boulder Ruckle favourite *Lightning Wall* (HVS 5a) - *page 391*.

Dorset Logistics

The Cove House Inn on the edge of Chesil Beach is a great après-climb pub and perfectly positioned for watching the sunset.

Emergencies

DIAL 112 and ask for the coastguard or other emergency services.
Poole Hospital A&E - Tel: 01202 665511 (24hr)
Dorchester Hospital A&E - Tel: 01305 255541 (24hr)
Weymouth Hospital (MIU) - Tel: 01305 760022 (NOT 24hr)
Portland Hospital (MIU) - Tel: 01803 614567 (NOT 24hr)
Swanage Hospital (MIU) - Tel: 01929 422282 (NOT 24hr)

Tourist Information Offices

For ideas on what to do on a rest day, accommodation advice, hiring a boat to look at some scary routes on Boulder Ruckle, or if you are just interested in local history; take a look at one of the Tourist Information Offices listed below. These offices can provide much more useful and extensive information than it is possible to provide in these pages.
Tourist Information Weymouth - Pavilion Theatre, The Esplanade. Tel: 01305 785747
Tourist Information Portland - Portland Bill Visitor Centre. Tel: 01305 861233
Tourist Information Swanage - Shore Road, Swanage. Tel: 01929 422885

When to Go

Portland and Swanage are both excellent year-round venues whilst Lulworth is best left for the period of late spring through to the onset of autumn. Summer is often too hot although the east and west coast of Portland means you can always find some shade. Swanage and Lulworth offer relatively little shelter from the hot sun. Some of the best conditions are found in spring and autumn. Fine climbing days in winter are also not that uncommon and can be pleasant in sheltered spots such as The Cuttings and at Winspit.

Temperature °C	Jan	Feb	Mar	Apr	May	Jun	Jul	Aug	Sep	Oct	Nov	Dec
Average Max Temp (°C)	8.4	8.3	10.0	12.5	15.4	17.9	20.3	20.4	18.3	15.0	11.5	9.3
Average Min Temp (°C)	3.5	3.1	4.3	6.6	8.1	10.3	12.5	13.3	11.6	9.3	6.2	4.5
Average Sun (hours/day)	2.0	2.8	3.9	6.2	7.2	7.1	7.6	7.0	5.4	3.8	2.7	1.8
Average Rain (mm/month)	76.6	64.3	62.9	47.6	46.6	47.0	35.6	52.2	66.4	77.4	84.5	90.9

Getting There

Trains

Regular train services from all over the country run to the closest stations to the cliffs - these are Weymouth (for Portland), Wareham (for Swanage) and Wool (for Lulworth). The best method of checking on times and prices is the website www.thetrainline.com

Buses

All of the climbing areas in this book are fairly easily reached by regular bus services. The best method of checking on times is the website www.traveline.info. **Portland** is serviced by bus routes that run close to all of the climbing areas via Easton, Weston and Southwell.
Swanage has a regular service from Wareham. For the eastern end of the Swanage cliffs (Subluminal and the Boulder Ruckle) it is a 1.5 mile walk to Durlston Country Park from the centre of Swanage. For the western end of the Swanage cliffs, a bus service runs from Swanage to Langton Matravers (for Dancing Ledge) and Worth Matravers (for Winspit). For **Lulworth** a regular bus service runs from either Wool or Wareham. Lulworth is also easily reached by bus from Weymouth.

Chris Weedon climbing *StuckOn* (E5 6a) - page 341 - at Fisherman's Ledge, Swanage. Photo: Oli Lyon

Portland Accommodation

No wild camping is allowed on Portland.

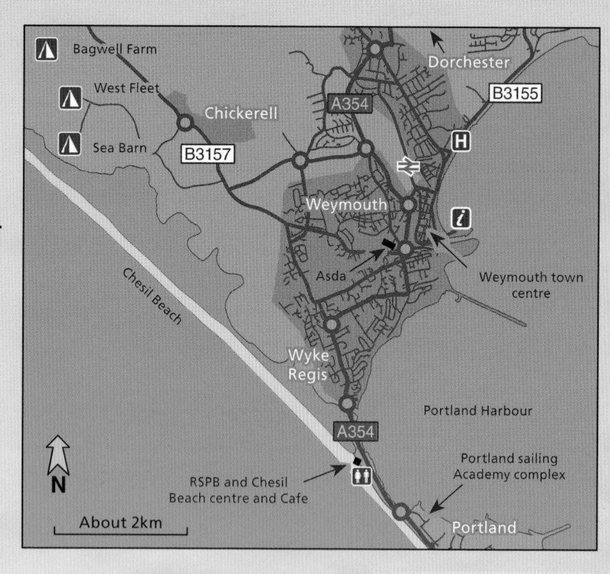

- Tents
- Caravans for hire
- Showers
- Walk to pub

Portland YHA -
Hardy House, Castletown, Portland.
Has rooms and limited camping that must be pre-booked.
Tel: 0845 371 9339
Open all year
www.yha.org.uk

Bagwell Farm Campsite -
Fleet, Weymouth.
Tel: 01305 782575
Open all year
www.bagwellfarm.co.uk
See advert opposite

Sea Barn Farm Campsite -
Fleet, Weymouth. Tel: 01305 782218. Open - Mar to Nov
www.seabarnfarm.co.uk
See advert opposite

West Fleet Holiday Farm -
Fleet, Weymouth. Tel: 01305 782218. Open - Mar to Nov
www.westfleetholidays.co.uk
See advert opposite

Also worth considering are the following:
The Aqua Hotel - Tel: 01305 860269 - Divers' hotel with good rooms.
Cove Holiday Park - Tel: 01305 821286 - Pleasant static caravans in a good location.
Glen Caravan Park - Tel: 01305 823548 - Very basic static caravans.
Dream Cottages - Tel: 01305 789000 - Holiday cottages on Portland and Weymouth.
Portland Holiday Homes - Tel: 01305 861044 - Holiday cottages on Portland.
Fathom and Blues - Tel: 01305 766220 - Bunkhouse and rooms.
YMCA - Tel: 01305 823761 - Rooms and good location.

Portland's east coast from near the Sunlovers Slab.

The Leeds Wall

Approx 200 Routes
Grades up to 8a+
Bouldering & Training Areas
Specialist Equipment Shop

www.theleedswall.co.uk
The Leeds Wall, 100a Gelderd Road, Leeds LS12 6BY. 0113 2341554

Because it's there...

From exhilaration on Dorset's Jurassic Coast, to rest and relaxation at your choice of three great camping parks by the Fleet Lagoon

www.seabarnfarm.co.uk
www.westfleetholidays.co.uk
www.bagwellfarm.co.uk

Ideal base-camps for Portland and other Dorset climbing routes

Great locations - Great facilities

Sea Barn and West Fleet: 01305 782218 *Bagwell: 01305 782575*

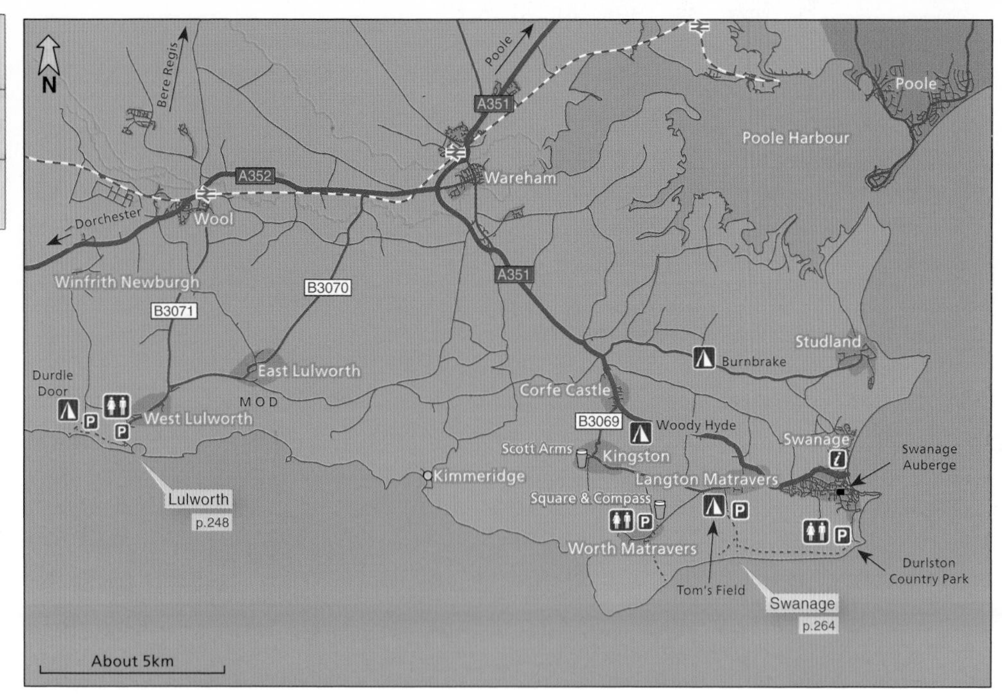

Swanage Accommodation

There are many camping and caravan sites in and around Swanage, several of the popular ones are listed below. Contact **Swanage Tourist Information** - Tel: 01929 422885 - for more information, including non-camping options.

Tom's Field Campsite -
Tom's Field Road, Langton Matravers, Swanage. Tel: 01929 427110.
Open - Mar to Oct.
www.tomsfieldcamping.co.uk
See advert opposite

Swanage Auberge -
45 High Street, Swanage. Tel: 01929 424368. Open all year. Bunkhouse accommodation in the centre of Swanage.
www.swanageauberge.com
See advert opposite

Acton Field Campsite -
Acton Field Campsite, Langton Matravers, Swanage. - 01929 439424. Open Summer and easter only. **www.actonfieldcampsite.co.uk**

Swanage Coastal Park -
Priests Way, Swanage. Tel: 01929 421822
www.shorefield.co.uk

Burnbake Campsite -
The Old Farmhouse, Rempstowe, Corfe Castle. Tel: 01929 480570. Open - Apr to Sept
www.burnbake.com

Woody Hyde Farm Camping Park -
Corfe Castle, Wareham. Tel: 01929 480274
Open - Apr to Oct
www.woodyhyde.co.uk

Lulworth Accommodation

Durdle Door Caravan Park -
West Lulworth. Tel: 01929 400200
Open - Apr to Oct
www.lulworth.com

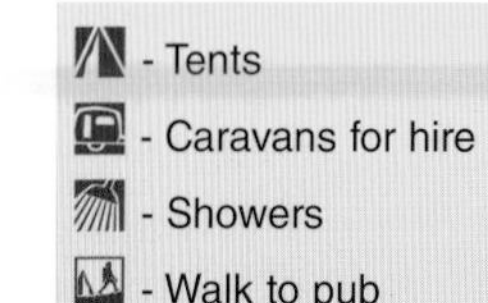

CLIMBERS • WALKERS • DIVERS WELCOME

45 HIGH STREET • SWANAGE • DORSET BH19 2LX

TEL: 07711 117 668

www.swanageauberge.com

OPEN ALL YEAR ROUND

LOOK ON OUR WEBSITE FOR SPECIAL OFFERS!

FROM £18.00 PER NIGHT

INCLUDING A HELP YOURSELF CEREAL BREAKFAST!

WARM, CLEAN, FRIENDLY & LAID-BACK

TOM'S FIELD CAMPSITE & SHOP

Classic Camping in Purbeck Dorset

Langton Matravers near Swanage

Tents & Motorvans only

Comprehensive Shop with local and Fairtrade products

Open Mid March to October end

The Walker's Barn & Stone Room
Available all year but by pre booking only

Tom's Field Road, Langton Matravers Dorset BH19 3HN

01929 427110

tomsfieldcamping.co.uk email: tomsfield@hotmail.com

'icture The Pool at Dancing Ledge

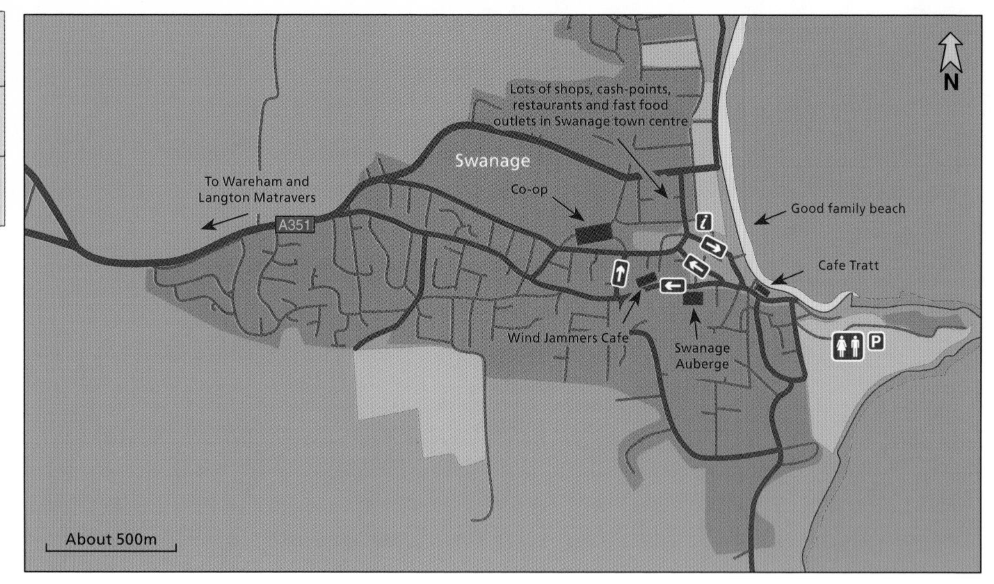

Shops

Portland Area

Weymouth is packed with every shop you could need. There is a large ASDA on the roundabout as you approach Portland. On Portland there are a couple of mini-markets in Weston and two Co-ops - one in Fortuneswell and one in Easton. There is a large Tesco in Easton, just off of the square. There are a number of post offices, cash machines and other small shops on the Isle.

Swanage Area

There is a large Co-op supermarket in Swanage centre and also shops in Wareham on the drive to the crags.

Lulworth Area

In Lulworth there is one local store. Wool, the main village on the way to Lulworth, has some shops.

Cafes

Portland Area

White Stones Cafe in Easton. Excellent food and coffee plus gallery, garden and WiFi.
The Sugar Loaf in Easton. Gives good service and does a decent fry-up.
The Blue Fish Cafe in Chiswell. Has very good coffee and breakfasts.
The Lobster Pot Cafe at Portland Bill. Useful for the Coastguard and Lighthouse cliffs.

Lulworth Area

Lulworth Cove has a very conveniently situated cafe, right in the middle of the car park. There are some tea shops in Lulworth village just up the road from Lulworth Cove itself.

Swanage Area

Swanage town has lots of cafes in and around the road that leads to Durlston Country Park. A couple of handy ones are listed below.
Wind Jammers Cafe on the high street. Good spot with WiFi.
Cafe Tratt on the road before turning up the hill from the seafront. Good street side location.
Durlston Castle Cafe (The Seventh Wave) near the car park. Recently refurbished.

Take-aways and Restaurants

Portland Area

There are a number of fish and chip shops on the Isle.
Balti Island in Chiswell is a good Indian and has a nice restaurant as well as a take-away menu.
The Peking Restaurant in Easton Square is a pleasant place to eat.
The Blue Fish Cafe in Chiswell is a fine restu-arant in the evening.
The Crab House Cafe has seafood and is located on the way onto the Isle.
The Cove House Inn on the seafront at Chiswell and *The George* at Easton do standard pub fare.

Swanage Area

Head for Swanage town centre where there is a good selection of take-aways and restaurants that cater for most tastes and budgets. If you are wanting to stop on the approach then try the Main Street in Wareham.

Good Pub Guide

Portland Area

The Cove House Inn on the seafront in Chiswell is a great place to sit outside as the sun sets over Chesil Beach and also has a convivial atmosphere. *The George* on the outskirts of Easton is a good traditional pub that often has live music. The bar at *The Portland Heights Hotel* has a great view out over Chesil Beach and Lyme Bay.

Lulworth Area

The Castle Inn is a nice pub with good food and a low-slung roof.

Swanage Area

In Swanage town there is a whole cluster of pubs near the end of the pier. If you are climbing at Dancing Ledge or Winspit you can head straight for *The Square and Compass* at Worth Matravers, which has a very 'olde worlde' atmosphere. *The Scott Arms* in Kingston (near Worth Matravers) is an excellent pub with good food and a lovely beer garden. Many of the pubs in Corfe Castle are excellent but possibly the best is *The Fox Inn*.

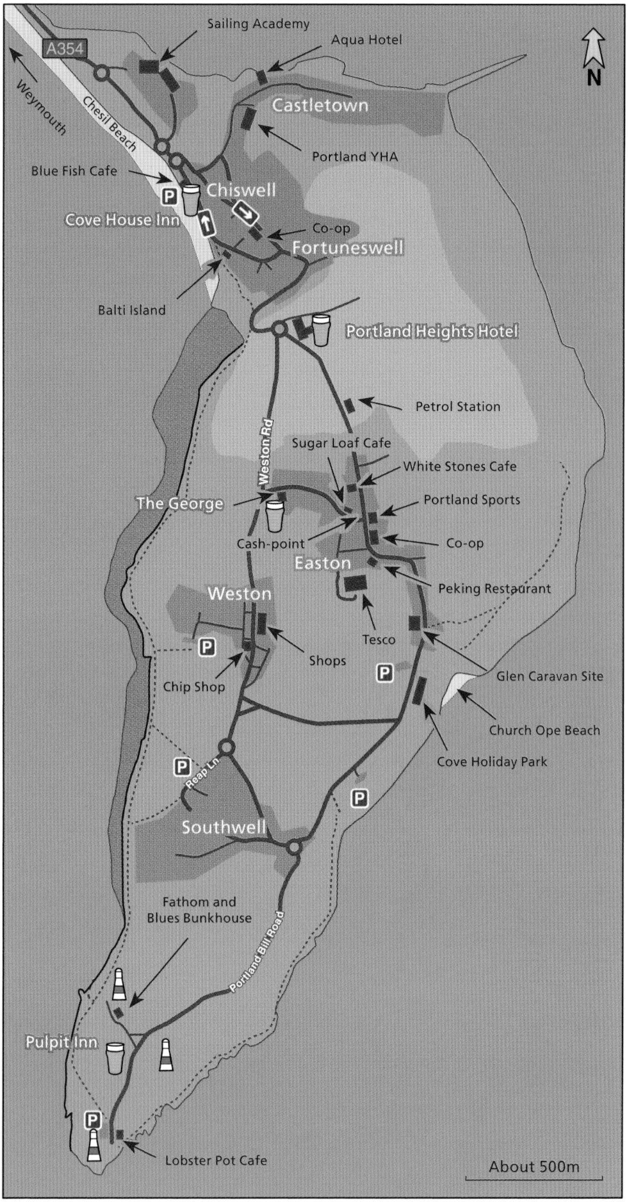

Beaches

Along the coastline the variety of scenery is quite remarkable. Beautiful, unspoilt sandy beaches occur at Studland, Sandbanks and Weymouth. There are also delightful stony coves at Lulworth and Worrbarrow Bay. The major venues have organised watersports such as water-skiing, parascending and windsurfing. Other areas which are popular for sunbathing and with families are Dancing Ledge Quarry, Swanage main beach and Church Ope Cove on Portland.

Climbing Shops

Portland
Portland Sports and Leisure Shop, 6 Easton Street, Portland - www.portlandsportsshop.co.uk
Sells climbing hardware and the guidebook.

Swanage
Jurrasic Outdoors, 11 High Street, Swanage - www.jurassicoutdoor.com
Sells climbing hardware and outdoor clothing.

Dorchester
Great Western Camping, London Road, Dorchester - www.greatwesterncamping.co.uk
Sells climbing hardware, boots, camping equipment, outdoor clothing and the guidebook.

Bournemouth
Cotswold Outdoor, Westover Retail Park, Castle Lane West, Bournemouth.
 - www.cotswoldoutdoor.com

Climbing Walls

Q.E. Leisure Centre (The Edge) -
Blandford Road, Wimbourne, Dorset. Tel: 01202 888208. 8m high lead and top-rope wall plus bouldering room. Open weekday evenings and weekends all day.

- Food/cafe
- Lead wall
- Bouldering

Calshot Activities Centre -
Calshot Spit, Fawley, Southampton. Tel: 023 8089 2077. A large centre with a 20m leading wall. Opening times vary, check before a visit.

Quay Climbing Centre -
Haven Road, Exeter, Devon. Tel: 01392 426 850. Large leading wall and bouldering sections. Open weekdays and weekends.

Bournemouth University Climbing Wall -
Bournemouth University, Talbot Campus. Tel: 01202 961677. Leading wall and bouldering.

Chesil Beach and Lyme Bay from the top of Portland.

The climbing Academy

The Climbing Academies are high class dedicated bouldering facilities with gourmet coffee, free wifi and good food. They are clean, brightly lit and have efficient chalk extraction coupled with 5 star toilets and showers.

And the climbing is pretty good too!

BRISTOL
Charlton St, Bristol, BS50AE
0117 907 2956 info@theclimbingacademy.com

GLASGOW
Portman St, Kinning Park, Glasgow, G411EJ
0141 429 6331 glasgow@theclimbingacademy.com

ONLINE CLIMBING SHOP
Fingerboards, campus rungs,mats, rehab etc
www.tca-climbingshop.com

SCARPA

www.theclimbingacademy.com

Dorset Climbing

Andy Schofield working on the very tenuous and sustained line of *Prison Sex* (7c+) - *page 171* - at Coastguard North.

Many of the climbing areas covered in this book have sensitive access but, thanks to the BMC and their local volunteers, most are currently accessible to all climbers - all areas with potential problems or actual bans are noted within the text. Climbers should be aware of their responsibilities and be careful not to abuse the access granted. In general, simple reasonable behaviour like not dropping litter, respecting restrictions, not making excess noise and using the described approaches is all that is required to ensure continued untroubled access to the climbing areas.
One notable area with a major access problem is Lulworth. This area is owned by the Weld Estate who in 1995 announced a total ban on climbing on their land for reasons of conservation and public safety. This ban continues to the present day. There are also some specific (non-bird) restrictions at Winspit Quarry, Dancing Ledge, Blacknor Far North and near the Godnor and Neddyfields cliffs that are covered in detail in their respective introductions.

Bird Nesting Restrictions

To avoid disturbance to nesting birds, seasonal climbing restrictions have been placed on certain sections of the Dorset coast. The nature of these restrictions varies from Portland to Swanage, but it is essential that climbers abide by the restrictions and also take note of any changes that may occur further to the information contained in this book. Note that the restrictions are not just no-climbing restrictions - please keep away from these areas altogether.
Portland - The restrictions on Portland are variable and reviewed each year and in general are only applied to the sections of cliff where the birds (often peregrines) have actually nested. The restrictions usually apply from the 1st March until 30th June but they are lifted if there are no nests or if the birds have fledged. The current practice is to mark the affected routes by fixing a sign on the bolts at the edges of the restricted area. There is also a permanent restriction on the far end of Coastguard South.
Swanage - Unlike the Portland restrictions, the bird nesting areas for Swanage are well established and seldom change. The affected routes are clearly marked in the text and all the bans apply from 1st March to 31st July. The crags with restrictions for nesting birds are Hedbury Big Cove, Smokey Hole, Guillemot West, some of Cormorant, some of Blackers Hole and several sections of the Boulder Ruckle.

All these restrictions can change so please check the BMC Regional Access Database (RAD) if you are unsure - www.thebmc.co.uk/modules/RAD/

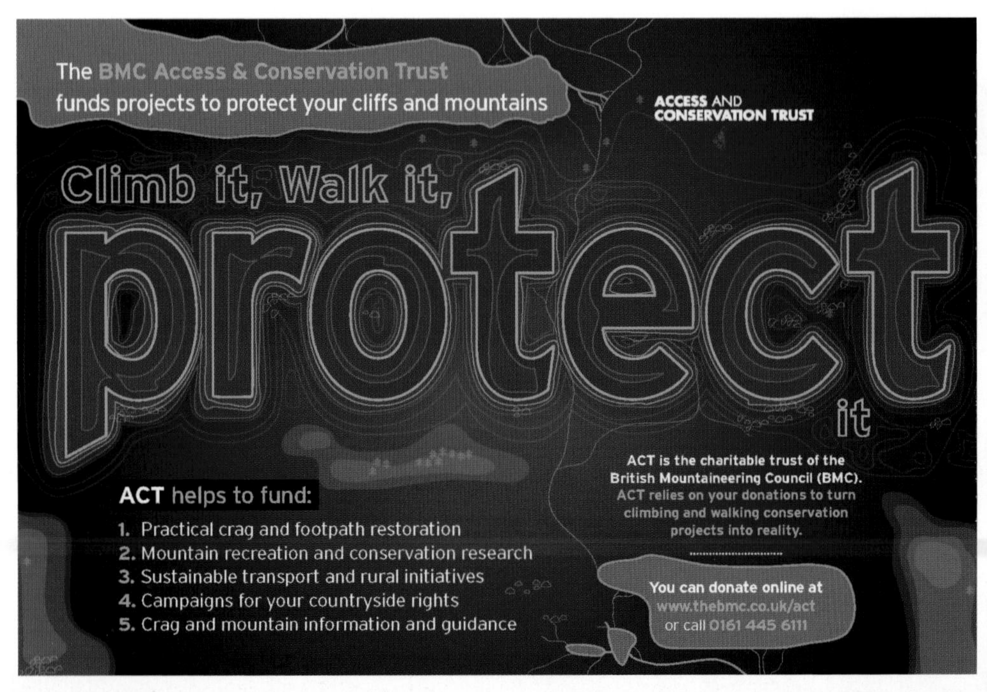

Brian Wilkinson on the first ascent of *Cruise Control* (6a+) - *page 212* - at Cheyne Cliff on the east coast of Portland. Part of Cheyne Cliff has a restriction on it due to nesting birds. Although this doesn't include this particular route it does affect the approach to the crag - see page 213 for details.

Parking

Only use the described parking places, these are clearly marked on all the approach maps. Please respect the local residents on Portland. Note that some of the places previously used for parking are now officially restricted and parking tickets are regularly issued.

Camping

No wild camping is allowed anywhere at Swanage, Lulworth or on Portland. Use one of the many local camp sites. All accommodation suggestions are on pages 18 and 20.

Cliff Plants

Minimise damage to fragile flora by not gardening routes. Check local information before developing any new areas. It is almost certainly the case that undeveloped areas on Portland have been left for a reason. Don't abseil over cliff-tops on Portland since this is where much of the rare flora grows on the Isle.

Sanctuary Zones and MOD Areas

Do not climb, or even enter, any of the sanctuary zones. Do not climb on any of the MOD property near Lulworth or on Portland.

On the fine line of *The Right Mix* (6b) - *page 139* - at the Unsung Area of Wallsend North.

Bolting

The bolting system predominantly used at the sport crags covered by this book is the U-bolt staple - see right. These are made from marine-grade stainless steel held in with a special epoxy glue. They provide inexpensive, corrosion-resistant protection with a lifetime in excess of 25 years.

When using these staples:
1) Use high-strength karabiners.
2) Carry a screwgate or sling to use on bolts which are close to edges or in uneven rock.
3) The staples can be lowered off directly or by abseil. When lowering always thread both belay staples.
4) Never top-rope or lower-off of a single staple.
5) Please don't top-rope directly through the lower-off anchors, instead, run your rope through karabiners to reduce wear and tear.
6) Always belay close to the rock face with the rope going straight up through the quickdraw clipped to the first bolt. Belaying a long way from the face puts a heavy outward loading on the bottom bolt which has caused problems with some bolts in the area. It is also a dangerous practice since both leader and belayer can get hurt in the event of a fall.
7) If bolts look suspect please report it to the BMC Southwest Area - **www.thebmc.co.uk/contact**

Nearly all of Portland and much of Swanage is now properly geared but there are places, such as Blackers Hole Quarry and The Promenade, that still need work. Additionally, existing routes need occasional maintenance and re-gearing.

The Dorset Bolt Fund

The DBF has been set up by a group of committed volunteer climbers with a passion for the climbing in Dorset. These volunteers raise funds for the purchase of bolts, and then do the hard work of equipping routes with them. The money raised is solely used for replacing old bolts on existing routes, in accordance with the Dorset Bolt Agreement.

The kit list for bolting is a big one - high-powered drills, spare batteries and drill bits, the bolts themselves, plus resin and glue guns for glue-in bolts. Then there is the climbing gear, ropes, pegs etc. All this adds up to a fairly hefty price tag per route, especially as bolting can trash kit pretty quickly.

How can I help?
The main way everyone can help is by making a donation. The simple gesture of a £5 online donation each time you go climbing in Dorset can go a long way to providing the necessary funding. If you want to get more involved then there is always a need for volunteers to help with the hard work. Bolting is a difficult and time-consuming activity. If you are an experienced climber, or have a background in rope access, you could be a real asset to the Dorset Bolt Fund.

For more information about the funding of bolting in Dorset and to donate to the DBF go to **www.ukboltfund.org** or to **www.dorset-climbing.com/dorset_bolt_fund/**

Piotr Wycislik on the tough central section of *Freaky Ralph* (8a+) - *page 69* - at Blacknor North on the west coast of Portland. Photo: Szymon Dziukiewicz

Sport Climbing

For the sport routes a single rope of 60m is advised since there are several areas on the east and west coast of Portland with routes close to 30m in length. It is possible to climb on many other areas with a shorter rope but please take special care and, no matter what length of rope you have, ALWAYS tie a knot in the dead end and stand close to the face when lowering off. For a number of the big lines at Blackers Hole a longer rope is necessary.

A rack of fourteen quickdraws is enough for any route on Portland, however some lines at Swanage require more, most notably once again at Blackers Hole. Certain sport routes require an abseil approach or are tidal as at White Hole, Coastguard South and The Promenade - again this is clearly indicated with the crag information and or route descriptions.

Trad Climbing

Double 50m ropes are required for virtually all the traditional climbs in this guidebook. In addition, a 50m abseil rope is essential for many of the crags at Swanage. Often these abseils are free-hanging so make sure a thick rope is used. Take a good selection of slings for belays and to help avoid rope drag from the ever-present overhangs at Swanage. For the big traditional routes take two sets of wires and some micro-nuts, plus a good selection of cams and some larger nuts. Include enough gear to belay yourself securely at the base of the cliffs (in case of a freak large wave).

Tides

The highest spring tides (new and full moon) have about a 2 to 2.5m range whilst neap tides (half moons) vary between 1 and 1.5m. Portland has a double tide, which is not really obvious to the eye but has the effect of prolonging the time the water level is high or low. Overall the changes in water level are slow when compared to Cornwall, Devon and South Wales. The tides advance by about 45 minutes a day and there are two highs a day some 12-13 hours apart. The flood tide flows to the east and the ebb to the west which are most apparent in the huge tidal race off of Portland Bill. At Swanage a knowledge of tides is essential for most of the cliffs although only a few areas are actually cut off by high water. For virtually all areas it is worth keeping well away when the sea is moderately rough or worse.

For sport climbing on Portland a knowledge of the tides is not essential unless visiting some of the cliffs on the east coast or Coastguard South. **The Portland deep water solos need the highest tides possible so look for spring tides of around 2m or greater**.

Tide tables can be bought in newsagents and post offices. There are different tables for Swanage and Portland. A rough guide to tides can also be gained from the surfing website at **www.magicseaweed.com**. This gives lots of data on sea swell, tides, wind strength and general weather conditions - just find a surfing location closest to the cliffs. Because of the very strong tidal races at Portland and Swanage swimming is not advised.

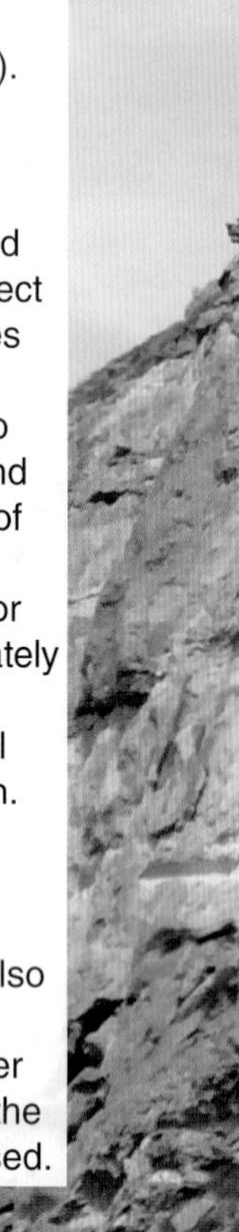

Ian Tsang tackling one of the most popular 7a sport routes on Portland *Wolfgang Forever* (7a) - *page 68* - at Blacknor North.

The Roped Climbing Safety Checklist

1) Wear a helmet - Because of the looseness of the rock and the unstable finishing slopes, helmets are very strongly recommended, particularly at Swanage.

2) Take care on the cliff top - When wet the grass and mud can be lethally slippery. This is also the case after long dry spells when the dry grass is frictionless.

3) Tie a knot in your rope - Take great care when lowering off and always have a knot tied in the dead end of the rope. *Tip - get into the habit of tying both ends of your rope to your rope bag each time you pack it away.*

4) Take an abseil rope with you - For crags requiring an abseil approach, do not assume that it is possible to abseil in on ropes you wish to use for climbing since frequently the abseil rope forms an integral part of the cliff-top belay.

5) Take Prusik loops - In most areas Prusik loops are essential since there is not always an easy escape route.

6) Watch your top-outs - Many of the Swanage trad routes finish on unstable earth and grass slopes that are often the most serious section of a climb. Place plenty of protection on the last sections of good rock and, if at all possible, consider locating the top of the climb prior to descending and fixing a short rope down the finishing slope.

7) Be careful when moving along the crag base - When above deep water, carry the rack and rope in a manner whereby they can be easily and quickly jettisoned. If you are hit by a big wave with them on you will sink VERY quickly if you are washed out of your depth.

8) Drop your grade - Remember that Swanage, and the Boulder Ruckle in particular, is a big and serious cliff. Until familiar with the place, it is highly recommended that you drop your leading grade by at least 2 notches when attempting a route there. Additionally, DON'T expect to instantly lead the equivalent trad grade as your best sport grade effort on a bolted route, especially if that bolted route was at a climbing wall!

9) Prepare to get hot - In summer many of the crags can be unbelievably hot so take lots of water, shades, a hat, and slap on the sun screen.

Cliff rescue practice at Hedbury Quarry, Swanage.

Beta Stick

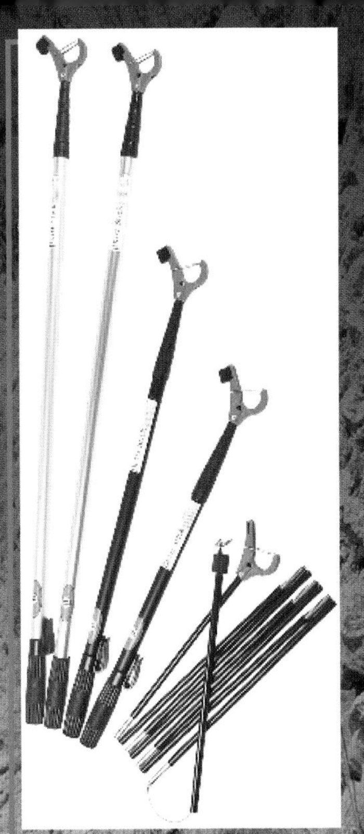

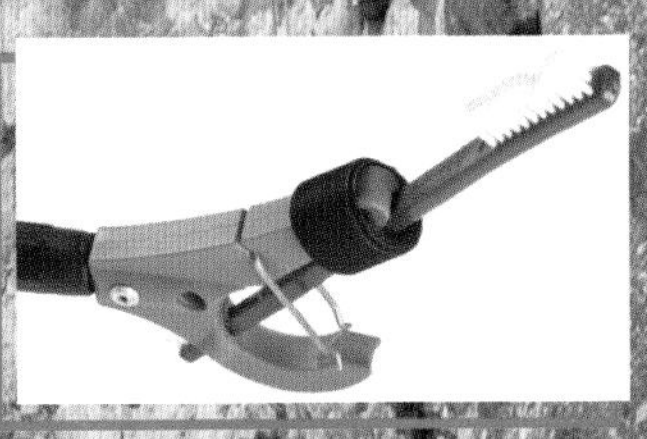

info@betaclimbingdesigns.com

0114 2558882

www.betaclimbingdesigns.com

In this book sport routes are given sport grades and traditionally protected routes are given trad (or British) grades. Deep water solos may have a trad grade or a sport grade, depending on whether the route is a bolted route or not, but they will also have an S-grade (see page 40). The grade table attempts to compare the main grading systems.

Sport Grade

A sport grade is simply a measure of how hard it is going to be to get up a certain bit of rock. It does not attempt to define how difficult the hardest move is, or how scary the route is. The routes in this book are graded for a first try by the easiest method, hence on-sights can seem harder if you miss the correct sequence.

Trad Grade

Trad climbing is where protection is placed whilst climbing (nuts and cams etc.) and there are usually no bolts to clip. The trad grading-system is divided into two parts;

The adjectival grade (Diff, VDiff, Severe (S), Hard Severe (HS), Very Severe (VS), Hard Very Severe (HVS), E1...E10). This gives an overall picture of the route including how well protected it is, how sustained and an indication of the level of difficulty of the whole route.

The technical grade (4a, 4b, 4c, 5a...7a). This refers to the difficulty of the hardest single move, or short section, on a route.

ROUTE GRADES

BRITISH TRAD GRADE

Grade	Name	Bold	Safe
Mod	Moderate		
Diff	Difficult		
VDiff	Very Difficult		
HVD	Hard Very Difficult		
Sev	Severe		
HS	Hard Severe	3c	4b
VS	Very Severe	4a	5a
HVS	Hard Very Severe	4b	5b
E1		5a	5c
E2		5a	6a
E3		5b	6a
E4		5c	6b
E5		6a	6c
E6		6b	6c
E7		6c	7a
E8		6c	7a
E9		7a	7b
E10		7a	7b

Sport Grade	UIAA	USA
1	I	5.1
2	II	5.2
2+	III	5.3
3-	III+ IV	5.4
3	IV+	5.5
3+	V-	5.6
4	V	5.7
4+	V+	5.8
5	VI-	5.9
5+	VI	5.10a
6a	VI+	5.10b
6a+	VII-	5.10c
6b	VII	5.10d
6b+	VII+	5.11a
6c		5.11b
6c+	VIII-	5.11c
7a	VIII	5.11d
7a+	VIII+	5.12a
7b	IX-	5.12b
7b+		5.12c
7c	IX	5.12d
7c+	IX+	5.13a
8a	X-	5.13b
8a+	X	5.13c
8b		5.13d
8b+	X+	5.14a
8c	XI-	5.14b
8c+	XI	5.14c
9a	XI+	5.14d
9a+		5.15a

Colour-coding

The trad and sport routes are all given a colour-coded dot corresponding to a difficulty band.

● **Green Routes** - Everything at grade **Severe** and under, and **4+** and under for sport routes. Good routes to kick off your climbing career.

● **Orange Routes** - **HS** to **HVS** inclusive, and **5** to **6a+** for sport routes. General ticking routes for those with more experience, a large range of excellent routes is available across this band.

● **Red Routes** - **E1** to **E3** inclusive, and **6b** to **7a** for sport routes. For the experienced and keen climber. Anyone operating at this level can expect to enjoy some of the best climbing in the book.

● **Black Routes** - **E4** and above, and **7a+** and above for sport routes. The hard stuff! Have a go at some major national testpieces, plus you can do all the red, orange and green routes as well. Can't be better than that!

Mark Glaister running both pitches of *Yellow Wall* (E1 5b) - *page 319* - together at Guillemot Ledge East, Swanage. Photo: Paul Cox

Deep Water Soloing

Routes that have been classed as deep water solos are indicated by the splash-down icon. These routes can be trad routes or sport routes, but some may also only have ever been done as deep water solos.

Little gear is needed for the actual climbing, apart from a good supply of spare boots and chalk bags in case of a wetting. For some of the routes it is necessary for an abseil to be made to reach sea level, for which you will need a harness and an abseil device (these should be left on the abseil rope when you set off on your solo so that you aren't weighed down if you end up in the water).

Deep Water Solo Grade

In addition to their normal sport grade, deep water solos are also given an S-grade at the start of the route description, this gives an indication of the seriousness of soloing the route under optimum conditions.
Routes given a trad grade that have also been climbed as deep water solos have been given a sport grade in blue next to the S grade (the sport grade is commonly used in deep water soloing).

An S-grade is **not** a green light to go ahead at any time for a deep water solo, as many factors will alter the seriousness of a route, such as the depth of water, height above water, sea state, strong currents, people in the sea below, swimming ability and water temperature.

The S-grade definitions are:
S0 - Can be undertaken at most tide states with normally plenty of water under all parts of the route. Low crux sections and an easy exit from the water.
S1 - Needs careful consideration of tides to ensure there is sufficient water under the route. Some climbing may not be above water. May have hard moves high up and/or some poor rock.
S2 - As for S1 but it may require high spring tides for sufficient water. Possible that water maybe too shallow for a safe entry. High hard sections. For the very experienced only.
S3 - Shallow water solos which are never really safe.

The Deep Water Soloing Safety Checklist

1) Always check tides before starting. Remember a neap high tide may not actually be that high. Check which routes need high spring tides carefully.
2) Never go deep water soloing on your own in case you get into difficulties in the water.
3) Before starting, always check the fall zone for ledges, reefs, boulders or any other environmental dangers. Just because a route has been soloed, it doesn't mean that there is always deep water beneath every section of it.
4) Check for exits from the water should you need them.
5) Keep an eye out for weather changes; a sudden change in wind speed or direction can quickly create rough and dangerous conditions.
6) In spring and early summer the water is very cold and it will suck the life out of you in no time at all. Make provision for getting dry and warm quickly if necessary.

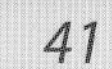

Neil Gresham deep water soloing the Fisherman's Ledge classic *Fathoms* (E3 5b) - *page 339* - at Swanage. Photo: Keith Sharples

Since 2000 the routes in Dorset have been open for voting on stars and grades on the ROCKFAX website and these graded lists have been based on the many votes we have received. The list on this page covers the sport routes at both Swanage and Portland. Some additional routes have been added if the online database consensus wasn't sufficient. If you disagree with the list then please let us know by visiting the website and placing your votes - **www.rockfax.com**

8 c

Stars	Route	Page
Top 50	Endeavour	328

8 b

Stars	Route	Page
Top 50	Lifeforce	349
Top 50	Vespasian	169

8 a +

Stars	Route	Page
***	Palace of the Brine	349
Top 50	Infinite Gravity	328
**	Fuel My Fire	364
**	Event Horizon	361
**	Freaky Ralph	69
***	Burn Hollywood Burn	256

8 a

Stars	Route	Page
***	Haka Pereperu	348
Top 50	Adrenochrome *S1*	256
Top 50	The Breathing Method	238
**	To Hungary for Love	141
**	Balance of Power	183
**	Solid State Logic	356
**	Fighting Torque	241

7 c +

Stars	Route	Page
***	Hell's Darker Chambers	305
Top 50	Forever Laughing	328
***	Never Kneel to Skeletor *S1*	254
***	Magnetic Pull	153
**	Under Duress	241
**	The Big Blue	188
**	Hurricane on a Millpond	239
**	Monoculture	116
**	Bar Room Brawl	169
***	Zen Zero	192
Top 50	The Schwarzechild Radius	328
**	Eternal Spider	169
***	Drunken Butterfly	349
**	The Mind Terrorist	237
**	Shock to the System	257
Top 50	King of the Swingers *S3*	192
**	Godfodder	355
**	Glycerine	168
**	Beautiful South	161
Top 50	Temple Redneck	348
**	Pandemonium	212
**	Legendary Shadows	305
**	Prison Sex	171
**	Journey to Eternia *S1*	254
**	Osaki Dolphin	192

7 c

Stars	Route	Page
**	Detonator	213
**	Boilermaker	76
**	Mirrorball	261
**	Clockwork Orange	169
**	Once Were Warriors	189
Top 50	Mark of the Beast *S1*	256
**	Atonement	354
Top 50	Tennessee	174
***	Total Seizure	356
**	Il Pirata	259
***	Screaming Skulls	174
**	The Font of Knowledge	172
**	Trance Mission	123
***	Illusions	213
***	Keyboard Wall	116
Top 50	Hall of Mirrors	238
**	Liquid Steel	361
**	Meridian Line	168
**	Crucifix Kiss	75
**	Nightmare Scenario	241
**	Shining Heart	171
**	Hong Kong Phooey	163
**	Cinderella's Big Score	289

7 b +

Stars	Route	Page
Top 50	Gates of Greyskull *S1*	255
**	Teenage Lust	141
**	Buried Violence	176
**	Corinthian Spirit	82
***	Waves Become Wings	355
**	Running It In!	170
**	Bust ya' Boiler	305
**	Subyouth	228
***	Zum Zeaux	153
**	Disintegration	153
**	Downhill Spiral	148
**	The Racing Line	123
***	Red Medicine	176
**	Headwall Emptiness	168
Top 50	Wax Museum	169
**	Fat Chance Hotel	303
***	Infernal Din	238
**	Sign of the Vulcan	234
**	In on the Killtaker	105
**	Frenzied Detruncation	171
Top 50	Realm of Chaos	153
**	Guardian Angel	172
Top 50	Zinc Oxide Mountain	123
**	Brooklyn Bimbo	172
Top 50	Road Rage	213
**	Reactor Meltdown	172
***	Colors	160
**	Coralized	211
Top 50	Cocteau Phenomena	83
**	Mr. Natural	151

7 b

Stars	Route	Page
***	Want Out	238
***	Frazzled	145
***	Avenging the Halsewell	278
**	Lulworth Arms Treaty	256
**	Down in the Sewer	356
**	Crest of a Wave	356
***	Birth Pains of New Nations	355
Top 50	Halfway to Heaven	159
**	Spanner Eyes	70
**	I Walk the Line	82
**	Think Black	105
**	Weakest to the Wall	139
**	Choco Loni	116
Top 50	Tessellations	355
**	The Fun Factory	123
**	Useless Generation	140
**	My Love of this Land	140
**	Sale of the Century	169
**	Topsy Turvy Land	138
**	Nihil	122
***	The Swinging Nineties *S1*	192
***	Genuflection	159
***	The Bad Seeds	162
**	Running Down a Dream	159
***	Ariane V	153
**	Dr Phibes	169
***	Twangy Pearl	76
***	Spacewalk	360
**	Ryme Intrinseca	103
**	Come In and Burn	177
**	Aeon Flux	176
**	Full Fathom Five	175
**	Spare Rib	170
**	Biscuits for Smut	172
***	Stay Golden	145
***	Outside the Gate	159
**	September Mourning	174
**	Prophets of Rage	302
Top 50	Sweet Smell of Success	145
***	Quick as Rainbows	176

7 a +

Stars	Route	Page
Top 50	Pump Hitler	122
**	Psychic EMF	126
**	Solstice	278
**	Damnation Game	283
**	The Pump Will Tear Us Apart	304
**	Song to the Siren	307
**	Mexican Stand-off	79
**	Dizzy up the Girl	81
**	Dogtown Skate Team	160
**	Cybernetic Orchard	82
**	Girl Power	170
**	Kendo Nagasaki	103
**	Crown of Thorns	104
**	The Singing Bush	102
**	Psychosomatic Addict	92
**	Troll Team Special	155
**	Barbed Wire Kisses	116
**	Ironhead	66
**	On the Wall	118
**	The Mouth Waters	239
**	Humanoid	118
**	Rocket from the Crypt	211
**	Dreams Burn Down	122
**	The Bigger Piece	150
**	Double or Quits	301
**	Bushwhacked	102
***	Mariner's Graveyard	304
**	Laughing Peter	150
**	Bend Sinister	230
Top 50	Victims of Fashion	116
Top 50	Animal Magnetism *S1*	254
**	Azymuth	177
**	Wax on Wheels	104
**	The Strobolising Scyphostoma	103
**	L'esprit du vent	177
**	Great Barrier Reef	104
**	Live by the Sword	240

Chris Weedon on his own new line *Slide Show* (E7 6c) - *page 341* - at the New Dawn section of Fisherman's Ledge. Photo: Ben Fordesman

This trad route graded list only covers routes at Swanage and Lulworth, including some deep water solos. Once again additional routes have been added if the online database consensus wasn't sufficient. If you disagree with the list then please let us know by visiting the website and placing your votes **www.rockfax.com**.

E8

E7

E6

E5

- ** The Fin ... 379
- Top 50 The Lean Machine ... 375
- *** The Vanishing S1 ... 344
- ** Sister of Night S3 ... 182
- ** The Brotherhood S2 ... 253
- ** Ice Queen ... 394
- ** Indian Pacific ... 377
- Top 50 Polaris ... 326
- Top 50 Wall of the Worlds ... 377
- ** Cave Rave ... 349
- ** Giantslayer ... 329
- ** Crazy Notion S1 ... 254

E4

- ** Bad Young Brother ... 346
- ** Magic Mountain ... 415
- ** Vikings ... 313
- ** Havana ... 333
- ** Water Wings S1 ... 191
- Top 50 Melpomene ... 412
- Top 50 Mother Africa ... 377
- ** Tempting Truancy ... 342
- ** Sting in the Tail ... 347
- ** Acapulco ... 393
- ** Cima Petite ... 379
- Top 50 Bare Reputation S0 ... 191
- Top 50 Impending Gleam ... 348
- ** Double 'ard Bastard ... 341
- Top 50 Warlord ... 313
- ** Singing Winds ... 391
- ** Dune Dust ... 391
- *** Barracuda ... 377
- *** The Great Shark Hunt S1 ... 344
- *** Crystal Voyager 2 ... 356
- *** Davey Jones' Lock-off S2 ... 338
- ** Tensile Groove Test ... 356
- Top 50 ...And Captain Blood's... S1 ... 338
- ** The Big Heat ... 317
- Top 50 Freeborn Man S1 ... 345
- Top 50 Crab Party S2 ... 191

E3

- Top 50 Facedancin' ... 313
- ** Howling Stone ... 361
- Top 50 The Ritz ... 347
- ** Moose's Tooth ... 395
- ** Limited Edition ... 347
- ** St Elmo's Firé ... 380
- Top 50 Mickey Mouse ... 385
- ** Marmolata Buttress ... 388
- ** No Mistaking ... 315
- ** Len's Rule of the Sea ... 357
- ** FAGI Code 65 ... 346
- ** Friends from the Deep ... 318
- *** Gorillas in the Mist ... 340
- * Blow Daddy-O ... 251
- ** The Planet ... 393
- ** Karma S2 ... 191
- ** Amazonia S1 ... 339
- Top 50 Ocean Boulevard ... 377
- Top 50 Soul Sacrifice ... 396
- Top 50 Russian Roulette S1 ... 191
- ** Leap of Faith S2 ... 343
- ** Philatus ... 409
- Top 50 Octopus Weed S0 ... 193
- Top 50 Fathoms S1 ... 339
- ** Damage Case ... 349

E2

- ** Squid ... 347
- Top 50 Ximenes ... 393
- ** Children of the Sun ... 387
- ** Vortices ... 392
- ** Ray of Sunshine ... 414
- Top 50 Gypsy ... 391
- ** Insecticide ... 398
- ** Oceanid ... 313
- ** Bert and Ernie ... 387
- Top 50 Buccaneer ... 385
- ** Grandma's Groove ... 409
- Top 50 Tudor Rose ... 313
- ** Mansion Pond ... 258
- ** The Tool ... 387
- ** Calcitron ... 349
- ** Mankini Biscuit ... 258
- Top 50 Mars ... 412
- ** The Adventures of Portland Bill 392
- ** The Peccary ... 412
- ** Ixtlan S1 ... 191
- ** Test Department ... 349
- Top 50 The Conger S1 ... 344
- ** Hung, Swung and... S1 ... 180

E1

- ** Sapphire ... 316
- ** Strongbow ... 392
- ** Yellow Wall ... 319
- ** Girl from the Snow Country ... 348
- ** Sinbad ... 385
- ** October Lady ... 394
- ** Dark Side of the Sun ... 378
- Top 50 Elysium ... 391
- ** Billy Pigg ... 384
- ** Stroof ... 406
- ** When Land Becomes Sea ... 341
- ** Chasm Groove ... 358
- ** Ganymede ... 397
- ** The Vapour Edge ... 333
- ** Bon Firé ... 346
- Top 50 Thunderball ... 380
- ** The Laws Traverse S0 ... 253
- ** Jurrasic Coast Pimps ... 259
- ** Rufty's Roll Up ... 333
- ** Eskimo Nell ... 367
- Top 50 The Spook ... 316
- ** Spittle 'n' Spume S0 ... 191
- ** The Big Easy S0 ... 190

HVS

- ** Fraggle Rock ... 415
- ** Buzz Light Year ... 387
- ** Argo ... 395
- * Baboon ... 405
- ** Dublin Packet ... 396
- ** The Golden Fleece ... 395
- Top 50 Jo ... 380
- ** Thunder Groove ... 391
- ** The God Slot ... 364
- ** Hyperbole ... 259
- Top 50 Lightning Wall ... 391
- ** Nutcracker Exit II ... 399
- Top 50 Behemoth ... 396
- ** Black Sunshine ... 378
- ** Prudence ... 397
- ** Strapiombo ... 317
- ** The Gift ... 259
- ** Valkyrie Buttress Direct ... 315
- ** Damson ... 364
- Top 50 Finale Groove ... 387
- * Transcript Direct ... 405
- ** Via Christina ... 404
- ** True Identity ... 315
- ** Astrid ... 412
- ** The Long Goodbye ... 399
- ** Aventura ... 379
- ** Ledgend Direct ... 318
- Top 50 Quality Street ... 321
- ** Aubergine ... 342
- Top 50 The Maypole S0 ... 253
- ** Troubled Waters S1 ... 345

VS

- Top 50 Tatra ... 388
- ** The Heidelberg Creature ... 387
- ** Sweet SA ... 387
- ** The Asp ... 382
- Top 50 Tensor II ... 317
- ** Revelation Chimney ... 355
- * The Coral Prison ... 364
- ** Wessex Hangover ... 365
- ** 'B' Line ... 387
- ** Isis ... 367
- ** Old Faithful ... 395
- * Spread Eagle ... 407
- Top 50 Freda ... 409
- ** Silhouette Arete ... 379
- ** Mojo-Pin ... 258
- ** Tobacco Road ... 333
- ** Mellow Yellow ... 414
- ** Batt Crack ... 318
- ** Mistaken Identity ... 315
- Top 50 Benny ... 354
- * Gimcrack ... 393
- ** Hangover ... 366
- ** Airy Legs ... 398

HS

- * Resurrection ... 366
- * Ledgend ... 318
- * Bottomless Buttress ... 379
- Top 50 Wall Street ... 321
- * Whynot ... 404
- ** Balcony ... 406
- ** Temporary Lifestyle S0 ... 190

S

- * Oran ... 320
- ** Cormorant Buttress West ... 321
- * Face ... 405
- ** Second Corner ... 409
- ** First Corner ... 408
- * Intersection ... 399
- * The Gangway ... 406
- Top 50 Avernus ... 410

VDiff

- * Double Chockstone ... 408
- * Grottle ... 365
- ** Felix ... 346
- * Chockney ... 366
- * The Chimney ... 366

Diff

- ** Helix ... 345
- ** Pulpit Route ... 367
- * High Street ... 407

Portland Destination Planner

Area	Destination	Routes	up to 4+	5 to 6a+	6b to 7a	7a+ and up
Blacknor Cliffs	Blacknor North	64	3	19	28	14
	Blacknor Central	74	1	10	39	24
	Blacknor South	53	8	11	29	5
	Blacknor Beach	28	22	4	2	-
	Blacknor Far South	55	2	6	26	21
Battleship	Battleship Edge	64	2	13	33	16
	Battleship Back Cliff	78	11	20	31	16
Wallsend	Wallsend North	126	8	21	53	44
	Wallsend South	115	1	4	56	54
Coastguard to the Bill	Coastguard Cliff	107	-	8	34	65
	White Hole	40	1	7	15	17
East Coast	Lighthouse Cliffs	65	5	10	23	27
	Cheyne Weares Area	224	37	81	78	28
	The Cuttings Area	134	28	37	38	31

Approach	Sun	Tides	Abseil	Multi-pitch	Restrictions	Summary	Page
12 to 15 min	Afternoon					One of the best and most popular areas with some spectacular flowstone formations. Long routes, a good grade spread and easy access make this a must-visit sector.	62
12 to 20 min	Sun and shade					Good long routes and the first spot to get the morning sun on the west coast. It can be dusty at times, although the well-travelled lines are all clean.	74
8 to 12 min	Afternoon					An extensive area with some of the longest mid-grade routes on Portland. There is also a good set of easier climbs. It is close to the descent path and on the path to other sections of Blacknor.	88
15 to 20 min	From mid morning					Located down by the sea are a number of huge boulders that are home to some fine lower-grade sport climbs. The rock and setting are superb. The descent needs care.	96
10 min	Afternoon					A superb set of face climbs on fine rock. A great place for technical routes in the 6s and 7s. The crux sections are usually short and intense. Easy and quick access.	102
10 min	Afternoon					An appealing wall with excellent rock and many routes. Most of the routes are technical and fingery. The base of the crag is a very pleasant spot. A fine quick-tick crag with easy access.	114
10 to 14 min	Afternoon					In contrast to its neighbour, the Back Cliff has some long stamina pitches in the mid-to-high grades. Nearby are some small venues with lots of popular easier lines.	122
10 to 20 min	Afternoon					A series of fine walls perched above vegetated slopes that gradually trail down to the boulder beach. Lots of routes to go at in the mid-to-hard grades. The approaches can be tough going.	136
15 to 20 min	Afternoon	Tidal				The best of the Wallsend cliffs, including one of the finest walls on Portland. Long and pumpy routes in the mid-to-high grades. A longish approach walk and slightly tidal access.	150
12 to 20 min	Afternoon	Tidal				The north section of the cliff has magnificent harder lines, whilst to the south the walls are plastered with lots of mid-grade classics. The southern end is tidal.	168
5 min	Sun and shade	Tidal	Abseil in			Shorter routes and deep water solos near Portland Bill. Easy to reach, though abseil approaches are needed for most routes.	178
5 to 15 min	Morning	Tidal	Abseil in			An atmospheric series of caves and walls. Huge roof-climbs plus some good deep water solos both hard and easy. Condition dependant and requires the highest of tides for the DWSs.	186
2 to 15 min	Sun and shade	Tidal	Abseil in			A collection of cliffs with great variety. The best has hard and steep sport routes, but the others have popular low-to-mid grade lines. Sheltered and gets the sun from first thing.	196
5 to 13 min	Sun and shade					Compact rock and some fine tough and technical climbs on one of Portland's most popular cliffs. Many easier sport routes and it is the best place for morning sun or shelter from the wind.	226

Faded symbol means that only some of the routes - are tidal / require and abseil / are multi-pitch / are restricted

Destination Planner

		Routes	up to S up to 4+	HS to HVS 5 to 6a+	E1 to E3 6b to 7a	E4 upwards 7a+ upwards
Lulworth	Durdle Door to Church Rock	20	-	5	9	6
Lulworth	Stair Hole	49	-	4	9	36
Lulworth	Lulworth East	35	1	11	10	13
Swanage	Winspit Quarries	79	4	26	31	18
Swanage	Hedbury and Smokey Hole	41	6	5	14	16
Swanage	Dancing Ledge	86	-	13	40	33
Swanage	Guillemot and Cormorant Ledge	46	2	14	16	14
Swanage	Blackers Hole	46	-	5	9	32
Swanage	Fisherman's Ledge	95	3	6	43	43
Swanage	The Promenade	106	1	10	36	59
Swanage	Cattle Troughs	36	8	13	10	5
Swanage	Boulder Ruckle	123	2	32	51	38
Swanage	Subluminal	83	16	35	22	10

Approach	Sun	Tides	Abseil	Multi-pitch	Restrictions	Summary	Page
10 min	Sun and shade		Abseil in		Restrictions	A collection of sport climbs on a number of very spectacular rock formations. Church Rock has a good line-up of mid-grade sport routes. Climbing is banned on these cliffs.	250
5 min	Lots of sun	Tidal			Restrictions	Two super-steep sea caves with a large collection of hard sport pitches and deep water solos. There are also a few easier DWSs. Climbing is banned on these cliffs.	252
15 min	Lots of sun	Tidal	Abseil in		Restrictions	A long cliff, topped-off with a large roof along most of its length. The harder lines are sport routes whilst a good number of mid-grade lines are also available. Climbing is banned on these cliffs.	258
20 min	Sun and shade				Restrictions	A collection of quarried walls and bays with many fine technical and strenuous sport routes. More sheltered from the wind than other Swanage crags with easy access and a level base.	274
30 min	Sun and shade	Tidal	Abseil in	Multi-pitch		Hedbury Quarry is a long sheltered quarried wall, with a collection of good sport lines. Hedbury Big Cove and Smokey Hole are a pair of big adventurous sea cliffs located just around the corner.	286
25 min	Sun and shade		Abseil in			One of the most popular sections of cliff at Swanage. A sport climbing quarry and some steeper routes on the sea-level roofs. Non-tidal, and it has its own swimming pool cut into the rock.	296
25 min	Lots of sun	Tidal	Abseil in	Multi-pitch		Three huge walls with several of the longest routes at Swanage. The top-outs are more-reasonable than many of the other Swanage cliffs. Abseil approaches.	310
45 min	Sun and shade	Tidal		Multi-pitch		A varied area with a huge and spectacular cave, home to the most impressive and toughest routes in Dorset. There is also a sport quarry and trad wall with some good hard routes. Mostly non-tidal.	324
40 min	Lots of sun		Abseil in			A varied area with superb deep water soloing and a magnificent cave with some hard, bolted roof-climbs. Easy access.	336
30 min	Lots of sun		Abseil in			The best sport climbing crag at Swanage with routes mostly in the higher grades. An easy abseil approach and access via a non-tidal ledge.	352
25 min	Lots of sun		Abseil in			Four contrasting trad sections of sea cliff with Cattle Troughs itself being a great beginners' area. Most routes start from a non-tidal ledges. Abseil approach.	362
10 to 20 min	Lots of sun	Tidal	Abseil in	Multi-pitch		The most extensive section of Swanage has classic trad routes across the grades. It is a big and committing area with free-hanging abseil approaches and loose top-outs being the norm.	372
10 min	Lots of sun		Abseil in			A great cliff for a first taste of Swanage. Short routes above a large ledge - mostly at very reasonable grades. Quick access from the car park. Also includes the more serious Black Zawn.	402

Faded symbol means that only some of the routes - are tidal / require and abseil / are multi-pitch / are restricted

Portland

John Warner on *Escape from the Dwaarfee Room* (6a) - page 106 - one of many fine grade 6 routes at Blacknor Far South on Portland's west coast.

Jutting out into the English Channel, the Isle of Portland is one of the United Kingdom's most recognisable coastal features, its only link to the mainland being via the narrow pebble-strip of Chesil Beach. Portland is part of the Jurassic Coast World Heritage Coastline, however, in the climbing world, Portland's famous white cliffs are better known as Britain's biggest and best sport climbing destination.

Circling the Isle's lofty fringes are around six kilometres of virtually unbroken limestone cliffs, a good proportion of which has been developed with hundreds of well-bolted sport routes throughout the grades. Early exploration focussed on traditionally protected routes, but Portland's true appeal came about with the development of its sport climbing potential. This evolution has been dramatic in the last 25 years or so and continues to this day with new routes still being put up on a regular basis. Deep water soloing and bouldering have also been very much part of this evolution, and have grown in popularity to the point where they have now been moved out of this guidebook and into other publications, although a good number of the more established DWSs are included.

Portland itself is a place of rich history riddled with folklore about smugglers, quarrymen and shipwrecks. These legacies are now reflected in its unique population and oddly-constructed terraces of stone cottages. Modern times have seen the closure of the local naval base coincide with the development of a tourist industry based around sport diving, wind surfing, kite surfing and sailing. The last Rockfax guide to Dorset was published six years ago, and in the intervening period the port has changed radically with the addition of vast facilities to cater for the Olympic sailing competition. Portland's expansive land-scape also provides an important habitat for a wide variety of plants and animals, some of which are nationally or even globally scarce. As a result, the coastline is designated a Site of Special Scientific Interest (SSSI) and is a European Special Area of Conservation (SAC) as well as also having its own dedicated warden. Often such designations bring with them problems for climbers, but thankfully this area is not burdened by excessive access problems and there are only a few small issues to be aware of.

The climate on Portland is mild and there is the possibility for year-round outdoor climbing. None of the cliffs suffer greatly from seepage, and they all get lots of sunshine during the winter months. Either sun or shade can almost always be found, and, unlike most sea cliffs, tides are not such a big concern here with only a few sections being affected.

The majority of the routes are well bolted with long-life staples throughout, so it is normally possible for climbers to push their grade to the limit without too much in the way of fear. Whether you are a dedicated local, beginner, old hand, winter-sunseeker or holidaying family climber, Portland has something for all.

Portland Bill

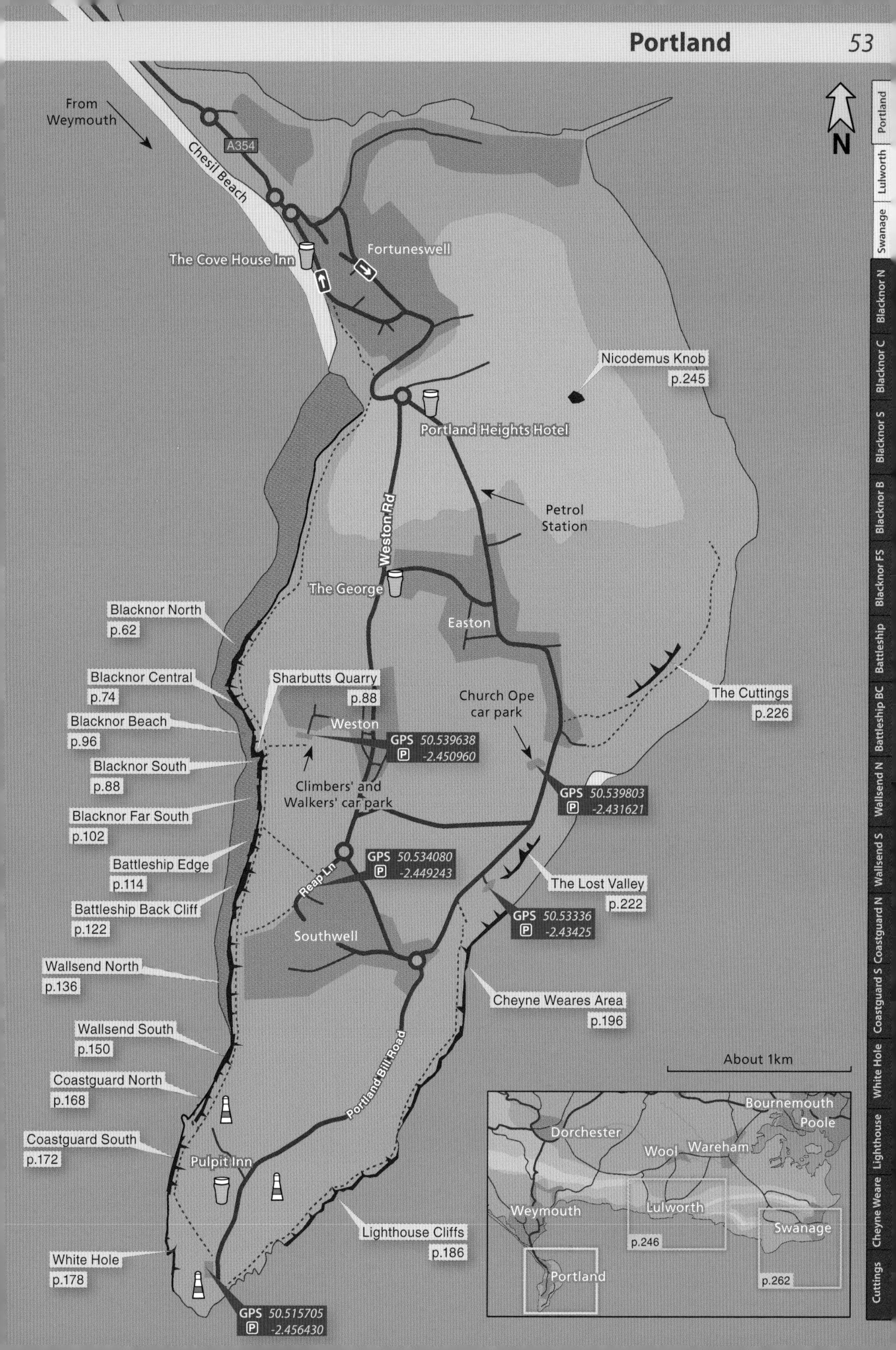
From Weymouth
A354
Chesil Beach
The Cove House Inn
Fortuneswell
Nicodemus Knob
p.245
Portland Heights Hotel
Weston Rd
Petrol Station
The George
Easton
Blacknor North
p.62
Blacknor Central
p.74
Sharbutts Quarry
p.88
Weston
Church Ope car park
The Cuttings
p.226
Blacknor Beach
p.96
GPS 50.539638 -2.450960
Blacknor South
p.88
Climbers' and Walkers' car park
GPS 50.539803 -2.431621
Blacknor Far South
p.102
Battleship Edge
p.114
Reap Ln
GPS 50.534080 -2.449243
The Lost Valley
p.222
Battleship Back Cliff
p.122
GPS 50.53336 -2.43425
Southwell
Wallsend North
p.136
Cheyne Weares Area
p.196
Wallsend South
p.150
Portland Bill Road
About 1km
Coastguard North
p.168
Coastguard South
p.172
Pulpit Inn
Lighthouse Cliffs
p.186
White Hole
p.178
GPS 50.515705 -2.456430
Bournemouth
Poole
Dorchester
Wool
Wareham
Weymouth
Lulworth
p.246
Swanage
p.262
Portland
N

Helen Heanes enjoying the fruits of her labour on an evening ascent of her now well established route *Ocean Drive* (6b) - page 103 - at Blacknor Far South on Portland.

Pre 1967 - Portland is ravaged by inland quarrying and the coastal crags were left to the peregrines and seagulls. A small band of locals establishes many of the easier routes at The Cuttings.

1967 - Reverend Bob Shepton records the first routes of real significance such as *Vesuvius*. Many loose cracks are ascended around the coast, often involving horrendous top-outs. The first E1s and E2s are recorded by Shepton accompanied by Ian Kestin.

1972 - Murray Hodgson adds many routes to Blacknor South.

1977 to 1981 - Shepton's reign continues, sometimes in the company of George Hounsome. This pair add several strenuous E2s. In 1980 Dave Jones climbs *Kate* (E4) and a year later Pat Littlejohn climbs *Bad Dream* (E4) at The Cuttings.

1983 - Pete Oxley puts up his first new line - *Two Fingers* at The Cuttings.

The Minimalist Drilled-Peg Era

The clean white walls of Portland were first climbed using limited numbers of stainless steel pegs drilled into the rock, however most of the routes still required a very bold approach on mainly trad gear. Portland's early reputation was as a place to be wary of and nobody visited to repeat the routes.

1988 - Oxley puts up the first hard routes *Superfly Guy* (7a) and *Nothing, but the Groove* (6c+) at Coastguard North, both with the odd drilled peg runner. *Colors*, the first E6 6b is climbed in Wallsend Cove. 7c arrives in the shape of *Keyboard Wall* at Battleship Edge which sees many new routes.

1989 - Martin Crocker opens up Blacknor Far South and Nigel Coe adds some easier lines. Oxley adds *Realm of Chaos* (7b+) and Crocker *Zum Zeaux* (7b+) to the Wallsend Area. *Cocteau Phenomena* (7b) at Blacknor South by Oxley is the first pure sport-climb on drilled pegs throughout. Late in the year On The Edge magazine profiled 'the new Pen Trwyn', as Portland was dubbed.

1990 - The Cuttings gets developed with some hard test-pieces from Oxley and Crocker. Battleship Back Cliff is opened up by Oxley with the likes of *Zinc Oxide Mountain* (7b+). Crocker puts up the second full sport-route with *Wax Museum* (7b+).

1991 - Coastguard South receives attention from Oxley with some classics such as *Quick as Rainbows* (7b).

The Modern Staple Bolt Era

Despite the wealth of new routes, Portland continued to be an unpopular backwater, considered as having only bold, hard climbs on suspect rock. The decision was made by Oxley to fully bolt all his subsequent new routes. To do this required a cheap and long-lasting bolt system. Oxley introduced the first home-made U-staples into Britain which were based on a system seen in Spain.

Retro-bolting: Many of today's classic clip-ups used to be gnarly trad routes. As the number of fully-bolted new routes increased it seemed logical, albeit controversial, to start retro-bolting the older, neglected lines. Initially this was done on the routes that had drilled pegs, and has since spread to virtually all the lines. The general rule was to only retro-bolt with the first ascensionist's permission. Pete Oxley led the way with the retro-bolting over the next few years, and set up the Dorset bolt fund. Thanks are due to all who have contributed in any way.

1992 - Oxley opens up Blacknor North with popular classics such as *Reptile Smile* (6a+) and *England's Dreaming* (7a+). Word spreads and other locals join in such as the Cook brothers and Steve Taylor. 8a arrives in November with *Freaky Ralph* (now 8a+), by Oxley - after 5 days of effort.

1994 - Bay of Rainbows is opened up by Steve Taylor. Damian Cook lands his best route in the shape of *Hong Kong Phooey* (7c). Mike Robertson, with support from Oxley and Taylor, develops the atmospheric White Hole. Cheyne Cliff is opened by Oxley with classics such as *Road Rage* (7b+). Just before the 1994 ROCKFAX goes to press Oxley climbs *Vespasian* (8a+ - now 8b) the hardest route to date.

Bruce Walker on a typically technical and sustained Cuttings grade 6 *Old Buffer* (6b) - *page 240* - on Portland's sheltered east coast.

1995 - Neal and Helen Heanes become regular new-routers at the Blacknor crags, and eventually open Rockies Climbing Shack (now closed). Oxley turns his attention to the east coast with some super-steep routes in Cave Hole such as *King of the Swingers* (7c+).

1996 - Londoner Nic Hellyer begins his campaign on the Blacknor crags. More hard routes in the 7c/8a range are added by Oxley. Sector Pom Pom is given the treatment by Oxley and Luc Percival, with his superb *Big Blue* (7c+). *Illusions* (7c) at Cheyne Cliff gives Jon Cook his finest new climb.

1997 - Mike Vaicaitis (with members of the Basingstoke M.C.) put up some easier climbs at Godnor Far North. Heanes, Hellyer and Oxley all very active and Guy Dixon creates a test-piece with his *Detonator* (7c) at Cheyne. Chris Cubitt makes the first repeat of an 8a - *Breathing Method*.

1998 - Wallsend North has many easier lines added by Neal and Helen Heanes whilst Coastguard North and South are plundered of many last remaining hard classics by Oxley. Andy Long bags the best line left with his brilliant *Tennessee* (7c) at Coastguard South. James Dunlop, Jim Kimber and Oxley develop White Hole North.

1999 - Gav Symonds helps clean up some projects with *Clockwork Orange* (7c) at Coastguard North. Neal Heanes gets his *Wasted* (7b+) at Coastguard North and Oxley completes *Balance of Power* (8a) at White Hole. Late in the year a bouldering wave, centred on The New Cuttings, Sector Pom Pom and the Lost Valley, takes place with two V10s from Oxley and Jimbo Kimber.

2000 - Dave Pickford makes an impressive flash ascent of *Zen Zero* (7c+) and repeats many of the harder lines. Dorset Rockfax, 2000 edition published. Steve McClure flashes *The Breathing Method* (8a) at The Cuttings.

2001 - The arrival of the Gary Gibson new-route machine sees a rapid cleaning up of outstanding lines all down the West Coast, particularly at Coastguard South. The Cuttings Boulderfield is developed by Ben Stokes, Tim Crawshaw and friends with over 50 problems added up to V6. Martin Crocker returned climbing many serious shallow-water solos at Beeston culminating with *Extreme Lives*, the Isle's first E7. Elsewhere Andy Long bagged a major classic prow aptly calling it *Beautiful South* (7c) (now 7c+) at Wallsend.

2003 - A busy year with the prolific Gibson discovering many decent pitches and the odd classic. Gavin Symonds completes the late Damian Cook's project naming it in his memory *To Hungary for Love* (8a) in Wallsend North. Other locals, Mick Ward and Neal Heanes, plug away with *Vin Chaud* and *Sang Chaud* standing out at 7a+. Liam Halsey makes the second ascent (in a day) of *Vespasian* (8b) where many had failed before.

2004 - Yet more Gibson activity, especially at Battleship and Blacknor. Mick Ward fills in a few other gaps and Taylor and Mark Williams develop Beeston South.

2005 - Rockfax Dorset, 2005 edition published.

2005/06 - Gibson continues to visit and mops up some gaps as soon as the latest Rockfax guidebook is published with *Sanfte Kuss* (7a+), *I Walk the Line* (7b) and *Crocadilia* (6a) being among the best. Symonds heads down to Wallsend again and climbs the long line of *Cloud Atlas* (7b+).

2007/08 - Taylor points the way to future new development with his lines *Euphemism* (6b) and *The Good Life* (5+) at Godnor South and North. Tom Beaumont starts his new routing push at Sharbutts Quarry and Dungecroft Quarry. John Leonard and Ward open up more lines at The Bower only metres from The Cuttings main cliff and at the isolated Nickodemus Knob. Gavin Symonds boldly solos *Balance of Power* (8a) at White Hole over some not so deep water.

2009 - Brian Wilkinson shows that good easier lines lurk amongst the tough stuff with *Cruise Control* (6a+) at Cheyne Cliff. Ward tidies up his last long lines on the Enchanted Path Area of Wallsend.

2010 - Andy Lamont and Bob Hickish establish two of the harder lines on the Isle since the last Rockfax with *Amber Vibe* (7c+) and *Under Duress* (7c+) respectively. Andy Dunford and Adam Perrett discover the instantly popular Veranda only a quick stroll from The Back Cliff. Perrett, Ward and Leonard uncover more of The Lost Valley, The Nook and fully develop Dungecroft Quarry.

2011 - Perrett and co add some short lines at The Attic and The Balcony whilst Ward and Leonard find Sunlovers Slab and The Rampart.

February 2012 - The new Rockfax is published.

The Blacknor Cliffs

The strange flowstone and conglomerate of Blacknor North is made for climbing on. The two classics of *Reptile Smile* (6a+) and *Slings Shot* (5) - *page 70* - get the attention they deserve.

	No star	1 star	2 stars	3 stars
up to 4+	10	21	3	2
5+ to 6a+	16	18	13	3
6b to 7a	22	62	33	7
7a+ and up	6	26	30	2

The first climbable sections of cliff-line that stretch virtually unbroken along the full length of the west coast of Portland are the Blacknor Cliffs. These are also some of the most impressive and intensively developed cliffs on the Isle, with routes of all grades and, for the most part, on vertical rock. The style of climbing is typically fingery and technical, sometimes on flowstone, and at others on crimpy faces of fossil fragments. All of the routes are easily accessed along the cliff-base paths, and the area should be high on every visitor's hit list.

Blacknor North is justifiably one of the most popular areas on Portland, with fine lines in abundance that ascend some of the most amazing flowstone formations to be found anywhere in the UK. Blacknor Central continues to be the scene of a good deal of new routing. Blacknor South has some magnificent wall pitches on delicate flowstone, plus a number of well frequented lower-grade routes. Below Blacknor South and Central are four popular slabby areas, with a much-travelled set of easier climbs in a fabulous seashore location. The Far South area has received a complete overhaul, and is now one of the best sections of Portland for mid-grade routes.

Conditions

Blacknor Central, and some of Blacknor South, face south-west and are good late-morning sun venues. The other cliffs are all west facing, and get plenty of afternoon sun, with Blacknor North staying in the shade the latest. There is little seepage, apart from a few drainage streaks on the Niagara Wall section of the Go With The Flow Area, by *The Oldest Profession* on the Medusa Falls Area (also Blacknor South) and on the central section of Blacknor Far South - all are usually dry in the summer. The Blacknor cliffs are fairly exposed to the wind, but can offer shelter if the wind is blowing straight onto, or over, the cliff-line.

Access

The main access problems here are to do with parking. Please follow the parking instructions described below, this will avoid the problems that have been created in the past by climbers parking randomly in the Weston Estate. **Only one short section of the Blacknor Cliffs has a restriction due to nesting birds; no climbing from March 1st to July 31st.**

The area to the north of Blacknor Far North is a sanctuary zone so please keep out.

Approaching the upper section of the exposed wall climbing on *Cocteau Phenomena* (7b+) - *page 83* - at Blacknor Central.

Approach Also see map on page 53

All the Blacknor cliffs are approached from the designated Climbers' and Walkers' car park (fee) at the far south west corner of the housing estate in Weston. **Do not park anywhere else in the housing estate**. If the car park is full, please park on the main street in Weston, and walk through the estate to the car park. It is also possible to park in Reap Lane.

The four main approaches to the crags are described below. Individual area details are included with the route pages.

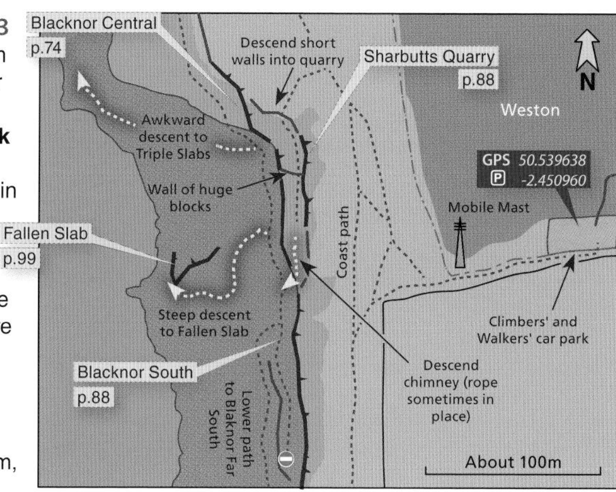

Blacknor North Approach

Walk towards the cliff-top path, and turn right (looking out). Continue for about 500m, past an old concrete-wall on the cliff edge, before the path drops down slightly into a quarried area. Locate a small path that drops steeply at a break in the cliff-line, and doubles back leftwards (facing out) down the hill. This leads down to the first routes on the Death of Cool Area.

Blacknor Central, South and Quarry Approach

From the car park, walk to the cliff-top path and walk right for 80m. Scramble down into a quarry, walk through a large block wall and then down a narrow gully at the far end of the quarry (rope sometimes in place). This gully emerges below the Medusa Falls Area on Blacknor South. Blacknor Central is accessed by a small track that contours underneath the crags eventually joining up with the path beneath Blacknor North.

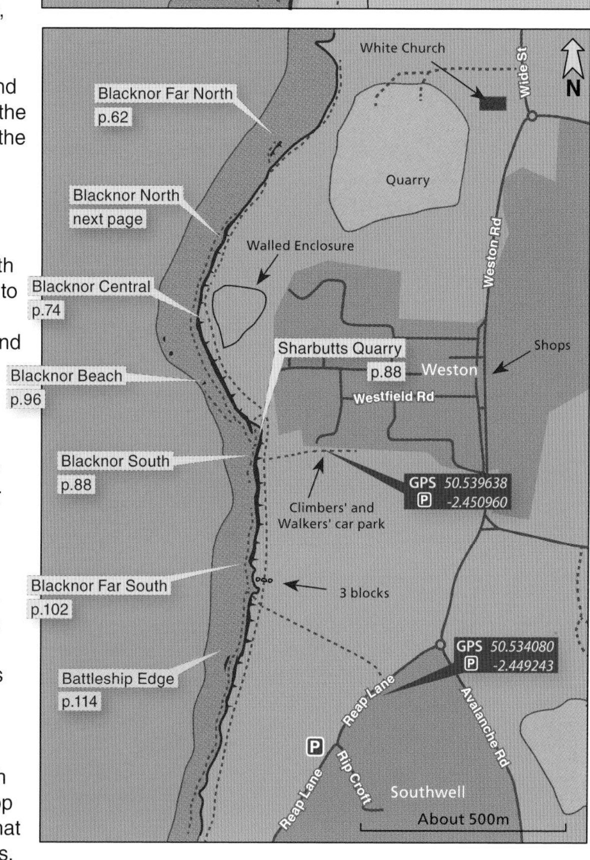

Blacknor Beach Approach

From the car park, follow the approach to the base of Blacknor South/Central. From here various steep paths descend to the cliffs at sea level. See the individual areas for the location of each descent path.

Blacknor Far South Approach

From the car park walk to the cliff-top path and turn left (looking out) along the cliff-top path. Continue for 400m to three blocks that lie across the path. Just beyond the blocks, descend steeply down a rough path and walk back right to below the crag. Blacknor Far South can be easily approached from the parking in Reap Lane.

Portland
Lulworth
Swanage
Blacknor N
Blacknor C
Blacknor S
Blacknor B
Blacknor FS
Battleship
Battleship BC
Wallsend N
Wallsend S
Coastguard N
Coastguard S
White Hole
Lighthouse
Cheyne Weare
Cuttings

Far North

A small, isolated block north of the main Blacknor cliffs. **Approach (see page 61) -** From the cliff top above the main descent to Blacknor North. Walk 40m further along the cliff top footpath until just before a quarry track on the right, a tiny path drops steeply down to the block.

The cliffs further north of this point are within a sanctuary zone so please keep away.

1 Reinheitsgebot 4

The line on the far left-hand side of the buttress. This pitch has cleaned up slightly, although some loose rock remains.

FA. Helen Heanes 7.5.1995

2 Another One for the Pot . . . 6a+

A pocketed sheet in the middle of the face. Avoid a large detached block near the top of the pitch.

FA. Neal Heanes 7.5.1995

The wide crack is the trad line of **Enlightenment, HVS 5b**.

Afternoon 15 min

11m

3 Slim Fingers' Revenge . 1 7a

A pleasant pitch in a quiet setting. Finish with hands on top.

FA. Neal Heanes 27.5.1995

4 Boiled Lobster 1 6b

The wall and groove on the right-hand end of the wall. Make sure you climb past the belay for the full tick.

FA. Neal Heanes 7.5.1995

Opposite the path that drops down to Blacknor North is a quarry entrance. At the back of the quarry is a bolted arete that gives two lines that may prove useful if the routes on the main cliff are wind blown, as the quarry is sheltered. Not shown on any topo.

5 Mystery Stripper . . . . 5+

Climb the arete on the left-hand side without barn-dooring.

FA. Mick Ward 3.7.2010

6 Ghost Writer . . . . 5+

Climb the arete on the right-hand side without barn-dooring.

FA. Mick Ward 6.6.2010

7 Absolute Beginners 2

The first bolted line on the approach to Blacknor North. Climb the arete of the gully with a square capstone wedged at the top. Not shown on any topo.

FA. Mick Ward 2002.

8 No Name Corner . . . . 3+

The bolted line to the right of *Absolute Beginners*. Not shown on any topo.

FA. Unknown

17m

Death of Cool Area

The first walls feature a number of large blocky roofs and some excellent long pitches on good rock. This area is often less busy than the sections further to the right.

Approach (see page 61) - The first climbs are reached after walking 150m along the path from the base of the approach descent.

9 Chin Reaction 6c
The loose wall and rib to an exposed finish over the roof.
FA. Gary Gibson 10.2005

The wide twisting crack is **San Andreas, E1 5b**.

10 Meltdown . . . . ☆2 7a
Good climbing with a fine bulge and upper crack. Don't walk by this one, it is well worth doing.
FA. Neal Heanes 2.7.1995

11 Quakin' in My Bones ☆1 7a+
Worth a look with rock as good as anything else on Portland. The upper groove is height dependant, however this does not detract from the quality of the climbing.
FA. Pete Oxley 4.10.1992

12 Sellerfield. . . . . ☆1 7b
A good pitch with a long reach to gain the upper break.
FA. Gary Gibson 10.2005

13 The Taylor Show . . . . 6a+
The crack and groove right of *Sellerfield*. An initially dirty section gives way to excellent climbing up the flowstone groove.
FA. Steve Taylor 9.6.2007

The chimney to the right is **Speleo Joy Toy, VS 4b**.

14 Living the Dream . . . . 6b+
Some nice positions.
FA. Mick Ward c.2008

Restriction (routes 15 and 16) - *No climbing from 1st March to 30th June due to nesting birds.*

15 Death of Cool . . . . ☆1 7a+
Good climbing with an entertaining crux move. No lower-off in place, reverse and lower from the last bolt.
FA. Pete Oxley 20.9.1992

16 Drag Racing Underground
. . . . ☆2 6c+
A fine pitch that passes a cave entrance at mid height. A tough finishing move and a holdless flowstone groove are the main problems to be encountered.
FA. Pete Oxley 28.4.1993

The corner to the right is the trad route **Poppadom, E1 5a**.

Seattle Be the Day - p.64

Portland
Lulworth
Swanage
Blacknor N
Blacknor C
Blacknor S
Blacknor B
Blacknor FS
Battleship
Battleship BC
Wallsend N
Wallsend S
Coastguard N
Coastguard S
White Hole
Lighthouse
Cheyne Weare
Cuttings

Seattle Be the Day Area

The first walls have some large blocky roofs and a number of excellent, long routes on good rock. This area is often less busy than the sections further to the right.

Approach (see page 61) - The first climb is reached after walking 200m along the path from the base of the cliff on the approach.

Restriction (Routes 1 to 5) - No climbing 1st March to 30th June due to nesting birds.

1 Seattle Be the Day . . . . 1 star 6b+
Some fine flowstone is the reward following on from a hard start.
FA. Pete Oxley 4.9.1992

2 The Fabulous Bakery Boys . . . . 1 star 6c
A fine face of perfect flowstone. The crux is a bit bold.
FA. Paul Twomey 9.7.1995

3 Captain Lob Meets the Nipple Pincher . . . . 2 star 6b
A pleasant, open groove. Super-technical and imaginative moves on the crux. High in the grade, and a touch run-out.
FA. Neal Heanes 9.7.1995

4 Grease Paint and Monkey Brains . . . . 1 star 6a
A long arete, well endowed with some good jugs leads to a ledge with two technical options above. The best is to use the flake on the right.
FA. Neil Burton 14.10.1996

5 Indian Summer . . . . . . 1 star 6a
A very nice climb. The long flake and groove with a juggy finish over a roof to a lower-off 3m above.
FA. Helen Heanes 9.1996

Afternoon 12 min

The corner and crack is the line of the trad route **The Curler, VS**.

6 Blowing Chunks 6c
A slabby wall, thin crack and a roof. It involves some good climbing, but is unfortunately a touch dusty.
FA. Neal Heanes 1997

7 Where's Blue Hippo 1 7a+
The thin wall with an entertaining mid-height crux. The rock is a little on the crumbly side.
FA. Neal Heanes 15.8.1996

8 Beer and Corruption . . . 1 7a
An excellent wall-climb and a good route for those looking to break in to the 7th grade.
FA. Pete Oxley 20.9.1992

9 Henry Rollins for President . . . . 7a+
Remember to break left early up the crack.
FA. Pete Oxley 12.9.1992

The chimney line is **Shatter My Illusions, but Don't Break My Heart, VS 4a.**

10 Wynona's Big Brown Beaver . . . 6c
A poor route. Traverse left from the second bolt on *Ximenesque*.
FA. Paul Twomey 19.7.1995

11 Ximenesque . . . . 6b+
A very thuggy roof crack not too dissimilar to its near-namesake away to the east in the Boulder Ruckle at Swanage (page 393).
FA. Joff Cook 5.9.1992

12 In Dust We Trust . . . . . 6c+
Break right out of *Ximenesque* after its second bolt.
FA. Paul Twomey 3.8.1995

20m
Ironhead - p.66
12
10
11

Portland
Lulworth
Swanage
Blacknor N
Blacknor C
Blacknor S
Blacknor B
Blacknor FS
Battleship
Battleship BC
Wallsend N
Wallsend S
Coastguard N
Coastguard S
White Hole
Lighthouse
Cheyne Weare
Cuttings

Portland | Lulworth | Swanage | Blacknor N | Blacknor C | Blacknor S | Blacknor B | Blacknor FS | Battleship | Battleship BC | Wallsend N | Wallsend S | Coastguard N | Coastguard S | White Hole | Lighthouse | Cheyne Weare | Cuttings

Captain Klutz Area

This section of the cliff has some excellent long routes on good rock. The conglomerate at the start of the right-hand lines needs to be handled with care, although it has now cleaned up considerably. This area is often less busy than the sections further to the right.

Approach (see page 61) - The climbs are on a steep wall just around a prominent arete reached after walking 250m along the cliff base path.

1 Ironhead ...... 2 stars, 7a+

The tall arete is photogenic and very good, if rather unbalanced. The last few moves make up the reach-dependent crux.

FA. Pete Oxley 4.9.1992

2 Meg's Got Leukaemia .. 2 stars, 6a

Great jug hauling to a fingery finish.

FA. Simon Vaughan 10.1992

3 Cinema Paradiso ..... 1 star, 6a

Begin just to the right of *Meg's Got Leukaemia*. A very enjoyable companion route, although the start is a little dirty.

FA. Mick Ward 2002

4 Skin Flick 7a

The bolt line directly to the right of *Cinema Paradiso*. Care needed with a loose block and dusty band at the start, continue to challenging climbing above.

FA. N.Gault 8.2010

A wandering trad pitch - **Hangman's Loose, HVS** *- tackles the wall rightwards to finish up the flake-crack just to the right of the next line.*

5 Captain Klutz and the Sailors of Fortune

.... 1 star, 6a

An incredible conglomerate formation at the start gains more conventional rock and climbing on the upper wall. Take care at the start, as the rock is less than perfect.

FA. Steve Taylor 20.3.1993

6 Major Mushrooms and that Mentally Muffled Mentality

.... 1 star, 6c

The conglomerate wall right of *Captain Klutz* to a ledge. Difficult moves up a groove lead onto a wall via a slim overlap.

FA. Gary Gibson 9.5.2002

7 Unknown 6a

Climb the loose, dirty slab to a high first bolt. Step left and climb a corner until a traverse right reaches the first lower-off. There is a higher lower-off but the moves to reach it are hard, loose and dirty.

FA. Unknown

Afternoon | 15 min

22m

Unused lower-off

1 2 3 4 5 6 7

Kimberley Waldron tackling the final steepening on the Portland flowstone classic *Slings Shot* (5) - *page 70* - at Blacknor North.

Wolfgang Forever Area

A long and sparsely featured wall that has a good selection of wall pitches in the 7s. The rock itself on the hard upper regions of the climbs is excellent, although the lower sections of the wall can be slightly dusty.
Approach (see page 61) - Continue along the cliff base from the approach descent. The cliff can be easily identified by the small stone shelter at its base.

1 Is Vic There? 2 **7a**
A particularly good wall climb that, if caught in prime condition, warrants an extra star. Thin moves to a jug at the break are immediately followed by a stretchy move to get established on a stuck-on block. Some great flowstone finishes the pitch.
FA. Steve Taylor 3.10.1992

2 Sanfte Kuss . . . . . . 1 **7a+**
A useful addition to the wall that delivers some worthwhile and difficult climbing, although the top section is a little crumbly.
FA. Gary Gibson 10.2005

3 Wolfgang Forever . 2 **7a**
A good and popular climb. A sustained pitch that contains an array of perplexing sequences split by good shakeouts.
Photo on page 35.
FA. Pete Oxley 4.10.1992

4 Popeye Doyle 2 **7c**
Climb the lower wall to the centre of the roof. Pull powerfully through and finish steeply leftwards on pockets and edges.
FA. Andy Long 3.2007

5 French Connection UK . 2 **7b+**
Climb the lower wall and first bulge as for *Popeye Doyle*, then finish on the right of the steepest section of the upper bulge.
FA. Yann Genoux 17.3.2007

6 Appleturnoverload . . . 7a+
An exciting pitch that is steady at the grade. Follow the gently leaning lower wall to a small ledge below the steep upper section. Pull through a bulge and up the wall with difficulty to a flowstone shelf and the top just above.
FA. Joff Cook 11.10.1992

7 Very Sleepy River 6b
Superb flowstone formations on the fingery and technical upper wall. Climb the fist-sized, overhanging crack to a point where the enticing drape of flowstone on the right can be accessed. Climb slightly rightwards up the tricky flowstone whose difficulty gradually eases.
FA. Damian Cook 12.9.1992

8 Edge Hog . . . . 7a+
A loose start and a contrived crux section have failed to promote this line to classic status.
FA. Steve Taylor 28.8.1993

The wide crack up which Edge Hog starts is the trad line of **Klepto Krack, HVS 4c**.

9 Toes Curl . . . . 6c+
Great technical face moves, but the contrived start spoils the overall feel of the route. Don't touch the chimney, it is off limits.
FA. Will Jones 1996

10 Freaky Ralph . . . 8a+
A test-piece of the area with a long reach to a pocket at half-height being the crux. The long reach can be climbed by a short person's sequence. *Photo on page 33.*
FA. Pete Oxley 3.10.1992

11 Aim High, Shoot Low . . . . . 6a+
Not as dirty as it once was, but the line is prone to dust being washed down from above. A tricky rightward finish to the lower-off of *Downtown Julie Brown* - is 6c+.
FA. Nic Hellyer 4.4.1997

Reptile Smile Area

A wall of absolutely stunning flowstone and one of Portland's finest sections of crag. The flowstone provides holds of all shapes and sizes, but can prove slick if damp. **Approach (see page 61) -** This is the section just before the Blacknor Pinnacle and has a well used gearing-up spot below it which is right under the popular climbs. Care should be taken not to sit directly beneath climbers in case of rockfall.

1 Downtown Julie Brown . . . . Top 50 **6c**
A fingery climb, and the first of the superb flowstone pitches on this section of the crag. Start by climbing the wall just right of the bolts to good holds. Ascend the increasingly-technical wall via a thin move and small undercut to an easier finish on the left.
FA. Pete Oxley 12.9.1992

2 Reptile Smile . . . . Top 50 **6a+**
A well-established and testing classic that features climbing on an amazing set of flowstone organ pipes. Move up easily rightwards, and pass a thread (sometimes missing) to the first bolt. Climb the flowstone pipes which gradually ease off after some difficult pulls low down. *Photo on page 59.*
FA. Pete Oxley 12.9.1992

3 Talking Smack . . . . 1 **5+**
Although only a linking section of climbing it provides a surprisingly good and quite long section of independent moves. From the second bolt on *Reptile Smile*, climb up and right to join *Slings Shot*.
FA. Will Jones 5.1996

4 Slings Shot . . . . Top 50 **5**
An extremely popular classic that follows the beautiful central section of flowstone on very good holds. Climb up to a huge flake of flowstone, and make the crux moves to get established above, where easier climbing leads to the lower-off.
Photo on pages 67 and 59.
FA. J.Tookey 1975. FFA. Nigel Coe 24.9.88. The line was bolted by Pete Oxley 11.5.94 and claimed as The Scales of Balance.

5 Crocadilia 1 **6a**
Climb the wall just right of *Slings Shot* to below a bulge. Follow the line right to a narrow shelf of flowstone and finish up the short wall above it.
FA. Gary Gibson 10.2005

6 Spanner Eyes 2 **7b**
Move up and then left to beneath a thin crack. Ascend the crack and move left to more hard moves and a precarious rockover before easier ground is encountered.
FA. Will Jones 8.1996

7 England's Dreaming Top 50 **7a+**
A southern sport climbing classic with stunning moves on magnificent flowstone. Climb the fingery lower wall to a powerful midway stretch for good holds. Swing left and finish steeply up yet more flowstone.
FA. Pete Oxley 4.9.1992

Portland
Lulworth
Swanage
Blacknor N
Blacknor C
Blacknor S
Blacknor B
Blacknor FS
Battleship
Battleship BC
Wallsend N
Wallsend S
Coastguard N
Coastguard S
White Hole
Lighthouse
Cheyne Weare
Cuttings

8 Cake Walk **6a**
A well-travelled and very good route. Climb the lower wall via a wide crack before moving up and left to below a big pillar of flowstone. Climb the pillar and finish leftwards through the final overhangs in a great position.
FA. Steve Taylor 11.10.1992

The wide crack come chimney is the trad line **Dirt Track, VS 4b**.

9 The Tea-Cake Path **6b**
The line to the right of the crack of *Cake Walk* finishes up a short tufa-flecked wall.
FA. Gary Gibson 8.9.2010

10 Californian Hot Licks . . **6a+**
A good line that has unfortunately been affected by rockfall near the top, and the final bolt is not in place. However, the line gets climbed regularly. The thin wall and crack above lead to another short wall prior to the finish up steep ground.
FA. Gordon Jenkin, Andy March, Keith Marsden 26.11.1994

11 Doughnuts and Duvets . **6b**
The technically-awkward direct line up the slabby wall and overhang to finish.
FA. Steve Taylor 10.6.1995

12 Apfelstrudel **6a**
A steady little face-climb that heads right from *Doughnuts and Duvets* and then up the wall to the first roof and break.
FA. A.Jende 13.3.1993

13 Dwarf Lops . . . . **6b+**
The slightly overhanging groove and blunt arete.
FA. Nic Hellyer 5.4.1997

14 Suck, Don't Blow **6c**
Has a frustrating move high up.
FA. Aiden Cook 31.10.1992

15 Mother's Milk **6a**
A top crack climb that is both fun and pumpy. Keep an eye out for the bolt hidden within the crack.
FA. Simon Cook 8.11.1992

16 Do You Like Our Owls? **6b**
A weird conglomerate-crack that is topped off with a committing roof finale.
FA. Nic Hellyer 27.6.1996

17 Hot From the Forge . . . **7a**
Sustained climbing on orange flutings. High in the grade.
FA. Pete Oxley 13.2.1992

18 Onto the Ice Flow. **7a**
Good climbing with a hard, but short-lived crux section. Things are much easier above, with the biggest jug in the world at the lower-off.
FA. Damian Cook 5.9.1992

Blacknor Central

Neal Heanes making the most of some late evening sun on the technical *Hysterical Solitude* (6c) - *page 75* - at Blacknor Central.

Portland
Lulworth
Swanage
Blacknor N
C
Blacknor S
Blacknor B
Blacknor FS
Battleship
Battleship BC
Wallsend N
Wallsend S
Coastguard N
Coastguard S
White Hole
Lighthouse
Cheyne Weare
Cuttings

Hysterical Solitude Area

This is a fine sector with some interesting flowstone that is especially useful as a late morning crag on this side of the Isle. Some of the routes have a tendency to be dusty.
Approach (see page 61) - This wall is just around the corner from Blacknor North. It can be approached from there or from the Blacknor South Quarry Approach.

1 Imbolc . . . . 1 ☐ **7b**
A well-regarded pitch that is both sustained and fingery.
FA. Nick White 7.2.1993

2 The Hong Jagged Flake of Death (Retired) . . . . 1 ☐ **6b+**
A great line, but the rock is fragile in the lower section. Care required with the first couple of clips.
FA. Nic Hellyer 8.2004

3 Distanced . . . . ☐ **6b+**
The long blunt rib will clean up in time.
FA. Gary Gibson 6.9.2010

4 Dudas sin nombres . . . 1 ☐ **6b+**
A pleasant and worthwhile route. The start is a bit indifferent, but the climbing then becomes an absorbing and technical challenge up the fossils to a hardish finish on the headwall.
FA. Nic Hellyer 20.3.1999

The huge and very loose flake-line is the trad route **Dreamer, HVS 5a.**

5 When This Hits the Fan 1 ☐ **6b+**
A very appealing line. Climb the low bulge and sustained arete on slightly friable rock.
FA. Gary Gibson 6.9.2010

6 Shit Happens, Actually . . . . 2 ☐ **6a**
A little gem that is low in the grade and has a cunning finish. The moves flow nicely and the rock is excellent.
Photo on page 89.
FA. Mike Robertson 17.2.1993

7 Unstuck On You (Flowstone Shuffle) . . . . ☐ **7b**
A pumpy eliminate. It is difficult to avoid using holds on *Shit Happens, Actually*.
FA. Joff Cook 1995. FFA. Pete Oxley 25.6.1995

8 21½ Weeks . . . . 1 ☐ **6b+**
Fine climbing, but it has become a bit unbalanced since losing a hold. The crux is now much harder than the rest of the climbing.
FA. Mike Robertson 17.2.1993

9 Birthday Girl . . . . ☐ **5+**
Follow the line of staples on the wall to the left of the chimney to a cave. Move left out of the cave and up to a lower-off.
FA. Meilee Rafe 30.5.2008

10 Divine Comedy 5
Break right onto the wall from *Birthday Girl*. Ascend diagonally rightwards by a series of delicate mantels.
FA. Mick Ward 15.5.2010

The chimney itself is the trad line of **Bag End, HS**.

11 Hysterical Solitude. . . . . . . 1 star 6c
A good route that has some great moves, although it can be dusty from time to time. *Photo on page 73.*
FA. Mike Robertson 20.2.1993

12 Crucifix Kiss . . . . . 2 stars 7c
An excellent route featuring a powerful crux and an interesting groove to finish. The groove can be a bit dusty.
FA. Pete Oxley 6.3.1993

13 Choc Speedway . . . . 1 star 6b+
A worthwhile route, which has now cleaned up with use.
FA. Gorden Jenkin, Francis Haydn 16.8.1998

14 Nothing is Cool . . . . . . 2 stars 6c
Virtually a slab climb, although there is a roof at the top.
FA. Steve Taylor 6.3.1993

15 Protein Delta Strip . . . . 2 stars 6c
Great positions higher up with an exposed crux and a slightly committing section.
FA. Joff Cook 2.1993

16 That Honeycomb Centre 7a
The wall right of the leaning corner.
FA. Gary Gibson 8.9.2010

17 Kit Kat . . . . 2 stars 6b
A super climb up a strong natural line. Some strangely shaped holds aid progress on the powerful crux section.
FA. J.Walker 2.2.1993

18 Whilst the Cat's Away. . . . . 1 star 7a+
A good crux move, but still a touch friable. Clip the bolt on the headwall and then move left immediately.
FA. Neal Heanes 3.1997

19 The Launch . . . . . . 1 star 7b+
Dynamic moves to cross the steep section give the hardest climbing. High in the grade.
FA. James Dunlop 14.9.1999

From mid morning | 20 min

Portland | Lulworth | Swanage | Blacknor N | Blacknor C | Blacknor S | Blacknor B | Blacknor FS | Battleship | Battleship BC | Wallsend N | Wallsend S | Coastguard N | Coastguard S | White Hole | Lighthouse | Cheyne Weare | Cuttings

The twin wide cracks in the corner on the left of this area make-up the line of the trad route **Struggling Jim, VS**.

1 Fat Falling Pigs . . . . 1 star **6b**
A good line that is low in the grade and can be dusty. Weird tufa pipes and formations show the way to a fairly tiring finish. Use the lower-off to the right.
FA. Gorden Jenkin 10.7.1993

2 Twangy Pearl . . . . . 3 stars **7b**
A well-travelled route now promoted to three stars by popular demand. Superb fingery flowstone climbing that has a technical lower wall and a powerful finish over the bulge.
FA. Damian Cook 6.3.1993

3 Boilermaker . . . . . 2 stars **7c**
Sustained climbing with a bouldery crux up a very blank looking wall. From a good hold, move up leftwards over a bulge from where hard and sustained climbing eventually gains a ramp and easier climbing.
FA. Pete Oxley 14.2.1993

4 Into the Sun . . . . 1 star **6c**
A dusty slab which is unlikely to clean up, but still has some good climbing. Climb the wall to the right of the grey streaks passing a welded-on flake to a lower-off in the groove above the upper breaks.
FA. Neal Heanes 24.3.1996

The wide loose crack to the right is the start of two trad lines - **Second's Swing, HVS 5a** *climbs to the upper break and traverses left to finish, whilst* **Poison Tip, E1 5b** *moves right and over the overhang.*

5 Bring on the Night . 1 star **6c+**
The middle of the blank wall has some nice climbing. Climb the rib to a thin wall and finish up an easier flake.
FA. Gorden Jenkin 22.6.1997

6 Does Trunky Want a Bun? . . 1 star **6b+**
A good pitch that should clean up. Ascend the wall to the left of the arete of *Monsoon Malabar*.
FA. Gaz Fry 1.5.2011

7 Monsoon Malabar . . . . 2 stars **6a**
A great outing with an easy start and an intricate finish up the striking, angular arete in the centre of this area. Move right around the top roof. Atmospheric and exposed positions.
Photo on page 1.
FA. Gorden Jenkin, Mike Robertson 22.6.1997

From mid morning | 20 min

20m

The Launch - p.75

1 2 3 4 5 6 7 8

The wide chimney-crack is the line of the two pitch trad route **Nomad, VS**.

8 Inbreeding 6b

The arete and slab to the right of the deep cleft has some dubious holds and has, unfortunately, still not cleaned up like many of the routes on this wall have.

FA. Gorden Jenkin, Francis Haydn 16.8.1998

9 We Are Not Men, We Are Roto. . 6c

A dusty pitch up the wall just right of a blunt arete. Old bolts mark the line.

FA. Will Jones 6.1994

10 The Stal's On Me, Pal. 7a

Good, but loose climbing that breaks right out of *We are Not Men We Are Roto.* Follow a weird conglomerate ramp of poor rock.

FA. Francis Haydn 16.8.1998

Monsoon Malabar Area

An good section of cliff-line that offers routes throughout the grades and some striking lines. The rock is generally good, but some of the routes can be a be touch dusty.

Approach (see page 61) - This wall is easily accessed by walking around the corner from Blacknor North. It can also be approached from the Blacknor South Quarry Approach.

The crack to the right is the trad line **Mirage, HVS 5a**.

11 Toothless Vampire 7b

The big flowstone pillar right of a large groove. Start by scrambling up to a bolt below and left of the corner. It has some friable holds so don't pull too hard.

FA. Will Jones 7.6.1994

The ramp and face to the right is the line of a three pitch trad line **Fond Farewell, E1 5b**.

Pregnant Pause Area

This wall has some scrappy routes on its left-hand side, but is dominated by the magnificent arete of *Pregnant Pause*.

Approach (see page 61) - This wall is now best approached via the good cliff-base path from the Blacknor South Quarry Approach.

1 Keeping Abreast of Things . . . . 6b+
The huge face just left of the big arete.
FA. Gary Gibson 5.2007

2 Paws for Thought . . . . 1 6b+
Climb the left-hand side of the *Pregnant Pause* arete, starting as for *Pregnant Pause*.
FA. Gary Gibson 5.2007

3 Pregnant Pause . . . . . . Top 50 6a+
The biggest arete on the island is a wonderful climb in an eye-catching situation. Start up cracks, then climb the right wall of the arete to some technical moves above a hand ledge to gain the arete itself. Climb to a ledge, then the final section above to a lower-off.
FA. J.Robertson, Mark Courtier 1993

The massive corner to the right of the arete of Pregnant Pause is the three pitch trad route **Big Corner, HVS 4b.**

4 Suenos de España . 1 7a+
A good pitch up the wall to the right of the massive corner. Start from a high ledge gained via a fixed rope.
FA. Jason Pickles 4.5.2006

5 Valerian 1 6a
The line up the buttress left of a steep grassy ramp. It has some superb flowstone on the upper wall. However, the first half of the route has a good deal of loose and dusty rock. Care required.
FA. Mick Ward 2002

6 The Viper's Tale. . . . . 1 7a+
The line to the left of *Natural Born Drillers*. Use a knotted rope to gain a grassy ledge. Climb the line of very dusty stuck-on holds to a hard move to gain a ledge at the top. Very good, but also very dusty.
FA. Gary Gibson 5.5.2006

28m
2
4
1
3
5
Approach via rope to ledge

7 Natural Born Drillers . . 1 6c
A nice flowstone face requiring some balance, but the lower section is awkward to cross. Gain the start via a knotted rope.
FA. Pete Oxley 4.3.1995

The chimney crack to the right is the trad line of **Flake Out, VS 4c**.

8 The Long Walk 2 6c
A great route; the tufas are steep and juggy, and the climbing is more exposed than your average Portland 6c.
FA. Mike Robertson 8.12.1995

9 Mexican Stand-off . . . . 2 7a+
A quality route, but it can be dusty. An easy, but snappy start leads to interesting flowstone in the centre of the huge face.
FA. Pete Oxley 4.3.1995

10 One Fine Day . . . . 1 6a+
The right-hand side of the wall. Start up broken rock and gain the better upper wall. Finish via a long reach or a dynamic move.
FA. Mick Ward 2002

The arete to the right is the line of the trad route **The Prow, E1 5b.**

Go With the Flow and Niagra Area

The Go With the Flow section of cliff has some good flowstone. The right-hand side of the wall - The Niagra Area - is defined by a water-stained long dark streak which is often wet and is generally only dry in the summer months.

Approach (see page 61) - This wall is now best approached via the good cliff-base path from the Blacknor South Quarry Approach.

1 Skank Central . . . . 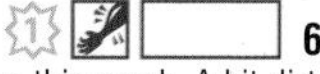 **6b+**

The right-hand arete is tackled via a thin crack. A bit dirty low down, but better than it looks. The top crack and arete are exciting. Start up the right-hand side of the arete.

FA. Damian Cook 11.6.1995

The large chimney in the corner to the right is the intimidating trad line of **Bob's Big Mistake, HVS 4c**, *whilst the cleaner chimney on the wall to the right is the line of* **Slim Jim, S 4a**.

From mid morning | 16 min

2 Go With the Flow 2 **6a**

One of the best bits of flowstone on Portland. Scramble easily to a high ledge to start, but gear up first. Climb the black wall to a series of incredible stuck on flakes, follow these to the top.

FA. Pete Oxley 6.5.1995

Go With The Flow includes part of the older trad route **Last of the Summer Wine, HVS 5a**. *This starts to the left of the bolted line and joins it at the stuck on flakes and finishes rightwards at the upper horizontal break.*

3 Ocean Rock . . . . 2 **6c+**

A fabulous pitch which follows another series of stuck on flakes to the right of *Go With the Flow*, but at a higher level of difficulty.

FA. Mick Ward 2002

The vegetated ramp, chimney and wall to the right is the line of the trad route **Pedestal Crack, HS**.

4 Best Destiny . . . . 2 **4+**

The right-hand arete of the great flake is a popular line with some excellent positions on the arete. Start up some awkward ledges.

FA. Mick Ward 2002

The next three lines all share a common start which climbs a dirty wall at 4+ to a belay below the water-stained Niagra Wall.

5 Aeroforce . . . . 2 stars **7b**
A tremendous find that, when in condition, has both excellent rock and pumpy climbing. From the belay blast direct up the leaning rib on some weird flowstone holds.
FA. Joff Cook 6.1995

6 Blame it on the Drain . . 1 star **7a+**
A tricky number, breaking left out of *Niagara Wall* at its second bolt via some pockets and flowstone to a final bulge.
FA. Damian Cook 5.1995

7 Niagara Wall . . . . 1 star **7a**
Climb from the right-hand side of the belay ledge up slabby rock past an amazing welded boulder. Finish up a flake.
FA. Mike Robertson 6.1995

To the right of the wet streaks the wall gains height as it rounds a blunt arete. On its left is a line of bolts that run up leftwards towards the wet streaks - this is a project.

8 Dizzy up the Girl . . 2 stars **7a+**
Break left out of *Gaze of the Gorgon,* on pockets, and fire up the groove on good clean rock.
FA. Gavin Symonds 7.2004

9 Gaze of the Gorgon . . . 2 stars **6a+**
A major crack-line that is both strenuous and sustained.
FA. Tim Dunsby 3.10.1992

Portland Lulworth Swanage Blacknor N Blacknor C Blacknor S Blacknor B Blacknor FS Battleship Battleship BC Wallsend N Wallsend S Coastguard N Coastguard S White Hole Lighthouse Cheyne Weare Cuttings

1 Sniffin' Glue . . . . 1 star, 7a+
Takes the blunt arete right of *Gaze of the Gorgon*. The crux has possibly lost a hold in recent times.
FA. Gary Gibson 2.5.2006

The wide crack/chimney to the right is **Insistence, HS 4b**.

2 Athenian Tactics . . . . . 1 star, 7b+
Climb up the big crack to a foot-ledge. Continue over some flowstone bulges on undercuts and smears to a hard and reachy finish over the final bulge. Low in the grade.
FA. Steve Golley 8.2004

3 Corinthian Spirit . . 2 stars, 7b+
Fine rock and a bouldery crux. Start as for *Cybernetic Orchard* before swinging left up a ramp at its fifth bolt.
FA. Pete Oxley 13.8.1995

4 Cybernetic Orchard . . . 2 stars, 7a+
A good, strong line that gradually increases in difficulty with height gained. Start left of a low overhang, at a bolt above a vegetated ledge. Climb up vegetated ground to a long groove line and follow it, passing a bulge on the left, to the top.
FA. Pete Oxley 29.5.1995

5 I Walk the Line . . . 2 stars, 7b
Intricate and sustained climbing up the wall just to the right of the long groove of *Cybernetic Orchard*. Start right of a low overhang below a difficult-to-see bolt. Climb up broken ground to the main wall. Climb the wall directly via some hard climbing in its mid section.
FA. Gary Gibson 4.5.2006

6 Portland Heights . . . 3 stars, 7a
A popular and sustained face climb. Start right of a low overhang below a difficult-to-see bolt. Climb up broken ground, then head up right. Sustained climbing up the bolt-line, past a fingery and technical section at mid-height, gains a fine finish.
FA. Pete Oxley 14.5.1989

7 Grand Larceny. . . . . . . 1 star, 7a+
An eliminate line. Start at a bolt-belay above broken ground, which is gained by abseil. Alternatively, climb up the initial broken wall of routes either side and traverse to the low belay. Take the steep prow on small pockets and edges to a slabby finish, without straying across to *Portland Heights*.
FA. Dave Pickford 9.1999

8 Burning Skies . . . . 3★ 6b+

A first class climb that features some great climbing on very good rock. Start at a horizontally-placed staple, just to the right of a crack. Climb up to a steep groove and continue with difficulty to a less steep, but still high-quality finish.

FA. Pete Oxley 18.6.1995

9 Isle of Slingers . . . . . . 2★ 6c+

A popular line with good moves and rock. Start at a crack-line in the lower wall. Move up the lower wall and climb directly up the wall above to a technical finale.

FA. Nic Hellyer 18.4.1999

10 Lord Stublock Deepvoid Breaks the Chain of Causation . . . . Top 50 6b+

A really good, long wall-pitch on fine rock. Start at a crack-line in the lower wall. Climb the gradually-steepening wall to a thrilling finish.

FA. Pete Oxley 18.6.1995

Portland Heights Area

This area has now been completely developed to yield some excellent long pocketed wall climbs. It is one of the first and best west coast crags to receive the sun in the morning. Some of the rock is a little crisp and shelly.

Approach (see page 61) - Use the Blacknor South Quarry Approach and head right (looking out).

11 Dusty Bedrock in Need of Careful Preparation . . . . 1★ 7a+

A big pitch that crosses the wide chimney. Start left of the wide crack that becomes a chimney higher up. Climb the wall via cracks to a ledge. The upper wall on the opposite side of the chimney provides the meat of the pitch.

FA. Gary Gibson 4.5.2006

The wide crack and chimney system is the trad line of **Persistence, HS 4a**.

12 Cocteau Phenomena Top 50 7b+

An impressive line up the steep wall to the left of the dominating arete. Start just to the right of the wide crack. Climb up and rightwards into the centre of the wall, then climb this to a hard finish. Finishing on the right is 7b. The lower-off is situated on the ledge above the route. *Photo on page 60.*

FA. Pete Oxley 11.5.1989

13 The Chronicles of Vladimir . . . . 6c+

A steep start gains the hanging arete. Start below the roofs. Climb up through the stack of overhangs and then climb the arete all the way to a difficult finish.

FA. Gary Gibson 2.5.2006

14 Ausfahrt . . . . 2★ 6b+

A much-travelled favourite. Start below a wide crack on the right of an overhang at 4m. Climb up past the overhang, and then pursue a line leftwards to a long groove just right of the arete. Follow this to an overhang and finish via some difficult final moves.

FA. Mike Robertson 6.5.1995

28m

11 12 13 14

Return to Roissy Area

Like its adjoining neighbour this is a fine towering wall of crisp and shelly rock, that provides a wide choice of face climbing classics and some very long pitches. It is one of the first and best west coast crags to receive the sun in the late morning.

Approach (see page 61) - Use the Blacknor South Quarry Approach and head right (looking out).

The wide crack that defines the left side of the wall is the trad line **Port Wine, VS 4c**.

1 Screw the Roses, Send me the Thorns . . . . 1 star **7a+**
Sustained wall climbing on a direct line at the lower limit of the grade. Start at the wall just right of an overhang at 4m. Climb the wall and broken ground to the upper face which gives some blind and fingery climbing.
FA. Nic Hellyer 1998

2 The Shells, The Shells . . . . 1 star **7a**
Eliminate in style, but worthwhile climbing. Start below a diagonal crack and a bolt between two staples. Climb the lower dirty wall and continue to the upper face, which gives good moves, though on a very tight line.
FA. Gary Gibson 16.9.2004

3 Driven Like the Snow . . 2 stars **6b+**
A Portland gem. Start at a boulder on the path. Climb the lower wall to below a long crack-line. Move up the crack until a line leads out left onto the wall and small ledge. Climb the slabby wall above the ledge until a tricky mantel move gains the lower-off.
FA. Pete Oxley 14.9.1991

4 Return to Roissy . . . . 2 stars **6b+**
The long crack is a good route. Start at a boulder on the path. Climb the lower wall to below a long flake-crack. Climb the accommodating crack to a tricky bulge at its end. Finish up a perplexing groove in the headwall. *Photo on page 11.*
FA. Pete Oxley 13.8.1995

5 Last Rose of Summer . . 2 stars **7a**
Pleasant climbing punctuated by some fairly tough moves. Start below a semi-circular cut-out above the first break. Climb to below the upper wall. Sustained climbing gains a small ledge from where one last blind move reaches easier ground and the top wall.
FA. Pete Oxley 21.8.1988

6 Through the Barricades . . . . 2 stars **7a+**
Fine climbing with the crux in the final groove giving a sustained section of thin climbing. Low in the grade. Start below a cave at 3m and climb up passing it on its left.
FA. Mike Robertson 19.4.1998

7 Step Away from the Gingga . 1 star **7a**
A good pitch. Climb to the third bolt of *Babelicious Redhead* then step left and climb the steepening shallow groove on shell pockets and edges to a slabby finish.
FA. Neal Heanes 14.10.2009

28m
4
1
2
3

8 Babelicious Redhead . . 1 6c
A friendly climb. Start below a cave at 3m, and climb up past it. Follow the steep wall above on crimps and pockets.
FA. Mike Robertson 1.12.1995

9 Chasing the Sun . . . . . 6c+
A worthwhile climb that gives some good wall climbing after a rather dirty initial section.
FA. Mick Ward 2002

A trad line **Jezebel Spirit, E1 5b** *follows the narrow, right-leaning corner crack.*

10 The Angry Sea 6c
An easier diagonal line linking into *Chasing The Sun*..
FA. Mick Ward 23.2.2003

11 The Wrecked Finger . . . . . . 6a+
An interesting line that has a section of crack climbing in its upper reaches (this is a bolted section of the trad line *Jezebel Spirit*).
FA. N.Gault, P.Flecks 12.2006

The huge chimney on the right-hand side of the wall is the trad route **Blockhead, HS 4b**.

From mid morning
12 min

28m
Blacknor South Sacred Angel Area
p.90

4 8 10 11 9 7 6 3 5

Portland | Lulworth | Swanage | Blacknor N | Blacknor C | Blacknor S | Blacknor B | Blacknor FS | Battleship | Battleship BC | Wallsend N | Wallsend S | Coastguard N | Coastguard S | White Hole | Lighthouse | Cheyne Weare | Cuttings

Blacknor South

Si Rooms moving up the fine flowstone flutings on *Medusa Falls* (7a) - page 92 - at Blacknor South.

Sharbutts Quarry

The first section of Blacknor South might be a bit short, but the climbs are on good rock, well bolted and offer some shelter from the wind.

Approach (see page 61) - The climbs are on the low, west-facing wall that is encountered in the quarry on the descent to the main Blacknor South cliffs. The climbs lie on either side of the quarried wall.

1 Sunseeker . . . . 2+
Climb the first line of flowstone encountered on the approach.
FA. John Leonard 2008

2 Meatjam . . . . 6a+
Climb over a small overhang and make a couple of fingery moves.
FA. Tom Beaumont 2008

3 Sunset Sessions . . . . 6c+
Climb the little overhang to a short, but technical face.
FA. Steve Muncaster 2007

4 Sunny Side Up 5
Climb the conglomerate rail to a lower-off on the ledge above.
FA. Josh Leonard 2008

5 Don't Kill Me 4
Good flowstone to finish via cleaned ledges.
FA. Tom Beaumont 2008

6 Vertically Challenged 3
The groove direct.
FA. Tom Beaumont 2008

7 Sunny Delight . . . . 3+
Climb flowstone to a lower-off on the ledge on the left.
FA. Steve Muncaster 2007

8 Surf, Sun and Just Having Fun . . 3+
Climb the flowstone groove and pillar.
FA. Josh Leonard 2007

9 The Mighty Bush . . . . 4+
The flowstone passing a small overhang.
FA. Vic Middleton 2008

10 Casting at the Sun 5
Climb to the large conglomerate crimps on the upper wall.
FA. John Leonard 2007

11 Memories of Blue 5
Climb the small overhang via a long reach to a flowstone finger-ledge on the upper wall.
FA. Mick Ward 2007

Quarried block wall

7m

5 6 7 8 9

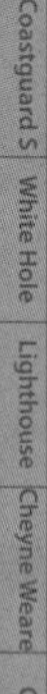

Jason Ahmed pulling through the crux of the popular Blacknor Central pitch *Shit Happens, Actually* (6a) - *page 74*.

Portland | Lulworth | Swanage | Blacknor N | Blacknor C | Blacknor S | Blacknor B | Blacknor FS | Battleship | Battleship BC | Wallsend N | Wallsend S | Coastguard N | Coastguard S | White Hole | Lighthouse | Cheyne Weare | Cuttings

Sacred Angel Area

A fine wall of vertical rock, suited to those with a technical bent and strong fingers. Some of the lines are useful for groups looking for climbing in the lower grades.
Approach (see page 61) - Descend through the quarry and down the chimney/gully. The wall is to the right when exiting the base of the chimney/gully.

1 Dirty Cow . . . . 1 ☐ **7a**
A decent wall pitch, although the rock is snappy. The bolts are spaced, but not dangerously so.
FA. Damian Cook 9.10.1993

2 Spontaneous Cattle Combustion
. . . . 1 ☐ **6c+**
A pleasing pitch which is fairly reasonable at the grade if the correct sequence is unlocked. Toughest at the top.
FA. Pete Oxley 2.2.1991

3 How Now Brown Cow . . 1 ☐ **6c+**
An eliminate straight up the wall to a fingery finale.
FA. Gary Gibson 16.9.2004

Afternoon 12 min

4 Talk . . . . 2 ☐ **6a+**
An enjoyable route with interesting moves up the lay-back crack with the added extra of an exciting finish.
FA. Nic Hellyer 22.2.1998

5 Toe the Line . . . . 2 ☐ **6b**
Much easier than first appearances would suggest. Good, fun climbing which can be finished straight up or out right.
FA. Joff Cook 1.12.1995

6 Sacred Angel. . . . . 2 ☐ **7a**
Another quality line that is at the bottom of the grade.
FA. H.Venables 15.4.1989. FFA. Steve Taylor 3.10.1993

A trad line **Reunion, E2** *started up Sacred Angel and traversed left to finish up Talk - it is now possible to climb it at 6a+ clipping the bolts on the nearby lines. Another trad line* **String of Pearls, HVS 4c** *starts up Sacred Angel and then traverses vegetated ground rightwards to finish up a flake-crack.*

7 Pining for Glossop . . . . 2 ☐ **7a**
Similar to *Sacred Angel*, but slightly better and tougher.
FA. H.Venables 8.7.1989

8 I Love the Smell of Resin in the Morning
. . . . 1 ☐ **6c**
The wall left of a big corner is a bit of an eliminate and features a tough finish.
FA. Nic Hellyer 25.7.1998

20m

1 2 3 4 5 6 7 8 9

Blacknor Central Return to Roissy Area
p.84

9 Love in the Mist. 6a
A short line up the arete and wall to a mid-height lower-off.
FA. Mick Ward 10.6.2010

The narrow corner and flake above where it fades is the trad line of **The Devil, HVS 5b**.

10 Draper's Henchmen . . . 7a+
An easy start leads to a step left to jugs at the bulge then back right immediately.
FA. Pete Oxley 19.8.1995

11 Oblivion is Forever. 6c
The belay is a bit too low, so top-out first to get the tick. Only 6a if not climbed past the belay.
FA. Pete Oxley 8.8.1988

The thin slanting crack is the trad route **Equinox, E2 5c**.

12 Silent, but Deadly . . . . 6c+
A technical slab. Climb the top crux direct, since it is probably only 6c if you escape to the left or right.
FA. Pete Oxley 19.8.1995

13 Hot Pants Explosion . . . 6b+
The small bulge near the top gives the crux. Take it on the left via a tiny seam.
FA. Neal Heanes 25.7.1992

14 Well Done Poppet 5
A very popular introduction to the climbing in this area. The finish provides the crux.
FA. Jane Wylie 30.4.1995

15 Do Ixtlan. . . . . 4+
A good pitch that has some excellent wall-climbing and a perplexing finish, especially if the hard-to-see hold is missed.
FA. Damian Cook 30.4.1995

A trad line **Scoop, HVS 4b** *goes up the wall to a grassy ledge and then finishes rightwards.*

16 Imperfect . . . . 3+
Once the start is dispatched, cruise to the lower-off which is located some way below the top of the cliff. A good first lead.
FA. Joff Cook 30.4.1995

The trad route **Jutland, VS 4b** *follows the arete on its left-hand side.*

17 Lifeline. . . . . 6a+
The photogenic arete. Climb steep ground on pockets to an easing midway up the arete. Move up and step left to finish up the crack pulling back right to the lower-off. Climbing directly up the right-hand side of the arete is a thin and fingery 6b+ variation finish.
FA. D.Glover 25.7.1996

18 It's My Life 5
A good, well-trodden line, with interesting moves.
FA. Jane Wylie 30.4.1995

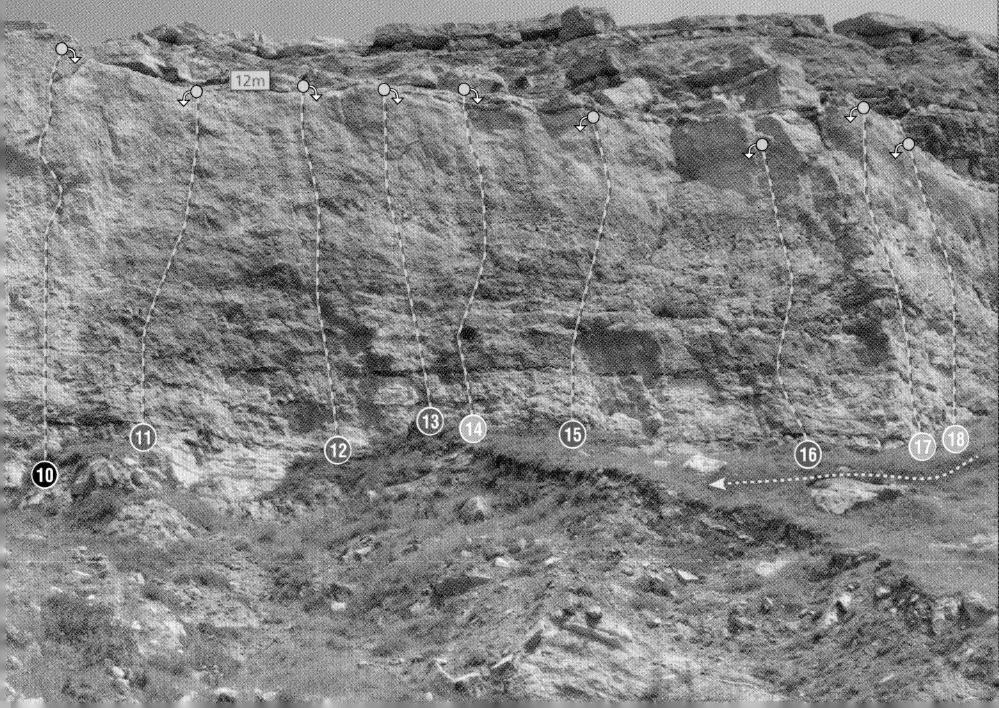

12m

10 11 12 13 14 15 16 17 18

Portland Lulworth Swanage Blacknor N Blacknor C Blacknor S Blacknor B Blacknor FS Battleship Battleship BC Wallsend N Wallsend S Coastguard N Coastguard S White Hole Lighthouse Cheyne Weare Cuttings

Medusa Falls Area

A superb wall with stunning flowstone that is also slightly less exposed to the weather than the other Blacknor crags.
Approach (see page 61) - Walk through the Blacknor South Quarry and descend the chimney/gully. The *Medusa Falls* wall is above and left (facing out) from the base of the chimney.

1 The Lizard of Oz. . . 2 stars 6a+
Great fun. A popular introduction to the flowstone experience. The start is the crux, but save something for the strenny finale.
FA. Jan Rostron, Pete Oxley 24.8.1995

2 Snakes Alive . . . . . 1 star 6b
A very good series of moves. The fourth bolt is difficult to clip.
FA. Pete Oxley 16.4.1994

3 Slither . . . . 1 star 7a+
A tight line. Crimps on the steep lower wall lead to long and balancy moves up a faint crack in the upper slab.
FA. Gary Gibson 2006

4 Medusa Falls . . . . 3 stars 7a
An incredible frozen sheet of flowstone pipes. The initial section is insecure and slippery if taken direct. *Photo on page 87.*
FA. Crispin Waddy (soloed onsight) 8.8.1987

Afternoon 12 min

5 To Wish the Impossible Top 50 7a
A superb pitch. Sustained and delicate climbing with a strenny finish.
FA. Pete Oxley 18.4.1994

6 Psychosomatic Addict. . 2 stars 7a+
Very similar to *To Wish the Impossible*, with escalating difficulties up the wall, narrow groove and headwall.
FA. Marty Hallett 16.5.1998

7 Crack My Bitch Up . . . . 1 star 6b
An easy corner leads to a hard, exposed finish.
FA. Marty Hallett 6.1998

8 Kamikaze Moped . . 1 star 7a
A short-lived fingery section and a good finish.
FA. Pete Oxley 10.7.1994

9 The Oldest Profession . . . . 2 stars 7a
Sometimes wet, but it is worth waiting for.
FA. Pete Oxley 10.7.1994

10 Loose Cannon . . . . 2 stars 7a
The black rib has some good moves.
FA. Mike Robertson 7.1998

11 Turned to Stone . . . . . . Top 50 6c+
One of Portland's finest routes. Some thin pocket moves and a great finish all on immaculate flowstone.
FA. Pete Oxley 22.4.1989

20m
1 2 3 4 5 6 7 8 9 10 11
Base of approach chimney/gully

12 Skids of Mark .... 1 star, 7b
The smooth wall has difficult moves over a bulge. Finishing up the upper section of *Turned to Stone* gives a worthwhile 7a+.
FA. Gary Gibson 24.8.2002

13 Bum Droplets .... 2 stars, 6b+
An exciting route that looks like its name. The upper layback section takes a little working out.
FA. Martin Crocker 23.4.1989

14 Cut Throat Jake ...... 2 stars, 6b
Quality climbing with a pocketed lower wall.
FA. Helen Heanes 4.9.1997

15 Cute Ass .... 1 star, 7a
A fingery headwall similar to the Battleship Edge routes.
FA. Pete Oxley 10.7.1994

16 No Ifs, No Butts ...... 1 star, 6c
The wall right of *Cute Ass* direct to a slim finishing groove and headwall.
FA. Gary Gibson, Hazel Gibson, Gordon Jenkin 15.9.2004

17 Seaman Stains ...... 1 star, 6c
Similar to the others on this section of the crag. Go careful with the clips and rock low down.
FA. Neal Heanes 23.7.1997

18 Hello Sailor. ..... 1 star, 6c
A good line up the shallow arete.
FA. Gary Gibson 2005

19 Master Bates........ 1 star, 6b+
A fine sustained groove leads to a swing left at the mid-height crux shelf.
FA. Helen Heanes 1.8.1997

20 Kite Marks .... 1 star, 7a
The wall, narrow groove and upper overhang.
FA. Gary Gibson 2005

21 Captain Pugwash..... 1 star, 6c+
Varied with a balancy start leading to a wild finish through the roof on buckets. It is worth trying to add a bit to the finish by getting your hands on top first before grabbing the belay.
FA. Neal Heanes 29.7.1997

22 Roger the Cabin Boy... 1 star, 6b+
Similar climbing to *Captain Pugwash*. The flake on the crux is suspect so treat it with care. Low in the grade.
FA. Neil Burton 1.8.1997

23 The Black Pig .... 1 star, 7b
The huge leaning arete at the end of the raised ledge is split by a rest ledge. Photogenic with fine moves high up.
FA. Neal Heanes 4.10.1997

The next route is up a huge corner to the right. To reach the start, follow a rough path around the very base of the cliff.

24 Still My Bleeding Heart.... 6a+
The long corner flake is dirty and loose.
FA. Nic Hellyer 26.1.1997

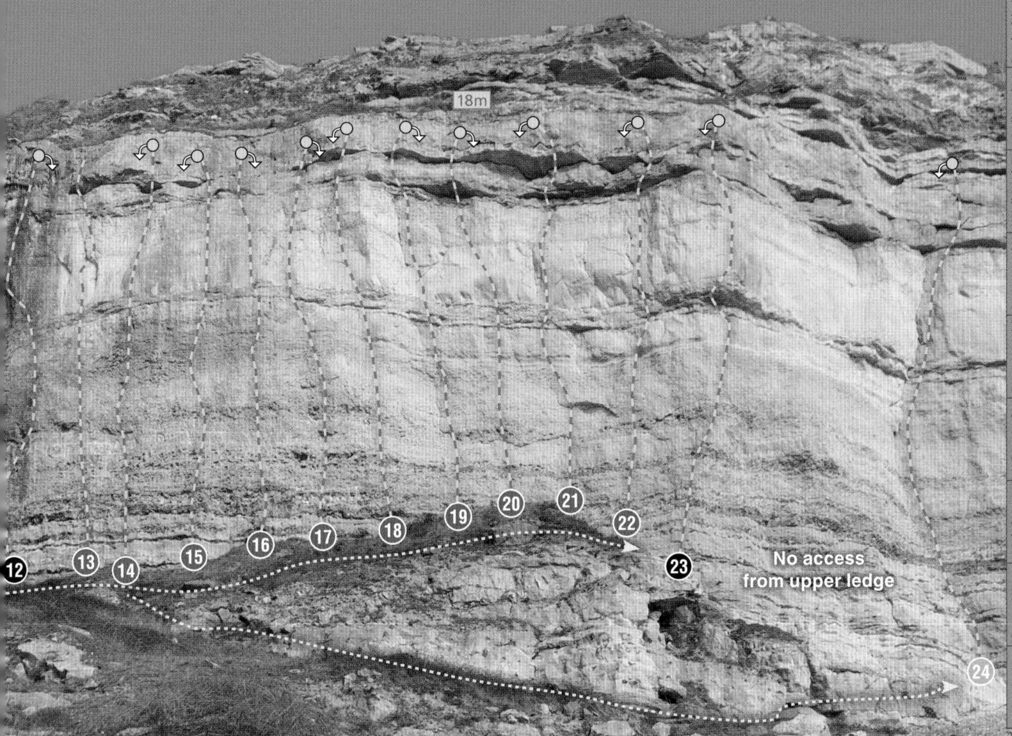

Blacknor Beach

Beth Woodley on the seaside *Fallen Slab Arete* (3) - *page 99* - at Blacknor Beach. The Triple and Diamond Slabs are in the background.

1 Solar Flare . . . . 3+
Follow the line of large pockets.
FA. Jimbo Kimber c.2002

2 Sun Spot 5
The tricky groove.
FA. J.Pullin c.2002

3 Sea of Tranquillity . . . . S
Start left of the large ammonite fossil. Not bolted.
FA. Jimbo Kimber c.2002

4 Moonshine 3
Start using the large ammonite fossil. Climb the wall on small fingery holds then move left into a shallow groove.
FA. Ben Thorne c.2002

5 Walking on the Moon 4
A diagonal line across the slab. Start as for *Moonshine* and finish close to *Half Moon*.
FA. Jimbo Kimber c.2002

6 Dark Side of the Moon . 4
A smooth face is climbed on slopers.
FA. J.Pullin c.2002

7 Lunar Eclipse 2
The massive pockets just right of the middle of the slab.
FA. Jimbo Kimber c.2002

The Lunar Park

The Lunar Park consists of two boulders on the beach below Blacknor Central - The Solar and Lunar Boulders. The routes are of similar difficulty and style to those on the nearby Diamond Slabs and Triple Slabs. The central lines are slightly tidal and all routes finish at bolt-belays.
Approach (also see page 61) - The quickest route of access is to descend the scree slope and boulders below the route *Toothless Vampire* (see the Monsoon Malabar Area at Blacknor Central). Also boulder-hopping from the Triple Slabs is not too problematic.

8 Half Moon . . . . 2+
A variation on *Lunar Eclipse*. Step right after 2m and foot traverse the lip until large holds are reached. Finish up a scoop.
FA. Jimbo Kimber c.2002

9 Full Moon . . . . 5+
A direct start to *Half Moon*.
FA. Jimbo Kimber c.2002

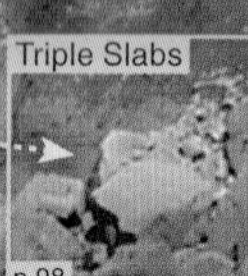

Diamond Slabs

Two clean and well-bolted slabs that are popular with those after some easier lines in a lovely setting.

Tides - The lower slab is very slightly tidal.

Approach (also see page 61) - The quickest route of access is to descend the scree slope and boulders below the route *Toothless Vampire* (see the Monsoon Malabar Area at Blacknor Central). Alternatively boulder-hopping from the Triple Slabs is not problematic.

10 Rough Diamond . . . . 1 star, 4

Start at the large flake under the overhanging left edge of the slab. Use this to gain the slab and climb direct to a lower-off.

FA. John Leonard 18.4.2008

11 Diamond Geezer . . . . 1 star, 5

The left-hand line of bolts up the attractive easy-angled face to a lower-off. Low in the grade.

FA. Steve Taylor 22.2.2005

12 Diamond Boulder . . . . 2 stars, 4

The central line via the flake to a lower-off.

FA. Scott Titt 26.3.1994

13 Diamond Edge . . . . 1 star, 4

Move out right and then back left to the lower-off.

FA. Steve Taylor 2005

14 The Hardye Girls . . . . 6c+

Start on the overhanging south face. Make a hard move to gain an overhung groove. Make a rightward rising traverse to a tricky move to pull out onto the back of the slab.

FA. John Leonard 4.10.2009

15 Diamond Solitaire . . . . 1 star, 3

The left-hand line on the smaller Diamond Slab.

FA. Steve Taylor 1996

16 Portland Snowshine . . . . . . 1 star, 3+

The right-hand line up the slab to a lower-off.

FA. Steve Taylor 27.2.2005

Blacknor South/Sharbutts Quarry approach-path - p.61

Best Destiny - p.80

Imperfect - p.91

Babelicious Redhead - p.85

Fallen Slab

p.99

The first line on the slab is a trad solo, **Retraction, VDiff**.

1 My Little Buddha . . . . 1 star 2+
The left-hand bolted line is a very easy but pleasing plod.
FA. K.Little 1995

2 Slabtastic . . . . 1 star 3
As the name suggests. AKA *Sunday Swing*.
FA. John Fletcher 1995

3 Suburban Dave . . . . . . 1 star 3
Another fine outing at the grade. Start from a boulder.
FA. M.Bateman 1995

4 Mystical Gill . . . . 1 star 3+
Pull onto the slab as for *Suburban Dave,* then follow the right-hand of the bolted lines on pockets and good friction.
FA. Pete Oxley (solo) 10.8.1988

The slab 2m left of the wide crack is the unprotected line of **The Erogenous Stone, VS 4b**.

The seaward boulder is reached by a scramble through a rock corridor and contains three more bolted routes.

5 A Nuggett of Purest Green . . 4
The left-hand line up the slab.
FA. Tom Beaumont 2006

6 Vertical Thrill . . . . 1 star 4
Climbs the slab just left of centre.
FA. Nigel Coe 15.10.1988

7 The Bolt Factory . . . . . 1 star 4+
The right-hand bolt line is just a touch harder.
FA. Steve Taylor 26.8.1993

The unprotected slab traversing out rightwards is **The Last Suitcase before the Holocaust, HVS 5a**.

The cherty crack on the left is the trad line **Crack Minuit, HS**.

8 Six Good Biceps . . . . 2 star 4+
A line of steep buckets. One pair of biceps should suffice.
FA. Joff Cook 28.5.1995

9 Losing My Sad Tomato . . . . 1 star 6c
An Interesting and technical line that is surprisingly sustained.
FA. Mike Robertson 27.5.1995

The shallow, cherty corner to the right is the poorly-protected trad line **Broken Trail, VDiff**.

Triple Slabs

The third of the sea-level sectors is located 100m north of the Fallen Slab area (see opposite). It consists of three huge slabs, all facing out to sea. The middle slab is the largest, and forms a deep gully that keeps the routes out of sight until you are right on top of them.
Tides - The main slabs are non-tidal, but the seaward face is slightly tidal.
Approach (see page 61) - Cross beneath the Sacred Angel Area and locate a path beneath *Babelicious Redhead.* This leads down to the slabs - awkward. Alternatively, boulder-hop along the beach from the Fallen Slab.

⑩ Le Cranium Cassé . . . . 1 6a+
The groove left of the arete is now adequately bolted, but it still has a sizeable fall potential.
FA. Damian Cook 27.5.1995

⑪ Fallen Slab Arete . . . . . Top 50 3
The huge ship's keel is exhilarating and photogenic. Stay as close to the arete as possible for maximum exposure.
Photo on page 95.

⑫ Fallen Slab 3 3
The centre of the slab is a lovely outing. A classic in a beautiful location.

Either side of Fallen Slab are two serious VDiffs.

From mid morning
15 min

Fallen Slab

The Fallen Slab is located within the mass of huge boulders downstairs from the main Blacknor South cliff. Since it was re-discovered and given a sport climbing overhaul, the area has become very popular.

Tides - The slabs are slightly tidal on the seaward face.

Approach (see page 61) - The Fallen Slab is reached by a steep track that leads straight down from below the route *Imperfect*. A pinnacle marks the top of the buttress which forms a mammoth slab and starts at sea level.

Blacknor Far South

Jude Summers on the upper wall of *Punter's Way* (6a+) - *page 106* - on the long unbroken cliff-line of the superb Blacknor Far South cliff.

Fear's Younger Brother Area

A great section of the cliff that is packed with flowstone and pocketed walls, giving some very technical and often sustained routes with the odd bulge and overhang thrown into the mix.

Approach (see page 61) - From the car park walk to the cliff-top path and turn left (looking out). Continue for 400m to some blocks that lie across the path then descend steeply down a rough path and back right to below the crag. Alternatively it is possible to walk around from below Blacknor South or via a path from Battleship Edge.

1 Where's My Washboard . . . 1 star **6b+**
An overhanging groove with a tricky roof move.
FA. Neal Heanes 4.1998

2 Castle Anthrax. . . . . 1 star **7a**
A left-hand variation to the route *An Arse With a View* . Move left at the first break and climb up to and over the final roof.
FA. Gavin Symonds, Ben Stokes 5.1998

3 An Arse With a View. . . 1 star **7a**
A flaky, technical groove to the smooth roof on its right.
FA. Neal Heanes 4.1998

4 The Singing Bush. . . . . 2 star **7a+**
One of the best on this section of wall. A pumpy and technical route following a faint rib.
FA. Joff Cook 2.6.1996

5 Bushwhacked . . . . 2 star **7a+**
Tasty-tufa-technicalities on the black wave. A good pitch.
FA. Damian Cook 1.6.1995

6 Chaos UK . . . . 2 star **7a+**
A fine twisting groove packs in some good hard moves.
FA. Martin Crocker 19.5.1989

7 AKA UK OK **7b**
Climb the easy wall to the bulge. Good holds gain access to the upper wall which provides a fine fingery finale. It borrows holds off other routes.
FA. Gary Gibson 9.5.2003

8 UK Subs . . . . . . 1 star **7a+**
A very rewarding pitch that ascends the blank wall, via some hard and sustained moves.
FA. Pete Oxley 2.2.1991

9 The Unknown Soldier . . 2★ 6b+
Good climbing up flowstone above the mid-height break. Anyone going to own up to it?
FA. The Phantom Bolter (still no claims 2012)

10 Read the Small Print . . 2★ 6b
The wall and baffling upper groove is one of the more popular lines at this end of the cliff.
FA. Steve Taylor 24.5.1995

11 Fear's Younger Brother . 2★ 6a
A Far South favourite. The crux takes a bit of working out, but the rest is steady and all on good rock.
FA. Steve Taylor 2.2.1991

12 Ocean Drive . . . . 2★ 6b
A superb sustained line with a stiff finish if taken direct.
Photo on page 54.
FA. Helen Heanes 4.1998

13 Kendo Nagasaki. . . 2★ 7a+
Challenging climbing with some blind moves at the bulge. Finish leftwards.
FA. Martin Crocker 7.5.1989

14 Ryme Intrinseca . . 2★ 7b
A direct and fingery test-piece. Keep right at the overlap.
FA. Martin Crocker 26.3.1989

15 The Strobolising Scyphostoma
. . . . 2★ 7a+
Steep and varied climbing. A hard move to gain the roof is followed by a pleasant groove then a taxing finish.
FA. Martin Crocker 26.3.1989

16 Kill a Gent's Tart . . . . . 1★ 6c+
Take the easy flake to a hard pull to gain an unrestful groove. Swing right below the roof.
FA. Pete Oxley 12.6.1994

17 Rag 'n' Bone Man . . . . 1★ 6b
A very nice climb up the wall, scoop and roof.
FA. Pete Oxley 14.10.1990

18 Steptoe and Son . . . . . 1★ 6c
Pleasant climbing with an impressive finish. Climb the tricky initial wall to the roof. Take this head-on to finish.
FA. Gary Gibson, Phil Gibson, Hazel Gibson 7.5.2003

Mechanoids Area

The mid section of Blacknor Far South is home to a line-up of high quality grade 7s and some tough grade 6s. The rock is well featured; the left side being peppered with fossil and conglomerate whilst the right-hand side is distinguished by its dark, vertical walls of smooth flowstone.

Approach (see page 61) - From the car park, walk to the cliff-top path and turn left (looking out). Continue for 400m to some blocks that lie across the path, then descend steeply down a rough path and back right to below the crag. Alternatively, it is possible to walk around from below Blacknor South, or via a path from Battleship Edge.

1 Sparkling Bone Chamber 1 star **7b**
Intense and blind climbing with a hard crux. The upper section is much easier.
FA. Martin Crocker 26.3.1989

2 Reality Bites . . . . 2 stars **6b+**
A stopper start that needs some luck to find the correct sequence. The remainder is delightful, assuming you find the good holds at the top.
FA. Janet Horrocks, George Ridge 6.4.1998

3 Slumberland Direct . . . 1 star **6b+**
A worthwhile line past a stuck-on ledge to a hard groove. A variation, *Slumberland,* avoids the hard mid-section by moving left into *Reality Bites* and then back right at the break.
FA. Steve Taylor, Joff Cook, Damian Cook 10.6.1995

4 Nobody's Hero . . . . 2 stars **6c**
A highly-rated outing up the juggy bulge and balancy upper section.
FA. Martin Crocker 19.5.1989

5 Great Barrier Reef . . . . 2 stars **7a+**
Superb and intense moves up a short groove above the fossilised coral ledge.
FA. Martin Crocker 30.4.1989

6 Crown of Thorns . . . . 2 stars **7a+**
Take the thin, blind seam high on the face to a fine finish on the headwall.
FA. Pete Oxley 26.2.1995

7 Wax on Wheels . . . 2 stars **7a+**
A big reach and high step above the mid-height ledge gain the beautiful rising seam and flowstone finish. Up-graded due to the loss of a hold.
FA. Martin Crocker 7.5.1989

8 Cerebellum . . . . 1 star **6c+**
A fine flowstone sheet with a couple of brain-like holds.
FA. Pete Oxley 26.2.1995

9 Hollow Ground. . . . 1 star 6b+
The long-admired thin flake right of *Cerebellum*. The flake is very thin, but has been tested by some heavy climbers.
FA. Ben Stokes 22.3.2002

10 So Special . . . . 1 star 7b
A testing route that is now climbed direct. Can be done by the short with a dyno.
FA. Martin Crocker 23.4.1989

11 Mechanoids . . . . 2 star 7a
Another vertical challenge taking a gritstone-like sequence up the ramp.
FA. Martin Crocker 23.4.1989

12 Cliché Upon Cliché. . . . 1 star 6c
A hard start and a hard finish. Move left to the lower-off.
FA. Martin Crocker 7.5.1989

13 Senseless Thing . . 1 star 7b
An reasonable pitch with a distinct crux.
FA. Martin Crocker 19.5.1989

14 In on the Killtaker . 2 star 7b+
A very good route taking in some unlikely climbing and with a sting in the tail.
FA. Pete Oxley 28.5.1993

15 Think Black. . . . . . 2 star 7b
Climb *In on the Killtaker* to the break and traverse right to below a bulge and shallow black groove. Pull the bulge and crimp and balance up the wall to a final easier finish around the upper overhang.
FA. Pete Oxley 23.4.1989

16 Paint a Black Picture 2 star 7c
An almost impossible rockover move (ok for shorties). It is often wet since it is on a drainage streak.
FA. Pete Oxley 28.5.1993

17 Look on the Bright Side 1 star 7a+
Start up *Paint a Black Picture* and break out right.
FA. Pete Oxley 1999

18 Amber Vibe. . . . . 1 star 7c+
Climb to the second bolt on *Boom-Boom Boom Box* and then head left up the smooth wall. This may get a direct start up the lower wall.
FA. Andy Lamont 19.9.2010

19 Boom-Boom Boom Box . 1 star 7a+
Take the lower wall past a difficult move to the midway ledge. Continue up the vertical wall above via hard moves to a steep finish.
FA. Gary Gibson 30.4.2006

Portland | Lulworth | Swanage | Blacknor N | Blacknor C | Blacknor S | Blacknor B | Blacknor FS | Battleship | Battleship BC | Wallsend N | Wallsend S | Coastguard N | Coastguard S | White Hole | Lighthouse | Cheyne Weare | Cuttings

Master of the Rolls Area

The tapering wall passed first on the approach has a number of excellent and popular routes, predominately in the grade 6s. The climbs are mainly wall and groove lines on some well-featured rock.

Approach (see page 61) - From the car park, walk to the cliff-top path and turn left (looking out). Continue for 400m to some blocks that lie across the path, then descend steeply down a rough path that goes rightwards beneath the crag. Alternatively, it is possible to walk around from below Blacknor South, or via a path from Battleship Edge.

1 Carlos Fandango Belay. 2 stars — **6b**

Climb the fingery lower-wall on positive, but hard-to-see holds to the break. Follow the easier, but enticing groove to finish.

FA. Neal Heanes 3.2002

2 Ghetto-Blaster Master 1 star — **6b**

The lower wall to the midway ledge provides the crux via a couple of fingery pulls. The upper wall is easier, but excellent.

FA. Gary Gibson, Hazel Gibson 30.4.2006

3 Paying It Forward .... 2 stars — **6a+**

A very good pitch from start to finish. The technical wall and pleasant groove culminate in a final pull onto the headwall using a vertical runnel.

FA. Neal Heanes 3.2002

4 Escape from the Dwaarfee Room .... 2 stars — **6a**

Varied climbing starting up the slightly left-trending line on the lower wall and passing a tufa shield just above mid-height. *Photo on page 51.*

FA. Ailsa Newcombe 8.4.1999

5 Punter's Way..... 2 stars — **6a+**

A much-praised pitch, one of the wall's best. The blank-looking lower wall has a few good pockets and edges that are hard to see. The upper section above the break is also excellent, and easier to read. *Photo on page 100.*

FA. Steve Taylor 2.5.1997

6 Blackthorn Winter .... 1 star — **6c**

Climb the lower wall rightwards to a thin crack and climb this to the midway break. Pull up to a small ledge at the base of a wide groove and follow it with difficulty to the upper breaks. Swing left and up to finish.

FA. Steve Taylor 28.5.1996

18m

1 2 3 4 5 6 7 8

Boom-Boom Boom Box- p.105

Project

7 Mistress of the Baps. . . . . . 1 6c+
Follow the wall and blind groove just to the right of *Blackthorn Winter*. Finish by grabbing the large lower-off ring.
FA. Neal Heanes 9.5.2008

8 Master of the Rolls . . . 2 7a+
A long, classy route with an exciting finish through the roof.
FA. Martin Crocker 23.4.1989

The next line is an open project.

9 The Loneliness of the Long Distance Driller 2 6b
A very worthwhile climb that takes on a bouldery lower wall to a superb upper section of brilliant rock.
FA. Nic Hellyer. 7.12.1996

10 The Sponginess of the Wrong Mixture Filler 2 6b
Climb the awkward wall, then step rightwards to the break. Move powerfully through the overhang and finish up the testing leaning wall.
FA. Gary Gibson 9.2005

11 If You Should Go Skating . . 1 6c
The butch overhang is followed by a thin wall crack. The start has become overgrown with ivy so start up either of the adjacent lines.
FA. Nic Hellyer 19.10.1996

12 Pulling Daisies . . . . 1 6a+
The rather dodgy-looking tufa shield and wall above direct.
FA. Gary Gibson 9.2005

13 Skating on Thin Ice . . . 1 5
A good variation moving left out of *Spare the Fern*.
FA. John Leonard 3.4.1997

14 Spare the Fern. . . . . . . 1 4+
Follow the groove and rib past a flowstone boss to a lower-off.
FA. John Leonard 30.7.1996

15 Desireless 1 4
The wide crack and wall. The initial bolt is high.
FA. Nigel Coe 13.5.1989

12m

Project

16 Good Lay 2 6b
A brief, but fine exercise up the wall and steep groove/flake.
FA. Martin Crocker 27.3.1989

The bulging crack is the trad line **The Enema Within, E4 6b**.

17 Shoobedoobabadah . . . . . . 6c+
The short peapod-groove provides plenty of interest.
FA. Steve Taylor 14.6.1995

18 Blood and Chocolate 6c
A thin and technical problem up the left wall of the arete.
FA. Nigel Coe 27.3.1989. Bolted and straightened by Neal Heanes.

The Battleship Cliffs

The popular Battleship Block is the first section of cliff to get the morning sun. Here teams take on the short, but intense lines of *Braer Rabbit* (4), *Wake Up, Time to Die* (6a) - and *Listing Badly* (6c+) page 128.

The Battleship Cliffs are some of the most popular on the whole Isle. There are two main sections - The Battleship Edge and the Battleship Back Cliff - and for most people the Battleship Edge is the starting point for exploring the west coast of Portland's huge supply of routes. It is an extremely friendly and inviting place. The gleaming white and grey-streaked faces and striking grooves are peppered with bolts. The crag base makes a pleasant place to sunbathe, picnic or relax, and it is possible to get a lot of mileage in here by nipping up and down the lines. The Battleship Back Cliff offers some superb stamina pitches with well-positioned crux moves, often high on the wall. The left-hand side of the Battleship Back Cliff is a favoured place for those seeking out long sustained pitches in the mid to upper grades whilst its right-hand side is slightly shorter and has some easier, but still high quality lines. The Block lies in front of the Back Cliff and has a number of good, slabby pitches at friendly grades, although they are a bit polished. Further on are the newly-developed areas of The Attic, The Balcony and The Veranda. These are smaller cliffs, but have a good line-up of mid-grade lines that are destined to become popular.

Conditions

The Battleship Edge and the Battleship Back Cliffs face due west, so get the afternoon and evening sun. The Block itself receives some morning sunshine and gives some useful shade on summer afternoons. The rock dries very quickly and there is no seepage. All the Battleship Cliffs are slightly more sheltered from the wind than the Blacknor Cliffs, as they are set back into the hillside.

Approach Also see map on page 53

The Battleship Cliffs are easy to reach from parking spots on Reap Lane, just to the south of Weston. Drive through Weston to a small roundabout and turn right into Reap Lane and park on the roadside beyond the traffic-calming installation (150m after the roundabout). **Do not park directly outside the houses if at all possible and do not change clothes or loiter in front of the houses**. From the first traffic-calming installation, pick up a fenced path that heads towards the cliff-top. At the junction with the cliff-top path, head slightly rightwards, and then take one of two steep paths down the hillside. The Battleship Edge is on the left. All the rest of the cliffs are reached from here - see individual approaches. It is also possible to approach from the Walkers' and Climbers' parking in the Weston Estate using the cliff-top path.

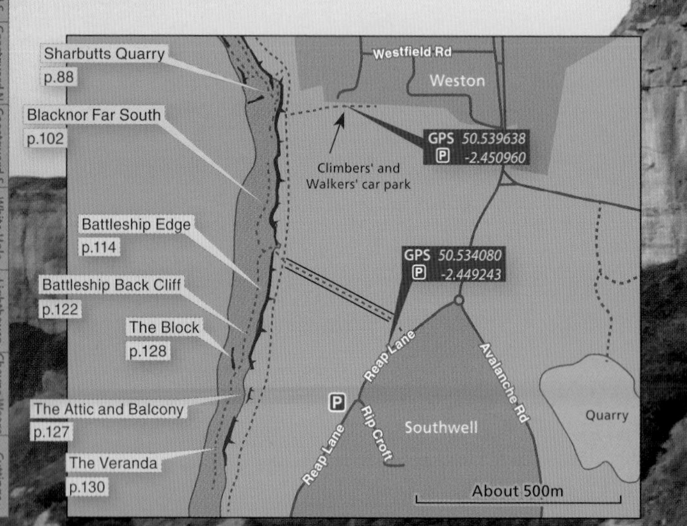

	No star	1 star	2 star	3 star
up to 4+	10	3	-	-
5+ to 6a+	15	12	6	-
6b to 7a	18	35	10	1
7a+ and up	4	12	12	4

Making the thin leftward traverse at the start of the hard climbing on the brilliant *Zinc Oxide Mountain* (7b+) - *page 123* - at Battleship Back Cliff.

Battleship Edge

Paul Cox nears the top of *Margaret on the Guillotine* (6a) - *page 117* - at Battleship Edge.

Portland Lulworth Swanage Blacknor N Blacknor C Blacknor S Blacknor B Blacknor FS Battleship Battleship BC Wallsend N Wallsend S Coastguard N Coastguard S White Hole Lighthouse Cheyne Weare Cuttings

Drive a Car Area

The first section encountered on the approach has a tall central section tapering off to either side. The central routes are very good and popular.

Approach (see page 110) - Follow the well-trodden path down and turn left just before the large grass mound.

1 Another Trojan Horse . . . . . 6b+
The left-most line up the wall past a reachy move to the break. The bulge above needs another long reach.
FA. Gary Gibson 14.9.2004

2 The Black Pariah . . 1 7a
The wall with a technical move to leave a ledge and fingery moves to reach easier ground slightly right.
FA. Gary Gibson 14.9.2004

3 The Misanthrope . . 1 7b+
A ferociously hard pitch which needs a dry spell.
FA. Martin Crocker 1.4.1989

4 Silage Clamp . . . . 1 7a+
Two very technical moves into and out of the scoop.
FA. Martin Crocker 1.4.1989

The wide crack is the trad line of **The Sheer Weight of Prague, VS 4c**. *To its right is a thinner crack of* **Kicking Steps, E1 5b**.

5 Never Drive a Car When You're Dead
. . . . 2 6a
A delightful route, friendly, well-bolted and sustained, but never desperate. It is also sheltered from the wind. *Photo opposite.*
FA. Steve Taylor 17.4.1993

6 Wind in the Riggin' . . . 2 6c
A gnarly, but rewarding pitch. There is at least one awkward clip high on the route.
FA. Martin Crocker 1.4.1989

7 Bawdy House 7a
A fierce start which is trickier for the short, this can be avoided by making a rightward detour.
FA. Martin Crocker 1.4.1989

8 The Ghost of Saturday Night
. . . . 1 5+
An enticing and subtle line starting near the top of the slope. Climb up a crack and then out leftwards to a groove and follow this to the top. Good climbing.
FA. Steve Taylor 6.1996

The open groove between The Ghost of Saturday Night and Borstal Breakout is the trad pitch **Sugar 'n' Spikes, E1 5a**.

9 Borstal Breakout 1 6c
A square-cut groove at the top of the grass bank leads to a tricky finish directly through the upper overhang. Finishing on the left-hand side of the overhang is an equally good 6b variation.
FA. H.Venables 17.12.1988

The left slanting flake is the central section of the wandering trad line **Stripped for Action, E1 5b**.

10 The Kane Mutiny 1 6b
A direct line that follows the shallow scoop and technical wall.
FA. Gary Gibson 3.5.2006

11 The Best Men . . . . 1 6c+
An entertaining and thin eliminate with a short lived crux direct up parallel blind cracks to the left of the groove of *Citizen Dust*.
FA. Steve Taylor 6.1996

12 Citizen Dust. . . . . 1 6a+
A good pitch up the groove and headwall gained from the left.
FA. Nigel Coe 9.4.1989

13 Meet the Manatees . . . 1 6b+
Follow a vague crack-line up the wall, to the right of *Citizen Dust*.
FA. Gary Gibson 7.5.2003

Afternoon 10 min

15m

1 2 3 4 5 6 7 8 9 10 11 12 13

Bilboes - p.116

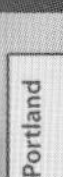

Barry Kerslake and Tammy Pay tackle the sustained crack and wall climbing on *Never Drive a Car When You're Dead* (6a) - *opposite* - at Battleship Edge.

1 Bilboes . . . . 1 star **7a**
Good technical climbing, although the sequence takes a bit of unlocking. Low in the grade.
FA. Martin Crocker 9.4.1989

2 Keyboard Wall . . 3 stars **7c**
A superb sequence of tenuous moves on flowstone ripples.
FA. Pete Oxley 10.12.1988

3 Choco Loni . . . . . . 2 stars **7b**
White hot fingery climbing on tiny holds. Steel fingers and good conditions are a must.
FA. Martin Crocker 9.4.1999

4 Wurlitzer Jukebox . . . . 1 star **7a+**
A good pitch that features a hard start and a stopper finish. It gets a little close to *Evening Falls* in its mid reaches.
FA. Martin Crocker 9.4.1989

5 Evening Falls . . . . 2 stars **6a+**
A strong line and popular pitch. Move up the initial wall to the corner proper, then climb to beneath the roof. Traverse rightwards along the horizontal break and make a steep move up to a jug. Linking into the last moves of *Wurlitzer Jukebox* is 6c.
FA. Pete Oxley 17.12.1988. Link Nic Hellyer 1998

6 Victims of Fashion . Top 50 **7a+**
A finger-stamina test of the highest calibre. Move up the pocketed lower wall. Then, from a small finger-ledge, make some tricky moves up to a shallow groove in the final section of the rib. Make a couple of blind moves to reach the horizontal break.
FA. Pete Oxley 10.5.1989

Victims of Fashion Area

The central section of Battleship Edge is one of the most popular areas on Portland, with a good supply of technical face and groove pitches. This is a great place to get a lot of mileage in if the grade range is right for you.
Approach (see page 110) - Follow the well-trodden path down and around the grassy mound to the base of the wall.

7 Barbed Wire Kisses . . . 2 stars **7a+**
Another strong corner-line with a hard crux sequence midway. Climb the lower wall into the base of the corner-line. Move up and make a hard move through a slight bulge to gain easier ground.
FA. Pete Oxley 13.11.1988

8 Monoculture . . . 2 stars **7c+**
A classic tendon-stretching testpiece. The lower wall sets the scene prior to the technical, and extremely fingery, blind moves over the upper bulge.
FA. Pete Oxley 12.1988 (1pt aid). FFA. Pete Oxley 17.4.1993

9 Reve d'un Corbeau . . . . 1 star **7a**
The hard lower wall has a stopper move. Difficult moves going left to the base of the interesting upper groove prove to be the undoing of many.
FA. Pete Oxley 19.11.1988

10 Lazy Days and Summer Haze 2 stars **6a+**
A testing pitch that is rounded off by a steep and exposed finish. Move up to the right and then back left to a shallow corner below a flake. Climb the layback-flake to the horizontal break. Move leftwards through the upper flowstone bulge to a lower-off.
FA. Pete Oxley 8.5.1989

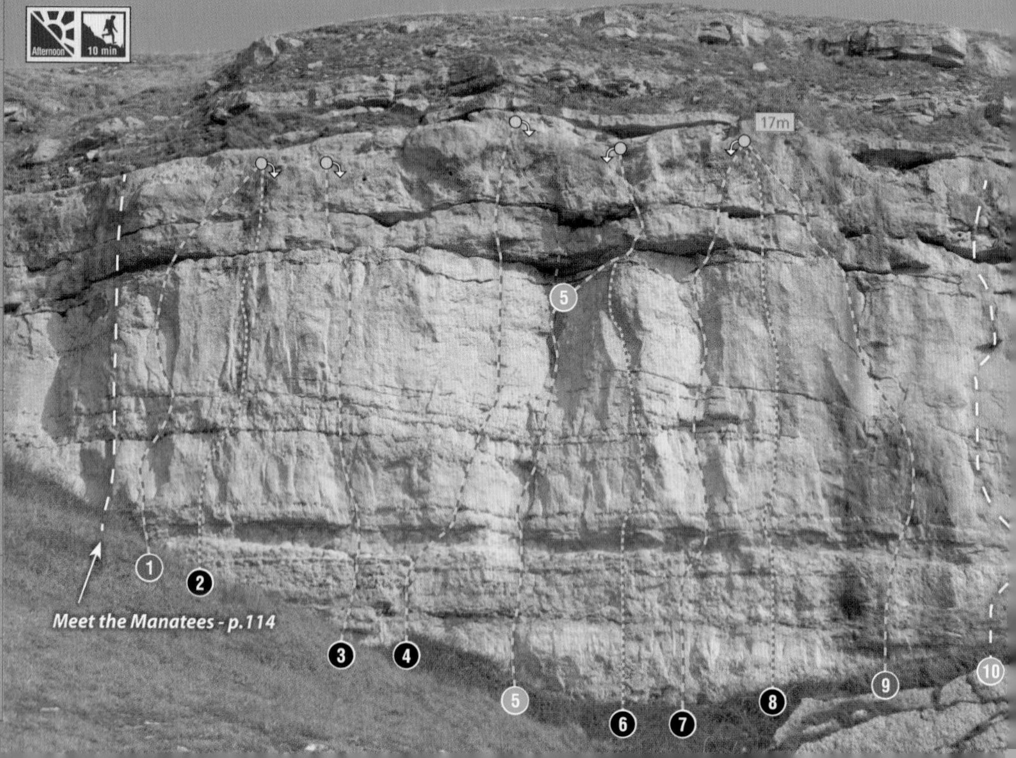

Afternoon 10 min

17m

1 2 3 4 5 6 7 8 9 10

Meet the Manatees - p.114

11 Norfolk Coast . . . . 1 star 7a+
An eliminate. Technical moves up the slab lead to a tricky finish.
FA. Gary Gibson 4.5.2003

12 Pinch an Inch . . . . 2 stars 6a
Pleasing and precise climbing on great rock. Move up the wall to a small corner and make some long moves to an easing at a thin crack. Climb the thin crack to a ledge at the horizontal break from where one last move up gains the lower-off.
FA. Pete Oxley 21.8.1988

13 Inch Perfect, Inchworm. 2 stars 6b+
An equally good experience to *Pinch an Inch*. Climb to positive holds in the groove. Make a series of technical moves up and right and then back left before easier ground and a lower-off.
FA. Crispin Waddy 8.8.1987. Direct Pete Oxley 21.8.1988

14 Serious Music . . . . 1 star 6c+
Intricate and well-positioned climbing. Move up to a high bolt and make a powerful pull to better holds. Traverse rightwards to the arete and climb it and the wall to a lower-off. The lower section can be climbed direct at 7a+.
FA. Pete Oxley 19.11.1988

15 Margaret on the Guillotine
. . . . 2 stars 6a
Surprisingly varied climbing which requires an eye for route finding. Start left of the first bolt, then move up and traverse rightwards before stepping back left to the shallow corner above. Climb the corner to a horizontal break where a long move gains the next break and a lower-off on the wall above.
Photo on page 112.
FA. Pete Oxley 22.4.1989

16 Gratuitous Lies Here . . 6c+
Good, hard climbing, but unfortunately rather runout. Move up to the first bolt which is shared with the previous route. Follow the thin groove up right to the break and finish via some difficult and bold moves through the overhang.
FA. Martin Crocker 22.4.1989

17 Keel Haul 7b
A good, but escapable eliminate. Climb the blunt arete via some hard pulls.
FA. Damian Cook 16.2.1993

18 Out of Reach, Out of Mind 2 stars 6c
The rounded groove is a fine climb. The pocketed groove passing - but not using - the doorknob, leads to the upper break. Make some steep and committing moves to finish.
FA. Pete Oxley 13.11.1988

19 No me Comas el Coco . 2 stars 7a
A good, varied pitch with a fingery start and, butch finish. Climb the thin groove and wall above it to the upper break. A powerful sequence up the bulging headwall gains the top and a lower-off.
FA. Jon Biddle 7.2.1993

20 Come, Armageddon, Come . 1 star 6c+
Unusual moves on the lower wall. Layback the chunky pinch-grips, to a steep finish.
FA. Pete Oxley 22.4.1989

21 Defcon One . . . . 2 stars 6c+
Climb a tricky initial groove to a testing stretch for the break. Swing left on the flowstone to finish.
FA. Pete Oxley 17.7.1990

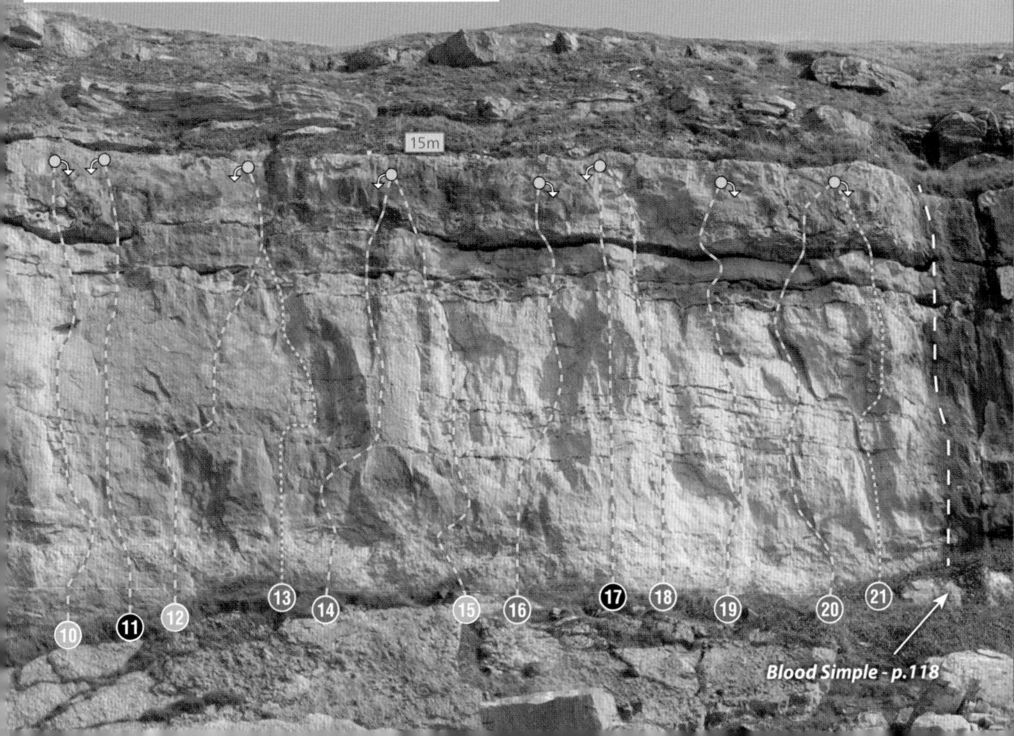

15m

10 11 12 13 14 15 16 17 18 19 20 21

Blood Simple - p.118

Portland Lulworth Swanage Blacknor N Blacknor C Blacknor S Blacknor B Blacknor FS Battleship Battleship BC Wallsend N Wallsend S Coastguard N Coastguard S White Hole Lighthouse Cheyne Weare Cuttings

Humanoid Area

An area with lots of vertical lines on some good rock, and a number of real tests of finger stamina. It is often empty when the lines to the left are crowded.

Approach (see page 110) - This is the far right-hand end (looking in) of Battleship Main Edge.

1 Blood Simple .... 1 star 7a
The scoop and slight groove to the right of *Defcon One* are gained via steep moves over the low bulge. Good rock.
FA. Gary Gibson 4.5.2003

The flake to the right is the trad line of **Eighth Wonder, HVS 5a**.

2 The Barton Fink 7b
The wall just to the right of the wide black streak, with desperate moves at half-height. Easier for the tall.
FA. Gary Gibson 14.9.2004

3 Hipnition. .... 1 star 7a
A hard boulder problem start is worth persevering with to access the nice upper groove.
FA. Pete Oxley 22.4.1989

4 Master of Ape Science .... 1 star 7a+
Like its near neighbours, this line has a bouldery start, but also hard moves on the upper wall.
FA. Martin Crocker 22.4.1989

5 A Taste of Honey ..... 1 star 7a+
The line to the right of *Master of Ape Science*. A tough sequence for the first couple of clips leads to pleasant 5+ climbing above.
FA. Mick Ward 19.3.2009

6 Dripping with Blood ... 6c+
It's all over after the vicious start. Finish up the crack and flowstone.
FA. Gorden Jenkin 5.8.1989

The flake-line to the right is the trad line of **Skateboard to Oblivion, HVS 5a**.

7 Maud in Memoria . 1 star 6c
Once again, the hard climbing is short-lived, but worthwhile. Follow edges and flakes to a short corner.
FA. M.Ford 20.12.1990

8 On the Wall...... 2 star 7a+
The entertaining, lichen-stained groove is often passed by, but is one of the finest on this section of the cliff.
FA. Pete Oxley 25.11.1989

9 Trance Dance .... 1 star 7a
The hard-won low crux passing a pocket is very bouldery. Finish up the shallow groove above.
FA. Pete Oxley 8.11.1988

10 Art For Art's Sake..... 1 star 7a+
Climb *Judge Jeffreys* for the first two clips, then follow the finger ledge left to the centre of the wall. Climb this direct to the break, then make tricky moves to gain the lower-off above.
FA. Mick Ward 7.4.2009

11 Judge Jeffreys.... Top 50 6c
Connecting the two flakes is a bit of a stopper move. From a small ledge above the flakes finish direct.
FA. Pete Oxley 19.11.1988

12 Humanoid....... 2 star 7a+
Fun and fingery from the word go, but it is a skin-eater.
FA. Pete Oxley 19.11.1988

13 One for the Gipper .... 1 star 6b
Don't miss the nicely-technical and balancy moves on this line.
FA. Pete Oxley 19.11.1988

14 President Elect ...... 1 star 6b+
A hard start to easier stuff above. High in the grade.
FA. Pete Oxley 19.11.1988

15 Chappaquiddick 6b
Climb the thin wall to the upper breaks.
FA. M.Ford 6.1990

16 Coastguard Ron 7a
A small, bouldery route with a number of possible sequences.
FA. Mark Williams 26.4.1998

17 April Skies . . . . 4+
The corner groove to the right of *Coastguard Ron*. Care needed with some of the rock.
FA. John Leonard 7.4.2009

18 Pyramid 6b
Climb the technical slab to the break. The headwall is climbed left of the bolts with a tricky move back right to the lower-off.
FA. John Leonard 5.4.2009

Middle Cliff

To the right of a wide crack/gully is a raised section of wall that has a selection of good, technical pitches.
Approach (see page 110) - A short steep path gains the base of the wall. Some of the lines have belay bolts at their bases.

19 Serendipity 4
The arete. Start up the first two bolts of the next route.
FA. Mick Ward 10.8.2011

20 Mr Dudley Meets Ting Tong Macadangdang
. . . . 6a
The wall and flakes on the left-hand side of the wall.
FA. Gary Gibson 5.2008

21 Flickhead Goes Boing, Boing
. . . . 7a
A good, bouldery crux with a blind reach.
FA. Steve Taylor 1996

22 Cruel Mistress . . . . 6c+
The hanging flake, rib and scoop.
FA. Mick Ward 7.8.2011

23 Hats off to the Insane . . . . . 6b+
Probably the best route here with pleasant wall climbing.
FA. Steve Taylor 1996

24 Trashcan Man 6b
Also a worthy pitch, which follows the thin flake-line.
FA. Steve Taylor 1996

The next lines have a bolt-belay on the raised ledge.

25 Dirty Filthy Rich 6a
Climb the blunt rib and groove right of *Trashcan Man*.
FA. Gary Gibson 10.9.2010

26 Setting the Date . . . 6b+
An unusually-wide groove. Passing the final roof to its left reduces the grade to 6a.
FA. Steve Taylor 1996

27 Sealed with a Kiss 6a
The slim groove and seam right of *Setting the Date*.
FA. Mick Ward 7.8.2011

28 Champagne Supernova
. . . . 6a
The narrow groove is short and awkward to both enter and exit.
FA. Steve Taylor 1996

29 Dishing the Dirt 6a
The groove line and short wall to the right of *Champagne Supernova*.
FA. Gary Gibson 10.9.2010

30 Andy Wallhole 6a
Short and sweet, and also low in the grade.
FA. J.Waddington 1996

Afternoon 10 min

12m

15 16 17 18 19 20 21 22 23 24 25 26 27 28 29 30

Battleship Back Cliff

Gaz Fry dodging the showers on the finely-positioned line of *Jurassic Shift* (7a) - *next page* - at the Battleship Back Cliff.

Portland Lulworth Swanage Blacknor N Blacknor C Blacknor S Blacknor B Blacknor FS Battleship Battleship BC Wallsend N Wallsend S Coastguard N Coastguard S White Hole Lighthouse Cheyne Weare Cuttings

Battleship Back Cliff - Left

This much-photographed wall features some brilliant climbs crossing the flint knobs and breaks that cut across the face. The climbing tends to involve technical moves on vertical rock - more sustained than cruxy. That being said, there are still some very hard moves! Many of the routes are more than 25m long, so take great care when lowering off.

Approach (see page 110) - Follow the crag-base path below Battleship Edge until it drops down towards the Back Cliff which towers above The Block.

1 Pol Pot Had the Lot 6b
Climb up dirty rock to the headwall.
FA. Gary Gibson 5.2008

2 Sex Cauldron. 7b
Move left and climb the upper arete and wall on the left.
FA. Joff Cook 2.5.1998

3 Even Better than the Beatles 1 7b
Good climbing in the high groove with a very blind crux.
FA. Steve Taylor 19.4.1997

4 Arc of a Fridge. . . . 1 7b
A very technical crux pulling through the mid-height bulge.
FA. Pete Oxley 1.12.1991

5 Dreams Burn Down . . . 2 7a+
A direct assault on the left-hand side of the massive wall, finishing up the corner. An often-overlooked pitch with a tough crux.
FA. Pete Oxley 27.1.1991

6 Nihil. 2 7b
The well-defined rib in the upper wall has good climbing and plenty of exposure. Climb the lower wall past a bulge to a rest below the upper wall. Make difficult moves through a larger bulge above, then climb the arete on its right-hand side.
FA. Pete Oxley 16.4.1993

7 No Man is an Island . . . Top 50 6c
A long-established Portland favourite. Climb to the narrow roof and pass it on the right before making some fingery moves back left above it to an easing. Continue to the base of the upper corner and follow cracks up this, exiting leftwards.
FA. Pete Oxley 10.7.1990

8 Always Have the Edge 2 6c
Another gem. Climb through the low overhangs with difficulty, then continue up the sustained wall above to a wide corner. Follow this to a steep finish past a pocket.
FA. Pete Oxley 10.7.1990

9 Pump Hitler. . . . . . Top 50 7a+
Exciting situations combined with technical climbing. Climb up and stretch past the low roof. Continue up the sustained wall to a blanker section of rock. Clip a high bolt, then traverse left on finger pockets before rocking up into a small corner. A final balancy wall and roof round off this great pitch.
FA. Pete Oxley 14.4.1993

10 Buoys Will Be Buoys . . Top 50 6b+
A long stamina-route that is one of the region's best grade 6 sport climbs. Move up to the overhang and negotiate it on the right before heading up the wall above to a corner with a good crack in it. Climb the corner and the left-trending groove above to a roof and swing right along the breaks until it is possible to pull up onto the headwall and finish rightwards.
FA. Pete Oxley 10.7.1990

11 Shape Shifter 1 7c
A hard upper wall. Climb easily to the mid-height ledge. Step left and climb direct up the wall via a powerful sequence to finish at the lower-off of *Buoys Will Be Buoys*.
FA. Bob Hickish 31.8.2008

12 Jurassic Shift 2 7a
A well-positioned route. Climb easily to the mid-height ledge, as for *Shape Shifter*. Ascend the groove above to a steep finish.
Photo on previous page.
FA. Pete Oxley 16.4.1993

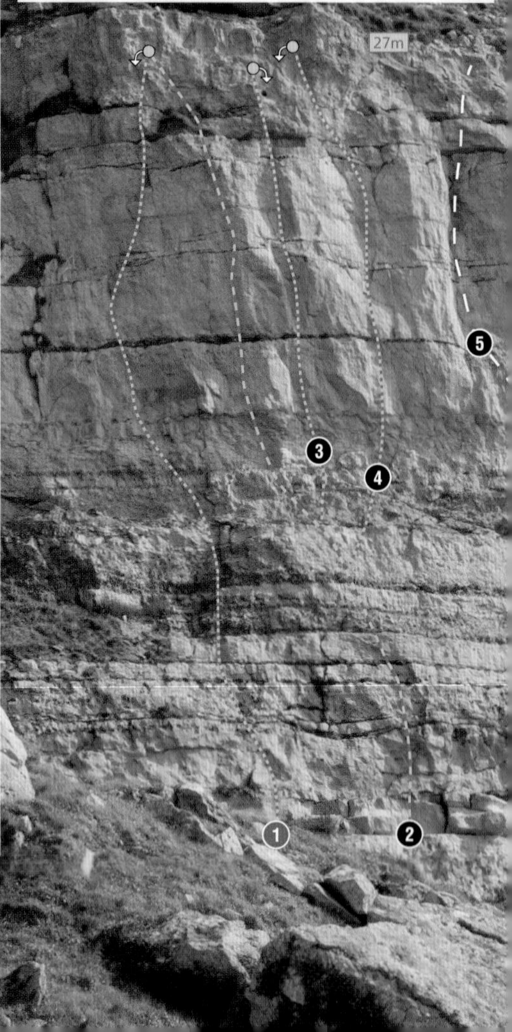

27m
5
3
4
1
2

⑬ The Fun Factory. . . 7b

Excellent and varied groove climbing with an almost gritstone-like mid-section. Climb poor rock until above the wide chert band. Move up and then left into a corner/groove and follow it to a steep finish that is overcome by a big reach.

FA. Pete Oxley 4.6.1997

⑭ Info Freako . . . . 7b+

Varied and technical moves up a thin crack in the impressive headwall. Climb the easy lower wall on poor rock to below the start of the thin crack. The crack succumbs to a series of precarious moves until better holds are gained in the upper break. Finish up the steep bulge via an enormous reach, the short-of-arm may prefer to finish up the arete to the right.

FA. Pete Oxley 18.7.1990

⑮ The Racing Line . . 7b+

An excellent climb. Climb the lower wall past a flake to a shallow, left-facing groove. Make technical moves up this and then right to a thin crack and tiny corner. Climb the crack and left-hand bolt-line up the wall to finish.

FA. Pete Oxley 4.6.1997

⑯ Trance Mission . 7c

A very technical hybrid. Start up *The Racing Line* and make a hard traverse to gain *Info Freako* below its crux.

Rave Mission 7c is another link-up from *Info Freako*, reversing the traverse on *Trance Mission* and finishing up *Racing Line.*

FA. Pete Oxley 1.7.1997. FA. (Rave Mission) Jim Kimber 12.9.1998

⑰ Zinc Oxide Mountain Top 50 7b+

One of Portland's very best routes, ascending the white headwall via some exquisite moves. Low in the grade. Start at a bolt-line just to the right of a low corner. Climb the lower wall and then make a rising traverse left to a thin crack and tiny corner. Climb the thin crack and finish up the right-hand bolt-line.

Photo on page 111.

FA. Pete Oxley 25.7.1990

⑱ Bending the Rules . 7b+

A long rising-traverse that forges a diagonal line starting up *Lost Army Expedition* (next page) and finishing up *Jurassic Shift.* Take a few long extenders. Hard for the grade.

FA. Pete Oxley 4.10.1997

Portland | Lulworth | Swanage | Blacknor N | Blacknor C | Blacknor S | Blacknor B | Blacknor FS | Battleship | Battleship BC | Wallsend N | Wallsend S | Coastguard N | Coastguard S | White Hole | Lighthouse | Cheyne Weare | Cuttings

1 Lost Army Expedition . . 1 star 6c+
Tough in the top groove and a bit run-out to boot.
FA. Brian Tilley 1992. Reclimbed after a rockfall by Steve Taylor 25.9.1993

2 Scapa Flow . . . . . . 2 star 6c+
A technical test-piece. Precarious groove climbing with nowhere near enough footholds for the right foot.
FA. Pete Oxley 6.1990

3 Koenig Class . . . . 1 star 7a+
The prow just to the right of *Scapa Flow* is climbed via a wandering line, but has some good, hard moves.
FA. Gary Gibson 2010

4 Raise the Titanic . . . . . 1 star 6b+
The open groove is a tricky proposition, and has a number of blind moves. Finish at the lower-off of *Scapa Flow*.
FA. Steve Taylor 4.9.1993

5 The Price of Silence . . . 2 star 6a
A pleasing and very popular route. You need to search around a bit on the top section for the best finishing holds.
FA. M.Bateman 21.4.1993

6 Wave Dodging 7a
This is a bold pitch if climbed direct - 6c+ indirect.
FA. Joff Cook 25.9.1993

7 Sink the Bismarck . . . . 1 star 6c
Quality climbing. It is possible to finish on the ledge of *Wave Dodging*, but if you add the extra 5m it is probably worth 6c+. Two old bolts.
FA. Pete Oxley 11.7.1989

Battleship Back Cliff - Right

Although shorter than the left-hand side of the cliff, this sector has a number of worthwhile climbs, and the friendlier grades tend to mean that it is more popular. The far right-hand end has a set of slightly steeper routes which have names that are almost longer than the routes themselves.

Approach (see page 110) - As for Battleship Edge, then continue underneath it to a path which drops down. The Battleship Back Cliff is opposite the jutting block that is detached from the main cliff-line.

Afternoon 11 min

19m

Zinc Oxide Mountain - p.123

1 2 3 4 5

8 Big Fish 7a
A tight line featuring three hard sections, though it has good rests in between. Finish to the right of a blank section.
FA. Gary Gibson 14.9.2004

9 Wiggi and Mopoke's Excellent New Hilti . . . . 5+
Climb the left side of the pillar and finish up the wall above.
FA. Nic Hellyer 28.9.1996

10 A Dream of White Porsches. 5
A good route up the right-hand side of the pillar.
FA. Pete Church 28.9.1996

11 The Sound of One Hold Snapping . . . . 6b+
A tough little number up the narrow groove.
FA. Nic Hellyer 5.4.1997

12 Electrically-Injected Shed Head . . . . 6b+
One of this wall's better routes. Good pocket pulling.
FA. M.Ford 16.12.1990

16m

6 7 8 9 10 11 12 13 14

13 Splat the Cat . . . . 6c+
The short scoop is a desperate problem, which has lost holds over time. Possibly harder.
FA. Pete Oxley 16.12.1990

14 Shallow End of the Gene Pool . . . . 6b+
An extended boulder problem followed by an easier finish.
FA. Nic Hellyer 30.11.1997

Battleship Back Cliff - Right

The furthest right of the lines on the Battleship Back Cliff itself are less popular, but very good and well worth a look should those on the more popular areas be occupied.

Approach (see page 110) - As for Battleship Edge, then continue underneath it to the path which drops down. The Battleship Back Cliff is opposite the jutting block that is detached from the main cliff-line.

1 Project 'A' .... 1 star 7a
Greasy even on good days, but the climb is okay.
FA. Aiden Cook 25.6.1995

2 Searing Tunnel of Re-injury. 1 star 6b
The groove is pleasant and the rebolted line now climbs direct to a lower-off above the capping overhangs.
FA. Pete Oxley 11.7.1990

3 The Cones of Stress .... 7a+
A poor eliminate to an old lower-off.
FA. Pete Oxley 16.1.1994

4 Psychic EMF ..... 2 star 7a+
The best route on this wall. The fine white dome is finger-wrenchingly good.
FA. Pete Oxley 11.7.1990

Afternoon 11 min

5 God Told Me to Skin You Alive
.... 1 star 6c+
Good climbing on very pocketed rock, but a touch snappy.
FA. Pete Oxley 11.7.1990

6 Roadkill on the Information Superhighway
.... 6b
The left-leaning groove is awkward low down.
FA. Nic Hellyer 16.3.1997

7 Error 404 .... 6a+
Very short and awkward.
FA. Nic Hellyer 26.1.1997

Up and right is the short wall of The Attic.

8 Unload the Fun Bags .. 6b+
Climb the fingery wall direct to easier moves at the break.
FA. Andy Dunford 3.6.2011

9 It's all a Bunch of Tree Hugging Hippie Crap
.... 5+
The faint crack to the overhang and pass it on the left.
FA. Sarah Perrett 2.7.2011

15m

To The Attic, The Balcony and Veranda

The Attic and The Balcony

Two small sections of cliff that provide a number of intense climbs on good rock and with a great outlook.
Approach (see page 110) - As for Battleship Back Cliff and continue a short way along from it to below the two areas that lie above a short but steep approach path.

10 Jurassic Bark . . . . 6c+
Tackle the overhang direct. Very reach-dependant.
FA. Adam Perrett 21.6.2011

11 High Flyer 6b
The right-hand line needs a dynamic approach at the overhang.
FA. John Leonard 3.6.2011

12 Lola 5
The left-hand line starting on some knobbly footholds.
FA. Andy Dunford 2.6.2011

13 Pretty Flamingo . . . . 6a+
A tricky start gains a crimp from where good climbing ends at a square-cut top.
FA. Mick Ward 31.5.2011

14 A Groovy Kind of Love 6c
The appealing groove is very hard to start.
FA. Mick Ward 31.5.2011

15 Itchycoo Park . . . . 6c+
A hard start leads to much easier ground above.
FA. Mick Ward 31.5.2011

16 Spear of Destiny . . . . 5+
The left-hand side of the arete provides some reachy moves.
FA. Adam Perrett 31.5.2011

17 Spear of Broccoli . . . . 5+
The right-hand side of the arete starting from flakes. Delicate and balancy climbing.
FA. Sarah Perrett 31.5.2011

18 Heart of the Sun 6a
Fingery climbing on the right-hand side of the wall. There is a move left to a chert lump, then head back right to the lower-off.
FA. John Leonard 31.5.2011

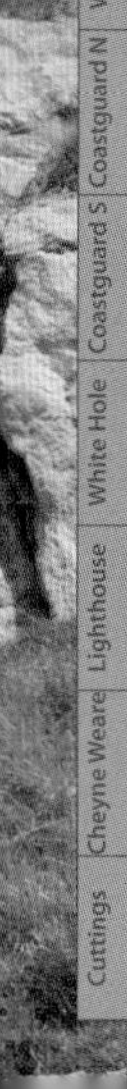

The Block

The Block is the huge detached lump of rock that stands in front of the Battleship Back Cliff itself. The short and slabby landward facing side of the The Block has some very popular routes which are useful for shade on summer afternoons or sun on cool summer mornings. The seaward face of the block has a small number of lines.
Approach (see page 110) - As for Battleship Edge, then continue underneath it to the path which drops down. To access the seaward face, walk around the south end of The Block.

The sharp southern arete of The Block is the trad line of **U-143, HVS 5a** *and is started via the crack leading up to it. This line will not be bolted.*

1 Coming Unstuck. . . 1 6a+
A testing series of moves on tiny pockets single out this line that is short on length, but great in difficulty.
FA. Steve Taylor 18.9.1993

The left facing corner and flakes is **Block 1, VDiff**. *The trad line of* **Block 2 Diff** *links the start of* **Block 3** *with the top of* **Block 1**. *The poorly-protected grooves are the line of the trad route* **Block 3, VDiff.**

2 Braer Rabbit 4
A shallow groove is a touch polished. *Photo on page 109.*
FA. Steve Taylor 18.9.1993

3 This is This. . . . . 1 4+
A very pleasant introduction to slab climbing.
FA. Pete Oxley 22.7.1990

4 Wake Up, Time to Die . . . . 1 6a+
A bit short on bolts at the bottom. A large hex or nut may be needed by some to protect the easy bottom section.
FA. Pete Oxley 22.7.1990

5 No Smears Here . . . . . 1 6a+
The line right of *Wake Up, Time to Die* is pretty tough.
FA. Gary Gibson 5.2006

The crack in the middle of the face is the trad line **Block 4, Severe**.

The face and flake to the right is the line of the trad route **Block 5, HS**.

6 Like a Drowning Man 1 4
The grade depends on where you climb - left of the bolts is **5**, the layback seam is **4**.
FA. Pete Oxley 22.7.1990

7 Hang Onto Your Ego . . . 1 6b
The second bolt is a tricky clip for shorties. A very thin, slabby number.
FA. Steve Taylor 18.9.1993

8 She's Going Down . 1 6b+
A good test of your off-vertical ability.
FA. Pete Oxley 22.7.1990

9 Listing Badly. . . . . 1 6c+
A wicked test of technique that has seen some tears over the years.
FA. Pete Oxley 22.7.1990

10 I'm Doing it Anyway 1 4
The flake-crack is a slick favourite that requires good footwork and technique on the polished holds to guarantee a tick.
FA. Steve Taylor, Mark Williams 18.9.1993

11 Hate the Sin and Love the Sinner
. . . . . 4+
The arete on the right-hand end of The Block.
FA. Nigel Coe 1995

Morning 11 min

The next two routes lie on the seaward side of The Block, which is steep and loose in places.

12 Another Stone on the Pile of Choss .... ☆1 ☐ 6c+

Walk down to the base of the highest section of the face. The steep, undercut arete is a touch loose at the bottom, but solid higher up.

FA. Jim Kimber 4.8.1996

13 Welcome to the Gravity Program ☐ 6c

The wall and arete 5m right of *Another Stone on the Pile of Choss.*

FA. Nic Hellyer 28.9.1997

There is a lone bolt further right again. The next routes start from a half-height ledge.

14 She's Dancing Tonight .... ☐ 5

Climb the exposed groove just right of the far arete of the ledge. There is a belay staple on the back wall.

FA. John Leonard 15.4.2009

15 Small is Beautiful .... ☐ 6b

Climbs the main corner of the ledge. There is a belay staple on the wall to the right.

FA. Mick Ward 15.4.2009

16 Tiny Goddess .... ☐ 5

Layback the seaward side of the southern arete. Exposed, photogenic and high in its grade.

FA. Mick Ward 18.4.2009

The Veranda

The Veranda is one of the wave of smaller crags that are now being developed all over Portland. Many of these smaller venues are remarkably close to some of the more popular areas and cater for climbers looking for routes in the lower-to-mid grades. The rock is often good and, although the routes have taken some unearthing, the lines will clean up quickly as the cliff becomes more popular. The Veranda has a great location with an expansive grass base.

Approach (see page 110) - From below the Battleship Back Cliff continue along the path for around 100m, passing below The Balcony and The Attic, to a small cairn that marks the top of the short descent path.

1 Dr. Sole and Mr. Sole 3
The left-hand route of the crag finishes with a delicate layaway up its top groove.
FA. Andy Dunford 25.9.2010

2 Never Lead a Numb Existence . . 4
Climb the wall to finish up the top flake of *Phil's Route.*
FA. Andy Dunford 25.9.2010

3 Phil's Route 4
Climb the crack, trending leftwards before making some big moves up the flake above to finish.
FA. Phil Bache 28.4.1990

4 Days of Heaven . . . . 4+
Pleasant climbing up the wall.
FA. Mick Ward 12.9.2010

5 Love on the Rocks ;) 5
Straight up over the grey band to a scoop. *Photo opposite.*
FA. Adam Perrett 10.10.2010

6 Absent Friends, Here's to Them . 5+
Climb the wall trending right at the grey band of rock. A hidden pocket may help to access the ledge above.
FA. Adam Perrett 25.9.2010

7 Limestone Cowboy . . . . 4+
Follows the crack-line. Named after a local entrepreneur.
FA. John Leonard 28.4.1990

8 One Flew Out of the Cuckoo's Nest . . . . 5+
Technical moves up the slight groove.
FA. Sarah Perrett 25.9.2010

9 When You Were Little You Dreamed You Were Big . . . . 6b+
Climb the brown flowstone stain between *One Flew Out of the Cuckoo's Nest* and *Hanging Out with Halo Jones.* The finishing hold is at the very top of the hanging groove.
FA. Adam Perrett 24.12.2010

10 Hanging Out with Halo Jones 6a
Good moves on the lower wall lead to a surprisingly tricky groove.
FA. Adam Perrett 25.10.2010

11 I Get High With A Little Help From My Friends 5
Climb the wall from the ledge. The finish may be awkward for the short. Care needed with the rock.
FA. Sarah Perrett 20.11.2010

12 Cat Juggling . . . . 4+
Climb from the right hand side of the ledge. The finish is height-dependant and maybe 6a for the short.
FA. Andy Dunford 19.11.2010

Julie Ashmore enjoying the initial fingery wall of *Love on the Rocks ;)* (5) - *opposite* - at The Veranda.

Wallsend Cove

Above the initial thin moves at the start of the Wallsend classic *The Watchman* (6b) - page 156 - at the Enchanted Path Area of Wallsend South.

	No star	1	2	3
up to 4+	9	-	-	-
5+ to 6a+	18	6	-	1
6b to 7a	36	46	22	5
7a+ and up	10	31	41	16

The largest cliff on Portland is the huge arc of Wallsend Cove which has two distinct sections - North and South. The routes here combine some superb climbing with bundles of atmosphere. The routes at Wallsend North are set back from the sea, in a short series of bays; varying from around 10m to 20m high, with some larger walls toward the centre of the cove. The spectacular Wallsend South areas are located at sea level and rise to around 30m. The climbs at Wallsend Cove span the grades well, providing many climbs that cater for most teams visiting the area.

Approach Also see maps on pages 53 and 166

There are two main approaches, both of which can be hard going, especially the sections along the boulder beach; this is not somewhere to bring non-climbing friends.

Wallsend North Approach (all areas up to the Laid Black Area) - Drive through Weston and, at a roundabout, turn right into Reap Lane and park after the first traffic-calming installation. From here go past the second traffic-calming installation, and pick up a footpath/track on the right (opposite Rip Croft) that heads towards the huge Southwell Business Park complex. At the massive fence, turn right and follow it to the coast path. Once at the coast path turn left (looking out) and walk on for 30m. Descend a path, which cuts back right, and at the end of this, head left to the So Hardcore Area. Further on are more sectors prior to the path dropping down to the boulder beach.

Coastguard Approach to Wallsend South (all areas from Bigger Piece south) - Drive to Portland Bill and park in the car park (fee). Walk back up the road past the Pulpit Inn and head out leftwards up a minor road towards the Coastwatch Lookout. Just before the Coastwatch Lookout, go down a grass slope to the cliff edge (see map on page 166) then descend a steep and precarious path (rope sometimes in place) onto a promontory and then continue down right to below Coastguard North. Walk north under this, past a gully, to reach Wallsend South. This approach is affected by high tide - see map opposite.

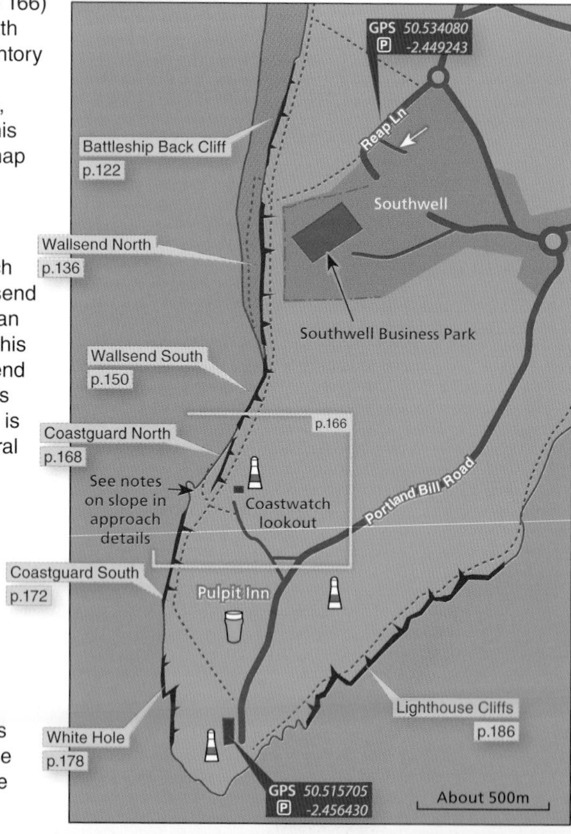

Conditions

All the Wallsend cliffs face west and catch the afternoon sun. The proximity of Wallsend South to the sea means that the holds can be greasy until the sun burns them dry; this may take longer when it is humid. Wallsend North is set well back from the sea and is therefore less prone to dampness. There is little seepage, although the Downhill Spiral Area suffers badly in winter.

Access

The only bird restriction currently on Wallsend affects the routes from *Empire State Arete* to *Beautiful South*. **No climbing from March 1st to July 31st.**

Tides

There are two tidal sections below Colors Area and Hong Kong Phooey Area. These cut off access for a short time at high tide and longer in rough seas.

Ed Babbington on *Some Velvet Morning* (7a) - *page 156* - at Wallsend Cove. Photo: Marti Hallett

Portland Lulworth Swanage Blacknor N Blacknor C Blacknor S Blacknor B Blacknor FS Battleship Battleship BC Wallsend N Wallsend S Coastguard N Coastguard S White Hole Lighthouse Cheyne Weare Cuttings

So Hardcore Area

Before the main cliffs start at Wallsend, there are a couple of isolated walls. Although very limited in height, the climbs are on good compact rock and offer very fingery and technical climbing. The small buttresses are sheltered and dry very quickly.

Approach (see page 134) - From the coast path, drop down a path that cuts back right and then left to the small walls. Two of the routes are on a short flowstone-wall below the main walls and are approached via a steep slope below the route *So Hardcore*.

1 Left Little Slapper . . . . . . 7b+
A direct line up the front face of the black-streaked arete.
FA. Pete Oxley 28.4.1996

2 Right Little Slapper . . . . . . 7a+
The right-hand variation.
FA. Pete Oxley 28.4.1996

3 Short Slutty Slab 6b
The short slab right of *Right Little Slapper*. One tricky move that may be easier for the short.
FA. Marti Hallett 5.5.2010

4 The Black Vegetable . . . . 5+
Climb the arete of the corner crack right of *Short Slutty Slab*. One for all fans of Black Adder.
FA. Adam Perrett 21.5.2011

5 The Dogging Spot 6c
The short, but technical wall.
FA. John Leonard 24.5.2011

6 Pearl Necklace 6b
Delicately climb the wall on the left side of the arete.
FA. Mick Ward 24.5.2011

7 Passing Bi . . . . 6a+
The flowstone wall before you walk around to *They Walked in Line* has some funky holds.
FA. Marti Hallett 5.5.2010

5m to the right is a short, clean wall.

8 They Walked in Line . . . 1 7b
Directly up the wall. Lower off the last bolt.
FA. Pete Oxley 5.7.1992

9 So Hardcore 1 7c
Utterly heinous and painful moves up the blank wall.
FA. Pete Oxley 11.5.1989

Afternoon 10 min

The next two lines lie below the main approach. Walk past the route So Hardcore and go down the slope rightwards to the orange flowstone wall.

10 Faith,Hop and Charity. 6a
Take the left-hand line on the flowstone sheet.
FA. Tom Beaumont 5.9.2006

11 Short 'n' Sexy 6a
Follow the right-hand line on the flowstone sheet.
FA. Tom Beaumont 12.12.2006

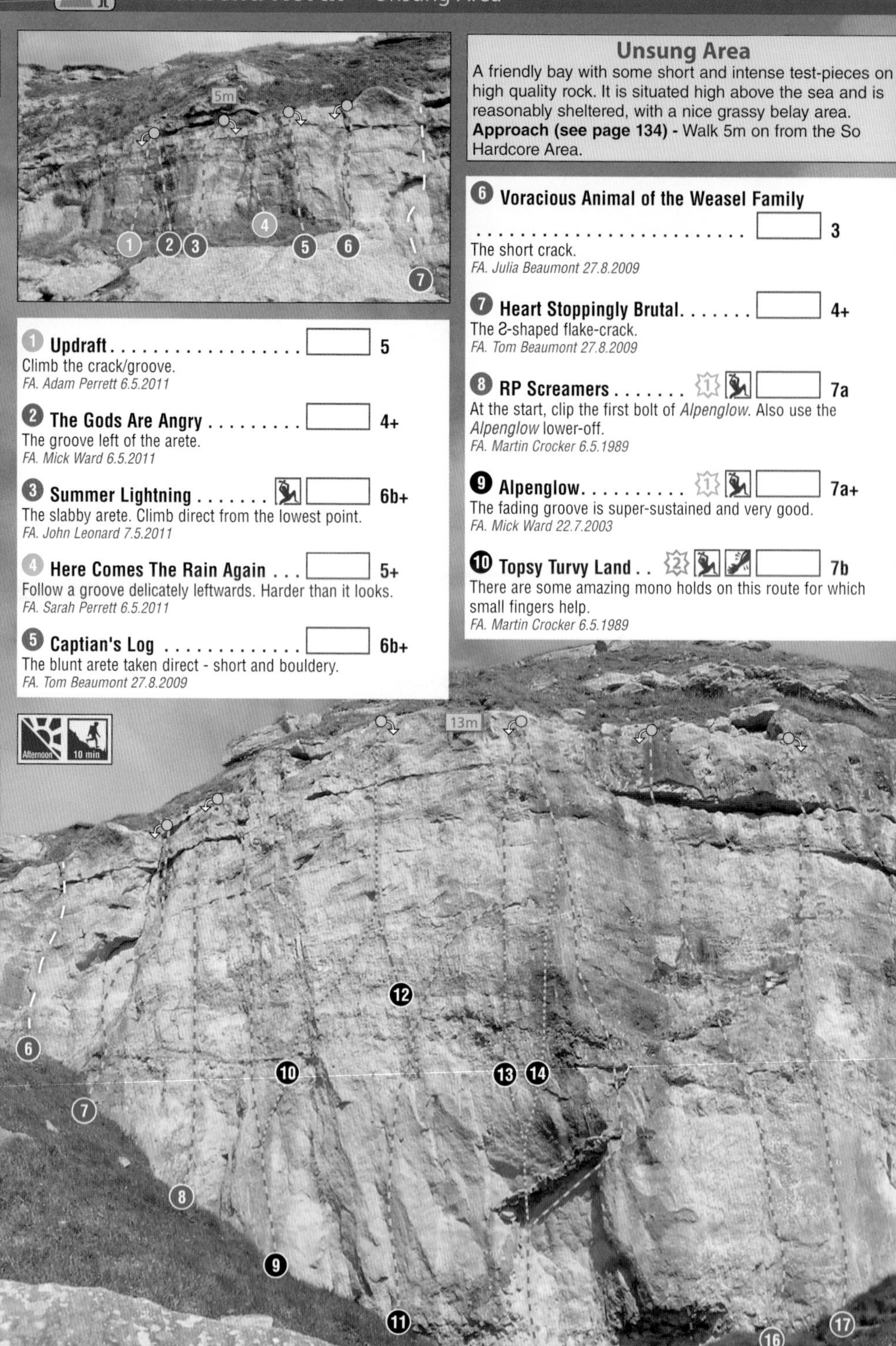

Unsung Area

A friendly bay with some short and intense test-pieces on high quality rock. It is situated high above the sea and is reasonably sheltered, with a nice grassy belay area.

Approach (see page 134) - Walk 5m on from the So Hardcore Area.

1 Updraft **5**
Climb the crack/groove.
FA. Adam Perrett 6.5.2011

2 The Gods Are Angry . . . . **4+**
The groove left of the arete.
FA. Mick Ward 6.5.2011

3 Summer Lightning . . . . **6b+**
The slabby arete. Climb direct from the lowest point.
FA. John Leonard 7.5.2011

4 Here Comes The Rain Again . . . **5+**
Follow a groove delicately leftwards. Harder than it looks.
FA. Sarah Perrett 6.5.2011

5 Captian's Log . . . . **6b+**
The blunt arete taken direct - short and bouldery.
FA. Tom Beaumont 27.8.2009

6 Voracious Animal of the Weasel Family **3**
The short crack.
FA. Julia Beaumont 27.8.2009

7 Heart Stoppingly Brutal . . . . **4+**
The S-shaped flake-crack.
FA. Tom Beaumont 27.8.2009

8 RP Screamers 1 **7a**
At the start, clip the first bolt of *Alpenglow*. Also use the *Alpenglow* lower-off.
FA. Martin Crocker 6.5.1989

9 Alpenglow . . . . 1 **7a+**
The fading groove is super-sustained and very good.
FA. Mick Ward 22.7.2003

10 Topsy Turvy Land . . 2 **7b**
There are some amazing mono holds on this route for which small fingers help.
FA. Martin Crocker 6.5.1989

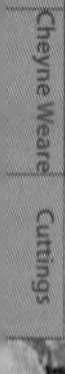

⓫ Weakest to the Wall . . . 7b
The superb, right-trending pocketed sheet is hard to flash.
FA. Pete Oxley 10.5.1989

⓬ The Magnificent 7 . 7b+
A leftwards link from the second bolt on *Weakest to the Wall* to the third bolt on *Topsy Turvy Land*, via a series of crimps and a committing move to the break. Includes the cruxes of both routes, plus a new crux.
FA. Andy Long 14.6.2009

⓭ Compromise . . . . 7b+
Use the same bolts as *Resisting Mutiny*, but climb to the left.
FA. Grant Wright 12.1995

⓮ Resisting Mutiny 7c+
A crimp-nasty sequence, directly above the shelf on *The Right Mix*, staying exactly on the bolt line. An eliminate.
FA. Grant Wright 12.1995

⓯ The Right Mix 6b
Well worth seeking out for the interesting geology. There is also a direct start, up the wall right of the arete, at about 7a.
Photo on page 31.
FA. Martin Crocker 6.5.1989

⓰ Never Lose that Feeling 6b
A technical delight with a low crux that stumps many.
FA. Pete Oxley 2.7.1992

⓱ Sing Something Simple . . . 6c+
The wall with a particularly hard move leaving a big ledge low down. Awkward to keep out of *Unsung*.
FA. Gary Gibson 20.5.2004

⓲ Unsung. 6b
A short, but action-packed line.
FA. Pete Oxley 18.8.1992

⓳ Come In Alone, Go Out Alone 6b
A bouldery start, followed by more hard climbing.
FA. Pete Oxley 6.5.1989

⓴ No Soft Option. . . . 7b
A very fierce crux, followed by an easier run-out section.
FA. Pete Oxley 10.5.1989

㉑ Dial-a-Cliché. . . . . 6c+
This attractive shallow groove is a touch bold, and has seen some nasty falls.
FA. Pete Oxley 6.5.1989

㉒ The Web. 6b
Move up to and follow the shallow groove.
FA. E. de Stefani 1994

㉓ Can't Stop the Bosch . . . . . 6b+
The short line on the right side of the bay.
FA. Joff Cook 8.5.1994

A two pitch traverse of the breaks starting up The Web and going leftward is the semi-trad line of **Sergeant Ford's Roving Truncheon, E3 6a**.

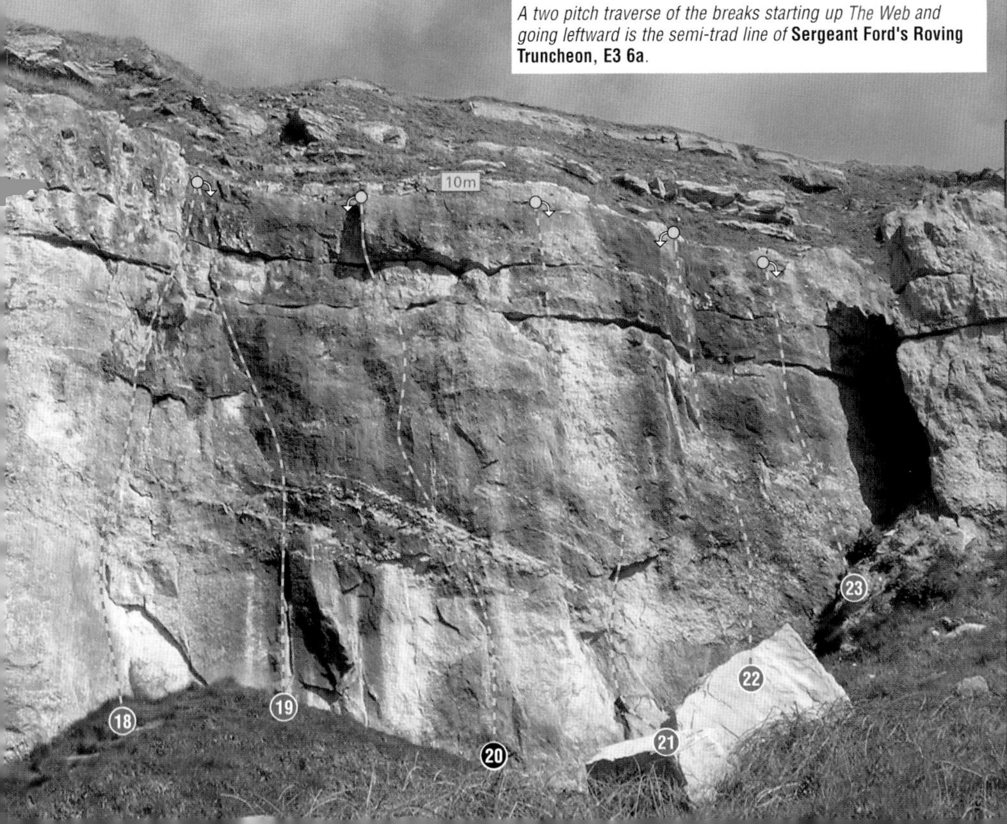

Acid Jazz Area

A fine, open face that, rather alarmingly, is gaining height due to slippage of the earth and ledges below. Take care when moving along the base of the crag. The first sections of the climbs are easy, but on crumbly rock.
Approach (see page 134) - Continue carefully along the path from under the Unsung Area. This path is liable to change as the slope slowly creeps seaward.

A number of short trad lines plus one sport route can be found just before the slope drops away.

1 Memories from the Fort 6c
Good pockets in the lower half gain crimpy side-pulls and then an easier upper wall follows.
FA. Philip Belcher, Mike Griffiths 24.9.2011

The next four sport lines are situated above a very active section of the earth slope, and the start has changed over time.

2 Sniper in the Brain . . . . 1 star 7a
Move left from the fourth bolt of *Holding the Zero*.
FA. Mick Ward 2003

3 Holding the Zero . . . . . 1 star 7a
Eases up after an interesting start.
FA. Mick Ward 2003

4 Stay on Target 7a
The original start was to the right, but this is now unclimbable due to earth slippage at the base. Start up *Holding the Zero* instead and move right.
FA. Joff Cook 28.4.1994

5 Dead Man's Click 7a
Move right from *Stay on Target* to reach the wall on the far right.
FA. Mick Ward 2003

The right-facing corner crack is the trad line of **Eternity's Toothpaste, VS 4c**.

6 Old Painless . . . . 7a+
The first route on the main wall has some spaced bolts.
FA. Joff Cook 30.5.1992

7 Useless Generation 2 stars 7b
Technical and fingery climbing.
FA. Pete Oxley 12.4.1992

8 My Love of this Land
. . . . 2 stars 7b
This has lost a hold and become a bit harder. The third clip remains as gripping as it has always been.
FA. Pete Oxley 14.5.1989

9 Treachery . . . . 1 star 7a+
Climb directly up the wall on some good rock, passing a small overhang midway.
FA. Gary Gibson 3.7.2009

10 Going Blank Again . . . . 1 star 7a+
There is only one hard move, but it's a tough one.
FA. Pete Oxley 12.4.1992

11 The Treacle Factory . . . . . . 1 star 6a+
The full-height groove and crack-system is worthwhile.
FA. Aiden Cook 30.5.1992

12 Alberta Balsam . . . . . . 1 star 7a
A good looking groove.
FA. Gary Gibson 3.7.2009

13 Montreal Protocol . 1 star 7b
A direct start has been added to straighten the route out.
FA. Martin Crocker 20.5.1989. Start - Pete Oxley 17.4.1993

Afternoon 12 min

14 Cosa Nostra . . . . 1 6a+
The corner line has a slightly dirty start, but gives good climbing above; however it is often damp and in such conditions the black lichen becomes dangerously slippy.
FA. E. de Stefani 24.4.1994

15 Acid Jazz Disco 2 7a
The fine arete has a slightly broken start, but improves dramatically higher up. The arete is climbed mainly on its right-hand side.
FA. Martin Crocker 20.5.1989

16 Eight-Bar Blues . . . 2 6c+
An excellent face of perfect blue rock. There is a handy belay-bolt at the base of the line.
FA. Joff Cook 1995

17 Precious to the Last 1 7c
Old bolts. Desperate grit-like palming which needs good conditions for a successful ascent.
FA. Pete Oxley 11.5.1990

18 Ecstasy . . . . 1 7a+
Old bolts. Trend rightwards up the wide open scoop.
FA. Pete Oxley 27.3.1990

19 Live Now, Pay Later . . . 1 7a+
Climb directly up the sustained, tilted wall.
FA. Pete Oxley 5.7.1992

20 John Craven's Jumper Contest 1 6c
Fine laybacking up the groove. Good moves.
FA. Pete Oxley 7.6.1992

21 The Watchmaker's Hands 2 7c
Some very intense moves on small side-pulls.
FA. Pete Oxley 8.7.1992

Teenage Lust Area

Some well-positioned routes above an elevated ledge.
Approach (see page 134) - From the Acid Jazz Area, the main path descends to the boulder beach. The ledges at the base of the climbs are reached via a series of knotted ropes. Take care with these and check the ropes are in good condition.

22 Breakfast of Champions 2 7b+
Follow the right-hand line of bolts at the crux.
FA. Damian Cook 29.8.1992

23 Youth Body Expression Explosion 1 7b
A good route with a witheringly hard crux right at the top.
FA. Pete Oxley 15.8.1992

24 To Hungary For Love 2 8a
The blunt arete has sustained moves on side-pulls and smears.
FA. Gavin Symonds 6.9.2003

25 So Shoot Me . . . . 1 7a+
Technical wall-climbing with some hard pocket-moves.
FA. Joff Cook 8.5.1994

26 Lolita . . . . 2 7b+
A big, sweeping line up the ramp and flake that breaks left from *Teenage Lust* at its third bolt. Some find a stick-clip necessary to extend the third bolt.
FA. Pete Oxley 17.5.1999

27 Teenage Lust . . . 2 7b+
There is a killer move off two monos. Slightly bold low down, with a tricky third clip (use a stick-clip if unsure) and exposed higher up.
FA. Pete Oxley 12.4.1992

Afternoon 16 min 26m

17 18 19 20 21 22 23 24 25 26 27

Approach scramble via knotted rope

The Rampart

A strip of excellent rock perched high above the beach which provides superbly-positioned and exhilarating climbing. The cliff is tricky to access but has a number of worthwhile climbs that are well bolted and on good rock.
Approach (see page 134) - Gain the base of the Sweet Smell of Success Area (page 144) and walk left (facing in) to where the ledge narrows and continue past a very narrow and exposed section - fixed rope - to below The Rampart.

1 Miss Jones . . . . 3+
The obvious cleft - very exposed.
FA Mick Ward, 17.6.2011

2 Ledge Shuffler's Delight . . . (1 star) 6c
The fine pocketed wall with a tricky start.
FA Mick Ward 12.7.2011

3 Guardians of Fate . . . . 5+
The centre of the flake, trending left at its top to the lower-off.
FA. John Leonard 12.7.2011

4 The Highwayman 6b
The right-hand side of the flake and the bulge above.
FA. Mick Ward 26.9.2011

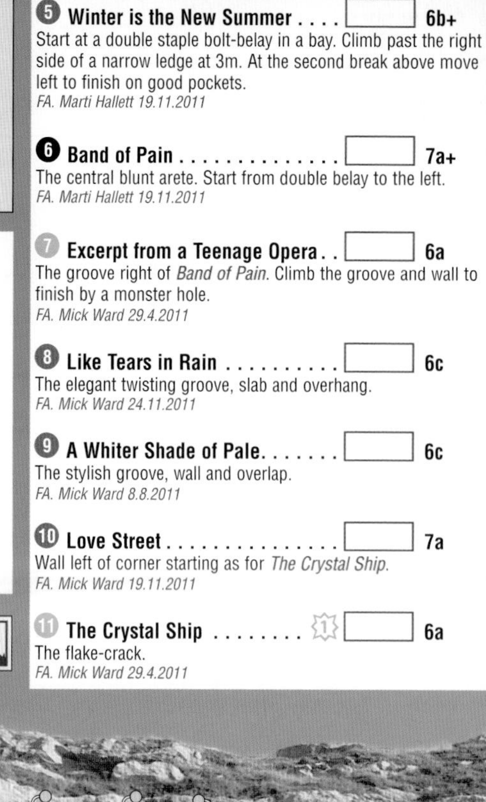

5 Winter is the New Summer . . . . 6b+
Start at a double staple bolt-belay in a bay. Climb past the right side of a narrow ledge at 3m. At the second break above move left to finish on good pockets.
FA. Marti Hallett 19.11.2011

6 Band of Pain . . . . 7a+
The central blunt arete. Start from double belay to the left.
FA. Marti Hallett 19.11.2011

7 Excerpt from a Teenage Opera . . 6a
The groove right of *Band of Pain*. Climb the groove and wall to finish by a monster hole.
FA. Mick Ward 29.4.2011

8 Like Tears in Rain 6c
The elegant twisting groove, slab and overhang.
FA. Mick Ward 24.11.2011

9 A Whiter Shade of Pale. 6c
The stylish groove, wall and overlap.
FA. Mick Ward 8.8.2011

10 Love Street 7a
Wall left of corner starting as for *The Crystal Ship*.
FA. Mick Ward 19.11.2011

11 The Crystal Ship . . . . (1 star) 6a
The flake-crack.
FA. Mick Ward 29.4.2011

12 Waiting for the Sun 1 6a
Follow the open groove.
FA. Mick Ward 29.4.2011

13 Black Slab . . . . 6b+
Technical black slab right of the groove of *Waiting for the Sun*.
FA. John Leonard 14.1.2012

14 Justin Credible 6a
The low slab and breaks in the upper wall.
FA. Richard Fox 17.11.2011

15 The Devil Came Down to Portland 6b+
The groove and breaks.
FA. Marti Hallett 19.11.2011

Seaside Slab

Under the main cliff-line is a large slab of good rock above the boulder beach. This has been developed and provides some easy bolt lines. They are all around 9m long.
Approach (see page 134) - Walk along the boulder beach to below The Rampart, The slab is directly below The Rampart at the top of the boulder beach.

16 Up the Apples and Pears. . . . . . 2+
The left-hand route.
FA. Sarah Perrett 1.5.2011

17 Sylvia Sunset . . . . 2+
Climb the faint groove to the right of the bolts.
FA. Sarah Perrett 1.5.2011

18 Magnum Farce . . . . 2+
To the right of *Sylvia Sunset* follow the line directly up the slab.
FA. Adam Perrett 1.5.2011

19 Easy Like a Sunday Morning . . . 2+
The right-hand route on the slab.
FA. Sarah Perrett 1.5.2011

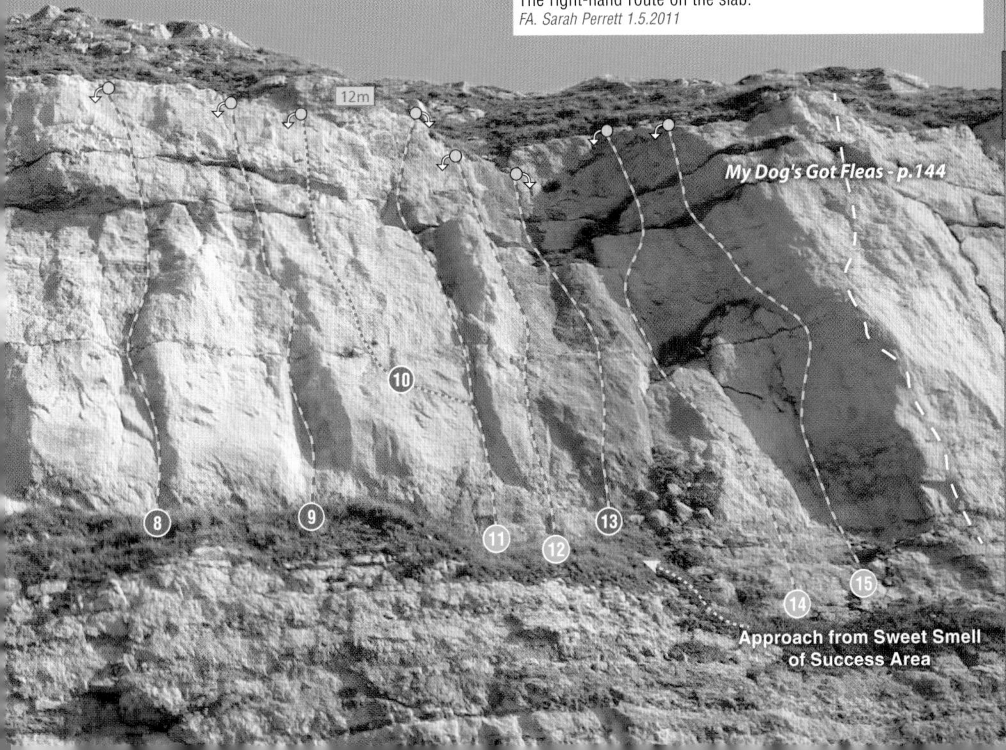

Sweet Smell of Success Area

A really good section of cliff with a handful of classic pitches. The base of the crag is grassy, stable and quite sheltered. Some routes can be dusty and *Sweet Smell of Success* suffers from seepage at times.
Approach (see page 134) - From the boulder beach, scramble easily up to the grass terrace below the wall.

There is a bolt-belay at an exposed ledge below the first lines.

1 My Dog's Got Fleas 2 stars **7b+**
Excellent rock and climbing up the rounded rib.
FA. Martin Crocker 12.8.1989

2 Poop Scoop......... 2 stars **6c**
Climb up to a flake-crack, then move left onto the arete.
FA. Martin Crocker 12.8.1989

3 Yikes Shaggy .... 1 star **6c**
A more direct version of *Poop Scoop.*
FA. Gary Gibson 2003

4 Pixie and the Milford Powerhouse
.... 1 star **6a**
The flake-crack starting up *Poop Scoop.*
FA. Tom Beaumont 29.1.2007

5 Scoobydoobydoo .. 1 star **6b**
The steep wall has a long move just before the roof finish.
FA. Gary Gibson 25.5.2003

6 Scooby Snacks .... 1 star **7a**
A striking arete. Climb the straightforward lower wall to a hand-ledge. Make a hard mantelshelf and further hard moves onto the arete proper. Fine, open climbing leads to the top.
FA. Gary Gibson 25.5.2003

7 The Heanous Quest ...... **6a+**
Climb over the flake to a short groove. Follow this to a handrail that leads up right onto the headwall.
FA. Neal Heanes 5.6.2003

8 Hen's Tooth......... **7b**
Tackle the bulge to gain a scoop. Leaving this requires a long reach. The bulging rib on the right provides the finish.
FA. Gary Gibson 27.5.2003

9 Sang Froid ...... 2 stars **7c**
A very good line. Climb the steep wall and arete on its right to a hard finish.
FA. Gavin Symonds 2010

Afternoon 18 min

20m

To The Rampart

10 So You Want to Be Happy . . . . . 7a+
Old/no bolts at the present time.
FA. Pete Oxley 17.7.1990

11 Up on the Hill . . . . 1 star 7a
Climb the wall and blunt rib then move onto the face above. Easier climbing remains.
FA. Gary Gibson 25.5.2003

12 Hallelujah. . . . . 1 star 7a
A good route that, despite being well-bolted, still feels bold.
FA. Pete Oxley 17.7.1990

13 Old Speckled Hen . . . . 1 star 6c+
A worthwhile pitch. Climb the wall to gain a prominent flake-hold. Reach the thin crack above and follow this to the slabby wall.
FA. Gary Gibson, Phil Gibson 2003

14 Stone Cold Sober. . . . . 2 stars 7b
A good climb, squeezed in just left of *Stay Golden,* and sharing its start. Quite blind on the crux.
FA. Mike Robertson 18.8.1998

15 Stay Golden . . . . . . 3 stars 7b
The first of three classics in this area features stylish climbing on great rock.
FA. Pete Oxley 17.7.1990

16 Sweet Smell of Success Top 50 7b
An outstanding route that overhangs gently all the way. One of the best lines on Portland.
FA. Pete Oxley 11.5.1990

17 Frazzled . . . . . . 3 stars 7b
A stunning and difficult line up the faint, streaked flake just right of the arete. There are three cruxes, each with its own character.
FA. Damian Cook 9.1994

18 Streaky. . . . . 2 stars 6c+
Not surprisingly, this follows the streaky wall.
FA. Mike Robertson 5.8.1994

19 Das Boot. . . . . 1 star 6c+
A good face-climb. Follow the line of conventional bolts up a short steep wall to gain the blackened upper face. Intricate climbing up this leads to a bulge and a big jug above. The finish is harder than it looks.
FA. Gary Gibson, Hazel Gibson, Phil Gibson 27.5.2003

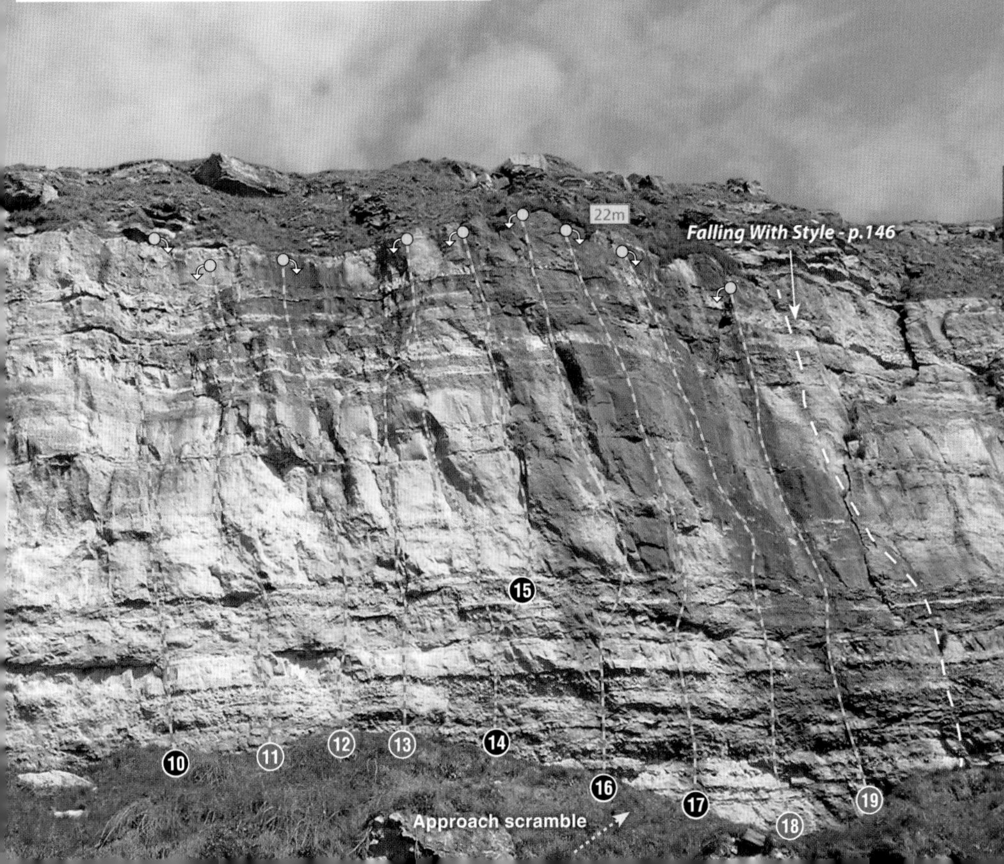

Portland | Lulworth | Swanage | Blacknor N | Blacknor C | Blacknor S | Blacknor B | Blacknor FS | Battleship | Battleship BC | Wallsend N | Wallsend S | Coastguard N | Coastguard S | White Hole | Lighthouse | Cheyne Weare | Cuttings

Bladerunner Area

This section of cliff occasionally suffers mudslides in the winter and as a result the routes can be dirty. The climbing here is definitely worth seeking out, especially on the upper sections, although the starts are tough.
Approach (see page 134) - Either walk along the grass bank from the Sweet Smell of Success Area (page 144), or scramble up direct from the boulder beach.

1 Falling with Style . . . . ☆1 ☐ **6b+**
Break left at a low shelf to a tricky groove. It can sometimes be very dirty.
FA. Neal Heanes 16.8.1998

2 Screw You Hippy . . . . . ☆1 ☐ **6a**
The best of the slabs has good orange rock. High in the grade and the start can prove to be a bit of a stopper.
FA. Neal Heanes 16.8.1998

3 Tanya's Sex Pot . . . . ☐ **6a+**
The steep wall, eventually gaining the finish of *Screw You Hippy*.
FA. Neil Burton 16.8.1998

4 Gay Dog . . . . ☐ **6a+**
After a crunchy start, this one has some interesting groove-climbing higher up.
FA. Neal Heanes 16.8.1998

5 Layback and Take It . . . . ☐ **6a**
A disappointing route up the flake.
FA. Neal Heanes 16.8.1998

6 Blackwind, Fire and Steel . . . . . ☐ **6b+**
A tricky line up the centre of the big flake.
FA. Neil Burton 16.8.1998

7 Beefcake, Beefcake . . . . . . ☐ **6a**
An unusually long and thuggy flake-climb.
FA. Neal Heanes 3.8.1998

8 Jungle Drums . . . . ☐ **6c+**
Some of the flakes ring hollow. A bold route.
FA. Joff Cook 29.8.1992

9 Aaron the Aardvark . . . . . . ☆1 ☐ **6b+**
Climb the centre of the face.
FA. Mike Robertson 6.5.1995

10 Bladerunner . . . . ☆2 ☐ **6b+**
Break right out of *Aaron the Aardvark* to an arete-hugging finish. A good route.
FA. Mike Robertson 6.5.1995

High on the fingery upper wall of *Opposites Attract* (6c) - *page 150* - at Wallsend North. Photo: Marti Hallett

Downhill Spiral Area

The Downhill Spiral Area routes start from a raised grass bank beneath heavily-stained black walls that are prone to seepage in the winter.

Approach (see page 134) - From the boulder beach, scramble up the bank to the grassy ledge below the face.

1 Fatal Fibre . . . . 1★ **6c+**
Start from a bolt-belay. The wall is followed with a hard move at the start to a lower-off on the right.
FA. Gary Gibson 4.5.2002

2 Billy Bob's Way . . . . 2★ **6b+**
Start from the bolt-belay of *Fatal Fibre*. Climb the prominent blackened-streak directly by pleasant, sustained moves.
FA. Gary Gibson Hazel Gibson 4.5.2002

3 The Man Who Wasn't There **7b**
Climb steadily up the wall to reach the left-hand side of the arete. Continue up this until a swing up and right onto the face is possible. The rib has some hard moves on its upper section and is a little loose lower down.
FA. Gary Gibson 3.5.2002

4 Hate Crime . . . . 1★ **7a+**
A fine, technical groove experience with one very hard move, but there are also a few rests to compensate.
FA. Neal Heanes 9.5.1998

5 Lefty Hoot 'n' Annie . . . 2★ **6c**
Good climbing up the yellow groove. It requires some wide bridging moves before the nifty finish.
FA. Neal Heanes 2.5.1998

6 And the Boat Sails By . . . . . 1★ **7a**
Sustained moves up the fine open face.
FA. Gary Gibson 30.3.2002

7 Downhill Spiral . 2★ **7b+**
Run-out and pumpy but the best climb hereabouts.
FA. Pete Oxley 19.4.1992

8 Everything's Eventual . . . . . 1★ **6c+**
A good pitch finishing up a shallow groove after a rather dusty start.
FA. Gary Gibson 1.4.2002

Afternoon 20 min

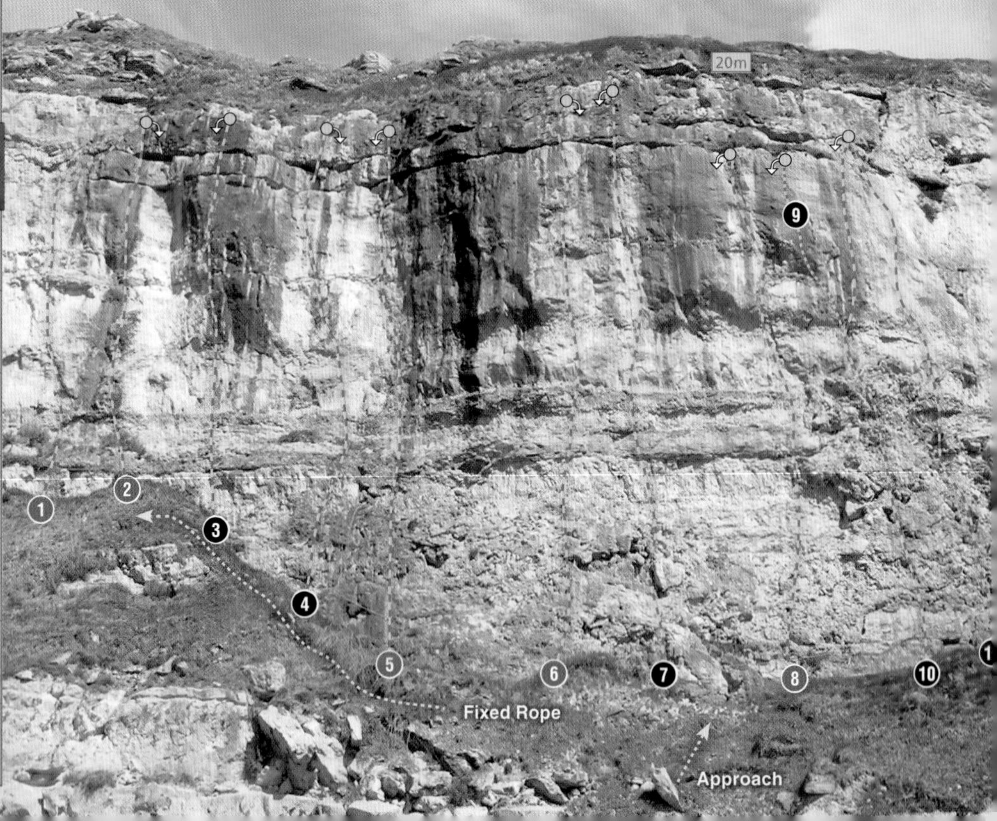

9 By Mistake . . . . 1 **7b+**
The thin left-hand finish to *More Than a Legend*.
FA. Andy Long 2005

10 More Than a Legend . . 1 **7b+**
A desperate technical sequence up the thin wall leading to a faint crack and more hard moves to the belay. Friable low down.
FA. Gary Gibson 1.4.2002

11 Under Crimson Skies . . 1 **7a+**
Surprisingly sustained climbing up the right-hand side of the flowstone. A friable lower wall.
FA. Gary Gibson 1.4.2002

Laid Black Area

This section of wall is the continuation rightwards from the Downhill Spiral Area and is just before the tall buttress of the Bigger Piece Area.
Approach (see page 134) - Continue along the boulder beach below the streaks of the Downhill Spiral Area. Then scramble up the grassy slope to the base of the wall.

The next route starts about 8m right of Under Crimson Skies.

12 My Figure Head **6c**
Climb dirty ground to a ledge. Gain the groove above with difficulty, then pull over the roof to the lower-off.
FA. Gary Gibson 11.5.2002

13 The Shipping News . . . 1 **7b**
From the ledge of *My Figure Head*, step right and climb the technical wall past a deep break to the lower-off.
FA. Gary Gibson 11.5.2002

14 Five Easy Pieces **6c**
A steep and intricate slab leads to a ramp and a steep, juggy headwall. Unfortunately loose low down and dirty higher up.
FA. Gary Gibson 3.6.2002

15 Laid Black . . . . 1 **6c+**
Climb over cleaned ledges to below the black wall. Tricky moves through the bulge lead onto the wall. Climb this leftwards to the lower-off.
FA. Gary Gibson 11.5.2002

The last two routes are around 25m to the right.

16 Wonderful . . . . 2 **7a+**
Climb a thin wall via a faint crack, then move left to good holds at the top. Continue direct to a ledge and an awkward finish. Excellent rock.
FA. Gary Gibson 1.6.2002

17 Wonder-Bra 1 **6b**
Trend right from the start of *Wonderful* and climb the scooped wall past a ledge to a steep finish.
FA. Gary Gibson 1.6.2002

Afternoon 20 min

20m
13
17
16
14
15
12
Approach

The Bigger Piece Area

An eye-catching, towering buttress, which is home to some exhilarating and exposed climbs that are well worth the long approach via the boulder beach.

Approach (see page 134) - The wall is about mid-way along Wallsend Cove, so it can be approached from either the north or south (it is cut off from the south at high-tide). Either start from the boulder beach, or scramble up the grass and vegetation to reach the routes on the right.

A two pitch trad line **Slice of Life, E2 5b** *takes the wall and left-hand side of the arete.*

1 The Bigger Piece . . . . . 2 stars — 7a+
One of the longest lines on Portland up a huge pillar. The reach symbol is for clipping the bolts (tip - do *No Place for Mambas* first and place the clips on your way down).
FA. Martin Crocker 13.8.1989

2 No Place for Mambas . . . . . 2 stars — 6b
Quality face climbing on the headwall and generously bolted.
FA. Martin Crocker 2.5.1992

3 Opposites Attract . . . . . 2 stars — 6c
Thin and sustained face climbing on quality rock high up.
Photo on page 147.
FA. Martin Crocker 2.5.1992

4 Mick Lovatt Stole My Trousers . . . . 1 star — 6b+
Follow the long layback crack at the top.
FA. Martin Crocker 2.5.1992

5 Cool to be Uncool . 1 star — 7b+
An unusual arete climb that feels bold. No lower-off.
FA. Martin Crocker 2.5.1992

6 Coconut Milk . . . . 2 stars — 7a
A worthwhile face route that follows the thin crack-line.
FA. Martin Crocker 16.7.1989

7 On a Desert Island Beach 2 stars — 7a+
The well-positioned arete. Start up *On a Desert Island Beach*.
FA. Martin Crocker 15.7.1989

8 Vin Chaud . . . . 2 stars — 7a
A fine left-hand finish to *Accordians Go Crazy* up some flakes.
FA. Neal Heanes 16.6.2003

9 Accordions Go Crazy . . . 2 stars — 6b+
Start to the left of the flake. Initially the rock is a bit crumbly, but it improves dramatically above.
FA. Martin Crocker 15.7.1989

10 Basrah Blues Band . . . . 1 star — 6c
Climb a flake to a ledge. Follow the groove above to a tricky bulge. The slab above this leads to the lower-off.
FA. Neal Heanes 14.6.2003

11 Laughing Peter . . . . . . 2 stars — 7a+
Climb the flake right of the bolts past a difficult second clip.
FA. Martin Crocker 15.7.1989

12 Sans Frontière . . . . 1 star — 6b+
A fine arete with a definite crux move at mid-height.
FA. Helen Heanes 2003

13 Charlton Mackeral, the World's Strongest Fish 6c
The left-facing flake-line has some hard moves.
FA. Neal Heanes 10.6.2006

Afternoon 20 min

30m 23m

14 Parkhurst Dozen . . . . . 1★ 6c
A good pitch up some layback flakes.
FA. Ben Stokes 26.3.2003

15 Sang Chaud. . . . . 3★ 7a+
Fine climbing up the wall and groove.
FA. Neal Heanes 16.6.2003

16 Son of Mustang Ford . . 1★ 7a
A thin and dirty wall with some good flowstone near the top.
FA. Pete Oxley 26.4.1992

17 Mr. Natural . . . . . . 2★ 7b+
An excellent, searing thin crack topped by a very hard move.
FA. Pete Oxley 19.4.1992

18 Catatonic . . . . 6b+
Some good, open face climbing in its upper half. Take care low down as the bolts are spaced and the rock friable.
FA. Pete Oxley 19.4.1992

19 Random Texter . . . . 6b+
Follow a direct line up the left-hand side of the arete.
FA. Gav Symonds 6.2006

20 Gravity Epiphany . . . . 6c+
The groove in the arete starting up *Random Texter*.
FA. Jane Weir 23.9.2006

The wide chimney is the two pitch line of **Family S, VS**.

21 Moan, Moan, Moan . . . 1★ 7b+
Climb to the roof and make a long move over it to an easy rockover using hidden holds above. Quality, sustained climbing remains to a one bolt lower-off.
FA. Martin Crocker 20.4.1992

22 Injury Encyclopaedia . . 1★ 7b
A fine white wall. The second piece of gear is a peg.
FA. Martin Crocker 25.4.1992

Afternoon 20 min

Mr. Natural Area

Like the Bigger Piece Area, the climbs on this wall are well worth the effort of the long approach.
Approach (see page 134) - The wall is about mid-way along the Wallsend Cove, so it can be approached from either the north or south (it is cut off from the south at high-tide).

Realm of Chaos Area

One of the biggest walls on Portland which has an array of top-notch pitches that will appeal to harder climbers. When in condition the climbs are some of the best on the coast. Due to lack of traffic they are more often than not a bit dirty and need a brief clean before an ascent. The pitches are long and sustained.

Approach (see page 134) - The quickest approach is from the south along the boulder beach, unless the tide is high, in which case a slightly longer approach can be made from the northern end of Wallsend.

1 Will 7b

Climb the wall left of the scruffy flake to a ledge. Step left and follow the elegant, technical groove.

FA. Mick Ward 4.4.2006

2 Michèle . . . . 6a+

Climb *Will* to the ledge; extend the third clip. The hanging groove and flake-crack give some excellent climbing.

FA. Mick Ward 4.4.2006

3 Shape of Tomorrow 6c
Start a metre right of the scruffy flake. Climb a steep wall to the halfway ledge, move left and head for the scary flakes.
FA. Mick Ward 4.4.2006

4 River of Dreams 7a
The crack left of the upper section of *Spinal Tap*, with a short sharp crux. Start as for *Shape of Tomorrow* with hard moves to gain the right side of the scary flakes.
FA. Mick Ward 13.4.2004

5 Spinal Tap . . . . 1 7b+
The long thin line has a safe, but scary run-out at the top.
FA. Pete Oxley 26.4.1992

6 Cloud Atlas . . . . . . 2 7b+
The steep wall and blind flake is powerful in its first half then technical in its upper reaches.
FA. Gav Symonds 6.2006

7 Million Watt Marshalls
. . . . 2 7b+
Continually absorbing and very sustained climbing, but unfortunately often dirty. Formally 7b.
FA. Pete Oxley 26.4.1992

8 Ariane V 3 7b
A direct and pumpy version of *Disintegration* with no real crux moves, but plenty of hard ones. A very good route.
FA. Pete Oxley 9.5.1996

9 Disintegration . . . . 2 7b+
An older line, but still excellent. Start up *Zum Zeaux* and link into the top of *Ariane V*.
FA. Pete Oxley 25.9.1989

10 Zum Zeaux . . . . 3 7b+
A tremendous route of contrasting styles. The initial leaning wall is burly whilst the upper wall is technical.
FA. Martin Crocker 16.7.1989

11 Magnetic Pull . . . . . 3 7c+
An extremely demanding direct on *Zum Zeaux* with a power-packed first 10m. Save some energy for the last moves.
FA. Pete Oxley 14.9.1996

12 Realm of Chaos . . . . . . Top 50 7b+
A superb and sustained route with a hard start up the shallow rounded weakness. One of the most impressive and best pitches on the Isle when in prime condition.
FA. Pete Oxley 24.9.1989

13 Hombre Solaire . . . 2 7c
Another huge stamina pitch. Start up *Realm of Chaos*, move out right at the fourth bolt for 4m, then climb direct to the top.
FA. Pete Oxley 6.6.1996. The old direct start has been abandoned.

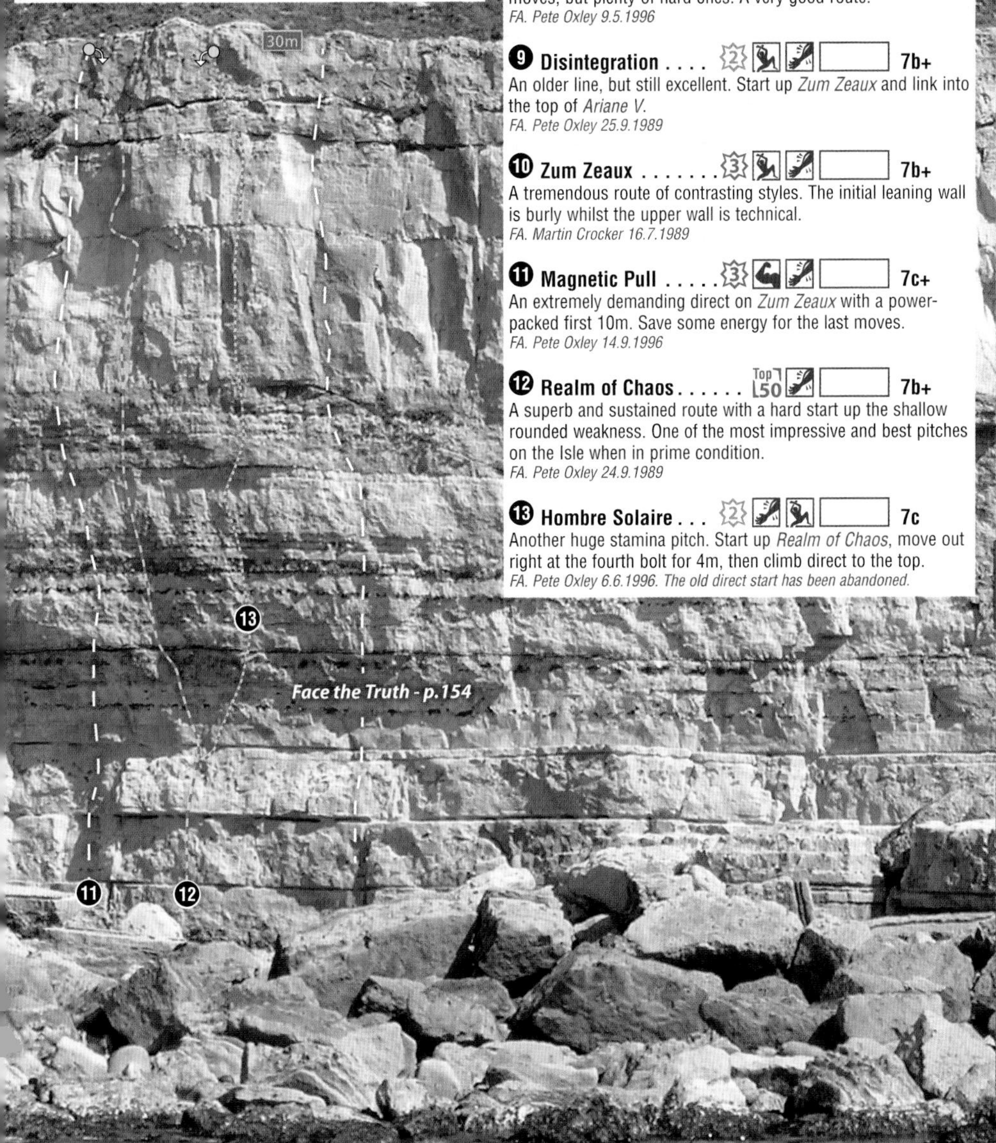

30m

13

Face the Truth - p.154

11 12

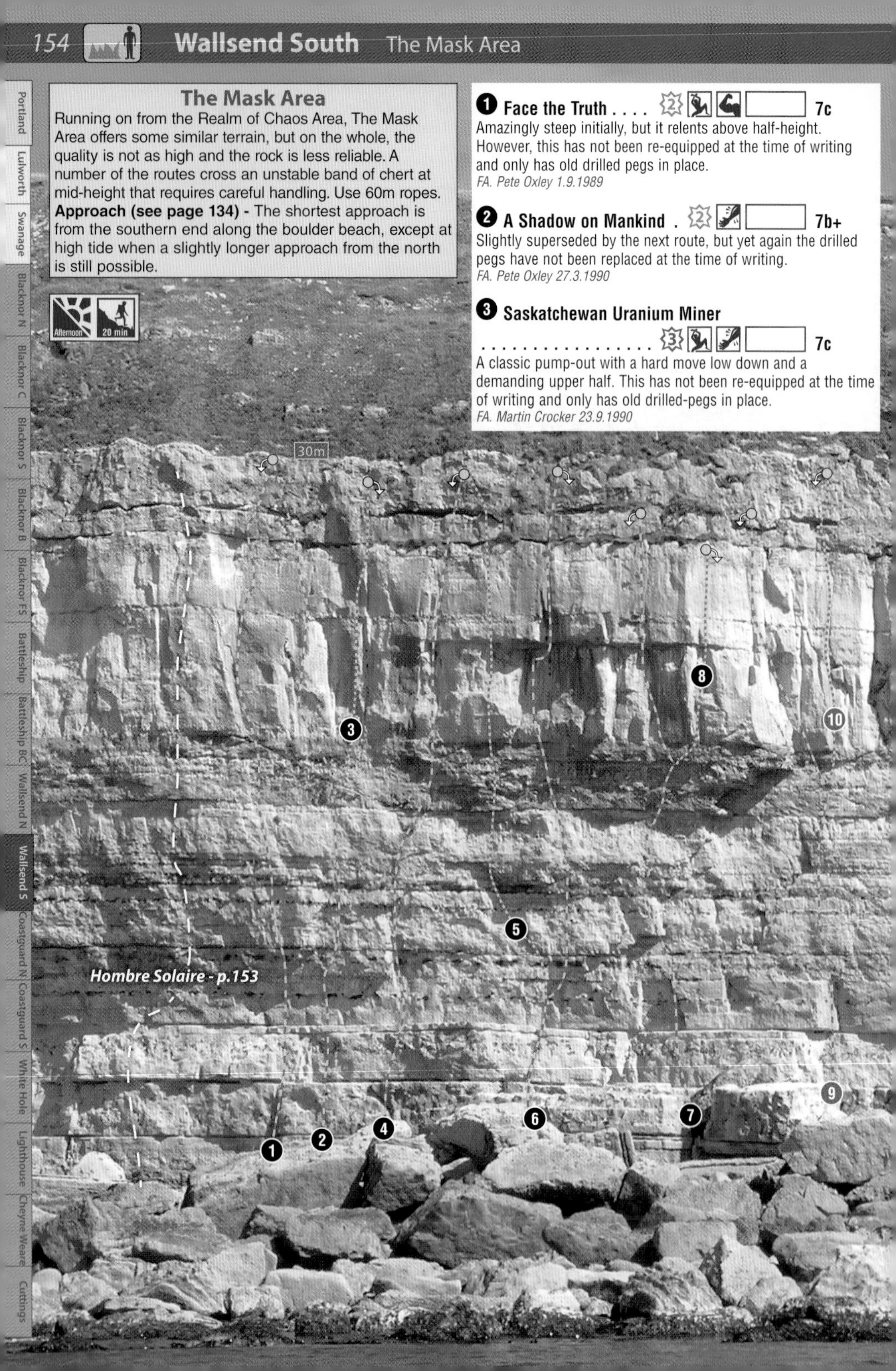

The Mask Area

Running on from the Realm of Chaos Area, The Mask Area offers some similar terrain, but on the whole, the quality is not as high and the rock is less reliable. A number of the routes cross an unstable band of chert at mid-height that requires careful handling. Use 60m ropes.
Approach (see page 134) - The shortest approach is from the southern end along the boulder beach, except at high tide when a slightly longer approach from the north is still possible.

1 Face the Truth 2 **7c**
Amazingly steep initially, but it relents above half-height. However, this has not been re-equipped at the time of writing and only has old drilled pegs in place.
FA. Pete Oxley 1.9.1989

2 A Shadow on Mankind . 2 **7b+**
Slightly superseded by the next route, but yet again the drilled pegs have not been replaced at the time of writing.
FA. Pete Oxley 27.3.1990

3 Saskatchewan Uranium Miner
. . . . 3 **7c**
A classic pump-out with a hard move low down and a demanding upper half. This has not been re-equipped at the time of writing and only has old drilled-pegs in place.
FA. Martin Crocker 23.9.1990

Heat Stroke Groove Area

A short and isolated section of good rock located 50m to the right of The Mask Area, and perched up above some unstable and vegetated low-angle rock which must be overcome to reach the base of the lines proper.

Approach (see page 134) - The shortest approach is from the southern end along the boulder beach, except at high tide when a slightly longer approach from the north is still possible.

4 Troll Team Special . . . . 2 — **7a+**
A good pitch with a low crux and great climbing above up the narrow corner.
FA. Pete Oxley 13.7.1989

5 The Pickford Files . . . . 2 — **7b+**
Start up *Breakbeat* then head left and up the fine slabby headwall.
FA. Dave Pickford 9.1999

6 Breakbeat . . . . 2 — **7b+**
A good sustained line with a fine upper groove. It does have a loose chert band but this may well now have cleaned up - best proceed with caution.
FA. Martin Crocker 19.8.1990

7 The Mask . . . . 2 — **7b**
Nice and exposed with some pumpy climbing.
FA. Pete Oxley 30.4.1990

8 Trent Reznor . . . . . 2 — **7b**
A wild version of *The Mask* with sensational exposure. Move out right from above the mid-height overhang.
FA. Pete Oxley 14.10.1995

A two pitch trad line **Kraken, HVS** *trends rightward across the wall and finishes up a corner to the right of the upper section of Moonfleet.*

9 Bevis . . . . — **6b**
The wall and soaring cracks give relatively easy access to some spectacular territory. However the rock is loose in the middle section of the pitch.
FA. Mick Ward 19.6.2004

10 Moonfleet . . . . — **6b+**
Interesting, sustained climbing above the loose start shared with *Bevis*. Care needed with some of the rock.
FA. Mick Ward 19.6.2004

The trad line of **Divine Madness, E1 5a/b** *goes up the wall to join the upper section of the trad line* **Kraken**.

The next three lines are located 50m to the right and all start up the same initial broken and vegetated wall.

11 Gossip and Drool . . . . . 1 — **7b**
Climb the blackened groove on the left-hand side of the upper wall. Good rock throughout.
FA. Martin Crocker 13.8.1989

12 Heat Stroke Groove . . . 1 — **6c+**
The fine, white groove with a reachy finish.
FA. Pete Oxley 7.9.1989

13 Summer Babe . . . . 1 — **7b+**
The right-hand rib has a slappy crux.
FA. Pete Oxley 21.5.1992

Portland
Lulworth
Swanage
Blacknor N
Blacknor C
Blacknor S
Blacknor B
Blacknor FS
Battleship
Battleship BC
Wallsend N
Wallsend S
Coastguard N
Coastguard S
White Hole
Lighthouse
Cheyne Weare
Cuttings

The Enchanted Path Area

One of Portland's finest mid-grade venues that has a number of fantastic wall climbs. The rock is generally excellent on the classic lines and the climbing sustained. The setting is stunning, and the base of the cliff is lined with good flat ledges - ideal for soaking up some sunshine between climbs.

Approach (see page 134) - The shortest approach is from the southern end along the boulder beach, except at high tide when a slightly longer approach from the north is still possible.

1 Eternal Peace **6c**
Climb the wall to a ledge and then head left and up the arete.
FA. Mick Ward 5.7.2003

2 Dark Play **6b**
A direct on *Eternal Peace* from the midway ledge. There is a line of taped-up bolts to the right that are on its old loose start.
FA. Mick Ward 2004

The wide crack is the two pitch trad line **Lacerations, VS.**

3 The Bog Man . . . . . **6b+**
The wall, overlap and flake-crack give good varied climbing. A long reach is useful at the top.
FA. Mick Ward 17.7.2003

4 Garstang . . . . **6c+**
The wall, groove and overlap. Good climbing with rests.
FA. Mick Ward 5.7.2003

The wall, wide crack and hanging block is the line of the two pitch **Boulder Crack, HVS.**

5 Shibumi 1 **7a**
Climb easy rock to a good wall high up.
FA. Mick Ward 2004

6 Slave State . . . . . . 2 **7b+**
Start by scrambling up to below the central gully. A bit run-out between bolts two and three.
FA. Pete Oxley 2.5.1992

The vegetated rightward-trending ramp and wide crack is the line of the two pitch trad route **Ferocity, VS.**

7 Child of Light . . . . 1 **6c+**
A left-hand finish to *Immaculata*. Climb to a groove high on the wall, then break out left and ascend the impending face.
FA. Mick Ward 10.9.2009

8 Immaculata 2 **6c**
Intricate climbing that builds to an exposed final wall. Climb, on slightly dusty rock to the upper wall. Move right into a corner, and climb this to a step left and the exposed headwall.
FA. Mick Ward 31.3.2003

9 The Watchman . . . Top 50 **6b**
A brilliant, testing line that features some hard moves low down. Start just to the left of a corner in the low overhang. Execute a technical, but short-lived sequence to better holds on the wall above, then follow this to the mid-height break. The clean-cut corner and headwall above are the icing on the cake.
Photo on page 133.
FA. Pete Oxley 31.12.1989

10 Waiting for the Barbarians . 2 **6b+**
The wall above the short corner is worthwhile. Start at the short corner in the low overhang. Move up through the overhang and pull left to a sloping ledge. Follow the shallow groove and wall above to a ledge below the upper wall. Climb direct to finish.
FA. Mick Ward 8.8.2008

11 Peace in the Nineties . . 1 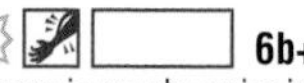 **6b+**
The rightward line above the short corner is much easier in its upper reaches. Start as for *Waiting for the Barbarians*. Move over the overhang and trend rightwards across the wall above it, until a direct line can be followed to the straightforward upper wall. A difficult direct start over the low roof is possible at 6c.
FA. Pete Oxley 31.12.1989. Direct start Pete Oxley14.10.1996

12 Some Velvet Morning 1 **7a**
The wall and blunt arete right of *Peace in the Nineties*. Start up *Peace in the Nineties* and continue beyond its traverse above the low overhang before ascending the face, blunt arete and headwall above to finish. *Photo on page 135.*
FA. Mick Ward 8.8.2008

13 The Enchanted Path . . . 2 6c

A powerful pull through the initial overhang is followed by far more pleasant climbing above. Start just to the left of an overhung sentry-box. Heave over the low overhang and ascend the wall above to twin corners in the upper wall. Finish via the left corner, turning the final overhang on the left.

FA. Brian Tilley 13.7.1989

14 Once Upon a Time in The West

. . . . 1 6c

A neat pitch. Climb *Best Fingers Forward* to clear the overhang, then weave up the wall to the groove. Climb the groove to an exit via some of the most amazing holds on Portland.

FA. Mick Ward 19.9.2009

15 Best Fingers Forward . . Top 50 6c+

A splendid pitch that features a forceful finger-crack. Start in an overhung sentry-box. Move up and right to clear the overhang and gain the wall above. Climb the wall rightwards on good finger-holds to the base of a thin crack in the upper wall. The fine, thin crack is climbed with difficulty to a short headwall.

FA. Pete Oxley 11.7.1989

16 Blue Faced Booby 2 6c

Exposed and committing climbing up the wall's right-hand arete. Start just to the left of the arete. Make a tricky series of moves over the low overhang and then climb rightwards up the wall to meet the upper arete. Make committing moves up the arete to an easier finish.

FA Martin Crocker 13.8.89. FA (with long direct start) Pete Oxley 14.10.95

Portland Lulworth Swanage Blacknor N Blacknor C Blacknor S Blacknor B Blacknor FS Battleship Battleship BC Wallsend N Wallsend S Coastguard N Coastguard S White Hole Lighthouse Cheyne Weare Cuttings

Trad Free World Area

Situated right in the centre of Wallsend Cove, this area has some of the best rock on offer on Portland, with long sustained pitches in an atmospheric setting. The only drawback is that some of the harder lines need good conditions to be climbable, especially the corner lines.

Approach (see page 134) - The southern approach to the base of the cliff is tidal and access is cut off for around 1 hour either side of high water.

The huge corner-crack that defines the left-hand side of the wall is the trad line of the three pitch route **The Gash, VS**.

1 Tea Cakes Calling . . . 7a

A pitch with a hard lower-crux. Start just right of the wide, broken corner-crack. Climb the wall direct with a bouldery move on the steep initial wall.

FA. Pete Oxley 21.5.1996

2 The Jewel of the Isle . . Top 50 . . 6b+

A magical wall climb. Start in the middle of the steepest section of the wall. Climb the fingery lower-wall with conviction to finish up a thin crack in the compact face above.

FA. Pete Oxley 25.6.1995

3 Stalker's Zone . . . . Top 50 . . 6a+

The right-hand line of the lower wall is another terrific face-climb. Start below ledges and a left-leaning corner under an overhang. Climb the gently overhanging wall on positive holds and finish up a flake-crack in the headwall. Stunning.

Photo on cover.

FA. Pete Oxley 30.4.1989

4 Trad Free World . . . . . . Top 50 . . 6b

A Wallsend classic that sees plenty of ascents. A lovely pitch on great rock. Start at the left-hand end of a high ledge below a shallow corner. Climb the rib just left of the corner to gain the wall proper and easier climbing. Follow the wall to a thin crack. Climb the thin crack to a final leaning headwall.

FA. Pete Oxley 7.11.1992

30m

9 5 12 4 6 7 8 10 11 13 1 2 3

5 Genuflection 7b
Gradually steepening climbing with an intense sequence midway. Start at the left-hand end of a high ledge, below a shallow corner. Climb the shallow corner for about 10m until a line of bolts on the left leads up to a bald wall, just above an overhang. Thin moves up the wall gain easier, but bulging ground that leads to the top.
FA. Pete Oxley 11.5.1996

6 Reverence . . . . Top 50 7a+
When in condition, the central depression and upper cracks offer a brilliant experience that is low in the grade. Start at the left-hand end of a high ledge, below a shallow corner.
Climb the technical central groove to a more defined section of the depression, where the difficulties build before the final impending headwall is reached and climbed on more-positive holds.
FA. Pete Oxley 5.7.1989

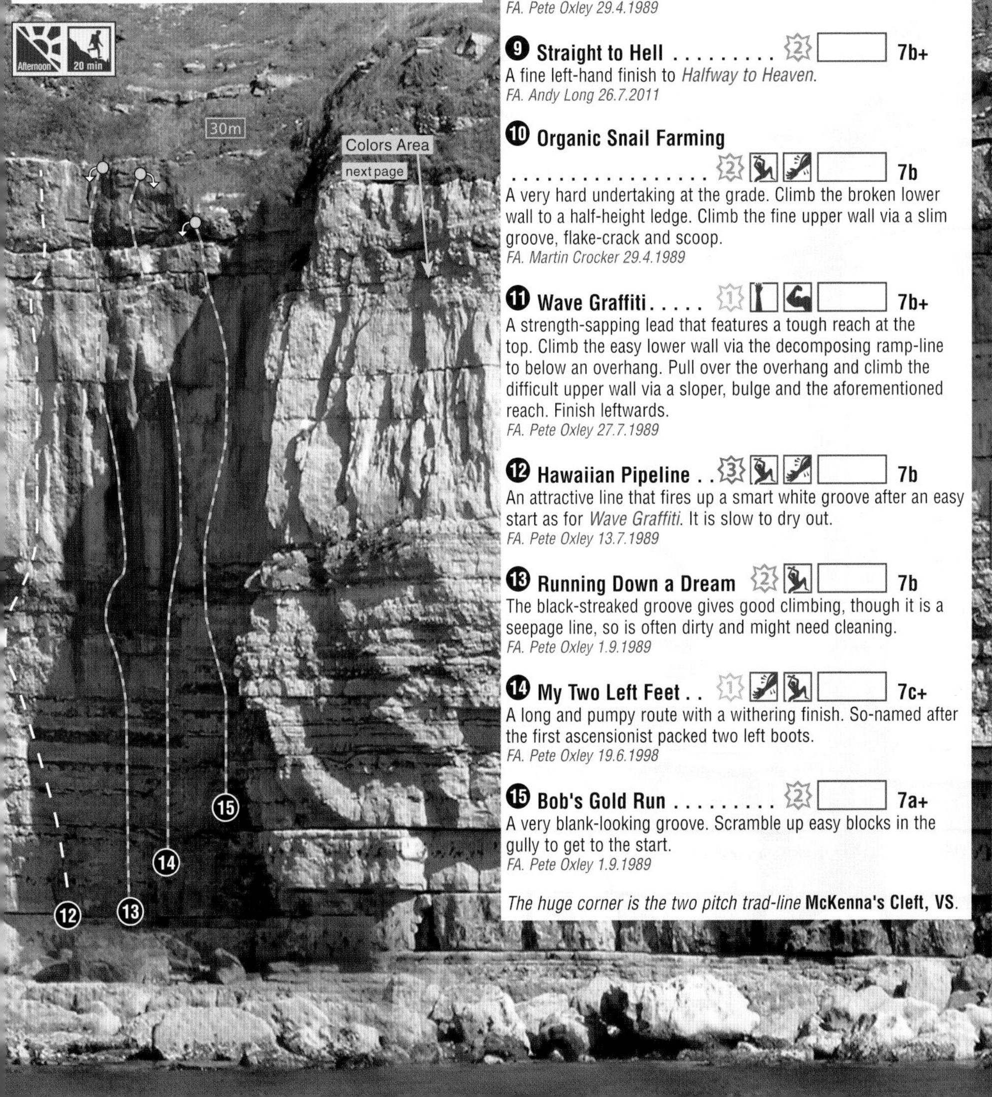

Afternoon 20 min

30m

Colors Area
next page

12 13 14 15

7 Outside the Gate . . . 7b
The routes's difficulties are split by the left-leaning, open corner in the middle of the bulging section of the upper wall. Start below the blank wall directly below the corner. Climb the fingery wall and flake to below the midway corner. Inch up to easier ground in the corner and climb this to more tricky climbing at its end, where the overhang and headwall provide a spectacular finale.
FA. Pete Oxley 5.7.1989

8 Halfway to Heaven . Top 50 7b
Another Portland classic, with continuously interesting and varied moves on superb rock. Start at a vertical wall directly below a clean-cut corner in the upper wall. A hard move to a good hold gains easier ground that leads to the midway horizontal break. Pull up leftwards into the base of the square-cut corner. Climb the corner steeply to a difficult exit out right and up to gain the finishing headwall.
FA. Pete Oxley 29.4.1989

9 Straight to Hell . . . . 7b+
A fine left-hand finish to *Halfway to Heaven*.
FA. Andy Long 26.7.2011

10 Organic Snail Farming
. . . . 7b
A very hard undertaking at the grade. Climb the broken lower wall to a half-height ledge. Climb the fine upper wall via a slim groove, flake-crack and scoop.
FA. Martin Crocker 29.4.1989

11 Wave Graffiti . . . . . 7b+
A strength-sapping lead that features a tough reach at the top. Climb the easy lower wall via the decomposing ramp-line to below an overhang. Pull over the overhang and climb the difficult upper wall via a sloper, bulge and the aforementioned reach. Finish leftwards.
FA. Pete Oxley 27.7.1989

12 Hawaiian Pipeline . . 7b
An attractive line that fires up a smart white groove after an easy start as for *Wave Graffiti*. It is slow to dry out.
FA. Pete Oxley 13.7.1989

13 Running Down a Dream 7b
The black-streaked groove gives good climbing, though it is a seepage line, so is often dirty and might need cleaning.
FA. Pete Oxley 1.9.1989

14 My Two Left Feet . . 7c+
A long and pumpy route with a withering finish. So-named after the first ascensionist packed two left boots.
FA. Pete Oxley 19.6.1998

15 Bob's Gold Run . . . . 7a+
A very blank-looking groove. Scramble up easy blocks in the gully to get to the start.
FA. Pete Oxley 1.9.1989

The huge corner is the two pitch trad-line **McKenna's Cleft, VS**.

Colors Area

A towering, tiered series of walls split by a number of gloomy north-facing corners. Some of the rock is not above suspicion, and a few of the climbs have had large sections and holds go missing since their initial ascents. Most of the climbs are very condition dependent.

Tides - The ledges below the face are covered for a short time at high tide and also during rough sea-conditions.

Approach (see page 134) - Walk in from the southern end along the boulder beach under Coastguard North.

Restriction (routes 7 to 10) - No climbing from 1st March to 30th June due to nesting birds.

1 Fleshworld . . . . . . 7b+

The holds can be soapy and sandy at times, but it's a cracking, if unbalanced pitch with a bouldery hard section and a much easier upper wall on excellent rock.

FA. Pete Oxley 8.8.1991

2 Colors . . . . 7b+

An incredible line that ascends a banded lower wall and long crack in the headwall. Low in the grade. Climb to the roof, pull over it to easier ground and move up to the long crack in the headwall. The crack is superbly positioned and on perfect rock.

FA. Pete Oxley 8.11.1988

3 Olympus Mons. . . . 7b

A fine route with a sting in the tail, that just merits the grade but at the present time has a huge loose block in its lower reaches. Start up the wide crack right of *Colors*. There is a much easier variant just right of the bolts.

FA. Gary Gibson, Phil Gibson 2003

4 White Unconquerable. . . . . 6b+

A huge line up a towering flaky corner. Much better value on your arms than its Stanage counterpart. Can be soapy and muddy.

FA. Pete Oxley 1.10.1995

5 Gedge . . . . 6b+

The overhangs, shallow groove and flakes in the wall just left of the central crack/chimney. Some of the rock is suspect.

FA. Pete Oxley 8.8.1991

6 Black'll do Nicely. . . . . 7a+

Good sustained climbing initially over bulges, then up the wall to a steeper finish. Close to *Gedge* on the crux.

FA. Gary Gibson 10.5.2003

The large, gloomy corner to the right is the three pitch trad line of **The Worm, VS.**

Restriction (routes 7 to 10) - *No climbing 1st March to 30th June due to nesting birds.*

7 The Empire State Arete. 6b+

A huge, adventure-style sport-route up the towering arete to the right of the gloomy corner. Start on the left of the arete and move up and around it at 8m onto its right-hand side. Climb direct to the top.

FA. Pete Oxley 27.9.1994

The next three lines start behind a large rock pinnacle that abuts the wall.

8 Dogtown Skate Team . . 7a+

The left-hand line is high in the grade. Carefully climb leftwards up the wall and pull over an overlap onto a slab. Move up the slab onto the headwall and climb it with difficulty.

FA. Andy Long 15.9.2002

p.158 Trad Free World Area

9 Rush . . . . 2 **7b+**
Start up *Beautiful South*. At the third bolt, move left to the flake-crack and follow it steeply to the top.
FA. Andy Long 25.4.2002

10 Beautiful South . . . 2 **7c+**
The impressive prow is gained from the right, and gives a fine pitch that involves plenty of difficult and technical climbing.
FA. Andy Long 10.4.2002

11 Tarquill's Trollies. 1 **6c**
The left-hand side of the leaning flowstone wall. This line is reported to have lost holds and may be harder than the original grade given.
FA. Mike Robertson 2.5.1998

12 Flipper's Revenge . 1 **7a+**
A desperate, cruxy route and even harder for the short.
FA. Gary Gibson 29.3.2002

13 Walking on Sunshine 3 **7a**
A brilliant little pitch. Rebolted and reclimbed after rockfall.
FA. Mike Robertson 5.8.1994

The final pitch on this section of cliff is situated 30m to the right. There is a knotted rope in place to reach the start.

14 No Victory In Europe **6c**
This line suffers from mud slides. Line not on topo.
FA. Pete Oxley 7.5.1995

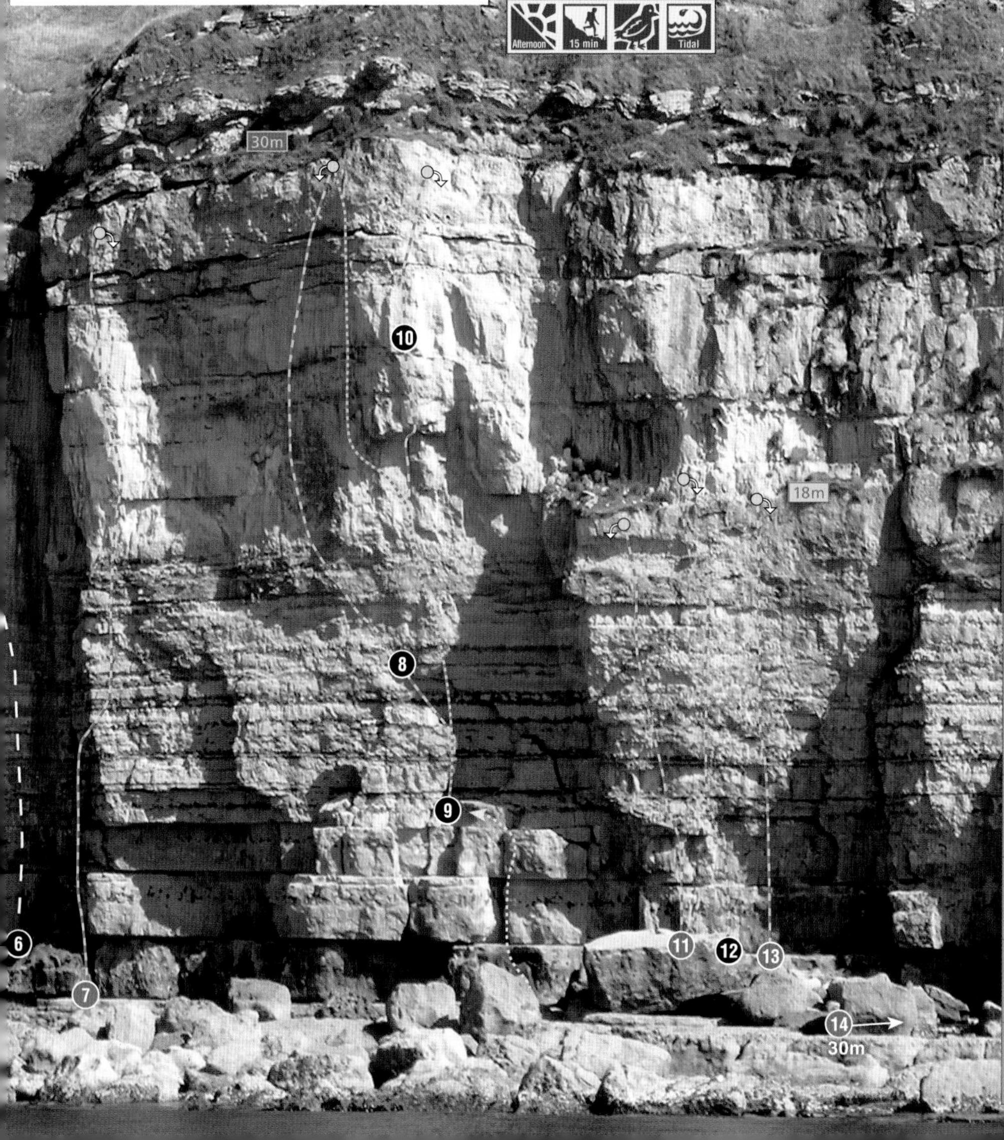

Afternoon 15 min Tidal

30m 10 18m 8 9 6 7 11 12 13 14 30m

Portland Lulworth Swanage Blacknor N Blacknor C Blacknor S Blacknor B Blacknor FS Battleship Battleship BC Wallsend N Wallsend S Coastguard N Coastguard S White Hole Lighthouse Cheyne Weare Cuttings

Hong Kong Phooey Area

An extensive section of cliff that has a number of good climbs on its various buttresses and walls. Good conditions are usually found late in the day on the shadier sections of the cliff.

Tides - The ledges below the left-hand section of the area are sea-washed at high tide and in rough seas.

Approach (see page 134) - Walk in from the southern end along the boulder beach under Coastguard North.

The wide crack, and vegetated rightward-trending line to the left of Critical Mass is the three pitch trad route **Sea Saga, HVS**.

1 Critical Mass 1 **6b**
Pleasant climbing up the arete and wall to a boldish finale.
FA. Gary Gibson, Hazel Gibson, Mick Ward 9.5.2003

2 Rapid Response 1 **7a**
A technical groove at the top of the climb makes up the meat of this route.
FA. Gary Gibson, Mick Ward 9.5.2003

3 Chert Noble . . . . . . 1 **7a+**
The right-hand pillar is a good climb with slightly blind climbing.
FA. Gary Gibson 10.5.2003

The slab and cracks give the line of the trad climb **End of the Pier, E2 5a**.

4 Face in the Chert **6a**
A slight climb on snappy rock that is slightly run-out. It follows the flaky crack-line gained direct via a juggy wall and ledge.
FA. Gary Gibson, Phil Gibson 6.5.2003

5 Glamour Cat 2 **6b**
A great face climb with plenty of good climbing.
FA. Jan Rostron, Pete Oxley 25.7.1996

6 1789 . . . . 2 **7a**
Climb directly up the middle of the wall and finish direct over the top roof. High in the grade.
FA. Pete Oxley 11.7.1989

7 The Bad Seeds 3 **7b**
A top flight stamina wall and thin crack pitch.
FA. Martin Crocker 23.9.1990

8 Magical Mr. Mephistopheles
. . . . 2 **6c**
Good climbing, heading for the open scoop right of *The Bad Seeds*. Swing left at the top to shared lower-off with *The Bad Seeds*.
FA. Pete Oxley 1.11.1994

9 Clacichew 1 **6b**
Traverse in carefully to the base. Follow the left-hand line past the dripping collar of flowstone. Slightly lichenous.
FA. Gary Gibson, Hazel Gibson 22.5.2004

10 Calcite Compliment 1 **6c**
The right-hand line has a testing central section.
FA. Gary Gibson, Hazel Gibson 22.5.2004

Afternoon 15 min Tidal

25m
3
10 11 12
1 2 4 5 6 7 8 9
Knotted rope

11 Jazz It Up . . . . 1★ 7a+
Start at a bolt-belay on a high ledge, accessed by a knotted rope. Worthwhile climbing with a very short hard section.
FA. Gary Gibson, Hazel Gibson 22.5.2004

12 Razzamatazz . . . . . 1★ 7b
A snazzy wall pitch from the same ledge and belay of *Jazz It Up*.
FA. Pete Oxley 6.11.1994

13 We are Stardust 4
Head out left across the wall to arete and then follow grooves and ledges to finish.
FA. Mick Ward 2009

14 We are Golden . . . . 5+
Break out right from midway up *We are Stardust*.
FA. Mick Ward 2009

The two pitch trad route **Stylus, HVS** *takes the wall and crack left of The Great Pretender.*

15 The Great Pretender 1★ 6c+
The well-positioned wall and blunt arete are sportingly bolted.
FA. Mike Robertson 5.8.1994

The long crack is the trad route **After the Gold Rush, E2 5c**.

16 Totally FOO to You . . . . 1★ 6c
A prominent arete, gained by tricky moves over an overlap which leads to fine open climbing above.
FA. Gary Gibson 22.5.2004

17 A Perfect Afternoon . . . 1★ 6b+
The pocketed wall to the right of the *Totally FOO to You* arete.
FA. John Leonard 9.9.2009

The vegetated ramp and chimney is the two pitch trad line of **Half-Way House, HS**.

18 Tunnel Vision . . . . 2★ 7b+
A sister route to *Hong Kong Phooey* keeping close to the bolt line. No escaping left at the top. Needs dry conditions.
FA. Pete Oxley 2.4.1999

19 Hong Kong Phooey . . . . 2★ 7c
A sustained route which needs dry conditions, and can be terminally damp without them. Plan for an afternoon ascent.
FA. Damian Cook 20.3.1994

20 Doolittle . . . . 2★ 6b+
A great line. Climb the scoop and crack to the upper roof and pass it on the left. Sustained.
FA. E.deStefan 2.2.1994

21 Jane Says . . . . 1★ 6b+
Start up *Doolittle* and break right up a crack which becomes increasingly steep as height is gained.
FA. Joff Cook 1994

22 Relax . . . . 1★ 6b+
Stay left of the bolts at the bottom for the best climbing.
FA. Nic Hellyer 10.1999

Afternoon 15 min

25m

Portland Lulworth Swanage Blacknor N Blacknor C Blacknor S Blacknor B Blacknor FS Battleship Battleship BC Wallsend N Wallsend S Coastguard N Coastguard S White Hole Lighthouse Cheyne Weare Cuttings

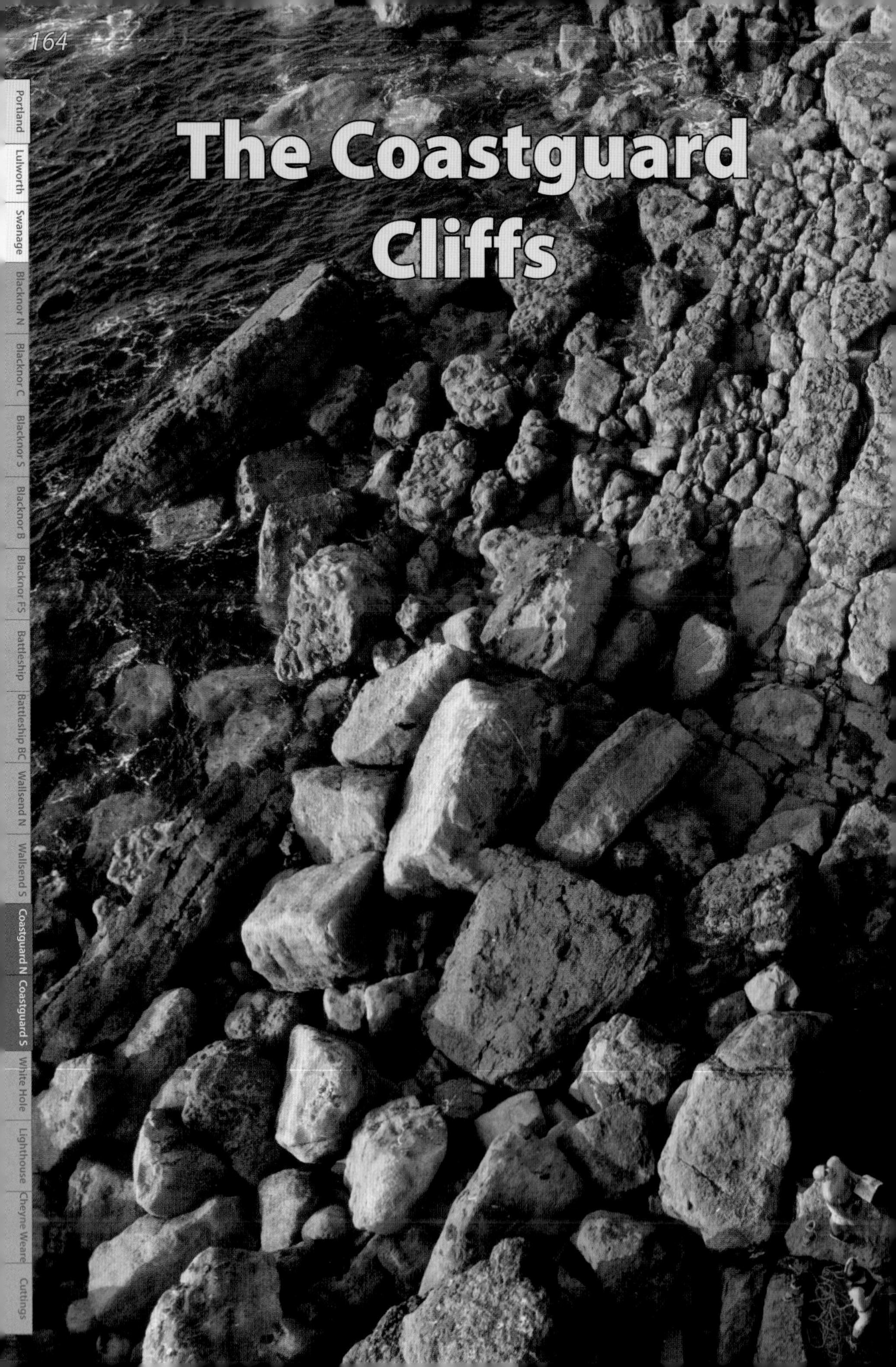

The Coastguard Cliffs

Sport climbing down by the sea doesn't come much better than this. Si Rooms midway on *Xavier's Wall* (6a) - *page 174* - one of a number of superb grade 6s at Coastguard South.

	No star	1	2	3
up to 4+	-	-	-	-
5+ to 6a+	-	1	6	1
6b to 7a	1	11	17	5
7a+ and up	5	23	30	7

The Coastguard Cliffs run south towards the Bill of Portland and possess a wealth of excellent routes set in a remote and beautiful environment. Unlike much of the rest of the west coast of Portland, the Coastguard Cliffs have an authentic sea-cliff feel about them, with all that this entails - tidal approaches, slippery boulders and the constant accompaniment of the sea close by.

Coastguard North is best known for its collection of steep, powerful and hard climbs, many in the high 7s. It is also the setting for Portland's hardest route - *Vespasian* at 8b. Coastguard South offers more in the mid-grades, including the very popular Xavier's Wall Area - home to a great spread of mid-grade routes. The rock at both the North and South Cliffs is some of the best on the Isle, and is furnished with some fantastic flowstone-sheets.

Approach **Also see map on page 53**

Drive to the southern end of the Isle and park at the Portland Bill car park (fee). Walk back up the road, and, just after the Pulpit Inn, take a minor road on the left. As the road starts to level out, just before the Coastwatch lookout, go left and down a grass slope to the cliff edge, then drop down a steep and precarious path onto a promontory (rope often in place - take care). The path gains the boulder beach below the right-hand side of Coastguard North. To reach Coastguard South, continue down the boulder beach then double back left and scramble over huge boulders to a level platform beyond.

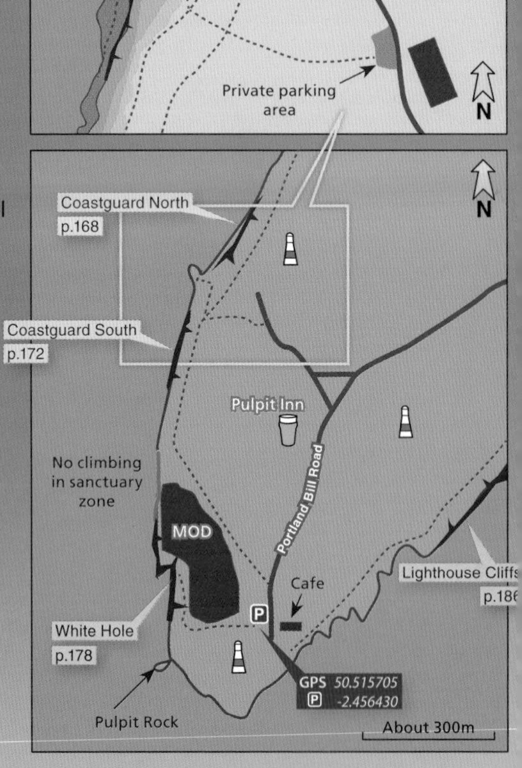

The Coastwatch lookout (left) directly above the descent to the Coastguard Cliffs.

Portland | Lulworth | Swanage | Blacknor N | Blacknor C | Blacknor S | Blacknor B | Blacknor FS | Battleship | Battleship BC | Wallsend N | Wallsend S | Coastguard N | Coastguard S | White Hole | Lighthouse | Cheyne Weare | Cuttings

On the leaning upper wall of *Tennessee* (7c) - *page 174* - deep in the heart of the Coastguard South cliff. Photo: Tom Beaumont

Access

There is a seasonal nesting-restriction at the very far end of the Azymuth Area at Coastguard South. **No climbing from March 1st to June 30th.** Slightly further south is a sanctuary zone where there is a total ban on climbing.

Conditions

The cliffs receive sun in the afternoon from about 2pm onwards. Dampness can be a problem in the morning and on humid days, and the area is best visited in bright, fresh weather and/or late in the day. There can be seepage on the right-hand side of Coastguard North and on the black streaks to the right of *Xavier's Wall*.

Tides

The first areas of Coastguard South are only affected for a very short time at high tide. Beyond Xavier's Wall Area, the tide time-window decreases, and there is a low tidal-trench before the Quick as Rainbows Area that only allows access for 2 to 4 hours at low tide. The Azymuth Area is only really accessible for any significant time at low spring-tide. Coastguard North is non-tidal.

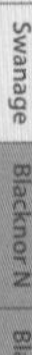

Wax Museum Area

These clean and appealing walls are home to some great stamina test-pieces. One drawback is that most of the routes are condition dependent and need sunshine and minimal humidity. The first four routes are situated 30m north of the main crag above a grass slope.

Approach (see page 166) - From the base of the approach to the boulder beach, head right (looking out) for 100m.

1 El Poder de un Coño . . . 2 stars **6c+**
The open groove just right of a huge prow has an airy climax.
FA. Mike Robertson 5.2.1994

The finger crack to the right is the **Explorator Motivator, E3 6a**.

2 100% Colombian . . 1 star **7a+**
The white wall has a stopper mid-height move and a tricky finale.
FA. Pete Oxley 19.3.2000

3 China White . . . . . 2 stars **6c+**
An appealing thin seam up the white wall. A fine pitch.
FA. Brian Tilley 11.7.1989

4 Pure Shores . . . . 1 star **6c**
A varied wall pitch that starts up the easy flake-crack.
FA. Pete Oxley 1.5.2000

5 Meridian Line . . . . 2 stars **7c**
Directly above the pillar, a blind crack leads to finger-burning mini-flakes. Fantastic climbing in the right conditions.
FA. Pete Oxley 3.10.1998

6 Ming the Merciless 1 star **7c+**
Very pumpy, with a desperate start.
FA. Pete Oxley 7.11.1998

7 Headwall Emptiness. . . 2 stars **7b+**
A classic on a dry, sunny day, and well worth waiting for.
FA. Pete Oxley 12.7.1992

8 Glycerine . . . . 2 stars **7c+**
A big stamina pitch with a complicated lower section and a hard finish. No cheating with long slings on the belay!
FA. Pete Oxley 17.10.1998

9 Sand Castles. . . . . **7a+**
The line of flakes left of *Wax Museum*.
FA. Paul Twomey 9.7.1995

Afternoon 13 min

10 Wax Museum .... Top 50 7b+
A magnificent line up the eye-catching sheet of orange flowstone.
FA. Martin Crocker 1.4.1990

11 Dr Phibes 2 7b
More brilliant flowstone finger-flakes after an awkward start.
FA. Pete Oxley 28.4.1993

12 Clockwork Orange 2 7c
The power-packed blind crack leads to a blank headwall.
FA. Gavin Symonds 4.1999

The next line of bolts is an old project (potential 8a)

13 The Nth Degree ... 1 7c
Blast up the overhanging scoop and big flake. Continue just right of the bolts, jumping to gain the break. Step back left to finish.
FA. Pete Oxley 4.6.1998

14 Wasted .... 1 7b+
The open scoop leads into a left-trending undercut. Can be greasy.
FA. Neal Heanes 28.3.1999

15 Last Orders 1 7c
A right-hand finish to *Wasted*. Move diagonally right on small holds then up to the finish of *Bar Room Brawl*.
FA. Pete Oxley 10.5.1999

16 Bar Room Brawl 2 7c+
An overhanging groove next to the huge black streak. So named after a couple of knee-bars on the route.
FA. Pete Oxley 23.4.1995

17 Vespasian .. Top 50 8b
The line of shallow open grooves is the hardest route on Portland that requires a BIG span for success.
FA. Pete Oxley 1.10.1994

18 Sale of the Century 2 7b
The central blind crack gives some very varied climbing. Hold something in reserve for the last moves.
FA. Pete Oxley 8.9.1996

19 Zero Tolerance ... 1 7b+
A rightward line from the ledge on *Sale of the Century*, up an overhung ramp. Needs good conditions.
FA. Pete Oxley 23.9.1998

20 Mid-Strife Oasis 1 7c
Very hard climbing in its lower half.
FA. Pete Oxley 18.9.1994

21 Eternal Spider .. 2 7c+
This brilliant and powerful pitch surges violently up the imposing white wall.
FA. Pete Oxley 18.4.1993

The next line is an open project (potential 8a+).

22 Happy to Go Blind . 1 7b+
A climb of two halves. Follow a tricky calcified crack to a grass ledge, then contort up the innocent-looking blank groove.
FA. Pete Oxley 12.12.1997

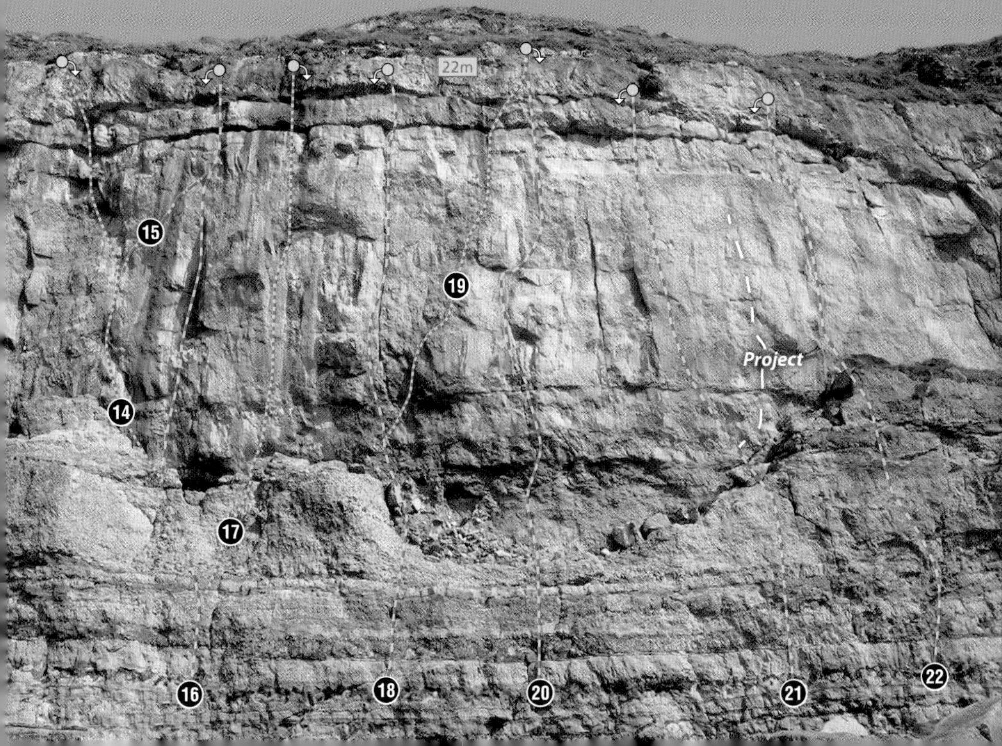

22m
15
19
Project
14
17
16
18
20
21
22

Portland
Lulworth
Swanage
Blacknor N
Blacknor C
Blacknor S
Blacknor B
Blacknor FS
Battleship
Battleship BC
Wallsend N
Wallsend S
Coastguard N
Coastguard S
White Hole
Lighthouse
Cheyne Weare
Cuttings

Portland Lulworth Swanage Blacknor N Blacknor C Blacknor S Blacknor B Blacknor FS Battleship Battleship BC Wallsend N Wallsend S Coastguard N Coastguard S White Hole Lighthouse Cheyne Weare Cuttings

Nothing but the Groove Area

A large, grey-streaked wall with many excellent and sustained wall pitches. Its proximity to the parking and the spread of quality routes across the grades make it quite a popular spot. Seepage can be a problem.

Approach (see page 166) - From the lookout, drop carefully down the main approach path. This wall is the first encountered above the path as you descend to the boulder beach.

1 Spare Rib 2 **7b**
Fine climbing, following a clean white tower of rock.
FA. Mike Robertson 6.5.1995

2 Girl Power . . . . 2 **7a+**
A bouldery crux on compact rock up the right-hand side of the arete.
FA. Pete Oxley 2.12.97

3 Steve's Route 1 **7b**
After an easy start, the central scoop gives an absorbing climb.
FA. Chris Cubitt 5.1998

4 Retaining the Ashes . . . 2 **6b**
A testing pitch that follows a leaning, thin crack up the wall.
FA. Steve Taylor 7.3.1993

Afternoon 12 min Seepage

5 Into the Groove . . . . . . 1 **6b+**
A short, but useful link-up. Start as for *Retaining the Ashes.*
FA. Pete Oxley 2000

6 Nothing but the Groove . Top 50 **6c+**
The soaring groove on the left-hand side of the wall is a fine line, although the groove itself is relatively easy. Move up with difficulty to the groove proper and continue up it more easily. *Photo on page 3.*
FA. Pete Oxley 8.8.1988

7 Running It In! . . 2 **7b+**
A very direct line that involves a good deal of fingery and technical moves with little in the way of respite.
FA. Martin Crocker 10.6.1990

8 Superfly Guy . . . . Top 50 **7a**
A quality pitch. Climb up and then left, past some good pockets to a large hold below the upper wall. Make some difficult moves to a slim groove. Follow this, and the wall to its right, to the top.
FA. Pete Oxley 8.8.1988

9 Lost in Rock . . . . 2 **6c+**
Good technical moves are the main ingredients of this often-overlooked route. Climb the initial wall, then pull rightwards over the bulge. Make some perplexing moves up and across the left-leaning groove before finishing up a thin crack.
FA. Pete Oxley 17.7.1992

22m
13
5
1 2 3
4
6 7

⑩ The Man Who Never Found Himself . . . . 2 stars **6a+**
An enjoyable climb. Ascend the steep lower wall and bulge to the base of the corner. Follow the corner to the top.
FA. Pete Oxley 15.8.1988

⑪ Van People . . . . 2 stars **7a**
A fine climb, although a little run-out in places. Climb straight up the wall and bulges to meet a very shallow depression on the upper wall. Climb the shallow depression to a hard finish.
FA. Brian Tilley 20.8.1989

⑫ Fantasy Island . . . . 1 star **6c**
An unusually tough layback which is sometimes damp.
FA. Mark Higgs 28.5.1993

⑬ Dosvadanya . . . . 1 star **6c+**
A diagonal traverse from *Fantasy Island* to the lower-off on *Retaining the Ashes*. A sling is needed to extend the 2nd bolt. 35m of climbing so make sure your rope is long enough.
FA. Pete Oxley, Brian Tilley 27.11.1999

⑭ La Usurpadora **7c**
An artificial eliminate up the wall right of *Fantasy Island*. Climb the fingery wall direct until a traverse rightwards joins the finish of *Shining Heart*.
FA. Pete Oxley 25.5.2000

⑮ Heartland . . . . 1 star **7c**
A short, but significant link-up. Move a little way up the wall and break right to join *Shining Heart* at its powerful crux.
FA. Pete Oxley 17.5.2000

⑯ Shining Heart . . . . 2 stars **7c**
A well-positioned power problem. Move up the wall and step left. Powerful moves up the rib allow a crack to be grasped. Climb this awkwardly and finish up the easier wall above.
FA. Pete Oxley 20.8.1989

⑰ Frenzied Detruncation . 2 stars **7b+**
A tough start is the entry price to the fine groove line above. Make technical and fingery moves on tiny crimps and smears to the overhang, then continue up the groove to the top.
FA. Pete Oxley 27.7.1989

⑱ Prison Sex . . . . 2 stars **7c+**
The shallow arete is completely desperate from start to finish.
Photo on page 27.
FA. Pete Oxley 28.5.1993

⑲ Midnight Oil . . . . 1 star **7a**
Considered to be a worthwhile line.
FA. Brian Tilley 5.1989

⑳ Hang 'em High . . . 1 star **7b**
A smart test-piece which supersedes an older route called *Gunbarrel Highway* that gained the line by stepping out right from *Midnight Oil*.
FA. Pete Oxley 2000. FA. (Gunbarrel Highway) Brian Tilley 5.1989

㉑ Gun Runner . . . . 1 star **6a**
Occasionally wet due to a drainage streak, but a good line.
FA. Pete Oxley 19.3.2000

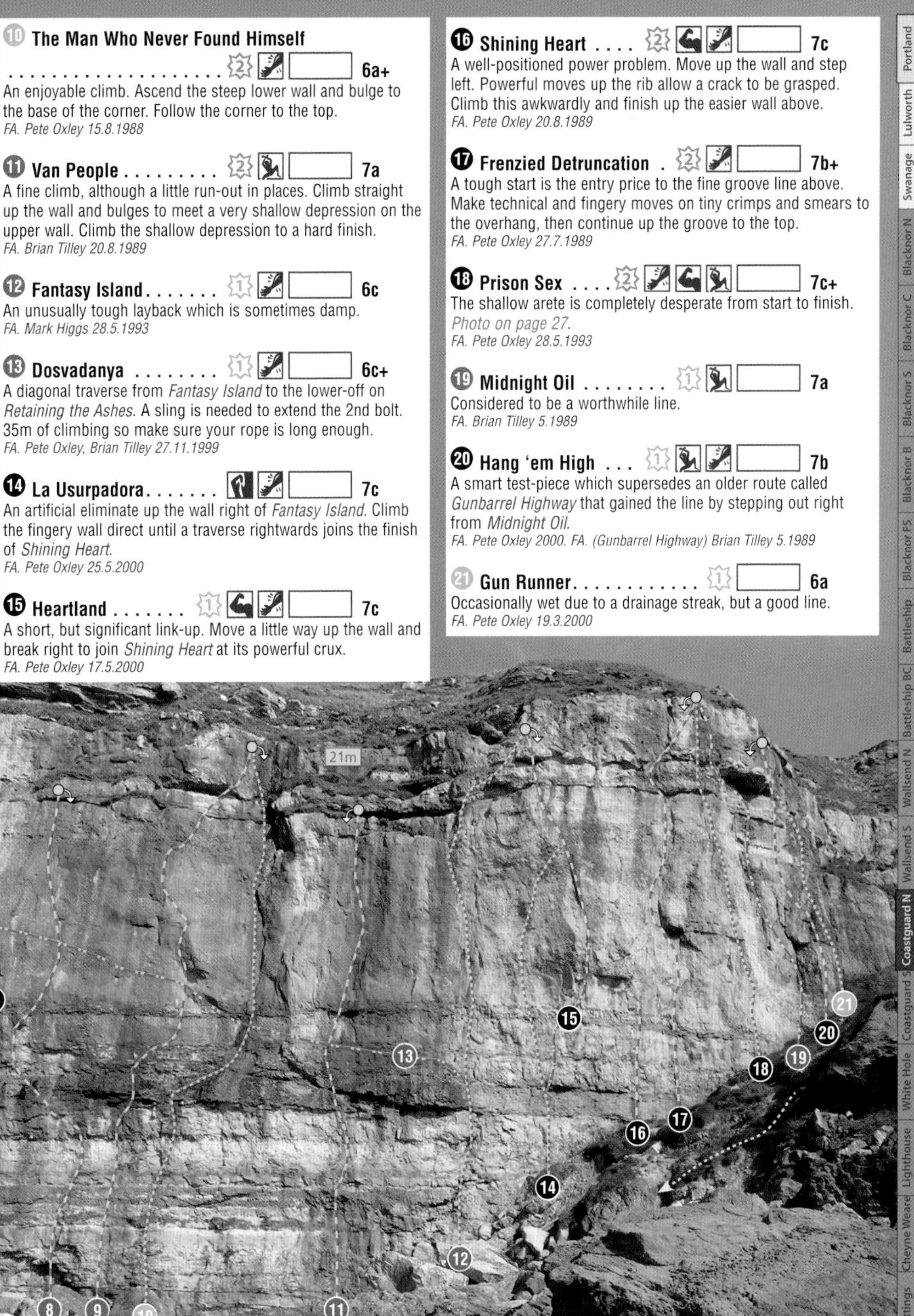

Portland
Lulworth
Swanage
Blacknor N
Blacknor C
Blacknor S
Blacknor B
Blacknor FS
Battleship
Battleship BC
Wallsend N
Wallsend S
Coastguard N
Coastguard S
White Hole
Lighthouse
Cheyne Weare
Cuttings

Grip '89 Area

This excellent area is easy to reach and has some great rock. Sadly the central section fell down in the winter of 2000/01. It contained several routes including *Grip '89*, the route this sector took its name from.

Approach (see page 166) - As for Coastguard North, but turn left (facing out) at the bottom of the descent path and scramble past some huge boulders to ledges.

Tides - The left-hand side of the wall is pretty much non-tidal, although it is best to keep away in rough seas.

Just above the base of the approach slope is an isolated slabby boulder with some short bolted lines on it - not listed here.

The first few routes lie 150m south of the approach slope, above a conglomerate-filled gully that lies behind a detached pillar. The most obvious feature is a weird suspended pillar of fused calcite and welded rubble on the left-hand side of the wall.

1 Seat of Learning 1 — 7c
Super technical and powerful climbing up a surprisingly difficult scoop on small layaways. Follow *Font of Knowledge* for the first 8m and stay just right of bolts 5 and 6.
FA. Pete Oxley 27.5.1998

2 The Font of Knowledge . 2 — 7c
A big line direct up the impending face with some tough moves at the top.
FA. Pete Oxley 18.5.1998

3 Biscuits for Smut . . . . . 2 — 7b
An attractive hanging groove which requires some thought and is difficult to flash.
FA. Pete Oxley 30.9.1994

4 Reactor Meltdown . 2 — 7b+
Start up *Biscuits for Smut*, via its conglomerate, then move right to a hidden flake. Follow the arete above on its left-hand side in a great position. Technical and superb.
FA. Pete Oxley 27.5.1998

The next section is where the huge rockfall occurred. The rock here has not yet stabilised sufficiently to offer any new routes.

5 Guardian Angel . . . 2 — 7b+
Superb face work with a complex blind crack in the headwall. Pass the third bolt directly for the 7b+ grade.
FA. Pete Oxley 2.5.1998

6 Brooklyn Bimbo . . . 2 — 7b+
The lower half packs it in on amazing flowstone while the upper arete is exhilarating. It is slightly spoilt by a mid-height ledge and is much harder in greasy conditions.
FA. (Original) Martin Crocker 29.6.1991. FA. (Direct) Pete Oxley 12.5.1998

Afternoon | 15 min | Tidal

Manhattan Skyline Area

The continuation wall running right from the Grip '89 Area has a number of strong lines on good rock. The area has suffered the loss of one route due to rockfall.

Tides - The base of the routes are covered at high tide. Keep away in rough seas.

Approach (see page 166) - Continue along the boulder beach and platform from the Grip '89 Area.

7 From a Buick Eight. 1 — 7b
Immaculate rock and climbing, taking the undercut arete and then the right-hand side of the sharp upper arete.
FA. Gary Gibson 7.5.2002

8 New York Dolls . . . . . . 2 — 6a+
Exciting, clean and open climbing up the lovely grey groove which gets harder towards the top. High in the grade.
FA. Pete Oxley, C.Collins 9.5.1998

9 The Devil's Work . . . . — 6b+
The recessed flake-line in the corner is dirty.
FA. Neil Burton 6.10.1996

10 Marshalling Amps . . . . 1 — 7b
An impressive pitch up the finger-crack and wall. Split at half-height by a resting ledge, but still high in the grade.
FA. Gary Gibson 15.9.2002

The long crack is the line of the trad route **Broadway, E3 5c**, *whilst the arete to its right is the trad line of* **Manhattan Skyline, E4 6a**.

11 Skyscraper . . . . 1 — 7a
A sustained route following the crisp grey wall.
FA. Gary Gibson 28.8.2002

12 H'electric Boogaloo . . . 2 — 6b
Start in a cave and climb out along the left wall. Pull around into a crack and follow this into a scoop. The groove above leads to the lower-off.
FA. Neal Heanes, Gavin Symonds 4.5.2000

13 The Bronx . . . . 2 — 6c+
Climb up leftwards to a good ledge. The arete above gives the main interest of the route.
FA. Gary Gibson 7.5.2002

The full-height wide crack is the trad line **Easy Cleft, HS 4a**. *To its right are the remains of the route* **American Beauty, 6c**, *the first 3 of its lower bolts are still in place.*

Right is a twisting flake-line of the trad route **Vesuvius, VS**.

14 California Dreams . . . . 1 — 6b+
A low and reachy crux. The first bolt is at 4m on the right.
FA. Alan Betts, Andy Long 25.5.2000

Portland
Lulworth
Swanage
Blacknor N
Blacknor C
Blacknor S
Blacknor B
Blacknor FS
Battleship
Battleship BC
Wallsend N
Wallsend S
Coastguard N
Coastguard S
White Hole
Lighthouse
Cheyne Weare
Cuttings

Xavier's Wall Area

A fine wall with a handful of the best lower 6s on the Isle, plus a few steep lines through overhangs.

Tides - The platform below is covered for a few hours at high tide which cuts off access to all the routes.

Approach (see page 166) - Continue under the main Coastguard South cliffs along the wave-washed platform.

1 September Mourning . . 2 **7b**

A hard fingery start over the overlap leads to open climbing above, finishing up a thin crack in the headwall.

FA. Gary Gibson 15.9.2002

2 Wharfedale Boyz . . 1 **7c**

The huge leaning wall and roof above the tidal shelf is very sustained and needs good conditions.

FA. Pete Oxley 30.4.1995

3 Screaming Skulls. 3 **7c**

A long and sustained pitch with a succession of bouldery moves between jugs in evermore spaced-out situations.

FA. Pete Oxley 10.12.1999

4 Tennessee . . . . Top 50 **7c**

A brilliant route direct up the bulging face, starting from the tidal trench. *Photo on pages 9 and 167.*

FA. Andy Long 7.1998

5 Darkest Before Dawn . . 1 **7b**

A desperate bouldery start stops most attempts. Above is an unusual long layback.

FA. Pete Oxley 23.5.1997

6 Actions Speak Louder 1 **7a+**

Hard and fingery moves over the roof are followed by great climbing up the wall and rib.

FA. Pete Oxley 21.9.1994

7 L'Odyssee Noire . . . . . 2 **6c+**

Climb the technical wall to an overlap. Pull over and climb the shallow groove above to good holds. Move right to the lower-off.

FA. Gary Gibson, Jean Marc Anagnostidis 7.5.2002

8 Xavier's Wall. . . . . Top 50 **6a**

Superb climbing. Follow a crack and groove left of an arete. There is a tricky move near the top. *Photo on page 164.*

FA. Pete Oxley 21.9.1994

The next two routes share a lower-off which can cause problems when the wall is busy. Avoid top-roping them if possible.

9 Coming of Age. 2 **6a**

The black wall gives a good pitch with an awkward start.

FA. Jan Rostron, Pete Oxley, Mark Higgs (all led) 8.9.1996

10 Underage . . . . Top 50 **6a**

The direct line up the black wall has fine climbing throughout and a blind crux move. High in the grade.

FA. Jan Rostron 5.1997

11 Xavier Zoo 2 **6a**

A pleasant route taking a direct line up the wall to finish at a shallow groove.

FA. Gary Gibson 8.5.2003

12 Young at Heart. . . . . 2 **6a+**

The right-hand line wanders around a bit.

FA. Pete Oxley 6.1997

Afternoon 17 min Tidal

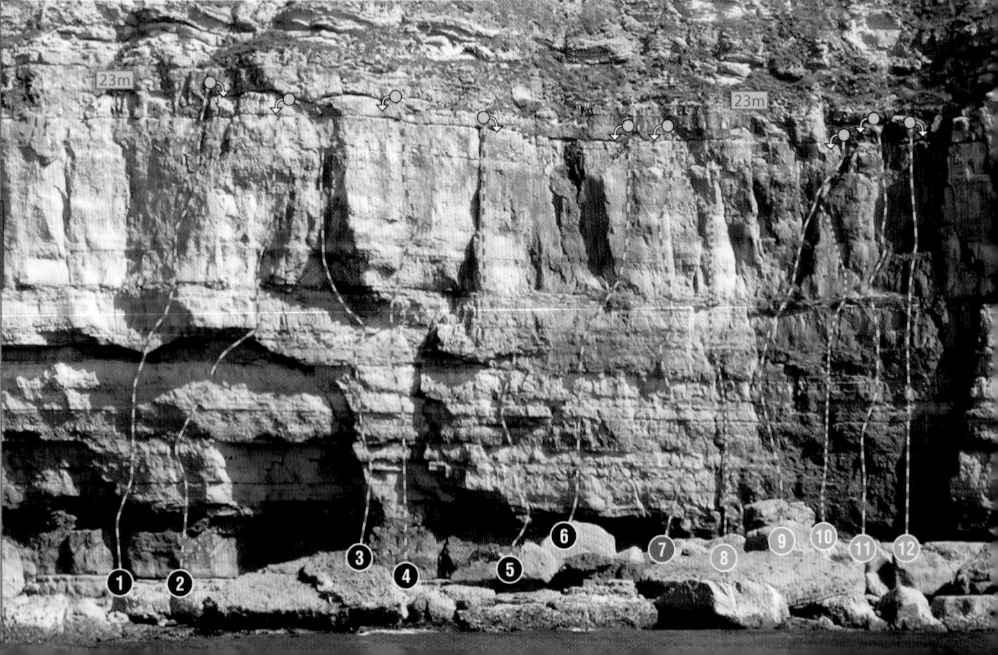

23m 23m

1 2 3 4 5 6 7 8 9 10 11 12

Bad Moon Rising Area

Lots of long, sustained wall climbs and some mean roofs are the main ingredients of this section of crag.

Tides - The platform below is covered for a few hours at high tide.

Approach (see page 166) - Continue along the wave-washed platform.

The chimney on the right is the trad line **Lucky Dip, HS**. *To the chimney's right the disjointed crack-line in the wall is* **What Gives My Son, E3 5c**.

13 Wavewatch . . . . 1 star **7b**
Climb the straightforward wall to a final steepening. A hard sequence gains the lower-off.
FA. Gary Gibson 9.5.2002

14 Full Fathom Five . . 2 stars **7b**
The steady lower wall gains a difficult and bouldery finish.
FA. Pete Oxley 13.4.1991

15 Bad Moon Rising . . . . . 3 stars **7a**
An impressive pitch up the blunt arete which gets harder as you get higher. Can be dusty and the first bolt is high.
FA. Pete Oxley 12.4.1991

16 A Ship Load of Moonies . . . 2 stars **6c+**
A fine pitch moving right from the start of *Bad Moon Rising* and finding a surprisingly easy way up this steep wall.
FA. Gary Gibson 15.9.2002

17 Dead by Sunset . . . 1 star **7b**
Very sustained climbing which overhangs all the way. There is a difficult step left onto a shelf near the bottom.
FA. Pete Oxley 28.9.1996

18 Witchdoctor. . . . . . 1 star **7b**
A route of two sections, pumpy low down and a technical headwall. At present it is a bold lead and deserves E6.
FA. Dave Pickford 3.5.1998

19 Vampire Killers . . . . . . 1 star **7b**
Another pumper with a delicate yet powerful scoop high up. Good climbing, but it can be dirty.
FA. Pete Oxley 23.5.1997

20 The Lost Buoys . 1 star **7c+**
A 7a first half leads to desperate crimping up the leaning rib to reach an easier crack to finish. Needs cool conditions.
FA. Pete Oxley 14.9.1997

21 No Survivors . . . . **7b+**
Worthwhile climbing which is spoilt by a rest at half-height. Can get dusty at the top.
FA. Pete Oxley 15.9.96

22 A Meeting of Minds . . . **7a+**
A massive roof test-piece at the bottom makes this one an unusual outing. A big half-height rest is the reward.
FA. Pete Oxley 15.9.1996

23 Lip Service . . . . 1 star **7a**
Great rock and a swing left on the lip of the roof provide the fun.
FA. Pete Oxley, Mark Higgs 15.9.1996

24 Bermuda Triangle . . . . 2 stars **6c**
Start as for the last route, but climb straight over the bulge and up the lovely grey slab. Super climbing on great rock.
FA. Pete Oxley, M.Higgs (both led) 8.9.1996

25 A Bird in the Hand . . . . **7a+**
A crimpy lower wall leads to an easy upper slab. A bit unbalanced, but great rock.
FA. Pete Oxley 14.9.1996

26 Hasta La Vista. . . . 1 star **6b+**
A fine steep start leads to a good slabby finish, but unfortunately it is spoilt by the big ledge in between.
FA. Gary Gibson 4.5.2003

Afternoon | 18 min | Tidal

Quick as Rainbows Area

A magnificent wall of immaculate flowstone. It sometimes suffers from seepage, can be dusty and is only accessible for a limited period.

Approach and Tides (see page 166) - Continue past the tidal trench, which is uncovered for 2 to 4 hours at low tide. Wading in could gain you an extra hour. In calm seas, it is possible to traverse the back wall to get in early, or out late, but take great care!

1 Small Talk Costs Walls . . . . 1 6c+
The roof, juggy wall and flowstone tufa left of *Smashing Orange*. Start in a small alcove above the tidal trench. Best done at dead-low tide, otherwise the rope will get wet when pulled.
FA. Pete Oxley 27.5.1998

2 Smashing Orange 2 7a
Classy crack climbing after a hard bulge above the trench.
FA. Pete Oxley 11.5.1991

3 Drive Blind 2 7a
A tough lower wall and a fine, easier, upper groove.
FA. Pete Oxley 11.5.1991

4 Forensic Scene . . . . . . 2 7a+
A lovely flowstone arete. A useful rest before the top move is the well-deserved reward after the steep start.
FA. Pete Oxley 14.5.1995

5 Quick as Rainbows. . . . 3 7b
A beautiful, frozen wave of flowstone. Brilliant as long as the top is clean, but if not climbed regularly, it can be dirty.
FA. Pete Oxley 17.7.1991

Afternoon | 20 min | Tidal

6 Red Medicine . . . . . 3 7b+
Sustained and unobvious climbing on immaculate flowstone.
FA. Pete Oxley 14.5.1995

7 Aeon Flux 2 7b
A hard lower half. Good rock all the way.
FA. Pete Oxley 17.7.1991

8 Under the Sky, Inside the Sea 2 7a
Steep moves on the sharp arete lead to a finishing corner.
Photo on page 5.
FA. Pete Oxley 17.7.1991

9 Forget Columbus . . . . . 3 7a+
Magnificent tufa-curtains and a huge flake.
FA. Pete Oxley 6.6.1993

10 Buried Violence . . . . . . 2 7b+
Very hard moves on the lower wall lead to an amusing finish on organ pipes.
FA. Pete Oxley 2.11.1993

11 Walking the King . . . . . Top 50 6b+
A classic pumpy wall of steep cracks and flowstone with the crux at the top. The best 6b+ on Portland.
FA. Pete Oxley 20.4.1993

12 An Ideal for Living . 2 7a+
More quality rock. Pumpy and technical all the way.
FA. Pete Oxley 21.8.1995

13 Time Bomb 2 7a
The central line on the coral wall finishes up a slab. This line has lost a hold on the lower wall and may now be 7a+.
FA. Pete Oxley 21.8.1995

24m

1 2 3 4 5 6 7 8 9 10 11 12 13 14 15 16

Tidal trench access 2 to 4 hours at low tide

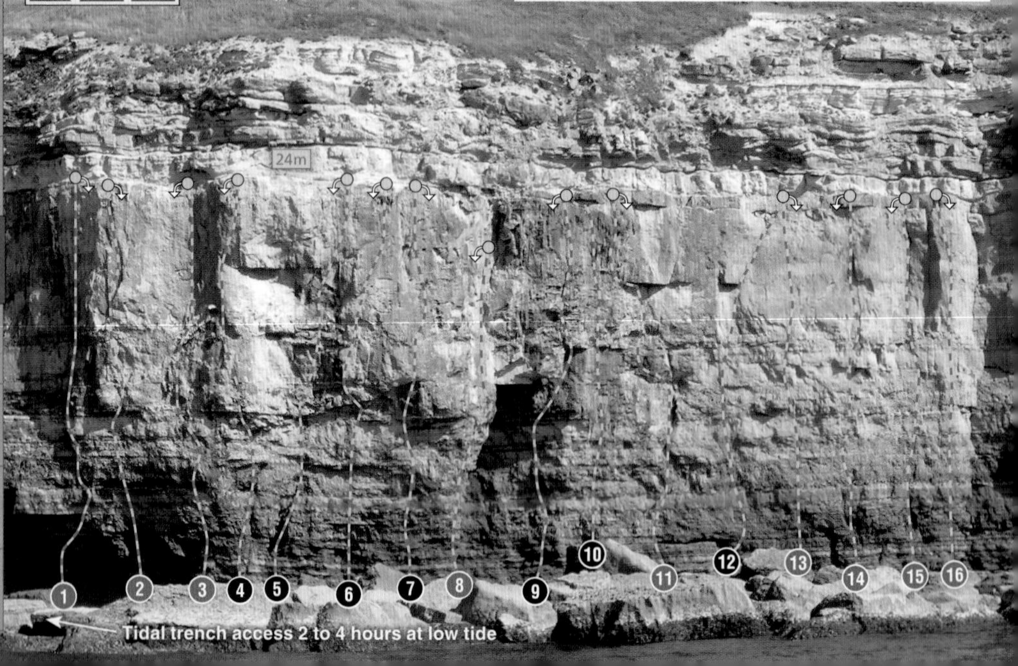

Azymuth Area

The final batch of routes on Coastguard South is on a superb steep buttress.

Approach and Tides (see page 166) - Approach as for the Quick as Rainbows Area, and continue along the platform. This area is only accessible for 2 to 3 hours at low tide.

14 Winning at Rodeo . . 3 stars — 7a
An enticing line with an intriguing corner high up.
FA. Mark Higgs 21.8.1995

15 Chevette de la Mer. . . . 2 stars — 6b
More great rock in the pocketed groove above the initial wall.
FA. Andy Bell 9.5.1998

16 Swimsuit Issue . . . . . . 1 star — 6c+
The arete is followed direct with some blind palming 'à cheval' to pass the mid-height bulge.
FA. Pete Oxley 9.5.1998

17 Xistenz . . . . 1 star — 7a+
A worthwhile climb direct up the wall and arete.
FA. Gavin Symonds 2002

The next two full-height cracks are the trad lines of **Razor Laugh, E1 5b** *and* **Hell Razor, E3 5c**.

18 Space Shanty . . . . 2 stars — 6b
Fine and varied climbing tackling the shallow groove on the left of the buttress.
FA. Chris Parker, Pete Oxley 23.5.1997

19 Astra Blaze . . . . 2 stars — 6c
A sustained and well-positioned climb direct up the arete.
FA. Pete Oxley 23.5.1997

20 Come In and Burn . 2 stars — 7b
Climb the wall to mid-height, and continue up the difficult groove.
FA. Pete Oxley 5.7.1997

21 Azymuth . . . . 2 stars — 7a+
The pumpy arete is an exciting pitch.
FA. Pete Oxley 23.5.1997

22 L'esprit du vent . . . 2 stars — 7a+
Entertaining climbing. It follows a big arching line up the side wall with a definite crux move.
FA. Pete Oxley 28.5.1997

8m right again, past a shallow cave, is a pillar of excellent white rock above a flat platform.

Restriction (routes 23 and 24 to project) - *No climbing from 1st March to 30th June due to nesting birds.*

23 Down to the Wire . . 2 stars — 7b+
A fine pitch directly up the arete above an easy starting groove. There is a long reach from an undercut at mid-height which is probably only 7b for the tall.
FA. Pete Oxley 12.2.2000

24 Dawn of a New Age 2 stars — 7b+
Starting 2m right of a flake-line. Hard, blind climbing on perfect rock follows the direct line up the front face of the white pillar. Very fingery and powerful on the crux.
FA. Pete Oxley 26.1.2000

The final line of bolts is an old project.

Restriction - *Directly below the large fence, where the boulders run out, is the beginning of a no climbing sanctuary zone that continues for 300m to White Hole.*

Afternoon — 20 min — Tidal

	No star	1	2	3
up to 4+	1	-	-	-
5+ to 6a+	5	2	-	-
6b to 7a	8	9	3	-
7a+ and up	3	10	5	1

White Hole is unique to the west coast of Portland, being an area of well-defined and deeply-incised zawns. The walls of the zawns are relatively short compared to the neighbouring Coastguard Cliffs, but have a set of good routes with an atmosphere that is out of all proportion to their size. The rock is solid, but also extremely rough and it can be a bit tough on finger skin. Many of the lines are climbed both as sport climbs and deep water solos. For a full picture of the deep water soloing see the Rockfax book Deep Water www.rockfax.com.

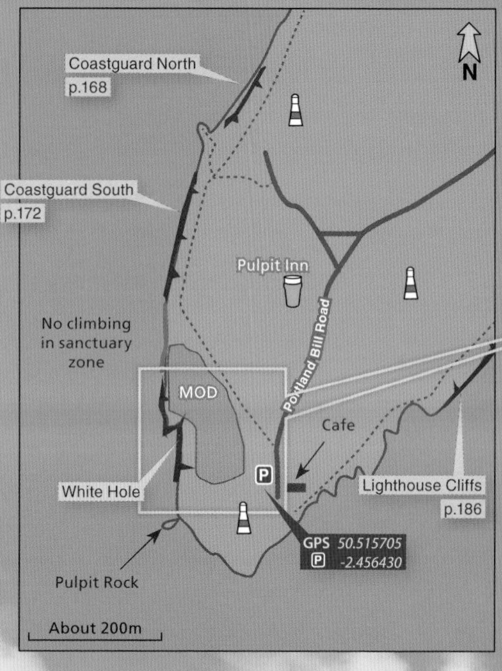

Approach Also see map on page 53

Drive to Portland Bill and park by the lighthouse (fee). Walk westwards (right - looking out) next to a fence and above an old quarry for 200m. Turn right at the cliff top and follow the fence. The South Cliff is just below the top after 20m. Mirthmaid Zawn is the large square-cut prow further into the bay. It is reached by following the fence closely past a pipe, before dropping down onto a large rock platform (see map). To reach Memories Zawn and the Faceache Area, continue from the large rock platform by scrambling up to the top of the Mirthmaid promontory. Move along a narrow cliff-top ledge that runs right (looking out) around a square-cut zawn to a narrow rift beneath the weird conglomerate rock bridge. More details are given with the route pages for the approaches from the cliff-top.

Portland | Lulworth | Swanage | Blacknor N | Blacknor C | Blacknor S | Blacknor B | Blacknor FS | Battleship | Battleship BC | Wallsend N | Wallsend S | Coastguard N | Coastguard S | White Hole | Lighthouse | Cheyne Weare | Cuttings

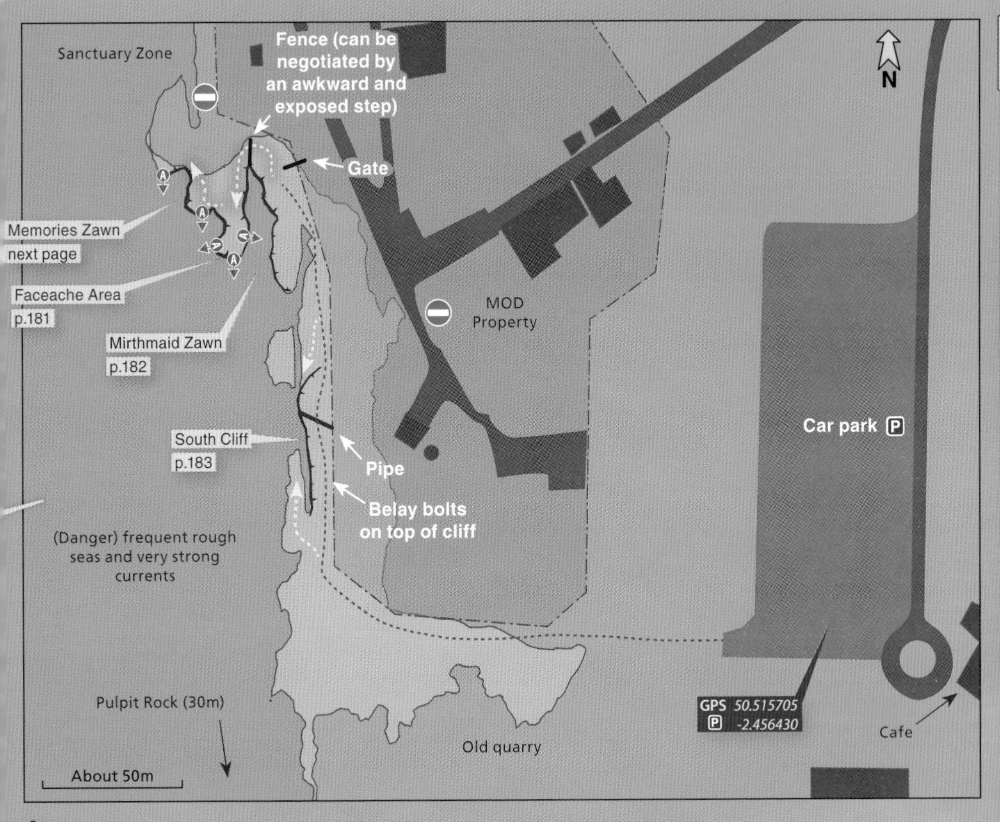

Portland
Lulworth
Swanage
Blacknor N
Blacknor C
Blacknor S
Blacknor B
Blacknor FS
Battleship
Battleship BC
Wallsend N
Wallsend S
Coastguard N
Coastguard S
White Hole
Lighthouse
Cheyne Weare
Cuttings

Access

The weird conglomerate mentioned in the approach is of geological importance and should not be damaged. **No climbing to the north of the cliff in the sanctuary zone.** Do not interfere with MOD property.

Conditions

The routes can be damp so only visit in dry and sunny conditions. A calm sea is vital for abseiling into most of the lines. The routes are nearly all non-tidal. Keep well away if the sea is even remotely rough. For the deep water solos a high tide is essential and be aware of the extreme currents that are in evidence hereabouts.

Special Note - Only a selection of the deep water solos recorded at White Hole are described. For a comprehensive guide to all of the deep water soloing available see Deep Water - www.rockfax.com

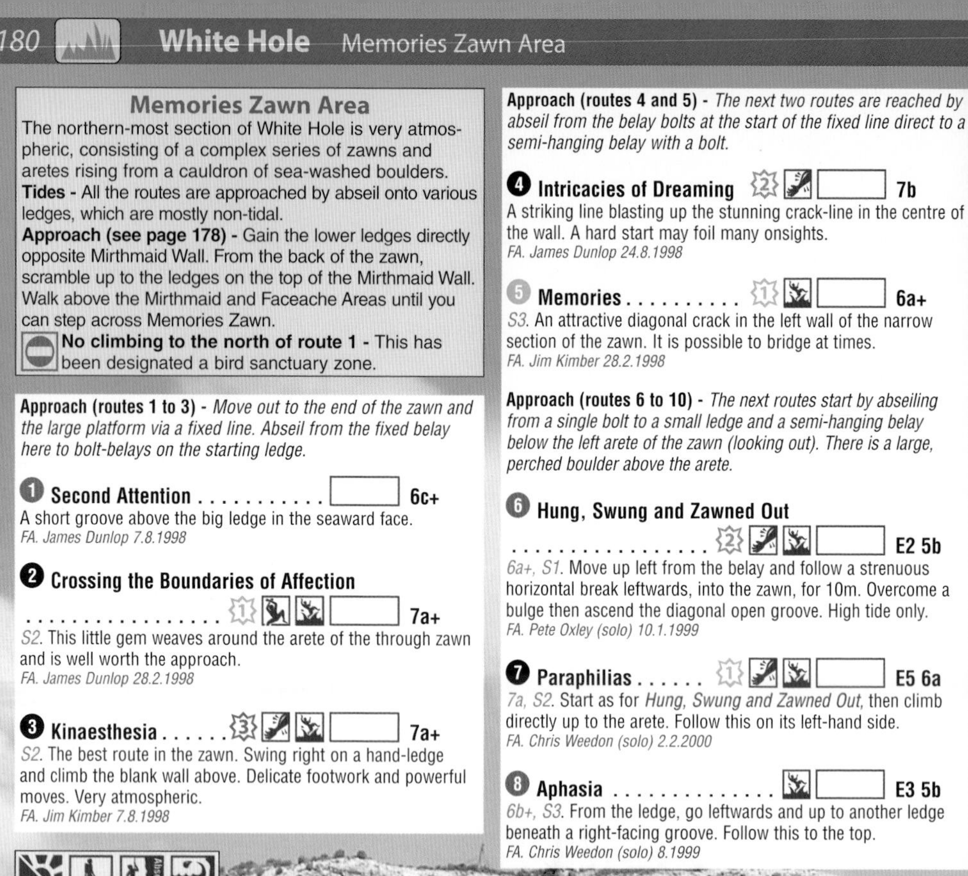

Memories Zawn Area

The northern-most section of White Hole is very atmospheric, consisting of a complex series of zawns and aretes rising from a cauldron of sea-washed boulders.

Tides - All the routes are approached by abseil onto various ledges, which are mostly non-tidal.

Approach (see page 178) - Gain the lower ledges directly opposite Mirthmaid Wall. From the back of the zawn, scramble up to the ledges on the top of the Mirthmaid Wall. Walk above the Mirthmaid and Faceache Areas until you can step across Memories Zawn.

No climbing to the north of route 1 - This has been designated a bird sanctuary zone.

Approach (routes 1 to 3) - *Move out to the end of the zawn and the large platform via a fixed line. Abseil from the fixed belay here to bolt-belays on the starting ledge.*

1 Second Attention . . . . 6c+
A short groove above the big ledge in the seaward face.
FA. James Dunlop 7.8.1998

2 Crossing the Boundaries of Affection . . . . 7a+
S2. This little gem weaves around the arete of the through zawn and is well worth the approach.
FA. James Dunlop 28.2.1998

3 Kinaesthesia . . . . . . 7a+
S2. The best route in the zawn. Swing right on a hand-ledge and climb the blank wall above. Delicate footwork and powerful moves. Very atmospheric.
FA. Jim Kimber 7.8.1998

Approach (routes 4 and 5) - *The next two routes are reached by abseil from the belay bolts at the start of the fixed line direct to a semi-hanging belay with a bolt.*

4 Intricacies of Dreaming 7b
A striking line blasting up the stunning crack-line in the centre of the wall. A hard start may foil many onsights.
FA. James Dunlop 24.8.1998

5 Memories . . . . 6a+
S3. An attractive diagonal crack in the left wall of the narrow section of the zawn. It is possible to bridge at times.
FA. Jim Kimber 28.2.1998

Approach (routes 6 to 10) - *The next routes start by abseiling from a single bolt to a small ledge and a semi-hanging belay below the left arete of the zawn (looking out). There is a large, perched boulder above the arete.*

6 Hung, Swung and Zawned Out E2 5b
6a+, S1. Move up left from the belay and follow a strenuous horizontal break leftwards, into the zawn, for 10m. Overcome a bulge then ascend the diagonal open groove. High tide only.
FA. Pete Oxley (solo) 10.1.1999

7 Paraphilias E5 6a
7a, S2. Start as for *Hung, Swung and Zawned Out,* then climb directly up to the arete. Follow this on its left-hand side.
FA. Chris Weedon (solo) 2.2.2000

8 Aphasia E3 5b
6b+, S3. From the ledge, go leftwards and up to another ledge beneath a right-facing groove. Follow this to the top.
FA. Chris Weedon (solo) 8.1999

Afternoon | 5 min | Abseil In | Tidal

9 The Drill Sergeant . 1 6c+
S2. Swing up left from the belay to climb the left-hand side of the arete. Finish up an absorbing technical crack.
FA. Pete Oxley 11.1.1999

10 Until the End of Man 2 7a
S2. A stunning climb up the outer arete of the zawn on the edge of everything.
FA. Pete Oxley 1998

Approach (routes 11 and 12) - *The next routes start from a belay on a recessed ledge 5m above the sea reached by abseil.*

11 Karate Kid. . . . . 6a+
A pleasant corner split by a couple of ledges.
FA. Pete Oxley, Jon Biddle 25.2.1998

12 Bar, Bar, Black Sheep. . 1 6c+
An intriguing crux in the roof involving a bomber knee-bar.
FA. Pete Oxley, Jon Biddle 25.2.1998

13 Excalibur's Edge . . . . . 2 6b+
An unusual and photogenic route up the right-hand side of the steep arete, starting up a free-standing sword of rock in the zawn. Abseil in to a small ledge to start.
FA. Pete Oxley 25.2.1998

14 The Labyrinth 1 7b
An exciting route, taking a sweeping diagonal line leftwards from the belay ledge on *One Life.* Swing left along a handrail to gain a hanging ledge above a roof. Move up and left to pass a bulge, before finishing up a pocket-laced slab. Fence belay.
FA. Pete Oxley 8.2000

There is a poor project here which needs debolting.

Faceache Area
These walls are peppered with a number of quality harder lines. The routes on the inside walls need evening sun to dry them.
Tides - All the routes are approached by abseil onto ledges that are non-tidal.
Approach (see page 178) - Gain the lower ledges directly opposite Mirthmaid Wall. From the back of the zawn, scramble up to the ledges on the top of the Mirthmaid Wall and walk above this to locate some abseil bolts at the end of the headland.

15 One Life 2 7b
S3. The finely-positioned arete can be started from the higher belay ledge on the right.
FA. Gav Symonds 9.5.2000. FA. (Direct start) Pete Oxley 9.6.2000

16 Faceache 2 7b
S3. Probably the best route here, giving superb face climbing up the right-hand side of the arete.
FA. Mike Robertson 16.7.1994

17 The Code Breaker and the French Teacher
. . . . 1 7a+
Blind climbing up the groove in the centre of the face.
FA. Mike Robertson 26.6.1994

18 Obscene Gesture (Part 2)
. . . . 1 7a+
Climb rightwards up the face. Shares the first bolt with *The Code Breaker and the French Teacher.*
FA. Mike Robertson 13.6.1994

19 The Skin Trade . . . 1 7a+
S2. Traverse the lower break rightwards then climb the arete. Left of the bolts gives a less-good 6c+.
FA. Mike Robertson 26.6.1994

Mirthmaid Zawn Area

The south wall of Mirthmaid Zawn gives some challenging climbing above an undercut through-cave.

Tides - The various starting ledges are non-tidal, though do not come here when the sea is rough, and always bear in mind that the abseil in will commit you to your chosen route, so take Prusiks down just in case.

Approach (see page 178)

Approach (routes 1 to 6) - *Access the lower ledges opposite Mirthmaid Wall, then from the back of the zawn, scramble up to the ledges on the top of the wall. Abseil in from here.*

The first 6 routes start from a ledge left of the through cave.

1 Sad Young Biscuits . . . 7a+
S1. Starting from a sentry box under the arete, climb up the right-hand side of the arete. An alternative start can be made from *the Splendid Isolation* ledge at the same grade.
FA. Mike Robertson 13.6.1994

2 Dead in Europe . 1 star 7a+
S1. The blank wall leftwards from the belay.
FA. Mike Robertson 6.8.1994

3 Splendid Isolation . 1 star 6c
S2. Pull over the roof and then climb the crack to a hard finish.
FA. Steve Taylor 26.6.1994

4 Just for a Day . . . . 1 star E4 6a
7a, S2. The steep blunt rib. Start up *Splendid Isolation* and move right on the lip of the roof to gain the rib.
FA. Pete Oxley 15.5.2000 (solo)

5 Mirthmaid. . . . . . . 1 star 7a+
S1. Head rightwards over a roof and up an easier crack.
FA Damian Cook 6.1994

6 Nightmirth . 1 star 7c
S1. A wild roof traverse extension to *Mirthmaid.*
FA. Pete Oxley 7.4.96

The next three lines start from a small foot-ledge in the middle of the east face to the right of Nightmirth, and need a high spring tide.

7 Sister of Night . . . . 2 star E5 6b
7a+, S3. Traverse left from the foot-ledge for 8m until under the blank-looking banana-shaped groove. The groove requires a series of blind and bouldery moves.
FA. Pete Oxley (solo) 24.6.2000

8 Any Last Requests? . . . E4 5c
6c, S3. Traverse left from the foot-ledge for 3m to reach the central groove. A hidden pocket near the top helps reduce the difficulties at the finish.
FA. Pete Oxley (solo) 7.2000

9 Spanish Air. E3 5b
6b, S3. Fairly straightforward climbing up the shallow groove directly above the foot-ledge. Short but serious.
FA. Pete Oxley (solo) 24.6.2000

10 Tiny Smiles. . . . . 7a+
Start from ledges in the back left-hand corner of the zawn.
FA. Pete Oxley 24.6.2001

South Cliff

This short wall of tough routes lies underneath the approach path. Most of the routes don't have lower-offs, but there are belays above including some staples.

Tides - The ledge below the wall is non-tidal, but keep away in rough seas.

Approach (see page 178) - Scramble down easy ledges on either side of the cliff. The first six routes need to be approached from the left-hand side (looking in) and start in the cave.

11 Evening Delight 4
The first line on the wall.
FA. Mick Ward 3.2011

12 Song of the Sea . . . . 5+
The wall left of the pillar.
FA. Mick Ward 3.2011

13 Balance of Power . . 2★ 8a
The pillar above the cave offers a fine technical challenge. Has been soloed above shallow water but is not really a DWS.
FA. Pete Oxley 21.11.1999. Soloed by Gavin Symonds 2007

14 The Pipers of Portland . 1★ 6c
Pull out of the cave and climb the groove to the left of the large pipe. A very strenuous outing.
FA. Pete Oxley 16.9.1994

15 Funnel Web . . . . 1★ 6b
Climb the groove just right of the streak below the cliff-top pipe.
FA. Pete Oxley 16.9.1994

16 End of Season Sale 6b
Shares the first two bolts with *Funnel Web*. Traverse right from the cave into a hidden groove.
FA. Pete Oxley 16.9.1994

The rest of the routes are approached by scrambling down the right-hand side of the cliff (looking in).

17 The Reign of Steel . . . . 1★ 6b+
Clip the first bolt on *Red Raw* then break left and climb a groove.
FA. Pete Oxley 16.9.1994

18 Red Raw . . . . 7a+
Move leftwards to the blank rib and climb it with great difficulty.
FA. Pete Oxley 5.9.1994

19 Tickled Pink . . . 1★ 7c
The short groove capped by a twin roof is desperate.
FA. Pete Oxley 5.9.1994

20 Wafer Thin . . . . 1★ 6b
From a higher ledge, climb a flake to a tricky finish.
FA. Pete Oxley 5.9.1994

21 Run, Rabbit, Run . . . . 6b+
Pull over a low bulge and then climb direct up the steep slab via a shallow groove and blank headwall.
FA. Pete Oxley 5.9.1994

22 Staple Diet . . . . 1★ 6b
The blank slab is not as tricky as it looks. Climb the slab passing a small ledge near the finish.
FA. Steve Taylor 1.10.1994

23 Painted Lady . . . . 6a+
Good climbing between jugs on the faint rib. Pull over the low overhang to a good hold and then gain the flake by a big move.
FA. Mick Ward 9.8.2003

24 The Feather 6c
Another thin, slabby wall on slightly crumbly rock.
FA. Steve Taylor 1.10.1994

25 Rust Never Sleeps 6a
Delicate and fingery climbing up the wall.
FA. Mick Ward 1.9.2011

26 The Cruel Sea . . . . 5+
The shallow corner/flake has a surprisingly awkward move.
FA. Steve Taylor 1991. Bolted and claimed by mistake by Mick Ward 2003.

27 Adonis Blue . . . . 6b+
The centre of the wall with a grit-like crux. Use an undercut to reach a flat hold, from where a difficult mantel accesses a flake. A reach gains the top.
FA. Mick Ward 15.8.2003

28 Chalk-hill Blue . . . . 1★ 6a+
Innocuous-looking, but looks can be deceptive. Make a long reach to a rail and then make an even bigger one to respite - or improvise.
FA. Mick Ward 15.8.2003

Afternoon 5 min

The East Coast

An early morning at Godnor Far North is the ideal choice for lots of warmth and sun and, in common with most of the East Coast cliffs, is well-sheltered from westerly winds. Bridget Collier climbing *Tombstone* (3+) - *page 205*.

	No star	1 star	2 star	3 star
up to 4+	5	-	-	-
5+ to 6a+	5	4	1	-
6b to 7a	7	10	4	2
7a+ and up	4	11	6	6

Running up the east coast from the southern tip of Portland is a series of low, waterside walls and severely overhanging sea caves topped by a landscape of beach huts and old quarry cranes. This area has now become the haunt of the deep water soloist, however dotted along the cliff-line are some sport routes that are very different in style to those found elsewhere on the Isle. Most of the better climbs - both sport and DWS - are hard and very steep and require good conditions and favourable tides. Sector Pom Pom is a delightful little bay that contains a frozen wave of grit-like stone, pitted with infrequent pockets; the climbs being in the style of extended boulder problems. The rest of the Lighthouse Cliffs are composed of an intriguing labyrinth of caves, ledges and tunnels that are worth exploring for their scenic value alone. For the climber however, the Cave Hole Area dispels the myth that Portland is all about vertical walls full of crimpy holds. Many powerful routes cross the banded roofs, and although not much more than ten metres in height, the nature of the climbing packs in the moves. The area is also worth exploring if a break from climbing is needed, as the small coves and inlets are sun-traps, and great for relaxing and swimming.

Special Note - Only a selection of the numerous deep water solos recorded on the East Coast are described in the following chapters. For a comprehensive guide to all of the deep water soloing available see Deep Water www.rockfax.com

The long line of low cliffs that run up the east side of the Isle from The Bill are some of Portland's steepest. In this picture the severely undercut cliff-line of the Lighthouse Cliff Area is capped by ancient quarry cranes and stacked dressed stone. In the distance is Beeston Cliff and The Cuttings.

Approach Also see map on page 53

All of the areas are best approached from the Portland Bill car park (fee).

Sector Pom Pom - Walk along the coast path in front of the beach huts to a cliff-top crane. Sector Pom Pom is 70m further along the coast path.

Too Funky Beach Area to Octopus Weed Area - Walk along the coast path in front of the beach huts to Sector Pom Pom and continue for 300m to reach the last trio of beach huts. This is above the Too Funky Beach Area.

Tides and Conditions

Sector Pom Pom is great sun-trap with little seepage. which makes it a fine venue to get some early season action on crisp winter mornings when the friction is good. Sector Pom Pom requires a very low tide and it is worth noting that the beach height changes from time to time as does the amount of seaweed deposited below the cliff. The rest of the Lighthouse Cliffs require morning sunshine, which is essential to dry the rock out. Avoid the area completely on humid days. Seepage can be a problem on some sections. The whole area requires careful judgement and knowledge of the tides; mid-to-low tide will give enough time for the sport routes, whilst a high tide is required for the DWSs.

Sector Pom Pom

A pleasant bay with some short, hard routes that are very bouldery, including the fabulous traverse of *The Waveband*. There are a number of very short bouldery routes bolted around the cove that are not recorded here. Good conditions are needed and are at their best in winter. The beach level varies.

Tides - Only come here at very low tide. Dog Rock can be approached at mid-tide.

Approach (see page 187) - Walk along the coast path from the car park to a cliff-top crane. 70m further on is Sector Pom Pom.

The first two lines are situated in a corner, just past an undercut buttress, on the right side of the bay (looking out).

1 El Scorchio . . . . 1 star — 6c
Start just right of a big cave and climb the short bulging wall slightly leftwards. There are two ways of climbing the crux.
FA. Rob Godfray 23.1.2000

2 Maximum Grrr... . . 1 star — 7b
Make fierce moves up the blank wall, starting from a slot near the corner and finishing via a short layback.
FA. Pete Oxley 23.1.2000

3 L'eau Profile . . . . 1 star — 7c
Make contorted moves directly over the roof on the front of the undercut buttress.
FA. Pete Oxley 4.4.1996

4 Private Dancer 6b
The short and technical groove on the right of the buttress. Top-out or lower off the last bolt.
FA. Pete Oxley 4.4.1996

5 Jug City 4
Climb to a juggy headwall. There is a staple belay on block.
FA. Mick Ward 1.10.2011

6 Jugalicious 3
Break right at *Jug City* ledge. There is a staple belay on block.
FA. Mick Ward 1.10.2011

A small sea stack known as Dog Rock has four lines on its landward face.

7 Matt's Dilemma 3
The left-hand line on the seaward face. The left side of the arete has been climbed using the same bolts at 6a.

8 Games Without Frontiers 4
A faint groove. Climb left of the bolts and then back right to the lower-off.
FA. Mick Ward 9.9.2011

9 The Dog's Bollocks 6a
Intricate moves up the wall to the left of the arete.
FA. John Leonard 10.9.2011

10 Tide and Time . . . . 4+
The surprisingly awkward groove.
FA. Mick Ward 11.9.2011

All the remaining climbs are situated on the wave of rock on the left side of the bay (looking out).

11 Burbage Belle . . . . 1 star — 7c
Pure bouldering. Jump to the break to start then tackle the Fontainebleau-like bulge.
FA. Pete Oxley 27.3.1996

12 The Big Blue . . . . . 2 star — 7c+
A tremendous test-piece that blasts up the central hanging groove by some very hard moves. Probably 8a for the short. Jump to the break to start.
FA. Luc Percival 26.10.1996

13 Ninth Wave . . . . 1 star — 7a+
A very aesthetic problem taking the hanging crack right of the prow. Jump to the break to start. It has been soloed, but it isn't a deep water solo.
FA. Luc Percival 6.1995

14 Zimmerframe with Attitude 7c
A desperate V8 boulder-problem start leads to the awkward corner. Used to be 6c, but a rockfall altered the start.
FA. Luc Percival, Neal Heanes 6.1995. Reclimbed by Andy Long 2004.

15 The O'lympets . . . . 6c+
A pleasant climb taking the vague crack in the side-wall after a hard start.
FA. Neal Heanes, Luc Percival 6.1995

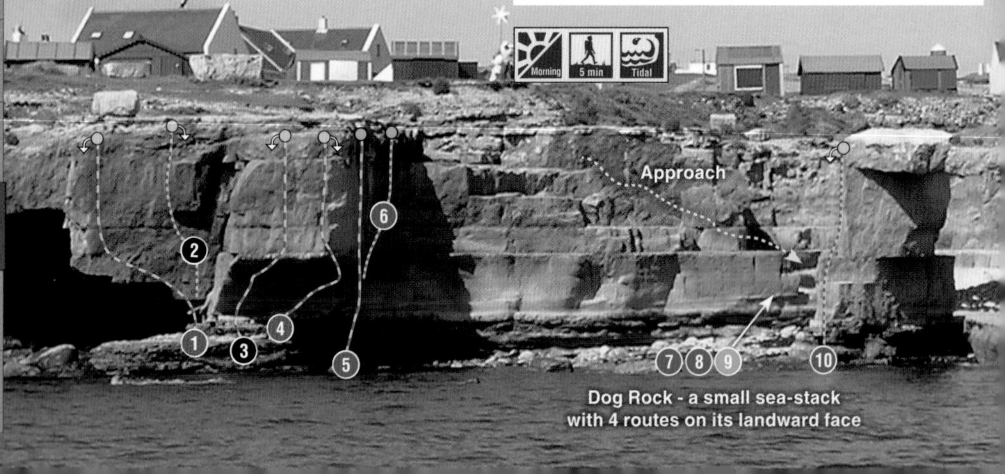

Dog Rock - a small sea-stack with 4 routes on its landward face

Too Funky Beach Area

A secluded little bay with a couple of sport lines.

Tides - *Once Were Warriors* can be done at any tide. *Too Funky For Me* and *Marine Boy Direct* need low tide.

Approach (see page 187) - Head up the east coast to the last group of three beach huts situated behind a rocky bay. Descend easily into the bay and the low cave is found on the left.

16 The Waveband . . 3 stars — **V9**

14m. The best boulder traverse on the Isle - more of a journey than a boulder problem. Start from a hand ledge below *Zimmerframe...* then traverse the break leftwards with hard moves out of *Ninth Wave* (spotters needed). Then the desperate finish where you eventually body-bridge onto the far ledge.

FA. Pete Oxley 6.11.1999

17 Honorary Froggatt . 1 star — **7b+**

A hard bulging start then teeter up an 'Artless-style' ramp.

FA. Pete Oxley 19.3.1996. Artless is a famous route at Froggatt.

18 Pocketful of Shells **7b**

A strenuous start then technical stuff up the corner.

FA. Pete Oxley 19.3.1996

19 A Girl of the Limberlost **6b**

Start at a short crack to the right of an arete. Move left around the arete and finish directly.

FA. Mick Ward 4.3.2010

20 The Huts Have Eyes . . . . **6a+**

Further right from *A Girl of the Limberlost* another wall rises from a low ledge. Climb the crimpy wall before the arete.

FA. John Leonard 2.3.2010

21 Somewhere West of Laramie . . . **6a+**

Right of *The Huts Have Eyes*. Climb the left-hand side of the arete above a ledge.

FA. Mick Ward 2.3.2010

22 Not in Kansas Anymore . . . . **6a+**

The wall just right of the right-hand side of the arete.

FA. Mick Ward 3.3.2010

23 Once Were Warriors 2 stars — **7c**

A memorable test of strength and ingenuity which takes the central 10m roof. Reverse to retrieve the gear.

FA. Pete Oxley 16.9.1995

24 Too Funky For Me . . . . 1 star — **6b+**

Only possible at low tide and in calm seas. Stake belay.

FA. Mike Robertson 6.8.1994

25 Marine Boy Direct . . . . **6b+**

Started direct at low tide only. This is the bolted method of climbing *Marine Boy*. The indirect is a DWS.

FA. Luc Percival 6.1995

Portland Lulworth Swanage Blacknor N Blacknor C Blacknor S Blacknor B Blacknor FS Battleship Battleship BC Wallsend N Wallsend S Coastguard N Coastguard S White Hole Lighthouse Cheyne Weare Cuttings

Portland Lulworth Swanage Blacknor N Blacknor C Blacknor S Blacknor B Blacknor FS Battleship Battleship BC Wallsend N Wallsend S Coastguard N Coastguard S White Hole Lighthouse Cheyne Weare Cuttings

Ixtlan Area

A good area of deep water solos on an atmospheric series of steep walls and buttresses. Only a small selection of the best routes on this section are included.

Approach (see page 187) - From the Portland Bill car park, gain the coast path and continue for 300m beyond Sector Pom Pom to reach a jib crane. Descend leftwards (looking out) towards ledges below. The first route has a slightly different approach.

Tides - All routes need a very high tide and calm seas.

Approach to route 1 - *Drop down a fixed ladder directly beneath the a jib crane.*

1 Temporary Lifestyle . . . 2 **HS 4b**
4+, S0. A spanking little route that is easy to find and gives a very good introduction to the fine art of deep water soloing. Descend the fisherman's ladder to the ledge and then drop down the iron rungs to a point where a traverse left can be made to a groove. Climb this and then head merrily off leftwards under the capping overhangs, to a point where the top can be gained.
FA. Mike Robertson (solo) 31.7.1994

2 Foxy Chicks. 1 **E2 5c**
6a+, S0. A cracking, but short-lived problem. From the ledge, reach the only crack you can find and yard up it.
FA. Mike Robertson (solo) 6.8.1994

3 Reel 'em In. 1 **E2 6a**
6b+, S0. Make a reach around the lip and campus or heel-hook away to the top. Not one for the weak.
FA. Damian Cook (solo) 21.5.1995

4 Aquamarina . . . 1 **E4 6b**
7a+, S1. A full-on bouldery wall climb with tiny crimps. Make sure the water underneath is adequate and pick your landing.
FA. Steve Taylor (solo) 11.8.1995

5 The Little Hard . 1 **E3 5c**
6a+, S2. Climb *The Big Easy* past its hard moves and then take a deep breath and fire up the weakness 2m left of the arete.
FA. Mike Robertson (solo) 15.5.1995

6 Big Easy Arete. . . . 1 **HVS 5a**
5, S1. Climb the arete past a sloper to arrive at the top shelf.
FA. Unknown

7 The Big Easy. 2 **E1 5c**
6a+, S0. The approach traverse to the following routes is a great outing in its own right. The wall to the arete is the crux. Once the arete is rounded, steep juggy moves lead past ever-more impressive ground. Continue as far as you like and then retrace your steps back again, or swim.
FA. Mike Robertson (solo) 6.8.1994

Crab Party Area

A brilliant area of bicep-busting deep water solo pump-outs on excellent rock. Not for the faint hearted. The wall right of *Crab Party* offers a nice contrast with its technical and fingery climbing, also on excellent quality rock.
Tides - All routes need a very high tide and calm seas.

8 Ixtlan . . . . 2 — E2 5b
6a, S1. Not too fluttery, but it is worth checking out the final holds on the ledge before starting out. From the end of *The Big Easy,* move right to the steep corner with flowstone at its top, just beneath the capping roofs. Good holds make upward progress rapid. Once your chin is over the top the fun begins.
FA. Damian Cook (solo) 23.4.1995

9 Karma . . . . 2 — E3 5c
6b, S2. A more serious undertaking. From 3m right of the corner of *Ixtlan,* climb the wall to a flowstone crack in a roof. Move over the roof to a flake and finish via a hard rockover.
FA. Mike Robertson (solo) 8.5.1995

10 Mad About You . 1 — E3 6a
6b, S2. A fine, but serious trip. Traverse about 7m beyond the corner of *Ixtlan* and climb the increasingly difficult, yellow and grey groove to a tough move and then a jug. Carry on up steep rock before a move left below the capping overhang allows access to the top. Take care there are some large boulders below.
FA. Mike Robertson (solo) 15.5.1995

11 Russian Roulette . . Top 50 — E3 6a
6b+, S1. A wonderful climb in a great location. Crank it out along the base of the face beyond the corner of *Ixtlan* until all looks lost at an overhanging arete. The flowstone crack above is climbed with difficulty to more friendly ground. At the top of the wall move left and pull through the final overhangs on good holds.
FA. Mike Robertson (solo) 11.6.1995

Approach (routes 12 to 16) - *Locate the chunky knotted down-climb rope roughly 60m north of the jib crane.*

12 Captain Haddock . . 1 — E2 5b
6b, S1. A good route for a first taster of this area. Climb across the rope and scuttle up the wall just right of the rope to a slightly crunchy finish.
FA. Mike Robertson 19.5.1995

13 Flipper Force. . . 1 — E3 6a
6c, S0. Move up the arete and then pull around left onto the face. Follow this to the top.
FA. Damian Cook (solo) 19.5.1995

14 Water Wings . . . 2 — E4 6b
7a+, S1. A crowd pleaser up the arete with a very on/off move to finish.
FA. Gavin Symonds (solo) 27.7.2001

15 Ooh, Lovely! . . . 1 — E3 5c
6b+, S0. Start right of the arete and climb leftwards through steep territory to the more reasonably angled upper face. A right-hand finish is also possible.
FA. Mike Robertson (solo) 19.5.1995

16 Crab Party. . . . Top 50 — E4 6a
6c, S2. A fantastic expedition which is one of the best deep water solos around. Check the water depth below the lip before starting out. Make a long traverse to below the roof rail. Climb up to and out along the rail to the lip. A contorted move gains the flat top.
FA. Mike Robertson (solo) 19.5.1995

Approach (routes 17 to 19) - *Abseil (staple at ground level) or down climb roughly 50m north of the chunky descent rope.*

17 Robertson's Jam 1 — HVS 5a
6a, S1. A good line up the vertical wall.
FA. Steve Taylor (solo) 13.6.1993

18 Spittle 'n' Spume 2 — E1 5c
6a, S0. Lots of fun is to be had on this super little rightward traverse on the lip of the roof. The wall looks totally blank, but has some small positive holds.
FA. Mike Robertson (solo) 13.6.1993

19 Bare Reputation. Top 50 — E4 6b
7a+, S0. Extend the traverse of *Spittle'n' Spume* via more brilliant and intense climbing.
FA. Mike Robertson (solo) 15.5.1995

Cave Hole Area

This area has some of the best roof climbing on Portland. In winter a spectacular cascade pours over the lip, whilst in the summer it is a good swimming and jumping spot.

Approaches and Tides (see page 187) - The Waterfall Cave is most easily reached by descending via the amphitheatre to the Cool Vibe Area and then making a short traverse around the promontory at low-to-mid tide and during calm sea conditions only. This gives access to the routes 9 and 11. Low tide is needed to cross the tidal trench below *King of the Swingers*. Beyond here there is a hidden through-cave which leads to the rest of the routes. Alternatively, abseil directly into the left-hand side (looking in) at low-to-mid tide, from the bolt at the back of the ledge or from blocks.

1 The Green Bearded Roof 7a+
Start at a single bolt-belay. Belay at the back of the cliff-top ledge.
FA. Pete Oxley 6.6.1996

2 Supergeek . . . . . . 1 star 7b+
The best of the routes hereabouts. Start from a single bolt-belay at the base. Belay at the back of the cliff-top ledge.
FA. Pete Oxley 28.7.1996

3 Pilot of the Future 7b
A very unlikely hanging roof on which shorties may need a bunk up to attain the first holds on the lip. Start from a single bolt-belay at the base. Belay at the back of the cliff-top ledge.
FA. Pete Oxley 18.7.1996

4 Zen Zero . . . . 3 stars 7c+
A great route for roof thugs with 15m of escalating bicep death. It needs good dry conditions. Start from a single bolt-belay and finish at a block belay.
FA. Pete Oxley 28.8.1996

5 Zombie Nation . . . . 1 star 7c
Features an arm-stretching bouldery start. Block belay.
FA. Pete Oxley 12.8.2000

6 Air Hoodlum . . . . . 2 stars 7b+
A dramatic grooved arete which needs calm seas. Gets plenty of sun into late afternoon and early evening.
FA. Pete Oxley 7.5.1995

7 The Cult of John Craven 1 star 7b
The fierce wall left of the escape route.
FA. Pete Oxley 24.1.2005

An escape route is up the wall at HVS 5a - not bolted.

8 Osaki Dolphin . . . . 2 stars 7c+
An 8m roof with wild moves. Needs dry conditions.
FA. Pete Oxley 7.8.1995

Law of the Jungle and King of the Swingers start from a communal single-bolt belay just inside the cave. The Swinging Nineties starts from a ledge just below the cliff-top.

9 Law of the Jungle . 1 star 7b+
S0. Short and hard. Head right over the 3m roof to emerge on the promontory ledge.
FA. Pete Oxley 6.5.1995

10 The Swinging Nineties . . . . 3 stars 7b
S1. Good fun. Reverse down the last jugs of *Law of the Jungle* then swing along the 8m roof to emerge on the cliff-top. Reverse to get the gear. Block belay at the start and finish.
FA. Pete Oxley 29.5.1995

11 King of the Swingers Top 50 7c+
S3. The biggest roof challenge on Portland. Start up *Law of the Jungle* then continue along the horizontal break to a no-hands knee-bar rest. Finish diagonally leftwards over the big roof. Reverse to retrieve the gear.
FA. Pete Oxley 27.8.1995

12 Different for Girls . . . . . 1 star 5+
A neat little pitch on some excellent rock.
FA. Mike Robertson 10.6.1995

13 Kisses and Lies . . . . . . 1 star 6a
More flowstone fun.
FA. Mike Robertson 10.6.1995

14 High Klicks . . . . 1 star 6b
A fine little route on flowstone pockets. Quite beefy.
FA. Mike Robertson 10.6.1995

15 100 Reasons to be Cheerful 6c+
A powerful roof problem. Lower-off from the wall well below the top or continue to belay on blocks.
FA. Mike Robertson 10.6.1995

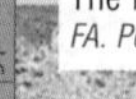

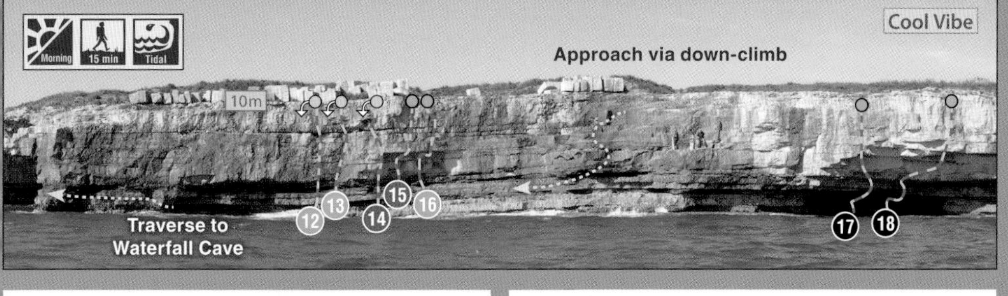

16 Bachelor Boy and the SR 500 5+
Steep climbing over the right-most roof.
FA. Mike Robertson 10.6.1995

17 Fly the Friendly Skies ☆2 7c
The biggest line here tackles the 8m cave roof. Best to reverse for the gear.
FA. Pete Oxley 13.5.1995

Cool Vibe and Octopus Weed Area

These are the tiered, overhanging bays immediately south of the next jib, on from the one above the Temporary Lifestyle area. Some reasonable sport lines and one very popular DWS.

Tides - Calm seas and low tide are necessary for the lead routes. High tide is needed for the solos.

Approach (see page 187) - For the Cool Vibe Area, walk and then scramble down rock steps in the second amphitheatre to the right (looking out) to a wide belay ledge beneath the roofs. For the Octopus Weed Area, go down rock steps in the first amphitheatre to the right (looking out) of the jib crane.

18 Seeing is Believing ☆1 7c
An impossible-looking double roof stack. Reverse for the gear.
FA. Pete Oxley 31.5.1995

19 Staring at the Sea 7a
A big roof challenge taking the left-hand line in the first cave below the jib crane. Low-tide required.
FA. Pete Oxley 8.1996

20 Underwater Love 7a
The right-hand roof line is the most aesthetic.
FA. Pete Oxley 8.1996

21 Octopus Weed . . . . Top 50 E3 6a
6c, S0. Gain the hanging shelf and crawl along this until at the midway point. Swing out across the roof and up the wall beyond.
FA.Damian Cook 1.5.1995

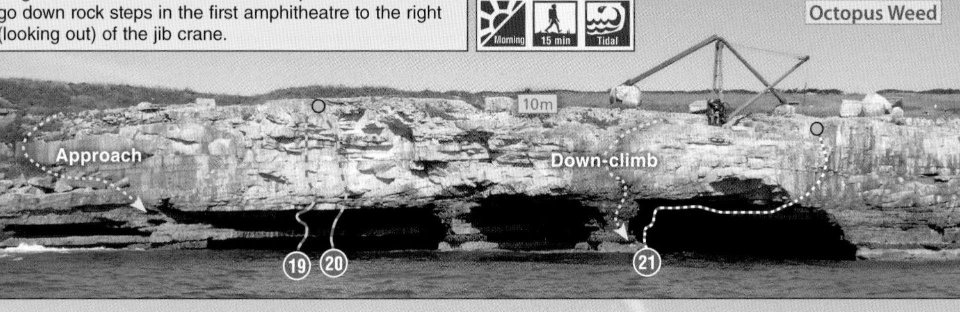

Emma Anderson making good use of the flowstone holds on *Etna* (3) - *page 200* - at the Bay of Rainbows Area. Photo: Tom Beaumont

Cheyne Weares Area

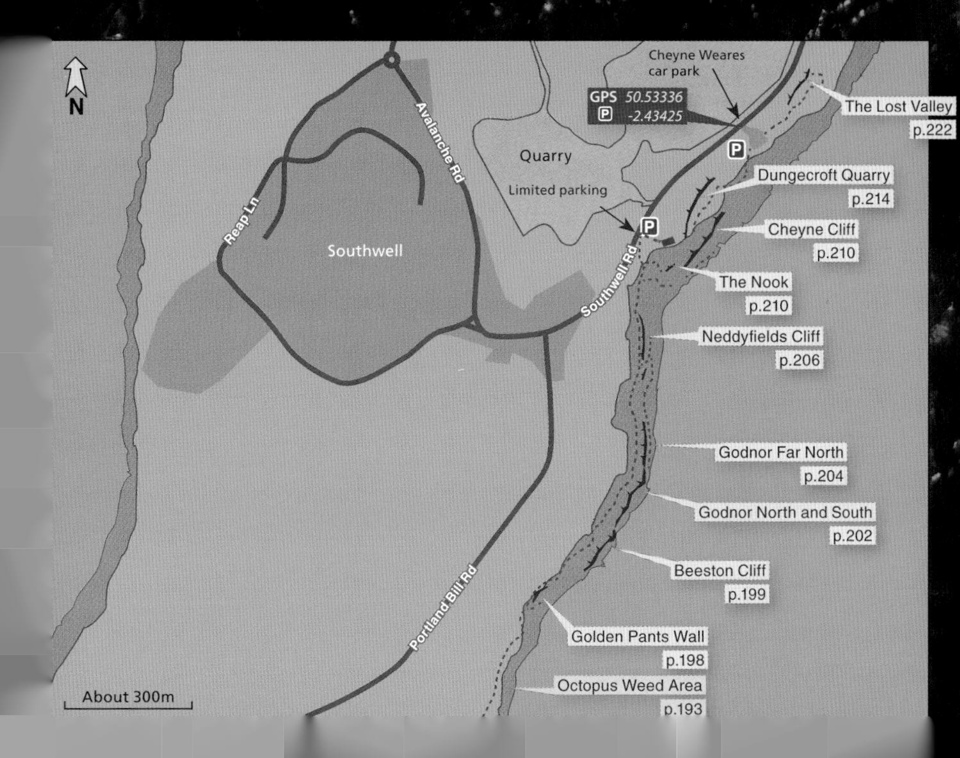

	No star	1	2	3
up to 4+	21	15	1	-
5+ to 6a+	40	36	5	-
6b to 7a	31	39	8	-
7a+ and up	8	7	11	2

The section of coast either side of the Cheyne Weares car park has nine individual cliffs that offer a wide range of grades and climbing styles.

Beeston Cliff is a little-frequented series of interesting and secluded bays with some short, quality routes on excellent rock and some particularly good easier and mid-grade lines. This is a quiet area that is often overlooked and is consequently worth considering on busy Bank Holidays.

Godnor South and its more extensively-developed Far North neighbour are a seaside low and mid-grade sport climbing playground.

The Neddyfields Main Cliff offers a similar line-up of climbing, although the cliff is set further from the sea and is more sheltered. Both these cliffs have become extremely popular, although it should be noted that the easier lines at Neddyfields Cliff can be over-run by outdoor groups at times.

High above the sea are two much shorter crags - Dungecroft Quarry and The Nook. Whilst these sections of cliff don't look very impressive, a good deal of decent rock and quality climbing can be found here.

The biggest crag in the area is Cheyne Cliff, which looks scruffy and unstable from a distance, but in fact harbours some fine flowstone faces and orange coral. The routes here are mostly for the fitter climber looking for fingery stamina-tests.

The Lost Valley is a sheltered location in a deep inland ravine with a quiet atmosphere. The Lost Valley has been cleaned and developed further in recent years and the number of lines has doubled - a bonus for those looking to escape gale force winds.

Access

There is a variable climbing restriction on The Nook and the left-hand section Cheyne Cliff (from the route *Drowning on Dry Land* to *Van Life*) because of a nesting peregrine. **No climbing from March 1st to June 30th**. The Road Rage section of wall is not restricted, although it should only be approached by abseil from above during the restricted times. Please do not top out or abseil at Godnor Far North as cliff-top fauna will be disturbed. Climbing is banned on the cliff with a large pipe next to it. It is situated between Neddyfields Cliff and Godnor North.

The Cheyne Weares cliffs give some of the widest choice of climbing on Portland, and are good spots to pick up some morning sun or afternoon shade.

Conditions

All the areas face east, so get the morning sun, which is great in winter, but can be hot on summer mornings, though they offer some welcome shade in the afternoons. There is no seepage, and all the cliffs dry quickly after showers. The Lost Valley is particularly sheltered. The sea-level crags can be greasy, especially Godnor South and Far North, so avoid these on humid summer days. Cheyne Cliff can become dusty in the summer.

Tides

Godnor South is tidal and only accessible at lowish tide. The Bay of Rainbows area is non-tidal owing to the raised belay ledge. Limekiln Cave needs a very low tide to expose the boulder beach.

Approach See map on page 195

The two main parking areas for these crags lie on the main road between Easton and Southwell. The first is the main Cheyne Weares car park which is clearly marked - park here for The Lost Valley and Dungecroft Quarry. The second limited spot (2-3 cars) is in a short track, on the seaward side of the road, 300m south of Cheyne Weares car park - park here for Beeston Cliff, Godnor South and Far North, Neddyfields Main Cliff, The Nook and Cheyne Cliff (this parking quickly fills up, although the large Cheyne Weares car park is only a couple of minutes walk back up the road). Good footpaths lead to all the cliffs. More details of the approaches to the individual crags are included with the relevant sections. Note that Beeston Cliff, Neddyfields, Cheyne Cliff, The Nook and Godnor Cliff are **not** accessible from Dungecroft Quarry.

Portland
Lulworth
Swanage
Blacknor N
Blacknor C
Blacknor S
Blacknor B
Blacknor FS
Battleship
Battleship BC
Wallsend N
Wallsend S
Coastguard N
Coastguard S
White Hole
Lighthouse
Cheyne Weare
Cuttings

Golden Pants Wall

This outlying area is a short, smooth, non-tidal wall of good rock which faces southeast. The routes are pretty fierce and fingery.

Approach (see page 197) - Walk along the coast path for 15 minutes, above Godnor, until a dome-shaped spoil heap is reached above a promontory. The Golden Pants wall is a further 200m along the coast path situated above a boulder beach.

1 Online . . . . 3+
The short, easy line finishing on the arete.
FA. Tom Beaumont 25.9.2008

2 Always a Little Further . . . 6b
Interesting moves between prominent jugs.
FA. Mick Ward 20.6.2003

3 Social Lepers . . . . 7a+
The blank wall is much harder for the short.
FA. Neal Heanes 1.1997

4 Suits you Sir! 7a
Tough stuff up the crack.
FA. Neal Heanes 5.1996

5 Winterset 6c
The prominent crack has a testing move.
FA. Mick Ward 26.2.2002

6 Skin Up . . . . 6a+
Climb the bulge and crack. A good one to get started on.
FA. Alan Ashmore 9.1996

7 Sea Pink 7a
The beautiful pink wall, with a brutal move. Lower-off shared with *Skin Up*.
FA. Mick Ward 26.2.2002

8 Eva Luna . . . . 7a+
The faint weakness has some elegant moves.
FA. Mick Ward 12.3.2002

9 Fight the Good Fight . . . . . . 7a+
Another weakness featuring combative moves.
FA. Mick Ward 15.6.2003

10 Strategem . . . . 6b+
Climb the wall.
FA. Mick Ward 15.6.2003

11 Burnt Sienna 6b
The wall past an oblique move.
FA. Mick Ward 12.6.2003

There has been a rockfall hereabouts that has destroyed a couple of lines. Also the boulder beach has a tendency to vary radically making the bases of the climbs either easy or nails.

12 East Coast Epic 1 6b
Climb up the small corner just right of the arete to the tricky headwall.
FA. Steve Taylor 16.9.2004

13 Return to Form 1 6a
The flake-crack just left of the large corner to a long move on the headwall.
FA. Steve Taylor 11.9.2004

14 Rusty Wall 1 6b
The weakness just right of the arete is followed by some difficult moves on the headwall. A very intense pitch.
FA. Steve Taylor 16.9.2004

15 Dirty Dog 1 6c
Climb the blank wall direct via a precarious move into the scoop.
FA. Steve Taylor 16.9.2004

16 Pavane 1 6a
The corner and wall is best climbed direct.
FA. Mick Ward 16.9.2004

*All of the remaining routes have **very** tidal bases and ascents are rare. It is possible that the boulder beach has receded and that the base is now only exposed at low spring tides, or not at all.*

17 Aquaserene 1 7a
A smart test-piece with a blind crux.
FA. Pete Oxley 6.7.1997

18 Te Taniwha 1 6b
Climb the blind crack and groove.
FA. James Dunlop 9.8.1997

19 Silence of the Deep . . . 1 6b
The calcite-encrusted face is nicely sustained.
FA. Pete Oxley 20.7.1997

20 Lucky Day in Hell . . 7b+
A very tough boulder problem which needs good conditions. Shares the final moves of *Silence of the Deep*.
FA. Pete Oxley 9.9.1997

21 Heart Full of Nails . 1 7a+
A miniature pump route up a steep leaning face.
FA. Pete Oxley 20.9.1997

22 Konked Out 1 7a
The bulging nose is very photogenic.
FA. Pete Oxley 9.9.1997

23 Rags to Rags, Rust to Rust 5
An amenable wall pitch past two old mystery pegs.
FA. Pete Oxley 9.9.1997

24 The League of Gurus . . 7a
Avoid the tricky crux on the left for an overall grade of **6c**.
FA. Pete Oxley 27.9.1997

Morning | 15 min | Tidal | Abseil in

Limekiln Cave Area

This is a series of low, tidal cliffs. Most of the routes are on compact rock, although limited access to many of the routes means that a visit must be well-timed.

Approach and Tides (see page 197) - From the promontory above *Bay of Rainbows* (see page 200), walk right (looking out) around the amphitheatre. By a block wall, head out to another promontory which overlooks the *Limekiln Cave*. Abseil from blocks to the boulder beach below, which is only really advisable at low spring tides. For the right-hand routes (looking out), walk another 50m and locate a good ledge just beneath the cliff-line which has a large rusty chain hanging from above it. It is best to abseil to the boulder beach from the staple in the back wall.

Portland | Lulworth | Swanage | Blacknor N | Blacknor C | Blacknor S | Blacknor B | Blacknor FS | Battleship | Battleship BC | Wallsend N | Wallsend S | Coastguard N | Coastguard S | White Hole | Lighthouse | Cheyne Weare | Cuttings

The Great Escape Wall

This snaking, block-topped wall has a number of unusual lines, including a fully-bolted traverse. However the boulder beach has dropped since the routes were established and the starts are now significantly different - there have been no known ascents in recent times. There are a number of difficult DWSs not described in this book - for details see *Deep Water* www.rockfax.com.

Tides - The first two lines require an abseil approach and very low spring tide. The remaining routes are non-tidal.

Approach (see page 197) - Walk along the coast path for 15 minutes, above Godnor, until a dome-shaped spoil heap is reached above a promontory. The Great Escape Wall is to the left of the earth mound (looking out). All the routes require an abseil approach from locations on the topo.

1 Sea of Tears . . . . 1★ **6c**
A photogenic arete with a blind crux.
FA. Pete Oxley 27.9.1997

2 The Underhill Mob . . . . **6a+**
A strenuous layback. Bolts reported missing.
FA. Pete Oxley 27.9.1997

Approach (routes 3 to 5) - *Abseil from bolts in the blocks to the non-tidal beach below in the amphitheatre.*

3 The Great Escape . . . . . 1★ **6c**
An atmospheric traverse. Unfortunately the boulder beach has dropped and the start is not possible at the present time.
1) 6c, 15m. Climb the pocketed wall above the roof, then traverse left along the lip to a hanging stance near the arete.
2) 6c, 15m. Continue traversing left around the arete, then trend upwards to a large square block.
FA. Mike Robertson 19.3.1994

4 Beach Madness **6c**
Follow the *The Great Escape* to the 6th bolt, then climb direct through the roof to a belay on a block. Note that the crux is on *The Great Escape*.
FA. Mike Robertson 19.3.1994

5 Esmeralda's Monkey **7b**
50m. An extension to *The Great Escape*. From the belay at the end of pitch 1 of *The Great Escape* , drop down and follow the line around the headland through caves and bays, eventually emerging on to a promontory overlooking Limekiln Cave. A great expedition. **Pitch grades - 6c, 7b, 7b, 6a+**.
FA. Mike Robertson 16.3.1996

Approach (routes 6 to 12) - *Abseil to a ledge with a bolt-belay.*

6 Stromboli . . . . 1★ **6a**
From a small ledge (belay staple) climb the slightly impending groove on flowstone crimps and flakes.
FA. John Leonard 29.9.2011

7 Krakatoa . . . . 1★ **4**
S3. Follow a diagonal line leftwards off the ledge.
FA. Steve Taylor 23.4.1994

8 Etna . . . . 1★ **3**
S3. Climb the flake above the ledge. *Photo on page 194.*
FA. Steve Taylor 23.4.1994

9 Popacatapetl . . . . . 1★ **6a**
S3. The wall and small roof.
FA. Steve Taylor 23.4.1994

10 Fifteen Minutes to Fame 1★ **6a**
S1. Start on the right of the ledge and climb up trending right.
FA. Steve Taylor 21.8.1994

11 Bay of Rainbows . . 2★ **6c+**
S1. From the right side of the ledge head rightwards up the wall.
FA. Damian Cook 4.1994

12 Belly Button Traverse 2★ **6a+**
S0. Traverse the low break to the far ledge and finish *up Bungle, Zippy and George*, or reverse the traverse. Great fun.
FA. Mike Robertson 25.4.1994

13 Cornflake Girl . . . . 6b+

S1. A tricky pitch. Start from near the end of *Belly Button Traverse*.
FA. Mike Robertson 25.4.1994

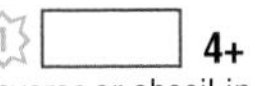

14 Bungle, Zippy and George. . 4+

S2. Start from the end of *Belly Button Traverse* or abseil in.
FA. Mark Williams 21.8.1994

Bay of Rainbows Area

A fine wall of flowstone with some pleasant and well-bolted lower-grade climbs. A great place to spend a sunny morning. This area is also a popular deep water soloing venue.

Approach and Tides (see page 197) - Walk along the coast path for 15 minutes, above Godnor, until a dome-shaped spoil heap is reached above a promontory. The Bay of Rainbows is situated on the promontory below and left (looking out) of the earth mound. All routes start from non-tidal ledges that are accessed via a short abseil from bolts in blocks.

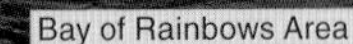

Godnor South and North

The adjoining sections of Godnor South and North are an isolated section of cliff which has been developed for sport climbing, and now provides a number of good pitches on sound rock. Although tidal, the climbs are worth venturing to and can be easily accessed from Godnor Far North. The area is unlikely to be very busy, and is a charming location dominated by a large sea-arch. The cliff has potential for more sport climbs.

Approach and tides (see page 197) - There are 2 options:
1) From the limited parking spot, walk 200m down the coast path to where a long, low bouldering wall appears on the right (2 mins from the road). The Neddyfields Main Cliff lies directly below the bouldering wall. Opposite the far end of the bouldering wall, use a good steep path which cuts back left (looking out) along the cliff base. At the bottom of the cliff, descend to the beach boulders then head right (looking out) for 150m along the boulder beach, past a large outfall pipe, to where the main crag of Godnor Far North starts. The boulders can be greasy and eventually they become tidal. At around 1 or 2 hours either side of low spring tides you can continue under the cliff (Godnor North) to quickly access a large tank-shaped boulder and a little further on a rock arch. The route *Euphemism* starts from the top of the tank-shaped boulder.
2) From the path above Neddyfields Main Cliff, continue for approximately 200m and locate the top of the cliff and abseil from boulders. This approach is only recommended for those familiar with the area.

An isolated bay containing four sport routes is located approximately 100m south of the topo on this page, and can be reached at low tide along the base of the cliff, or more easily via abseil from some huge, stacked blocks. There is a good number of trad lines all along this section of the cliff - not described.

1 Portland Exclusion Zone 6c
Climb the steep corner and wall to a niche at 3m - no bolts - and continue via a flake to blocks and a single-bolt lower-off.
FA. Steve Taylor 26.3.1995

A project takes the wall between Portland Exclusion Zone and Leonardo starting up Leonardo.

2 Leonardo . . . . 6a+
Climb the steep crack and groove before a balancy move rightwards around the arete joins the wall of the next route. Shared lower-off.
FA. Mick Ward 9.2011

3 Mona Lisa . . . . 5+
A tricky start leads to pleasant wall climbing.
FA. Mick Ward 9.2011

4 Whitestones . . . . 3+
Two huge white pebbles mark the start of the wall. A stiff start leads to nice slabby climbing. It is possible to top-out on this line.
FA. Mick Ward 9.2011

5 The Good Life . . . . {2} 5+
The well-positioned crack and left arete of the small bay south of the arch. High in the grade.
FA. Steve Taylor, John Howells, Gavin Symonds 9.6.2007

Approach
Abseil from blocks
12m
Rock arch
1 2 3 4
5 6

Just to the right is the crack of **Break-Over Crack, E1 5b**.

6 Enter Shikari 6c
Starts up the hanging flake immediately south of the arch.
FA. Gavin Symonds, Rob Kennard 9.6.2007

7 Short, but Perfectly Formed 1 6a
A short, but difficult pitch that has a blind move through the bulge at mid-height.
FA. Steve Taylor, Gavin Symonds, John Howells, Rob Kennard 9.6.2007

8 Big Slab Variant . . . . 1 4+
A short lived, but worthwhile little pitch in an interesting location. From a small ledge, swing right on good holds and get established on less-steep ground. Continue up the slab to a lower-off.
FA. c2001

9 Unnamed . . . . 1 6a+
A longish line that climbs the steep wall right of *Big Slab Variant* and finishes with a pull up on the jutting block.
FA. c2001

10 Loving the Moment 6a
Climbs the grooves and cracks right of the jutting block of *Unnamed*.
FA. Mick Ward 8.9.2011

11 Euphemism 1 6b
Start from the centre of the tank block. Climb the groove direct with a hard move to finish.
FA. Steve Taylor, Gavin Symonds, John Howells, Rob Kennard 9.6.2007

12 Prisoners of Gravity 1 6b
Start from the boulder beach below the tank-shaped block. Follow staples up to a big move onto the jutting prow.
FA. Mick Ward 30.11.2009

13 Island in the Sun 1 6a
The slab to the right of *Prisoners of Gravity*. Start up a tricky little groove to gain an easy slab, move up and finish on steeper ground.
FA. Mick Ward 30.11.2009

The next two lines are the first to be encountered when scrambling along the tidal cliff-base from Godnor Far North.

14 Private World 6a
Start about 30m along the tidal section of the cliff and follow a diagonal line leftwards.
FA. Mick Ward 23.9.2011

15 Stress Test 6a
Start just right of *Private World* and climb steeply past overlaps.
FA. Mick Ward 23.9.2011

Godnor Far North

Godnor Far North has become a popular section of cliff that receives plenty of early morning sun, and has lots of easily accessible lines, mainly in the low to mid-grades.

Tides and Conditions - The whole of the cliff base although close to sea level is non-tidal. Can be very greasy in humid conditions.

Approach (see page 197) - The cliff is passed on the approach to Godnor South - see previous page. **Do not abseil in or take short-cuts due to rare fauna on the slopes around the cliff.**

1 Gi' It Laldy . . . . 1 star **6c**
Make a hard start over the undercut roof (boulder missing at present). Steep, blind climbing and much harder than its neighbour.
FA. George Ridge 15.8.1997

2 Harpies and Quines . . . 2 stars **6b+**
A good atmospheric little route which is worth seeking out. Pumpy all the way. The first bolt is high.
FA. Janet Horrocks 22.8.1997

3 Any Day Mike? . . . 1 star **7b+**
Start as for *Harpies and Quines* and continue directly up the shallow rib.
FA. Jimbo Kimber 7.2000

4 One Day, James . . . . . 1 star **6b+**
A good route featuring a nice crack that has now cleaned up.
FA. A.O'Boyle 21.9.1997

5 Pathfinder. . . . . 1 star **6b**
An excellent little pitch which is quite tricky at the top.
FA. Mike Vaicaitis 14.9.1997

The flake right of Pathfinder is the trad line **Snatch Squad, HS 4b.**

6 Sidewinder **6a**
A good, subtle line up a series of thin flakes and cracks.
FA. Mike Vaicaitis 20.9.1997

7 Dreamscape . . . . 1 star **6a**
A popular route that can be made harder by climbing direct past the first bolt at 6b.
FA. Mike Vaicaitis 20.9.1997

The next five routes all have technically difficult moves at mid-height.

8 Ben . . . . 1 star **5**
The central section of the route is the difficult bit.
FA. P.Cunningham 10.8.1997

9 Willem. . . . . 1 star **5**
A tricky mid-height move again.
FA. P.Cunningham 10.8.1997

10 Jasper . . . . 1 star **4+**
A more sustained pitch that still has a tricky mid-section. Perhaps the easiest line on this section of the crag.
FA. P.Cunningham 20.4.1997

11 Jody Sunshine. . . . . . . 1 star **4+**
Beware of the crux move (about half way) it is harder than you might expect, although the top half is straightforward.
FA. P.Cunningham 20.9.1997

12 Wave Warrior . . . . 1 star **4+**
High in the grade. Start at a crack and finish at a jutting block on the skyline.
FA. S.Robbins 20.9.1997

13 Valerie's Patio. **3**
The right-to-left rising diagonal line.
FA. P.Cunningham 25.8.1997

Morning | 10 min | Sheltered

15m

3

1 2 4 5 6 7 8 9 10 11 12 13 14 15 16

14 Garden Party .... 1 star 6a
The wall above *Valerie's Patio*. Start up *Valerie's Patio*.
FA. Mick Ward 21.5.2010

15 Starbuck 6a
A tricky move at mid-height, involving crimpy holds to the left, gains easier climbing above.
FA. Mike Vaicaitis 25.8.1997

16 Last Human 6c
Thin wall climbing.
FA. Mike Vaicaitis 26.8.1997

17 Tin Man .... 1 star 5+
The flowstone flecked shallow arete.
FA. Mike Vaicaitis 25.8.1997

18 Tombstone .... 2 star 3+
A beauty for the grade which is a nice relaxing climb for a hot summer day. The start looks unlikely, but persevere.
Photo on page 185.
FA. S.Robbins 20.7.1997

19 Where Silence Has Lease
.... 2 star 6c
The best pitch here up the blunt arete on its right-hand side. Tough at the top and requiring a long reach.
FA. Mike Vaicaitis 31.8.1997

20 Wedding Daze .... 1 star 6b
Clean climbing throughout. One brief hard move at the top to a massive jug.
FA. J.Parsons 10.8.1997

21 Future Imperfect ..... 2 star 6a+
A highly regarded route. Straightforward moves leading to a nice finishing crack.
FA. Mike Vaicaitis 10.8.1997

22 Jacob's Ladder ...... 2 star 5
A fine pitch that finishes at the jutting block.
FA. Mike Vaicaitis 3.5.1997

23 The Truth is Out There . 2 star 6b
A good jug-haul to start with gains a delicate top section. The small crimpy stuck-on bits at the top are the key to success.
FA. Mike Vaicaitis 20.4.1997

24 Resistance is Futile 1 star 7a+
A good, technical roof and wall problem that gives by far and away the hardest move (or two) at the cliff.
FA. Mike Vaicaitis 20.7.1997

25 Car Parts, Bottles and Cutlery. 1 star 6b+
Keep left near the top, out of the groove.
FA. Nic Hellyer 22.2.1998

26 Factor 15 .... 1 star 6a+
A reasonable pitch which can be a bit dusty.
FA. Pete Church 8.2.1998

27 Net Asset .... 5+
Tackle the overhang to the right of *Factor 15*. Move diagonally left to turn the overhang on its left-hand side and then head back right to finish on the final clip and lower-off of *Kung Fu Panda*.
FA. Andy Dunford 19.5.2010

28 Kung Fu Panda .... 1 star 4
Climb to the right end of the overhang and then up the corner and wall above.
FA. Adam Perrett 21.8.2009

29 Nonnie and the Pulp Fiction Tantrum
.... 1 star 4+
The crack and wall.
FA. Andy Dunford 20.8.2009

Morning | 10 min | Sheltered

17m

16 17 18 19 20 21 22 23 24 25 26 27 28 29

Neddyfields Main Cliff

The Neddyfields Main Cliff is a popular morning crag with plenty of friendly grades. It is quick to reach, has a pleasant outlook, is sheltered from strong westerly winds and offers shade on summer afternoons and evenings. There is good bouldering on the short wall above the Main Cliff.

Approach (see page 197) - From the limited parking spot, walk 200m down the coast path to where a long low bouldering wall appears on the right (2 mins from the road). The Neddyfields Main Cliff lies directly below the bouldering wall. Opposite the far end of the bouldering wall, use a good steep path which cuts back left (looking out) along the cliff base. For the first five routes cut back south (right - looking out) along the boulder beach. The cliff base is in a hollow 10m above beach level, attained by a short scramble.

Morning | 5 min | Sheltered

1 **Return of the Rice Bandit** 6a
The left-most route on the wall. Keep right at the top.
FA. Sam Ferguson 10.12.2012

2 **Midday Massacre** 5
A little dirty, but with nice moves on big holds.
FA. Sam Ferguson 9.9.2011

3 **La Fievre Spiteuse** . . . . 5+
A difficult start and a hard move higher up.
FA. Sam Ferguson 10.1.2012

4 **Lucy's off the Wall** 5
A stout route that requires a lot of effort between the mid-height breaks.
FA. P.Cunningham 13.8.97

5 **Nothing's Shocking** . . . 6a+
A fun climb. The last few moves often provide an anxious moment.
FA. Steve Taylor 1995.

6 **First Contact** 6b
A clean pitch tackling the front face of the buttress.
FA. Mike Vaicaitis. 13.8.97

7 **Brace Yourself Sheila** . . 5
The vague undercut arete. A lovely climb with a top section that may catch you out.
FA. P.Cunningham 13.8.97

The next lines are on the Neddyfields Main Cliff itself.

8 **Conquistadors of the Useless** 6c
Ascend the not quite blank wall via a bouldery sequence.
FA. Mick Ward 7.5.2010

9 **Small object of Desire** . . . . 6a+
Another shorty. Tricky moves gain a sloping scoop.
FA. John Leonard 8.5.2010

10 **Annapurna, Mon Amour** . . . . . . 6a+
Move up the wall via an overlap.
FA. Mick Ward 9.5.2010

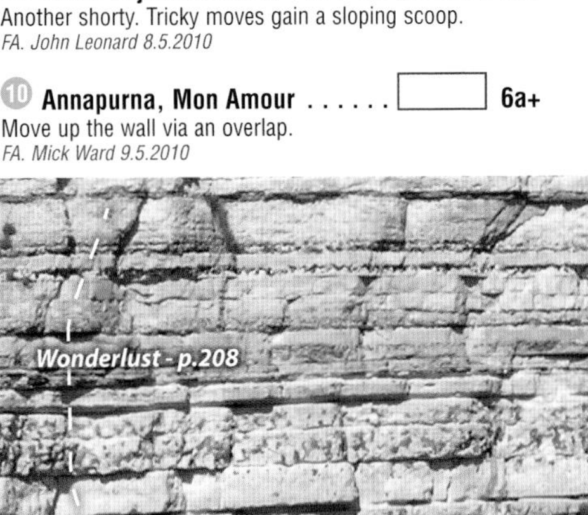

11 **The Accelerator** . . . 7a
This micro-route starts halfway down the descent. Don't be deceived by its length; it packs a lot in. Low in the grade.
FA. Mike Vaicaitis 10.8.97

12 **Nameless** 6c
A very bouldery route with just the one hard move. It is easier to top-out and walk around than lower off.
FA. Mike Vaicaitis 1997

13 **Born to Hunt** 6c
A fierce and sequency wall climb that gradually builds in difficulty.
FA. Mick Ward 10.2010

14 **Thick as Thieves** 6c
Easy climbing to one nails move.
FA. Guy Dixon 1995

15 **Three in a Bed** . . . . 5+
Start next to an old rusty ring. Make hard initial moves to gain the easier upper face.
FA. Steve Taylor 1995

A trad line **Frank's Effort, HS 4a** *follows the wall just right of Three in a Bed, starting as for that line.*

Just right again another trad line **Steve's Wall, VS 4b** *tackles the wall to join, and finish up the line of Frank's Effort.*

16 **I Wish I Was In Steve's Shoes** . . 5+
A difficult start leads to a steep bulge - take care with the rock.
FA. Brian Wilkinson, Steve Thorpe 16.4.2010

17 **Felix Navidad** . . . . 6a+
Easy lower ledges lead to a fingery mid-section.
FA. Unknown

18 **Infelicity** 6a
Move up past a low bolt and small pedestal. Finish up the pleasant wall.
FA. Unknown

19 **Milly Vanilly** 6a
Make a stiff pull at a head-height bolt and climb the sustained wall above.
FA. Unknown

20 **Books Across the Sea** 6a
The wall and overlap.
FA. Mick Ward 9.4.2010

21 **Puppet Show of Memory** 6a
The crack, wall and rib at the right-hand end of the wall.
FA. Mick Ward 9.4.2010

A trad line **Inertia, VS 4b** *takes the overhangs and vegetated wall above, starting at a low overhang at the base of the slope.*

Neddyfields Main Cliff

The Neddyfields Main Cliff is a popular morning crag with plenty of friendly grades. It is quick to reach, has a pleasant outlook, is sheltered from strong westerly winds and offers shade on summer afternoons.

Approach (see page 197) - From the limited parking spot, walk 200m down the coast path to where a long, low bouldering wall appears on the right (2 mins from the road). The Neddyfields Main Cliff lies directly below the bouldering wall. Opposite the far end of the bouldering wall, use a good steep path that cuts back left along the cliff base (looking out).

1 Damn These Electric Sex Pants . 6a+
Bolted line to the left of *Kate*. Start by an iron stake.
FA. Marti Hallett 20.9.2010

2 Kate . . . . 6b+
One of the old trad-lines on the cliff - now bolted.
FA. Dave Jones, J.Kenton 21.6.1980

3 Wonderlust . . . . 2★ 6b
A very popular line. Low in the grade, but don't underestimate the finish, which has a hard move.
FA. Pete Church 26.2002

The line of **Intimidation, E1 5b** *starts to the right of Wonderlust and works left crossing Wonderlust at mid-height.*

4 Shit Route 7a
Now considered to be better than the route name it was originally given. A difficult bulge and finishing crack supply the interest.
FA. Andy Long 7.2001

5 Julie Ocean . . . . . . 2★ 6c+
Well-positioned moves on the headwall. The lower moves are easy, but the climbing builds up nicely to a first-class crux sequence.
FA. Mike Vaicaitis 28.3.1997

6 Northern Invasion 7a
Start easy and finish with difficulty, the headwall is hard to read.
FA. Sam Ferguson 21.9.2011

7 Bigus Dickus 6b
An old trad line that has been retro-bolted.
FA. Dave Jones, J Kenton 22.6.1980

8 Lugwiler's Dismal Itch . 1 star 6c
A worthwhile route with good moves all the way and with the harder climbing based around its mid-section. The moves on the bubbly wall can sometimes be damp.
FA. Nic Hellyer 14.2.1998

9 Ecosystem . . . . 1 star 6b+
Quite a pleasant climb with some interesting moves over the roof on clean rock. Low in the grade.
FA. Mike Vaicaitis 26.7.1996

10 Time of the Month . 1 star 6b+
A lovely climb which has an intricate middle section. Much easier at the top.
FA. Nic Hellyer, Christine Forkin 18.4.1999

11 Inception . . . . 1 star 5+
The mid-height bulge gives food for thought, but keep something in reserve for the last move.
FA. B.Slattery 1996

12 The Screwfix Escourt Agency 1 star 6a+
The wall and tricky headwall.
FA. Unknown

The wall next to The Screwfix Escourt Agency is climbed by the **The Scoop, S 4a**.

The corner-line right again is the route **Better Things, HS 4a**.

13 Ocean Boulevard . . . . . 1 star 4+
Start by a low overhang and an iron ring on the ground. There is a difficult opening move over the roof. The wall above is still tricky. It may be a poor relation to its Swanage namesake, but it is not a bad route at all.
FA. B.Slattery 20.7.96

The corner just to the right is taken by the trad climb **Outside Left, S 4a**.

The wall to the right is climbed by the trad line **Crush with Eyeliner, E1 5b**.

14 Bundle of Joy . . . . 1 star 4
Climb diagonally leftwards to good fingery moves through the knobbly band of rock.
FA. John Leonard 11.5.2010

The left-trending ramp is **Sunday Rake, S**, *and the depression to the right is* **Spider Cracks, HVS**.

The last route on the wall is the wide crack of **Butterfly Crack, S**.

From parking
15m
14
9 10 11 12
8 13
13

Cheyne Cliff

The main section is a superb wall, covered in fantastic flowstone and orange coral sheets. The harder routes have been used for training purposes and many variations have been done over time. There has been a large rockfall at the southern end in recent times that has destroyed the starts of three lines recorded in previous guidebooks.

Approach (see page 197) - The crag can be approached from either of the two parking spots. Head toward the Neddyfields Main Cliff, but double back down a steep slope which leads to the crag base. All the sectors can be reached from here.

Restriction (From the Nook and all routes up to *Van Life*) - No climbing between 1st March to 30th June due to nesting birds. The Road Rage wall must only be approached by abseil from above during this period. The abseil point is in Dungecroft Quarry see page 213.

The Nook

A tiny, wedged-shaped wall perched above the large neighbouring cliff. It has a number of short climbs on solid and well-bolted rock, a quick approach and is very sheltered.

Approach (see page 197) - The crag can be approached from either of the two parking spots. Head toward the Neddyfields Main Cliff, but double back left after 50m along a low quarried terrace to arrive at the crag.

Restriction - No climbing 1st March to 30th June due to nesting birds.

1 Leering Crack **5**

The headwall crack left of *Air Kisses*. Climb the short lower wall - no bolt - and then move left to climb the crack on its right.

FA. Mick Ward 30.1.2010

2 Air Kisses .... 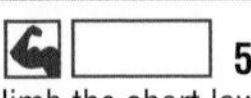 **6c**

Start below the widest overhang of the headwall. Packs in a lot of tricky moves.

FA. Mick Ward 12.12.2009

3 My Pashminas Got Caught in the Gri-gri

.... 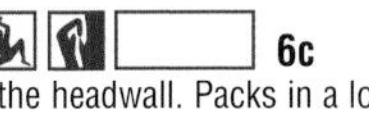 **6a**

From the corner created by the pedestal, climb up to the V-notch in the headwall.

FA. Mick Ward 14.12.2009

4 East Side Story . . . . 5+
From the corner created by the pedestal, climb up and move right at the break to enter the slanting groove in the headwall from its right-hand side. This can be done direct at about 6a+.
FA. John Leonard 14.12.2009

5 Chill Dementia . . . . 4+
Right of the pedestal. A tricky start on the lower wall accesses the blocky corner in the headwall where good holds are found.
FA. Adam Perrett 20.12.2009

6 Sinister Dexter . . . . 1 6a+
The left-hand of three routes that climb the flowstone headwall at the right end of the crag. Good moves on the lower wall lead to a tricky sequence above.
FA. Adam Perrett 10.1.2010

7 Bring Me Sunshine. 6a
Climb the middle of the flowstone headwall. Start from the base of a rightward-sloping ramp and climb straight up to a surprisingly pumpy sequence on the wall above.
FA. John Leonard 23.1.2010

8 It's a God Awful Small Affair . . . 2
Climb the sloping ramp or the wall to its right to gain the conglomerate groove above. Some amazing holds.
FA. Sarah Perrett 10.1.2010

The rest of the routes are on the tall orange wall reached by descending down to the left and walking right - see page 197.

9 Drowning on Dry Land . 2 6c
A flowstone classic taking a long line up the calcite face and high groove.
FA. Mike Robertson 9.1994

Coralized Area

The massive wall encountered first on the approach is encrusted with orange flowstone and has a few decent sustained wall climbs. The left side of the wall has suffered a recent rockfall and three routes have been lost.
Approach (see page 197) - The crag can be approached from either of the two parking spots. Head toward the Neddyfields Main Cliff, but double back down a steep slope which leads to the crag base. All the sectors can be reached from here.
Restriction - No climbing 1st March to 30th June due to nesting birds.

10 Rocket from the Crypt. . 2 7a+
A big pitch that is worth seeking out as a first sample of the harder routes hereabouts. Start 6m right of the tunnel.
FA. Pete Oxley 22.7.1994

11 Coralized . . . . 2 7b+
A good, sustained climb with amazing coral on the lower wall and more good rock above.
FA. Pete Oxley 22.7.1994

12 Heartbeats . . . . . . 1 7a+
Climb the lower half of *Coralized* then take the line that heads off to the right on the upper wall.
FA. Andy Long 31.1.2008

13 Van Life . . . . 2 7a+
Climb the lower wall to a tough slim flake-line on the headwall.
FA. Gavin Symonds 31.1.2008

Morning | 10 min | Sheltered

Portland | Lulworth | Swanage | Blacknor N | Blacknor C | Blacknor S | Blacknor B | Blacknor FS | Battleship | Battleship BC | Wallsend N | Wallsend S | Coastguard N | Coastguard S | White Hole | Lighthouse | Cheyne Weare | Cuttings

Pigskin Bus Area

A narrow section of continuous rock is sandwiched between the two main walls. The climbs are worthwhile, but care is needed with some of the holds. There is no restriction on this wall, but please only approach these routes from above (abseil in from above *Road Rage* in Dungecroft Quarry) when the restriction is on the rest of the crag - 1st March to 30th June.

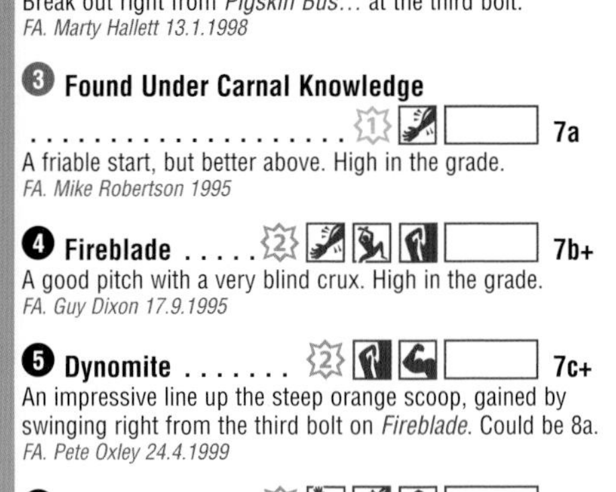

1 The Pigskin Bus Pulls Into Tuna Town 1 **6a**
It is worth persevering with the dirty start, since the rest of the pitch gives good flowstone climbing.
FA. Pete Oxley 22.7.1994

2 Dutch Courage 1 **6c**
Break out right from *Pigskin Bus...* at the third bolt.
FA. Marty Hallett 13.1.1998

3 Found Under Carnal Knowledge 1 **7a**
A friable start, but better above. High in the grade.
FA. Mike Robertson 1995

4 Fireblade . . . . . 2 **7b+**
A good pitch with a very blind crux. High in the grade.
FA. Guy Dixon 17.9.1995

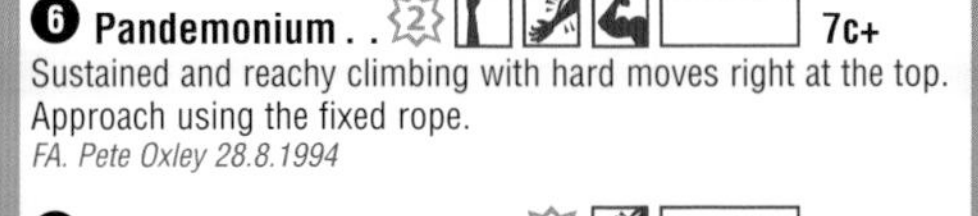

5 Dynomite . . . . 2 **7c+**
An impressive line up the steep orange scoop, gained by swinging right from the third bolt on *Fireblade*. Could be 8a.
FA. Pete Oxley 24.4.1999

6 Pandemonium . . 2 **7c+**
Sustained and reachy climbing with hard moves right at the top. Approach using the fixed rope.
FA. Pete Oxley 28.8.1994

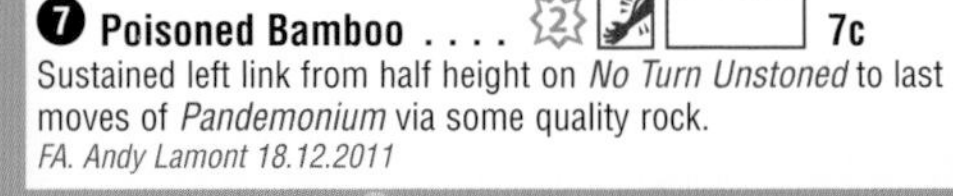

7 Poisoned Bamboo 2 **7c**
Sustained left link from half height on *No Turn Unstoned* to last moves of *Pandemonium* via some quality rock.
FA. Andy Lamont 18.12.2011

Morning | 10 min | Sheltered

8 No Turn Unstoned . . 7a
A good pitch on excellent rock that follows the right-hand side of the face. Approach using the fixed rope.
FA. Rob Kennard 23.1.2011

9 Cruise Control . . . . 6a+
The fine crack and steep corner to a lower-off. Can be continued to the top. *Photo on page 29.*
FA. Brian Wilkinson 25.3.2009

10 Road Rage . . . . . . Top 50 7b+
A fine climb - one of the best on the east coast - that climbs the orange sheet of flowstone which is usually chalked up.
FA. Pete Oxley 18.7.1994

11 Detonator 7c
Hard and pumpy climbing up superb flowstone. High in the grade, especially for the short.
FA. Guy Dixon 1997

12 Illusions 7c
Another fantastic stamina-test with a debilitating reach near the top - shorties beware.
FA. Joff Cook 30.4.1996

13 Yesterday's Dreams
. . . . 7b+
The wall and V-groove on the far right-hand side of the face, starting as for *Illusions* then breaking right at its second bolt. The original start collapsed, but it is still a very good pitch.
FA. Mike Robertson 10.12.1995. Reclimbed by Pete Oxley 18.11.1996

14 Rememberance Sunday 6b+
From a belay bolt, climb the thin blind crack and pillar.
FA. Rob Kennard 17.4.2011

The next lines are reached via a fixed line up a steep, unstable slope around 20m to the right.

15 Italian Eighth. . . . . 6b+
Climb up and slightly leftwards to side-pulls, then continue up the vague arete to a tricky finish.
FA. Tom Beaumont 17.10.2008

16 Threatening Speedos . . 6c+
The smooth, blank-looking wall.
FA. Tom Beaumont 17.10.2008

17 Pouch of Douglas. . 5
The cracked flowstone arete gives pleasant juggy climbing - exposed and high in the grade.
FA. Tom Beaumont 17.9.2008

18 Bariatric 4
Climb the flowstone crack-line at the right-hand end of the wall.
FA. Tom Beaumont 24.6.2008

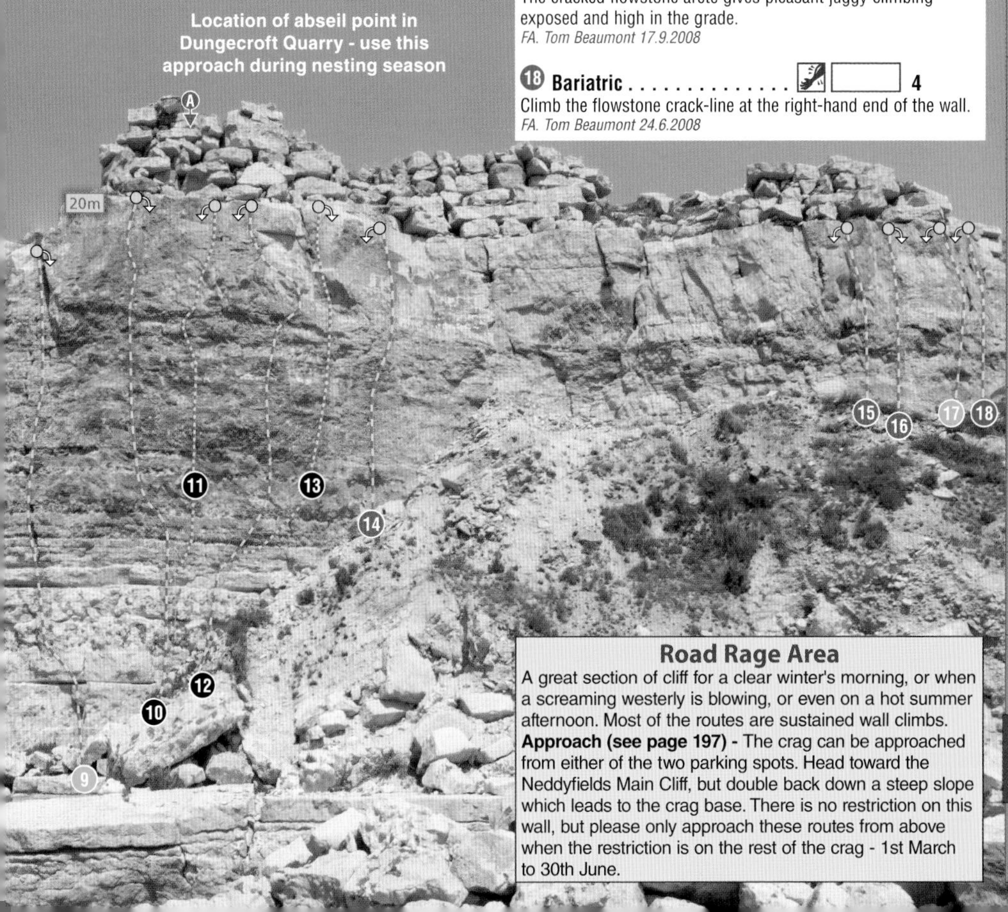

Location of abseil point in Dungecroft Quarry - use this approach during nesting season

A

20m

11 13 14 15 16 17 18 12 10 9

Road Rage Area

A great section of cliff for a clear winter's morning, or when a screaming westerly is blowing, or even on a hot summer afternoon. Most of the routes are sustained wall climbs.
Approach (see page 197) - The crag can be approached from either of the two parking spots. Head toward the Neddyfields Main Cliff, but double back down a steep slope which leads to the crag base. There is no restriction on this wall, but please only approach these routes from above when the restriction is on the rest of the crag - 1st March to 30th June.

Dungecroft Quarry

Dungecroft Quarry is a very long, but short escarpment composed of, for the most part, compact vertical rock and some excellent flowstone. Dungecroft has been heavily developed in recent times, and now has plenty of well-bolted lines that are worth a look. The climbs are generally pretty tough for the grade, and some of them surprisingly pumpy given their lack of height. The other advantage of this area is its very sheltered aspect and extremely convenient location - only a minute or so from the parking.

Approach (see page 197) - Park in Cheyne Weares car park, and walk south for 50m until the quarry comes in to view. Walk down to the quarry floor, from where all the sectors are easily accessed.

Note - The following areas are **not** accessible through Dungecroft Quarry: Neddyfields, Cheyne Cliff (except by abseil), The Nook, Godnor Cliff Cliffs and Beeston Cliffs.

At the far end of the quarry, on the cliff edge overlooking the sea, is the abseil bolt in a block used to descend to the base of the route *Road Rage* during the bird ban on Cheyne Cliff.

Sarah and Adam Perrett on *Crazy Old Hippies* (4+) - *page 217*
- one of many short and intense lines at Dungecroft Quarry.

Wind Dog Sector

A small wall with a handful of well-bolted lines.

Approach (see page 197) - Park in Cheyne Weares car park, and walk south for 50m. The quarry is on the right and the Wind Dog Sector is at the far end of the quarry.

1 A Ying and a Yang and a Yippiedeedoo . . . . 1 ☐ 5+
A steep and juggy line, one of the best in the quarry.
FA. Tom Beaumont 1.8.2010

2 The Lesser of Two Weevils . 1 ☐ 6b+
The overhang followed by the crimpy and reachy headwall.
FA. Tom Beaumont 1.8.2010

3 Wind Dog . . . . 1 ☐ 6b
A boulder-problem headwall involving a difficult-to-spot undercut mono pocket.
FA. Tom Beaumont 1.8.2010

4 Never Ignore A Pooh-Pooh . . . . ☐ 2+
The ledges and brown flowstone.
FA. Jeremy Whittles 1.8.2010

5 Trust me I'm a Doctor . . . . . ☐ 3
The short corner, ledges and juggy headwall.
FA. Jeremy Whittles 1.8.2010

Wind Dog Sector
8m
1 2 3 4 5
Morning 3 min Sheltered

Ultrasonic Shoulder Sector
8m
6 7 8

6 T-Muffhundred . . . . 4+
Climb the corner/offwidth to ledges then step round the overhang onto the flowstone headwall.
FA. Tom Beaumont 17.4.2010

7 Sping Nol . . . . 1 4+
The flowstone slab with some unobvious and reachy climbing.
FA. Julia Beaumont 17.4.2010

8 Julio's Ropeladder . . . . 1 6a+
The fingery and balancy flowstone slab - good climbing.
FA. Tom Beaumont 17.6.2010

9 Die Screaming with Sharp Things in your Head . . . . 1 5+
The flowstone and conglomerate to a hard finish at a jug right of the lower-off.
FA. Jeremy Whittles 29.4.2007

10 Ultrasonic Shoulder . . . 1 6a+
A bouldery route on quality flowstone. Finish at poor holds on the top of the wall.
FA. Tom Beaumont 10.4.2007

Ultrasonic Shoulder Sector

A wall of steep and good quality flowstone.
Approach (see page 197) - Park in Cheyne Weares car park and walk south for 50m. The quarry is on the right and the Ultrasonic Shoulder Sector is at the far end of the quarry.

11 Death Star Canteen . . . 1 5+
The steep flowstone groove has a tricky start. Start in the ditch.
FA. Tom Beaumont 17.6.2010

12 Crazy Old Hippies . . . . 1 4+
The juggy flowstone. As with all the routes on this wall start in the trench for the full tick. *Photo on page 215.*
FA. Tom Beaumont 8.4.2007

13 Crowbar Assassin . . . . 6a+
A fingery and bouldery flowstone route. Jugs to the left are out of bounds at this grade. Keep an eye on the boulder to the right if you fall off.
FA. Tom Beaumont 29.4.2007

8m

9 10 11 12 13

Portland Lulworth Swanage Blacknor N Blacknor C Blacknor S Blacknor B Blacknor FS Battleship Battleship BC Wallsend N Wallsend S Coastguard N Coastguard S White Hole Lighthouse Cheyne Weare Cuttings

1 Covert Strike . . . . 1 ☐ **6b**
This is the farthest left of this set of routes, technical flowstone-climbing, which is steeper than it first appears.
FA. Tom Beaumont 29.5.2007

2 The Epicurean Paradox . . . . 1 ☐ **6b+**
Start up *Dungecroft Delight*, then, at the first bolt, move left to good holds in the fault. Continue steeply via a long reach or a small crimp to an easy finish. For a 6a+ variation, don't move left until the second bolt of *Dungecroft Delight*.
FA. Tom Beaumont 29.5.2007

3 Dungecroft Delight . . . . 1 ☐ **5**
Start up the left side of the conglomerate, continue on good flowstone jugs, hardest at the top.
FA. Tom Beaumont 26.5.2007

4 The Alpha and The Omega . 1 ☐ **3+**
Climb onto the flowstone ledge, then follow the flake-crack to the top of the slabby wall.
FA. Jeremy Whittles 26.5.2007

5 Dirty Bertie . . . . ☐ **4+**
The start is 30m to the left of *Hayabusa*. The left-hand line has a hard start with easier climbing above.
FA. Andy Dunford 13.7.2010

6 Doris Does Dungecroft . . . . ☐ **3**
Climbs to the right of *Dirty Bertie* on big jugs.
FA. Sarah Perrett 13.7.2010

South of the pit is a large undercut boulder with a good wall to its right.

7 Hayabusa . . . . ☐ **6a**
A technical lower wall to the ledge leads to a good flake above.
FA. Adam Perrett 19.6.2010

8 Fix It Duck . . . . ☐ **6b**
Climb the technical groove below the ominous hanging block and the left-hand side of the arete above.
FA. Andy Dunford 10.7.2010

9 We Apologise for the Inconvenience
. . . . ☐ **5**
Climb the slab on its right to the ledge then take the left-hand side of the corner above.
FA. Adam Perrett 19.6.2010

10 Gecko Wall . . . . ☐ **6a**
At the left-hand side of the pit is a hanging slab. Climb up under the slab and pass it on its left by an awkward mantel. Move back right on to the slab to finish. Shares staples of *Wall Lizard*.
FA. John Leonard 26.6.2010

Covert Strike Sector

The tallest section of the quarry and its steepest. The lines are all on steep flowstone and amongst the best on offer at Dungecroft.

Approach (see page 197) - Park in Cheyne Weares car park and walk south for 50m. The quarry is on the right and the Covert Strike Sector is midway along the wall.

11 Wall Lizard . . . . 6c+
The hanging slab at the left-hand side of the pit. Climb the hanging slab direct. No crafty feet on the ledges at either side for this grade. Just like being on the gritstone.
FA. John Leonard 1.7.2010

12 The Cookie Monster 3
The left-hand of two easier lines follows the corner right of the hanging slab.
FA. Madi Leonard 23.6.2010

13 Make Cookies Not War 4
The right-hand of two easier lines tackles the wall via ledges and flakes to a lower-off on the top wall. Quite good.
FA. Madi Leonard 23.6.2010

14 Rai 6a
Crimpy moves up the left wall. More physical than *Julia*.
FA. Mick Ward 3.6.2010

15 Julia 6a
Left of *Peace* is a large open pit with a grey pillar on its right. Delicate moves up the gritstonesque slab. More elegant than *Rai*.
FA. Mick Ward 3.6.2010

Wall Lizard Sector

An open section of the cliff with a good spread of grades.
Approach (see page 197) - Park in Cheyne Weares car park and walk south for 50m. The quarry is on the right and the Wall Lizard Sector is midway along the cliff-line.

16 Peace . . . . 6a+
Climb the slightly-blind, faint groove left of *Love*.
FA. Mick Ward 4.6.2010

17 Love 6c
Climb the middle of the white wall left of the rift area, past a block leaning against the wall. A few technical moves based on the obvious shot hole.
FA. Mick Ward 4.6.2010

18 Return of the Gecko 6c
Climb the wall right of *Love*. Essentially a direct finish to *I Learned to Swim at Dunkirk*.
FA. Mick Ward 18.8.2010

19 I Learned to Swim at Dunkirk . . 4+
The shothole line at the right-hand side of the wall. Climb to the break and sidestep the bulge by stepping onto the huge, seemingly-detached flake. The name commemorates a great line from one of the old Portland quarrymen.
FA. Mick Ward 18.8.2010

Morning | 3 min | Sheltered

8m

7 8 9 10 11 12 13 14 15 16 17 18 19

Heroes of Swanage Sector

A steep wall of reasonable rock that provides some stout challenges. There is a trench in front of the lines which makes belaying awkward and some extra care is needed on a couple of the routes to prevent falling off the ledges.
Approach (see page 197) - Park in Cheyne Weares car park and walk south for 50m. The quarry is on the right and the Heroes of Swanage Sector is the first section of the cliff encountered.

The first couple of lines are located on the wall to the left of the large rift which contains the majority of the routes in this sector.

1 Well 'ard . . . . 7a+
Just as the name says, the short blank wall is tough.
FA. John Leonard 16.8.2010

2 Little Terror . . . . 1 star 5
A sporting mantel into the corner groove leads to powerful moves on big holds to gain the ledge above. Great fun on excellent rock.
FA. John Leonard 24.5.2010

3 Blood on the Rocks . . . 1 star 6a
Step across the rift to a faint groove, climb this and move right to cross the overhang. Take care with the conglomerate on the upper wall.
FA. John Leonard 24.5.2010

4 The Clicking of Her Needles Spelled Doom . . . . 6b+
Step across the rift, crimp to the break and then step left and follow flowstone to the top.
FA. Mick Ward 30.5.2010

5 Can You See Scratchy Bottom? . 6a+
Climb the crack and wall above. Well, can you?
FA. Mick Ward 30.5.2010

The next route is on the tall boulder just opposite the face.

6 Dad Gets Another Monkey Bite . 2
A large sloping boulder facing the rift area has been stapled to give a practice spot for beginners.
FA. Rhys Dunford 19.6.2010

7 Truly, Madly, Steeply 7b
A neat tufa. Unusual climbing, but with some good moves.
FA. Mike Vaicaitis 1997

8 Heroes of Swanage . . . . . . 5+
Make some difficult layback moves to the break and continue up the steep crack.
FA. Mick Ward 19.5.2010

9 Heroes of Portland 6b
Start up *Heroes of Swanage*, but step rightwards for more technical fare. A tough little number.
FA. Mick Ward 19.5.2010

10 Lifesigns . . . . 7a+
Blind and very fingery moves.
FA. Mike Vaicaitis 1997

11 Sex, Lies and Videotape . . . 7a
The gritstone-like grey wall on the far right of the rift.
FA. Mike Vaicaitis 1997

Morning 3 min Sheltered

8m

Lost Valley

A hidden ravine with a good selection of sheltered sport routes that are worth a look in windy weather. The rock is good, and the routes, although short, offer some intense sequences.

Approach (see page 197) - From Cheyne Weares car park, walk north for 150m (left when looking out), until a rocky ravine on the left is reached - this is the Lost Valley. Drop down a steep chute at the far end to gain the right-hand side of the cliff.

The first line is an uncompleted project.

1 Tug on this Jody. 7a
A bouldery start gains some monos on the top wall to finish.
FA. Marti Hallett 10.12.2009

2 Look West & Find Salvation 7a+
A hard start gains an easing prior to a reachy finishing move.
FA. Marti Hallett 22.12.2009

3 Quite Nice Actually . . . . . . 6b+
Climb the flake to a grunt through the upper overhang.
FA. Neal Heanes 17.3.1996

4 Little Pinky . . . . 6b+
Ascend some flowstone to a hard move using a mono undercut.
FA. Mike Robertson 9.4.1994

5 Drilling in the Name. . . . . . 1 6b+
Climb the blunt buttress left of *Robin Crack* directly.
FA. Marti Hallett 22.12.2009

6 Robin Crack 1 5
Climb the crack via a loose, but well keyed-in hold.
FA. Marti Hallett 22.12.2009

7 Clamped Aggression 1 6b+
A good route. Powerful climbing on slopers and finger pockets.
FA. Mark Williams 9.4.1994

8 Bastard Crack 7a
The name says it all. The thin crack in the arete.
FA. Steve Taylor 9.4.1994

9 Plystalker 7c
A hard boulder problem past the first bolt.
FA. Dave Henderson 2.1997

10 No Chutney on His Ferret . . . . . 5+
An awkward crack - one for those with some crack technique.
FA. Neal Heanes 17.3.1996

11 Chapter and Verse 6a
The very short groove has gained a grade or two.
FA. Helen Heanes 17.3.1996

12 Oatsheaf, Chief . . . . 5+
A slight rib has also had a serious upgrade.
FA. Helen Heanes 17.3.1996

13 Training for Hubble 1 6a+
Good rock. Care needed clipping the second bolt.
FA. Pete Oxley 31.7.1992

14 The Stoning of St.Stephen. . 2 7b+
Tendon-stretching pocket-pulling with a bouldery start.
FA. Pete Oxley 31.7.1992

15 Mono y Mono . . . . 1 7a+
A bouldery route just right of *The Stoning of St.Stephen.*
FA. Jim Kimber 5.9.1996

16 Cadwallader . . . . 1 6b+
A strong line up the thin crack-line.
FA. Steve Taylor 10.4.1991

The next line is the trad route of **Redundancy Crack, E2 5b***.*

17 The Martyr . . . . 2 7a+
A good test-piece, but the old bolts are now rusting.
FA. Steve Taylor 5.7.1992

18 The Secret Garden . . . . 1 6b+
The steep wall and groove to the break, then easier ground.
FA. Steve Taylor 6.11.1993

19 The Beauty of Decay. . . . . . 6b+
The thin twin cracks.
FA. Mike Robertson 6.11.1993

20 Flake Away 4
The flake-line up the left-hand side of the pinnacle.
FA. Mick Ward 28.10.2009

21 Portrait of a Lady. . . . . 6c+
Take the centre of the pillar between *Flake Away* and *Flaked Out.*
FA. Mick Ward 18.11.2009

Bolted project

6m

1 2 3 4 5 6 7 8 9 10 11 12

22 Flaked Out . . . . 4+
A tricky crack leads to the right-hand side of the flake pinnacle.
FA. John Leonard 2.11.2009

23 Echoes of Trad . . . . 4+
The offwidth crack yields to some pleasant ledge shuffling.
FA. Mick Ward 2.11.2009

24 Test Pilot 1 6a
A technical delight up the corner groove.
FA. John Leonard 2.11.2009

25 Primordial . . . . 1 6a+
The wall to the right of *Test Pilot*.
John Leonard 18.11.2009

26 Touch the Earth 7a
The miniscule crack requires disproportionate effort.
Mick Ward 02.11.2009

27 Constant Companion 5
The arete to the right of *Touch the Earth*.
John Leonard 12.12.2009

There is a small wall opposite with a handful of routes.

28 Sweet Dreams are Made of This 3+
The first route on the small opposing wall.
FA. Sarah Perrett 21.3.2010

29 4, 8, 15, 16, 23, 42 . . . . 4+
A tricky start leads to good holds in the breaks.
FA. Adam Perrett 21.3.2010

30 Rhys Gets Another Monkey Bite . 5
The central line has a hard move to pass the upper break.
FA. Andy Dunford 15.3.2010

31 Not the Same Mistake Again Kath 5+
A hard-to-read sequence to reach the lower-off.
FA. Andy Dunford 15.3.2010

32 Plastic Tractor . . . . 3+
Another tricky start leads to good holds in the breaks.
FA. Michèle Ireland 15.3.2010

There are two more minor routes passed on the approach.

33 The Lost Domain 6a
The arete passed on the approach above the awkward step.
FA. Mick Ward 7.9.2009

34 Enjoy My Experience . . . . 6c+
On the front face of the ravine is a short route with rusting bolts.
FA. Jimbo Kimber 3.2000

Chris Barr nearing the final few metres of the fingery and bouldery classic *Brief Encounter* (6b) - *page 238* - at The Cuttings.

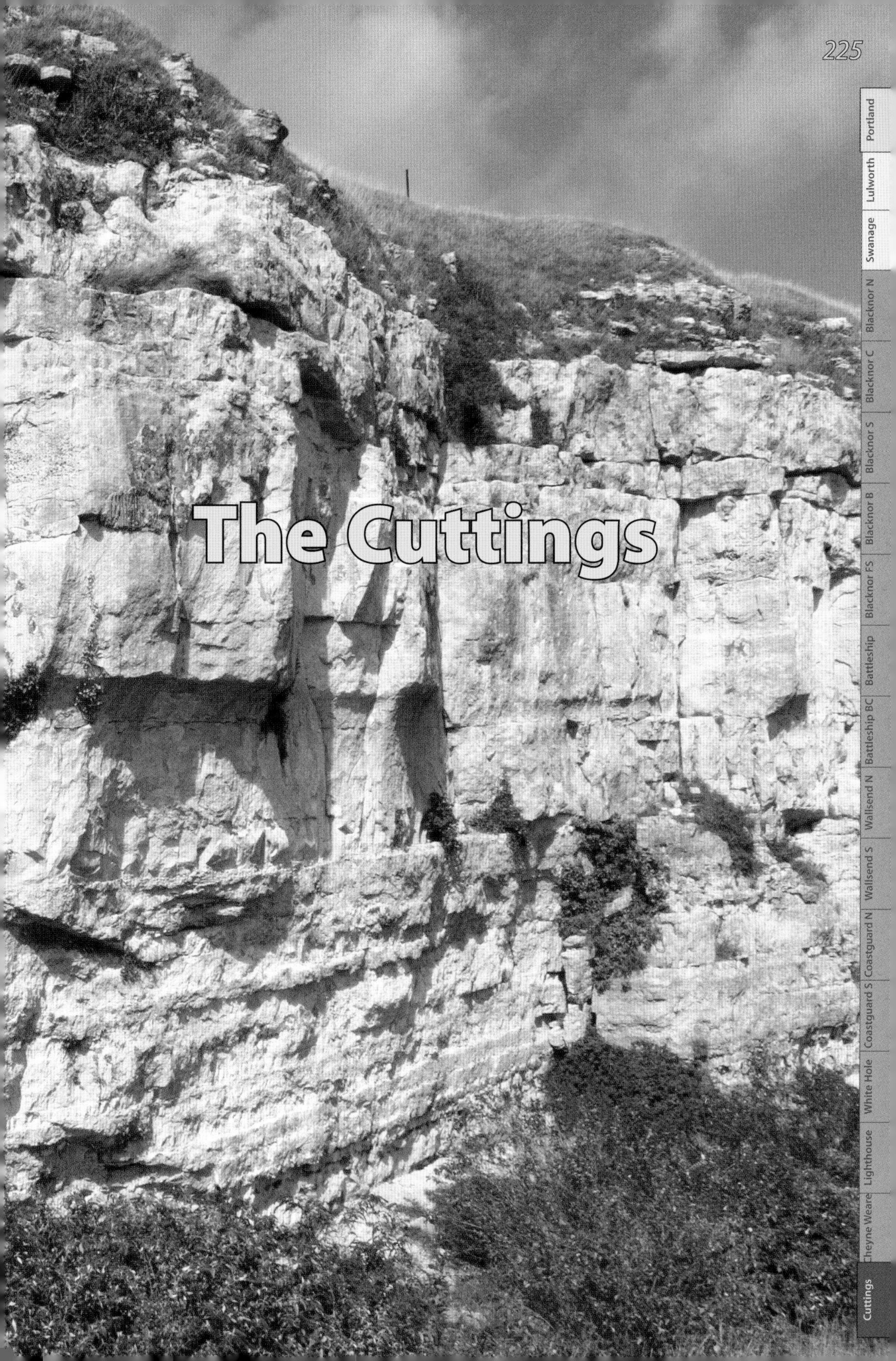

The Cuttings

	No star	1 star	2 star	3 star
up to 4+	19	7	2	-
5+ to 6a+	6	27	4	-
6b to 7a	5	19	13	1
7a+ and up	3	13	12	3

The Cuttings is an excellent and popular inland crag that holds some of Portland's most well-travelled lines. Its easy access, broad spread of grades and sheltered position ensure that there are few days in the year where there won't be someone climbing here. It is an old railway cutting that has left several walls rising directly from a flat quarried base. The walls yield climbing that is mostly sustained and technical in nature, on clean vertical rock. Many of the climbs need lots of finger strength and tenacity, although the profusion of cracks, corners and grooves that bisect the blanker walls give pitches requiring a full range of techniques. There is also a very well-used beginners' wall set up for groups and individuals to cut their teeth on, which has an array of short, bolted easier routes.

Over the last few years, a number of new sections of cliff have been opened up - The Bower, Sunlovers Slab and the outlying Nicodemus Knob have all become popular with their cache of routes between grades 3 and 6.

In front of The Cuttings is a massive area of boulders, scree and dense vegetation that runs down to the sea - this is the The Cuttings Boulderfield, which has many problems scattered over the larger boulders - see **www.rockfax.com** for a 2012 PDF MiniGUIDE (right). For those familiar with the area the small quarried crag called The Ditch in previous guidebooks has been blown up.

Approach Also see map on page 53

Drive through Easton towards Southwell to the Church Ope car park. Walk back up the road for 50m, and at the tiny Portland Museum, turn right onto Church Ope Road. Follow the road under an arch and down to a flat area with some benches. From here, take the coast path (not the path to Church Ope Cove) to a wide track which leads to The Cuttings in a couple of minutes. The New Cuttings is the first cliff reached, quickly followed by The Cuttings cliff itself. The Bower is well hidden only metres from The Cuttings. The Sunlovers Slab is down by the sea and Nicodemus Knob is approached from another parking area - for detailed approach descriptions see the relevant sections dealing with these cliffs.

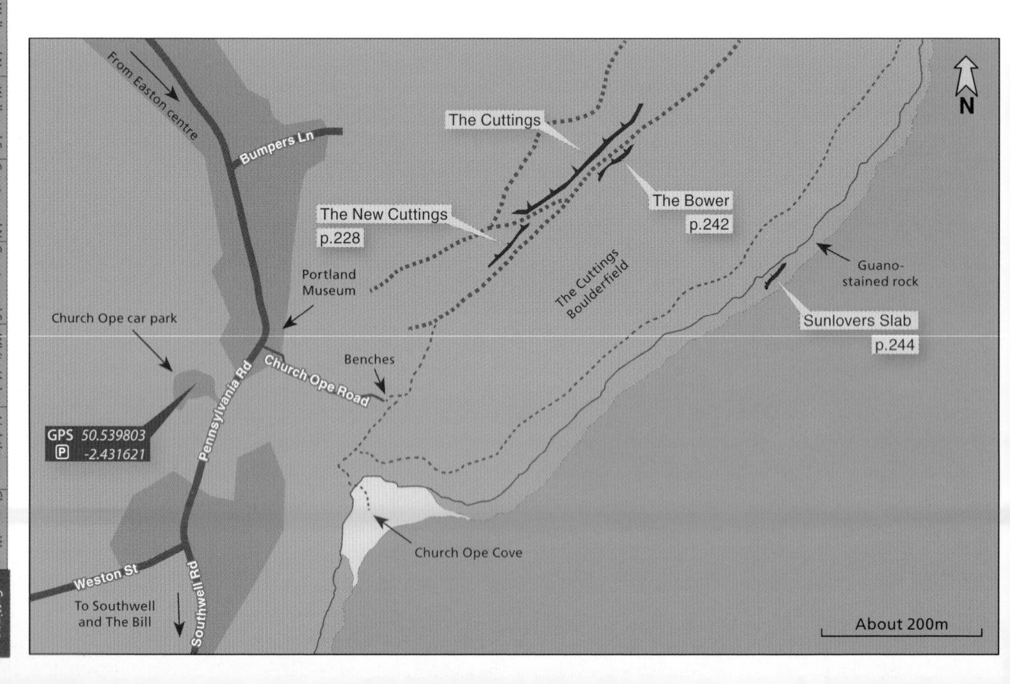

Portland
Lulworth
Swanage
Blacknor N
Blacknor C
Blacknor S
Blacknor B
Blacknor FS
Battleship
Battleship BC
Wallsend N
Wallsend S
Coastguard N
Coastguard S
White Hole
Lighthouse
Cheyne Weare
Cuttings

Conditions

The Cuttings provides an important cold weather venue for locals and visitors to Portland alike. When the wind is blowing a strong westerly or north westerly (not uncommon) this crag is the place to be. The Cuttings catches the morning sun, and is very quick drying, with virtually no seepage. In very hot weather, when the west-coast crags are like ovens, The Cuttings is a haven of shade from mid-afternoon. Much the same can be said of the rest of the crags, although Sunlover Slab is right next to the sea (not advised in rough conditions) and Nickodemus Knob is exposed, being on top of the Isle.

Access

There are no access problems, but the recent closure and redevelopment of the Mermaid Pub, where the old approach was described, has meant that parking on the main road and using old approach tracks may become an issue - please use discretion if following the old approaches.

Setting off up the tough finger crack of *Chalkie and the Hex 5* (5+) - *page 236* - one of a number of testing lines that span the grades at The Cuttings.

Portland | Lulworth | Swanage | Blacknor N | Blacknor C | Blacknor S | Blacknor B | Blacknor FS | Battleship | Battleship BC | Wallsend N | Wallsend S | Coastguard N | Coastguard S | White Hole | Lighthouse | Cheyne Weare | Cuttings

The New Cuttings

A great little crag that is almost always in condition and has a good set of short and technical routes in both the higher and lower grades. Some of the harder lines have boulder-problem starts that are often climbed/attempted in their own right and makes the grading of the lines slightly awkward. The crag is very sheltered, being well away from the sea and gets sun from early in the day. To the left of the route *Subyouth* the cliff falls away in height and has been developed as a good bouldering venue.

Approach (see page 226) - This wall is the first encountered on the approach track and is partially hidden by a low embankment on the left of the track.

1 Subyouth ..... 2★ 7b+

A hard and height-dependant start is followed by a pause at the break and a final heave over the roof. High in the grade.

FA. Pete Oxley 7.11.1990. Reclimbed in 1993 after losing a hold.

2 Flowers on the Razor Wire .... 2★ 6c

Climb the thin corner with difficulty and then take the roof and wall above via a troublesome sequence past a good hidden hold. *Photo on page 231.*

FA. Pete Oxley 7.11.1990

3 Stompin' with Bez . 2★ 7c

A hideously hard and bouldery start (V8) to a steep finish through the capping roof. It can be started direct by dynoing to the crimps and not swinging in from the pocket, at about V9.

FA. Pete Oxley 7.11.1990. Direct start Jim Kimber 11.1999

4 The Fibonacci Sequence .... 1★ 7c+

Climb direct up the arete right of *Stompin' with Bez* to a desperate move to gain the layaway on *Stompin' with Bez*, finish over the capping roof. The initial moves are V10.

FA. Jim Kimber 23.12.1999. Reclimbed after hold loss by John Gaskins 2004

Morning | 5 min | Sheltered

5 Lats, Babes and Bolts 1 ☐ 7b+
The flowstone pocked wall is both fingery and reachy. Finish over the roof as for *The Fibonacci Sequence*. The first 3m is V8.
FA. Pete Oxley 29.8.1992

6 Bogus Roof . . . . 1 ☐ 7b
Start up *The Unworthy* then fly leftwards over the roof.
FA. Pete Oxley 4.5.1998

7 The Unworthy . . . . 2 ☐ 6c
A cracker. Short but steep, varied and surprisingly pumpy.
FA. Joff Cook 29.8.1992

8 The Vulcanites. . . . . . . 1 ☐ 7a
A good alternative first half to *The Unworthy*.
FA. Pete Oxley 29.6.1996

9 Deadlosski Must Die 1 ☐ 7b
Unusual and awkward climbing up a layback pod.
FA. Pete Oxley 25.2.1995

10 Leer of Beethoven . . . . 1 ☐ 7b+
A very hard sequence from the mid-height undercut. Linking leftwards into *Deadlosski Must Die* is 7b and the variant using the upper right-hand arete is 7a+.
FA. Mike Robertson 7.5.1994. Variations - Pete Oxley 29.6.1996

11 Bunfight at the Portland Corral
. . . . 1 ☐ 5+
Climb up the wide layback crack and from its top move up and left to the lower-off at the top of *Leer of Beethoven*.
FA. John Leonard 19.5.2008

12 Buddleia Boulevard . . . . ☐ 4+
Up the left-hand crack behind the tree.
FA. Mick Ward 14.7.2011

13 Skaterdater. . . . . ☐ 4+
Up the right-hand crack.
FA. Mick Ward 14.7.2011

Andy Schofield makes the most of some low winter sun on the powerful start to the demanding line of *Bend Sinister* (7a+) - *next page* - at The New Cuttings.

The New Cuttings - Right

The right-hand end of the crag also has a good set of short and technical lines but lacks the capping roof. Like its neighbour the crag is very sheltered, being well away from the sea and gets sun from early in the day.

Approach (see page 226) - This is the right-hand end of the first crag encountered on the approach track and is partially hidden by a low embankment on the left of the track and bushes.

1 Elephant on Rollerskates 1 star 4+

An appealing climb that follows the flowstone sheet left of a shallow corner. Start on the left and move up to a good hold before stepping right into the corner. Continue up the corner and wall above to finish.

FA. Scott Titt 1990s

2 Limbo Dancer . . . . 1 star 5+

Start at the base of the shallow corner. Make a hard move up the corner and then climb the wall on the right via good small ledges just left of the arete to a big ledge. Move up and right to finish.

FA. Jon Howell 27.4.2008

The hairline crack to the right is the line of **Beeching's Track, E1 6a**.

3 Tipping the Scales . 1 star 7a

The short blank wall is a very tough little cookie.

FA. Steve Taylor 23.4.1994

4 Pop for the Top . . . 1 star 6c

The thin crack in the wall just right of *Tipping the Scales* is another short, but fingery exercise. Do what it says on the tin.

FA. Mick Ward 10.5.2008

5 Two Nuns, a Hang-glider and Jesus . . . . 1 star 4+

The steep corner with bolts on its right wall is more difficult than it first appears. Finish up the short wall above.

FA. Scott Titt 1990s

The wall and arete right of the corner of Two Nuns, a Hang-glider and Jesus is a highball V4 boulder problem which has a single bolt at its top.

6 The Running Man. . . . . 1 star 6c+

A tricky piece of climbing that heads up right to join the upper section of *Bend Sinister*.

FA. Mark Williams, Gavin Symonds 10.4.1998

7 Bend Sinister . . . . 2 star 7a+

A really good pitch that features a stout start and a technical sequence to surmount the flowstone. *Photo on previous page.*

FA. Pete Oxley 7.11.1990

8 Plyometrically Speaking . . . . 1 star 7b+

One for wood merchants. Good climbing.

FA. Pete Oxley 12.6.1994 (solo)

The straight finger crack in the groove to the right is the line of the trad route **Learning Curve, E1 5c**.

9 The Blandford Weasel 7b

A miniature grit arete with wicked moves just to the left of the ivy sheet. Lower off at the third bolt.

FA. Pete Oxley 28.4.1996

The trad line **Cold Fusion, E1 5b** *climbed the flake and wall to the right, but is now hidden under a thick coat of ivy.*

Bruce Walker on the initial thin layback of *Flowers on the Razor Wire* (6c) - *page 228* - at the sheltered New Cuttings.

Portland Lulworth Swanage Blacknor N Blacknor C Blacknor S Blacknor B Blacknor FS Battleship Battleship BC Wallsend N Wallsend S Coastguard N Coastguard S White Hole Lighthouse Cheyne Wears Cuttings

1 Eat, Stick, and Die . . . . ☐ 2
The first short line on the wall. Move up to the second bolt and using an undercut traverse up right to a lower-off.

2 We're Only Placing Bolts For Nigel . . . . ☐ 3
Climb up and move left to the second bolt to join the short traverse of *Eat Stick, and Die* to finish.

3 Cheese and Pickle . . . . ☐ 4+
A difficult and fluttery pitch. Move up onto a ledge and climb direct to a lower-off. Climbing up on the left is equally difficult. Watch out for the ledge below.

4 Parsnip Soup. . . . . ☐ 5
A testing little pitch. Climb the shallow rib and finish on some very sloping holds.

Bonsai Area

The far left-hand end of The Cuttings has lots of very popular lower-grade routes that are getting very polished. The difficulties keep themselves well hidden and some of the routes have been upgraded. It is worth noting that some of the bolts are not right next to the harder moves, and there is an unhealthy number of ledges, so care must be exercised when leading here. The routes (up to *Little Chef*) were bolted by members of Basingstoke M.C. The lines are slightly awkward to distinguish, so pause and check before you climb.

Approach (see page 226) - This wall is just above the track that drops down between The New Cuttings and The Cuttings.

5 Corporal Punishment 5
Move up onto a ledge. Climb the steep wall via some pockets and high friction crimps.

6 On Manoeuvres 3
Very polished. Gain a ledge with difficulty and finish more easily up the wall and breaks to a lower-off.

7 Arc Angel . . . . 2+
Make very difficult moves onto a ledge at 3m. Move up and right past a large pocket to finish.

8 Charity Work Mate 3
Make an awkward move up onto a ledge at 3m. Climb direct past a pocket as for *Arc Angel* to its lower-off.

9 Magical Misty Tour . . . . 3+
Climb the cracks, ledges and walls above the buddleia bush.

10 Bonsai . . . . 3+
Start between the two ground-level bushes. Climb to the left of the bolts all the way to the top and reach right to clip the lower-off.

11 Sting in the Tail . . . . 5+
Climb direct to a good break below the final wall. Climb the wall with difficulty, right of the bolts and reach left to clip the lower-off.

12 Baron's Revenge . . . . 3+
Climb a short technical corner and continue to the final delicate wall.
FA. Steve Taylor 11.4.2008

13 Chicken Boy . . . . 3+
Sustained climbing up the white wall on sloping holds.
FA. Steve Taylor 11.4.2008

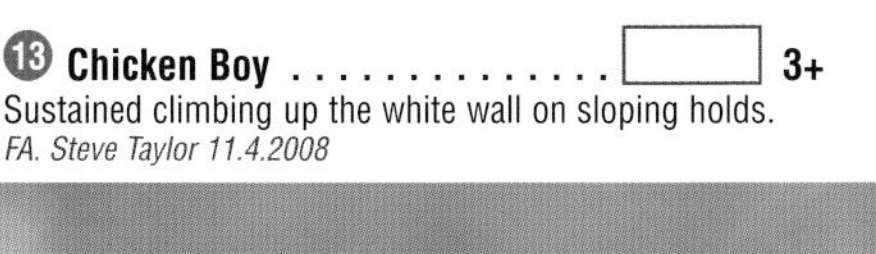

14 Tantrums and Tiaras . . . . 3+
Start up the narrow groove right of *Chicken Boy* and left of a shattered groove.
FA. Steve Taylor 11.4.2008

15 100 Sunny Days 3
Nice climbing to the right of the shattered groove.
FA. Steve Taylor 11.4.2008

16 Juggernaut 5
Climb up and right before making some hard moves up and right again to get established in the upper break. Finish Direct.

17 Rock Lobster . . . . 4+
The slim groove gives a sustained and demanding pitch with a hard initial 3m.

18 Amazonia . . . . 1 4+
A good climb. Start just right of the initial bolt and pull up into the corner. Follow the corner and flake-line to the top.

19 The Great Hamburger Disaster
. . . . 1 4+
An enticing line. Climb the crack-line past a small rattly hold - low in the crack - to an awkward exit below the short final wall.

20 Definitely Maybe . . . . 1 6a+
The narrow wall is best taken to the right of the bolts.

21 Little Chef . . . . 1 5+
The groove with an old peg is hard to enter.

Morning | 5 min | Sheltered

Portland | Lulworth | Swanage | Blacknor N | Blacknor C | Blacknor S | Blacknor B | Blacknor FS | Battleship | Battleship BC | Wallsend N | Wallsend S | Coastguard N | Coastguard S | White Hole | Lighthouse | Cheyne Weare | Cuttings

Mindmeld Area

A popular section of the cliff with a range of grades and a couple of the most attempted routes on Portland.

Approach (see page 226) - This wall is just above the junction of the track that drops down between The New Cuttings and The Cuttings and the main approach track.

1 Little Sod 1 **6b**

Climb up the right side of the arete, between *Little Chef* and *The Sod*. Do not start as for *The Sod* but start on the arete to the left.

FA. Steve Muncaster 2.2.2007

2 The Sod . . . . 1 **5+**

The big corner at the base of the track that runs down under this section of the crag has some long reaches. Although it has become polished, it is still about right at the grade, but perhaps is a little tougher for the short.

3 Lup Dup . . . . 1 **6a+**

Climb to the first bolt on *Mindmeld*, then traverse left to the second bolt on *The Sod*. From here, trend up and left using the undercut flake to gain the arete, clipping the 3rd bolt on *Little Sod* as you go. Finish up *Little Sod*. Sounds contrived, but is a pretty good route.

4 Mindmeld . . . . 1 **7a+**

Direct up the arete, keeping out of the corner all the way to the ledge. At the top, head left to join *The Sod*.

FA. Mike Vaicaitis 19.7.1995

5 Sign of the Vulcan . 2  **7b+**

A thin crux with a split pocket gives a terrific test-piece.

FA. Pete Oxley 4.9.1994

6 Hillman The Hunter . . . 1 **6b+**

Pass the brickwall with one peculiar hard move. Watch your leg behind the rope.

FA. Steve Taylor 13.1.1991

The crack and shallow groove on the right is the line of the trad route **Hole in the Wall, E1 5c**.

7 Flying Peach 1 **6b**

Follow the clean wall to the right of *Hillman the Hunter*.

FA. John Leonard 31.7.2007

8 Grapefruit takes a Whipper . 1 **6a+**

Start right of *Flying Peach* and climb above the rift via some good moves up the wall.

FA. Steve Muncaster 31.7.2007

9 Princess and the Pea . . . . **6b+**

The wall just right of the corner.

FA. Nick Hellyer 2000s

10 Pillow Talk **6c**

The wall just left of the arete.

FA. Nick Hellyer 2000s

Having negotiated the bouldery start, the climber is now facing the intricacies of the rest of the pitch on the hard, but brilliant *European Flavour* (6b) - *page 238* - at The Cuttings. Photo: Sarah Stirling/Glaister Collection

Cutting Edge Area

The left-hand end of the main section of The Cuttings has a few good hard routes, interspersed with some equally good easier corners, cracks and aretes.

Approach (see page 226) - The wall begins as the track below the crag comes close to the edge of the cliff. The first feature is the prominent square-cut arete of the excellent *The Cutting Edge* - a crag classic.

1 The Cutting Edge . . . . . Top 50 **6c+**
The much-fancied, striking arete is short, but immaculate. Most finish on the left at the top of the arete, but the right-hand side also goes, although it is a bit tougher. The direct start is 7a.
FA. Pete Oxley 18.12.1988

2 Dumbfounded . . 1 **7b**
The blank-looking wall just to the right of *The Cutting Edge* is possibly 7b+ for shorties, but only 7a+ for the tall.
FA. Martin Crocker 15.4.1990

3 Chalkie and the Hex 5 . 2 **5+**
The appealing full-height crack demands good technique.
Photo on page 227.
FA. C.Ellison, H.Venables 1981. Bolted in 2002.

4 The Ramp 1 **5**
The ramp right of *Chalkie and the Hex 5*. Pass the roof on its right and move up to a lower-off. Can be climbed left of the roof to reach the belay of *Chalkie and the Hex 5*.
FA. Unknown. Bolted in 2002.

5 Lusty Wedlock Needs Coil of Prevention
. . . . **7b**
A hard and fingery sequence well suited to the boulderer.
FA. Pete Oxley 27.10.1994

6 Rusty Chubblock Seeks Oil of Lubrication
. . . . 1 **7c**
This route has stumped many over the years. The first bolt is shared with *Lusty Wedlock Needs Coil of Prevention.*
FA. Martin Crocker 15.4.1990

7 Evening Mistress 1 **6b**
A very good little pitch. Climb the blank dihedral by some technical bridging and strenuous layback moves.
FA. Pete Oxley 18.12.1988

8 Men Behaving Badly 1 **7a+**
Climb the wall and flowstone rib right of *Evening Mistress.* Stepping in from the left lowers the grade to 7a.
FA. Rob Kennard 21.7.2010

9 Amen Corner. 2 **5**
The slim corner in the arete is the line of this intense pitch. Pull up steeply to gain the corner and follow it all the way to the top.
Photo on page 6.

10 Mousefolk. 1 **6c**
Delicate arete climbing. Keep out of the groove.
FA. Martin Crocker 15.4.1990

Morning 5 min Sheltered

11 Too Many Cooks Spoil the Broth 2 6b
A fingery and tenuous little wall climb with a distinct crux. Keep away from the crack of *Jam* on the right.
FA. Pete Oxley 5.11.1990

12 Jam . . . . 2 4+
Climb the jamming crack - that doesn't necessarily need to be jammed - right of *Too Many Cooks Spoil the Broth.*
FA. Unknown. Bolted in 2002.

13 Chips with Everything . . 1 5
The crack, small overhang and short corner.
FA. Dave Jones, J.Kenton 21.6.1981. Bolted in 2002.

14 Quality Family Day. . . . 2 4+
A very pleasing climb that tackles the flake and flowstone corner to a high lower-off.
FA. Marti Hallett, Paul Fields 16.2.2008

15 True Love . . . . 6b+
Move up over ledges and climb the committing arete direct on its left side. Move right at the top to a lower-off.
FA. Marti Hallett 16.2.2008

A good trad line **Bridget Riley, E2 6a** *follows the very technical corner left of the arete of The Mind Terrorist, past good nuts and a peg to a lower-off on True Love.*

16 The Mind Terrorist . 2 7c+
The flying arete is bouldery, powerful, hard and very good.
FA. Pete Oxley 13.1.1991

17 Knockout Punch . . . 1 7b+
A short-lived, but intense test-piece direct up the centre of the face.
FA. Pete Oxley 2.10.1996

The trad line of **Spicer, E2 5c** *takes the crack right of Knockout Punch.*

The next two lines incorporate sections of an old trad line **That Divine Chill, E2 6a**.

18 Levitation by Proxy . . . 1 6c
Take the pleasant wall to a narrow corner/groove and climb this via some extremely technical moves to a steep final move.
FA. Mick Ward 19.10.2008

19 Finesse 7a
The arete right of *Levitation by Proxy*, starting up the wall to its right. Climb to a ledge, then step left to climb the arete direct, keeping well to the left of the bolts.
FA. Mick Ward 29.11.2008

20 Hidden Treasure 1 6a
Using the bolts of *Finesse,* climb the same lower wall, then the left side of the three-part flake to join *Finesse* on top of the arete.
FA. John Leonard 3.12.2008

The ivy-coated corner just right of Hidden Treasure is the trad line **Kestrel, VS 4c** *and the arete to its right another trad line* **Looking for Love, E2 5b**.

Hall of Mirrors Area

The centrepiece of The Cuttings has the best climbing, with some great routes across the grades. The rock is clean, and the sheltered location makes this a prime venue for hot summer afternoons or cold winter mornings. With the harder routes, good conditions are usually crucial for a successful ascent, since the climbing is technical, and requires good finger friction.

Approach (see page 226) - This is the central section of the main Cuttings area.

On the far left of the wall is a short corner leading to dense ivy and bushes - this is the line of the old trad route **Dee, HS**.

1 Blowing the Gimp . 1 star **7a+**
A difficult-to-read crux on hard-to-see holds in its mid-section.
FA. Pete Oxley 23.11.1994

2 The Sears Tower . . 1 star **7b+**
Sustained crimping and smearing up the bald, grey wall.
FA. Pete Oxley 4.11.1990

3 The Holy Hand Grenade . . . . 2 stars **7a**
Fine, sustained climbing up an open groove. High in the grade.
FA. Mike Robertson 26.11.1995

4 Brief Encounter . . . 2 stars **6b**
A great piece of climbing. The wide groove, mainly on its right-hand side. The start is a boulder problem at about V2.
Photo on page 224.
FA. Tim Dunsby 6.10.1991

5 Infernal Din . . . . 3 stars **7b+**
A hard and technical route with three difficult sections.
FA. Pete Oxley 2.10.1996

6 European Flavour . . . . . 2 stars **6b**
A fantastic route that features a lot of varied and tough climbing. The start is a powerful boulder problem at V2.
Photo on page 235.
FA. Pete Oxley, Barry Clarke 2.10.1996

7 Europe Endless . . . . 2 stars **6b+**
Climb the steep wall with a hard move to gain the corner.
FA. Pete Oxley 3.11.1990. This was originally a trad route which straightened an older route called Gourmet which avoided the bulge on the left.

8 The Breathing Method . Top 50 **8a**
A sequency power-problem through the mid-height overhang. Originally the second crux was done as a layback all the way up the groove, harder. Many now use a small crimp to rock up and leftwards to overcome this section.
FA. Pete Oxley 24.4.1994

9 Hall of Mirrors . . . . . 3 stars **7c**
An impressive route that needs crisp conditions and features some unusual moves to gain and climb the shallow groove.
FA. Pete Oxley 3.11.1990

10 Want Out . . . . 3 stars **7b**
The overhang-dotted corner is an excellent route with both technical and strenuous climbing. High in the grade.
FA. Martin Crocker 24.3.1991

Morning 5 min Sheltered

20m

1 2 3 4 5 6 7 8 9 10 11 12

11 New Saladin . . . . {2} 6c
Wild moves up the crack and hanging corner above the start of *Want Out*. A fine pitch, but avoid the prickly bush on the right.
FA. Pete Oxley 13.1.1991

12 Hurricane on a Millpond {2} 7c+
One of the most technical face-moves in the area, best accomplished on an ice-cold day.
FA. Pete Oxley 21.11.1996

13 Consommé . . . . . . {2} 6a+
The long, thin layback flake is an outstanding line.
FA. Unknown. Unearthed and reclimbed by Jim Kimber 6.9.1997

There is a project line here.

14 Haute Cuisine . . . . {2} 7a
Technical face moves based around a very thin crack.
FA. Martin Crocker 16.4.1990

15 The Mouth Waters . {2} 7a+
A pleasant, crimpy face climb with some good rests.
FA. Martin Crocker 16.4.1990

An excellent low-level boulder traverse climbs from Haute Cuisine to Blowing the Gimp (V7). Stay low on crimps below the juggy break. Great stamina-training.

16 Two Fingers . . . . {2} 6a
Climb easily to a ledge. Make a difficult pull across a gap into the base of a corner and then follow it to a final fingery wall.
FA. Pete Oxley, Tim Dunsby 16.10.1983

17 Three Fingers . . . . {1} 6a
Climb easily to a ledge. From the right gain a smaller ledge on the left with difficulty and then move up the small groove above precariously to an easing below the final wall. Previously given 4, but now much harder due to the loss of one of the finger tips.
FA. Unknown. Bolted in 2002.

18 Opus . . . . {1} 5
The wide corner/groove right of *Three Fingers*. A long and interesting pitch that culminates in a spectacular pull over the final roof on a good pocket.
FA. Unknown. Bolted in 2002.

19 Rusty the Red Neck Takes one for the Team . . . . {1} 6a+
Start up *Opus* and move right onto the wall and up the arete.
FA. Neal Heanes 2002

20 Perihelion. . . . . {2} 6b
The overhanging flake-crack provides a stiff obstacle.
FA. George Hounsome 7.5.1979

21 Disobedience Contest. . . . . {2} 6b
One for the old school who revel in jamming. Climb the crack, and at its top, swing out left and finish up the wall and horizontal breaks.
FA. Mike Robertson 17.11.1995

22 The Potting Shed . . . . {1} 6a
The corner right of *Disobedience Contest*.
FA. Scott Titt 1991

23 Rules is Rules. . . . . 6b+
An eliminate up the short arete.
FA. Marti Hallett 29.12.2011

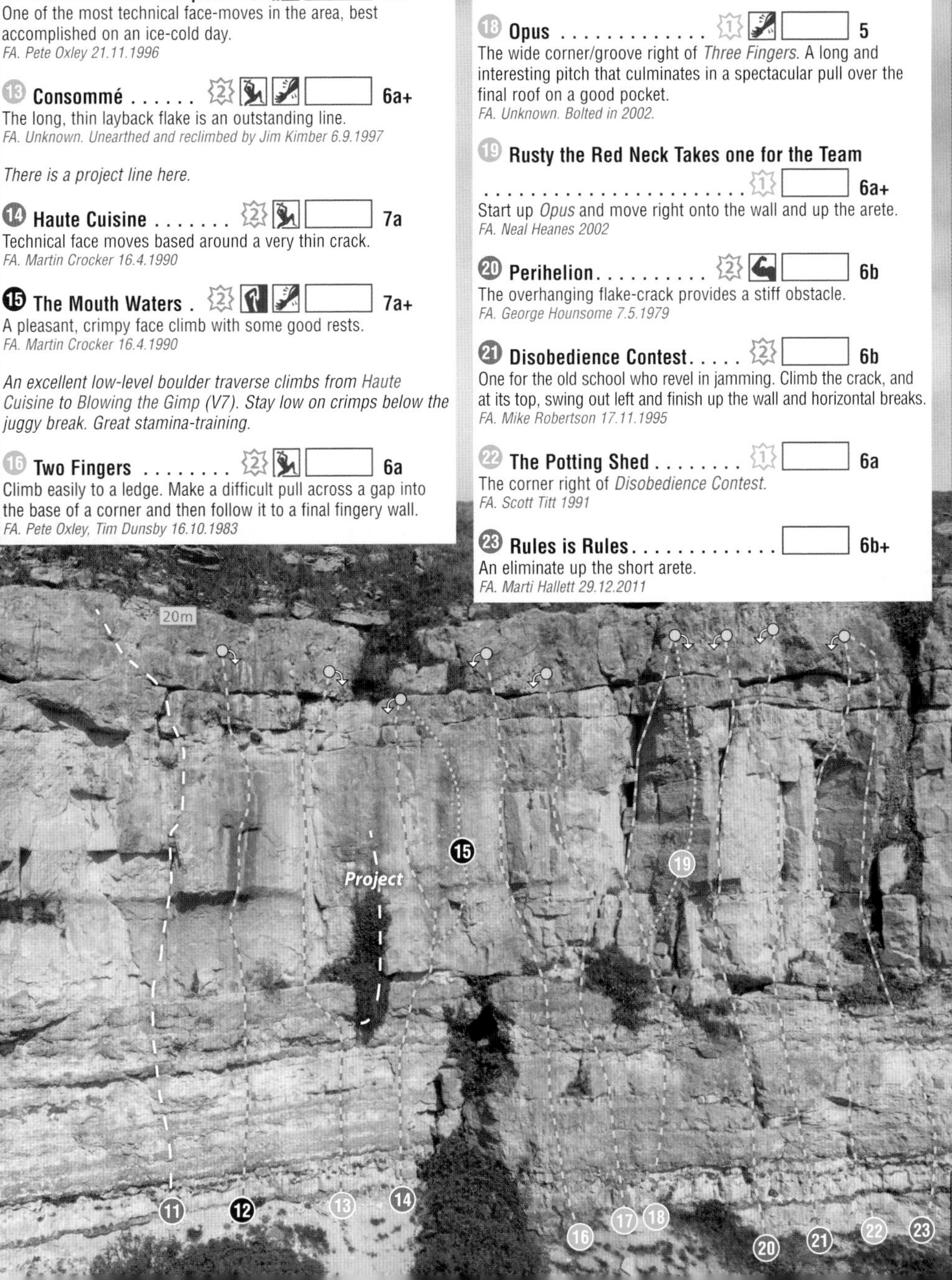

Portland Lulworth Swanage Blacknor N Blacknor C Blacknor S Blacknor B Blacknor FS Battleship Battleship BC Wallsend N Wallsend S Coastguard N Coastguard S White Hole Lighthouse Cheyne Weare Cuttings

Modern Nightmare Area

At the far end of The Cuttings is a large roof-capped corner flanked by some clean walls and aretes. Most of the routes here are in the higher grades, consequently the area is not often busy, however there are a few grade 6s to the left that are worth a look.

Approach (see page 226) - Continue under the Main Crag to the far end, where the long corner taken by *Modern Nightmare* is a prominent feature.

Morning 5 min Sheltered

21m

1 2 3 4 5 6 7 8 9 10 11

1 Life is Life . . . . 1 star **6b**
A steep and powerful start gains the upper arete.
FA. Marti Hallett, Steve Hau 21.12.2011

2 Old Buffer . . . . 1 star **6b**
The groove left of *Live by the Sword* is a varied pitch.
Photo on page 56.
FA. Tim Dunsby, Nigel Coe, Scott Titt 2.11.1991

3 Live by the Sword . . . . 2 star **7a+**
Fine, crimpy wall climbing on the headwall.
FA. Pete Oxley 5.2.1994

4 Another Notch in the Gun 2 star **6b**
Good climbing all the way. The first bolt is right of the crack because of suspect rock.
FA. Pete Oxley 14.1.1991

5 Figgy Dropwise . . . . . . 1 star **6c+**
Technical moves, but spoilt by the possibility of escape onto *Another Notch in the Gun* when the going gets tough. Try to keep right. Start from the high ledge.
FA. Mike Robertson 23.11.1995

6 Dusty Fred's Winter Collection **6c**
A varied climb which has lost holds at the start and is still a bit loose.
FA. Joff Cook. 23.11.1995

7 Ectomorph .... 1 ☐ **6a**
Move up and left to a ledge and then follow the undercut line left to a crack and finish up it. A wandering line with a big feel to it.
FA. Unknown. Bolted 2000s

8 Aperitif .... ☐ **5+**
Climb to the first ledge on *Ectomorph* and continue up the corner to a lower-off.
FA. Unknown. Bolted 2000s

9 Unknown Arete .... ☐ **7a+**
Tackle the square-cut arete above the ledge of *Ectomorph.*

10 The Bournemouth Flyer 1 ☐ **6b**
Good at bridging? If so, this is the route for you. There is one desperate clip for shorties.
FA. Tim Dunsby 29.4.1990

The first bolt on the next two routes is shared and is also a karabiner snapper - use a long sling.

11 Nightmare Scenario 2 ☐ **7c**
Very sustained and technical, especially on the crux.
FA. Pete Oxley 25.2.1995

12 Modern Nightmare .... 2 ☐ **7a**
The big corner has a hard start and a superb, pumpy finish. High in the grade. The ivy needs stripping back from time to time.
FA. Pete Oxley 29.4.1994

13 Fighting Torque . 2 ☐ **8a**
A ferocious test-piece with unlikely moves. Possibly 7c+.
FA. Pete Oxley 14.4.1994

14 Under Duress .. 2 ☐ **7c+**
A tight, but inescapable line. Start up *Fighting Torque* and continue direct with some hard moves over the bulge and up the arete.
FA. Bob Hickish 14.9.2010

15 Shiver Me Timbers. 1 ☐ **7a**
The finger-crack. Loose at the bottom, painful at the top.
FA. Pete Oxley 7.12.1985

16 Weird Shit, Keep Drilling 2 ☐ **6b+**
Fine climbing on the arete.
FA. Joff Cook 14.3.1994

Morning | 5 min | Sheltered

21m

10 11 12 13 14 15 16

Portland | Lulworth | Swanage | Blacknor N | Blacknor C | Blacknor S | Blacknor B | Blacknor FS | Battleship | Battleship BC | Wallsend N | Wallsend S | Coastguard N | Coastguard S | White Hole | Lighthouse | Cheyne Weare | Cuttings

The Bower

Well-hidden, but only metres away from the main action at The Cuttings, is this excellent section of cliff. The Bower sits in front of the track that runs through The Cuttings, and is split into two sections. The Bower itself is tucked away in a secluded dell, and has gained a reputation for good lower-grade lines on sound and well-bolted rock. The second section - the so-called Bottom Deckio - is a more substantial chunk of rock that has a limited, but good selection of grade 6s.

Approach (see page 226) - Climb over the col via a short crack, directly opposite the route *European Flavour* on The Cuttings itself. A short, steep path gains The Bower. To access the Bottom Deckio, walk down a steep scree-path just beyond the end of the seaward cutting, this leads quickly to the base of the wall.

1 Whispering Gallery 2

The first line of bolts encountered on the descent path. Climb on good holds to a final steepening that is climbed using some stuck-on blobs.

FA. Michèle Ireland 27.1.2009

2 Queen of the New Year . . . . 2+

Climb the line of bolts just right of *Whispering Gallery* to a final sequence on the wall to reach the lower-off.

FA. Sarah Perrett 7.2.2009

3 Sun Trap 3

Start in the corner at a block. Move up the corner - bolt on the left - and gain and climb the narrow left-facing corner to a lower-off.

FA. Mick Ward 2.1.2009

4 The Bumper Fun Book . . . . ⭐1 4

Climb the corner - bolt on the right - to where it fades. Continue up the wall to a lower-off.

FA. Mick Ward 2.1.2009

5 Tinkerbell . . . . ⭐1 6a

The arete right of the corner is a brief, but excellent little climb. Move up the right-hand side of the arete - technical - to a small overhang, pull through this and climb a short wall to finish.

FA. Mick Ward 2.1.2009

6 Far From The Madding Crowd ⭐1 5+

Climb the wall, passing the right-hand side of a stuck-on block, to an overhang. Pull through on good holds, and make a couple of final moves to gain a lower-off.

FA. John Leronard 2.1.2009

7 Six Finger Exercise . . . . . . ⭐1 6b+

A good, and quite stiff, line. Ascend the crack to the overhang, then pull through it with difficulty.

FA. John Leonard 7.2.2009

8 Godbeams . . . . ⭐1 4

Climb the crack.

FA. John Leronard 2.1.2009

9 Ladybower . . . . ⭐1 3

The grooved arete. There is a belay bolt at waist height. This is the upper section of the full version of the route *Voices in the Bower* which starts on the Bottom Deckio.

FA. Mick Ward 24.3.2009

⑩ Voices in the Bower 3
A long line starting at the base of the wall. Climb leftwards on the left-most bolts to the edge of The Bower. It can be continued up the arete as for *Ladybower* to give a one-star outing.
FA. Mick Ward 1.4.2009

⑪ Up the Junction . . . . . . 1★ 6b
A very good climb with a series of excellent moves in its middle section. Start up *Voices in the Bower*. The small, detached-looking hold proves to be solid.
FA. Neal Heanes 4.2008

⑫ Round the Bend . . . . . . 1★ 6b
Fine climbing that has a teasing crux. Start as for *Up the Junction*, then break right over a bulge before tackling the slim groove.
FA. Tim Dunsby 1993

⑬ Winter Sun . . . . 1★ 6a
A little gem. Climb up through the low bulge, and follow the open corner to the final, short wall.
FA. John Leonard 14.12.2008

⑭ Time Out of Mind 5

The right-hand line of the buttress has a difficult lower bulge followed by easier climbing above. The lower bulge is 6a if climbed direct.
FA. Mick Ward 8.12.2008

⑮ Voices in the Mind . . . . 1★ 5+
A girdle of the Bottom Deckio Wall. The traverse pitch is great.
1) 3. Climb *Voices in the Bower* to the Bower belay ledge.
2) 5+. Step back down and traverse right across the wall to a hanging belay on *Time Out of Mind*.
3) 3. Climb *Time out of Mind* to the top.
FA. Andy Dunford, John Leonard (alts) 4.5.2010

Portland Lulworth Swanage Blacknor N Blacknor C Blacknor S Blacknor B Blacknor FS Battleship Battleship BC Wallsend N Wallsend S Coastguard N Coastguard S White Hole Lighthouse Cheyne Weare Cuttings

Sunlovers Slab

The Sunlovers Slab is an isolated, leaning boulder perched next to the sea. The rock is solid, and the climbs feature steep starts followed immediately by delicate slab climbing above. The slab, as its name suggests, gets plenty of sun and is next to the sea and convenient for a dip.

Approach (see page 226) - Drive through Easton towards Southwell to the Church Ope car park. Walk back up the road for 50m and at the tiny Portland Museum turn right onto Church Ope Road. Follow the road under an arch and down to a flat area with some benches. From here, walk right, down the path towards Church Ope Cove. A little way down cut left along the seaside path for around 400m until level with the far end of The Cuttings (set back up the hill). Locate a white guano-stained rock on the edge of the sea, the Sunlovers Slab is around 50m to its right. Walk and scramble down to the base of the slab.

1 Come on Eileen . . . . 1 6a+
Start on the far left of the block and pull up and right with difficulty on to the slab. Finish more easily.
FA. Adam Perrett 26.2.2011

2 Grand Tour . . . . 1 6a+
Gain the slab as for *Come on Eileen,* and traverse the block, finishing at the top of *The Portland Crowd*. It is probably wise to move up and clip the second bolt on the top slab of *Come on Eileen* before making the exposed traverse. Bring up your second to retrieve the gear.
FA. John Leonard 19.3.2011

3 Boys Will be Girls . . . . 1 6c+
Cross the steepest part of the roof to powerful, fingery moves over the lip. Delicate slab climbing follows.
FA. Mick Ward 19.3.2011

4 Shockwave . . . . 1 5+
Enjoyable moves through a weakness in the left-hand side of the scoop in the roof. Pull on to the slab using cherty nodules.
FA. John Leonard 19.2.2011

5 Sunlover 1 5
Another good pitch pulling through the steep section and onto the slab. Similar to *Shockwave*.
FA. Mick Ward 12.2.2011

6 The Portland Crowd 1 5
The right-hand side of the scoop in the roof. The steep lower wall giving good climbing, but the best holds are not obvious.
FA. Mick Ward 15.2.2011

Nicodemus Knob

Set well away from the main climbing areas on Portland is this curious feature named in honour of a local man, Nick O'Demus, and his outstanding appendage (perhaps). The Nicodemus Knob is a squat pinnacle set high above the sea on the rim of the Isle's plateau. It has a beautiful outlook, as well as a quiet setting. Although only home to a small bunch of climbs 'The Knob' is an interesting spot and worth a visit.

Approach - Drive up the steep hill out of Fortuneswell. Turn left at the roundabout by the Portland Heights Hotel at the top of the hill. Follow the road past the viewpoint car parks and continue to a sharp left-hand bend going downhill. At the bend, take a right turn, and follow the road past the prison entrance and on to where the road becomes unsurfaced. A short distance down the wide track it is blocked by a gate, park here. Walk through the rough field leftwards until the summit of the pinnacle is easily seen. Follow paths leftwards down to the base of the pinnacle.

Conditions - The rock dries extremely quickly and gets plenty of sun from midday onwards. The Pinnacle is very exposed to wind and rain.

Afternoon | 5 min | Windy

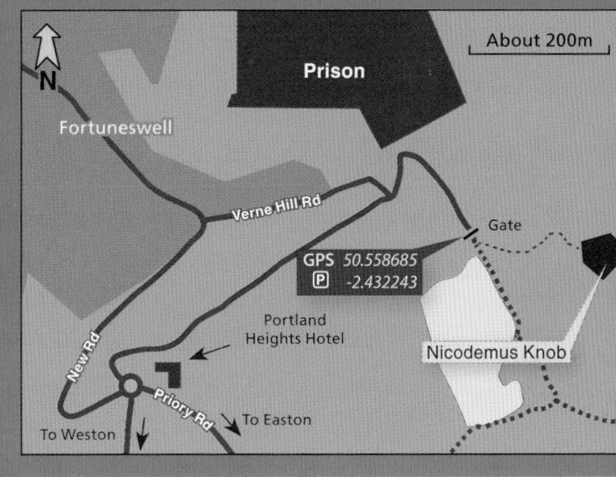

7 Nick's Bulge 1 **6b**

The left-hand line of the face has a hard pull to get established in the final shallow corner. The rock needs a bit of care at two-thirds height.

FA. Mick Ward 8.11.2008

8 Big Wall Dreams . . . . . 1 **6a+**

Sustained climbing up the lower wall culminates in a pressing finish through the upper bulge to reach a good hold near the top.

FA. John Leonard 8.11.2008

9 Nick O'Demus 1 **6a**

A good, but tough pitch taking on the steep lower overhangs, and then the technical upper wall which requires careful route finding.

FA. Mick Ward 8.11.2008

10 Wild Rover 1 **6a**

Another worthwhile line, but once again its benign appearance will catch out the unwary.

FA. John Leonard 8.11.2008

12m

7 8 9 10

The summit can be reached via a moderate scramble

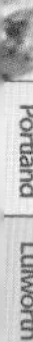

Lulworth

Steve McClure easing his way up *Animal Magnetism* (7a+) - *page 254* - in the West Cave at Lulworth Cove. Photo: Keith Sharples

	No star	1 star	2 stars	3 stars
Mod to S	1	-	-	-
HS to HVS	8	8	3	1
E1 to E3	3	16	7	2
E4 and up	2	18	22	13

The Lulworth area lies at the heart of the Jurassic Coast, and is popular with visitors attracted by the remarkable scenery, fine coastal walks and beautiful beaches. For the climber the main event is the fantastic overhanging faces and architectural rock arches. The position of the walls perched above the sea not only adds atmosphere to the bolted climbing, but also allows great deep-water-soloing, for which the area has become renowned in recent years.

On the eastern side of Lulworth Cove itself is another climbing area - Lulworth East, which has some worthwhile sport and trad pitches that usually involve spectacular roof climbing. To the west of Lulworth Cove lies a high ridge of steep pinnacles (Dungy Head) and a huge boulder on the seashore known as Church Rock. These provide a complete contrast in style with generally easier, pocketed wall climbs that may be an attractive option when the arms can no longer lock-off at Stair Hole, or for those in search of easier grades. The final area is Durdle Door, with its famous and much-photographed arch, which is home to several sustained pump-outs.

Approaches

Lulworth Cove is well sign-posted from the town of Wool on the A352, between Wareham and Dorchester. The main crags are approached from the large car park (fee) in West Lulworth.

Dungy Head/Church Rock - Walk up the road, past the Cove Centre, and continue up the steep hill on the right. After 200m, turn left up a hidden track, just past Stair House, and follow this steeply to gain a ridge. See approach details on the relevant crag page for approaches from here.

Stair Hole - Walk up the road, past the Cove Centre, and continue over a ridge to descend into the Stair Hole basin. Do not bear left towards the telescope on the hill. See approach details on the relevant crag page for approaches from here.

Lulworth East - These are the cliffs situated on the far side of the main Lulworth Cove. See approach details on the relevant crag page for approaches from here.

Conditions

All the areas are south-facing, so get plenty of sun. Stair Hole is a sun-trap that is sometimes climbable in mid-winter. In the summer months, the roofs at Stair Hole and Lulworth East shelter the face, which means you can find shade here when you might not expect to. The cliffs are well-drained and, there is little seepage, although they can hold dampness on humid days. The rock is a bit rough in places and can be harsh on the skin, especially at the Lulworth East.

Tides

Low tide is needed to access the ledge below the routes at Durdle Door, and to enable an easier sea-level approach at Lulworth East. The other areas can be accessed during all states of tide, but are best avoided in rough seas, except Dungy Head which is well clear of the sea. The traverse in at Lulworth East can be very dangerous unless the sea is calm. The beach approach to Stair Hole can also be awash at very high tide, but it is always possible to wade. The deep water solos generally are best tackled at higher tides.

Access

The Lulworth area is owned by the Weld Estate, who do not allow climbing to take place on their land. This is for reasons of conservation and public safety. The descriptions and information presented here are only included for reasons of completeness.

There is also a ban on climbing on the cliffs within the MOD range which starts to the right of the Lulworth East.

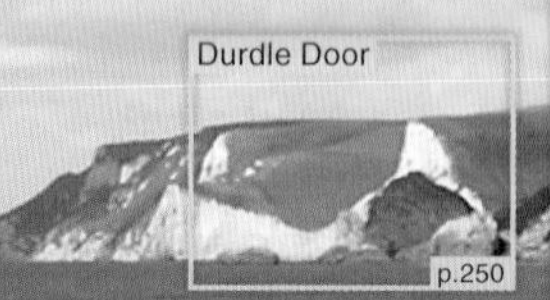

History

1987/88 - The first significant development takes places at Lulworth with the E7 trad-route *Mark of the Beast*.

1992 - Lulworth is extensively developed including *Adrenochrome* (8a).

1993/4 - Deep water soloing becomes more popular and Oxley DWSs *Mark of the Beast* (7c) .

1995/1996 - Lulworth East at Lulworth are developed by Oxley and Dominic and Damian Cook, whilst Joff Cook solos *Gates of Greyskull* (7b+).

1998 - The first deep water solo festival is organised by Robertson and results in a ground up of *Mark of the Beast* by Leo Houlding and others.

1999 - Rich Bingham DWSs *Adrenochrome* (8a).

2001 - Deep water soloing becomes even more popular with a yearly festival attended by 100s. The highlight is an astounding solo ascent of *Riding to Babylon* (E7 6a) at Durdle Door from Robertson. Oxley develops a multitude of hard sport classics at Lulworth East.

2003 - Oxley adds the excellent *Journey to Eternia* (7c+) at Stair Hole.

2004 - At Stair Hole, visitor Rob Sutton overcomes *Pump up the Beast* (E7).

2006 - Rob Kennard along with Steve Taylor, Dave Simmonite, Alex More and Marti Hallett continue the trad development of Lulworth East.

2007 - Gav Symonds climbs the tough *Windowchrome* (8a+) at Stair Hole.

2009 - Bob Hickish climbs a number of hard link-ups at Stair Hole.

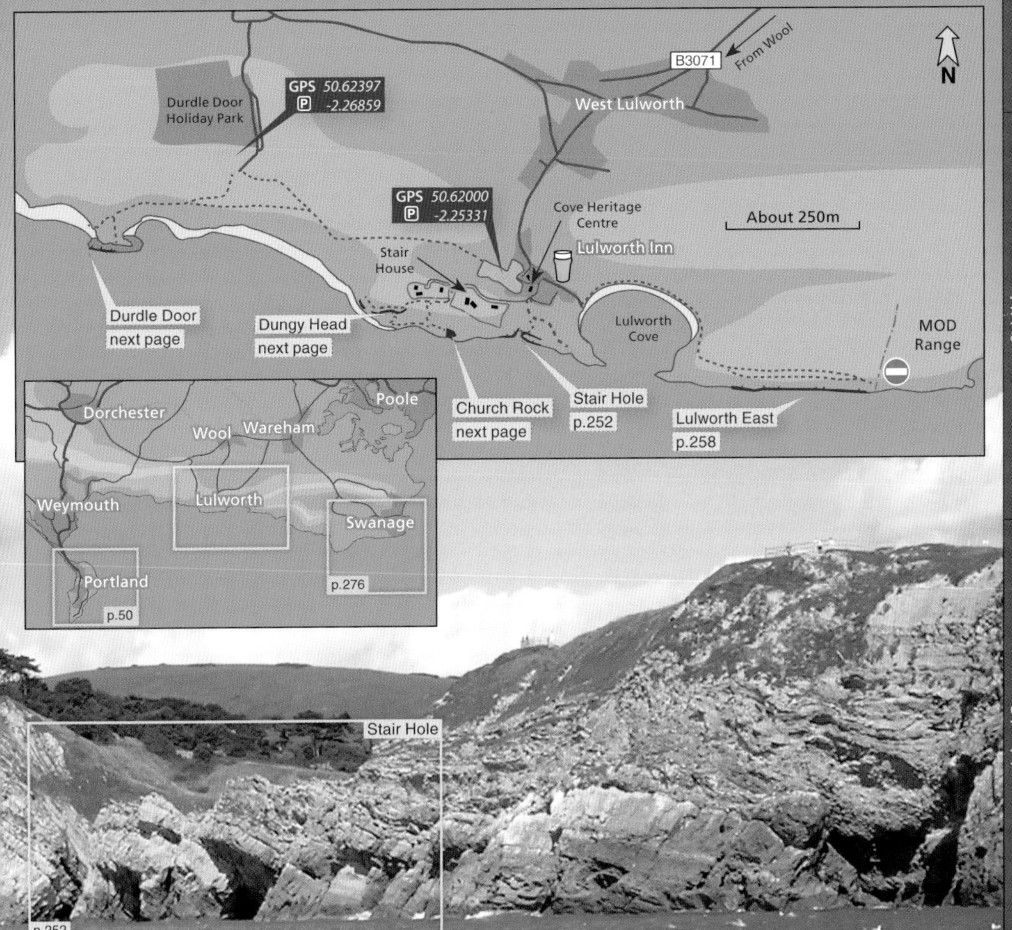

Portland
Lulworth
Swanage
Durdle Door to Church Rock
Stair Hole
Lulworth East

Durdle Door

Durdle Door has some fine, well-bolted sport routes that are located on the seaward face of the arch and should be regarded as serious undertakings.

Approach - Durdle Door can be easily reached from Lulworth Cove. A path leads down to the arch. Once on the ridge, scramble rightwards to the col before the final summit. Abseil down the seaward face to reach the platform from blocks and threads. There is a hidden ledge for gearing up on the far side of the ridge.

Tides - The start ledge is covered at high tide.

Access - Durdle Door is on the same estate as Lulworth Cove, so climbing is not allowed here. It is only included in this guidebook for completeness. Additionally, in the past there have been incidents where people on the beach have called out the coastguard to rescue climbers.

To get to the first route, abseil down the landward side of the arch to a bolt-belay on a small ledge at the base of the pillar.

1 Arcwelder . . . . 3 stars **7b**
S3. A hard start leads to a leaning wall above.
FA. Pete Oxley 25.4.1993

The next three routes are reached by a direct abseil from the col.

2 Riding to Babylon . . . . 3 stars **7a+**
S3. A magnificent route, which overhangs 10m in its 25m length and features a bit of a stopper move to finish.
FA. Pete Oxley 22.12.1992

3 They Call Me Tall Man . . . . 1 star **6b**
Short and steep, with the main difficulties at half-height.
FA. Joff Cook 13.12.1992

4 Unleash the Veins . 2 stars **7b+**
A gleaming white sheet of limestone. Follow good holds before more difficult moves lead eventually to jugs and a steep finish.
FA. Pete Oxley 16.10.1992

Approach (route 5) - *The first route lies about 300m further along the path. Walk up the hillside towards Durdle Door. After the first stile, drop down the hill towards the sea, where the ridge hits the beach level. The route lies on the wall up and left.*

Dungy Head and Church Rock

Church Rock is the isolated pinnacle down on the boulder beach west of Lulworth Cove. The rock has some decent short pitches. Dungy Head refers to the ridge of pinnacles situated high above the sea, just past Church Rock.

Dungy Head Approach - Walk along the main path above the pinnacles and drop down a gully, after walking past four pinnacles, and three boulder choked gullies.

5 Pickpocket **5**
Follow the line of old bolts up the central line.
FA. Tim Dunsby 5.4.1987

On the far (west) side of the main descent gully is a lone route.

6 Morris the Carnivore . . . . **6a+**
Varied climbing starting from a bolt-belay at the base. It is best approached by abseiling from a stake on the top of the crag.
FA. Mike Robertson 24.4.1994

The next routes are to the left (looking out) of the descent gully.

7 Beavis and Butthead **6a**
A poor and very loose route up the left-hand arete.
FA. Mike Robertson 19.2.1994

8 Beers, Steers and Queers 1 star **6c+**
The roof then a sustained wall above. The crux clip has seen some flyers. The lower-off is on a boulder.
FA. Steve Taylor 19.2.1994

9 Dungeons and Dragons. 1 star **7a+**
A roof leads to blind moves above and a shared lower-off.
FA. Pete Oxley 27.9.1987

10 Shoes for my Friends . . . . . 1 star **6a+**
The arete with thuggy moves low down and balancy moves higher up in a groove.
FA. Alex More 21.4.2011

11 Lost Souls. . . . . **6a+**
The exposed face left of the arete.
FA. Mike Robertson 5.12.1993

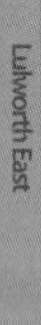

12 Looking Through the Infinity Window . . . . 3 stars 6c+
Good value. Move right onto the arete at the last bolt.
FA. Pete Oxley 23.12.1988

13 Closing Time . . . . . 2 stars 7a+
A stamina test up the leaning white wall. Start from a belay in the corner. Going left to the arete drops the grade to 7a.
FA. Steve Taylor 27.3.1994

Church Rock Approach - From the Cove Centre, walk up the road to Stair House. Turn left after the house and follow a steep path for around 100m to the cliff top. Drop down a steep slope direct to the rock at the water's edge.

14 The Debt Collector . . . . 1 star 6b
The left-hand side of the inland face via a shallow depression.
FA. Mike Robertson 10.7.1993

15 Wall of Feedback . . 1 star 6c+
A vague crack left of the right-hand arete is a good pitch.
FA. Pete Oxley 13.12.1988

16 Blow Me! 7a
The fingery wall just to the left of the arete.
FA. Marti Hallett 5.9.2007

17 Blow Daddy-O . . . . 1 star E3 5c
An eye-catching trad route up the spectacular arete.
FA. Clarke Alston 20.11.1988

18 House Nation . . . . 2 stars 6c
Excellent climbing up the steep pocketed wall, starting just right of the arete and moving rightwards.
FA. Pete Oxley 13.12.1988

19 Jugmaster Funk Meets M.C. Lane . . . . 2 stars 6b
The juggy vein in the centre of the west face. A micro-gem. Can be linked to *House Nation* by moving left on an undercut after the first bolt.
FA. Pete Oxley 13.12.1988

20 Turn It On . . . . 1 star 7b
A good but hard problem that takes on the leaning wall via some fingery moves. Shared belay.
FA. Steve Taylor 3.7.1993

Lots of sun | 10 min | Restrictions

Descent down gully
20m
14m
20m
A
5
6
7
8
9
10
11
12
13
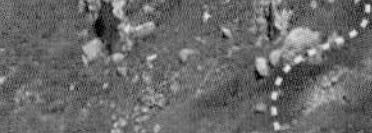

Church Rock 100m

Beach Bouldering
There is a decent amount of bouldering to be found on the beach boulders between Church Rock and Dungy Head. There are around 20 problems up to V9 in difficulty.

Stair Hole Approaches

The main climbing area is on the seaward side of Stair Hole, and has several approaches. There are a number of traditional easier pitches on either side of the caves that are not described.

Stair Hole West, Skeletor approach - From the beach, make a VDiff traverse around the end of the headland (this is part of *The Maypole*). There is a bolt-belay on a pedestal in the cave entrance below *Never Kneel to Skeletor*.

Stair Hole West, Greyskull approach - Climb up onto the ridge and scramble along it to the central area, just past an awkward slab. The gearing-up spot is further on. Descend to sea level down a steep VDiff ridge on the far side between the two caves, passing The Grotto on the right (looking in). At sea level, traverse back left (looking in) past various grooves to reach a bolt-belay below the right-hand side of the West Cave.

Stair Hole East, Stagedivin' approach - Climb up onto the ridge and scramble along this to the central area just past an awkward slab. The gearing-up spot is further on. Descend down a steep VDiff ridge on the far side to The Grotto. *Stagedivin'* starts here, the other routes are reached by VDiff scrambling down to sea level.

Stair Hole East, Mark of the Beast approach - Climb up onto the ridge and scramble along this to the central area just past an awkward slab and on to a gearing-up spot. Continue until it is possible to drop down a short groove onto a slab below (VDiff). Scramble back left (looking in) along this below the big roof of the East Cave.

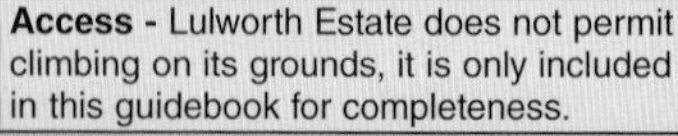

Access - Lulworth Estate does not permit climbing on its grounds, it is only included in this guidebook for completeness.

1 The Laws Traverse . 2 **E1 6a**
6b+, S0, **45m.** An enjoyable low-level traverse. Start by scrambling around to a ledge in the first cave. Make a wild swing onto the underside of a slab and then onto a boulder in the back of the second cave. Continue to the arete. Reverse the route.
FA. Pete Oxley and a team of locals 29.5.1993 (solo)

2 Trashy's Arete . . . . **VS 4c**
5, S2. The left side of the arete to a ledge. Reverse the route.
FA. Mike Robertson 7.9.2005 (solo)

3 The Brotherhood 2 **E5 6b**
7b+, S2. Direct up the buttress left of the diagonal break-line.
FA. Liam Cook 8.2009 (solo)

4 The Walkin' Dude . . **E4 5c**
6b+, S3. A pseudo deep water solo up the rising break-line.
FA. Mike Robertson 26.6.1993 (solo)

5 Skillfish **E3 5b**
6a+, S3. The higher diagonal break above *The Walkin' Dude.*
FA. Jon Biddle 1.9.2007 (solo)

6 The Maypole . . . . Top 50 **HVS 5b**
6a, S0, **80m.** A very good circular traverse, and a fun introduction to the area. Start on the beach and head round the west tip of the Stair Hole Promontory. Continue into the West Cave at, or very near sea level, to emerge back on the beach.
FA. Jon Williams 23.5.1990 (solo)

7 Thieving Gypsy . . . 1 **E5 6b**
7b+, S0. A tough mission with blind moves. From the beach traverse to the boulder at the start of *Window of Opportunity*.
FA. Gavin Symonds 13.8.2003 (solo)

8 Imp of the Perverse 2 **E6 6b**
7b+, S0. Follow *Theiving Gypsy* and then climb across a slab to gain the apex of the arch. Drop down and climb the underside of the arch to gain *Horny Lil' Devil.*
FA. Gavin Symonds 6.2006 (solo)

The Laws Traverse Buttress

A steep section of rock with one very popular DWS traverse and some serious DWS lines above it.
Approach - Start at the edge of the rocky beach.
Tides - High tide is essential for sufficient water.
Descent - Reverse *The Laws Traverse* back to the beach.

Morning | 5 min | Restrictions

West Cave

The west cave is somewhat overshadowed by its neighbour, but still offers some fine routes in a dramatic setting. A number of deep water solos have also been done inside the skull-shaped cave. These are very esoteric and usually greasy and green; best reserved for summer when it is too hot outside. See Deep Water www.rockfax.com for full details.

Approach - Use either the Skeletor approach or the Greyskull approach - see page 252.

Belays - Bolt belays are situated over the lip and below the ridge for bringing up the second, taking photos, or abseiling for gear.

Approach (routes 1 to 8) - *See the Skeletor approach on page 252.*

1 Cheddar Direct . . . 1 star — **VS 4c**
5, S2. Climb the steep nose and easy slab above.
FA. Unknown

2 Truth, Justice and the Raggamuffin Way . . . 1 star — **E2 5c**
6a+, S1. A touch friable at the top.
FA. Jon Biddle 20.7.1991 (solo)

3 Crazy Notion . . . 2 stars — **E5 6b**
7a+, S1. Climb *Animal Magnetism* to its second bolt, then move straight up the overhanging wall. A committing pitch.
FA. Mike Robertson 1990s (solo)

Access - Lulworth Estate does not permit climbing on its grounds, it is only included in this guidebook for completeness.

4 Animal Magnetism . Top 50 — **7a+**
S1. The ramp is short, but intense. *Photo on page 246.*
FA. Pete Oxley 4.6.1992

5 Journey to Eternia . 2 stars — **7c+**
S1. A left-to-right diagonal link-up giving superb climbing. Start up *Animal Magnetism*, reverse the crux of *Magnetic Gates* and finish up *Gates of Greyskull*.
FA. Pete Oxley Summer 2002

6 Never Kneel to Skeletor . . . 3 stars — **7c+**
S1. Start at a bolt-belay. Extremely technical and powerful.
FA. Pete Oxley 5.9.1992

7 Never Kneel to an Eternity of Mediocracy . . . 2 stars — **8a**
S1. Link up of *Never Kneel to Skeletor* into *Journey to Eternia*.
FA. Bob Hickish 4.9.2010 (solo)

8 Hurbot the Turbot 1 E4 6b
7a+, S1. A left-to-right line across the hanging ramp.
FA. Jon Biddle 22.7.1991 (solo)

Approach (routes 9 to 14) - *See the Greyskull Approach opposite.*

9 Skullthugery 3 E6 6b
7c, S2. Reverse *Hurbot the Turbot* until on the hanging slab in the middle of the arch. Make wild horizontal moves outwards towards daylight and the diagonal crack at bottom of the *Gates of Greyskull* face. Make a couple of moves up the crack to join *Gates of Greyskull*, and finish up it.
FA. Bob Hickish 28.6.2009 (solo)

10 Gates of Greyskull . Top 50 7b+
S1. A superb route direct through the cave roof.
FA. Pete Oxley 4.6.1992

11 Magnetic Gates . . . 1 7c
S1. An exciting right-to-left link-up. Start up *Gates of Greyskull* and break left, crossing *Never Kneel to Skeletor* via a tricky sequence, to finish up *Animal Magnetism*.
FA. Damian Cook 7.2000

12 Magnetic Skulls . . . 2 E6 6b
7c, S1. Link *Skullthugery* into *Magnetic Gates* taking in the crux of each.
FA. Bob Hickish 19.6.2010 (solo)

13 The Honorary Society of Self-Publicising Water Rats 1 E4 6a
6c+, S2. The short, overlapped roof into a groove right of *Gates of Greyskull*. Not one to fall off.
FA. Damian Cook 1990s (solo)

14 Hairy Clamber . . 1 VS 4c
5, S2. Follow the slabs diagonally rightwards under the roofs before pulling over the narrowest section on jugs. Finish leftwards.
FA. Damian Cook 7.2000 (solo)

Lots of sun | 5 min | Restrictions

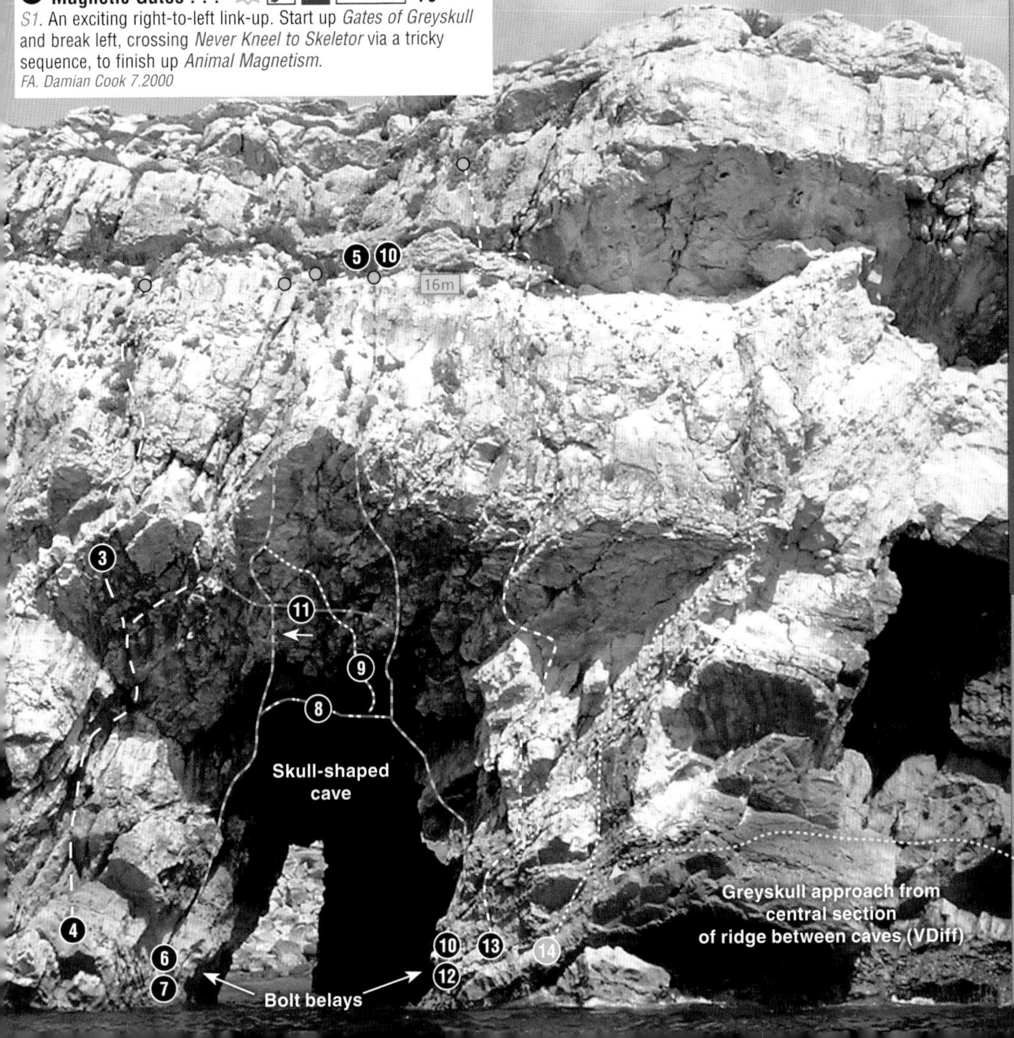

East Cave

An awesome venue packed with brilliant pitches on magnificent rock. Some of the routes are bolted but many have also been deep water soloed.

Approach - Use either the *Stagedivin'* or *Mark of the Beast* approach - see page 252.

Belays - There are bolt-belays in place over the lip.

1 Captain Bastard Got There First 1 E2 5c
6a+, S0. From sea level, move right and climb a blunt arete.
FA. Joff Cook 21.7.1991 (solo)

2 Despicable Terrier . 1 E3 6a
7a, S0. The arete to the right of *Captain Bastard Got There First.*
FA. Mark Williams 7.2004 (solo)

3 Anarchy Stampede 1 E3 6a
7a, S0. A steep blind crux not far above the sea.
FA. Jon Biddle 6.9.1988 (solo)

4 Stagedivin' . . . . 1 7a+
S1. Short and steep. Take care leaving the ledge if soloing.
FA. Pete Oxley 5.1992

5 I Love Eszter E3 5c
6b, S0. At low tide, traverse across to the left corner of the arch. Graunch up the greasy chimney to join *Horny Lil' Devil.*
FA. Damian Cook 1990s (solo)

6 Window of Opportunity 2 E5 6b
7b, S0. Follow *I Love Eszter* until a line of good holds joins *Horny Lil' Devil* from below.
FA. Mike Robertson 1990s (solo)

7 Hornier Than Thou . 2 E6 6b
7b+, S0. Climbs the arch from right to left below *Horny I'il Devil.* Reverse *Window of Opportunity* to finish. Strenuous.
FA. Joff Cook 1990s (solo)

8 Sliding Down the Banister 1 E4 6a
6c, S0. A wild and dark route, starting as for *Horny Lil' Devil,* and going through the arch to the beach in the cove.
FA. Pete Oxley 23.5.1992 (solo)

9 Horny Lil' Devil . . . Top 50 7a
S0. A brilliant, juggy traverse across the bottom of the wall.
FA. Pete Oxley 19.5.1992

10 Adrenochrome . . Top 50 8a
S1. A brilliant, sustained test-piece which involves some highly dynamic climbing.
FA. Pete Oxley 20.5.1992

11 Lord of Darkness 2 7c
S0. Start up *Mark of the Beast* to the big flake by its 3rd bolt, then traverse left across *Adrenochrome* to The Grotto ledge.
FA. Pete Oxley 1990s

12 Mark of the Beast Top 50 7c
S1. One of the best 7cs around. Good moves on large holds leading to a powerful crux at the lip. It is a popular route to attempt to solo.
FA. Pete Oxley 23.10.1987

13 Burn Hollywood Burn 3 8a+
A desperate crux above the 3 pockets. After the crux, it is just a matter of how long you can hang on for.
FA. Pete Oxley 10.5.1992

14 Lulworth Arms Treaty 2 7b
Direct and powerful.
FA. Pete Oxley 23.10.1987

15 Freed from Desire . 7a+
A smart addition with a low crux (left then right past the second bolt) to gain the big undercut on *Grimly Fiendish*. Continue leftwards to finish on *Lulworth Arms Treaty*.
FA. Jim Kimber, Pete Oxley 1990s

16 Grimly Fiendish 7a
A gentle warm-up? - no, not really.
FA. Pete Oxley 23.10.1987

The next routes link up sections of other routes already described and require intimate knowledge of the crag.

17 Pump up the Beast. E7 6b
8a, S1. An awesome link-up of *Window of Opportunity*, *Horny Lil' Devil* and *Mark of the Beast*.
FA. Rob Sutton 16.8.2003 (solo)

18 Windowchrome . E7 6c
8a+, S1. Link *Window of Opportunity* to *Adrenochrome*.
FA. Gavin Symonds 5.9.2007

19 Stage Fright 7b
S1. Reverse the last move of *Roof Predator* and finish up *Adrenochrome*.
FA. Pete Oxley 2000s

20 Centre Stage . . . . . 7b+
S1. Extend *Stage Fright* into *Mark of the Beast*.
FA. Pete Oxley 2000s

21 Z-Cars E6 6b
7b, S0. Follow *Hornier than Thou* past its crux before making a testing move to gain the large porthole on *Horny Lil' Devil*. Finish across *Horny Lil' Devil*.
FA. Joff Cook Summer 2001 (solo)

22 The Beast of Lulworth. . 7c
Start up *Mark of the Beast* to its niche. Swing right along a ramp to finish up *Lulworth Arms Treaty*. Worthwhile.
FA. Pete Oxley 29.7.2000

23 The Beast Goes East 7c
S1. Climb *Mark of the Beast* to where it moves slightly right to a flake at half height. Make an undercut move up right to a ramp, move right again and finish up *Burn Hollywood Burn*.
FA. Bob Hickish 4.9.2010

24 Taming the Beast. . 7b+
S1. Climb *Mark of the Beast* to a pocket at 3/4 height. Go up on edges until a move right gains a large porthole. Slap for the top.
FA. Bob Hickish 4.9.2010

25 Beast Club 7c
Start up *Lulworth Arms Treaty* through its first crux then traverse left to reach jugs on *Burn Hollywood Burn*. Continue diagonally leftwards to the high niche on *Mark of the Beast*. Finish up this.
FA. Pete Oxley 28.12.1992

26 Burning Arms 7c
Start up *Lulworth Arms Treaty*, clip its thread then move leftwards to join *Burn Hollywood Burn*. A good pitch.
FA. Pete Oxley 1990s

27 The Roof Predator . . 7c+
Start up *Grimly Fiendish* and over to *Lulworth Arms Treaty*. A sloping ramp leads past *Burn Hollywood Burn* to a hard move into *Mark of the Beast*. Follow this leftwards to a flake, then make a big move to a side hold on *Adrenochrome*. Go left again to a jug on *Stagedivin'*. Move down to The Grotto ledge to finish. **Reverse Predator, 7c**, is the pitch in reverse but traversing to easy ground once *Grimly Fiendish* is reached.
FA. Pete Oxley 28.12.1992.

Access - Lulworth Estate does not permit climbing on its grounds, it is only included in this guidebook for completeness.

Mojo-Pin and Il Pirate Area

A quiet section of cliff with a number of worthwhile routes on reasonable rock. There are some easier trad lines to the west, along with two big traverses that end in the restricted MOD area. These are not described.

Approach - Walk around the shingle beach of the cove and follow a steep track on the far side. Take the lower coast path, and, after about 150m, double back down the slope to a rock amphitheatre. From the far side of the amphitheatre, marked by a deep gully, scramble (Diff) or abseil down to just above the water line. The starts are reached by scrambling along the base of the cliff, which is easy at low tide, but tricky at high tide (VDiff). Leave gear well out of sight to avoid being rescued!

Tides - The starts can be reached at all tides, although it is more awkward at high tide. **Stay away in rough seas.**

1 Stalinist Regime . . 1 **HVS 5a**
Climb the prominent groove, then move left onto a slab. Continue on up to the roof, step left and pull over on accommodating flakes to finish at a ledge up on the left.
FA. Steve Taylor, Dave Simmonite 23.7.2006

2 Southern Stutter 1 **E1 5a**
Climb a flake up the left side of a slab past a detached spike to the roof. Make badly protected moves up rightwards to the finish of *The Poet and the Thief.*
FA. Dave Simmonite, Steve Taylor 23.7.2006

Access - Lulworth Estate does not permit climbing on its grounds, it is only included in this guidebook for completeness. Additionally no climbing is allowed on the Fossil Forest or any of the cliffs to the east of the MOD fence.

3 The Poet and the Thief . 1 **VS 4b**
Climb the centre of the slab and upper wall. Poorly protected in its upper reaches.
FA. Alex More, Rob Kennard 24.7.2006

4 Mojo-Pin. . . . . 2 **VS 5a**
A good slab route. Climb a groove on the right and at its end make thin moves up leftwards to the roof. Finish over the roof and up the wall on fossilised holds.
FA. Rob Kennard, Marti Hallett, Alex More 30.6.2006

5 Mansion Pond 2 **E2 5b**
A sustained and interesting route up the left-hand side of the bay, right of the *Mojo-Pin* slab. Technical bridging leads to a final difficult move to gain the roof. Swing right over the roof on deep pockets to a solid upper wall.
FA. Rob Kennard, Steve Taylor 27.9.2008

6 Mankini Biscuit . . . 2 **E2 5c**
Follow the line of the thin crack that crosses the roof left of *4 Years, 5 Months...*
FA. Rob Kennard, Steve Taylor 27.9.2008

7 4 Years, 5 Months and 15 Days and Still Missing You... . . . . 1 **E2 5b**
Bold climbing in its first half. Starting just left of an alcove, climb easily to some good gear. Harder and steeper climbing leads to the break under the roof. Finish over the roof via the crack-line.
FA. Marti Hallett, Alex More, Rob Kennard 30.6.2006

8 Fear of Litigation 1 **E1 5b**
Follow the easy wall to the roof, where some powerful moves gain a small alcove, and easier climbing to finish.
FA. Steve Taylor, Rob Kennard 27.9.2008

9 Extraordinary Rendition ⭐1 **E1 5c**
Climb easily up the left-hand side of an arete to the roof. Move left on good holds before making a hard move on small holds up onto the wall to finish.
FA. Rob Kennard, Alex More 13.5.2006

10 Hyperbole . . . . ⭐2 **HVS 5a**
Climb to the cave and follow a line of thin cracks to a niche in the roof - hard to place protection. Make a difficult move over the roof to finish at an unusual rounded fossil feature.
FA. Rob Kennard, Alex More 13.5.2006

11 MC Hammer . . . . **VS 4c**
An eliminate. Climb *Hyperbole* to the cave. Move up right to gain an undercut and finish just above.
FA. Rob Kennard, James Dunlop 24.6.2006

12 Too Driven . . . . **HS**
The arete immediately right of the descent. Good climbing, but escapable.
FA. Ben Stokes 17.6.2006 (solo)

13 Pussy Galore . . . . ⭐1 **VS 4c**
Start just right of the descent route, in a right-facing corner that forms the left-hand side of a bay. Climb the corner, taking care with some loose holds on the upper wall.
FA. Rob Kennard, Alex More 13.6.2006

14 Bad to the Bone . . . ⭐1 **7b+**
Start at a bolt-belay and make some reachy moves before powering up for some small holds at the lip.
FA. Pete Oxley 1990s

15 Il Pirata . . . . ⭐2 **7c**
The central line has lost holds (formerly 7a+). Cool moves and a definite crux at the roof.
FA. Pete Oxley 1990s

There is a right-hand finish to Il Pirata which is still a project.

16 Jurrasic Coast Pimps . . ⭐2 **E1 5b**
A very good pitch. Climb thin flakes and a slab just right of a corner to the roof. Follow jugs out to the lip of the roof and pull onto the finishing wall via undercuts.
FA. Ben Stokes, Mark Williams 17.8.2006

17 Svengali . . . . ⭐1 **E3 6a**
Tackle the roof to the right of *Jurrasic Coast Pimps* via a pancake feature.
FA. Rob Kennard, James Dunlop 24.6.2006

18 Bolt Free . . . . ⭐1 **VS 4c**
Climb easily to the prominent weakness in the overhang and climb steeply over it to a small niche. Finish up the wall above.
FA. Steve Taylor, Mark Williams 17.6.2006

19 Carbon Footprint . . . . **HVS 5b**
The steep left-facing corner and wide crack above the break is a struggle.
FA. Rob Kennard, James Dunlop, Jon Howell 17.6.2006

20 The Gift . . . . ⭐2 **HVS 5b**
A well-positioned pitch with good climbing. Follow the groove right of the arete to the roof. Move left to a steep crack and take this with difficulty to the top - well protected.
FA. Steve Taylor, Scott Titt 5.11.2006

21 Dry Your Eyes Mate . . . ⭐1 **7c+**
This is the right-hand line of the two that has some long reaches and sharp pockets. The left-hand line remains a project.
FA. Dan Knight 22.4.2005

22 Jay Kay . . . . ⭐1 **HVS 4c**
Follow the left-facing corner until a swing right gains a difficult wall that ends at a big overhang. Traverse left under the overhang and then up and left to finish.
FA. Rob Kennard, Scott Titt 5.11.2005

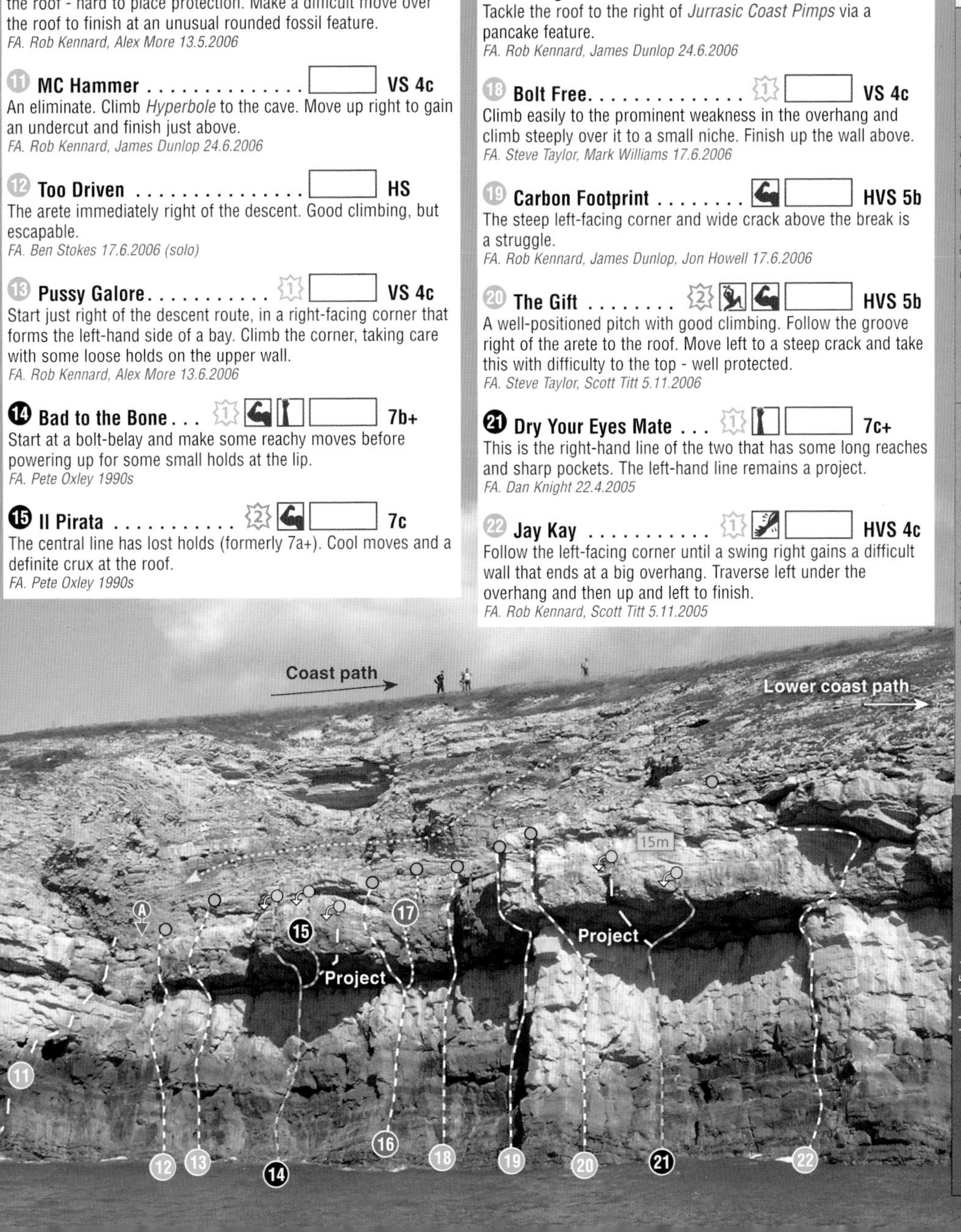

Amphitheatre Roofs

This roof playground gives similar routes to those at Stair Hole, only shorter and steeper. The rock is good, containing many pockets and flakes. The routes lie to the west of the MOD fence. The world famous Fossil Forest ledge is just beyond the fence.

Approach - Walk around the shingle beach of the cove and follow a steep track on the far side. Take the lower coast path, and after about 150m double back down the slope to a rock amphitheatre. From the far side of the amphitheatre, marked by a deep gully, scramble (Diff) or abseil down to just above the water-line. The starts are reached by scrambling along the base of the cliff which is easy at low tide but tricky at high tide (VDiff). It is also possible to abseil into the eastern end from a stake 40m from the MOD fence, or a bolt above the route *Mirrorball*. Leave gear well out of sight to avoid being rescued!

Tides - The starts can be reached at all tides, although it is more awkward at high tide. **Keep away in rough seas.**

Lots of sun | 15 min | Abseil in | Tidal | Restrictions

The first routes are 50m east of the descent gully.

1 The Lemon Express . . . 1 star — **7b**
Powerful moves on big holds. Pre-clip the first bolt in the roof on the next route then step left 2m to start.
FA. Pete Oxley 1990s

2 Breathe the Pressure 2 stars — **7b+**
Cross the central weakness. Full of variety.
FA. Pete Oxley 1990s

3 Ramases Cubed. . . . . — **7b+**
A powerful route that requires some inventive footwork to circumvent a blank section close to the lip of the roof.
FA. Pete Oxley 23.1.2005

4 Granny Lifts Car. . . . . . 2 stars — **7b+**
Climb to a hole in the roof. Difficult moves out of this gain better holds, from where a fierce sequence reaches the lip of the roof.
FA. Pete Oxley, Andy Bell 23.1.2005

5 Let Ya Bones Hang. 1 star — **7a**
A good introduction to the steep roofs. Start at a bolt-belay in the grooved rib. Climb the easy groove to the roof. Ape out across the roof on big pockets to jugs on the lip. Move slightly right on the rib to easier ground and the lower-off.
FA. Pete Oxley, Rob Godfray 18.2.2001

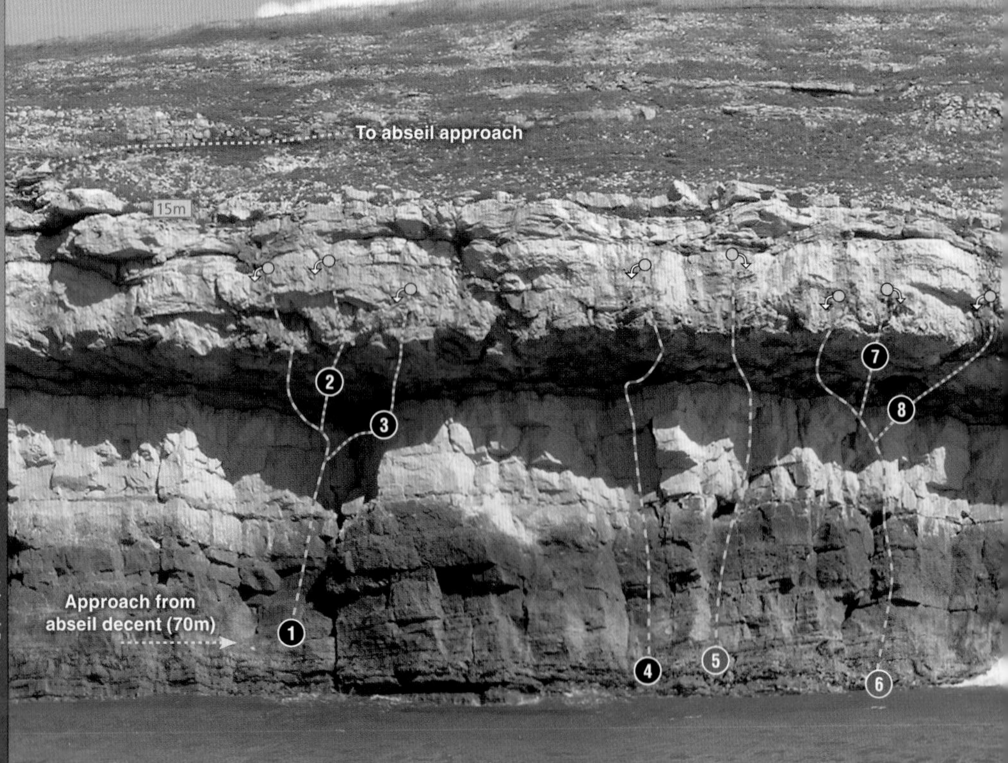

6 Rigor Mortise . . . . 2 stars 7a
Great fun on good holds (mostly). Climb to the roof, then move left and out through the roof direct past a small niche.
FA. Pete Oxley, Jon Biddle 1990s

7 A Storm in Heaven . 2 stars 7c
A very hard route with an amazing inversion at the lip. Brilliant moves on a central line. Start up *Rigor Mortise* to the roof.
FA. Pete Oxley 1990s

8 Eye of the Storm . . . 3 stars 7b+
A wild and acrobatic 10m roof. From the niche on *Storm in Heaven*, break right to an intermittent finger rail. Reach a big jutting ledge and pull through the lip to easier ground and a lower-off.
FA. Pete Oxley 25.2.2001

The next line of bolts is a project.

9 Language of Nature 1 star 7b
The obvious challenge of the diagonal crack in the right side of the roof finishing up *Eye of the Storm*. The bolt on the lip needs a long sling.
FA. Pete Oxley 25.2.2001

10 Weld's Mother . . . . 4+
An escape pitch if your elbows blow out. Follow the left-slanting rib between two bays.
FA. Damian Cook 1990s

11 Monolith Monsters . 2 stars 7b+
A blank-looking line through the widest part of the ceiling. Worth seeking out.
FA. Damian Cook 1990s

12 Mirrorball . . . . 2 stars 7c
Very powerful and graded for those with a big reach. Start up *Monolith Monsters*. Step right under the roof and make hard moves to cross the lip. Step right at the lip to finish on the difficult rockover of *Shining Path*.
FA. Pete Oxley 4.2001

13 Shining Path . . . . 1 star 7a+
Almost at the end of the cliff before the MOD fence. For guerrillas only.
FA. Dominic Cook 1990s

Beyond is the Fossil Forest, which marks the start of the MOD land. Do not climb here, or even enter when the ranges are closed, or you are likely to be escorted off and prosecuted.

Access - Lulworth East is on the Weld Estate so climbing is not allowed here. It is only included in this guidebook for completeness. Additionally no climbing is allowed on the Fossil Forest or any of the cliffs to the east of the MOD fence.

Mark Glaister embarking on the classic tour of the Boulder Ruckle offered by the excellent four pitch route *The Adventures of Portland Bill* (E2 5b) - *page 392*. Photo: Marti Hallett

Swanage

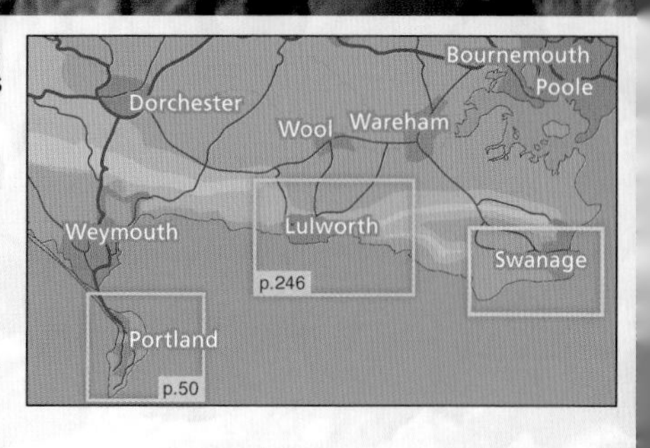

To the west of the bustling seaside town of Swanage - officially Britain's sunniest town! - lies the glorious Isle of Purbeck, a beautiful area famed for its gorgeous scenery, spectacular geology and stunning coastal cliffs. The countryside and coast are dotted with romantic little haunts and historic sites that include Corfe Castle and all things related to the novelist and poet Thomas Hardy. The whole area is an excellent holiday destination having a large choice of good beaches offering swimming and scuba diving, plenty of campsites, country pubs and places of interest to visit. These attributes, combined with the extensive climbing on the sea cliffs and quarries, puts Swanage high on the list of major UK climbing destinations.

For both traditional and sport climber, the limestone cliffs that run unbroken for five kilometres to the west of Swanage offer a unique climbing experience. Much of the rock is steep or overhanging, with many routes in the higher grades. For the accomplished climber, the style complements perfectly the more technical and fingery routes found on Portland. A good number of the crags, such as The Promenade, Palace of the Brine, Stair Hole and Blackers Hole offer huge roofs of a scale rarely encountered elsewhere in the country, whilst the Boulder Ruckle is Swanage's best known trad venue offering lots of mid to high grade climbs on its impressive walls. However many of Swanage's climbs are not on such powerful terrain, or of such an intimidating scale, and the more popular destinations are the bolted quarries at Dancing Ledge, Hedbury and Winspit. Also popular are the gentler trad sections of cliff such as Subluminal and the Cattle Troughs, which offer those starting out the chance to take their first steps on traditionally protected climbs at Swanage.

Another well-known draw of the area, and of great interest in the summer months, is the superb deep water soloing at Fisherman's Ledge - very probably the best in England.

Since the publication of the last Rockfax guidebook new route development at Swanage has continued apace, the most recent high-grade developments having been of both the more technical and serious head-point style most notably in the New Dawn Area, and the continued push for difficult sport climbs such as *Lifeforce*, and the very latest - *Endeavour* 8c - the first route to be climbed of this grade in Dorset.

Mike Hutton on the very popular Swanage classic *The Spook* (E1 5b) - page 316 - at the reliable Guillemot Ledge East. Photo: Dan Lane

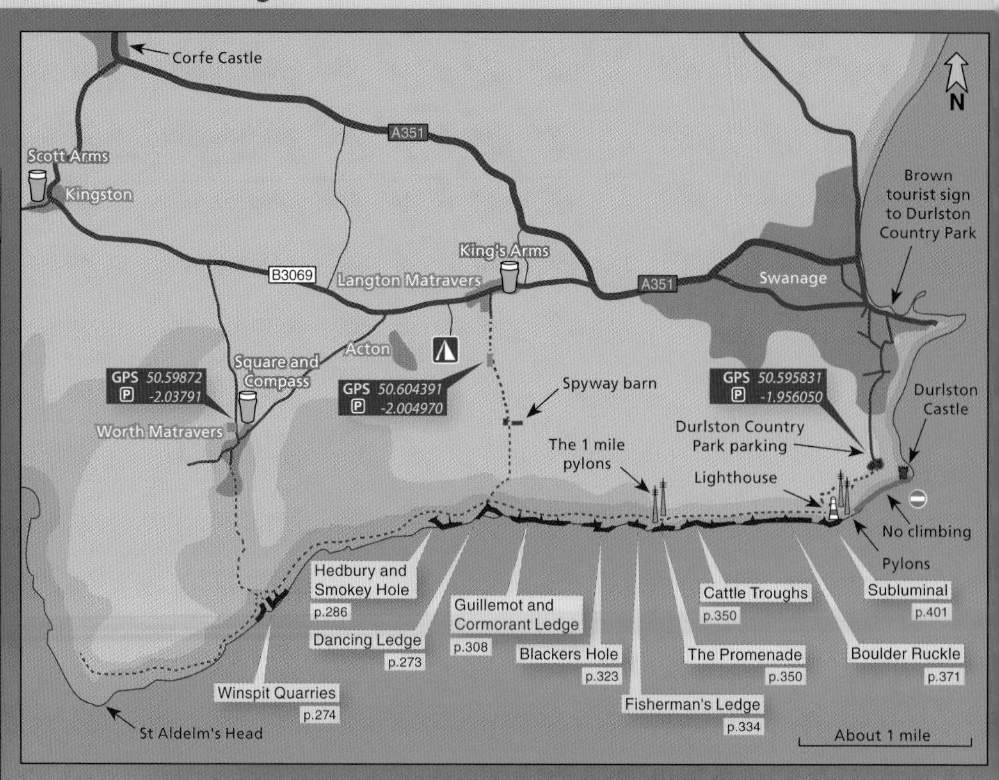

Swanage's climate is generally kind to the climber and more often than not is much better than elsewhere in the country. It is not unknown to be climbing in shorts in mid-winter, although the summertime heat can become unbearable at times. For the best conditions the cooler days in autumn and spring, and the crisp clear days of winter should be exploited and cherished. The majority of the Swanage cliffs face south and catch all the available sun. Hopefully the following pages will tempt all climbers to pay a visit, it is surely insane not to leave the cold and dark north and the wet west behind for a few days in the sun? Bring your shorts and some sunscreen, pack your quick-draws for the sport routes, a rack of gear for the trad lines, or at the very least a towel and a tankard of adrenaline for the odd deep water solo or two.

Corfe Castle - the gateway to the coast at Swanage.

High up on *Bert and Ernie* (E2 5b) - *page 387* - in the Boulder Ruckle. Chris Weedon making the first ascent. Photo: Oli Lyon

1900 to 1950 - Unrecorded wartime training ascents undertaken in the Boulder Ruckle.

1957 - The first recorded route *The Ramp* (Severe) at Boulder Ruckle by John Cleare.

Pre 1963 - Barrie Annette established the areas first classic *Tatra* (VS). Subluminal and Cattle Troughs are quickly developed, with some aid points used.

1963 - The first Swanage extreme *Apex Corner* is ascended by John Mustoe and graded HVS, which set a trend for undergrading.

1965/66 - Tony Wilmott raises standards with *Philatus* (now E3) and *Stroof* (E1 5c). George Smith finds classics in the Boulder Ruckle such as *Lightning Wall* (HVS) and *Finale Groove* (HVS).

1967/1972 - Richard Crewe becomes a major driving force establishing many classics such as *The Conger* (E2) and *Buccaneer* (E2). However *Oceanid* (E2) by Pat Littlejohn becomes the big test-piece. Swanage Climbing Club spearheads the group of active locals.

1973/1976 - Brian Snell climbs many lines at Guillemot Ledge whilst Crewe finds the perfect route with his *Tudor Rose* (E2). *Squid* (E2) is climbed free and demonstrates that the big roofs at Swanage, can be done without aid. George Hounsome, a bold climber nudges up the grade to E3 with *The Last Hurrah of the Golden Horde*.

1978 - Young outsiders from Bristol and Portsmouth raise the level to E4/5. Arnis Strapcans added the awesome *Polaris* (E5) and Littlejohn freed the pumpy *Melpomene* (E4). Other E4s were added by Nick Buckley and Kevin Turner, such as the future classic *Freeborn Man* (E4).

1982/84 - Martin Crocker enters the scene and raises the grade to hard E5 with *Fly Crazy but Free* and *Procrastinating Giant*.

1985 - Pete Oxley equals the hardest routes yet done with his *Punks in Power* (E5). Crispin Waddy joins in and explores some esoteric new stuff.

1986 - Oxley gives The Promenade some attention and produces many test-pieces including *Birth Pains of New Nations* (E6) and the first sport route, *Tessalations* (7b). Waddy begins deep water soloing at Connor Cove, Fisherman's Ledge.

1987/88 - Oxley adds numerous E6s and 7c+s then late in the year, Oxley completes the huge roof of *Laughing Arthur*, the first E8 in the South.

1989/90 - *Street Fighting Years* (E7) is climbed at Blackers Hole. Swanage quarries including Dancing Ledge and Hedbury are developed by Oxley.

1991 - Oxley adds the first 8a with *Solid State Logic* at the Promenade then pushes the standard to 8a+ with *Palace of the Brine*. An excellent batch of E6s and E7s go up at Smokey Hole, as well as *Godfodder* a big E7 roof at The Promenade.

1992 - *Infinite Gravity* (8a+) is put up to give one of the UKs most overhanging pitches.

1993 - A meeting decides which areas of Swanage are to be opened up for sport routes and which are to remain trad.

1993/4 - Mike Robertson opens up many sport routes at Winspit and Dancing Ledge. Deep water soloing becomes more popular. Crocker makes a return with the likes of *Deaf Mosaic* (E6) at Guillemot Ledge. The first Dorset Rockfax is published that covers the sport climbing areas at Swanage.

1996 - A 'last great traverse' around Hedbury Cove is completed by Crocker and Robertson.

1997 - Robertson adds a batch of necky E6s at Black Zawn and Connor Cove such as *Talisman* and *Terminal One*.

1998 - Oxley solos and straightens *Privateer* (E6) and adds *For Whom the Swell Tolls* (E6). The first deep water solo festival is organised by Robertson.

1999 - Oxley adds three E6s to Connor Cove including *The Drowning Pool*. Oxley returns to hard trad routes with *Full Circle* (E7) at Blackers Hole and later he adds *Mile High Club* (E6) to Conner Cove. Dave Pickford has an awesome summer repeating scores of routes and sets the scene for the next millennium by onsighting the *Schwarzechild Radius* (7c+) and *The Roaring Boys* E6.

2000 - A busy year of consolidation and repeats after the second Dorset Rockfax is published. Pickford repeats *Infinite Gravity*, and achieves a bolt-free ascent of *A Dose of the Malhams* (E6). The Promenade sees more development from Oxley with classics such as *Rise of the Robots* (7b+).

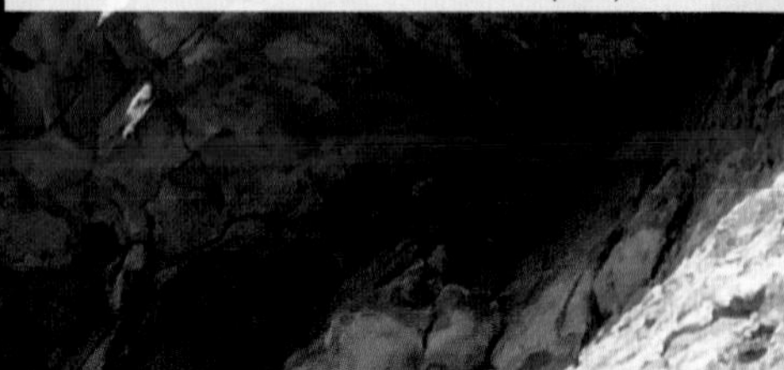

Carrie Hill bridging up the steep initial pitch of the wild and exposed *Heidelberg Creature* (VS 4c) - *page 387* - in the Boulder Ruckle.

2001 - Deep water soloing reaches a climax with a regular yearly festival attended by 100s on the Swanage cliffs. Products of this are the classic *Vanishing* at E6 6a. Oxley adds several routes to The Promenade up to 7c+ including *Eye of the Storm* and *The Incredible Hulk*.

2002 - Pete Finklaire and Sue Hazel add *Children of the Sun* (E2) in the Boulder Ruckle - one of a number of very good trad lines put up by Finklaire over the years such as *Buzz Light Year* (HVS) and *Dark Side of the Sun* (E1). Oxley finds some quality hard sport climbs such as *Atonement* (7c) and *The Futurist 2002* (7b+), both at The Promenade.

2003 - Highlight of the year is the superb *Event Horizon* (8a+) from Rob Kennard at The Promenade. Matt King spearheads a resurgence of new sport climbs at Winspit.

2004 - The Promenade receives one of its best with *State of Play* (7c+) from Oxley.

2005 - Local Dan Kennard sorts out two old projects, which both turn into powerful 7c+'s. Oxley manages once again to get the last new route in the new Rockfax (2005) guidebook just in the nick of time with his *Haka Pereperu* (8a) in the Palace of the Brine Cave. Late in the year Oxley finishes his long-standing project *Lifeforce* (8b) - a fitting final addition prior to his departure to live in New Zealand.

2006 - Dan Knight and Kennard complete the obvious roof challenge at Winspit with *Souls of Mischief* (7c+).

2008 - Over the winter Fisherman's Ledge suffers a massive rockfall and Marti Hallett adds the first line on the newly exposed cliff - the aptly named *When Land Becomes Sea* (E1).The popular *Larus* (HS) is also destroyed by another big collapse in the Boulder Ruckle.

2010 - Bob Hickish climbs an old bolted project at Unknown Ledge to produce *Fuel My Fire* (8a+) and with Tom Randall climbs a stunning, fully bolted version of *Laughing Arthur* at Blackers Hole - *Forever Laughing* (7c+). Chris Weedon turns his attention to the fresh rock exposed in the rockfall a Fisherman's Ledge and climbs a trio of bold, hard trad lines - *Slide Show* (E7) being the walls hardest offering at present.

2011 - Hallett climbs the steep wall of *No Mistaking* (E3) at Guillemot Ledge, whilst Pickford and Hickish paddled into the depths of Blackers Hole and emerged with the adventurous and super-steep trad line *The Aquatic Ape* (E6). Hickish completes his major project at Blackers Hole - *Endeavour* (8c) - and with it ushers in a new level of difficulty to the cliffs of Dorset.

February 2012 - The new Dorset Rockfax is published.

Marti Hallett on the first pitch of the fine new line of *Buzz Light Year* (HVS 5a). The tapering corner to the left is the Boulder Ruckle classic *Finale Groove* (HVS 5a) - *both on page 387*.

Winspit to Dancing Ledge

Dan Wicks on the stunningly-positioned sport route *Born Again* (6b+) - *page 307* - at Dancing Ledge.

Portland | Lulworth | Swanage | Winspit | Hedbury and Smokey | Dancing Ledge | Guillemot Ledge | Blackers Hole | Fisherman's Ledge | The Promenade | Cattle Troughs | Boulder Ruckle | Subluminal

	No star	1 star	2 star	3 star
Mod to S	2	2	-	-
HS to HVS	8	14	3	-
E1 to E3	7	14	9	1
E4 and up	2	5	9	2

Winspit Quarry is a very pleasant and sheltered sport climbers playground with an excellent set of routes that span the grades. It is now established as a popular and well-bolted venue, and one of the best places to climb during the winter months in the south of England. The climbs pack in the moves and progress is mostly made on positive, square-cut holds and in-cuts. The quarry is divided into two halves enclosing a rocky cove, which is a popular picnic and sunbathing spot throughout the year, making this one of the better family-friendly cragging venues in the Swanage area.

Conditions Also see map on page 266

Winspit's clement micro-climate often means that climbing is possible when conditions are poor elsewhere. Should the sea be rough making access to the main cliffs dangerous, Winspit is a good alternative, being set well back from the main cliff edge and consequently sheltered from southerly and westerly gales. The Quarryman's Wall/South Face have the best climbing with both faces receiving plenty of sun and the Quarryman's Wall in particular gets sun until late in the day. It is very sheltered and suffers hardly any seepage. The steep faces offer dry climbing in light rain, especially if the wind is blowing from the east or north. The very back of the Quarryman's Wall is sheltered from southerly gales. In showery conditions there are plenty of caves that provide shelter in the event of sudden downpours.

Approach

Also see map on page 266

Winspit Quarry is situated 1.5km south of Worth Matravers, and is reached by a pleasant stroll down a picturesque valley. Park in the main car park (fee) which is situated on the right as the village is entered. The approach path starts down a lane below the village pond.

Access

Winspit Quarry West is on private land, and the owners have requested that no more bolting is to take place as well as no group use. If you climb here, you may well be asked to leave. If this does occur, please leave without making any fuss so as not to jeopardise any future access negotiations. Winspit is only included in this book for completeness.

A climber midway up *Insect Graveyard* (6b) - *page 280* - at the Quarryman's Wall, Winspit. This wall offers some of the most consistently good climbing conditions in the UK and is a popular winter venue.

Portland
Lulworth
Swanage
Winspit
Hedbury and Smokey
Dancing Ledge
Guillemot Ledge
Blackers Hole
Fisherman's Ledge
The Promenade
Cattle Troughs
Boulder Ruckle
Subliminal

West Quarry

Winspit West is the least attractive of the quarries, and is characterised by some impressive man-made caves and a good number of square-cut overhangs. Much of the rock needs treated with care.

Approach - On entering the quarry, head rightwards towards some old buildings at the foot of the wall. The first routes are reached via an arch (see topo).

Access - No group use and no more new routes are allowed.

1 The Skin Room . . . 7a+
Steep and powerful climbing, but also dangerously loose.
FA. Jamie Hannant 10.5.2003

2 Warm Love . . . . 1 star 6a
The bolt line to the right of *The Skin Room* features gradually steepening climbing and a tough finish.
FA. Scott Titt 23.2.2008

3 Think About It . . . . 1 star 6a+
The wall and groove just left of the through-cave with the crux at the top. Take care with some suspect holds by the third bolt.
FA. Kevin Turner 1977

4 Things That Make You Go Hmmmm... . . . . 1 star 6c
A slightly friable route up the steep corner above the through-cave. The start has lost a hold which has pushed the grade up.
FA. Pete Oxley 22.9.1991

5 Restless Heart. . . . . . . 2 star 6b+
The wall right of the corner is nicely sustained with good climbing throughout. It is possible to get a no-hands rest in the niche.
FA. Mike Robertson 4.12.1993

6 Any Old Time 1 star 6b

Aim for the upper arete, which is followed on its right-hand side. Only short, but featuring some exposed positions once on the arete itself.

FA. Mike Robertson 11.8.1993

7 Bread Knife 1 star 4

Climb the well-defined corner to the right of *Any Old Time*. Starting to the right of an earth mound, climb a flake in the white wall and then move left to the corner and take this to a lower-off.

FA. Scott Titt 1.1.2006

8 Post-coital Snooze 1 star 6a+

The routes takes the cracks in the wall to the right of *Bread Knife* and features a distinct crux on smooth rock.

FA. Mike Robertson 18.3.1994

9 Iron Bar 1 star 5

Start just left of a small quarried cave and climb the line of bolts up the wall. Originally the line was graded 6a, but a block has come off and the route is now easier.

FA. Scott Titt 1.1.2006

10 The Chestnut Mare 1 star 7b+

A short but powerful line through the roof of the quarried cave.

FA. Rob Kennard 2005

11 Mini Line 6a

Short line up wall.

FA. Unknown

12 Book 3 6c+

The left side of the twin caves. Escapable climbing.

FA. Matt King 2003

To the right is a low quarried cave that has been the scene of some unusual activity for Dorset - dry tooling. The route **A Different Game, M10** *follows the roof crack, protection being supplied by clipping a rope rail that should be set-up along the line of bolts which follow the line.*

13 The Fantastic Mr Faz 6a+

Climb the central pillar, moving right to a lower-off.

FA. Jamie Hannant 2003

14 Idiot Village 1 star 6a+

Climb the large blocky overhangs to the right of a deep cave. A little careful route finding reduces the thuggery and once over the first roof the rest is straightforward, so long as you can jam.

FA. Mike Robertson 11.12.1993

15 Autumn Leaves 1 star 5+

This line has now cleaned up and provides a popular pitch that follows the steep groove to the right of *Idiot Village*.

FA. Scott Titt 1.8.2006

16 Flux Capacitor 1 star 5+

Climb the groove/crack-line 15m to the right of *Autumn Leaves*. The second bolt is a grip clip.

FA. Tom Beaumont 13.3.2007

17 Eroman 6c

Steep line 10m to the right of *Flux Capacitor*.

FA. Scott Titt 2000s

Morning | 20 min | Restrictions

Portland | Lulworth | Swanage | Winspit | Hedbury and Smokey | Dancing Ledge | Guillemot Ledge | Blackers Hole | Fisherman's Ledge | The Promenade | Cattle Troughs | Boulder Ruckle | Subluminal

Quarryman's Wall

The Quarryman's Wall is the most popular section of cliff at Winspit and is a very reliable venue being set well back from the sea and extremely sheltered from the wind. The routes are on good rock and the majority, clean and well bolted. The climbs furthest inland are overhanging, whilst the rest are vertical. This is an excellent place for teams of mixed abilities and a good venue to head for if sea conditions prevent access elsewhere.

Approach - On entering the quarry, bear left towards the wall, which is ahead and to the left of the track.

1 Free Entre-prises . . . . **5+**
The left-most line on the Quarryman's Wall which, tackles the short flake-crack and corner-line left of *The Genius of S.K.*
FA. Marti Hallett 27.1.2008

2 The Genius of S.K. **6a**
The groove toward the left-hand end of the wall has some poor rock and a very loose block between the second and third bolt. The climbing itself is reasonable.
FA. Mike Robertson 13.5.1994

3 Solstice . . . . 2 **7a+**
The groove to the left of *Avenging the Halsewell* is packed with some excellent climbing.
FA. Rich White, Rob Kennard 21.6.2006

4 Avenging the Halsewell 3 **7b**
A popular test-piece that lies at the upper end of the grade. A strenuous outing up a series of small overhangs that features three hard sections and a perplexing no-hands rest.
FA. Pete Oxley 30.7.1988

5 Ancient Order of Freemarblers
. . . . 2 **7a**
Steep stamina climbing. A powerful and technical sequence of moves gains a finger crack at mid-height.
FA. Pete Oxley 13.11.1987

6 Billy Winspit 2 **7b**
A relatively easy lower wall and flake lead to a hands-off rest. The next move is the crux and is very reach dependent.
FA. Steve Taylor 28.11.1993

7 Peppercorn Rate 2 **7a**
A quality pitch, tough and unyielding, with a pumpy top wall and a blind crack.
FA. Pete Oxley 23.12.1987

8 Smiling Assassin . . . . **7a+**
The line just left of the arete is an eliminate, and it is easy to drift off the line.
FA. Matt King 2003

Afternoon | 20 min | Sheltered

9 So Naughty . . . . 1 star — 5

A popular outing that shed a hold on its crux, but can still be climbed at grade 5 if a move right is made at the third bolt (6a+ if taken direct). Start up the arete, then make a tricky move into the corner which is followed to the top.

FA. Carol Robertson 5.12.1993

10 Insanely Yours. . . . . 1 star — 6c+

A short but interesting line. Originally climbed without using the arete at 7a+.

FA. Mike Robertson 20.3.1994

11 Jargon Eater . . . . 1 star — 6b+

At the roof, move left and finish with difficulty.

FA. Nigel Coe, Tim Dunsby 20.12.1987

12 Unseen Ripples of the Pebble 2 stars — 6a+

Nice climbing up the well-bolted crack-line.

FA. Nigel Coe, Pete Oxley 31.12.1987

13 I Thought You Had It! . . 2 stars — 7a

The crack and grooved arete to the right of *Unseen Ripples of the Pebble* has some decent climbing, although at the top some care has to be taken to stay on line.

FA. Rob Kennard, Matt Ridgeway 16.2.2008

14 Gallows' Gore . . . . 2 stars — 7a

Good climbing on some fine rock, with a boulder-problem crux, starting at the right edge of the cave.

FA. Pete Oxley 3.1.1988

15 Red Rain . . . . Top 50 — 6c+

A great route - nicely sustained and varied - that features a tricky no-hands rest and, near the top, one of the best finger locks around.

FA. Pete Oxley 3.1.1988

16 Queen Anne's Men. . . . 2 stars — 6c

Classy climbing with a definite crux section. Reaching the lower-off is a touch bold.

FA. Pete Oxley 31.12.1987

17 Exuberance. . . . . 1 star — 7a

Steady climbing leads to a crux move close to the top.

FA. Mike Robertson 5.8.1993

18 Stone Mason. . . . . 2 stars — 6a+

A fun, well-travelled pitch up the disjointed crack-line.

FA. Tim Dunsby 20.12.1987

19 Hitachi and Girls . . . . 6a+

Start up *7a+ Took Me Lung* then the wall on the left to a contrived finish.

FA. Patti Flecks, Niall Gault 12.2006

20 7a+ Took Me Lung . . . . 4+

The well-bolted line of flakes needs care with the rock.

FA. Bolted by Niall Gault in 2006 but it had been climbed before this.

Afternoon | 20 min | Sheltered

Portland | Lulworth | Swanage | Winspit | Hedbury and Smokey | Dancing Ledge | Guillemot Ledge | Blackers Hole | Fisherman's Ledge | The Promenade | Cattle Troughs | Boulder Ruckle | Subluminal

21 Resin Devotion 1 6a

Climb the line just right of *7a+ Took Me Lung*.

FA. Mike Robertson 13.5.1994

22 Insect Graveyard 1 6b

The centre of the wall provides a nicely sustained pitch.

Photo on page 275.

FA. Mike Robertson 5.8.1993

23 Know What I Mean Pal 1 6a

An enjoyable pitch up the right-hand side of the wall.

FA. Mike Robertson 5.11.1993

24 Playtime with Playtex. . 1 6c+

A mid-height traverse from *Know What I Mean Pal* to *Gallows' Gore*.

FA. Pete Oxley 30.7.1994

25 Tom's Patience 1 4

The flowstone groove gives a pleasing pitch at the grade.

FA. Matt King 2003

The Korean Route 5 *has been debolted as it was considered a potential death trap, the bolts having been placed in loose rock.*

26 Pump Me Tenderly . . . . 1 6c+

There is only one hard move but it's at the top.

FA. Mike Robertson 9.11.1991

27 Anne-Marie Paid my Fee . . 4+

Climb the corner to the left of *Nine Years Absence*.

FA. Scott Titt 1.1.2006

28 Nine Years Absence . . . 1 6a

Climb the wall to the right of a corner. Only short but worthwhile and enjoyable.

FA. Mike Robertson 1.9.1993

29 The Vixen Bitch from Hell . . . . 1 7a+

The last move will be dynamic for some.

FA. Mike Robertson 31.7.1993

Afternoon | 20 min | Sheltered

20m

The Korean Route

Dave Pickford pulling through the roof on the spectacular *Disbelief Suspended* (7b+) - *page 283* - at the super steep South Face of Winspit.

South Face

The South Face of Winspit is a steep and sunny section of cliff that has a number of good lines. Most of the better routes are steep and powerful, crossing low-level roof stacks before finishing up a vertical headwall. A few of the starts utilise cairns to reach the first holds, and these often need rebuilding.

Approach - On entering the quarry, bear left and continue around the corner from the Quarryman's Wall.

1 Agonies of a Dying Mind 1 star 7a
A powerful start and a friable finish. The start gives a good V4 boulder problem in isolation.
FA. Mike Robertson 4.3.1993

2 Dick Dastardly. . . . 1 star 7a+
A tricky route that is difficult to on-sight. There are only two or three hard moves, but they are tough.
FA. Mike Robertson 5.12.1993

3 Korean South Face Route . . 1 star 6c+
Good climbing with a tough finish. The bolts are placed in poor locations.
FA. c.2007

4 Lips of a Stranger . . . . 6c+
Surprisingly good moves over the shattered roof and up the groove.
FA. Mike Robertson 4.12.1993

5 Fragile Mind . . . . 1 star 6c+
The steep left-hand line up the impressive crack. Take care with a couple of holds at the start.
FA. Rob Kennard 2003

6 Card of Hearts . . . . 1 star 7a+
More strenuous stuff taking the right-hand bolt-line after starting up *Fragile Mind*, with a technical bridging finale.
FA. Rob Kennard 2004

7 Chrissy. . . . . 2 star 6c
A good thuggy start off a wobbly jug leads to a testing mid-section and some very fine bridging in the groove. Excellent and quite committing; one of the best on this wall.
FA. Mike Robertson 31.7.1993

8 Chick Power . . . . 2 star 7c
An eliminate that has a fierce boulder-problem crux midway.
FA. Rob Kennard 15.9.2008

9 Revhead's Hi-roller 2 star 7b+
A steep start leads to the exposed arete to finish.
FA. Pete Oxley 5.6.1994

10 First Dazes of Summer . . . . 1 star 6c
The steep groove and bulges above the roof right of *Revhead's Hi-roller*.
FA. Marti Hallett 18.9.2008

11 Mackerel . . . . 2 star 5
The groove and flowstone with the main difficulties at the start and finish.
FA. Matt King 2003

12 Stargazy . . . . 1 star 6a+
The thin crack to the right of *Mackeral* is tricky towards the top.
FA. Scott Titt 28.5.2006

13 Knickerless Crutches . . . . . 6b+
The thin crack, with one tricky move that is very run out.
FA. Mike Robertson 4.12.1993

14 Premenstrual Princess . . . . 6b+
Takes the short open corner that is gained from the left. Finish up the wall right of the bolts.
FA. Marti Hallett 12.12.2006

15 Damnation Game . . . . . 2 stars 7a+
A classy and sustained pitch to the left of the big cave.
FA. Mike Robertson 28.11.1993

16 Frightened of the Sun . . 1 star 7b+
A difficult start leads to steep moves around the lip of the large roof. Good wall climbing finishes this spectacular line.
FA. Rich White 2003

17 Disbelief Suspended 2 stars 7b+
Climb the same difficult start as *Frightened of the Sun* to a very spectacular roof. Finish up the wall above, joining *Frightened of the Sun*. Can also be finished out right as for *Souls of Mischief* as shown on topo. *Photo on page 281.*
FA. Rob Kennard 2003. FA. (RH Finish) Pete Oxley 2004

18 Disbelief Reinvented 2 stars 7c
Start up *Souls of Mischief* to the roof then climb left through the crux roof of *Disbelief Suspended* to finish.
FA. Jimbo Kimber 24.12.2005

19 Souls of Mischief . . 2 stars 7c+
The old project from the left-hand ground level cairn has now been completed. From atop the cairn, climb the bouldery crack to the roof, from where hard moves up and right gain an easier finishing groove. Low in the grade.
FA. Dan and Rob Kennard 29.1.2006

20 The Pizza Express . 2 stars 7c+
Follow *Souls of Mischief* to its 4th bolt, then, with hands on the lip of the roof, break right to the knee-bar on *Lunacy Booth*. Finish up *Lunacy Booth*.
FA. Bob Hickish 20.1.2009

21 Lunacy Booth . . . . . 3 stars 7c
An entertaining, big and burly roof climb starting from the right-hand pile of boulders in the centre of the cave. A good knee-bar above the large roof gives a quick hands-off rest. The first bolt might need to be stick-clipped by the short.
FA. Pete Oxley 5.6.1994

22 Nosey. . . . . 6a+
A short pitch with a bold finish.
FA. Mike Robertson 12.11.1993

Lots of sun | 20 min | Sheltered

20m

Portland | Lulworth | Swanage | Winspit | Hedbury and Smokey | Dancing Ledge | Guillemot Ledge | Blackers Hole | Fisherman's Ledge | The Promenade | Cattle Troughs | Boulder Ruckle | Subluminal

South Face - Right

The right-hand side of the South Face has become more popular recently after the addition of a few new lines. The face is well-sheltered and gets lots of sun. Some of the rock looks to be potentially unstable, so care is needed.

Approach - On entering the quarry, bear left and continue around the corner from the Quarryman's Wall to below the initial section of the South Face. Continue under the face to the climbs.

The first route is to the right of the route Nosey in a bay just before the large loose cliff left of the Fishy Business Sector is located.

1 Rampant Love Jugs . . . 1 star 6b
Start in the dip 8m right of *Nosey*. Highly enjoyable if a little runout in places. No piling rocks under the start - jumping is the whole point of the route name.
FA. Mike Robertson 12.11.1993

The following three pitches are on the Fishy Business Sector which is the section of corner-lined cliff to the right of a huge bay of unstable rock

2 Plaice a Bolt . . . . 1 star 5
Start up a corner, then move left to another corner and climb this to a lower-off.
FA. Scott Titt 25.7.2006

3 Fishy Business . . . . 1 star 5+
The right-hand corner gives some worthwhile climbing. Start up *Plaice a Bolt*.
FA. Scott Titt 23.6.2006

4 Silver Bream Machine . . . . 1 star 6c
The line of bolts to the right of the corner of *Fishy Business*. The top section gives the hardest climbing.
FA. Scott Titt 3.9.2006

The next set of routes are over in the far corner of the quarry.

5 Gorilla Tactics . . . . 2 star 6c
Good climbing. The route has cleaned up and has been rebolted.
FA. Mike Robertson 5.11.1993

6 Flash Heart Direct . . . . 2 star 6b
The buttress right of the cave entrance is taken by this steep and well bolted line.
FA. Mike Robertson 7.8.1993

7 On the List E2 5c
The arete to the right of *Flash Heart Direct*. Climb the arete and at the third bolt stretch left for a crack and good gear. Finish direct as for *Rubic's Hex*.
FA. Marti Hallett 20.5.2009

8 Rubic's Hex. . . . . VS 5a
A trad line up the steep loose crack and corner above.
FA. G.Jefferies, M.Dutson 12.1989

9 Hot Beef Injection 6b
Line to the left of *Birthday Treat*. From a boulder, climb direct up the face.
FA. Theo Elmer 27.8.2009

10 Birthday Treat . . . . 5+
Climb the corner right of *Flash Heart Direct* moving left on the upper wall to finish.
FA. Steve Newman, Scott Titt 22.7.2008. Subsequently bolted in error.

Portland
Lulworth
Swanage
Winspit
Hedbury and Smokey
Dancing Ledge
Guillemot Ledge
Blackers Hole
Fisherman's Ledge
The Promenade
Cattle Troughs
Boulder Ruckle
Subliminal

	No star	1	2	3
Mod to S	2	4	-	-
HS to HVS	1	3	1	-
E1 to E3	1	10	3	-
E4 and up	-	6	8	2

Meilee Rafe on the technical wall climbing of *Moves for the Masses* (6a+) - *page 288* - at the sheltered Hedbury Quarry. Photo: Mike Robertson

The Hedbury and Smokey Hole areas encompass four very different crags to the west of Dancing Ledge. The main interest for most climbers will be Hedbury Quarry, which is a similar but more compact version of the main quarry at Dancing Ledge. The rock here is steep and solid and dotted with flowstone holds. It is a good place for an afternoon's sport climbing in winter, getting lots of sun and being set back away from the sea. Just around the corner from the quarry is the atmospheric Hedbury Big Cove with its leaning walls, massive overhangs, slightly unstable rock and hard trad routes. Smokey Hole, on the other hand, is more solid and less steep than Hedbury Big Cove but has a similar set of high quality, high grade trad routes in a sensational setting. The tucked away Topmast Quarry has three steep and sheltered sport routes.

Approach Also see map on page 266

Hedbury is approached from Langton Matravers. From just outside Swanage town, turn off the A351 towards Langton Matravers. Once in the village, go past the post office and turn left into Durnford Drove. A free car park is 300m down the road (on a track for the last 150m) just beyond Langton House. From the parking, walk south on a good path/track to Spyway Barn. Continue through two fields until the cliff-top path is reached. Head down the big hill (via stone steps) to the coast path, which lies above Dancing Ledge.

For Hedbury Quarry and Big Cove (left) - Once on the coast path, above Dancing Ledge, turn right (looking out) and follow it for 500m over a gentle hill. At a stile, drop down a ridge path on the left into a huge open quarry with a large cannon in its base. The quarry routes are on the wall on the left (looking out). To get to Hedbury Big Cove, drop down some rock steps to a sea-level ledge that leads left (looking out) into a cave.

For Big Cove (right) and Smokey Hole - See page 292.

Tides and Conditions

All routes are non-tidal, but keep away from Hedbury Big Cove and Smokey Hole in rough seas. The central routes in the quarry have a waterfall running down them in winter, but the rest are seepage free and climbable all year round. It can get very hot in summer. Hedbury Big Cove and Smokey Hole both face south, so get lots of sun. Both are relatively unaffected by seepage.

Access

All the routes at Hedbury Big Cove and Smokey Hole are restricted because of nesting birds. No climbing from 1st March to 31st July.

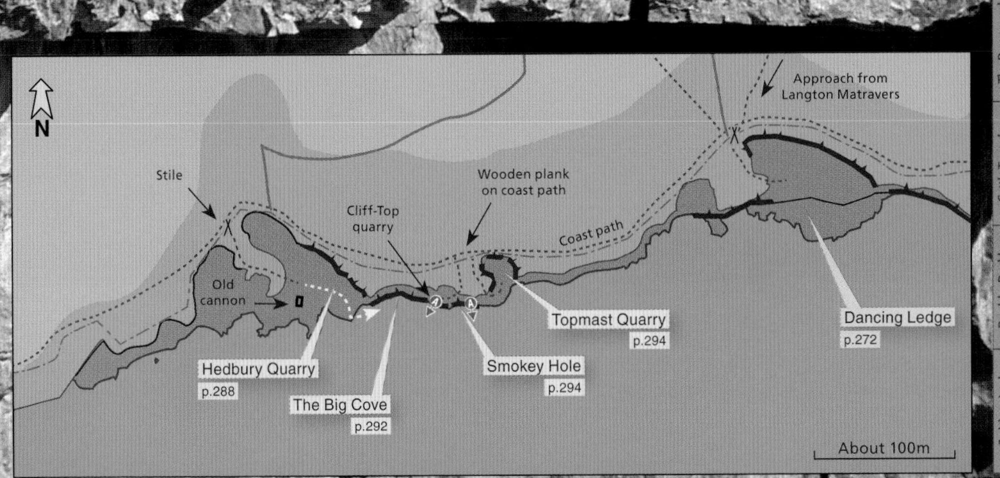

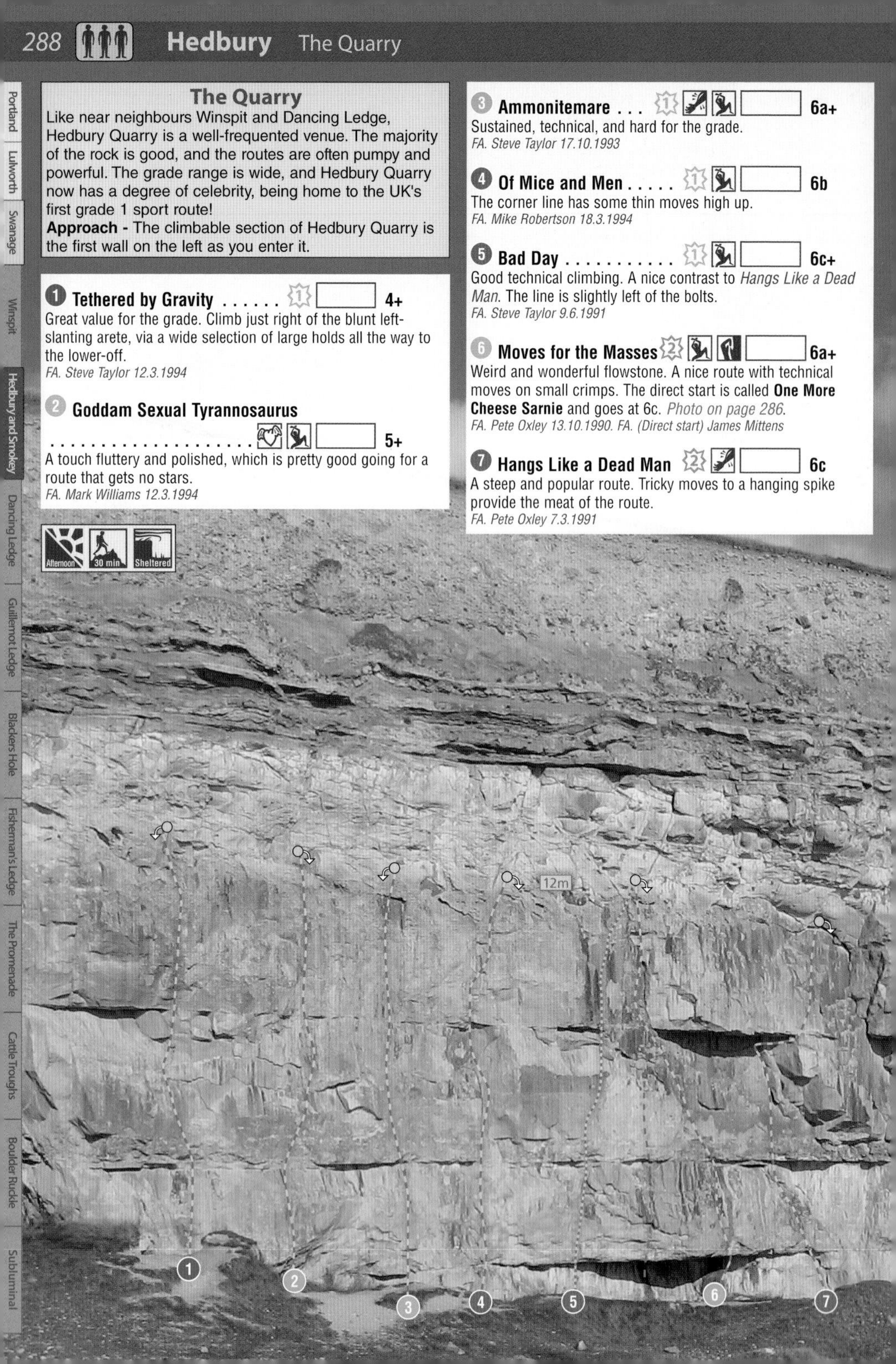

The Quarry

Like near neighbours Winspit and Dancing Ledge, Hedbury Quarry is a well-frequented venue. The majority of the rock is good, and the routes are often pumpy and powerful. The grade range is wide, and Hedbury Quarry now has a degree of celebrity, being home to the UK's first grade 1 sport route!

Approach - The climbable section of Hedbury Quarry is the first wall on the left as you enter it.

1 Tethered by Gravity . . . . . . 1 ☐ **4+**
Great value for the grade. Climb just right of the blunt left-slanting arete, via a wide selection of large holds all the way to the lower-off.
FA. Steve Taylor 12.3.1994

2 Goddam Sexual Tyrannosaurus . . . . ☐ **5+**
A touch fluttery and polished, which is pretty good going for a route that gets no stars.
FA. Mark Williams 12.3.1994

3 Ammonitemare . . . 1 ☐ **6a+**
Sustained, technical, and hard for the grade.
FA. Steve Taylor 17.10.1993

4 Of Mice and Men . . . . . 1 ☐ **6b**
The corner line has some thin moves high up.
FA. Mike Robertson 18.3.1994

5 Bad Day . . . . 1 ☐ **6c+**
Good technical climbing. A nice contrast to *Hangs Like a Dead Man*. The line is slightly left of the bolts.
FA. Steve Taylor 9.6.1991

6 Moves for the Masses 2 ☐ **6a+**
Weird and wonderful flowstone. A nice route with technical moves on small crimps. The direct start is called **One More Cheese Sarnie** and goes at 6c. *Photo on page 286.*
FA. Pete Oxley 13.10.1990. FA. (Direct start) James Mittens

7 Hangs Like a Dead Man 2 ☐ **6c**
A steep and popular route. Tricky moves to a hanging spike provide the meat of the route.
FA. Pete Oxley 7.3.1991

8 Under Starters Orders/Realm of Radical Cool . . . . 1 star **7a+**
The slight bulging groove left of *Jumping the Gun* to moves rightwards crossing *Jumping the Gun* to finish up rightwards.
FA. Pete Oxley 2004. FA. (RoRC) Mike Robertson 18.3.1994

9 Jumping the Gun . . . . . 2 stars **6b**
The big diagonal flake is a delight in good conditions but unpleasantly slick if at all damp or greasy. Not one for an unsure second as the start is tough and protection on the blunt end not good.
FA. Pete Oxley 7.3.1991

10 Mouth Breather . . . 1 star **7c**
Hard and painful undercutting through the roof. A good, tough Hedbury Quarry test-piece.
FA. Pete Oxley 9.5.1991

11 Sureshot. . . . . 2 stars **6c**
The big corner is often wet, but when dry is very good.
FA. Pete Oxley 8.10.1990

12 Sexy Beast . . . . 1 star **7a**
The striking leftward-slanting crack to the finish of *Sureshot*.
FA. Pete Oxley 2004

13 Alice In Pumpland . . . . 1 star **7a**
A short lived teaser taking the appealing steep crack over the roof.
FA. Pete Oxley 2004

14 Cinderella's Big Score . . . . 2 stars **7c**
Since the loss of a big spike, the route is now an archetypal fitness test with a fierce crux entering the lower groove and a technical bulge to finish. One of the best hard quarry routes at Swanage (when dry).
FA. Pete Oxley 6.5.1991

15 It Can't be Denied . 2 stars **7b**
A really good, short power endurance effort which joins *Cinderella's Big Score* near the top. A standing start off a boulder pile to reach the lip of the first roof makes it 7b; alternatively climb from the back of the roof from the ground at 7b+.
FA. Mike Robertson 22.10.1994. FA. (Direct) Pete Oxley 11.1994

16 Dry Time Climb . . . . **4+**
The black groove to the right of *It Can't be Denied*. Start part way up the grass slope and move left into the groove. The direct entry into the groove is 6a with a small pile of stones as an assist to start.
FA. Scott Titt 18.7.2010

15m
8 9 10 11 12 13 14 15 16
The Quarry - Right 20m

1 Bop Ceroc . . . . 1 6b+
A recently retro-bolted line with one hard sequence.
FA. Gordon Jenkin, Scott Titt, Tim Dunsby, Nigel Coe 20.4.1992

2 Glue Crux Clan 1 6c
A fine direct pitch with interesting moves all the way to the last bolt, but especially in the first 5m.
FA. Pete Oxley 26.9.1990

3 Produced by Fred Quimby . . . . 1 6b+
An easier diagonal start to *Glue Crux Clan* and once again features a tough finish.
FA. Mike Robertson 29.6.1991

4 Strange Devices 4
A new line that follows bolts right of *Produced by Fred Quimby* to moves right to finish at the lower-off of *Don's Long Gone.*
FA. c.2010

5 Don's Long Gone . . . . . 1 6b+
The roof crack. Good steep fun.
FA. Tim Dunsby 20.4.1992

6 Mindless Optimism . . . . . . 1 6b+
The short upper arete has some unusual moves utilising some stuck-on finger flakes on the very edge of the arete.
FA. Mike Robertson 29.6.1991

7 New Age, New Style . . . 1 5+
Slabby and with a distinct crux.
FA. Jim Titt 2004

8 Very Ordinary Route 1 1
Yes a grade 1! The left-hand line in the blocky groove.
FA. Jim Titt 2004

9 Another Contribution 1 2
The right-hand line in the blocky groove.
FA. Jim Titt 2004

10 Moral Flexibility 1 5
The next line on the right, with a good finish.
FA. Jim Titt 2004

11 Sea View 1 3
The far right line, closest to the cliff edge. A tough finish.
FA. Jim Titt 2004

Afternoon | 30 min | Sheltered

The Quarry - Right

A popular section of the quarry with some easier lines and a handful of tougher pitches on reasonable rock.
Approach - The climbs are on the wall to the right of the main section of cliff and closer to the sea.

16m
1 2 3 4 5 6 7 8 9 10 11
Hedbury Big Cove
Main Quarried Wall 20m

Bulging with Climbing Gear!

Many shops claim to be climbing specialists.
At Rock On we sell climbing/ mountaineering
equipment and books, and absolutely
NOTHING ELSE.
Now that's specialist.

Mile End Climbing Wall
Haverfield Road,
Bow, London,
E3 5BE.
Tel: 0208 981 5066

Craggy Island
9 Cobbett Park,
Slyfield Estate,
Guildford, GU1 1RU.
Tel: 01483 565635

Redpoint Climbing Centre
77 Cecil Street,
Birmingham,
B19 3ST.
Tel: 0121 359 8709

www.rockonclimbing.co.uk

Jess Garland on Tipping the Scales, 7a. The Cuttings

The Big Cove

This is a very intimidating cliff with huge, overhanging routes often on suspect rock. The routes are adventurous, and the lines that the climbs take are extremely impressive. This is a great place to hang out on a hot day; it is easy to get to from Hedbury Quarry, and has a secluded swimming spot in the cove.

Tides - All routes are non-tidal but keep away in rough seas when the place could be a bit too exciting!

Approach - Routes 1 to 4 are easily accessed from Hedbury Quarry by dropping down some ledges to gain a rock platform that stretches across to the sea cave.

Restriction - No climbing from 1st March to 31st July due to nesting birds.

1 Under the Sky, Above the Sea 1 E5 6b

An obvious challenge tackling the gymnastic roof crack above the centre of the platform. Start just right of a gap.

1) 6b, 18m. Follow a diagonal crack rightwards to a huge pedestal block. Power through the roof crack (small cams) and belay on a slab above.

2) 5a, 12m. Climb the easy groove and step right to a finish as for *Sheffield Uber Alles* (thread).

FA. Martin Crocker 27.8.1995

2 Sheffield Uber Alles . . . 2 E6 6b

A pump-out up a very overhanging wall giving sensational climbing. Start 8m right of the gap, at a short groove and thread at 5m. The first half is very steep (2 pegs) and leads to an open, left-facing groove. From halfway up this, a juggy line of left-trending flakes leads to the top.

FA. Pete Oxley 8.10.1990

Lots of sun
30 min

3 The Jesus Lizard 2 E6 6b

Another awesome climb which crosses even steeper ground than *Sheffield Uber Alles*. A big rack is needed. Start 3m right of *Sheffield Uber Alles* and climb a slight prow (2 pegs) into an open groove. Continue up the right-hand wall of a corner (peg) to a steep set of left-trending flakes parallel to *Sheffield Uber Alles*. Follow these to finish.

FA. Pete Oxley 24.3.1991

4 Once in the Jungle 2 E6 6b

A mercilessly steep and committing climbing. Start from the right-hand end of the access ledge.

1) 6b, 25m. Climb a short groove (thread) and from jugs swing right (thread) to a chert nose. Move up through bulging rock above to reach a rising handrail, which leads to a niche. Make powerful moves out right to a rest on a white projection. Traverse leftwards (peg) and move up and left over a bulge to a foothold stance in an open groove.

2) 6a, 25m. Climb a slab diagonally right, and continue to where it disappears between massive roofs (peg). Keep low until a bold swing right around a rib leads to a right-facing corner. Trend right up the corner to a broken finish. Belay and pull-out on a rope (pre-place from the fence posts).

FA. Martin Crocker, Mike Robertson 31.8.1996

Approach (routes 5 to 7) - *The Cliff-Top Quarry is situated 50m further on from the open Topmast Quarry, which in turn is 300m further on from Dancing Ledge. The abseil point is from the quarryman's thread in the right-hand (looking out) side of the cave. This leads to a ledge on the fault-line, just outside the cove and 15m above the sea.*

5 Nowhere to Run. 3 E6 6b

A fantastic voyage crossing the entire cove from right-to-left at roughly half height. Make sure you choose a long summer day since you will need plenty of time to complete the trip.

1) 6a, 27m. Traverse the break past a corner. Continue along a shelf in the fault-line until a drop down, and hand traverse, lead to a good stance on the lip of the cave. Peg and cam belay.

2) 6a, 15m. Traverse easily left until squeezed by steep rock, forcing a strenuous link (2 threads and a peg) to a superb stance on a perched slab in the centre of the cove. Peg, thread and nut belay.

3) 5c, 10m. Continue left with a tricky move to gain a slab. Follow this more easily to belay at its end. Nut and cam belay.

4) 6b, 28m. Climb down left to a thread jug then finger traverse left to a short groove. Ascend the groove and pass two 'leg-over' breaks leftwards, before making breath-taking moves left (peg) and over a bulge to gain an open groove. (Possible stance as on *Once in the Jungle*). Climb diagonally down for 5m then horizontally to a belay on a spectacular hanging arete. Thread and nut belay.

5) 5c, 20m. Follow the break leftwards past *Jesus Lizard* and the other routes, to a corner. Continue using a thin break to the arete and make a final haul up (thread) to a projecting belay on the edge of the cove. Scramble left into the quarry.

FA. Martin Crocker, Mike Robertson 25.8.1996

6 The Fabulous Professor Panic 2 E5 6a

An intimidating and exposed pitch with good gear. Ascend a deep crack on the left, but where that continues out right, pull left (thread) to a niche in a corner. Move up the corner then traverse left between roofs for 10m to a break in the roof (thread). Gain jugs above and a steep exit headwall. Belay to the fence.

FA. Martin Crocker, John Harwood 19.11.1995

7 Figurehead 1 E2 5b

Another exposed pitch but at a more friendly grade. Can be a bit dirty and dusty. Start as for *Professor Panic* by traversing left and up the deep crack. At its top, swing right to finish up the steep, hanging arete into the quarry.

FA. Crispin Waddy, Andy Ford 16.8.1985

Note - This is a bolt-free zone, although two routes were done here before it was declared as such. The bolts on these routes are still in place, however both routes have been done without clipping them. They may be removed sometime.

Portland Lulworth Swanage Winspit Hedbury and Smokey Dancing Ledge Guillemot Ledge Blackers Hole Fisherman's Ledge The Promenade Cattle Troughs Boulder Ruckle Subluminal

Smokey Hole

A huge leaning wall of good rock with routes to match those on the Lean Machine Wall in the Boulder Ruckle. It is hidden from view except for a sideways glimpse from Cliff-Top Quarry. This little quarry is the gearing-up point.

Approach - The Cliff-Top Quarry is situated 50m further on from Topmast Quarry, which in turn is 300m west from Dancing Ledge. The descent path is below some planks on the coast path that cross a dry stream bed. The four routes are gained by an abseil from a point 10m left (looking out) of the descent to the Cliff-Top Quarry. The abseil leads down *Diving for Pearls* to a solid bolt-belay just above the high water line (backed up by the abseil rope). It maybe necessary to swing-in on the abseil or place nuts on the way down to stay in contact with the rock. All four climbs can be gained from this belay.

Tides - The belay bolt is above the high tide mark but keep away in rough seas.

Note - This is a bolt-free zone but there is a useful bolt at the sea-level belay.

Restriction - No climbing 1st March to 31st July because of nesting birds.

1 Slow Dive . . . . . 1 star — **E6 6b**
A complicated and serious pitch on good rock. High in the grade. Trend left via a groove to a small ledge (runners on left). Boldly gain a layback edge above and step left (Rock 2). Make hard moves past a peg to a break then pull over a 2m roof (thread). Finish straight up the headwall (2 pegs) to a juggy break at the top (thread). Exit easily on the right.
FA. Pete Oxley 31.7.1991

2 Diving for Pearls . . 2 stars — **E6 6b**
The central line is very sustained, with a fairly bold start. From the bolt-belay, climb direct up a slight groove (RPs and peg) to arrive at the fault-line (large cam) Cross a tough bulge (peg) to a hand-ledge and then move left and back right to a jug (peg on right). Reach some large flakes (peg) and finish up slabby rock on the right.
FA. Pete Oxley, M.Ford 1.12.1990

3 Vapour Trail . . . Top 50 — **E7 6b**
The best route here. Start from a hanging belay, 5m right of the bolt-belay. Ascend the pillar (peg) past hard and serious moves to the fault-line (thread). Pass a peg to a spike then muscle left to a jug (peg). Move right to an alcove then climb through a series of bulges (peg and thread) to the headwall. More pumpy stuff leads to a solid top.
FA. Pete Oxley 13.12.1990

4 Rocket USA. . . . . 2 stars — **E6 6b**
Not as serious as *Vapour Trail* but steeper. It follows the groove system overlooking the zawn on the right. Start at a semi-hanging belay on the left arete of the zawn, 10m right of the bolt-belay. A right-facing corner leads past an overhang to reach the fault-line. Swing up left (thread) to a handrail then make some powerful moves right to jugs and runners. Continue up the groove, past a hole, and over a bulge to a jug (2 pegs). Finish up leftwards.
FA. Pete Oxley 31.7.1991

Topmast Quarry

This small quarry has a set of short and powerful lines that are very well sheltered from the elements.

Approach (see map on page 287) - Turn left before the planks and head down leftwards to the quarry.

5 Bar Code. . . . . 1 star — **7b**
The line on the left-hand side of the deep cave.
FA. Pete Oxley 2004

6 Bar King Mad . . . . 1 star — **7a+**
The central line links to the upper part of *Bar Code*.
FA. Pete Oxley 2004

7 Isobar. . . . . — **7a**
The right-hand neighbour, but finish by swinging left to the lower-off of *Bar Code/Bar King Mad*.
FA. Marti Hallett 2004

Norman Gilman on the intricate *Daylight Robbery* (6c) - *page 301* - Dancing Ledge Quarry. Photo: Dan Lane

	No star	1	2	3
Mod to S	-	-	-	-
HS to HVS	4	9	-	-
E1 to E3	12	18	10	-
E4 and up	4	16	9	4

Portland
Lulworth
Swanage
Winspit
Hedbury and Smokey
Dancing Ledge
Guillemot Ledge
Blackers Hole
Fisherman's Ledge
The Promenade
Cattle Troughs
Boulder Ruckle
Subluminal

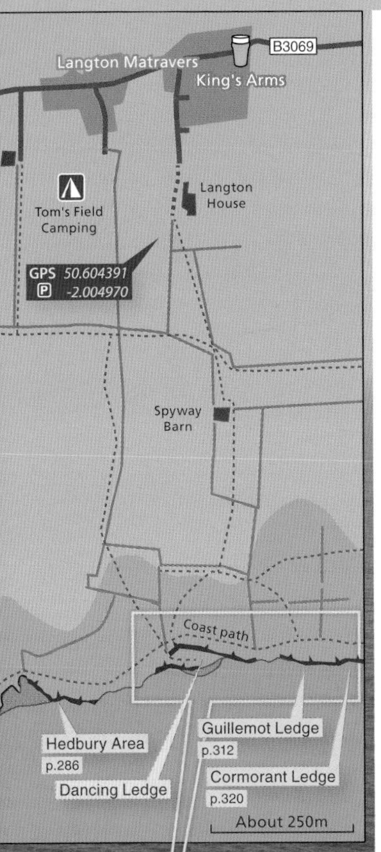

Dancing Ledge is one of the most important areas at Swanage for sport climbers. The quality and variety of routes is good and virtually all are fully bolted with solid staples. The quarry routes are mostly very solid and friendly outings, whilst the sea-level cave routes are intimidating, often committing and strenuous, though the rock and atmosphere are excellent. The picturesque setting makes this a great summer spot for picnicking and swimming.

Approach Also see map on page 266

Dancing Ledge is approached from Langton Matravers. From just outside Swanage town, turn off the A351 towards Langton Matravers. Once in the village, go past the post office and turn left into Durnford Drove. A free car park is 300m down the road (on a track for the last 150m) just beyond Langton House. From the parking, walk south on a good path/track to Spyway Barn. Continue through two fields until the cliff-top path is reached. Head down the big hill (via stone steps) towards Dancing Ledge which lies directly below the coast path. Steps lead down into the quarry.

Conditions

This can be considered a year-round venue that offers some of the most sheltered climbing in Dorset. The back wall of the quarry stays dry in light rain, and only suffers from seepage in mid-winter. The lower walls suffer more from drainage and dampness if it is humid or if the sun is not out. It can be unbearably hot here. Bring the sun-block and water.

Access

The National Trust has requested that no top-roping or abseiling takes place over the cliff-top.

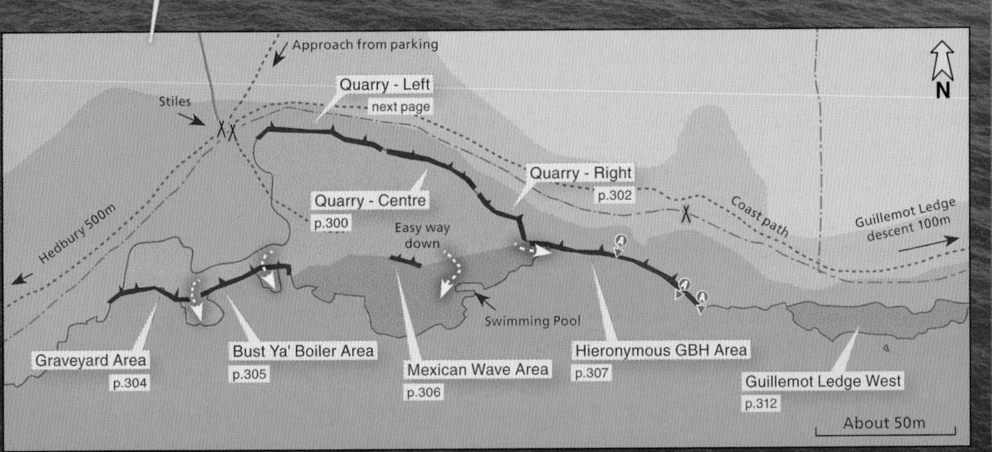

The Quarry - Left

The left side of The Quarry is split into two walls of compact, steep rock that see quite a lot of attention. The steepest area around *Sugar Ray* is extremely sheltered and may provide some dry rock during light rain, whilst to the right the less steep and easier lines dry very quickly. Some of the easier lines are a touch runout.
Approach - On entering the quarry, double back left towards the wall.

The first area of interest is the back wall of the quarry starting by the bricked-off cave. Two old routes, **For Your Arms Only** *and* **Volx with Friction***, which were on the wall above the cave, have been de-bolted because the cave has been declared unsafe by the National Trust.*

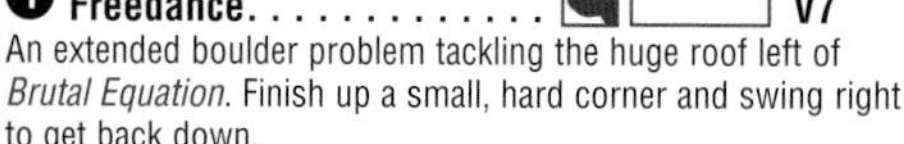

1 Freedance. V7
An extended boulder problem tackling the huge roof left of *Brutal Equation*. Finish up a small, hard corner and swing right to get back down.
FA. Pete Oxley 4.11.1999

2 A Brutal Equation. . 7a
Occasionally dusty. A boulder-problem start from the back of the low roof is also possible at V4.
FA. Pete Oxley 6.6.1991

3 Skinhead Clash . . . . . . 6b+
One of the steepest routes at this grade in the quarry.
FA. Mike Robertson 19.6.1991

4 Idiot Joy Showland. . . . 6c+
An excellent little pitch. Make a hard rockover above the low overhang, then climb direct up the leaning wall on incuts. The start in isolation is a good V4 boulder problem.
FA. Pete Oxley 19.5.1991

5 Sugar Ray. . . . . 7a+
A neat stamina pitch up the flowstone face that is deceptively tough. The start to gain a jug over the second roof is a V2 boulder problem.
FA. Pete Oxley 8.4.1992. The first route in the UK to have staple bolts.

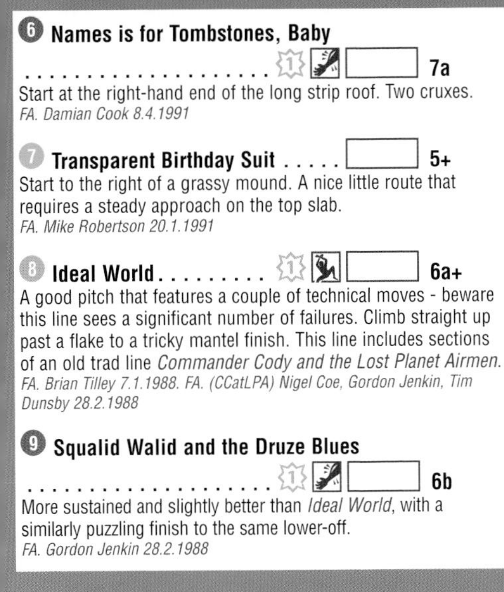

6 Names is for Tombstones, Baby 7a

Start at the right-hand end of the long strip roof. Two cruxes.
FA. Damian Cook 8.4.1991

7 Transparent Birthday Suit . . . . . 5+

Start to the right of a grassy mound. A nice little route that requires a steady approach on the top slab.
FA. Mike Robertson 20.1.1991

8 Ideal World . . . . 6a+

A good pitch that features a couple of technical moves - beware this line sees a significant number of failures. Climb straight up past a flake to a tricky mantel finish. This line includes sections of an old trad line *Commander Cody and the Lost Planet Airmen*.
FA. Brian Tilley 7.1.1988. FA. (CCatLPA) Nigel Coe, Gordon Jenkin, Tim Dunsby 28.2.1988

9 Squalid Walid and the Druze Blues 6b

More sustained and slightly better than *Ideal World*, with a similarly puzzling finish to the same lower-off.
FA. Gordon Jenkin 28.2.1988

10 Ozark Mountain Daredevils . 6a+

One of the better 6a+ climbs at Dancing Ledge.
FA. Tim Dunsby 28.2.1988

11 B4 Destruction. . . . . . . 6b+

A worthwhile line up the steep and crimpy wall.
FA. Marti Hallett 31.1.2007

12 Date with a Frog . . 6a

The interesting groove just left of the high roof is a good benchmark 6a.
FA. Mike Robertson 13.4.1991

13 Project . . . . 7c?

A reach-dependant move at the overhang.

14 Fear of a Black Planet . 7a

The bulges to a good finish on flowstone holds.
FA. Pete Oxley 26.9.1990

15 Today Forever . . . . 7a+

A lovely, balancy pitch up the black wall and roof that has a perplexing crux sequence.
FA. Pete Oxley 23.3.1991

Lots of sun | 25 min | Sheltered

Portland
Lulworth
Swanage
Winspit
Hedbury and Smokey
Dancing Ledge
Guillemot Ledge
Blackers Hole
Fisherman's Ledge
The Promenade
Cattle Troughs
Boulder Ruckle
Subluminal

Quarry - Centre

This section of the quarried wall is open, quick drying and offers up a good array of mid-grade lines. The routes are very popular and a little polished in places, however the quality of the rock and climbing make the routes worth tracking down. The wall is deceptively steep and along with the profusion of slopers means that the routes can feel quite tough and more of an undertaking than their modest height might suggest.

Approach - Turn left on entering the quarry and the centre of The Quarry wall is directly ahead.

1 Chicago Pipe Dreaming . . . 1 star **6a**
A popular climb starting just left of a well hole. Although the runout between the second and third bolt appears to be significant there are jugs all around.
FA. Jane Wylie 5.9.1993

2 Borra Ring . . . . 1 star **5+**
A neat route directly above the well hole.
FA. Jan Rostron 1.8.1996

3 Perpetual State of Confusion 1 star **6b+**
The wall to the ledge is the crux.
FA. Mike Robertson 26.8.1993

4 Hiccup **6c**
Climb the wall to an exit left at the roof.
FA. Mike Robertson 11.5.1991

5 Empty Promises. **6a**
A pleasing and quite technical wall climb.
FA. Steve Taylor 23.5.1994

6 All Fall Down . . . . 1 star **6a+**
A fun route up the centre of the white wall via some tempting, but at times blind, breaks.
FA. Steve Taylor 23.5.1990

7 Carol's Little Injection **6a**
A disjointed climb with a half-height rest.
FA. Mike Robertson 26.8.1993

8 Slopin' and Hopin' . . . . 2 star **6b+**
A fine pitch up a leaning wall on sloping holds. Best done on a cold crisp winter's day; then the slopers feel like jugs.
FA. Mike Robertson 26.8.1993

9 Mr Choo Choo . . . . 2 ☐ **7a**
Stylish moves up a shallow, leaning groove at the left-hand end of a low roof.
FA. Damian Cook 14.5.1991

10 Seven Year's Solitary 1 ☐ **7a+**
Make some hard starting moves over the big bulge.
FA. Pete Oxley 13.5.1990

11 Figure at the Base of a Crucifixtion
. . . . 1 ☐ **7b**
A hard test-piece with a tough crucifix move rightwards on to some poor slopers.
FA. Pete Oxley 28.10.2008

12 Disco's Out, Murder's In 1 ☐ **6c+**
A hard, bouldery start through the initial roof is not easy to read. Take care with some of the rock near the top of the pitch.
FA. Damian Cook 17.2.1991

13 Daylight Robbery . . . . . 2 ☐ **6c**
A varied and interesting route up the leftward-leaning groove. Keep an eye on the footholds or things can quickly feel a lot harder.
Photo on page 295.
FA. Steve Taylor 11.11.1990

14 Double or Quits . . . 2 ☐ **7a+**
The calcite wall just right of the bolt line. Further left is also an option at a slight increase in difficulty.
FA. Pete Oxley 7.1991

15 Rambling Moses Weetabix and the Secona Park Seven . . . . 2 ☐ **6b+**
The centre of the flat orange sheet is a fine route and one of the best of its grade in the quarry.
FA. Pete Oxley 27.6.1987

16 The Honey Monster . . . . ☐ **6c**
Climb up leftwards from the bottom corner of the orange face. Grabbing the lower-off is frowned upon.
FA. Steve Taylor 21.8.1993

17 The War of the Wardens . . . . . . ☐ **5+**
A well-loved and well-used line that has become polished.
FA. Mark Williams 17.5.1994

13m
8 9 10 11 12 13 14 15 16 17

The Quarry - Right

The overhang strewn right-hand side of the quarry has a number of excellent and powerful routes, a few of which offer the chance of climbing in light rain.

Approach - Turn left on entering the quarry and this is the seaward end of the quarried wall.

1 Negative Creep . . . . . . 1 star **6b+**
A butch pitch that ascends a shallow leftward-leaning flake and groove.
FA. Pete Oxley 8.4.1992

2 Slap, Bang on a Hang. **6c**
A very short route over a roof.
FA. Pete Oxley 22.12.1990

3 Corona Envelope 1 star **7b+**
The right-hand side of the scoop is very bouldery.
FA. Pete Oxley 22.12.1990

4 Corona Connection. 1 star **7b+**
A pumpy link-up from *Corona Envelope* into *Prophets of Rage*, via a short finger traverse.
FA. Pete Oxley 15.2.1996

Lots of sun | 25 min | Sheltered | Dry in the rain

5 Prophets of Rage . . 2 star **7b**
A tough but excellent route which has a right-hand variant on the mid-section also at 7b. The direct start is 7b+ ish.
FA. Pete Oxley 7.5.1990

6 Haunted by a Million Screams
. . . . 2 star **6c+**
An excellent jug haul up some steep ground and a slight groove through the overhangs. A Dancing Ledge classic.
FA. Pete Oxley 17.3.1988

7 The Ghost of Ian Curtis
. . . . 1 star **7c+**
Steep moves, knee-bars and a cornflake-sized crux hold.
FA. Pete Oxley 21.7.1992

8 Atrocity Exhibition . 1 star **7a+**
Some fierce moves up the blank groove.
FA. Pete Oxley 16.9.1990

9 The Wonders of Wallkraft 2 star **7a**
The steep crack-line. Use long slings on some of the bolts to prevent krabs bending over the roof edges.
FA. Pete Oxley 2.12.1990

The next line of bolts is an old project.

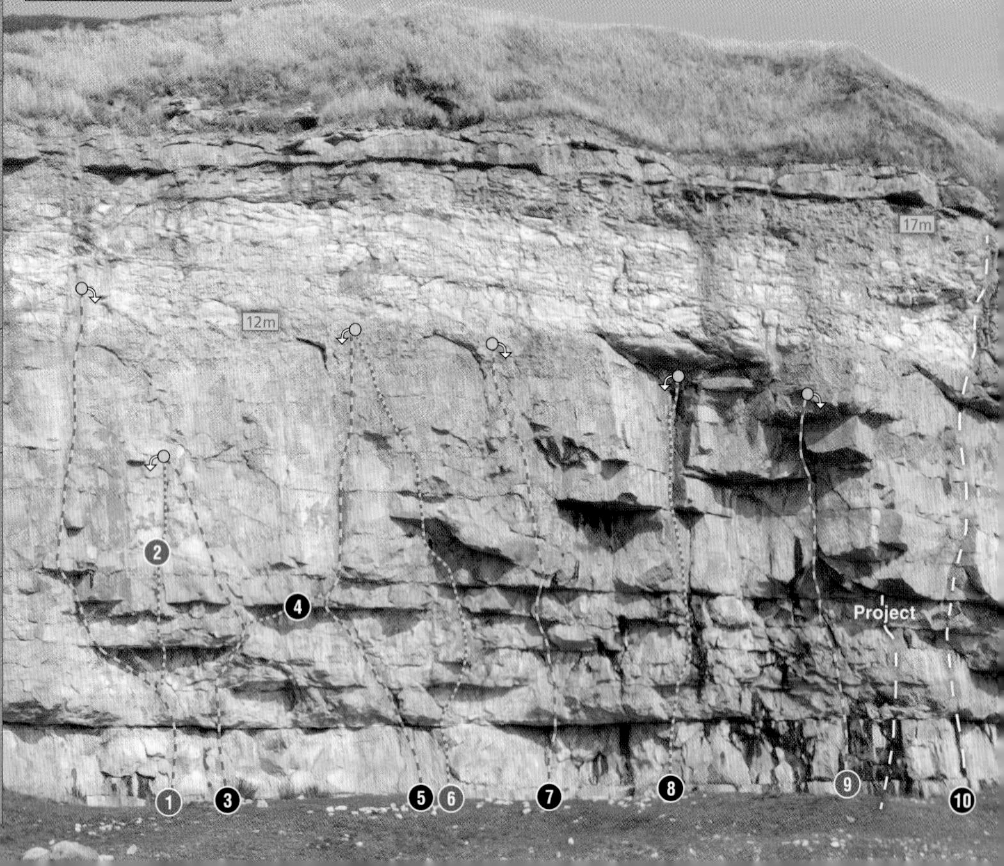

10 Fat Chance Hotel . . 2 stars **7b+**
A good test-piece with a distinct crux. Use a knee-bar at the roof. The extension is the longest and most pumpy route at Dancing Ledge Quarry - **Extremely Fat Chance Hotel 7b+**.
FA. Pete Oxley 20.4.1988

11 Day of the Lords **7a**
Use a long sling on the third bolt.
FA. Pete Oxley 13.5.1990

12 Minimum Maximum . . . 1 star **7b+**
Boulder out the bolt line exactly with no swinging in from the right at the start. High in the grade.
FA. Pete Oxley 4.11.2006

13 Ken Wilson's Last Stand 1 star **7a**
Steep climbing with a long reach to a flake.
FA. Pete Oxley 6.5.1991

14 With or Without You . . . . . . 1 star **6a+**
A pleasant technical pitch which climbs the grey wall to finish as for *Ken Wilson's Last Stand*.
FA. Jan Roston, Pete Oxley 29.10.2006

15 Cold Steal. **6b**
The staggered left-facing corner is awkward.
FA. Mike Ford 22.12.1990

16 John Craven's Willy Warmer 1 star **5+**
Subtle bridging makes this well worth doing. Probably the easiest route in the quarry - if you can get off the ground.
FA. Matt King 8.1992

17 Taylor-made Tracking Damage. . **6c+**
Now harder due to hold loss and extreme polish.
FA. Mike Ford 15.12.1990

18 Alienation. **7a**
A technical eliminate. Start up *A Sea Without Water* then break left immediately to climb the difficult blank groove - which becomes balancy - and ends in a steep finish over a capping bulge.
FA. Chris Weedon 7.2002

19 A Sea Without Water 1 star **6c**
A bouldery start gains some jugs from where increasingly technical and sustained moves lead with interest past a small roof to the belay shared with *Alienation*.
FA. Rob Godfray, C.Parker 2000

A line here has had the bolt holes drilled.

20 Option B . . . . **6c+**
The dusty shot-holed overhangs left of the arete.
FA. Damian Cook 6.9.1993

21 Eye am the Sky . . . 1 star **7a+**
Trend right around the arete and finish with a crux reach for the belay.
FA. Pete Oxley 11.4.1992

Graveyard Area

Hidden away under the west end of the quarry are two very eerie caves containing layers of tiered roofs. The rock is good with dramatic mega-steep pump-outs which are far more rewarding than the average clip-up in the quarry above, if you are up to them. This is also a great swimming and jumping spot for the hot summer days. Some of the routes here have been soloed, however most can not be considered as deep water solos.

Approach (route 3) - Requires a well-positioned abseil onto the start ledge, from bolts in blocks above.

Approach (routes 4 to 8) - Abseil to the ledge on the right (looking in) of the cave. Once acquainted with the area it is possible to solo down the abseil line at about VDiff.

Tides (all routes) - The cave is non-tidal but keep away in rough seas.

There are two isolated routes in the small quarry to the right of the approach path and above the Graveyard Area.

1 Birth, School, Work, Death V4
An extended boulder problem up the left side of the overhangs.
FA. Pete Oxley 16.9.1990

2 This Should Move Ya! 7a
The large rock stack just right of centre, with a jump for the lip.
FA. Pete Oxley 16.9.1990

Lots of sun
25 min
Abseil in

3 Corridors of Power . . . . 1 7a+
From the belay on the ledge at the end of pitch 1 of *Mariner's Graveyard,* swing out left and tackle the bulging wall.
FA. Mike Robertson 27.11.1993

4 Mariner's Graveyard. . . 3 7a+
A great traverse all the way across the narrow wall hanging above the zawn. Brilliant if you get good conditions.
1) 7a+, 25m. The long pumpy rail.
2) 6b+, 10m. Blast up the wall, or do *Corridors of Power.*
FA. Pete Oxley 19.10.1990

5 The Pump Will Tear Us Apart . . . . 2 7a+
Follow the monumental hand-traverse to halfway, then head upwards for the light. It has been soloed but is definitely not a deep water solo.
FA. Pete Oxley 7.10.1990

6 Lucretia, My Reflection 2 6c
S1. A cool route with great positions. Take a diagonal line through roofs onto a hanging slab.
FA. Pete Oxley 30.9.1990

7 F.Y.B. 1 6c
S1. Start as for *Lucretia, My Reflection* then move out right and up to the top.
FA. Mark Higgs 7.10.1995

8 Here Comes the Hezbollah . 6b+
S2. A direct line above the belay ledge, up a bulging wall.
FA. Mike Ford 22.2.1992

10m

Abseil in from ledge or descend via VDiff down-climb

Bust Ya' Boiler Area

This steep section of roofs gives some great traverse pitches which can be climbed at any tide state.
Approach - Up to mid-tide you can walk across from the lower ledges, by the Mexican Wave Area, to scramble across the seaward floor of the small zawn. At higher tides abseil from blocks or down-climb (a Diff).

The first five routes share a starting point and initial section. Start around the corner in the huge cave by a single-bolt-belay in the side wall. There are also two sets of bolt-belays on the top ledge for use with these routes.

9 Slave to the Cave. 3 7b

This big right-to-left traverse is poised above the lip of the cave, and is similar to *Mariner's Graveyard*. It is possible at any tide, and in rough seas for added adrenaline. Prusiks are advisable if you are uncertain.
1) 7b, 25m. The rail to a belay on small ledge.
2) 6c, 12m. Continue to a belay on the far side of the cave. Escape via an easy wall on the left or continue across *Mariner's Graveyard* if you aren't too pumped.
FA. Pete Oxley, Jon Biddle 3.2.1998

10 Hell's Darker Chambers . . . . 3 7c+

Extremely strenuous and spectacular roof-climbing. Belay on the top ledge. Reverse the route to retrieve the gear.
FA. Pete Oxley 3.5.1992

11 Legendary Shadows . . . . 2 7c+

A sensational addition which forges a radical path through a very unlikely set of roofs left of *Bust ya' Boiler*. Belay on the top ledge. Reverse the route to retrieve the gear.
FA. Pete Oxley 30.1.1998

12 Bust Ya' Boiler. . 2 7b+

Superb power-climbing. Pull over the roof and traverse along the hand rail for 3m, then climb direct through three roofs to a crux on the last lip. Belay on the top ledge.
FA. Pete Oxley 17.10.1993

13 Mucho Gusto! 1 7b

S2. A short, photogenic and very steep line across the roofs, passing a short crack. Belay on the top ledge (pre-place a sling over the edge to lower-off). If soloed, a spotter is needed for the first moves.
FA. Pete Oxley 23.1.1998

The next routes are in the small zawn crossed on the approach walk.

14 Hard Act to Follow 1 6c

Short, but very sweet, and far steeper than it looks.
FA. Pete Oxley 23.1.1998

15 Dancing Fool. 1 7a

A tough roof-problem on good rock.
FA. Pete Oxley 23.1.1998

16 Marianas Trench Coat. . . . . 1 6b+

Climb diagonally leftwards above the zawn.
FA. Pete Oxley 3.3.1991

17 Coprophobia . . . . 1 6b+

Start as for *Marianas Trench Coat* and then climb straight up to the top.
FA. Marti Hallett 18.5.2007

Portland
Lulworth
Swanage
Winspit
Hedbury and Smokey
Dancing Ledge
Guillemot Ledge
Blackers Hole
Fisherman's Ledge
The Promenade
Cattle Troughs
Boulder Ruckle
Subluminal

Mexican Wave Area

The clutch of climbs on the Mexican Wave offers a fine venue for muscle junkies who like a bit of air beneath their feet. There is a full grade spread from 7a to 7c+. The area is popular with non-climbers so watch your swearing.

Approach - From the main quarry, follow the easy way down to the lower sea-level ledges. The Mexican Wave Area is at the back of the non-tidal ledge in a small rectangular cave.

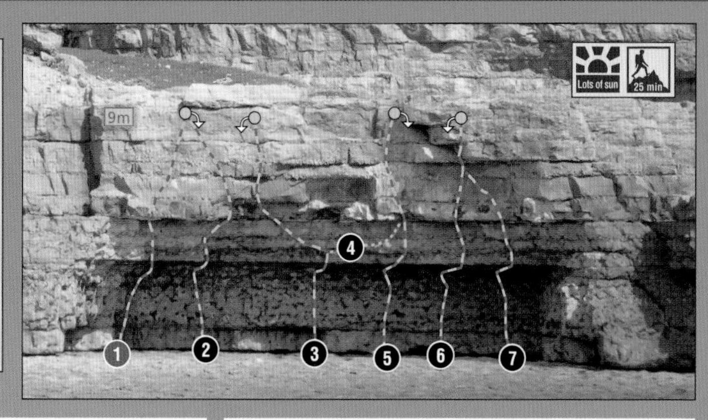

1 Whipping Boy 7a
Short and strenuous with a tough last move.
FA. Pete Oxley 8.2.1997

2 Mexican Wave . . . . 1 7a+
A fun jug-haul to a leg-over or heel-hook move near the top.
FA. Pete Oxley 22.3.1988

3 Armed and Dangerous . . . . 7b+
There is a large, dodgy block on the final roof so take great care.
FA. Pete Oxley 24.7.1987. Reclimbed - Mike Robertson 14.10.1996

4 A Short Story About Power 1 7b
Another route which has been cleaned up and now proves to be worthwhile.
FA. Pete Oxley 7.5.1990

5 Circus Beach . . . . . 1 7b+
Climb direct across the 3m roof to join *A Short Story About Power*. Superb acrobatic moves.
FA. Pete Oxley 1.2.1998

6 The Ringmaster . . . 2 7c
The longest and most involved arm-buster here, crossing a 7m roof stack. Top out or lower off the last bolt.
FA. Pete Oxley 26.1.1998

7 One Finger Trapeze . . . . 1 7c+
Desperate stuff over the first roof including a one-finger dyno. The second roof is also hard, taken direct past the bolt to join *The Ringmaster* at the third roof. Top out or lower off.
FA. Pete Oxley 28.2.1998

Approach (routes 8 to 12) - *Approach from the main quarry by traversing a thin ledge to belay bolts, or from the sea-level platform below, if the sea is calm.*

8 Now and Always . . . . . 2 6c+
An innocuous-looking route that is in reality quite steep, and has a tough crux. One of the better routes at Dancing Ledge.
FA. Pete Oxley 14.2.1998

9 Lover's Leap . . . . 1 7a+
From the bolt-belay 5m right of *Now and Always*, climb a series of bulges with a dynamic crux to a welded block.
FA. Pete Oxley 14.2.1998

The next 3 routes share a bolt-belay on the lowest ledge.

10 Born Again . . . . 2 6b+
An elegant groove-line. Worth seeking out - one of the best of the grade at Swanage. *Photo on page 273.*
FA. Pete Oxley 28.3.1998

11 Hieronymous GBH . . . . 2 6c+
An atmospheric climb tackling the wall above and right of the cave.
FA. Pete Oxley 15.12.1990

12 Dante's Inferno . . . 1 7a+
Climb to a hanging groove via a fierce, pocketed crack, then tackle the bulge and wall. Head left at the top.
FA. Pete Oxley 28.3.1998

13 Sea of Holes 1 6b
The line of this atmospheric route is completely hidden, just left of a big sea-cave. Start from a hanging belay, before some low roofs, directly below the line. Follow the line of big pockets and pull out on the abseil rope.
FA. Mark Williams 25.8.1994

14 Song to the Siren . . . . . 2 7a+
A great route which follows the huge pillar-face to some leaning tufas. Sadly, it is usually a drainage line in winter. To start, abseil to a hanging stance, with 2 bolts, just above the water line. Pull out on the abseil rope to finish.
FA. Pete Oxley 30.10.1991

15 White Rave . . . . 3 7a+
A hidden route up the pocketed wall and slab to the right of the green drainage streak. Abseil to a hanging stance, with 2 bolts, 4m above the water line. There is a belay in an alcove below the top. Pull out on the abseil rope.
FA. Mike Robertson 25.8.1993

16 Ten-K-Rig E4 6a
Start at the bolt-belay of *White Rave*. Traverse right to the base of a crack then follow the crack through a bulge to a niche. Take a continuation crack in the wall above (to the left of a spike) and bear leftwards to the belay niche of *White Rave*.
FA. Martin Crocker, Pete Finklaire 21.1.1996

Hieronymous GBH Area

The next set of routes is on the face to the east of the quarry. The first few can be reached from the quarry, though those further right require committing approaches by abseil. They offer rewarding outings in superb situations but see few ascents.

Approach (Routes 13 to 16) - The routes each require an abseil approach. The fence posts are located above and to the east (left - looking out) side of the quarry, just below the coast path. Take great care that you abseil in the correct place by using the detailed features on the photo. It may even help to have a friend back in the quarry to shout instructions. Take some Prusik loops in case things go wrong, and avoid in rough seas.

Tides - None of the routes are tidal (including those reached by abseil) however, keep away in rough seas.

Lots of sun | 25 min | Abseil in

Abseil from fence post
A
A
20m
16
15
14

Portland
Lulworth
Swanage
Winspit
Hedbury and Smokey
Dancing Ledge
Guillemot Ledge
Blackers Hole
Fisherman's Ledge
The Promenade
Cattle Troughs
Boulder Ruckle
Subluminal

Guillemot and Cormorant Ledge

Martin Kocsis finishing the difficult rightward traverse on pitch 2 of *Yellow Wall* (E1 5b) - *page 319* - Guillemot Ledge, after running both pitches together. Photo: Mike Hutton

	No star	1	2	3
Mod to S	-	1	1	-
HS to HVS	1	4	7	2
E1 to E3	1	7	5	3
E4 and up	-	9	4	1

Trevor MacAlonan and Phil Dawkins on the first pitch of the popular line of *Ledgend* (HS 4b) - *page 318* - at Guillemot Ledge.

Guillemot Ledge is a large and diverse area that is home to the highest section of cliff along the whole of the Swanage coastline. The big multi-pitch trad routes on the West Face are amongst the most challenging in the south, and almost all of them give tremendous climbing in wild and exposed situations. Across the two areas of the West and East Faces, there is a reasonable grade spread from HS to E6, but Guillemot Ledge should be recognised and treated as a serious cliff where experience of committing and difficult climbing is essential. The rock is usually sound, and the presence of a quarried top on the East Face will calm fears of potential loose finishes when topping-out. A number of the climbs in this area rely on fixed protection from pegs - these should be carefully inspected and backed-up where possible. Cormorant Ledge is an extensive section of crag with a small number of good low and mid-grade lines, including a couple of classics. It is possible to gain access to either end of the area by abseil, and a visit can be added on to a day at Guillemot East without the need to move gear or abseil station.

Approach Also see map on page 266

Guillemot and Cormorant Ledges are approached from Langton Matravers. From just outside Swanage, turn off the A351 towards Langton Matravers. Once in the village, go past the post office and turn left into Durnford Drove. Drive 300m to a free car park (on a track for the last 150m). From the parking, walk south on a good path/track to Spyway Barn. Continue through two fields until the cliff-top path is reached. Turn left and follow the path to just past the next stone wall. Drop diagonally right, down a steep hillside, to reach another stone wall. Follow the valley bottom to reach a rickety stile in the fence.

Guillemot Ledge - cross the stile to find the lower cliff-top quarry on the left. The main abseil and gearing-up ledge lies at the base of the deep gully on the right (looking out) of the stile. Steep rock steps lead down a gully to a small ledge. There is an abseil stake cemented into the ledge.

Cormorant Ledge - from the rickety stile, follow the fence line left to a wall. Continue along the fence line and cross the fence at the fourth wooden stile (about 150m from the wall). Drop down into a small quarry. An abseil stake is in the floor of the quarry 25m from where the path enters.

Tides and Conditions

The base of the cliffs at Guillemot Ledge are non-tidal, however the approach to Guillemot Ledge West is cut off for a short time around high water. The base of Cormorant Ledge can be accessed for 4 hours either side of low water in calm sea conditions. Both cliffs can get very hot.

Access

Some of the routes on Guillemot Ledge West cliff have restrictions as does the route *Cormorant Buttress West* due to nesting birds. **No climbing from March 1st to July 31st.**

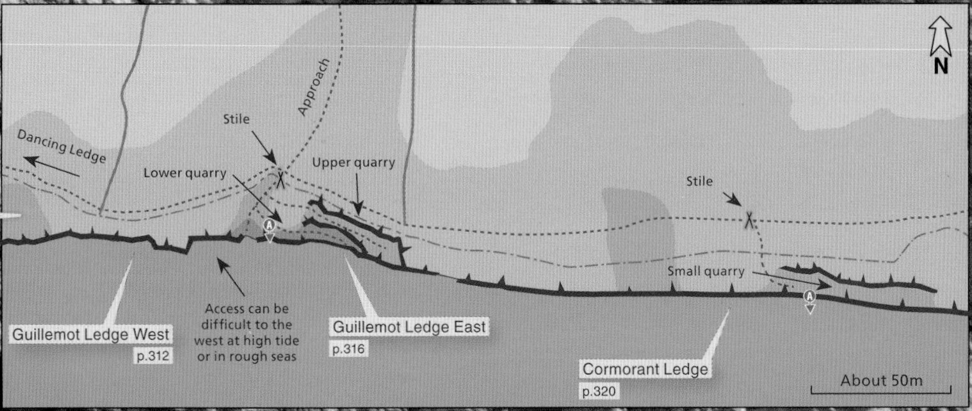

N
Approach
Dancing Ledge
Stile
Lower quarry
Upper quarry
Stile
Small quarry
Guillemot Ledge West
p.312
Access can be difficult to the west at high tide or in rough seas
Guillemot Ledge East
p.316
Cormorant Ledge
p.320
About 50m

West Face - Tudor Rose Area

This is one of the most impressive sections of cliff at Swanage, and also one of the most intimidating. The cliff's well-respected sheer white face and adjoining sea cave have an array of hard multi-pitch climbs that weave their way up and around its well-featured bulk. The rock is generally good, although the finishes need care.

Tides - The boulder beach below the face is non-tidal, but calm seas are needed to get to the face from below the abseil point.

Approach - From the abseil, boulder-hop rightwards (looking out) around the large Valkyrie Buttress for 100m to below the towering white face and the brooding sea cave.

Restriction - No climbing from 1st March to 31st July due to nesting birds.

1 Dougal the Great . . 2 E6 6c

A big route taking a huge diagonal line to finish at a high leaning chimney. Start near the right-hand side of the low cave roof.

1) 6c, 30m. Go direct over two roofs (peg and wedge) to join *Race for the Oasis*. Traverse 10m left under the roofs (thread and 3 old studs) to a peg. Power around the roof and continue up the steep wall (2 threads and a peg) to a small recessed ledge. Peg and nut belay. Watch out for rope drag.

2) 5c, 20m. Climb the bulging wall above from the left-hand side (thread) to a jutting ledge (thread). Finish diagonally leftwards, on shattered rock, to exit up the chimney.

FA. Pete Oxley, Jon Biddle 12.2.1988. Formerly an A3 aid route.

2 Race for the Oasis . . . . ☆1 **E5 6a**
A wandering outing but with good pitches. Start at the very right-hand side of the low roof.
1) 6a, 25m. Gain a chimney and traverse left for 8m (peg under the strip roof) then move up to a peg below another roof. Swing out to a bottomless small groove and climb its left-hand side via a fingery rib before trending right to join *Tudor Rose*. Hanging belay at the right-hand end of a narrow roof.
2) 5b, 10m. Move left for 3m and climb a shallow groove. At the top of this traverse left again, and down, to the recessed belay on *Dougal the Great*.
3) 5c, 30m. Head diagonally rightwards to the fault-line and swing along to a good ledge (peg). From the left-hand side reach a peg, step left and move boldly up the wall to good finishing holds. Exit right then left up an easy groove.
FA. Martin Crocker, Jim Robertson 27.11.1982

3 Sons of Pioneers . .  **E6 6b**
Very intricate route finding and another set of bold and interesting link-ups. Start as for *Race for the Oasis*.
1) 6a, 18m. A bold pitch. From the chimney, move left for 3m then drop out and around the roof (crucial medium cam) to follow a right-leading handrail for 3m. Cross the bulge above to the foot of a slight corner on *Tudor Rose*. Peg and nut belay.
2) 6b, 10m. From the top of the corner move up right to a horizontal break in a bulge (peg). Make wild moves over the bulge onto the lip. Multiple large to medium cam belay.
3) 6a, 20m. Just right of an ammonite, climb the bold wall to wires. Trend right to a square-cut niche below the headwall. Climb direct (peg) to the top ledge. Move right to an exit corner.
FA. Martin Crocker, Nigel Coe 28.8.1994

4 Tudor Rose . . . . Top 50 **E2 5b**
A remote route that takes a looping line across the hanging wall above the sea cave, then back across the capping white wall. Start at the right-hand end of the sea cave overhangs.
1) 5b, 42m. Move onto a ledge and pull up a short, steep wall to a slab on the right. Move steeply up left to a crack-line and jugs. Traverse left to a tiny short corner and rest ledge at its top. Move left to a short right-facing corner, then traverse left once again to the base of a corner/groove line. Climb this past the mid-height fault-line to a belay on ledges above.
2) 5b, 25m. From the right-hand end of the ledge move up a flake, and into a shallow groove on the left. Make a tricky move to a good horizontal crack above, then traverse rightwards to a narrow ledge. Move right along the ledge to a blocky corner and climb this with care to the top. Belay on fence posts.
FA. Richard Crewe, P.Charman 5.5.1974

5 Facedancin' . . . . . Top 50 **E3 6a**
Stupendous wall climbing up the best line on the face. The climbing is hard, and high in the grade, but the gear is very good on the hardest sections. Start as for *Tudor Rose* at the right-hand end of the sea cave overhangs.
1) 6a, 25m. Follow *Tudor Rose* to the good, small rest ledge on its traverse and then climb up to a narrow overhang. Move up to the groove above and make a very hard move to enter it and exit right to a good hold. Climb the short wall above to the fault-line and a hanging belay on nuts, cams and a thread.
2) 6a, 25m. From the fault-line, move up right for 5m and then step left to a foot-ledge. Move up to the base of the white wall, then climb thin breaks and flakes, past twin pegs, to another peg, and a final, long move to a good hold just below a long ledge. Stand on the ledge, and traverse rightwards to a blocky corner. Climb this with care to the top. Belay on fence posts.
FA. Martin Crocker, Jim Robertson 8.1.1983

6 Oceanid . . . . ☆2 **E2 5b**
The dominating central crack-line. Steep, strenuous and intimidating and with some loose rock on pitch two. Start 5m right of *Tudor Rose* on a boulder pile.
1) 5a, 20m. From the top of the boulders, move out left across a slab to the base of a broken crack-line. Follow the crack-line, past a niche, and move right to a thread belay on a ledge on the slab.
2) 5b, 30m. Climb up left to the fault-line and gain the wall passing a bulge on the left. Follow a steep groove direct, stepping left at its top. Pass a big wedged-in block to gain the exit corner. A couple of large cams are useful on this pitch.
FA. Pat Littlejohn, K.Goodman 5.8.1972

7 Fly Crazy But Free .  **E5 6b**
Technical and pumpy climbing blasting up the white face just right of *Oceanid* pitch 2. An airily-positioned top pitch that is high in the grade.
1) 5a, 20m. As for *Oceanid*.
2) 6b, 30m. Climb diagonally left then back right, above an overhang, to a small ledge (peg). Swing left and pass a niche to ascend twin cracks above. A hard move on the left gains a good horizontal break. Continue up the technical, leaning headwall (2 pegs) to the top.
FA. Martin Crocker, D.Light 26.9.1983

8 Warlord . . . . Top 50 **E4 6a**
A great top pitch that heads up the leaning white headwall at its highest point. Start on the huge boulders right of the sea cave.
1) 5a, 20m. As for *Oceanid*.
2) 6a, 24m. Move diagonally left, then back rightwards above an overhang to a small ledge and a peg. Follow the tapering crack above, past a large, wedged cornflake, to fingery moves that gain the final, slightly broken wall. Belay on fence posts. The crack has lots of pegs insitu, however some of them have very narrow eyes, so some narrow-nosed karabiners will be found useful to clip them.
FAA. Brian Snell, Keith Knight 21.2.1976
FFA. Steve Monks, Steve Findlay 28.11.1981

9 Vikings . . . . ☆2 **E4 6a**
Three fine pitches right of *Warlord*. Technical and sustained with small wires essential. Start 20m right of *Oceanid* at two converging cracks. The finish to the top pitch needs care.
1) 5a, 22m. Climb halfway up the right-hand crack, then step left into a scoop. Ascend a short corner to a slab, then traverse along until is possible to reach the higher slab (peg). Continue left to the belay on *Oceanid*. Friable rock.
2) 5c, 10m. Trend right to the roof (large cam) then move over this. Undercut right along the lip then move up to belay (peg) below a short corner in the next roof.
3) 6a, 20m. Gain a corner and pull over the roof onto a narrow ledge (peg). Climb the wall just right (bold) to a rest in a flake-crack, then tackle the steep white wall on the left.
FA. Martin Crocker, Jim Robertson 21.8.1983

West Face - Right

The first section of Guillemot West is close to the base of the abseil approach and rises dramatically to the summit of Valkyrie Buttress. There is a number of relatively popular routes and some harder ones - all have their fair share of poor rock and unstable finishes.

Tides - The boulder beach below the face is non-tidal but calm seas are need to get to the face from below the abseil point.

Approach - From the base of the approach abseil, boulder-hop right (looking out).

Restriction (routes 1 to 5) - *No climbing from 1st March to 31st July due to nesting birds.*

1 Caiaphas **E3 5c**

An adventurous route with a good bottom pitch. Start at a short corner 3m right of a huge pillar that leans against the cliff.

1) 5c, 25m. Climb the corner, then trend right to reach a white sheet. Traverse 3m left and climb a thin crack to pass a strip-roof at the fault-line. Follow a long diagonal flake rightwards to a stance after 5m.

2) 5a, 15m. Continue along a flake to finish up a loose corner.

FA. George Hounsome, Scott Titt 22.9.1979

2 Deaf Mosaic . . . 1 **E6 6c**
The blank white face right of *Caiaphas*.
1) 6c, 25m. Climb direct as for *Caiaphas* to a horizontal break beneath the wall. Mono-doigt holes lead up the centre (2 pegs) to the main break. A big undercut gains the shield above. From here, proceed more easily to belay on *Caiaphas*.
2) 5a, 15m. As for *Caiaphas*.
FA. Martin Crocker, Nigel Coe 28.8.1994

3 Valkyrie . . . . **VS 4b**
The huge corner is a major feature of the cliff but has a very loose top pitch. Not recommended. Start beneath the corner.
1) 4b, 20m. Follow the corner to a belay at the fault-line.
2) -, 11m. Traverse right and belay on the face of the buttress.
3) 4b, 20m. Move up left to a ledge at 7m and then traverse left to the arete. Move up the arete until a line leads left again to a loose and serious finish.
FA. D.Hadlum, G.Smith, P.Grainger, J.Midgley, A.Webster 11.4.1966

4 Be-Bop-Deluxe 1 **E2 5b**
The right wall of *Valkyrie's* first pitch, has open face climbing on mostly solid rock. The upper pitch is looser and airy but easy.
1) 5b, 25m. Climb a crack in a bulge to a horizontal break and traverse right to below a yellow face. Climb the bold wall past a peg to moves slightly rightward that gain a groove. Follow the groove to a belay.
2) 4c, 17m. Move left and follow a small corner to where moves right, around the arete, gain a slab. Climb the slab to the top.
P.Jarvis, Chris Flewitt 6.12.1983

5 Valkyrie Buttress Direct
. . . . 2 **HVS 5a**
A nice route with a fairly sound finish. Start at a steep wall below a big roof in the middle of the seaward face of Valkyrie Buttress.
1) 5a, 22m. Climb up the steep wall - towards the left side of the buttress - and pass the roof on its left. Bold climbing follows, up and slightly right, to a good belay ledge.
2) 4c, 18m. From the middle of the ledge, climb up leftwards to an overhung ledge and mantelshelf onto it. Continue straight up a good crack to a reasonable finish and belay on the fence posts.
FA. R.White, B.Wood 21.5.1967

6 Zo Zo . . . . 1 **VS 4b**
An impressive climb for the grade that has an excellent first pitch, but finishes on some poor rock, requiring care.
1) 4b, 25m. The large corner needs some big gear. At the fault-line move left to a large ledge and belay.
2) 4a, 17m. The wall and groove above and to the right of the corner is steady but has some loose blocks.

7 No Mistaking. 2 **E3 5c**
Climb straight up black pocketed rock, past an angular chockstone in a horizontal break to a thread. Pass the thread on the left over a bulge and move up into small corner. Step out left and continue boldly up the wall to a good horizontal break. Climb right then left between the breaks to gain a small sloping niche below the headwall. Pull up the headwall on good holds to finish past a big thread and broken ledge. Traverse off right (or leave a rope over loose ground) belay on fence post.
FA. Marti Hallett, Sam Ferguson 15.3.2011

8 Mistaken Identity. . . . . 2 **VS 4c**
A nice little route on good rock and with a relatively solid finish. Climb up the left side of the black overhang and continue up the vertical, cracked wall with interest to finish on a good ledge on the right.
FA. Pete Finklaire, B.Etheridge 1976

9 True Identity . . . . 2 **HVS 5a**
A good but forgotten route. Start as for *Mistaken Identity*. Follow *Mistaken Identity* until just passed the roof. Move right past a big thread and climb up to sloping ledges. Use a crack to pass an overlap on its right and then climb straight up the slabby wall to a shallow scooped headwall. Finish directly up the steep headwall to a sound finish.
FA. Pete Finclaire, N.Withers 9.10.1994

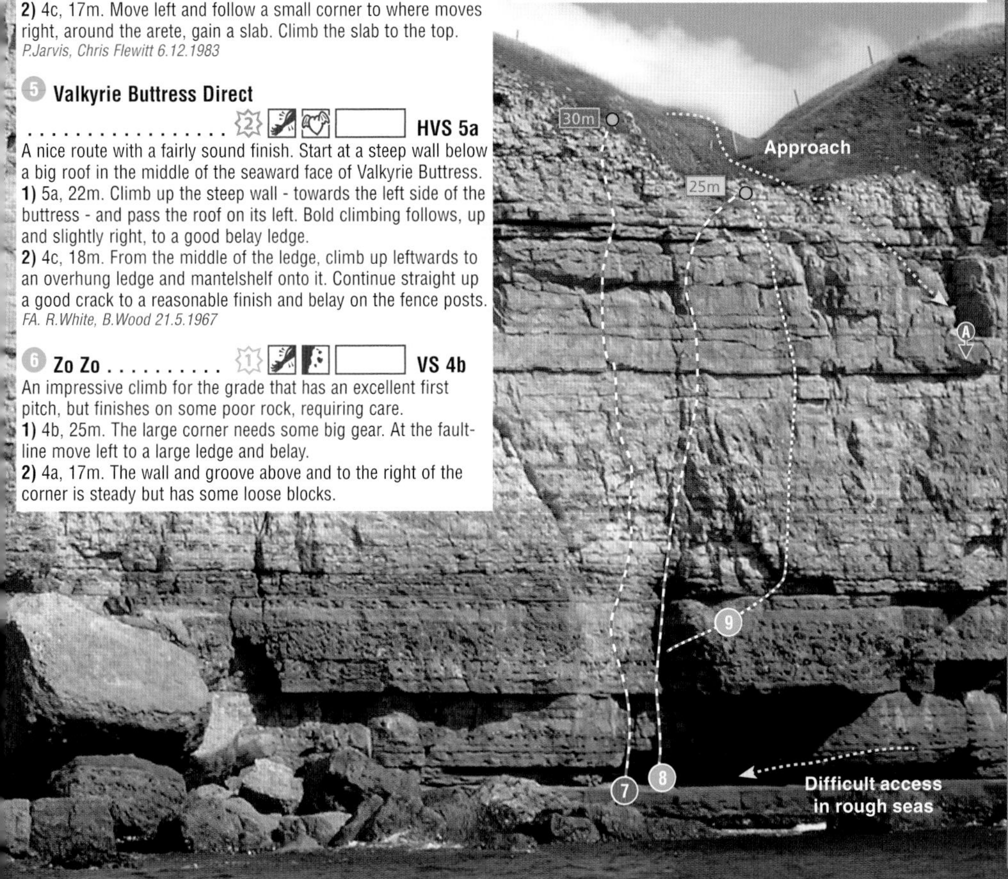

30m
Approach
25m
A
9
7
8
Difficult access in rough seas

Portland
Lulworth
Swanage
Winspit
Hedbury and Smokey
Dancing Ledge
Guillemot Ledge
Blackers Hole
Fisherman's Ledge
The Promenade
Cattle Troughs
Boulder Ruckle
Subluminal

1 Outside The Wire **E1 5b**

The line of the abseil. Climb up to twin cracks via the arete or the chimney (easier). Pull up into the cracks with difficulty, and finish up the friable corner.

FA. Marti Hallett, Steve Taylor, Mick Cooke 6.3.2011

2 Exit Chimney Two - The Sequel 1 **E4 6a**

Climb past a roof crack, then make bold moves up flakes to a mid-height roof (thread). Follow twin leaning cracks to the fault-line then climb direct on big holds to the top.

FA. Pete Oxley, J.Williams 5.12.1987

3 Sapphire 2 **E1 5b**

A much-attempted route that features a spectacular and powerful top pitch. Start beneath a huge rectangular depression that meets the overhangs at the fault-line.

1) 4b, 18m. From right of the low overhangs, move leftwards above them and climb the steady wall, with little in the way of gear, to a thread and nut belay in the rectangular depression.

2) 5b, 16m. Gain the fault-line beneath the overhang and move left to an arete (large cam useful). Pull over the roof (2 pegs) to reach the next roofs. Traverse rightwards underneath these and finish up a crack, past a bulge to the top.

FA. George Smith, Kenny Winkworth 3.4.1972

4 The Spook . . . . Top 50 **E1 5b**

A sustained, varied climb and one of the best E1s at Swanage. Start under a prominent, smooth-sided corner.

Photo on page 265.

1) 5a, 18m. Climb a corner to the roof, and swing right to beneath the smooth-sided corner. Climb the fine corner to the mid-height break and belay on a ledge to the right.

2) 5b, 15m. Step right onto the wall and climb easily, but boldly up to the chert band and roof - old hidden peg. Arrange good gear, then step left and climb the overhang to finish up the bold wall.

FA. Richard Crewe, P.Sharman 31.3.1974

5 Toiler on the Sea . . 1 **E5 6b**

Good, clean climbing. Start at the arete right of *The Spook*.

1) 6b, 18m. Serious. Follow the arete to the roof (peg and threads), then pull around past a niche (peg) to safer ground. Pass another peg to finish up a shallow groove to the fault-line. Belay as for *August Angie*.

2) 5b, 15m. Ascend diagonally left (peg) to reach a protruding ledge. Gain a nose and continue to the top.

FA. Pete Oxley, G.Anstey 6.6.1987

Lots of sun | 25 min | Multi-pitch | Abseil in

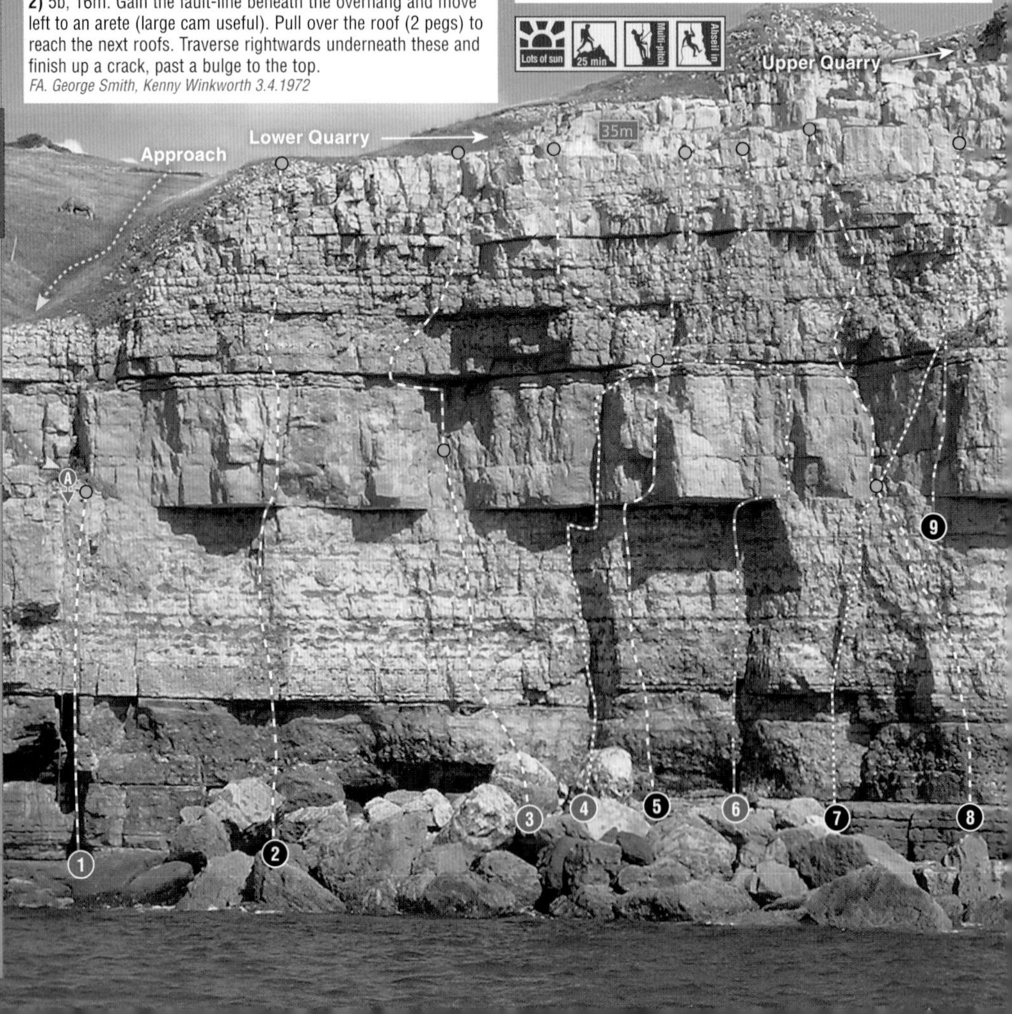

6 August Angie .... 1 star E1 5b
Sustained, nervy climbing. Start at the groove right of the arete.
1) 5b, 25m. Take the groove to the roof then traverse right to clear it. Follow a corner to the fault-line and take a stance 3m to the left. Take care with rope drag.
2) 5a, 12m. Climb the wall on the right to a roof. Swing right around an arete then climb through the weakness in the overhangs, to the top.
FA. Brian Snell, M.Colson. FFA. Richard Crewe 28.10.1973

7 Necromancy ..... 1 star E4 5c
Technical and bold wall climbing up the committing face 5m right of *August Angie*. Move up and pass a break in the roof. Trend right to a (peg) at a flake then run it out direct to a ledge (possible belay). Finish heading rightwards across a short blank wall to a clean-cut exit. Low in the grade.
FA. Pete Oxley 11.8.1990

8 The Heat .... 1 star E4 5c
A big pitch with quality moves but little gear. Start beneath a large roof at 15m.
1) 5c, 15m. A short wall leads to a ledge (peg). Move left (peg) then climb direct on blind edges to a ledge. Serious.
2) 5b, 20m. Follow a corner and trend right then left past a fault-line to a nose (peg). Traverse left to a V-shaped overhang.
FA. Brian Snell, W.Lyons 7.4.1974. FFA. George Hounsome, G.De Lacy

East Face - Tensor II Area

This is a justifiably popular section of cliff. With its easy access, good lower to mid-grade routes and clean-cut quarried finishes, it is a perfect place to sample the delights that Swanage has to offer. The routes are a bit shorter than on the neighbouring West Face, and many have a friendly feel to them.
Tides - All the climbs are non-tidal and are possible even during moderately rough seas because of the shelter afforded by the boulders along the base.
Approach - The Tensor II Area is situated to the left of the approach abseil (looking out), and the routes are reached along the boulders below the wall.
Belays - The belays are on wires in the back wall of the quarry. There are also some blocks and a few stakes.

9 The Big Heat ..... 2 star E4 6a
A logical direct version of *The Heat*. Climb the serious lower wall then press on (2 pegs) up the face left of the arete, in a good position. Finish up the final wall as for *Necromancy*.
FA. Pete Oxley, J.Williams 6.6.1987

10 Mañana .... 1 star HVS 5a
A worthwhile and slightly bold outing with good rock on the hardest climbing. Start below the large overhang.
Climb the unprotected wall below the capping overhang to a welcome peg runner. Continue up to a groove to the right of the roof, crux, and seek the most stable line up the final wall to the top.
FA. J.S.Cleare, A.G.Smythe (1pt) 5.5.1963

11 Funeral Pyre ...  E5 5c
Unprotected where it matters. The line follows the wall 8m right of *The Heat*, and 5m left of the corner of *Tensor II*.
1) 5c, 15m. Ascend right then left to foot-ledges. Go for it up the blank scoop to a good stance as for *Tensor II*.
2) 5a, 15m. Finish as for *Tensor II*.
FA. Pete Oxley, Steve Williams 6.5.1987

12 Tensor II ....  Top 50 VS 5a
One of the very best VSs at Swanage. Both technical and sustained, but furnished with good protection. Start at a raised ledge below a corner next to a massive boulder.
1) 4c, 20m. Climb the corner until level with an overhang on the left. Traverse beneath this and pull up the wall on good holds to a good ledge and huge flake belay.
2) 5a, 15m. Stand on the flake, then either climb with difficulty direct to the next wide break, or at about the same difficulty, step left and move up to the break. Climb past the overhang above on its left, and finish up the corner above.
FA. Brian Snell, W.Lyons 8.12.1973

13 Strapiombo .... 2 star  HVS 5b
A direct corner and crack climb starting as for *Tensor II*. Follow a corner past a spike and peg to pass a big roof on the right. A chimney allows access to the fault-line and a huge ledge (possible belay). Climb the continuation crack to the top. A helmet jam has been used to great effect by more than one team on this route.
FA. A.Webster, D.Hadlum 27.3.1967

Portland Lulworth Swanage Winspit Hedbury and Smokey Dancing Ledge Guillemot Ledge Blackers Hole Fisherman's Ledge The Promenade Cattle Troughs Boulder Ruckle Subluminal

East Face - Ledgend Direct Area

Running on from the Tensor II Area is a similar section of the East Face that also has a good number of mid-grade lines that see plenty of traffic and are blessed with quarried finishes.

Restriction (Route 11) - No climbing from 1st March to 31st July due to nesting birds.

1 Helen's Return 1 E2 5b

Nice climbing, however the gear is a bit fiddly on the lower wall. Start below the wall right of the corner of *Tensor II*. Make thin moves straight up until level with the roof of *Strapiombo*, arrange good gear, then move right on small holds to join the arete above the lower crack of *Ledgend*. Climb the arete to the ledge above. From here, climb straight to the top on good holds past a small overlap.

FA. D.Coley 5.1987

2 Ledgend . . . . 1 HS 4b

A popular but wandering outing. Start below a big flake-crack in a steep wall 60m east of the abseil (right - looking in).

Photo on page 310.

1) 4b, 25m. A crack leads up rightwards to gain a flake. Follow this to its top. Climb a corner on the right to the fault-line, then traverse right to belay on a ledge.

2) 4a, 15m. Step right off the ledge then move up for 5m. Traverse left to reach the quarry. Care required with loose flakes.

FA. D.Burgess, J.Allen, R.Colledge 11.4.1966

3 Graffiti Bombers of New York City 1 E2 5c

Start below a large thread. Boulder up to the thread and climb straight over a bulge to a blunt arete. Climb the arete, passing a ledge on the left. Continue up the wall and small groove past another thread to a good ledge (optional stance). Follow the shallow groove and easy stepped wall to finish.

FA. Pete Oxley, Richard Newey 20.12.1986

4 Ledgend Direct . . . . . . 2 HVS 5a

A popular route up a gear-packed corner 9m right of *Ledgend* that gives exhausting climbing. It has taken a lot of scalps over the years and now fully merits its HVS grade.

1) 5a, 18m. Climb a wall to gain the corner, which leads steeply to a ledge on the left, as for *Ledgend*.

2) 4a, 15m. As for *Ledgend* pitch two.

FA. P.Neame, A.Monnery 12.2.1967

5 Vampire Direct 1 E1 5b

A well-positioned pitch. Start just right of *Ledgend Direct*. Climb directly up the leaning arete to meet a crack in the arete. Follow this to the fault-line. Surmount the overhang using an ammonite hold, and continue straight to the top.

FA. Tim Dunsby, Nigel Coe 27.6.1982 Direct S.Lewis, J.Bentley 1982

6 Batt Crack. . . . . 2 VS 4c

A popular route. Start just right of *Ledgend Direct*.

1) 4c, 18m. Climb a short wall to a ledge, then move up rightwards to enter and follow a corner to an overhang. Go right to a ledge and belay.

2) 4a, 18m. Ascend a groove and flakes, then move right and up to a ledge. Pass another ledge and a small roof on the left.

FA. D.Hadlum, G.Reynolds 25.3.1967

7 Friends from the Deep . 2 E3 5c

An eliminate with an absorbing first pitch. Start just right of a chimney in an arete, 8m right of *Ledgend Direct*.

1) 5c, 25m. Gain a slot (thread) then pull out right to cross a bulge. Continue to a rest on *Yellow Wall*. Traverse left to a flake then follow the sustained crack (thread) to the fault-line. Belay on the left in the corner as for *Batt Crack*.

2) 4c, 15m. Move 2m right then finish rightwards through a V-shaped roof.

FA. Tim Dunsby, Nigel Coe 6.5.1987

8 Yellow Belly Wall. . 1 E5 6b

A fine, hard eliminate on *Yellow Wall*. Follow a shallow groove, left of the normal start, past a bulge. Continue more easily to the downward-pointing spike on *Yellow Wall*. Step right, boldly climb the wall to the fault-line, then pass the roof above (peg) to gain an undercut block on *Yellow Wall*. Finish direct, exiting up a white wall right of a broken groove.

FA. Martin Crocker, Nigel Coe 5.4.1997

9 Yellow Wall. E1 5b

Fine wall climbing on the initial pitch, rounded off by a challenging top pitch. Start just left of a big groove/corner.
Photo on pages 39 and 308.
1) 5b, 20m. Climb the wall, trending left to a down-pointing spike. Move left and up past a bulge (peg) into a shallow groove. Continue to a belay on the left at the fault-line.
2) 5b, 20m. Trend steeply rightwards under blocks, then over to a small ledge. Move on and rightwards, around an arete, into a corner with a large flake. Finish up this, exiting left.
FA. Richard Crewe, A.Wilde, P.Crewe 3.4.1972

10 Robud . . . . 1 HVS 5a

A good, but indirect line. Start below a big groove/corner.
1) 5a, 20m. Climb the corner/groove and move to the right-hand side of the overhang at its top. Climb the groove above to a small stance and belay.
2) 4c, 20m. Take a long diagonal line leftwards to the top.
FA. R.Wood, B.Metcalfe 26.3.1967

Restriction (route 11) - *No climbing from 1st March to 31st July due to nesting birds.*

11 Younger Days 1 E3 6a

The prominent arete 8m right of *Yellow Wall*. Start 3m right of the arete and climb easily until the arete steepens. Layback its right-hand side (thread) to the fault-line. Finish direct up the easy wall above.
FA. Matt Saunders 6.6.1987

Portland
Lulworth
Swanage
Winspit
Hedbury and Smokey
Dancing Ledge
Guillemot Ledge
Blackers Hole
Fisherman's Ledge
The Promenade
Cattle Troughs
Boulder Ruckle
Subluminal

Cormorant Ledge

The remote and isolated Cormorant Ledge has a limited number of worthwhile routes. The atmosphere and quality of the climbs are well worth the effort of the approach and can easily be combined with a visit to the close by Guillemot Ledge.
Tides - Low-to-mid tide and calm seas are required.
Approach - The routes are reached by abseiling in at either end and then by scrambling along the boulders below the wall.

Restriction (route 1) - *No climbing from 1st March to 31st July due to nesting birds.*

1 Cormorant Buttress West .. 2 ☐ S 4a

The best route of its grade in the area. A remote setting and the need for the right combination of tide and calm seas make this a serious undertaking. It is not a good route for the inexperienced. Start from a massive block below the large undercut buttress.
1) 4a, 16m. From the block, make a tough step-up onto the wall - crux. Good holds lead up left into a shallow groove. The groove provides steeper climbing to gain a large ledge and good belays.
2) 4a, 15m. Climb up rightwards to a huge flake-crack. Large nuts or cams protect the moves up the flake-crack. From the top of the flake-crack, move right to an easy-angled but unstable slope which, with great care leads to the top.
FA. J.Yaldren, Richard Crewe 11.10.1969

The next three routes are 100m to the right and best approached from the quarry abseil.

2 Quality Street .... Top 50 ☐ HVS 4c

A superb pitch packed with excellent holds and climbing and with the added benefit of a solid finish. One of Swanage's best HVSs. Move up the wall on great holds to a flake at 10m, before climbing rightwards on steeper ground to gain the fault-line (possible belay). Gain the steep wall on the left above the fault-line and take this to an overhang. Go left and up into a shallow corner with difficulty, before easier bridging and crack climbing finishes this memorable pitch. Low in the grade.
FA. Richard Crewe, P.Charman 10.2.1974

3 Wall Street .... Top 50 ☐ HS 4b

A great little expedition at the grade, once again featuring good rock, holds and a solid top-out. Start just right of *Quality Street.*
1) 4b, 17m. Good holds lead up and right to a crack. Keep going on the same line past a ledge to the fault-line. Traverse right to a stance on the arete just above the fault-line.
2) 4b, 15m. The narrow groove above gains a solid top-out.
FA. Richard Crewe, Kenny Winkworth 29.3.1970

4 Oran.............. 1 ☐ S 4a

Smart climbing on good rock. Low tide and a calm sea is required to reach the base. Start 10m right of *Wall Street.*
1) -, 17m. Climb to and up a corner just right of the low roof. At the fault-line, move right past an arete to a belay ledge.
2) 4a, 14m. Take the line above the stance, bearing right at the top.
FA. Kenny Winkworth, Richard Crewe 27.3.1970

Portland
Lulworth
Swanage
Winspit
Hedbury and Smokey
Dancing Ledge
Guillemot Ledge
Blackers Hole
Fisherman's Ledge
The Promenade
Cattle Troughs
Boulder Ruckle
Subluminal

35m

1

Approach from Guillemot Ledge - lowish tide and calm sea required

From quarry abseil access (100m) - lowish tide and calm sea required

Blackers Hole

Adam Bailles moves out into the sun on the upper section of the massive pitch *Infinite Gravity* (8a+) - page 328 - in the Great Cave at Blackers Hole. Photo: Mike Hutton

	No star	1	2	3
Mod to S	-	-	-	-
HS to HVS	1	3	1	-
E1 to E3	1	6	2	-
E4 and up	1	9	11	11

Tom Randall on the first pitch of *Forever Laughing* (7c+) - *page 328* - at The Great Cave, Blackers Hole. Photo: Mike Hutton

Portland
Lulworth
Swanage
Winspit
Hedbury and Smokey
Dancing Ledge
Guillemot Ledge
Blackers Hole
Fisherman's Ledge
The Promenade
Cattle Troughs
Boulder Ruckle
Subluminal

Blackers Hole contains some of the greatest challenges available to climbers along Britain's south coast, and for most, the view of the Great Cave's twenty five metre roof comes as a shock to the system on first acquaintance. This vast cavern provides the setting for cutting edge routes such as *Infinite Gravity* and *Endeavour*. Further east the cave gives way to slightly less-steep territory on its left-hand side, but the base changes from boulders to sea, making access difficult and the climbs even more adventurous. It is here that a number of long and difficult trad adventures wend their way, with the likes of *Polaris* and *The Aquatic Ape* being amongst Swanage's most serious undertakings. However, there is more on offer here, in the shape of roof-based sport routes in the quarry, and some secluded (though accessible) trad routes on the shorter walls to the east of the Great Cave.

Approach Also see map on page 266

The shortest approach is from the Durlston car park (fee). Walk west past the lighthouse and turn right (looking out) on to the coast path. Pass the distinctive mile pylons and continue around a wide bay, crossing over two stone walls. 200m past the second stone wall, locate a hidden descent ramp leading down to the left (looking out) side of the quarry. See the route pages for the specific approaches.

Tides and Conditions

The routes in The Great Cave and some routes on the Polaris and Centrepiece Areas are affected by the tide. More details are given with the route descriptions. Keep well away in rough seas. Most of the cliffs here get the sun all day except for The Great Cave which only receives some late evening light in the summer months. The quarry is a useful winter sun trap. There is little seepage except in The Great Cave where dampness can linger.

Access

Access to all the routes in the Polaris Area and Great Cave are restricted because of nesting birds. **No climbing from 1st March to 31st July.**

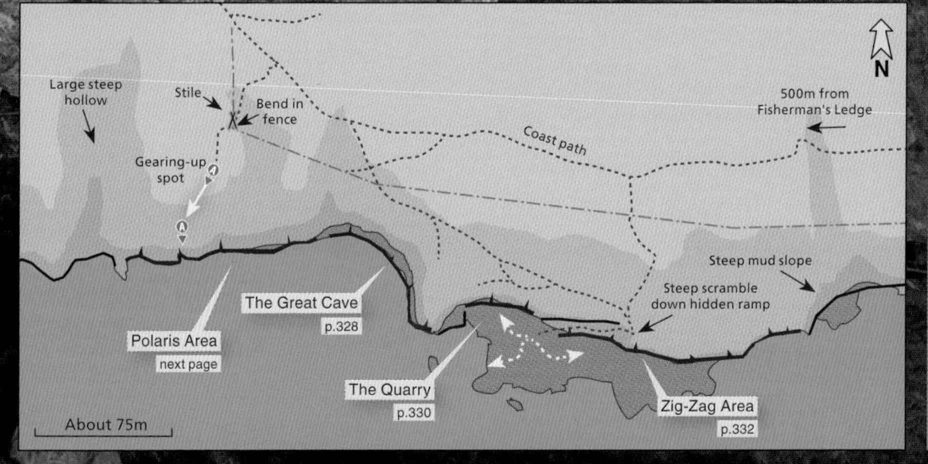

Polaris Area

Left of the great cave are some very impressive trad routes. All bar one are centred on a huge bottomless groove (the main pitch of *Polaris*). All are worthwhile expeditions in tremendously exposed positions. The rock quality is mostly good, and the gear reasonable. Prusik loops are strongly advised on all routes here.

Tides - Low tide is needed for the full versions of Routes 1 and 2. Routes 3 to 7 are possible at any tide, although they could be a bit too exciting in rough seas. Route 8 is approached by boat.

Belays - Final belays for all routes are on the abseil rope, or a pre-placed rope.

Restriction - No climbing from 1st March to 31st July due to nesting birds.

Approach (routes 1 and 2) - *150m west of Blackers Hole, locate a stile on a 90 degree bend in the fence, cross over the stile and go directly downhill for 40m to a big stake. Gear up and abseil down the very steep grass to a pair of stakes. From here, another abseil gains the base of the routes.*

1 Frank's Little Secret E1 5b

A fine climb on good rock, starting from the base of the abseil. Now described in a single pitch and upgraded from HVS. Climb the left-hand crack to a little overhang. Traverse right, go up to the bigger overhang and traverse left. Continue up the wall until a flake line appears on the right. Make a bold move to gain the line and continue to the abseil stakes.

FA. V.Dennis, Nick Buckley 7.8.1977

2 Polaris . . . . Top 50 E5 6a

A Swanage classic. The climbing on the upper pitches is steep and exposed, but the protection is reasonable.

1) 5b, 30m. Climb the left-hand crack past an overhang to the fault-line and traverse rightwards to the arete (or better, traverse rightwards at a slightly lower level). Continue the traverse to a belay below a large open groove.

2) 6a, 15m. A very exposed pitch. Move down onto the main arete and climb a steep thin crack to a hand-traverse line across a leaning wall. Follow this right to a final tough move onto a belay ledge above the huge roof.

3) 5c, 25m. Climb the wall 2m right of the corner to a hidden peg. Move left and follow a slanting crack to a rest at the bottom of the big upper corner. Climb the sustained corner past a bulge to a slab and finish up steep grass to a stake belay.

FA. Arni Strapcans, Gordon Jenkin, Frank Farrell 13.8.1978

Approach (route 3) - *Abseil down a groove just right (looking out) of the finishing corner on Polaris to a belay 10m above the sea on a scooped ledge just left of the lower arete. Nuts will need to be placed to keep in contact with the rock on the diagonal abseil.*

3 Exchange of Fire ..... 1★ E5 6a

A well-positioned route based on the left arete of the *Polaris* groove. It is steep, but has good rests. Dynamically climb the lower arete on its right-hand side to the fault-line. Follow *Polaris* up the steep thin crack, then go over its capping bulge to a niche. Continue up the blunt arete to finish up the flake of *Nuke*.
FA. Martin Crocker, Mike Robertson 1.9.1996

Approach (routes 4 to 7) - *Abseil down the final groove of Polaris to its second stance on the lip of the roof. Nuts will be needed on the abseil to stay in contact with the rock.*

4 Nuke .... 1★ E4 6a

An exposed climb up the flake, trending left onto the arete, and finishing more easily on slightly suspect holds.
FA. Dave Ivory, Ed Hart 1.3.1980
FFA. Crispin Waddy, Andy Ford 10.1987

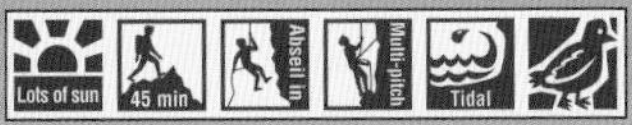

Lots of sun | 45 min | Abseil in | Multi-pitch | Tidal

5 Bolt the Blue Sea ..... 1★ E5 6b

A meaty number tackling a very steep crack in the left wall. Climb the back of the corner and pull over a bulge to join *Polaris*. Swing left (peg) and climb the thin crack steeply to good flake holds (peg). The flakes lead leftward onto the arete to easy ground beyond.
FA. Martin Crocker, John Harwood 15.10.1994

6 Weapons of Sound E5 6a

Well protected. From the right-hand side of the stance, move rightwards to a pocket-line (thread). Gain a hand ledge and go up a short groove. Launch right across the steep wall, on a pocket line, to a break. Continue direct to easier ground.
FA. Martin Crocker, John Harwood 2.10.1994

7 Enter the Void .... 2★ E6 6b

A superb climb in an awesome position, mainly on good pocket holds. Start out as for *Weapons of Sound* past the thread. From the hand ledge above, traverse right to another pocket line. This leads steeply (peg) to a good slot. Climb straight up the blunt white arete with hard moves to gain the ledge above. Step right to a broken, but easy finish.
FA. Martin Crocker, John Harwood 2.10.1994

8 The Aquatic Ape .. Top 50 E6 6b

The awesome undercut pillar and roof left of *The Schwarzchild Radius* provides one of the most outrageous trad routes at Swanage; a *Polaris* for the twenty-first century. The line cannot be realistically approached by abseil due to its extreme steepness (it overhangs around 18 metres) nor by traversing in. Approach by boat to a hanging belay. A pre-placed rope at the second belay may be a preferable exit to the route rather than climbing pitch 3 (pitch 4 of *Laughing Arthur*).
1) 6b, 25m. Contort up the chimney (very large cam useful at the top) and make wild moves out to good holds on the wall above. Move up and right across straightforward terrain (thread) to gain an overhung, guano-coated ledge (peg). Make steep moves up on guano and slime-covered holds to gain a severely-overhanging diagonal crack that leads directly to the roof (thread). Take a hanging belay here on the thread and a selection of cams in one of the wildest positions at Swanage.
2) 6b, 15m. Hand traverse out left from the belay (good small and medium cams) until level with the insitu thread hanging from the lip of the 2m ceiling. Make an ape-like span (crux) out to jugs on the lip, then cut loose and fly up the overhanging wall above (2 more threads) to gain a ledge. Belay here on a pre-placed rope and two threads, or traverse right to the third belay of *Laughing Arthur*.
3) 5b, 20m. Climb Pitch 4 of *Laughing Arthur*, or jumar up the chossy slab on the pre-placed rope.
FA. Bob Hickish, Dave Pickford 2.9.2011

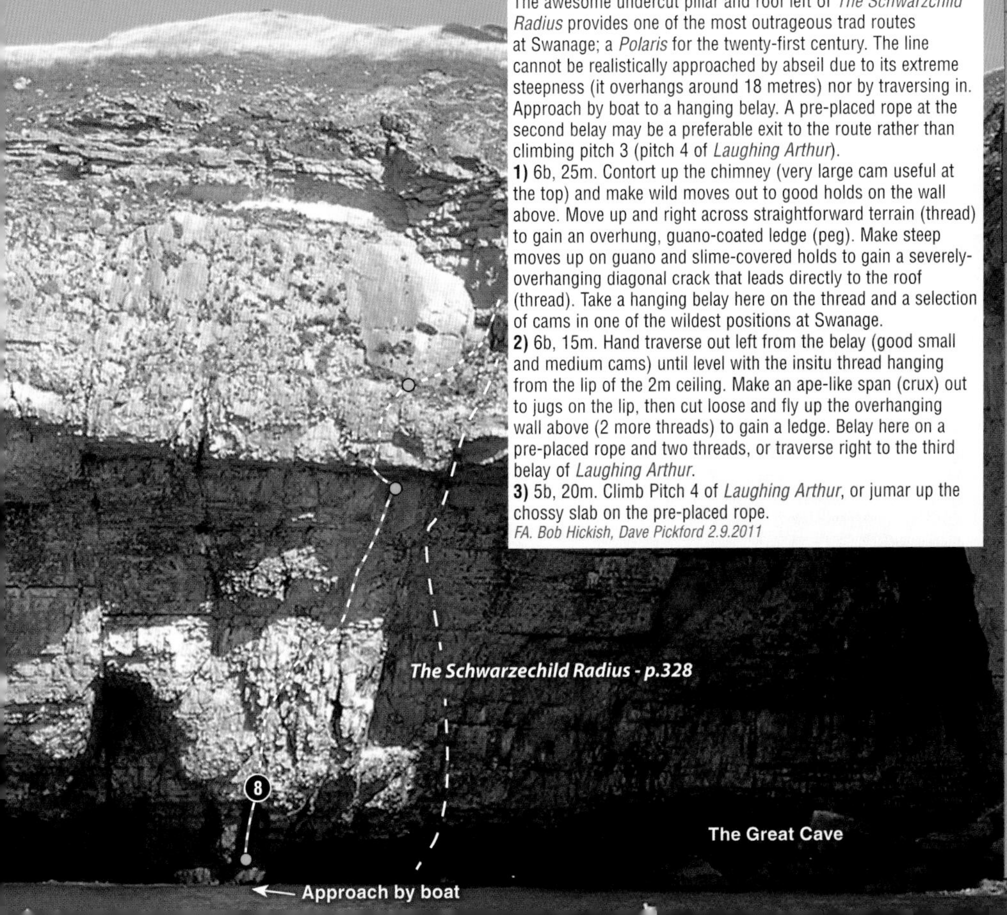

The Schwarzechild Radius - p.328
8
The Great Cave
Approach by boat

Portland
Lulworth
Swanage
Winspit
Hedbury and Smokey
Dancing Ledge
Guillemot Ledge
Blackers Hole
Fisherman's Ledge
The Promenade
Cattle Troughs
Boulder Ruckle
Subluminal

1 The Schwarzechild Radius
. . . . Top 50 7c+/A1
A vast, arching line through the overhangs on the left-hand side of the cave including an 8m roof crack. Crawl leftwards from the pebble beach to a small ledge. Non-tidal, but requires calm seas.
1) 7c+, 25m. The cave roof and leaning wall above provide a great pitch, which is worth doing in its own right.
2) 6b/A1, 15m. When eventually linked to the first pitch it will be a stunning 8a+.
3) 5b, 15m. Climb the easy bulging pillar on the right.
FA. Pete Oxley 23.2.1993

2 Laughing Arthur. Top 50 E8 6b
One of the largest roof climbs in Britain. The first and third pitches have not been repeated and the second pitch can still be climbed using trad gear although it is bolted.
1) 6b, 25m. Climb the bulges to a large flake and rest above. Traverse right into the groove, then surge out to good holds and follow the main groove on more big holds until a short traverse left. Guano-encrusted jugs above lead to ledges and a belay.
2) 6b (7c+), 15m. Climb the monumental roof crack, with occasional use of the side wall, to the lip. Pull around to a bolt-belay.
3) 6b, 10m. Follow the continuation crack, on blocky holds, to belay to the right of a slab (2 threads and a bolt).
4) 5b, 15m. Exit easily (as for *The Schwarzechild Radius*).
FA. M.Boater, P.Deketelaere 6-8.8.1970. FFA. Pete Oxley 3.12.1988

3 Forever Laughing. . Top 50 7c+
A safer and fully-bolted version of *Laughing Arthur*.
Photo on page 324.
1) 7c, 25m. Start up *Infinite Gravity*, then break left to climb the hanging ramp and steep groove to the roof. Bolt belay.
2) 7c+, 15m. As for *Laughing Arthur* pitch 2.
3) 7a+, 15m. Climb direct to the belay of *Infinite Gravity*. This is a fully bolted version of an older link pitch *Coma 2*.
FA. Tom Randall and Bob Hickish 23.9.2010
FA. (Coma 2) Pete Oxley 25.11.1989

4 Endeavour. . . . . Top 50 8c
Dorset's hardest. Start up *Infinite Gravity* until level with the 10th bolt, swing out left past a large hanging spike and underneath a big roof to gain the bottom of the hanging orange wall that forms the other side of the huge ship's prow. Climb this with hard moves on pockets to join the *Laughing Arthur* roof crack half way along. Finish rightwards along this to the belay at the end of *Laughing Arthur* pitch 2. *Photo on page 331*.
FA. Bob Hickish 15.9.2011

5 Infinite Gravity. . . . Top 50 8a+
The outrageous ship's prow arete overhangs at 45° for most of its length. It has three hard sections with shakeouts in between. The first is a radical groove, then a crack bisecting a series of huge roofs and finally a less-steep arching crack and bands of horizontals with tough moves to reach the belay. There are around 22 bolts.
Photo on page 323.
FA. Pete Oxley 4.1992

6 Naked and Savage . Top 50 ☐ **E7 6b**
A big, steep pitch. Well protected by nuts and a few pegs. Start on the right-hand side of the boulder beach, below the overhanging groove line. Climb a thin crack (2 pegs) then up a corner (peg) to a niche (pegs). Gain the steep corner above and follow it to a crux undercut (peg and thread) which leads, via a vertical crack, to an old bolt-belay.
FA. Pete Oxley 23.8.1990

7 Procrastinating Giant . . Top 50 ☐ **E6 6a**
A big challenge.
1) 6a, 25m. Start up *Naked and Savage* to its niche, then traverse out right via an overlap to a hanging stance at its end.
2) 5b, 10m. Climb a corner on *Monsters of Rock* past 2 pegs, and cross the right wall around the arete to a thread and peg belay.
3) 6a, 15m. Pull rightwards over bulges (thread) then climb up a left-trending crack (peg) to the fault-line. Surmount the capping bulge (peg) to reach a bolt-belay. Climb out or abseil off.
FA. D.Fell 11.8.1974. FFA. Martin Crocker, Jim Robertson 10.10.1983

8 Monsters of Rock. . . . . 3 ☐ **E7 6b**
A very impressive line taking the centre of the huge black wall and the groove above, bisecting *Procrastinating Giant*. Reasonable gear and low in the grade.
1) 6b, 15m. A very sustained pitch. Reverse the access traverse to the centre of the wall (old peg). Climb straight up past 3 pegs, moving right at the third to a flake (thread). Attain the overlap above and belay at its right-hand side.
2) 6a, 20m. Climb a steepening corner past old pegs. Near the top roof, swing out right in a dramatic position (peg) to pass the top bulge (peg and thread) to a bolt-belay. Lower-off or top out.
FA. Pete Oxley, Jon Biddle 3.9.1989

The next routes start 4m right of the cave edge, and are easily accessed by ledges from Blackers Hole Quarry.

9 Giantslayer . . . . 2 ☐ **E5 6a**
Really good climbing in an exposed position. Quite well protected but very pumpy with a strenuous finish. Watch out for rope drag. Climb a rib, then head diagonally leftwards to the arete. Follow a flake-crack just right of the arete to a thread and peg on *Procrastinating Giant*. Finish as for that route. There is a bolted direct start and finish to this line at around 7b.
FA. Martin Crocker, D.Light 24.9.1983

10 Cold Empty Gun. . . 1 ☐ **E6 6a**
A direct line avoiding the loop on *Giantslayer*. It is bold and sustained up the blind crack - take plenty of small wires.
FFA. Dave Pickford, Richard White 2000.

11 Coercri . . . . 1 ☐ **E4 6a**
A varied climb up the centre of the west-facing wall, starting at a groove/ramp just right of *Giantslayer*. Well protected.
1) 6a, 20m. Ascend the ramp to its top (peg). Make tricky moves to start the crack out right which leads strenuously to a ledge.
2) 5c, 10m. Climb another ramp up left (peg) then pull direct over an exposed bulge to easier ground. Stake belay.
FA. Kevin Turner, Nick Buckley 1980
FFA. Martin Crocker, Jim Robertson 28.8.1983

12 Cosa Nostra . . . . 1 ☐ **E2 5c**
Good exposed climbing up the right-hand arete of the west face. Climb a bulging crack on the seaward side, then move onto the arete. Step right, level with a ramp on the left, and follow the arete past a bulge and crack to easier ground.
FA. John Williams, Pete Oxley 21.4.1988

The Great Cave

The collection of awe-inspiring routes in the Great Cave are some of the most overhanging climbs in Britain. In recent years a number of new lines have been added, and re-bolting is ongoing.
Approach - Descend from the quarry to a sea-level ledge below *Giantslayer*. The routes to the left of this are reached by a traverse (fixed rope) along the low fault-line in the side wall.
Tides - You can reach the routes at high tide, but it is better and easier at low tide. Keep away in rough seas.
Restriction - No climbing from 1st March to 31st July due to nesting birds.

Portland
Lulworth
Swanage
Winspit
Hedbury and Smokey
Dancing Ledge
Guillemot Ledge
Blackers Hole
Fisherman's Ledge
The Promenade
Cattle Troughs
Boulder Ruckle
Subluminal

The Quarry

A worthwhile spot for some sheltered fun on sport roofs, plus one good trad line. The bolts on the routes to the left are all old, however a couple on the right have been re-equipped.
Approach - 200m past the second stone wall, locate a hidden descent ramp leading down to the left (looking out) side of the quarry. It is non-tidal and well-sheltered.

1 Freedom Fighter . . . 7a
Steep and entertaining. Old gear.
FA. Pete Oxley 3.2.1988

2 Crack Gang Killing 7b
There is also a desperate direct start V8-ish, on which no starting boulders are allowed. Old gear.
FA. Pete Oxley 18.11.1988

3 Roof Supreme . . . . 7b+
A bicep bulk-out. Old gear.
FA. Pete Oxley 11.6.1988

4 Sunyata 7b
A testing roof with a wild finish. Old gear.
FA. Pete Oxley 6.2.1988

5 The Energy, the Faith, the Devotion
. . . . 7c+
A desperate, reachy roof and it is still hard higher up. Old gear.
FA. Pete Oxley 12.3.1988

6 Plasma Stream . . . 7c
A hard roof to start, and nasty above as well. Rebolted.
FA. Pete Oxley 13.4.1989

7 The Nolans Meet Impulse Manslaughter
. . . . 7a+
A graunchy route which requires a huge reach. Rebolted.
FA. Pete Oxley 21.1.1988

8 Swimming in Jugs E3 5c
As fun as the name suggests. A good pitch that has a difficult start and sustained climbing above.
FA. Pete Oxley 6.2.1988

9 Les Hommes en Noir E3 5c
The diagonal flakes on the far right are poor. Finish on a pre-placed rope.
FA. Pete Oxley 3.2.1988

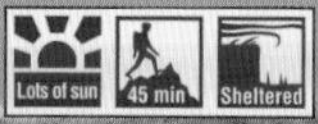

Lots of sun | 45 min | Sheltered

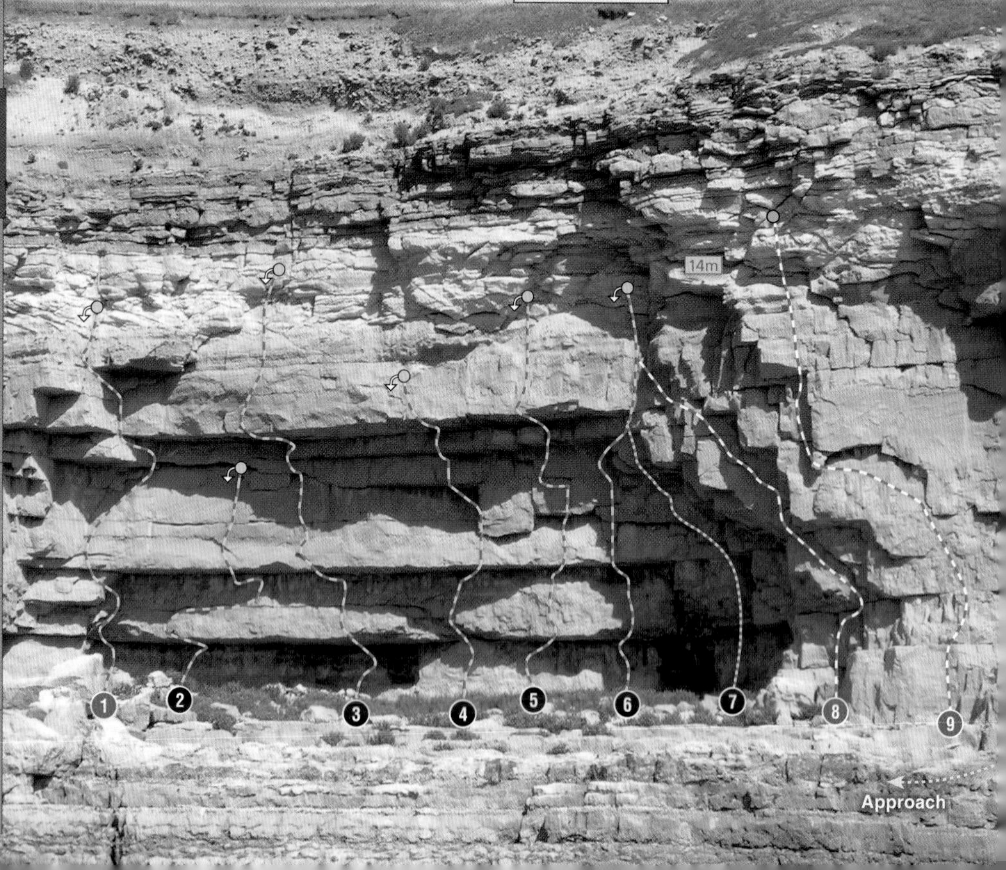

14m
1 2 3 4 5 6 7 8 9
Approach

Bob Hickish on his own line *Endeavour* (8c) - *page 328* - in the Great Cave at Blackers Hole. Photo: Mike Hutton

Zig-Zag Area

The lower walls at Blackers Hole have a good mixture of routes, although most have unstable exits.
Approach - A short scramble down from the left side of the quarry (looking out) leads to a wave-cut platform.
Tides - Most of the routes start from a non-tidal ledge below the wall. The final four routes need low to mid-tide.
Belays - All routes finish at cliff-top stakes, although most require pre-placed ropes on their upper sections.

1 Zig-Zag . . . . **VS 4c**
The top of the second pitch of this climb is reported to be in a very dangerous state. Start at the foot of a diagonal crack.
1) 4a, 15m. Ascend the crack rightwards and over a bulge to come back left up another crack. Belay at an overhung ledge.
2) 4c, 15m. Traverse a ledge on the right and climb a delicate slab rightwards to finish up a very unstable-looking flake.

2 Parallel Lines . . . . 1 **HVS 5a**
A nice, but run-out pitch on good, compact rock. Start 3m right of the diagonal crack of *Zig Zag*. Climb as directly as possible to the first stance of *Zig Zag*. Take a vague groove and the walls above to the top - bold.
FA. A.Hedger, D.Simpson 11.8.1992

3 Credit in the Straight World 1 **E4 6a**
A good, bold wall climb right of the slab. Start 7m right of *Zig-Zag*, at an alcove. Climb the left-hand side of the alcove, then go up a steep wall moving right to an undercut. Gain the slab and follow an easy flake before moving right and climbing another steep wall to a small groove. Move up left to finish.
FA. Martin Crocker, Jim Robertson 20.8.1983

For the remaining lines use a pre-place rope to lower-off/belay.

4 Absence Makes the Heart... 1 **E3 6a**
An enjoyable wall climb starting at a rib to the left of the roof stack. Climb the rib and a short groove to a ledge. Ascend rightwards, passing a groove, and follow the headwall (peg) trending rightwards to the top.
FA. Martin Crocker, Nigel Coe 23.2.1986

5 Street Fighting Years Top 50 **E7 6c**
A mighty challenge tackling the triple-roof-stack head on. The hardest roof at Swanage and possibly 7a. It is well protected.
1) 6c, 12m. Climb to the roof and contort through the right-hand ceiling crack to belay around the lip on threads and wires.
2) 6b, 10m. Cross the next 3m ceiling, past a large jug, into a small corner. Swing up right to a semi-hanging belay.
3) 6a, 15m. Go over the roof and up a groove in the headwall before going left to finish as for *Absence Makes the Heart.*
FA. Pete Oxley 22.8.1989

6 Full Circle 2 **E7 6c**
Another sizeable roof test-piece through the right-hand side of the cave. Good gear on the crux, but bold elsewhere.
1) 6c, 18m. Move easily up then continue boldly over the first roof (peg on left is out of reach, unfortunately) to enter a slight groove. At the roof (thread), lean out, then climb leftwards via a fading crack. Make hard moves past the lip to reach the next break. Semi-hanging belay as for *Street Fighting Years.*
2) 6a, 15m. As for *Street Fighting Years.*
FA. Pete Oxley 14.6.1999

The next two climbs may have been altered by rockfall.

7 A Dose of the Malhams 1 **E6 6b**
Climb the dramatic prow, then move through a 3m roof to the lip. Swing left and pull up flakes to the break. Belay on the left as for *Street Fighting Years*. Finish up this.
FA. Pete Oxley 7.8.1990. FA. (without bolt) Dave Pickford 2000

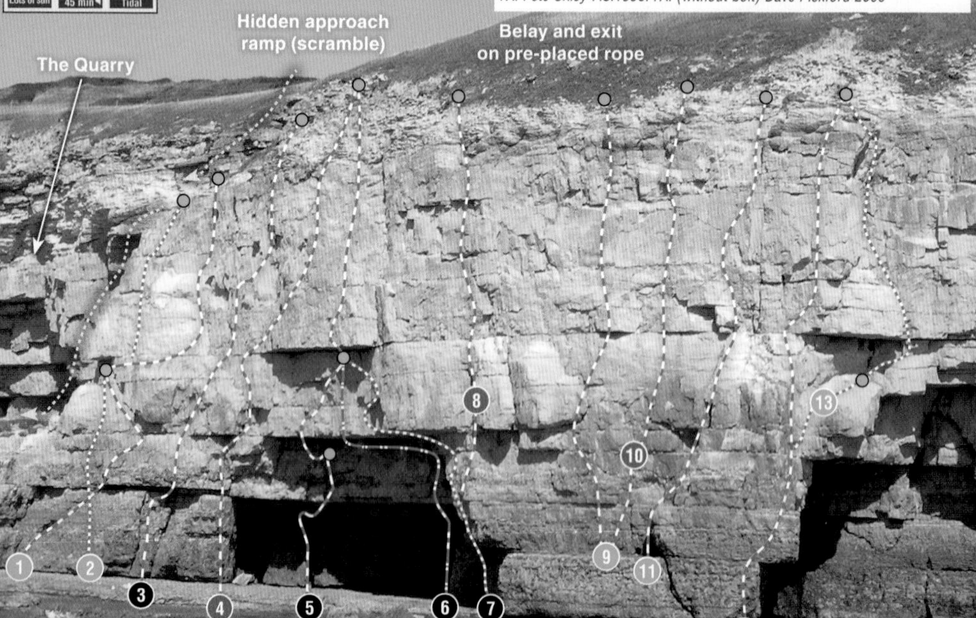

8 Sport Free World! . 1 star — **E3 5c**
A long line out of the right-hand side of the cave that may have been altered by rockfall. Start as for *A Dose of the Malhams*. Swing out and up the leaning prow before traversing boldly right to a peg. Ascend direct up a shallow groove to a ledge, then move leftwards via a short flake to a finger-crack. This leads with increasing difficulty to jugs just below the top.
FA. Pete Oxley, Brian Tilley 10.6.1999

9 Mr Fantastic Totally Stroptastic . . . . 1 star — **HVS 5b**
Start on a raised ledge at 2m. Climb straight up and over a small overhang at half height. Use cracks above to climb the headwall to sloping ledge. Finish up and right.
FA. Marti Hallett, Steve Taylor 6.2001

10 Rufty's Roll Up . . . . . . 2 stars — **E1 5b**
A pleasant pitch away from the crowds. Start from the right-hand side of a raised ledge at 2m. Climb the lower wall, past a prominent white jug, to finish up a vertical crack in the headwall.
FA. D.Simpson, A.Hedger 11.8.1992

11 Tobacco Road . . . . 2 stars — **VS 4c**
Varied climbing on good rock. Start at the same point as *Rufty's Roll Up*. Head rightwards and up two vertical cracks to a ledge below the headwall. Move left onto a ramp then out right to finish up cracks and a groove.

12 The Vapour Edge . . . . . 2 stars — **E1 5b**
Nicely situated climbing. Start below the arete, and climb it easily to a ledge at 15m. Trend rightwards and ascend a thin crack, just left of the upper arete, finishing up the wall above.
FA. Martin Crocker, Jim Robertson 27.3.1983

13 Parsons Pleasure . . . . 1 star — **VS 4c**
1) 4a, 15m. Climb the arete a short way, then move right to a corner and follow this to a sloping belay ledge.
2) 4c, 15m. Climb the chimney right of the roof to a ledge. Follow the corner strenuously to a ledge. Move left and up to finish.
FA. Scott Titt, Richard Crewe, G.Seymour 4.10.1975

The route **Snout** *takes the recess on the right but is reported to have suffered a rockfall recently and has been omitted.*

14 Havana . . . . 2 stars — **E4 6b**
Quality climbing throughout, including a technical crack up a flying headwall on the right. Well protected. Follow a direct line out of the right-hand side of the recess, passing a small roof crack to the undercut headwall. From good holds on the lip (thread) crank the thin crack to easier ground.
FA. Martin Crocker, John Harwood 15.10.1994

15 The Equalizer . . . . 2 stars — **E6 6b**
Climb an easy flake (peg), then pull right over a roof (2 threads). Climb the desperate layback-seam past a peg to a ledge.
FA. Pete Oxley 31.5.1987

16 Centrepiece . . . . 2 stars — **E5 6c**
A great test-piece taking the dominating central line. Climb past a thread into a pod, then make desperate moves up the calcite sheet. Pass a peg to a sloping ledge.
FA. Martin Crocker, Matt Ward 5.9.1986

17 Not Forgotten, No Fade Away 2 stars — **E5 6b**
Similar in quality to *Centrepiece*, but more difficult to protect. Climb a direct line through the bulges and up the smooth face 3m right of *Centrepiece*.
FA. Martin Crocker, Matt Ward 5.9.1986

Fisherman's Ledge

Pete Oxley making the first ascent of *Haka Peruperu* (8a) - *page 348* - at the Palace of the Brine Cave, Fisherman's Ledge. Photo: Mike Robertson

	No star	1	2	3
Mod to S	1	-	2	-
HS to HVS	1	3	2	-
E1 to E3	8	20	11	4
E4 and up	-	15	13	15

Adam Brown deep water soloing the pulse-enhancing *Freeborn Man* (E4 6a) - *page 345* - at Fisherman's Ledge. Photo: Daimon Beail

The climbing available at Fisherman's Ledge is undoubtedly the most diverse at Swanage and ranges from some of the UK's best deep water solos to some massive roof climbs that are tackled by both traditional and sport climbs. There is also a good number of traditional routes that are not as popular but span the grades from HVS to E7 - some being amongst the most serious pitches on the coast.

Approach

Also see map on page 266

Park at Durlston Country Park and take the tarmac road to join the coast path close to the lighthouse. Walk west along the coast path to the stile before the mile marker pylons. Cross the fence and continue along its seaward side for 250m, to where a slight ridge descends to the cliff-top ledges above *Helix* and *The Conger*. The various areas require different approaches from here, these are described in detail with each section.

Tides

Most of the areas are non-tidal apart from the Palace of the Brine cave which floods at mid-to-high tide, cutting off the approach to a number of the climbs. Many of the solos are safer at high tide although it is not essential for the majority of the routes. The area is worth keeping away from in rough seas.

Conditions

The cliffs get the sun for most of the day although the Palace of the Brine cave is so steep that no direct sunlight touches the routes that venture up and through its roof. It is usually considered as a summer venue because of the deep water soloing; however if the deep water soloing option is not picked, then it can be considered a year round venue and often benefits from crisper conditions in the cooler months. There is some seepage in the Palace of the Brine cave, on the roofs of the Conger Cave and around *...And Captain Bloods Cavern* but this has normally dried up by early summer.

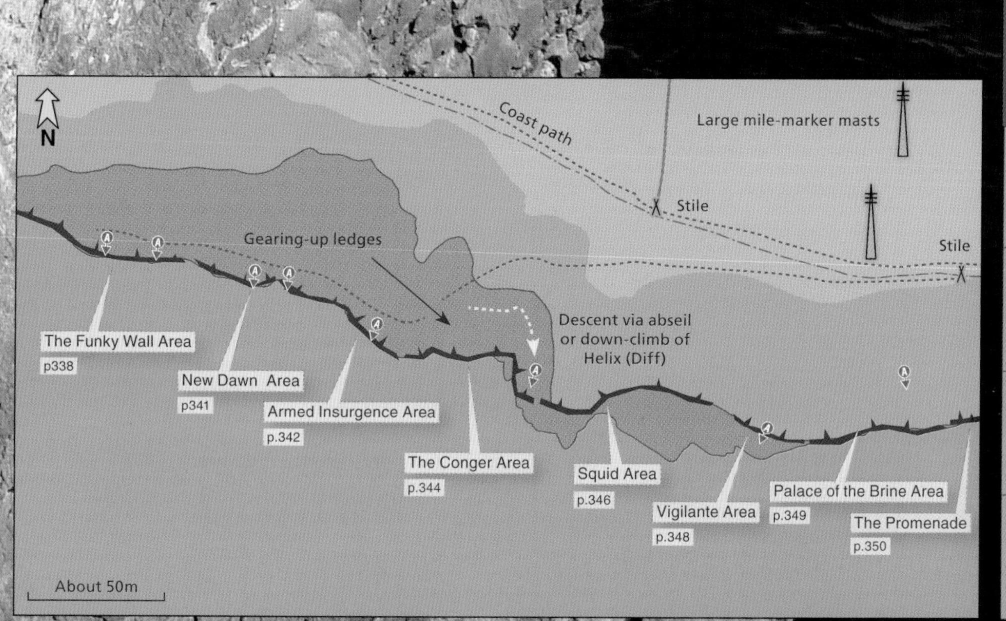

Portland
Lulworth
Swanage
Winspit
Hedbury and Smokey
Dancing Ledge
Guillemot Ledge
Blackers Hole
Fisherman's Ledge
The Promenade
Cattle Troughs
Boulder Ruckle
Subluminal

The Funky Wall

The western end of Fisherman's Ledge is a sheer wall of superb rock that drops straight into the sea and is the preserve of the deep water soloist. Any of the routes on this wall given an S (DWS) grade are best soloed although the option of a trad lead is always a possibility.

Conditions - The best conditions are to be found in the summer and autumn when the sea is at its warmest. There is some seepage on routes 1 to 4.

Tides - All the routes are possible at any tide but keep away in rough seas.

Approach (routes 1,2 and 5 to 9) - Abseil from a stake at the right-hand (looking out) end of the cliff-top ledge system to a sizeable ledge (The Funky Ledge), from where the routes start. For routes 3 and 4 abseil directly to a tiny ledge at sea level. Should a splash down occur, swim to the right-hand side (looking in) of the Funky Ledge to get out. Then either Prusik up the abseil rope, or solo out via *The Rise and Dear Demise of the Funky Nomadic Tribes* (HVS 5a) not a DWS. It is also possible to swim a couple of hundred metres rightwards (looking in) to *Helix* (Squid Area) and solo out.

Warning - Be careful here, this is a serious spot. It is probably best to stay away from the routes in this area if you aren't confident of soloing up a HVS 5a which is **not** a deep water solo and are a poor swimmer.

1 ...and Captain Blood's Cavern

Top 50 . . . . E4 6a

6c, S1. 40m. An atmospheric and beautifully structured classic poised over a hidden sea cavern. Seepage can affect this route. From the starting ledge, traverse the break leftwards, until almost at the sea cavern. Launch up the leftward-arching corner for 10m and overcome the bulge on the left to gain an easier exit on the right. A variation **The Strawberry that Killed the Seal** moves left 1m from the base of the arching groove and follows positive edges to rejoin the parent route (*7b, S1*).

FA. Joff Cook (solo) 8.8.1990. FA. (Variation) Andy Lamont 29.8.2011

2 Davey Jones' Lock-off

3 stars E4 6a

6c+, S2. 40m. At the end of the arch-traverse on *...and Captain Bloods Cavern*, step down and continue left to a jutting foot-ledge. Climb the bulge above on undercuts and side-pulls to a rest. Finish up left. A variation **DJ Bloods Mariana Variation** drops down to below the roof of the traverse and then heads left to pull back up over the roof to join the parent route (*7b+*).

FA. Crispin Waddy (solo) 8.1994. FA. (Variation) Andy Lamont 13.8.2011

Approach (routes 3 and 4) - *Abseil directly from two stakes above a large boulder, keeping a big swing going to reach a small foot-ledge at the base of a corner at sea level (good large nut placement).*

3 Privateer. . . Top 50 **E6 6b**
7b+, S2. ...and Captain Bloods Cavern big brother, which features a high and exposed crux. Climb the corner above the belay to join the *...and Captain Bloods Cavern* archway for 5m. Pull around a bulge and follow a tough right-facing groove which terminates in a committing finale to exit into a short crack.
FA. Martin Crocker 12.10.1996. As an E5 6b trad route with a different start. Line described above soloed by Pete Oxley 23.5.1998

4 For Whom the Swell Tolls 2 **E6 6b**
7b+, S2. Three cruxes with some steep stuff near the top for maximum pump. Swing right at sea level for 2m and ascend a hard scoop to the horizontal break. Continue up on good incuts then make extending moves leftwards to reach a giant undercut. Deep breath - go for it with full power direct to a mantelshelf exit, passing a big jug mid way. May have lost a crucial hold.
FA. Pete Oxley 23.5.1998.

5 In Too Deep 1 **E3 6a**
6c, S1. Link from the horizontal break on *For Whom the Swell Tolls* to *Fathoms*.
FA. Pete Oxley (solo) 8.1997

6 Fathoms . . . . . . Top 50 **E3 5b**
6b, S1. A rite-of-passage route with its crux at the top. From the starting ledge traverse the break left for 8m to a small ledge then climb the first big groove diagonally leftwards to its finishing bulge. Leaving the big jug may take some will power.
Photo on page 41.
FA. Crispin Waddy (solo) 8.9.1986

7 Feeding Neptune 1 **E6 6b**
7b+, S1. A steep, bouldery route with some big air potential. Start up *Donald, Where's Your Trousers* then break left across difficult terrain to a thin finger flake. Excitement is guaranteed.
FA. Pete Oxley (solo) 24.7.1999

8 Donald, Where's Your Trousers 1 **E2 5c**
6a+ S1. Follow *Fathoms* to the small ledge below the big groove. Then break right up a lovely wall to finish up a short flake.
FA. Crispin Waddy (solo) 8.9.1986

9 Amazonia 2 **E3 5c**
6c, S1. A great introduction to this sector for soloists. From the ledge gain a secondary small shelf then head leftwards to an arete and corner. Tricky low down.
FA. Joff Cook (solo) 4.6.1993

10 Amazon Emancipation 1 **E6 6b**
Not a DWS. Ascend the very narrow corner directly above the secondary ledge on *Amazonia*. Belay on this ledge then climb up to a desperate move over a bulge at 8m. Crucial Rock 2 at mid-height and hard won gear in general.
FA. Martin Crocker 15.9.1996

Funky Wall - Right

There are no deep water solos on this section of the cliff, it is back to trad lines on excellent quality rock.

Tides and Conditions - All the routes are possible at any tide - apart from *Charmed Life* - but keep away in rough seas.

Approach (routes 1 to 6) - Abseil from a stake at the right-hand (looking out) end of the cliff-top ledge system to a sizeable ledge (The Funky Ledge).

Approach (route 7) - Abseil to the right-hand side of the very lowest ledge at sea level - low tide and calm seas only.

Approach (routes 8 and 9) - Abseil directly down a rib, from a big boulder, to a semi-hanging stance, 4m above sea level.

1 The Rise and Dear Demise of the Funky Nomadic Tribes . . . . 1 HVS 5a

Make a tricky start up a slight groove starting from the left-hand side of the main ledge. Awkward to arrange protection.

FA. Kevin Turner, Frank Farrell 27.8.1979

2 Ten Thousand Spoons. . E2 5c

The wall above the middle of the ledge gives good face climbing on seams and cracks. Hard for the grade.

FA. Mike Robertson, Barry Clarke, Mark Williams 3.8.1996

3 The Friendly Ranger of Durlston Castle 1 E2 5c

A tricky face climb, starting from the right-hand side of the ledge. The finish is on poor rock but with good gear below.

FA. Kevin Turner, Frank Farrell 27.8.1979

4 Telomere 1 E1 5b

A very pleasant pitch. From the right-hand side of the ledge taking a rightward-trending line of holds into a small notch at the top. Take care with the rock near the top.

FA. Barry Clarke, Mike Robertson, D.Gilbert 3.8.1996

5 The Talisman 1 E6 6a

A serious eliminate. Start as for *Telomere* initially then head out right via a pocketed break (thread) to another thread and good wires. Step left and climb the blank unprotected scoop slightly left to good wires in a niche. Trend right easily to finish.

FA. Mike Robertson, James Dunlop 5.10.1996

6 Gorillas in the Mist 2 E3 5c

A quality line which starts as for *The Talisman*. At the thread at the end of the pocketed traverse, ascend a cracked layback rib to the top, exiting up a groove on the left. Small cams useful.

FA. Mike Robertson, Mark Williams 16.8.1996

7 Charmed Life 2 E6 6b

This route gives *The Talisman* a long direct start for a fine, balanced, hard route. Trend right to the low break (good wires) then make fingery pocket pulls (crux) above gear, to the thread on *The Talisman*. Finish as for that route.

FA. Pete Oxley 3.8.1999

Lots of sun | 40 min | Abseil in

Amazon Emancipation - p.339

8 The Slant . . . . 1 star E3 5c
The bold, left-trending ramp starting up *The Friendly Landlord of Durlston Castle*. Climb diagonally past two very thin threads to a finish on poor rock.
FA. Mike Robertson, Barry Clarke 17.8.1996

9 The Friendly Landlord of Durlston Castle . . . . 1 star E1 5b
Climb the right-hand side of the rib, 5m left of the huge rockfall scar. At two thirds height, move left 3m and finish past a thread on poor rock.
FA. Crispin Waddy (solo) 6.9.1986

New Dawn Area

This section of cliff suffered a massive rockfall in 2009 and has had a number of new routes added.

Tides - All the routes start from non-tidal ledges. Keep away in rough seas.

Approach - Abseil from stakes, boulders and threads on the cliff-top.

10 Where the Land Meets the Sea E2 5c
Follow a big diagonal flake to two sling placements. Finish direct via a run-out technical scoop. The start has changed.
FA. Pete Oxley (solo) 21.6.99

11 When Land Becomes Sea . . 2 stars E1 5b
The crack-line on the left-hand side of the rockfall. Can be started direct on right or moving in from the left.
FA. Marti Hallett, Trev Ford 9.10.2008

12 New Dawn . . . . 2 stars E6 6b
Start 8m right of the corner that marks the start of *When Land Becomes Sea*. Boulder past a small thread and then break left and up to an obvious stuck-on dinner plate hold. A hidden pocket leads up and slightly right to the top.
FA. Chris Weedon 11.9.2010

13 Double 'ard Bastard . . . . . . 2 stars E4 6b
Start as for *New Dawn*. Boulder past the small thread and gain the stuck-on encrusted slab on the right. Climb up on these to twin vertical slots under the sloping roof. Move out right until a good flake allows easy access to the top.
FA. Marti Hallett, Mick Ward 28.6.2010

14 Just as 'ard . . . . 1 star E4 6b
Follow *Double 'ard Bastard* to its sloping roof and finish straight over it directly to the top.
FA. Chris Weedon 5.9.2010

15 StuckOn . . . . 2 stars E5 6a
Start 12m right of *When Land Becomes Sea*. With a full rack of skyhooks, follow the stuck-on flowstone holds up and slightly left all the way to the top. *Photo on page 17.*
FA. Chris Weedon 5.9.2010

16 Slide Show . . . . 3 stars E7 6c
Start 18m right of *When Land Becomes Sea* at the base of a flake that finishes at half height. Place as much gear as you can, hold your breath and make hard moves on small crimps to the top. *Photo on page 44.*
FA. Chris Weedon 11.9.2010

Approach (routes 1 to 10) - *Abseil down Aubergine which follows a corner in the west (right - looking out) side of the central bay.*

1 Tempting Truancy . . 2 stars **E4 5c**
Excellent fingery wall climbing taking the face 4m left of *Aubergine* but with negligible gear.
FA. Crispin Waddy, P.Windall, Toby Foord-Kelsey 9.9.1986

2 Terminal One . . . . 1 star **E6 6a**
A very serious eliminate based on the grit-like arete just left of *Aubergine*. A skyhook and poor thread protect the upper section. No side runners at this grade. Very photogenic.
FA. Mike Robertson 6.10.1997

3 Aubergine . . . . 2 stars **HVS 5a**
Climb the big flake-crack in the corner past good gear and one stubborn section.
FA. R.Kent, Kenny Winkworth, P.Charman, Richard Crewe 1.3.1970

Armed Insurgence Area

A rarely travelled wall covered with some fairly hard trad routes and a trio of DWSs on its right-hand end.
Approach - Abseil to ledges from stakes, wires and threads.
Tides and Conditions - All the routes start from non-tidal ledges. Keep away in rough seas.

4 Mile High Club . 1 star **E6 6c**
A cracking test-piece. From the bottom of the ramp on *Aubergine*, step right and climb up flutings to the break (gear). Undercut a flake and make a very hard move slightly rightwards. Finish direct with no more gear. Serious.
FA. Pete Oxley, Brian Tilley 16.12.1999

5 Into You (Like a Train) 2 stars **E5 6b**
The steep, seamed bulge 3m right of *Aubergine* is very technical though with some good wires when really needed.
FA. Mike Robertson 3.9.1996

6 Armed Insurgence . 1 star **E3 5c**
The centre of the black wall trending right via an intermittent crack to a steep finish.
FA. G.Stace, S.Cook 15.4.1984

7 Pariah . . . . 1 star **E6 6b**
A good, bold line. From a small ramp 5m right of *Armed Insurgence* (wire), follow side-pulls direct until serious moves left gain a huge flake on *Armed Insurgence*. Finish up this.
FA. Pete Oxley, James Dunlop 3.5.1999

The wall is a bold project dubbed **Black Box Recorder, 7c-ish**.

8 A Taste for Danger . 1 star **E3 6a**
The shallow black corner rising above a break in the ledge is harder than it looks. The gear is sparse but good. Exit rightwards via an easy slab.
FA. Pete Oxley, Brian Tilley 20.5.1999

A
18m
2
4
1
3
5
6
7
8
9
10
Project
Wide ledge above high water mark

9 La Quebrada E3 6a
Strenuous but reasonably safe. Start at a corner 3m right of *A Taste for Danger* above a small belay ledge. Climb into the corner then move out left to follow a central rib through steep black overlaps to an exit flake. Finish as for *A Taste for Danger*.
FA. Pete Oxley, James Dunlop 3.5.1999

10 Whack your Porcupine E1 5b
Climb the steep, tapering groove 3m right of the area of steep rooflets. There is no real belay ledge at the bottom.
FA. Crispin Waddy (solo) 8.9.1986

Approach (routes 11, 12 and 13) - *After a gap of 5m, past an easy corner marking the end of the shallow bay, are the next routes. Abseil directly into these from awkward nut and drilled thread belays.*

11 Barry's Route E1 5c
Move left to the corner/groove.
FA. Barry Clarke 2002

12 The Caretaker 1 E6 6a
A serious headpoint taking a good line up the face left of *Ruurd Ruum* to arrive at an easy exit groove. Hard climbing above a nasty landing with no gear. A solo.
FA. Mike Robertson 6.1998

13 Ruurd Ruum 1 E4 5c
An underrated pitch that starts as for *The Caretaker* then takes a fine series of rightward-slanting cracks to an exit groove. Difficult to protect, take micro-wires.
FA. Crispin Waddy, Toby Foord Kelsey 8.9.1986

The final three lines are all commonly climbed as DWSs.

Approach (routes 14, 15 and 16) - *Abseil in directly to the base of the corner of A Bridge Too Far from wires and blocks.*

14 Leap of Faith. 2 E3 5c
6b, S2. The arete left of the cave gives fine climbing. Move leftwards around the bulge. Be aware of a submerged rock at the base and some loose rock near the finish.
FA. Damian Cook (solo) 6.1993

15 Tsunami . . . 1 E4 6a
6c+, S1. The direct finish to *A Bridge Too Far*. An exposed and bouldery crux through the roof at the top.
FA. Damian Cook 6.1993

16 A Bridge Too Far 1 E1 5b
6a, S1. A good line but with a friable finish. Start at the large corner left of the Conger Cave. Climb the corner to a roof then step down right to a foothold. Bridge the chimney then continue rightwards to the exit of *The Conger*.
Yawn Yawn, VS 4c - The chimney direct is accessed via a traverse right from the belay.
FA. Nick Buckley (solo) 9.1979

Lots of sun | 40 min | Abseil in

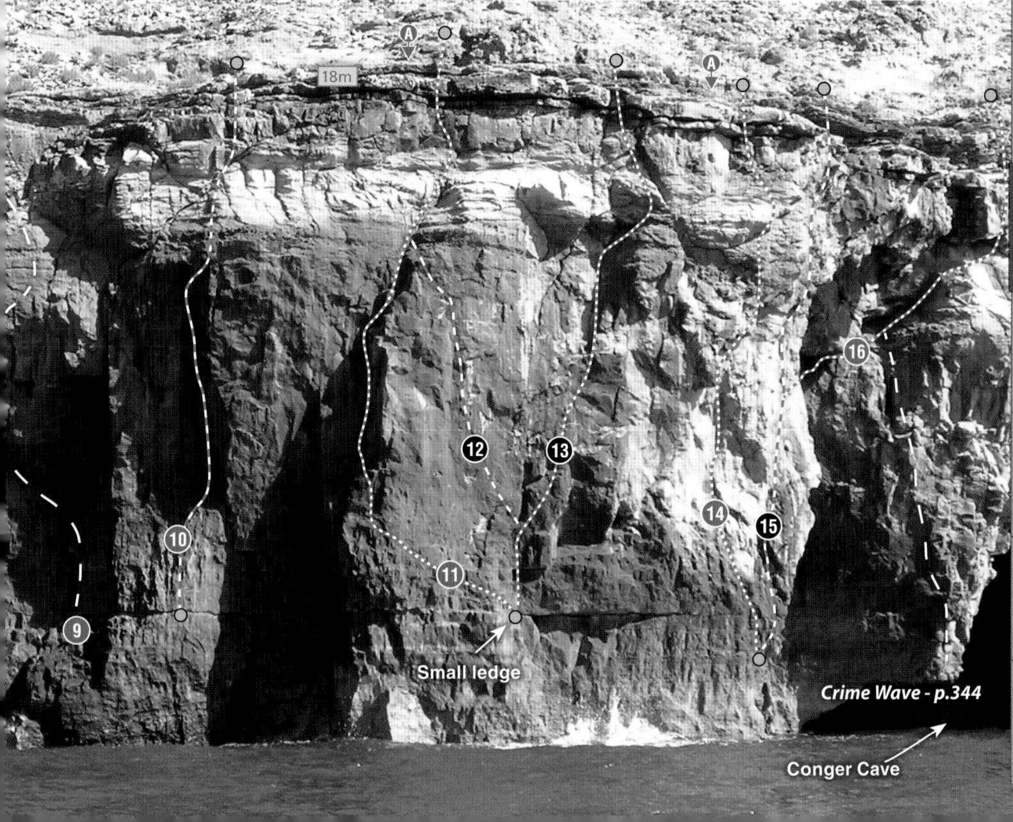

Portland Lulworth Swanage Winspit Hedbury and Smokey Dancing Ledge Guillemot Ledge Blackers Hole Fisherman's Ledge The Promenade Cattle Troughs Boulder Ruckle Subluminal

The Conger Area

The Conger Cave Area is the show-piece of all the deep water soloing venues in Dorset. The majority of the routes provide exciting challenges and have good viewing galleries for spectators, plus high diving areas, adding to the interest. Like the Funky Wall, this area is the preserve of the deep water soloist, and roped ascents are rarely, if ever, undertaken.

Tides and Conditions - High tide is preferred for the solo routes, though it is not a necessity. The cave takes time to dry out and seepage can be in evidence. Stay away in moderate or rough sea conditions.

Approach (routes 1 to 3) - *Abseil to a hanging belay on an undercut pillar below and left of The Conger exit (looking in). The same point can be reached by traversing the fine technical wall between the base of A Bridge Too Far and the hanging stance. This link is* **The John Williams Traverse, E1 6a,** *6b, S0.*

1 Crime Wave 1 **E2 5c**
6b, S1. The face left of *Furious Pig*. It makes a good descent solo when familiar with the area.
FA. Damian Cook (solo) 6.1993

2 Furious Pig 1 **E2 5c**
6b+, S1. Climb the left-hand pillar and flake to *The Conger* exit.
FA. Crispin Waddy (solo) 3.1989

3 The Great Shark Hunt . . 3 **E4 6a**
7a, S1. The right-hand groove from the hanging pillar start. One of the best deep water solos around.
FA. Crispin Waddy 3.1989

4 The Appearing 1 **E5 6a**
7a+, S1. Approach by boat. Start in the back of the cave at a bottomless chimney on the left. Climb to a good ledge where a winding series of cracks leads to the high point and finish of *The Vanishing*. A link-up - **Red Bully** *7a+, S1* - follows *The Appearing* to the good ledge, then moves leftwards over a slab and bulge to join *The Vanishing* just before it reaches daylight.
FA. (both) Adam Wainwright (solo) 31.8.2002

5 The Vanishing 3 **E5 6a**
7a+ S1. Approach by boat, or from below *The Conger,* enter the cave by ducking under a low roof and traversing wet rock to a ledge at the back of the cave. From the ledge, move up and left across a slab onto an arete (spotter needed). Climb the arete to the top of the cave and a good rest. Move down and out to *The Conger* chimney via complex moves. Finish as for *The Conger*.
FA. Mike Robertson (solo) 16.8.2001

Approach (routes 6 to 17) - *Solo or abseil down the route Helix to the sea-level ledge at its base.*

6 The Conger . . . . . . Top 50 **E2 5c**
6b, S1. Memorable. A fine climb in a very atmospheric position. Start by traversing in along the break to a niche just before the cave. Continue up past another corner and across slabs until stopped by a wall. Go round the rib and bridge out and up the chimney. Keep bridging, then pull out left and up to finish.
FA. Richard Crewe 7.9.1969. FFA. Frank Farrell 9.1979
First soloed by Nick Buckley 26.6.1983

7 Snap, Crackle and Plop **E3 5c**
6b+, S2. A direct finish above the chimney of *The Conger*.
FA. Damian Cook (solo) 11.9.1990

Lots of sun 40 min Abseil in

8 Jellied . . . . 1★ **E3 5c**
6b+, S1. Another variation finish above the chimney of *The Conger*. Break rightwards above the big roof to a prow.
FA. Jon Biddle (solo) 8.1990

9 The Drowning Pool. 2★ **E6 6b**
7b+, S2. Make some hard moves through the left-hand side of the roof, finishing on the last section of *Jellied*.
FA. Pete Oxley (solo) 27.3.1999

10 Swordfish Trombones 3★ **E5 6b**
7a+, S2. A wild trip through the roofs above the hanging slabs of *The Conger*. The big roof provides most of the excitement with a hard pull over to finish.
FA. Crispin Waddy (solo) 27.9.1987

11 The Musharagi Tree . . . 1★ **E2 5c**
6b, S2. The diagonal hanging slab which can be started direct via the hanging arete (harder). Start at the niche of *The Conger*.
FA. Jon Biddle, John Williams 1.8.1988

12 Halcyon Days . . . . 1★ **E2 5b**
Not a DWS. Tackle the fine overhanging corner above a good belay ledge to the finish of *The Musharagi Tree*.
FA. Gordon Jenkin, Frank Farrell 9.1979

13 Herman Borg's Basic Pulley Slippage . . . . 2★ **E6 6b**
7b+, S2. The left arete of the side wall is very technical.
FA. Pete Oxley (solo) 1996. Originally with a bolt by Pete Oxley in 1993.

14 Freeborn Man . . Top 50 **E4 6a**
6c, S1. A classic, with a soft landing. From halfway along the approach traverse, climb the slab and then the steep pocketed wall above to a big hole. Swing left and make some final tricky moves onto the top slab. Linking from just below the crux to *Herman Borg's Basic Pulley Slippage* is **Freeborn Borg,** *7a+, S1*, and continuing direct onto the slab is **Freeborn Direct,** *7a, S1*.
Photo on page 336.
FA. Nick Buckley, Kevin Turner 8.1979
FA. (Borg) Pete Oxley (solo) 19.3.1999
FA. (Direct)Mike Ford (solo) 1990s

15 Troubled Waters . . . . . 2★ **HVS 5a**
5, S1. A line up the wall right of *Freeborn Man* is popular as a warm-up for the bigger challenges to the left.
FA. Pete Oxley (solo) 15.7.85

16 Helix Direct. . . . . **S 4a**
The crack just right of *Troubled Waters* to join *Helix*.

17 Helix . . . . 2★ **Diff**
A superb climb for its grade - solid and varied. It spirals leftwards up a hidden slab above the Conger Cave.

18m

A

Descent - Abseil from twin stakes or down-climb the line of *Helix*

Approach traverse

9 10 11 12 13 14 15 16 17

Portland Lulworth Swanage Winspit Hedbury and Smokey Dancing Ledge Guillemot Ledge Blackers Hole Fisherman's Ledge The Promenade Cattle Troughs Boulder Ruckle Subluminal

Squid Area

This area is often ignored in favour of its more illustrious neighbours but it contains a good set of mainly harder routes that tackle the roof and overlap covered wall.

Approach - Reverse down *Helix* or abseil from stakes above the finish of *Quo Vadis*. The first route in this area is on the far left (looking in) of the sea-level ledges, just before the cliff turns a corner.

Tides and conditions - The ledges are just above high tide but keep away in rough seas. The roofs can be very greasy at times.

1 Felix . . . . **VDiff**
Pleasant climbing up the juggy wall and tricky high groove.

2 Rough Boys . . . . **HVS 5b**
Good but slightly escapable. Start 3m right of a wide crack. The hard bit is reserved for the upper crack.
FA. Nigel Coe, Frank Farrell 4.8.1984

3 Bon Firé **E1 5c**
A great little expedition. Climb *Rough Boys* then move right and up before traversing rightwards across the lip of the big upper roof. Finish straight up.
FA. Crispin Waddy, Dave Thomas 4.1989

4 The Wey of All Men **E3 6a**
Well protected and varied. Start as for *Rough Boys*.
1) 4c, 10m. Climb up to clear the first overhang then traverse right above it to belay near the end of a slab.
2) 6a, 15m. Climb the roof crack on the left (crux) then continue direct via a thin crack.
FA. Dave Thomas, Crispin Waddy 25.3.1989

Lots of sun | 40 min | Abseil in

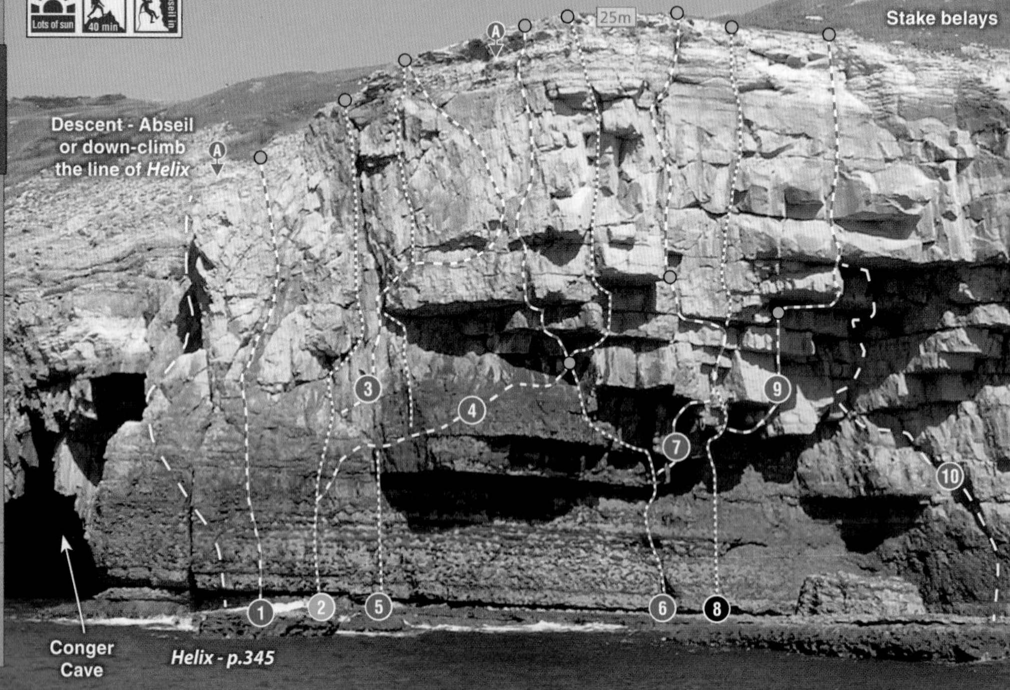

5 FAGI Code 65 . . . . **E3 5c**
Climb straight up to the corner of the roof and hand traverse the horizontal crack right for 2m. Ascend the flake-crack to a small niche under the roof and follow *Bon Fire* up the arete and right. Then instead of traversing forge straight up the wall to an overlap and shallow niche above. Finish past this and a ledge.
FA. Marti Hallett, Sue Hazel 11.7.2010

6 Quo Vadis Direct **E2 5c**
Despite the name, a wandering route up the buttress left of the impending roofs above the main ledge. The start is often wet.
1) 5c, 8m. Pull over the first roof then move out left and up a short groove. Continue through the next roof onto a slab and belay on *The Wey of All Men*.
2) 5b, 15m. Traverse right and break through the next overhang. Come back left to an arete then climb direct, via an open groove, past another overhang, to the top.
FA. Chris King, Pat Littlejohn 1.3.1979

7 Paternoster **E2 5c**
An awkward undertaking. Start as for *Quo Vadis Direct*.
1) 5c, 20m. Climb into a niche and then up into a chimney/slot (2 threads). Break right to gain a blocky corner then traverse left, 4m along a break, beneath a strip roof. Climb into an open groove and belay on a perched ledge on the left.
2) 5b, 8m. Ascend the groove above to a snappy finish.
FA. Martin Barnicott, R.Henderson 30.5.1976

8 Bad Young Brother **E4 6b**
A direct route with reasonable gear. From the first niche on *The Ritz*, break left (crux) around a bulge (2 threads on the left) to gain the blocky corner on *Paternoster*. Go direct over the roof (peg) then climb straight up twin cracks, passing a large flake. Follow a crack above (thread) to the top.
FA. Pete Oxley 28.5.1988

25m
Stake belays
Descent - Abseil or down-climb the line of *Helix*
Conger Cave
Helix - p.345

9 The Ritz . . . . Top 50 E3 6a

A brilliant outing for the grade, travelling through some awesome overhangs with good protection. Start below a niche.
1) 5b, 10m. Attain the small niche then move right into a chimney. Swing right along a roof and climb a groove to the next roof. Ape through this to an amazing hanging perch to belay.
2) 6a, 10m. Put on your cycle clips and power through the roof crack on the right to below another roof. Traverse left to an arete then climb the corner above to finish.
FA. Nick Buckley, Kevin Turner 11.1978

10 Squid 2 E2 5c

A tough roof crack. Start beneath the right wall of the roofed central bay at a diagonal crack.
1) 5a, 10m. Follow the crack up left to a ledge and take a small chimney to the left of a roof. Belay on a good ledge on the right.
2) 5c, 15m. Assault the brutal roof to a breather in a chimney below the next roof. Traverse left into the light to join *The Ritz* at the arete and finish as for that route.
FA. Richard Crewe, J.Yaldren 6.8.1967
FFA. Falco Rech, Howard Lancashire 1975

11 Crackers E3 5c

A bold undertaking skirting the right-hand side of the roofs.
1) 5b, 10m. Climb direct above the start of *Squid* via a short groove. Trend left to the *Squid* belay.
2) 5c, 15m. Climb rightwards to make difficult and scary moves over the roof into a small groove. Finish straight up.
FA. Kevin Turner, Nick Buckley 9.1979

12 Mental as Anything 1 E4 6b

A safe and strenuous undertaking. Climb past a ledge then up a groove to tackle the first overhang (2 threads). Pull straight over another roof to a scoop. Undercut rightwards and cross a final overhang to finish up an easier cracked corner on its right.
FA. Pete Oxley 22.12.1987

13 Rock Around the Block Direct 1 E3 6a

An enjoyable outing which is more sustained than cruxy. Start at the left-hand side of a rock pool. Trend right to gain a chimney then pull over the block roof directly on its left-hand side. Continue to the top via the big groove.
FA. Pete Oxley 15.2.1988

14 Sting in the Tail . . . 2 E4 5c

Bold but with great rock. Reported to have lost a hold and maybe harder. Start on the right-hand side of a rock pool. Climb past a roof and up a flake on its left-hand side. Move rightwards up a wall passing a shallow groove to gain the upper corner. Weave up this, first rightwards, then finish back left (poor peg). Save some umpf for the final moves.
FA. Crispin Waddy, Pete Oxley 11.7.1986

15 Limited Edition 2 E3 5c

Start just right of an arete. Climb to a shallow right-facing corner. Climb this easily to a roof then move direct up the impending wall above to the top. The original start has suffered a rockfall and is now much bolder above the low hard section.
FA. Gordon Jenkin, Frank Farrell 17.5.1980

Portland
Lulworth
Swanage
Winspit
Hedbury and Smokey
Dancing Ledge
Guillemot Ledge
Blackers Hole
Fisherman's Ledge
The Promenade
Cattle Troughs
Boulder Ruckle
Subluminal

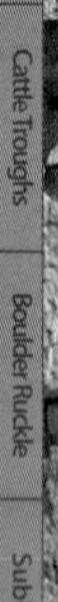

Vigilante Area

The right-hand end of the Squid Area has a couple of huge boulders on the platform. The wall above these has a few routes that are of interest to the enthusiast.
Approach and Tides - Climb or abseil down *Helix* and walk right along the ledge. The routes all start from a raised ledge well above the sea, and can be done in moderate seas or at any tide by abseiling in directly.

1 Aquascrotum II . . . . **HVS 5a**
Climb the corner, moving left around the bulge at the top.
FA. R.Snell, I.Howell 12.2.1967

2 Slow Road to Ruin . 1 **E5 6a**
After an easy start, follow the bold, right-trending groove to finish on the last moves of *Vigilante* (shared peg).
FA. Mike Robertson 11.7.1997

3 Vigilante. 2 **E6 6b**
The central line direct up the wall gives intricate climbing that does not relent. It is bold low down, then continues direct before trending left (peg) near the top. Small wires needed.
FA. Pete Oxley 3.4.1988

4 Sue's Route 1 **E2 5b**
Enjoyable. Climb the technical cracks and flakes that form a long shallow groove on the right.
FA. W.Church, R.Houston 1968

5 Girl from the Snow Country . 2 **E1 5c**
A hidden gem. From *Sue's Route,* follow a diagonal flake onto a slab and the lovely calcite pocket vein above. This leads straight through the roof and direct to the top.
FA. Pete Oxley 3.4.1988

6 All Quiet on the Southern Front
. . . . 1 **E3 5c**
An absorbing climb with tricky gear. From the right-hand end of the ledge, swing out right to a spike and then continue fairly directly up the vague rib on finger flakes.
FA. Pete Oxley 20.6.1987

Palace of the Brine Area

A massive cave that is home to some of the biggest and hardest overhangs around. Good conditions are hard to come by, although there is little seepage.
Approach and Tides (routes 7 to 21) - At low tide, walk to the routes from the Squid Area. At high tide, abseil directly to the ledge below *Calcitron*. The abseil is from 2 stakes found about 20m below and east of the pylon. For Routes 11 to 16, traverse leftwards to two small stances 5m up the wall.

7 Impending Gleam . . . . Top 50 **E4 5c**
A tremendous climb up the huge, towering groove.
FA. Nick Buckley 1993

8 Temple Redneck . . Top 50 **7c+**
A sensational and highly-rated route up the arete on the left-hand side of the cave. Climb the right-hand side of the arete and over a large roof. Continue up the steep wall to the break on *The Mind Cathedral.* Swing out left to insitu lower-off krabs, or belay and finish as for *The Mind Cathedral.*
FA. Pete Oxley 22.2.1993

9 Haka Peruperu. 3 **8a**
A major stamina pitch. Start up *Temple Redneck* to its break, and have a shake out. Pull up rightwards to a haven with a difficult kneebar shake out. Drop down and execute a complex series of swings rightwards under the roof, passing a strange fang to join the last section of *Lifeforce.* From big flakes at the lip, more tricky moves lead up a short groove to the top.
Photo on page 335.
FA. Pete Oxley 12.6.2005

10 The Mind Cathedral . . . Top 50 **E6 6b**
The big groove in the roof creates some well protected and outrageous climbing. A proper classic.
1) 6b, 30m. Climb the groove (2 threads) to a belay on the lip.
2) 5b, 8m. Finish straight up a short wall.
FA. Pete Oxley 21.5.1988

Lots of sun | 40 min | Abseil in

Stake belays
18m
Palace of the Brine Area
Limited Edition - p.347
Ledge well above high tide level

11 Lifeforce . . . . Top 50 8b
One of the biggest free overhangs in the UK. The quality of the rock and creative movement are magnificent. The route takes the arcing central line across the great cave. Good cool conditions essential.
FA. Pete Oxley 2.10.2005

12 Palace of the Brine . . . 3 8a+
A huge climb taking an amazing line through the roof of the cave. Start from a non-tidal ledge, and trend right up a blank wall. Then ape out left to tackle the horizontal groove in the 15m roof.
FA. Pete Oxley 21.9.1991

13 Drunken Butterfly . . . . . 3 7c+
The hanging V-groove gives another big roof climb in an outrageous position. Quite intimidating.
FA. Pete Oxley 25.3.1993

14 Paparazzi News . . . 2 E6 6b
A sensational pitch. Climb a blank groove above the belay to undercuts, then blast out rightwards through the roofs into a shallow groove. Exit via a corner on the left, as for *Drunken Butterfly*.
FA. Pete Oxley 17.2.1988

15 Cave Rave 2 E5 6a
A wild pump-out up the steep groove 4m left of a deep chimney. Start from a ledge at 6m. Climb the groove and roofs (thread) before moving left to a corner (peg). Finish up this.
FA. Pete Oxley 14.11.1987

16 The Beautiful and the Damned 1 E5 6a
Start as for *Cave Rave*, but ascend the serious slab on the right to a peg. Pull over the roof and up a short hard groove to a thread. Finish rightwards (thread) to a pre-placed rope.
FA. Pete Oxley 12.6.1988. Reclimbed after a rockfall by Dave Pickford

17 D Sharp . . . . 1 HVS 5a
A good line at a bargain grade for this area. Climb the groove right of the big chimney to a niche then move right to finish up some steep cracks.
FA. George Hounsome, T.Daniells 1980

18 Test Department 2 E2 5b
Fine climbing up the left side of the wall. Lots of threads.
FA. Pete Oxley 10.7.1986

19 Damage Case 2 E3 5c
The straight crack. Many threads are in place.
FA. Pete Oxley 11.7.1986

20 Calcitron 2 E2 5b
The crack in the middle of the wall has 3 threads. A classy mid-grade route and much better that it looks.
FA. Pete Oxley 11.7.1986

21 Stress Fracture E3 5c
A sustained line (just off of the topo). Start by a thread and some slots. Move up to a finger jug and continue up and slightly right to a juggy protrusion. Trend up leftwards and take a shallow groove to the bulge above. Pass the bulge to reach easier ground. Trend left to *Calcitron* and then back right to finish.
FA. Matt Perks, Andy Lamont 24.4.2011

Lots of sun | 40 min | Abseil in | Tidal

The Promenade to Cattle Troughs

Taking a breather midway up the steep crack of *Lobster* (HVS 5b) - *page 365* - at Flake Ledge. Flake Ledge and its near neighbour, Unknown Ledge, have some good atmospheric pitches, and are less frequented than some of the more popular sections of Swanage. The walls of Unknown Ledge and the large overhangs of The Promenade can be seen in the middle distance.

Portland
Lulworth
Swanage
Winspit
Hedbury and Smokey
Dancing Ledge
Guillemot Ledge
Blackers Hole
Fisherman's Ledge
The Promenade
Cattle Troughs
Boulder Ruckle
Subluminal

	No star	1	2	3
Mod to S	1	-	-	-
HS to HVS	-	8	1	1
E1 to E3	7	19	10	-
E4 and up	9	23	21	6

Harry Massey on the classic sport climb *Tessellations* (7b) - *page 355* - at The Promenade, Swanage. Photo: Marti Hallett

The Promenade is the first of the predominantly sport climbing crags passed on the approach from Durlston Country Park and is one of the best roof climbing crags in the south of England. The savage bulging walls here give a host of powerful pitches that hit you from the first move and keep going until you heave yourself around the final lip to clip the lower-off - exhausted but satisfied. Whilst most visitors will come here for the excellent bolted roofs, the trad lines that sit comfortably between the bolts should not be ignored. Many of these also take on the stacked roofs at some impressively big grades.

There isn't too much here for those leading in the mid and lower grades though although the routes described are worthwhile and you can also easily combine a visit with the nearby Unknown Ledge. A handful of the recorded boulder problems have also been included, as they stay dry in the rain.

The big flat belay ledges at the base of the crag are another of The Promenade's enticing features although they are prone to being wave-washed even in moderate seas - watch where you leave your rucksacks!

Approach Also see map on page 266

From Durlston car park, follow the road towards the lighthouse then turn west (right - looking out) along the coast path. Continue to a stile just before the two mile pylons. From here, drop down a steep grass gully to a ledge above a large rock amphitheatre. Descend this (Diff) past a tricky step at the bottom to gain the platform. There are abseil bolts if required (the rope can be pulled down afterwards) and this is probably advisable on a first visit.

Tides and Conditions

Conditions are often favourable in this area as the severely-overhanging nature of the rock keeps many of the routes dry, and numerous east and west-facing buttresses mean that sun and shade can be found in about equal measure. The sea-level platform is non-tidal, however the odd section becomes wave-washed in even moderate seas. Keep well away in rough seas or on windy days. The Promenade receives all the sun that is going and is best visited on bright, fresh days to avoid the dampness that can linger on some of the holds. There is a little seepage on some of the steeper roof routes but most of the area is unaffected. The main roofs are always dry by the middle of summer and are in the shade because of their steepness.

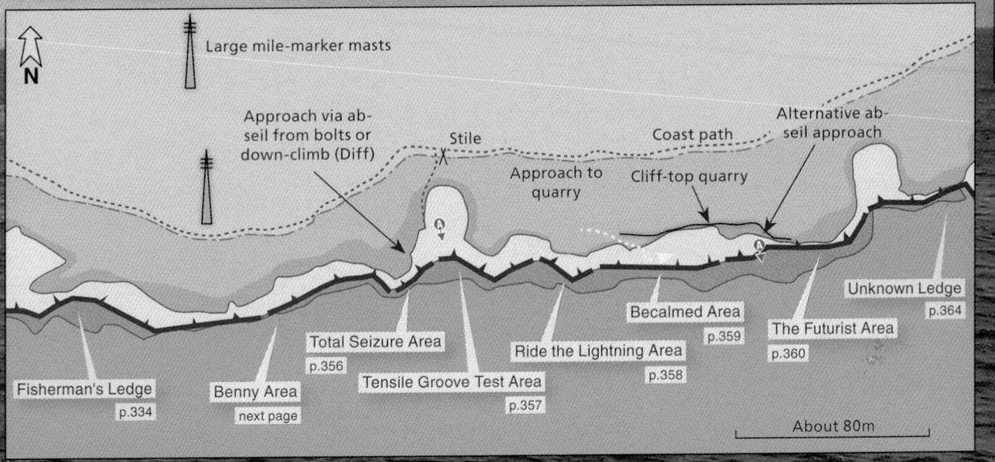

Benny Area

The far western end of The Promenade is a fine section of cliff that has high quality, well-bolted lines which give powerful routes above ledges.
Tides - Non-tidal, but keep away in rough seas.
Approach - The first routes start at the west end of the ledge (left - looking in), where further progress is prevented by the deep sea-cave of *Benny*. Stake belays are in place for all the routes that top-out.

1 Benny . . . . Top 50 **A1/VS**
This popular but serious undertaking delves into the deep zawn at the western limits of The Promenade. Calm seas are essential for the first pitch - **if it is remotely rough then keep away**.
1) A1, 15m. Drop down and follow the side wall of the zawn just above the water, pulling on fixed threads and nuts to gain a rock bridge at the back of the zawn.
2) 4b , 15m. Climb the dark chimney above on good holds, until you are spat out of the blow hole, belay immediately. Lots of slings for threads needed.
3) 4b , 20m. Traverse awkwardly right to the arete, where a ledge leads right to easy ground.
FA. Scott Titt, Dave Gumn, Richard Crewe 24.4.1976

2 Atonement 2 **7c**
A series of huge bulges above *Benny*. Start from the westerly edge of the platform. Lower off the single-bolt belay once easy ground is reached. In a great position.
FA. Pete Oxley 13.8.2002

3 Air of Detachment . 2 **7b**
An independent direct version of *Crimes Against the Soul*, gaining the groove direct from the overhung slab, via some wild moves.
FA. Rob Kennard, Bernard Exley, Rich White 31.5.2008

4 Crimes Against the Soul . . . 1 **7a**
The steep rightward line leading into a deep groove.
FA. Pete Oxley 8.4.1989

5 Hot Flush Down Under **7b**
A desperate chimney. Trend right to finish up the fine wall.
FA. Pete Oxley 24.9.1993

6 Hot to Trot . . . . 1 **7b+**
A powerful roof to start, then take the upper wall of *Hot Flush Down Under*.
FA. Pete Oxley 19.6.1994

7 Gangster Lean 2 **6c**
After a hard pull over a roof, the route follows a fantastic sustained leaning face, with no hard moves.
FA. Pete Oxley 22.7.1986

8 Seppukku 2 **6c**
Climb direct past two roofs to undercuts in a third roof. Move left to a vague rib that leads to the lower-off.
FA. Pete Oxley 3.1989

9 Chicago Peace . . . . 2 **6b+**
Climb over bulges then trend right into a left-facing groove, which leads to the lower-off.
FA. Pete Oxley 31.1.1987

Lots of sun | 30 min | Dry in the rain | Abseil in

⑩ Clamp Down . . . . 2 **6c+**
Climb up to the roof and then boulder over it to the upper wall.
FA. Pete Oxley, Andy Bell 19.11.2005

⑪ J.J.Burnell, King of the Bass
. . . . 1 **6b**
Above a break in the ledge, move right up a slab then layback around the roof and climb the easier wall. Unlikely looking territory for a 6b.
FA. Pete Oxley 7.4.1989

⑫ Just Another Victim 2 **7b+**
Super-steep climbing with wild moves. Initial bulges lead to a roof crack that requires good footwork.
FA. Pete Oxley 10.6.1994

⑬ Godfodder. . . . . . . 2 **7c+**
A good route through the mighty 4m roof crack. Impressive. The easy second pitch requires gear.
FA. Pete Oxley 27.5.1991

There is an open project to the right of Godfodder.

⑭ A Bosch Boy, a Trad, and a Funky Dredd
. . . . **E4 6b**
A short roof problem. Swing left to a lower-off. Old bolts. 7a+ if re-bolted
FA. Pete Oxley 14.4.1991

⑮ Show of Hands 1 **7a**
Start up a shallow groove and gain the edge of the huge ceiling before making a hard rockover to finish.
FA. Pete Oxley, Rich White 20.7.2002

⑯ Empowerless. 1 **7a**
Short, sharp roof climbing around the overhang left of the zawn.
FA. Brian Tilley 29.8.1994

⑰ Community Service . . . 1 **7a**
A neat eliminate. Start up *Empowerless,* before moving right onto the prow proper. Climb this without bridging across the chimney.
FA. Pete Oxley, Rich White 20.7.2002

⑱ Revelation Chimney . . . 2 **VS 4c**
Great rock and a superb line. This trad classic tackles the huge chimney right above the zawn via some sustained bridging and back-and-footing.
FA. George Hounsome, Scott Titt 28.3.1976

⑲ Waves Become Wings . 3 **7b+**
A superb leaning wall. Best conditions are in the afternoon when the wall gets the sun.
FA. Pete Oxley 19.6.1994

⑳ Birth Pains of New Nations
. . . . 3 **7b**
The centre of the leaning face, joining *Waves Become Wings* at half-height. Another high calibre line that again needs the sun on it for the best conditions. High in the grade.
FA. Pete Oxley 8.10.1986

㉑ Tessellations. . . . . Top 50 **7b**
The overhanging arete right of *Revelation Chimney* is a majestic route that doesn't let up. Start direct up the lower arete.
Photo on page 352.
FA. Pete Oxley 10.7.1986

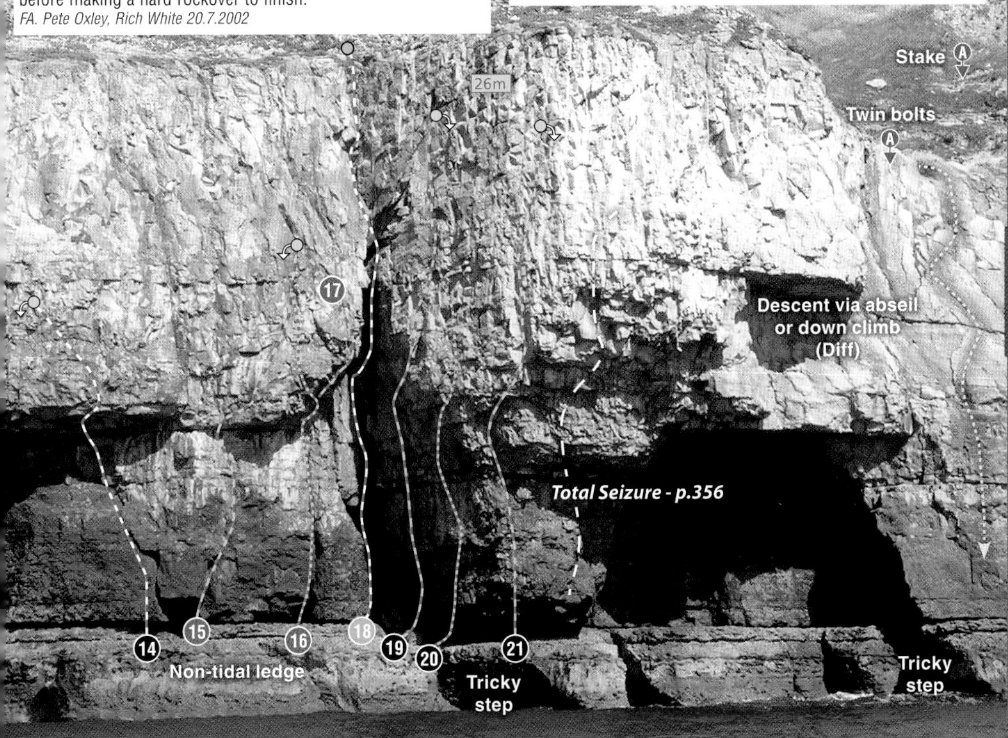

Total Seizure Area

The best section of the Promenade for spectacular climbing out over the sea. The routes are all worthwhile and require both power and stamina. The belay ledge is a little uncomfortable and care is needed when lowering off to avoid going over-board!

Tides - Non-tidal but keep away in rough seas.

1 Carpe Diem . . . . . . 7b+

An excellent, steep line. Start up an easy groove and then climb a roof to gain a groove. Move leftwards on a steep and natural line to join *Tessellations*.

FA. Pete Oxley, Rich White 21.9.2001

2 Total Seizure 7c

A great route which tackles a set of huge bulges. Often in condition. Start as for *Carpe Diem*, then weave through the bulges to a lower-off where the angle drops back.

FA. Pete Oxley 28.11.1987

3 State of Play . . . . . 7c+

Super-steep moves that break rightwards over the wide roof right of *Total Seizure* to eventually finish up *Solid State Logic*.

FA. Pete Oxley 2004

4 Solid State Logic . . 8a

A brief but powerful climb over a 6m overlapping ceiling, that is easier for the short. Reverse to retrieve the gear.

FA. Pete Oxley 12.5.1991

There is an open project over the roof above the belay.

5 Defining Moment 7c+

Very powerful climbing up the right-hand side of the *Solid State Logic* cave. Needs good conditions. The nearby ledge is strictly out of bounds if you had any ideas about sneaking a rest.

FA. Pete Oxley 21.9.2001

6 The Flail Trail 6a

One of the few easier routes at The Promenade.

FA. Pete Oxley 29.5.1985

7 My New Top . . . . 6b+

A short direct line below *Flail Trail* is not bolted.

FA. Danny Woodward 12.7.1996

8 Violent Breed . . . . 7b+

A good hard power problem. Photogenic and not to be missed. Start up the wall and then swing left and up over the bulges.

FA. Pete Oxley 23.5.1987

9 Down in the Sewer . 7b

A striking line up a leaning groove that features sustained and powerful climbing on great rock. Climb the hanging groove line, starting up the first few feet of *Violent Breed*.

FA. Pete Oxley 23.5.1987

10 Elements of Abstraction 7c

An extension to *Down in the Sewer*. Head right under the top roof across *Tensile*. Then swing along the lip of the roof with hard moves to exit up its right edge.

FA. P.Oxley 2006

11 Tensile Groove Test . . . E4 6a

A big overhanging trad line starting at the back of the cave. Good steep moves that are well protected. Can be damp.

FA. Pete Oxley 11.10.1986

12 Crest of a Wave . . . 7b

An audacious line that swaggers leftwards through the roofs to finish next to *Tensile Groove Test*. The start is very technical.

FA. Pete Oxley 12.6.1996

13 Crystal Voyager 2. . . . . E4 6a

Reclimbed after the crux roof collapsed. Start via an awkward crack to jugs, then, using huge undercuts, initiate hard moves rightwards up a blank wall (peg) to the roof above. Further difficult undercut moves lead rightwards past the final two roofs. Finish up a pleasant groove. Stake belays.

FA. Pete Oxley 28.12.2005

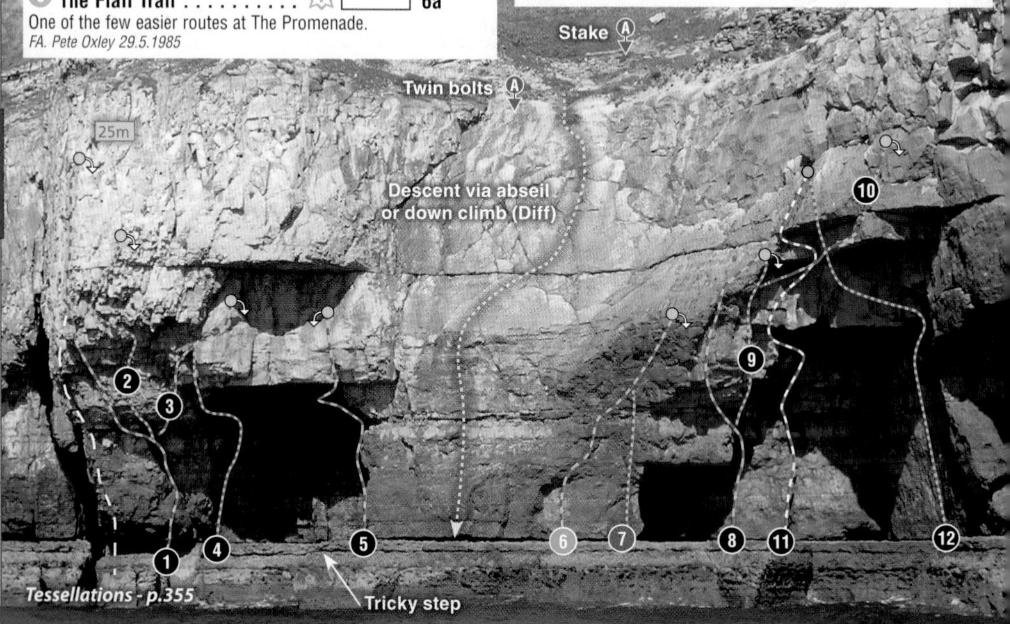

14 Star of Africa . . . . . 1 star 7b+
Reclimbed since rockfall. Start easily up the slab and cross the roof before heading diagonally rightwards up the blank headwall to lower off the last bolt.
FA. Pete Oxley 29.8.2001

15 Len's Rule of the Sea . . . . 2 stars E3 6a
Another worthy trad line that tackles the staggered flake-line above a break in the ledge. The start is bold and at times wet.
FA. Dave Ivory, A.Ivory 2.8.1983

16 Yorkshire Talk . . . . 2 stars 7b+
The photogenic arete right of *Len's Rule of the Sea*. A quality route, with a campus-style crux.
FA. Pete Oxley 12.6.1996. Re-climbed post rockfall in 2001 by Pete Oxley.

17 Shock to the System 2 stars 7c+
The heinous blank roof is very powerful.
FA. Pete Oxley 1999

18 The Resistor . . . . 1 star 7c
Great moves over the big bulging overhang just left of *Electric Circus*. Start up *Electric Circus* and share its belay.
FA. Pete Oxley 20.8.2002

19 Electric Circus . . 2 stars 7b+
A fine route with an intense sequence on small holds. Pass a short, left-facing corner low down. Very technical.
FA. Pete Oxley 27.2.1996

20 Volts Discharge . . . . . . 1 star 7a
Bulging rock and hidden pockets 2m right of *Electric Circus*. Easier when you know where the holds are.
FA. Pete Oxley 2.11.1986

Tensile Groove Test Area

A popular section of the cliff that has a trio of good trad lines, along with some powerful roof climbs that are often accessed by technical faces. The caves can be damp and greasy.
Tides - Non-tidal but keep away in rough seas.

21 Mr. Gymnasia . . . . 1 star 7a
Fun moves following the slight crack.
FA. Pete Oxley 16.6.1985

22 Gym'n'Tonic . . . . 7b+
A bouldery link-up from the first holds on *Load it for Me* leftward over the big roof to join *Mr. Gymnasia*. Good climbing, but it is a bit of an eliminate.
FA. Pete Oxley 14.9.2001

23 Load it for Me . . . . 2 stars 7b
After a hard start, move rightwards into a shallow groove with a seepage streak.
FA. Pete Oxley 4.10.1986

24 Load it for Me Direct . . 2 stars 7b+
A direct start is also possible.
FA. Pete Oxley 27.2.1993

25 Deep Puddle Dynamics. 1 star 7c+
The tough roof and wall above.
FA. Dan Kennard 2.2005

26 The Garage Mechanic 1 star 7c
A powerful problem starting just left of a small pool.
FA. Pete Oxley 10.5.1993

27 The Undertow Traverse. 2 stars V6
18m. Start beneath *Volts Discharge* and traverse powerfully right around the roofed bay to a slab at the start of *Chasm Groove*. Can be linked to *Fat Lip*. Not marked on the topo.
FA. Pete Oxley 8.2001

Lots of sun | 30 min | Dry in the rain | Abseil in

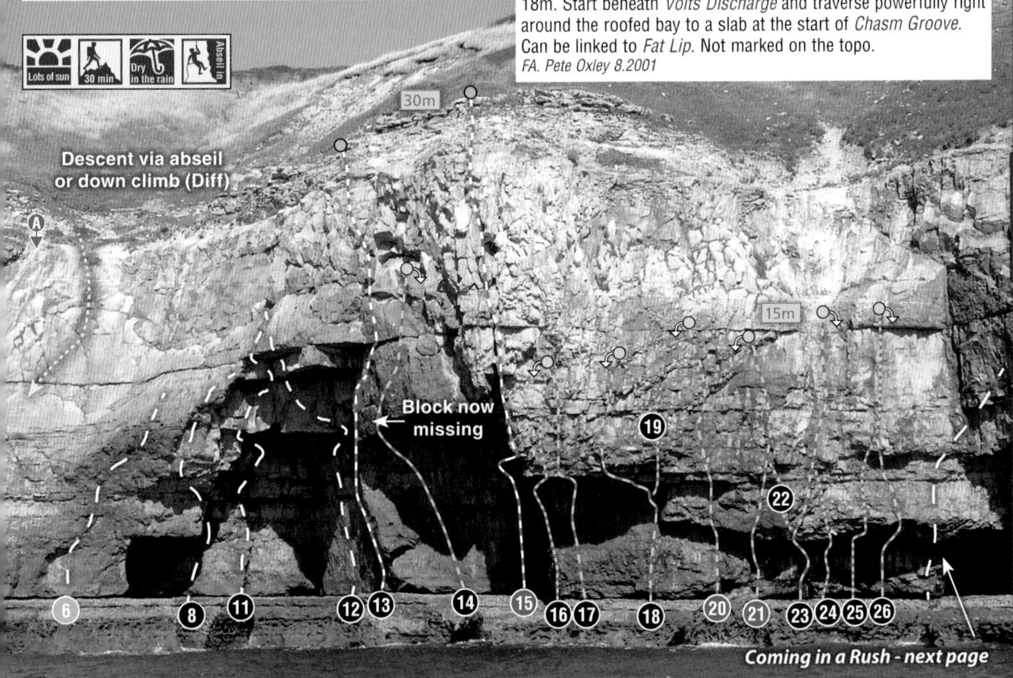

Portland Lulworth Swanage Winspit Hedbury and Smokey Dancing Ledge Guillemot Ledge Blackers Hole Fisherman's Ledge The Promenade Cattle Troughs Boulder Ruckle Subliminal

Ride the Lightning Area

This deep recess has been developed mainly as a bouldering area. The problems here are short, powerful and mostly hard and are included as they are often dry.
Tides - Non-tidal but keep away in rough seas.
Approach - At the base of the descent, turn left (looking out) and continue to the roofed recess.

1 Coming in a Rush . . . . 7b+
A hard roof to start before trending rightwards across *Chasm Groove* to climb the wall. 2m to the right, the roof can be crossed by **Jump Camp, V6**. One for the tall only.
FA. Pete Oxley 21.2.1987

2 Fat Lip . . . . 1 star V6
Squat start at a huge jug low on the left. Move up right along the lip of the roof before slapping up the hanging arete. Reverse back down *Chasm Groove*. Bold, so come with a spotter.
FA. Pete Oxley 9.9.2001

3 Chasm Groove . . . . 2 stars E1 5b
The break in the crag angle above the pool on the ledge. Start to the right and traverse left above the overhang until the groove can be accessed and then climbed to a slabby exit out left.
FA. M.Boater, D.Fell 19.4.1969

4 Ride the Lightning . 2 stars V10
A long boulder traverse from left to right.
FA. Pete Oxley 3.1993

5 Drive By . . . . 1 star V6
Tackle the big bulge to a high pointed jug 3m left of *Juggernaut*.
FA. Pete Oxley 1.9.2001

Lots of sun · 30 min · Abseil in

6 Juggernaut V7
A boulder problem to link two jugs, over the largest roof in the cave. The right-hand start - **Jack Knife** - is the same grade.
FA. Pete Oxley 28.2.1993. FA. (Jack Knife) Pete Oxley 3.1993

7 Techno Sketching V6
Boulder up the blank groove 5m left of the seaward arete.
FA. Pete Oxley 3.1993

8 Puddle Jumper V5
Climb the right wall of the blank groove.
FA. Pete Oxley 3.1993

9 Baby-faced Assassin 1 star 7a+
A well-positioned steepy just inside the cave, starting via a short crack.
FA. Pete Oxley 25.6.1996

10 Boongary . . . . 1 star HVS 4c
Climb steeply up left to the easier upper wall.
FA. Scott Titt, Brian Tilley 13.2.1978

11 Hip Hop . . . . 1 star HVS 5a
Start up *Boongary* and then follow a small ramp right and make a powerful move over the roof. Finish up the clean slab.

12 German New Order 1 star 7b+
The hard wall 5m right of the cave to a juggy roof.
FA. Pete Oxley 18.9.1986

13 Blitzkrieg . . . . 7b+
A hard and fingery problem with a crux at the roof. Old bolts.
FA. Pete Oxley 14.12.1986

14 Big Brother Is Watching . . . 1 star 7a
Some big pulls on jugs through the roof.
FA. Pete Oxley 14.3.1987

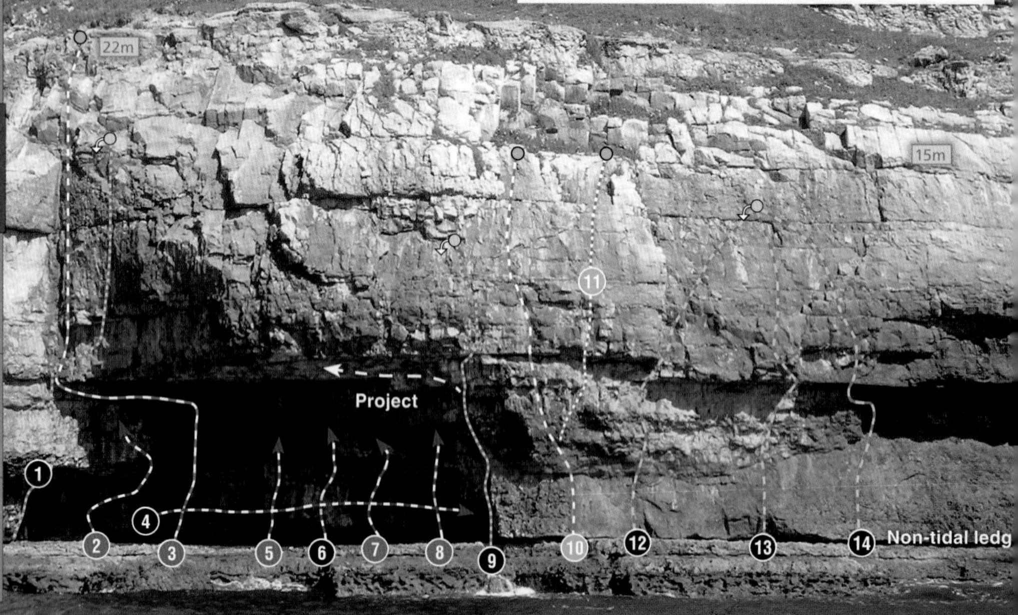

Becalmed Area

This section of cliff provides a welcome respite from the very hard routes encountered on The Promenade with something of interest for most tastes.

Tides - It is non-tidal but keep away in rough seas.

Approach - At the base of the descent, turn left (looking out) and continue past the recess to an area of staggered roofs directly below the cliff-top quarry.

15 Ju An Si Wei . . . . VS 5a
Start at a roof capped left-facing corner. Climb the corner and traverse right onto the front face. Finish direct.
FA. Marti Hallett, Jonny Murrey 28.3.2011

16 Kangaroo . . . . HS 4b
A good climb that features a start for those with strong arms.

17 Spray Fever E1 5a
The leaning wall right of the start of *Kangaroo* is bold.

18 Distant Early Warning . . E1 5c
The bold, juggy roof leads to much easier climbing.
FA. Matt Ward 6.9.1986

19 Original Route . . . . S 4b
Move up the corner and traverse leftwards to clear the roof. Finish rightwards with care up the easy but bold slab and corner.

20 Kool and the Gang E1 5b
The corner of *Original Route* and its continuation leads to a steep pull through the roof.
FA. Pete Oxley 26.4.1986

21 Playing With Fire 6c
The slabby wall and roof right of *Kool and the Gang*. A weird crux that involves a swing leftwards over the roof.
FA. Pete Oxley 13.6.1996

22 Genetix 6b
A black groove leading through four roofs is quite a tough little number. Good rock and climbing.
FA. Pete Oxley 12.4.1987

23 Seratonin . . . . . 7a+
The easy slab and 3m roof to good holds. Tough.
FA. Pete Oxley 18.12.2005

24 Boiling Point 7a
The bouldery roof right of *Genetix*, starting at a hanging, left-facing corner. Hard.
FA. Pete Oxley 13.6.1996

25 To Fever Pitch . . . . 7a+
A multiple roof stack with great moves.
FA. Martin Crocker 6.9.1986. Rebolted direct by Pete Oxley 18.12.2005

26 Becalmed . . . . 7a+
Good cranky stuff over a few bulges.
FA. Pete Oxley 27.2.1996

27 Stakk Attakk E2 5c
A few tricky reaches past a small roof are gained by a short traverse from the left.
FA. Pete Oxley 29.5.1985

28 Geordie Pride 7a
A strenuous diagonal over the flying roof right of *Stakk Attakk*. Finish via a rockover onto the upper slab.
FA. Pete Oxley 27.2.1996

29 DWM E2 5c
The innocuous-looking corner is good but hard won.
FA. B.Thomas, S.Lowe (1pt) 1963. FFA. George Hounsome 15.5.1977

30 Peggy's Cove . . . . 6c+
A very hard pull to distant holds over the low overhang.
FA. Pete Oxley 27.2.1996

31 Zeitgeist . . . . 7a+
The sustained open corner has good rock and climbing.
FA. Crispin Waddy, Pete Oxley 12.7.1986

32 Spirits Rising 7b
The reachy roof and fingery wall just right of *Zeitgeist*.
FA. Pete Oxley 3.6.2001

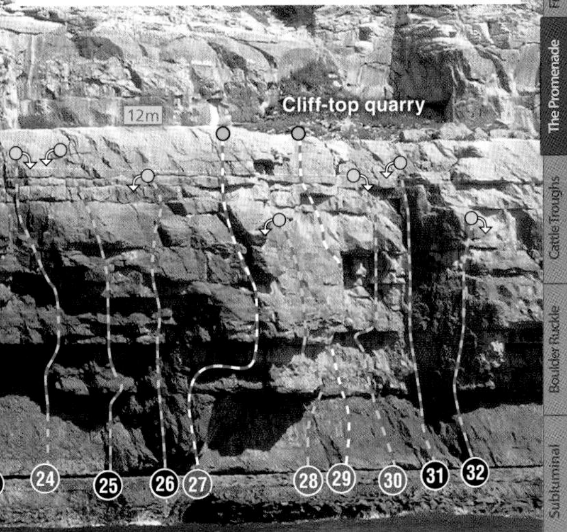

The Futurist Area

The final section of The Promenade contains more of the same - big steep roof routes with powerful lines, along with some good trad routes.
Tides - Non-tidal but keep away in rough seas.
Approach - Either walk left from the base of the descent (looking out), or abseil direct to this section from a belay in the quarry above.

1 A Quantum Jump for Apekind . . . E4 6a
Back to the roof stacks. Start just right of the arete.
FA. Pete Oxley 26.11.1987

2 Dafinko. . . . . . . 1★ 7c
A powerful and unusual roof problem. Very reachy.
FA. Martin Krasnansky 19.8.2009

3 The Calling . . . . . . 1★ 7b
The central overlap with irresistible moves - acrobatic.
FA. Pete Oxley 25.6.1996

4 Guided by Voices 1★ 7b+
Sustained, gymnastic, and tough, especially on those without arms like a baboon.
FA. Pete Oxley 25.6.1996

5 Ocean of Violence E3 6a
The very steep crack.
FA. Pete Oxley, Tim Dunsby 16.6.1985

6 Grossville . . . . 2★ 7a
The huge ship's keel direct has some wild moves.
FA. Pete Oxley 18.10.1986

7 Spacewalk . . . . 3★ 7b
A modern classic - very steep and pumpy. Start as for *Grossville*, before trending rightwards up the bulging wall to a roof crack. Cross the roof and swing out to the apex of the buttress.
FA. Pete Oxley 3.6.2001

8 Sea Ride. . . . . 1★ HVS 5a
A worthwhile route with a safe crux. Start at the right-hand of two cracks in the back of the bay. Climb a slab and corner to a well-positioned roof crux. Block belay in the quarry above. This also acts as an abseil approach point if needed.
FA. M.Boater, R.Shergold 31.5.1969

9 Hackney's Hammer . . . 1★ HVS 5a
Varied climbing up the groove system parallel to *Sea Ride*, with a tough step left to attain the quarry. Block belay.

The next two routes start from the top of a huge block.

10 Sexaphone . . . . . . 2★ E6 6b
A wild roof crack that requires specialist knowledge to overcome. Good gear but hard to place (1 thread and a peg in the upper groove). Stake belay.
FA. Pete Oxley 13.10.1987

11 Space Threshold . . . . 1★ E3 6a
A right-trending line through the roofs right of *Sexaphone*, finishing up a big flake. Stake belay.
FA. Pete Oxley 23.3.1986

12 Edward's Effort . . . . 1★ E1 5b
Start just right of the huge block. Climb a slabby ramp to a small sentry box under a roof. Make some fingery moves across the white wall on the right to a foot-ledge. Balance up to jugs over a flake and then romp to the top, passing three roofs. Either top out or use the lower-off on a slab to the right just below the top.
FA. B.Heard 16.6.1974

13 All Apologies. . . . . 1★ 7a+
A long bulging arete with a low crux and a tenuous rounded rockover to finish.
FA. Pete Oxley 29.6.1994

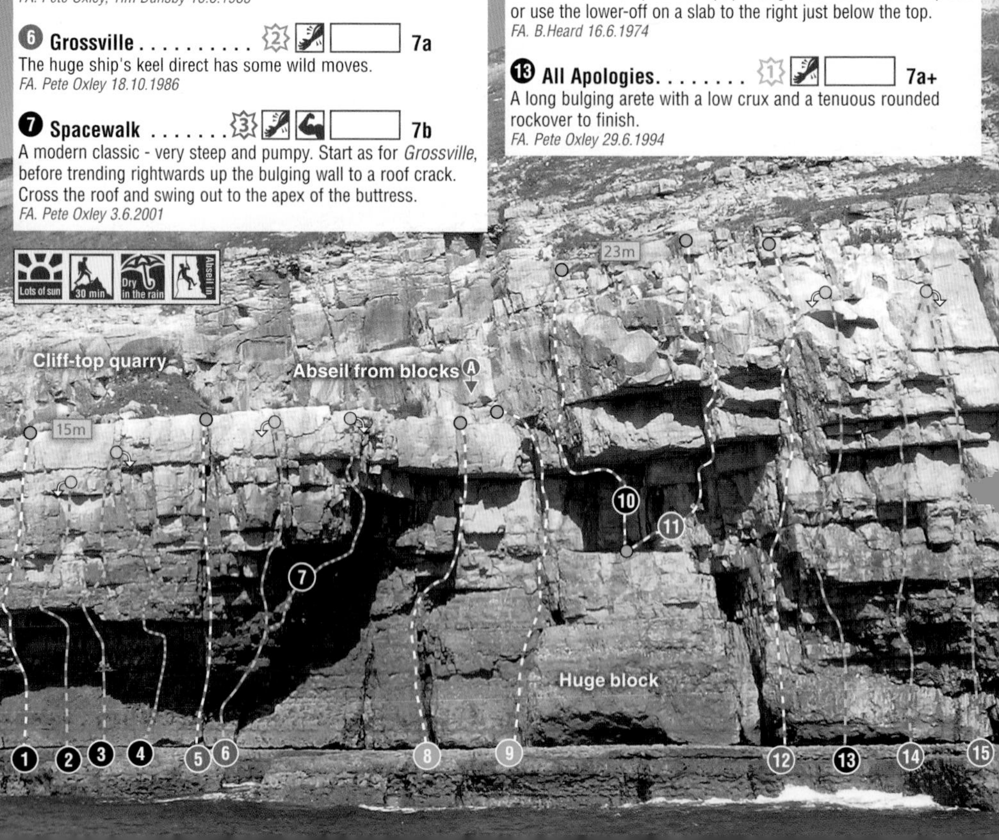

⓮ Strangled in Black . . . 7a
A good line up bulges and a steep crack in the centre of the buttress. High in the grade.
FA. Pete Oxley 18.10.1986

⓯ Titter Ye Not Mrs! . . . 6b+
Climb up a slight groove after a steep start through the bulges.
FA. Pete Oxley 4.1990

⓰ Two Tickets to the Gun Show 7a+
Start at a big black jug on the nose. Pull up and follow the overhangs out right using holds on the lip.
FA. Marti Hallett 20.4.2011

⓱ Fat Necrosis E4 6b
The first crack breaching the long, low level roof.
FA. Martin Crocker 6.9.1986

⓲ Rise of the Robots . . . 7b+
A superb power endurance line. Explosive moves cover unlikely ground to a jug rail. Overcome the last bulge to a shared belay.
FA. Pete Oxley 8.2000

⓳ Liquid Steel 7c
A fine anaerobic challenge across the 6m roof.
FA. Pete Oxley 13.7.1994

⓴ The Futurist 2002 . . . 7b+
Spectacular moves rightwards gain the roof crack. Follow the crack with increasing difficulty to easy ground.
FA. Pete Oxley 4.11.1986. Extended in 2002

㉑ Event Horizon . . 8a+
The awesome line out of the cave to the right of *The Futurist 2002*. Steep ground accesses the lip where thin cruxy moves may allow the belay to be gained.
FA. Rob Kennard 10.2003

㉒ Berserka E4 6b
Climb rightwards to a gap in the ceiling then finish direct up the wall above.
FA. Pete Oxley 12.7.1986

㉓ The Shape of Roofs to Come
. . . . 7b
A fun, bicep-bulging test over the 4m roof right of *Berserka*. A long quickdraw is needed for the fourth bolt. No sneaking off rightwards at the top.
FA. Pete Oxley 24.6.2001

㉔ War of Attrition . . . 7c+
A desperate extended boulder problem over the double roof-stack. Essentially a V8 with bolts.
FA. Pete Oxley 17.9.2000

㉕ The Incredible Hulk . . 7c
An excellent line over the five metre triple roof stack. Great climbing in a good situation.
FA. Pete Oxley 24.7.2001

㉖ Howling Stone E4 6a
A strength-sapper up the final leaning pillar. Climb a crack in the arete and move right around an overhang to a rest below a roof. Climb the roof and continue up the arete on good holds to the top.
FA. Pete Oxley 7.7.1985

㉗ Grockles Passage . . . . VS 4c
A good climb in an atmospheric location. Start 3m left of the cave.
1) 4c, 16m. Climb for 5m to a chimney and take this to a ledge. Move left under a block to a ledge and belay on the arete.
2) -, 10m. Climb the right side of the gully to the top.
FA. P.Scott, R.Crewe 27.7.1975

23m
15m
5 16 17 18 19 20 21 22 23 24 25 26 27

Nearing the upper corner crack of the popular *Grottle* (VDiff) - *page 365* - at Flake Ledge. Photo: Marti Hallett

	No star	1	2	3
Mod to S	3	4	1	-
HS to HVS	2	6	5	-
E1 to E3	2	7	1	-
E4 and up	-	1	4	-

The Cattle Troughs routes are easy to reach and have generally sound rock. However, gear can be a bit sparse on some climbs and it is a dangerous venue in rough, or even moderate, seas. The Cattle Troughs Area is popular with novices and beginners, although for a first taste of Swanage, Subluminal may be a better bet.

The Unknown and Flake Ledges are very quiet venues that have a number of interesting and varied climbs spanning the grades. Amphitheatre Ledge Area has some quality harder climbs on reasonably good rock, whilst the slabs and short friendly walls of the Hangover and Isis Areas are favourites with those looking for good easier and mid-grade routes.

Approach Also see map on page 266

From Durlston car park, follow the road towards the lighthouse then turn west along the coast path (right - looking out). Continue to 150m beyond the fourth stone wall from the lighthouse, where the cliff-top path dips into a small valley above a slabby cove. Cross the fence here at a small stile. This is Amphitheatre Ledge. For the **Isis, Hangover and Flake Ledge Areas** follow a narrow, exposed path that contours rightwards along the cliff-top (looking out). Pass several belay stakes until a large gearing-up ledge is reached after 200m (just beyond a large amphitheatre known as the Lecture Theatre). Alternatively, continue along the main coast path, cross a stile and follow a steep path leading down to the cliff-top gearing up ledge. See route pages for further approaches from here.

Tides and Conditions

All the climbs start from non-tidal ledges, however, keep away in rough seas since freak waves can wash high up the walls. Always take a belay at the base of the routes. The Cattle Troughs' cliffs are fast drying sun-traps, and there is no seepage; this can be considered a year-round venue. Beware of the cliff-top path if it is at all muddy, as well as the descent into the Hangover Area, which is a bit polished, fairly steep and can be covered in mud from other people's boots. Cattle Troughs has almost nowhere to get out of the sun on hot days. Bring plenty of water and sunscreen.

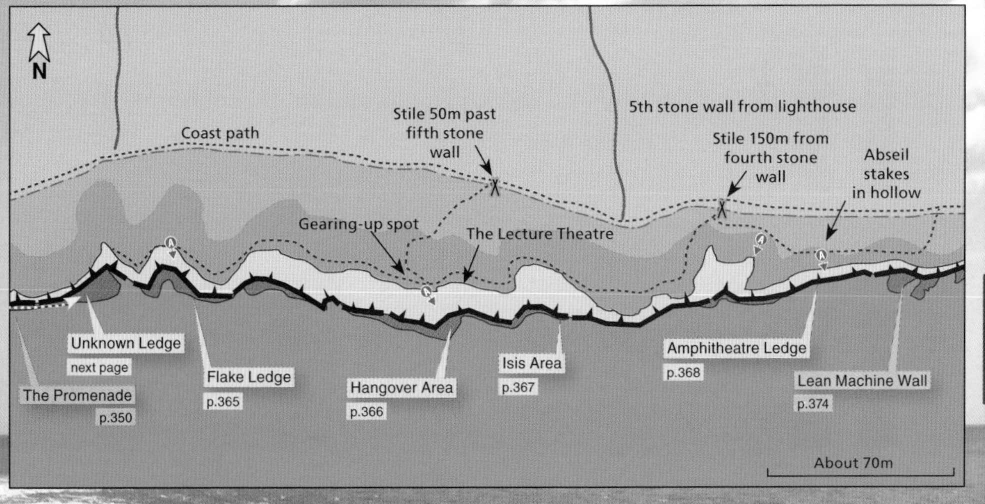

Unknown Ledge

Unknown Ledge is a little-visited section of Swanage. The climbs are steep, strenuous and single pitch. Those that top-out finish at a clean, but narrow ledge which requires care to set up a safe belay.

Tides - Non-tidal but keep away in rough seas.

Approach - As for The Promenade (p.353), then walk back east to cross to Unknown Ledge and pass behind the huge detached pillar to reach the first routes. Alternatively, an approach from Flake Ledge via a sea-level traverse (S) can be made (in calm seas only).

Lots of sun | 25 min | Abseil in

1 Jesus and Mary Chain . 2 stars **E3 6a**

Start at a hole. Follow a thin crack up onto a wall and gain a block up on the right. From the block, climb rightwards to a groove right of the overhangs. Take the groove and wall above to a clean ledge and belay on small and medium nuts. Scramble easily off right along the ledge.

FA. Pete Oxley, Jon Biddle 29.9.1986

2 Fuel My Fire . . . . . 2 stars **8a+**

An incredibly good power-endurance route with great moves and rock. The first couple of bolts have been chopped, so a clipstick is useful as the first bolt is now at 3.5m. Start on the left and traverse up and rightwards to the arete, move leftwards then upwards to the other arete and easy ground.

FA Bob Hickish 3.6.2009. Bolted by Pete Oxley.

3 The God Slot . . . . 2 stars **HVS 5a**

A challenging pitch worth searching out. Start at the east-facing wall that leads up towards The Slot. Climb the wall 3m right of the arete to a point level with the overhang. Traverse left to a corner and climb The Slot - an exposed chimney - to a thread and continue to a clean ledge and belay on small and medium nuts. Scramble easily off rightwards along the ledge.

FA. Jim Titt, Scott Titt 5.12.1976

4 Damson . . . . 2 stars **HVS 5a**

A fine, remote lead up the east wall above the small zawn that separates Unknown Ledge from Flake Ledge. Start at the far west limit of Flake Ledge. Traverse left on good holds to a diagonal crack that heads up to a roof. Climb the crack to the roof, step left and up into a chimney. Climb the chimney and wall above to the top and stake belays.

FA. Jim Titt, Scott Titt 21.11.1976

5 The Coral Prison . . . . . 1 star **VS 4b**

Some fine rock and a stunning setting, although the climbing is bold to start with. There has been a small rockfall but the line has been reclimbed since. Start at the far west limit of Flake Ledge (as for *Damson*). Gain the ledge at 3m and move up and left to a good horizontal crack. Pull up and left boldly to good, well-weathered holds, and continue leftwards more easily on good rock with better protection to a final short wall and the top. Stake belays above and to the right.

FA. Pete Oxley, D,Sharman 7.7.1985

6 Hell's Teeth . . . . 1 HVS 5a
A good honest pitch with a tough initial overhang. Start 3m to the right of the far west limit of Flake Ledge. Move up to the overhang and climb the crack over it with difficulty and continue to a block. Now move up and right to a steep groove and follow this to the top. Stake belays on the ledge.
FA. A.White, R.Black, A.Mannery 9.1963

7 Moonstone 1 E1 5b
Sustained with good protection. Start right of *Hell's Teeth* and climb the long crackline up the leaning buttress to the top and stake belays.
FA. George Hounsome, Richard Crewe 13.11.1976

Flake Ledge

An appealing cliff with a handful of reasonable climbs that take on some exposed and exciting ground. Some of the rock above half height needs careful handling.
Tides - Non-tidal but keep away in rough seas.
Approach - From the top of the descent to Cattle Troughs, walk west along the rocky edge of the cliff for 70m to the second of two large blocks (these are above a section of cliff called The Jumble). Move up onto a path that continues west for another 70m to an amphitheatre and a good gearing-up ledge. To descend to the base of the cliff, set up an abseil or down-climb leftwards from the centre of the amphitheatre (Diff) - see topo for line.

8 Grottle . . . . 1 VDiff
A steep pitch that finishes up a well protected slim corner. Start on the upper ledge at the base of the descent down-climb/abseil. Move up right on to the stepped arete and climb this to below a left-facing, well-defined slim corner crack. Climb this with difficulty - well protected - to the top and stake belays well up the slope to the left. *Photo on page 362.*
FA. R.White, G.Davis 10.1963

9 Lobster . . . . 1 HVS 5b
Wild climbing that requires a determined approach - well protected. Start at an undercut crack/chimney above a block in the bay right of the base of the descent. Climb the crack in its entirety, with a welcome rest at 8m on the left. The second half of the crack has some useful holds on the left. Where the crack ends, finish up the much easier wall above, taking care with a couple of big semi-detached flakes. *Photo on page 350.*
FA. Nigel Porter, Richard Crewe 4.8.1974

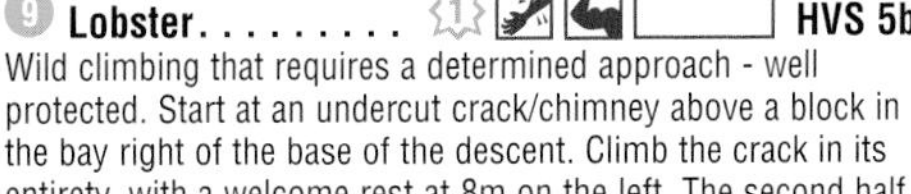

10 Wessex Hangover . . . . 2 VS 4c
Exposed and atmospheric climbing that traces a line up the side of a deep inlet and finishes with a breathtaking stride over the void. At the far east end of Flake Ledge is a narrow zawn that has a wide corner crack in its west wall, start here. Climb the awkward corner to a roof and step right to below a crack. Climb the crack with difficulty to another overhang and move right to above the zawn. Bridge out right and pull up to easier ground that leads to the top and stake belays.
FA. A.Hall 1971

Hangover Area

The cliff-line at Cattle Troughs comprises two semi-circular amphitheatres with a broken ledge system running along their base, allowing easy access. The first few routes lie just west of the descent above a flat ledge system.

Tides - The area is non-tidal but keep away in rough seas.

Approach - Descend down into the Lecture Theatre amphitheatre on its west side (right - looking out), below the cliff-top gearing up ledges. There is a stake in place for abseil but most experienced climbers will be able to scramble down. The first routes lie just to the right (looking out) of the descent.

1 Inspiration . . . . **S 4a**
A pleasant line up the centre of a flat face. Start just right of a large boulder. Easy but poorly-protected climbing gains a ledge at half height. Climb the groove above and exit right.

2 Consolation. . . . . **S 4a**
The right-hand side of the face via a short groove.

3 Chockney . . . . 1 **VDiff 4a**
A classic corner problem just left of the descent route makes a good first lead - if you can get off the ground.

The Lecture Theatre - *Right of the way down (looking in) and past the easy slabs, is the first route above the east side of the amphitheatre. The following four routes finish at a ledge above the wall or, further back and safer, a stake belay by the cliff-top path.*

4 The Chimney. . . . . 1 **VDiff**
The Chimney is one of Swanage's most popular climbs and is the first introduction to the delights of the Swanage sea cliffs for many climbers. The start of the climb is close to the low-angled descent line that gains the base of the unusual cliff feature - The Lecture Theatre. The climb is actually only a chimney for the first half of its height and it is this section that is the sternest section of the route which requires some strenuous back-and-footing on some slippery rock to overcome it. At the top of the chimney a traverse right accesses easier ground that leads to the cliff top and an iron-stake belay. Finishing straight up is a good and well-protected alternative finish at S 4a.

5 Hangover . . . . 2 **VS 5a**
A great little route up the steep wall and bulge 2m right of *The Chimney* to a large ledge. It has lost holds over the years, hence the upgrade.

6 Resurrection . . . . 1 **HS 4b**
A fairly serious climb that needs care to search out the spaced-protection opportunities available. Although the climbing is on good holds throughout it is a fairly steep experience. Start up a steep wall to a recess and then continue up the wall before exiting rightwards near the upper section.

7 Perfection . . . . **S 4a**
Follow the arete out right and finish up a groove.

8 Old Lag's Corner . . . . 1 **VS 4c**
The corner above a large pedestal block. By-pass the top overhangs on the right to a good ledge. Direct is 5a.
FA. Frank Farrell, Gordon Jenkin 13.8.1984

Just before the end of the Lecture Theatre is a good bouldering wall.

9 Bunney's Wall . . . . 1 **VS 5a**
This climb takes the central line to the top with good moves finishing up a slanting crack. The start is tricky. A good alternative is to swing right and climb the headwall. Nut and block belays.

Isis Area

Around the corner lies the second hollow, known as The Pulpit Amphitheatre. All the routes finish at stake belays.
Tides - It is non-tidal, but keep away in rough seas.
Approach - Descend down into the Lecture Theatre on its west side (right - looking out) below the cliff-top gearing-up ledges. There is a stake in place for abseils, but most climbers will be able to scramble down. The Isis Area lies to the left of the descent (looking out).

10 Fallen Block Climb . . . . 1 **VDiff**
Take an easy line up the wall on the far side of the bay. The route is well protected and has some fine positions.

11 Pulpit Route . . . . 2 **Diff**
A superbly-positioned climb on good rock. One of the best and most travelled sea cliff climbs at the grade on the coast. The line of the climb takes the easy-angled slab via a steep entry move to a point near the slab's top where it steepens up. Move left to easier ground and continue to the top and a stake belay.

12 Pearly Gate . . . . **HVS 5a**
Climb a crack on the right of the slab, then follow flakes leading to a roof. Move left to finish via a groove. Serious above half height.

13 Eskimo Nell 2 **E1 5b**
An excellent pitch. Climb onto a huge block just right of *Pearly Gate,* then head up and follow a groove just left of the half-height overhang.
FA. H.Evans, P.Deketeleare 16.2.1969

14 Isis . . . . 2 **VS 4c**
A popular route with varied climbing in good situations. Start at the left-hand side of a high, arched recess 5m right of a large block. Climb the groove on the left until moves left gain the lip of an overhang. Ascend a bulging groove on the left, trending right then back left and finish up two short walls.
FA. D.Rowlands 1963

15 Archangel **E3 6a**
This line has been affected by rockfall and may not have been re-climbed since.
FA. S.Evans, R.Evans 5.5.1974

16 Peacemaker 1 **E1 5b**
The last good route in this area is a serious undertaking. Climb up the right-hand corner of the arch to a foot-ledge near the top. Step up right onto a slab for a tricky and bold finish.
FA. Pete Oxley 8.2.1989

Portland Lulworth Swanage Winspit Hedbury and Smokey Dancing Ledge Guillemot Ledge Blackers Hole Fisherman's Ledge The Promenade Cattle Troughs Boulder Ruckle Subluminal

Amphitheatre Ledge

Amphitheatre Ledge is a quiet and secluded area that deserves more traffic. The climbing is invariably steep with good rock, but the finishes require caution. Some of the routes are awkward to approach.

Tides - The area is generally non-tidal, although some of the starts are much easier to reach at low tide. Keep away in rough conditions.

Approach (routes 1 to 5, and 10) - *Abseil from two stakes above The Amphitheatre on its east side (left - looking out). The abseil ends on a ledge system that leads along the base of the cliff.*

1 Varina . . . . **HS 4a**
A pleasant, though serious, route up the arete of The Amphitheatre, finishing up a short groove. Sparse protection from small wires. Belay on the abseil rope. Take care as the route has lost a large block high up and maybe harder now.
FA. R.Heigh, W.Church 1968

2 Uncry These Tears 1 **E2 5c**
A strong line up the face right of *Varina*. Climb to an overlap (small thread) then onwards to a larger overlap. Pass this on its left (thread) and continue - peg - to reach an exit ramp on the left.
FA. Mike Robertson, Barry Clarke 2.5.1997

The next three routes are situated on the gloriously-steep orange wall to the right. For those who have enjoyed Lean Machine, these give similar super-strenuous pump-outs. Pre-place a belay rope from the abseil stakes.

3 Atomic Road Hero . 1 **E5 6b**
Climb straight up an easy lower wall and attack the technical and intricate face above (3 threads, 1 peg) to a large undercut. Move diagonally left (thread) to a slight corner and continue rightwards to the top.
FA. Pete Oxley 14.12.1986

4 Theory of Everything 2 **E5 6b**
This is the central line and has the most sustained climbing. Start 3m right of the last route and ascend the easy lower wall to beneath some spidery cracks. Power up these past a peg and continue in a direct line to a good finish.
FA. Pete Oxley 23.3.1990

5 Zoolookologie 2 **E5 6a**
A full-body work-out with reasonable gear. Start easily as for *Theory of Everything* then take the big cracks to the right up the steep wall (thread) pulling over a bulge to a ledge. An easy groove leads to the top.
FA. Pete Oxley 8.8.1986

Lots of sun | 25 min | Abseil in | Tidal

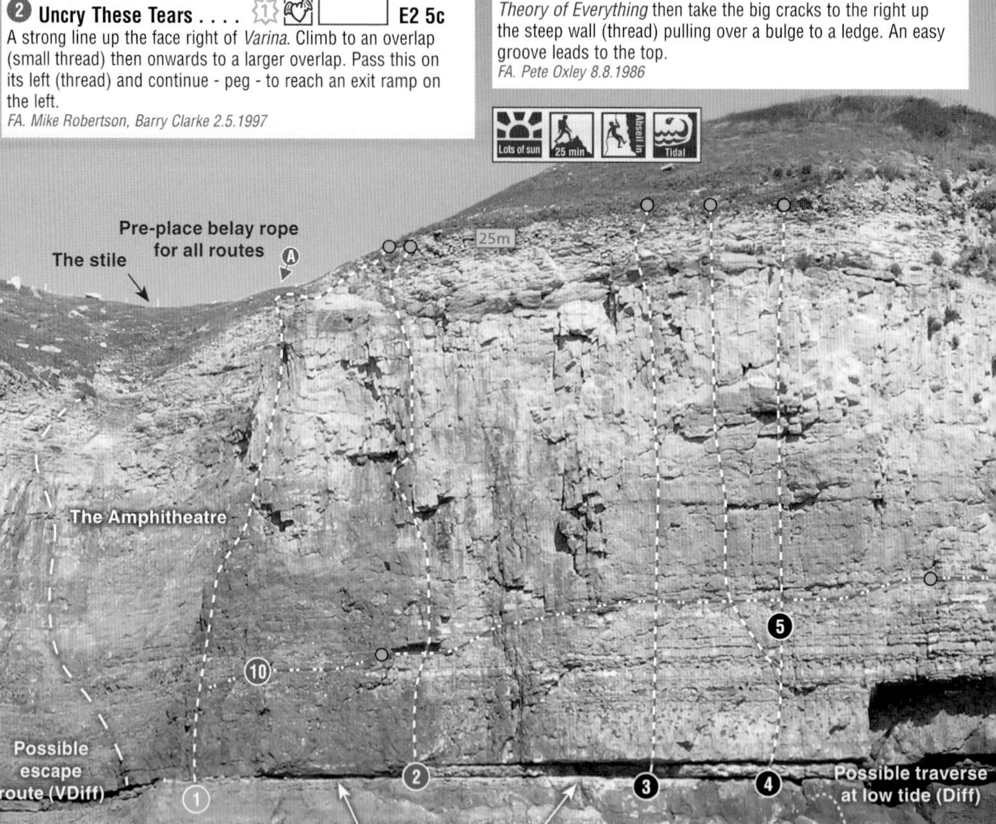

Approach (routes 6 to 9) - *Abseil from a stake, below a thorn bush, to the left of a hollow (looking out). This is 30m left of the Amphitheatre. Leave the abseil rope in place as a belay point at the top of the routes. Take Prusik loops down in case of problems. Routes 6 and 7 can be reached by a sea-level traverse at low tide (Diff).*

6 In a Big Sky. E2 5c
Start from a large sloping ledge, at a flake, 15m right of the big leaning wall. Move straight up to follow thin cracks past 5 threads. Near the top, move right with difficulty to an easier finish and a ledge.
FA. Pete Oxley, Gordon Jenkin 8.6.1986

7 Land of the Leaning 1 E2 5b
1) -, 8m. Start as for *In a Big Sky*. Climb the flake then move right easily for 3m to a ledge above the zawn. Thread and nut belay.
2) 5b, 20m. Climb cracks rightwards then step left and back right at their end. Finish up easier rock.
FA. Pete Oxley, Jon Biddle 7.6.1986

8 World in Action . . . 2 E5 6b
A peach of a climb. It needs a direct abseil approach to reach a small isolated ledge at the fault-line 5m above the sea, 5m right of the ledge of *In a Big Sky* (looking in). Climb the bulging arete above (peg and thread) to easier ground (thread), then move slightly left to beneath the orange headwall. Surge up a thin crack, past lots of wires and 2 threads, to a jug. Before the pump wins, finish up the technical shallow groove to a cleaned exit.
FA. Pete Oxley, Steve Williams 11.4.1987

9 Arapiles Syndrome. . . . 1 E3 5b
Reminiscent of *Ocean Boulevard*. Abseil directly, from the stake, to a ledge beneath a diagonal crack, 5m right of *World in Action*. Start up a short groove, then swing out left to reach the crack and follow it diagonally right to an overlap. Make two short staggered traverses rightwards again to gain an exit ledge. Belay on the ab rope.
FA. Pete Oxley, Nigel Coe 5.4.1986

10 Mr Ruckle 1 E1 5a
A fine, mid-height traverse of this exciting area all the way from *Varina* to finish right of *Arapiles Syndrome*. It can be done in rough seas. Before starting you need to pre-place a rope on the twin stakes above the Lean Machine area, for the last belay.
1) 5a, 18m. From 8m up *Varina*, traverse right (small thread) past a groove to belay on a cracked prow. This is reported to be a serious pitch with ground-fall potential and it can be avoided.
2) 5a, 30m. Drop down and rightwards across the *Zoolookologie* bay thread. Continue past a slight prow and vague scoop. Belay down and right of a cracked pillar.
3) 4c, 35m. Climb down and right to traverse a weakness past various old threads, in the centre of a bay, to a comfortable stance on the far side in a groove.
4) 4c, 15m. Follow the corner to the top and a terrace where you hope to find your pre-placed rope. Pull out on the rope to finish.
FA. Mike Robertson, Brian Tilley 28.8.1997

Portland
Lulworth
Swanage
Winspit
Hedbury and Smokey
Dancing Ledge
Guillemot Ledge
Blackers Hole
Fisherman's Ledge
The Promenade
Cattle Troughs
Boulder Ruckle
Subluminal

Boulder Ruckle

Lee Proctor starting up the magnificent and very pumpy *Ocean Boulevard* (E3 5b) - page 377 - in the Boulder Ruckle.

Portland
Lulworth
Swanage
Winspit
Hedbury and Smokey
Dancing Ledge
Guillemot Ledge
Blackers Hole
Fisherman's Ledge
The Promenade
Cattle Troughs
Boulder Ruckle
Subluminal

	No star	1	2	3
Mod to S	1	1	-	-
HS to HVS	-	11	16	5
E1 to E3	6	21	16	8
E4 and up	3	18	11	6

The white and yellow striped walls of the Boulder Ruckle make up the showpiece crag of Swanage. The Ruckle, as it is affectionately known, runs westwards from Subluminal, unbroken for over a kilometre and, at over forty metres in height, it offers fear, exhilaration and many sensationally-positioned routes. The grade range of Severe to E6 means that it will appeal to most, however, with the seriousness of the free-hanging approach abseils, the awkward escape routes and the broken finishes, it becomes a less attractive option for inexperienced teams. Nevertheless, for those in search of an adventurous mission, don a helmet, dust off the Prusik loops and prepare to do battle on some fine atmospheric classics with little likelihood of having to queue.

The walls of The Ruckle are especially good for those operating in the HVS to E3 range. Fortunately, protection possibilities are usually in good supply with the unrelenting steepness of the rock accounting for the grade on most climbs, rather than any great technical difficulty or terrifying bold run-outs.

Approach Also see map on page 266

Walk down the tarmac road from Durlston car park, then head west along the coast path (right - looking out). A cliff-top track runs below this and the abseil stakes are found near this lower path. The first area arrived at is a ten minute walk, and the furthest area takes around twenty minutes. Precise details of the various approaches are listed on the area pages.

Tides and Conditions

Most of the areas are untroubled by the tides due to a large boulder beach that runs along the bottom of the cliff, however avoid the whole place if the seas are rough. There are a few isolated spots which require low tide; these are mentioned in the area notes. The full length of the cliff faces due south so is a huge sun-trap. This is good in winter, but may become too hot in the summer, although it is shady in the evening. It can be greasy in hot weather, though the rock is rough and there is little polish. There is no seepage.

Access

There are bird restrictions in place from **1st March to 31st July** on some of the areas. Check the access notes on individual area pages.

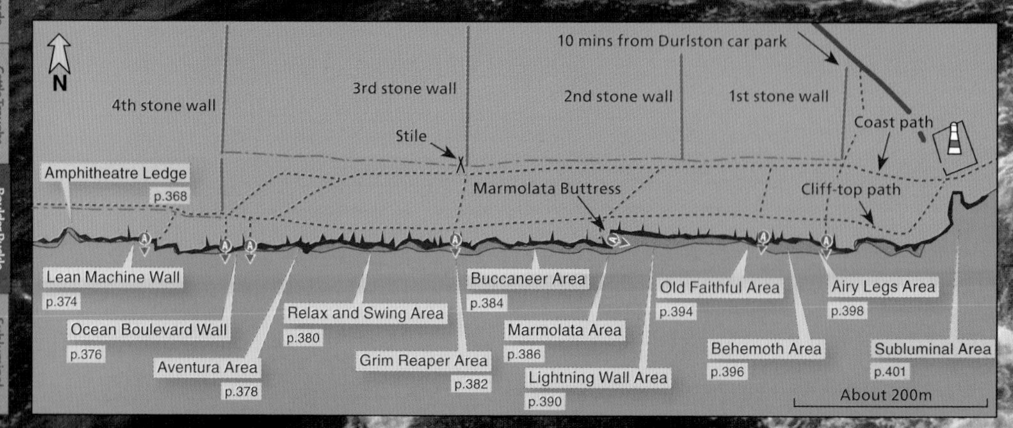

John Samways getting stuck-in to the initial crack of *Airy Legs* (VS 4c) - *page 398* - at the fine eastern end of the Boulder Ruckle.

Portland
Lulworth
Swanage
Winspit
Hedbury and Smokey
Dancing Ledge
Guillemot Ledge
Blackers Hole
Fisherman's Ledge
The Promenade
Cattle Troughs
Boulder Ruckle
Subluminal

Lean Machine Wall

The furthest west area of the Boulder Ruckle is a very secluded section of the cliff, and its base is quickly cut-off from easy exit options. Most of the climbs are steep and pumpy experiences, though the gear is usually good.
Approach - Walk 50m (17 fence posts) beyond the 4th wall encountered on the coast path when walking west from the lighthouse, then climb over the fence and head down through a break in the bushes to the cliff edge. 5m to the right are 2 stakes directly above *The Lean Machine*. Make a free-hanging abseil to boulders. Access to the boulder beach is only possible if the sea is calm.
Tides - Climbing on this wall is not advisable in rough seas, although the approach described above is possible at high tide during calm seas. The wall can also be accessed from the Ocean Boulevard Area at low tide.
Note - The easiest solid route out of this area is E3 and sea-level escapes are very awkward. Be sure that both leader and second can climb out comfortably and take Prusiks just in case things go wrong. On most of the routes the abseil rope is essential to assist in finishing the top slab and/or for belaying on.

1 Sirius 1 E3 5b
The first of the mega-pumpy lines on this wall has good gear and good holds although care is required with the rock.
Climb to and over a roof at the low fault-line and then follow an obvious crack-line marking the left edge of the face to a final steep pull around an overhang at the top. Finish by pulling up the abseil rope.
FA. George Hounsome, Scott Titt 10.5.1980

2 Wild at Heart. E4 6a
A tight eliminate variation on *Sirius*. Start as for *Sirius*. Climb to the low roof but swing right and then up left into the parallel crack just to the right of *Sirius*. Climb the crack and its thinner continuation to a roof. Cross the top roof leftwards. Finish by pulling up on the abseil rope.
FA. Tim Dunsby, Nigel Coe 19.9.1992

3 Punks in Power . . .  **E5 6b**
A hard pitch with good but spaced protection. A real arm destroyer. Start as for *The Lean Machine*. Follow *The Lean Machine* to a good hold 2m above the low fault-line. Move left on big handholds to a crack and take this to a move up left to a flake. Continue to below a blank calcite sheet near the top. This provides a testing climax. Exit right through the upper overhang and climb a thin slab rightwards to a ledge. Finish by pulling up on the abseil rope.
FA. Pete Oxley 15.9.1985

4 The Lean Machine . . . . Top 50 E5 6a
An incredibly steep and pumpy climb that wends its withering way up a series of well-protected cracks in the centre of the wall. Start on top of a massive boulder at the base of the abseil. From the boulder, climb a thin crack to the low horizontal break. Move left and climb the accommodating crack-line rightwards on good holds until a move up left gains a small right leaning overhang. Move out right up the wall via a thin crack and then up to belay on the abseil rope where the angle drops back. Pull out on the abseil rope to finish.
FA. Martin Crocker, Jim Robertson 11.6.1983

5 Surge Control . . . . Top 50 E5 6b
A superb stamina-test that follows the cracked face right of *The Lean Machine*. It shares the middle section of *The Lean Machine* and has a tough start and finish. Start at a thin crack.
Climb to the low fault-line and then follow a thin crack with difficulty to a slot. Continue to join *The Lean Machine* and follow it to a shallow horizontal break. Climb out rightwards to a small recess and move up out of it with difficulty until a move left gains a flake. Join and finish up *The Lean Machine*. Finish by pulling up on the abseil rope.
FA. Pete Oxley 18.7.1985

6 The Roaring Boys. . 1 E6 6b
The hardest route on the wall - almost E7 for effort. Start as for *Surge Control*. Climb *Surge Control* to the slot at the end of its thin crack. Swing right and follow the edge of the wall (crux at the top - thread). Finish by pulling up the abseil rope.
FA. Pete Oxley 1.8.1987

The big corner to the right of the main wall is an E1 but is a very poor and loose route (not described). The last two routes described are on a slab, just right of the corner. They both have loose finishes.

7 Charge of the Wild Horsemen E1 5b
Climb the groove then the slab diagonally right, up a crack, to the fault-line. Take the groove above to the right of the prow to finish.
FA. Pete Oxley 29.8.1988

8 Charge of the Light Brigade. E1 5b
A counter diagonal to *Charge of the Wild Horsemen*, starting at a small groove near the arete. Finish by pulling right onto the final prow from the groove to its left.
FA. Tim Dunsby, Nigel Coe, Scott Titt 19.5.199

Ocean Boulevard Area - 50m (low tide only)
next page

Portland Lulworth Swanage Winspit Hedbury and Smokey Dancing Ledge Guillemot Ledge Blackers Hole Fisherman's Ledge The Promenade Cattle Troughs Boulder Ruckle Subliminal

Ocean Boulevard Wall

A fine, leaning wall mostly composed of excellent rock that is home to a number of Swanage's finest single pitch Extremes. The routes are sustained and although generally well protected, are very pumpy. The wall is a little featureless save for some thin crack-lines and the odd peg and thread. This makes route finding slightly problematical although the major lines of *Ocean Boulevard*, *Mother Africa* and *Wall of the Worlds* are easily identified.

Tides - The boulder beach at the base of the cliff is above high tide.

Approach - Follow the coast path to the 4th stone wall, when walking west from the lighthouse. The abseil stakes are hidden above an earthy ramp 15m back towards the lighthouse from this stile. The abseil takes you down the upper part of *The Ramp*. **Note -** The abseil/belay stakes in the gully below the stone wall itself are directly above the route *Ocean Boulevard* and are often used as an alternative approach.

1 Le Jaune Mechanique . E4 5c

Good climbing that weaves up the left edge of the huge Ocean Boulevard Wall. Start at a step in the rock platform. The pegs are now rusty.

1) 5c, 22m. Climb onto the left wall of the arete (thread) and continue (thread) to a shallow groove. Step right and up the left side of the arete (thread) to a belay on the fault-line (peg and thread).

2) 5b, 24m. Pass the overhang above on the right (peg) to join *Barracuda* to finish.

FA. Pete Oxley, Crispin Waddy 21.6.1986

2 Barracuda E4 5c

A mean fish which is steeper than first appearances might suggest. It tackles the first big crack-line on the wall and never lets up. Safe, pumpy and excellent.

FA. Arni Strapcans, Gordon Jenkin 1.4.1979
FFA. Dave Ivory, P.Preston 1.4.1983

3 Tuna Lick E5 6a

An eliminate pitch just to the right of *Barracuda*, joining it near the top. Very strenuous.

FA. Pete Oxley 4.10.1987

4 Ocean Boulevard . . . . . Top 50 E3 5b

An outstanding Swanage classic. It follows the steep cracks and mid-height bulge towards the left-hand side of the wall. Very pumpy but also very well protected. Start at a slab just right of the base of the unrelenting crack-line. Follow the slab easily left to the base of the crack-line and climb it to the mid-height horizontal break. Pull through the steep bulge above to a shake out at a good hold on the left. Continue up the thinner, but less-steep crack above the good hold to a point where a step left gains easier climbing and the top. *Photo on page 371.*

FA. Kevin Turner, Nick Buckley, S.Bartlett (with a belay midway) 3.1979
FFA. Steve Monks, Gordon Jenkin 21.11.1981

5 Mother Africa . . . . Top 50 E4 6a

Superbly-sustained climbing that tracks an intricate line up the centre of the wall. Start at the base of the wall, below a thin crack with a rope sling at the midway horizontal break. Climb the first few easy-angled metres to the start of the thin crack. Make hard but well protected moves up the crack to the horizontal break - an insitu rope sling. Move left, then up, past good holds and a peg before gaining a thin crack-line on the left. Follow the crack-line past four more pegs to finish.

FA. Martin Crocker, Jim Robertson 5.6.1983

Lots of sun | 20 min | Abseil in

6 The Great Hunter House Milk Robbery
. . . . E5 6a

Follow *Mother Africa* to the fault-line and then climb direct up a blank wall (peg). Step left into the parent route near the top.

FA. Ben Moon (1pt aid) 23.10.83
FFA. Pete Oxley 16.10.1985

7 Wall of the Worlds . Top 50 E5 6a

A truly fantastic pitch. Sustained, well protected and with a pressing crux move high on the wall. Start below the very thin line of cracks in a slight depression on the upper wall and just right of the rope sling at the midway break on *Mother Africa*. Move up the wall on good holds to a narrow ledge. Harder climbing past white blotches gains the horizontal break above. Sustained climbing through the bulge and up the line of thin cracks leads past a jug, but without much respite, to another bulge. A hard couple of moves up and right past a peg gain a thread and the final short wall.

FA. Martin Crocker, Jim Robertson 12.6.1983

8 The Last Hurrah of the Golden Horde
. . . . E3 5c

An impressive line but although the protection is adequate has its fair share of poor rock. Start at the base of *The Ramp*. Climb to a large ledge then traverse left to ascend a crack to the fault-line. Follow the dodgy pillar and crack with care to the top.

FA. Jim Titt 19.2.1972. FFA. George Hounsome 1976

9 The Ramp . . . . S 4a

A poor and loose escape route from the western section of the Ruckle. Follow the easy, stepped ramp heading diagonally right underneath the right-hand side of the wall. Pull out on the abseil rope - don't try and climb out.

10 Indian Pacific E5 6a

A tremendous right-to-left girdle traverse of the upper section of the Ocean Boulevard Wall. Start as for *The First Och Aye of the Tartan Army*. Move out left to a peg, then follow a vague break (peg) to a niche on *The Last Hurrah of the Golden Horde*. Continue across (peg) to good holds on *Mother Africa* and climb up until a move left accesses *Ocean Boulevard*. Finish up the last few metres of *Ocean Boulevard*.

FA. Pete Oxley 15.3.1986

11 The First Och Aye of the Tartan Army
. . . . E3 5b

Start from a stance two thirds of the way up *The Ramp* (there is a poor lower pitch). Move up and traverse out left to a peg. Ascend the wall above, trending left to a shallow groove.

FA. Martin Crocker, Jim Robertson 23.7.1983

12 Screaming Blue Messiah . . E3 6a

Start from the block belay on *The Ramp*. Climb steep thin cracks past a thread and peg.

FA. Pete Oxley 18.5.1986

13 Queen of Carp E5 6b

An eliminate up the face just right of *Screaming Blue Messiah* past 2 pegs. Requires small wires.

FA. Mike Robertson, Mark Williams 28.7.1997

Aventura Area
next page

Aventura Area

An intimidating section of cliff that features numerous roofs and corners and is home to the popular *Aventura*, along with a handful of other worthwhile lines. The right-hand side of the area has some bird restrictions.

Tides - The boulder beach is above high tide.

Approach - As for Ocean Boulevard Area, then walk left (looking out) along the boulder beach for 25m to the start of the first route below a huge mid-height roof.

Restriction (routes - 8 to 10) No climbing from 1st March to 31st July due to nesting birds.

1 Jericho Groove . . . . . . 1 HS 4b

A fairly popular expedition that provides a good alternative to *Bottomless Buttress*. Start at a crack in the wall around 25m right of the base of the abseil line, below a huge roof at the fault-line - not shown on the topo.

1) 4b, 21m. Climb up the crack and then move leftwards to a corner below the roof. Climb the corner, over a bulge and traverse left to a belay on a big jammed boulder.

2) 4a, 18m. Climb up a groove for 5m and move left to ledges. Move along the ledges to a crack in a wide groove and take this to the top.

FA. J.F.Clarke, A.G Smythe c.1963

2 Black Sunshine . . . . 2 HVS 4c

A well-travelled and solid route. Upgraded from VS.

1) 4c, 20m. Climb a scoop, just left of the big boulder, then move leftwards around a roof. Traverse 8m back right to a corner and slab. The slab leads to a belay on the left at the fault-line.

2) 4b, 18m. Climb to an overhang, traverse 3m right and pull over. Continue to the top and an earthy finish.

FA. Jim Titt, J.Thornby 24.10.1971

3 Dark Side of the Sun . . 2 E1 5b

An excellent new route on superb rock and with good protection. Start 3m right of *Black Sunshine* at an overhang leading to a thin crack underneath a gap in the overhangs at 10m. Surmount the overhang and climb the crack to just below a bulge. Traverse left a couple of moves to a flake-crack leading up to the overhang forming the left side of the gap. Pull rightward round the overhang with conviction and into the gap. Bridge this to jugs and continue to the corner on *Black Sunshine*. At the top of this take a direct line on excellent rock to a small overhang. Pull through this on good holds and finish up a delightful prickly rib.

FA. Simon Laker, Pete Finklaire 12.6.2010

4 Nassty Spider 1 **E2 5c**

A typical Swanage roof test-piece. Start right of the large roof.

1) 5c, 15m. Climb a wall and crack to the right-hand side of the roof. Swing out past an old peg and surmount the roof leftwards with difficulty into a crack leading to the fault-line.

2) 5a, 17m. Head diagonally right via two stepped roofs. Move right again and over a bulge to finish up a solid corner.

FA. Brian Snell, K.Knight 26.7.1975

FFA. Gordon Jenkin, Tim Dunsby 10.6.1984

5 Aventura . . . . 2 **HVS 4c**

Good climbing and very exposed. Start at a cave just west of a huge undercut buttress. Low in the grade.

1) 4c, 15m. Climb the corner above the cave, then at the fault-line, move right to belay on a thread around an ammonite.

2) 4c, 15m. Ascend leftwards to a crack in the roof and pull around in a sensational position to continuation cracks. These lead to a ledge and the exit corner as for *Nassty Spider*.

FA. Pete Crew, P.A.Bell 29.8.1964

Lots of sun | 20 min | Abseil in | Multi-pitch

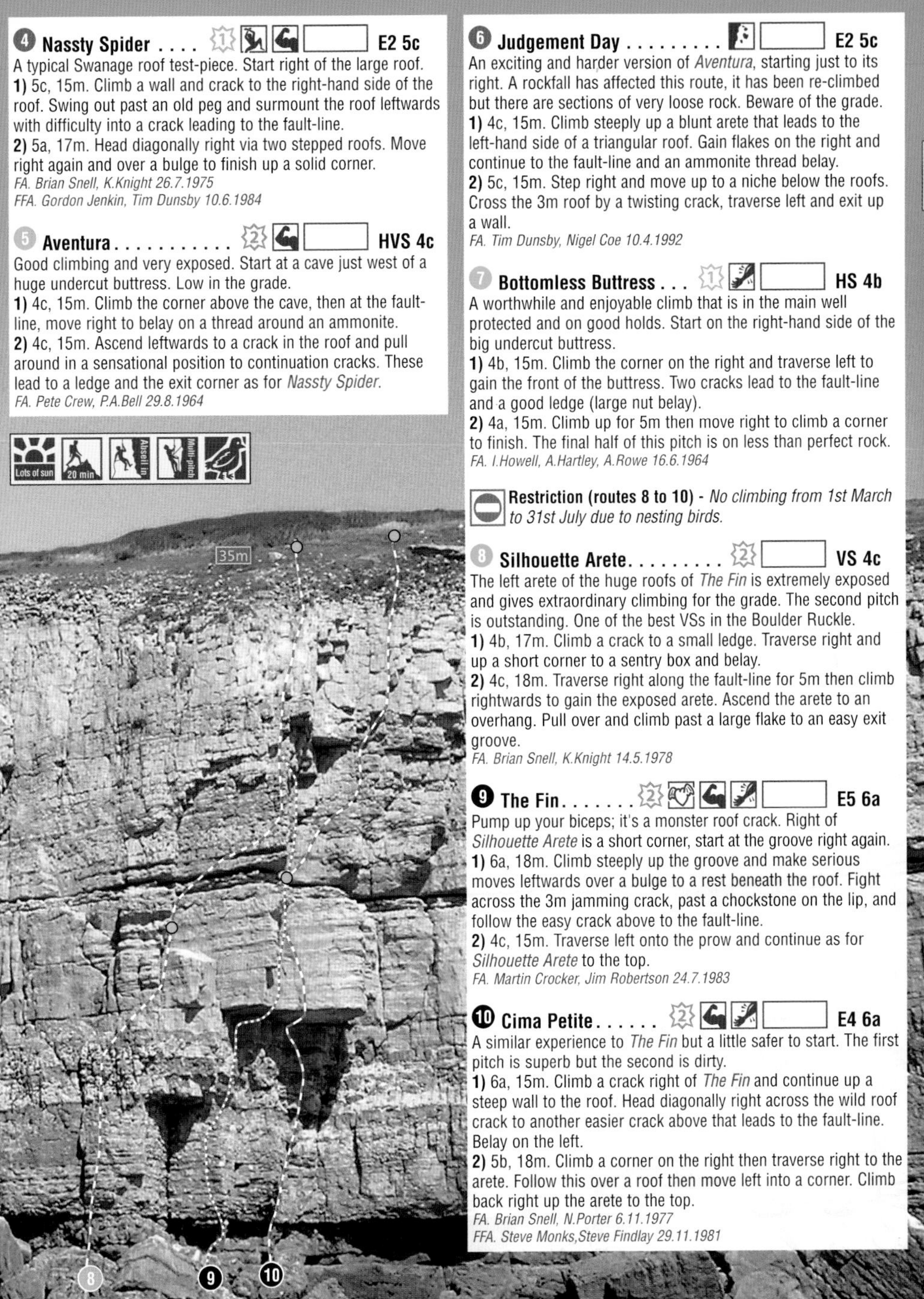

6 Judgement Day **E2 5c**

An exciting and harder version of *Aventura*, starting just to its right. A rockfall has affected this route, it has been re-climbed but there are sections of very loose rock. Beware of the grade.

1) 4c, 15m. Climb steeply up a blunt arete that leads to the left-hand side of a triangular roof. Gain flakes on the right and continue to the fault-line and an ammonite thread belay.

2) 5c, 15m. Step right and move up to a niche below the roofs. Cross the 3m roof by a twisting crack, traverse left and exit up a wall.

FA. Tim Dunsby, Nigel Coe 10.4.1992

7 Bottomless Buttress . . . 1 **HS 4b**

A worthwhile and enjoyable climb that is in the main well protected and on good holds. Start on the right-hand side of the big undercut buttress.

1) 4b, 15m. Climb the corner on the right and traverse left to gain the front of the buttress. Two cracks lead to the fault-line and a good ledge (large nut belay).

2) 4a, 15m. Climb up for 5m then move right to climb a corner to finish. The final half of this pitch is on less than perfect rock.

FA. I.Howell, A.Hartley, A.Rowe 16.6.1964

Restriction (routes 8 to 10) - *No climbing from 1st March to 31st July due to nesting birds.*

8 Silhouette Arete. . . . . 2 **VS 4c**

The left arete of the huge roofs of *The Fin* is extremely exposed and gives extraordinary climbing for the grade. The second pitch is outstanding. One of the best VSs in the Boulder Ruckle.

1) 4b, 17m. Climb a crack to a small ledge. Traverse right and up a short corner to a sentry box and belay.

2) 4c, 18m. Traverse right along the fault-line for 5m then climb rightwards to gain the exposed arete. Ascend the arete to an overhang. Pull over and climb past a large flake to an easy exit groove.

FA. Brian Snell, K.Knight 14.5.1978

9 The Fin. 2 **E5 6a**

Pump up your biceps; it's a monster roof crack. Right of *Silhouette Arete* is a short corner, start at the groove right again.

1) 6a, 18m. Climb steeply up the groove and make serious moves leftwards over a bulge to a rest beneath the roof. Fight across the 3m jamming crack, past a chockstone on the lip, and follow the easy crack above to the fault-line.

2) 4c, 15m. Traverse left onto the prow and continue as for *Silhouette Arete* to the top.

FA. Martin Crocker, Jim Robertson 24.7.1983

10 Cima Petite 2 **E4 6a**

A similar experience to *The Fin* but a little safer to start. The first pitch is superb but the second is dirty.

1) 6a, 15m. Climb a crack right of *The Fin* and continue up a steep wall to the roof. Head diagonally right across the wild roof crack to another easier crack above that leads to the fault-line. Belay on the left.

2) 5b, 18m. Climb a corner on the right then traverse right to the arete. Follow this over a roof then move left into a corner. Climb back right up the arete to the top.

FA. Brian Snell, N.Porter 6.11.1977

FFA. Steve Monks,Steve Findlay 29.11.1981

Portland
Lulworth
Swanage
Winspit
Hedbury and Smokey
Dancing Ledge
Guillemot Ledge
Blackers Hole
Fisherman's Ledge
The Promenade
Cattle Troughs
Boulder Ruckle
Subluminal

Relax and Swing Area

An intimidating section of cliff that sports lots of large overhangs, both at the bottom and top of the wall. The area (aka Thunderball Bay) is very atmospheric, and the routes all have a remote and committing feel about them.
Tides - Non-tidal, but rough seas can be a problem.
Approach - As for the Ocean Boulevard Area, then scramble left along the boulder beach (looking out) for about 200m, passing the Aventura Area en route. All routes finish at stake belays.

Restriction (routes 1 and 2) - *No climbing from 1st March to 31st July due to nesting birds.*

1 Sun Streets 1 E2 5b

An exposed climb in a good position.
1) 5b, 15m. Ascend a short groove to the right of the pointed block to its capping roof. Move out left and up before climbing back right to a hanging arete. Climb up this to the fault-line and poor belay. Better to move right and belay in the corner of *Snowdrop*.
2) 5b, 15m. Pull over a roof and climb a crack, just right of the arete, to a roof. Step left onto the arete and follow it and the short rib to the top.
FA. Pete Oxley, Crispin Waddy 31.8.1986

2 Snowdrop 1 E1 5b

An intimidating route with lots of exposure on its second pitch. Start under the perfect groove on the edge of the bay.
1) 4c, 15m. Climb the groove to a hanging stance at the fault-line.
2) 5b, 18m. Move up to the roofs then make an airy traverse left to the arete which is then followed to the top. Intimidating.
FA. Pete Holden, Howard Lancashire 31.3.1975

3 St Elmo's Firé 2 E3 5c

An exposed arete with quality climbing tempered by a necky start. Starts 3m right of *Snowdrop*.
1) 5c, 15m. Launch out over a low roof and up the left-hand side of the arete to the fault-line.
2) 5c, 15m. Climb the crack right of the arete, then the arete itself steeply all the way to the top.
FA. Crispin Waddy, Pete Oxley 13.7.1986

4 Thunderball. . . . . Top 50 E1 5b

An incredibly intimidating line that requires good route finding on the second pitch, which snakes through the upper overhangs. Start 7m right of a large roof-capped corner.
1) 5a, 16m. Pull up through bulges to a rest above. Climb rightwards to an arete, then move around it to a corner that ends at the fault-line and a belay.
2) 5b, 19m. Climb the wall on the left, past a small overhang, then move right to below a roof. Pull strenuously through the roof at a break to a corner. Follow this to a final overhang which is passed on its left side. Stake belays in place above.
FA. P.Bell, T.Goodfellow 11.7.1963

5 Jo . . . . Top 50 HVS 5a

A brilliant climb. Varied, well protected and in a remote location. Start at the back of the bay at a cave.
1) 4c, 17m. Climb the right wall of the cave to a ledge. Bridge up past a roof and continue up a corner to a belay at the fault-line.
2) 5a, 19m. Move up onto the wall above the stance and head rightwards (thread) to a bulge. Pull over the bulge to a corner and finish up this. Stake belays in place above.
FA. Richard Crewe and Team 16.6.1968 - Pitch 1. Howard Lancashire, Pete Holden 31.3.1975 - Pitch 2.

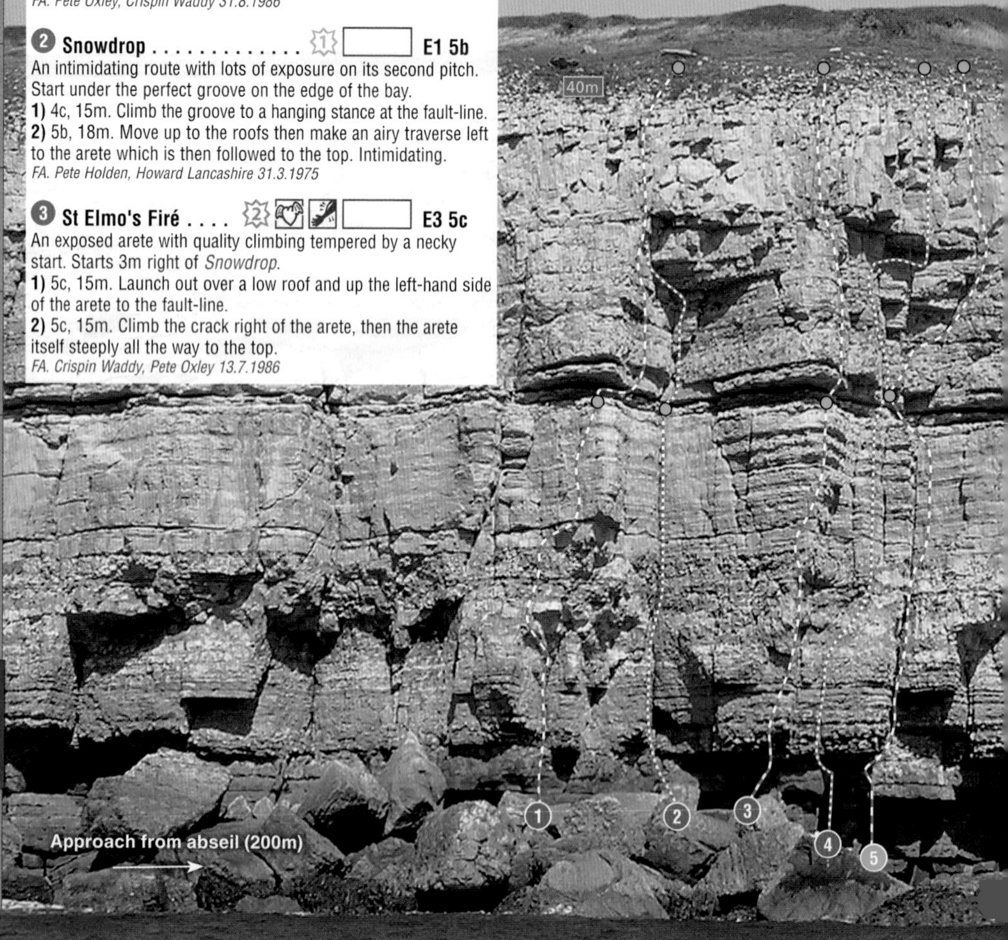

40m
1 2 3 4 5
Approach from abseil (200m)

6 Relax and Swing . . . 3 E5 6a

A mind and body-blowing experience. The highlight is a Separate-Reality-style ceiling crack. Start 5m right of *Jo* at the large roof.
1) 6a, 10m. The big pitch. Gymnastically power out along the 7m horizontal jamming horror (great gear) to reach a hanging belay in a square-cut corner.
2) 5b, 12m. Traverse left to miss the next roof and follow an easy corner crack to the fault-line.
3) 5c, 20m. Climb a shallow groove then move rightwards beneath a blank headwall. Climb a thin technical crack, stepping left at the top to finish.
FA. Martin Crocker, Jim Robertson 23.7.1983

Restriction (routes 7 to 9) - *No climbing from 1st March to 31st July due to nesting birds.*

7 Sardine Special 1 E5 6b

More roof work - not as wide as *Relax and Swing,* but harder.
1) 6b, 12m. The original starting boulder has moved, so combined human tactics are required to reach the first finger-locks in the roof seam. Battle it out into the corner above, then traverse right just below the next roof to a crack. Strenuously pass the roof to gain the left-hand groove. Belay.
2) 5a, 25m. Climb the groove, past the fault-line, to a roof. Move out right into a short exit groove.
FA. Brian Snell, K.Knight 19.9.1976. FFA. Pete Oxley, Steve Williams 7.6.1987

8 Jug Index 1 E4 6b

Another fun roof problem.
1) 6b, 12m. From the raised ledge, cross the centre of the 2m ceiling (thread) past the jug, to a corner. Climb this in more normal fashion to the fault-line.
2) 5a, 15m. Move right along the fault-line to ascend a crack. This leads into a long groove that goes all the way to the top.
FA. Pete Oxley, John Williams 29.11.1987

9 Future Primitive. . . 1 E4 6b

A real beauty but the serious start puts off many attempts.
1) 6b, 20m. Gain a groove and follow it to a small roof. Swing right to undercut around to a friable ledge. Swing left and attack the perfect 2m roof crack. An easy groove leads to the fault-line and belay.
2) 5a, 12m. Take a groove on the right to a ledge then move back left to another groove system right of the arete.
FA. Martin Crocker, D.Light 5.11.1983

Portland
Lulworth
Swanage
Winspit
Hedbury and Smokey
Dancing Ledge
Guillemot Ledge
Blackers Hole
Fisherman's Ledge
The Promenade
Cattle Troughs
Boulder Ruckle
Subluminal

The Grim Reaper Area

This section of the Boulder Ruckle has its fair share of loose rock and is rarely climbed on.

Tides - The boulder beach is above high tide.

Approach - Directly below the 3rd stone wall - when walking west from the lighthouse - a small path leads down from the coast path to twin abseil stakes (these are painted in fading yellow paint). The free-hanging abseil is down the line of *Prayers for Rain*. The routes in this sector are either side of the huge and unstable corner of *Scythe*.

Restriction (route 1) - *No climbing from 1st March to 31st July due to nesting birds.*

1 The Asp . . . . 2 VS 4c

A worthwhile climb, however the finish is very unstable and a pre-placed rope should be left down the final slope. The finish is found 5 fence posts west of the 3rd wall, where a gap through the gorse leads to stakes on the right. Run the rope over a semi-buried boulder in the top of the slope. Start at a pointed boulder.

1) 4b, 17m. Climb the short rounded arete and then move up and right to a corner which is followed to the fault-line.

2) 4c, 18m. Move back left to the corner and climb to a roof. Traverse right carefully to a ledge on the arete. Traverse back left over the roof to another ledge and climb the groove above (peg).

FA. Richard Crewe, P.Charman 24.6.1973

2 Prayers for Rain 1 E3 5c

A worthwhile route that follows a line just right of the abseil, starting 10m left of the huge groove of **Scythe** (not described). Climb on good holds to a thin crack in a smooth wall and follow it to the fault-line. Continue direct to cross a strip-roof. Use a crack to reach a short flake. Swing left then make a hard move through another overhang via a steep groove to an exit corner.

FA. Pete Oxley 29.10.1989. Using a self-belay system.

3 The Grim Reaper 1 E1 5a

A fine sustained route that begins just left of the huge groove.

1) 5a, 20m. Gain a small ledge (poor peg). Pass a bulge and follow a crack-line to a small, scary stance, 3m above the fault-line.

2) 5a, 20m. Traverse left under roofs and pull over, as for *Prayers for Rain*, at a good block. Skirt the roofs above and right, then move back left to a short corner. Swing right then pass some final roofs by another hand traverse rightwards to easier ground. Stake on the upper slope.

FA. Tim Dunsby, R.Lovett 6.6.1984

4 Alas, Poor Yorick . .  E4 6a

A great first pitch that tackles the bold arete. The second pitch is loose - *The Grim Reaper* provides an alternative finish.

1) 6a, 20m. Climb to a small roof, then move right to a steep flake. Gain jugs above that lead to the arete. Technical and bold moves lead to the fault-line. Belay a little higher on *The Grim Reaper.*

2) 5c, 18m. Ascend rightwards to a roof on the arete. Pull over leftwards and finish past hollow rock up the exposed top wall.

FA. Crispin Waddy, John Alcock 5.6.1987

5 Razor Blade Smile .  E5 6c

The only route to breach the strip-roof takes a line 5m left of the square-cut recess in the right-hand side of the bay (looking in). Pull onto the roof via juggy pockets and pass a blind crack by desperate moves to a thread belay in the break above. Continue up *Gold Fever* or lower off.

FA. Pete Oxley 16.10.1989

6 Blow the House Down. .  E3 5c

An intimidating route taking a leftward traverse line above the low-level roof.

1) 5c, 25m. Climb into and around the square-cut recess (tricky). Follow the horizontal break left into a groove. Ascend this to a small stance below the fault-line.

2) 5b, 25m. Climb the groove above the fault-line then move out left (thread) to gain an arete. Exposed moves up the long flake above lead to the top.

FA. Pete Oxley, Nigel Coe 10.11.1985

7 Gold Fever . . . .  E4 5c

Varied and sustained with a pumpy top pitch. A good route.

1) 5c, 10m. Start as for *Blow the House Down* by negotiating the square-cut recess. Then head diagonally left 5m to belay in the centre of the wall.

2) 5b, 30m. A big pitch. Pass a small ledge, then climb the wall to the fault-line. Step right and then up, on small holds, to a metal spike. Step left and pull into a steep corner, which leads strenuously to the top.

FA. Martin Crocker, Jim Robertson 23.10.1983

Buccaneer Area

A fine sector, which has some superb corner and roof climbs, pride of place being that taken by the magnificent *Buccaneer* and the nearby duo of *Sinbad* and *Mickey Mouse*.
Tides - The boulder beach sits above the high tide mark.
Approach - Walk west from the lighthouse as far as the third stone wall. A small path leads down from the coast path to twin abseil stakes (these are painted in fading yellow paint). The free-hanging abseil is down the line of *Prayers for Rain* (Grim Reaper Area). Walk left (facing out) for around 60m to the first routes. This area is also easily accessed from the *Marmolata Buttress* Abseil.

A popular route **Larus, HS 4b** *climbed up the cliff to the left of Joe 90 but a large rockfall has destroyed the lower section of the line. It has been re-climbed at E1, but is loose.*

1 Joe 90 . . . . 2 E5 6a
A fine sustained pitch. Climb past a roof and trend left to the fault-line. Continue to another roof, then climb over and right up a flake to a further roof. Finish up a long flake.
FA. Crispin Waddy, Dave Thomas 4.1989

Lots of sun · 15 min · Abseil in · Multi-pitch

2 Flying Finish 1 E2 5b
A varied route starting under the left end of a long roof at 10m.
1) 5b, 15m. Ascend to the roof then take a crack on the left to the fault-line. Hanging belay.
2) 5b, 20m. Follow a groove to a high roof. Swing right and over it leftwards finishing via a crack to the top.
FA. Arni Strapcans, Gordon Jenkin 31.3.1979
FA. (Pitch 2) Crispin Waddy, John Vlasto 28.3.1985

3 Billy Pigg 2 E1 5b
A great introduction into the art of roof thuggery with good gear.
1) 5b, 15m. Climb to the break in the roof and pull over it. Continue to the fault-line and step right to a belay ledge.
2) 4c, 18m. Follow a wall and groove to a roof. Go left then back right and climb a corner to the top.
FA. Richard Crewe, Kenny Winkworth 28.7.1968
FFA. George Hounsome 11.3.1978

4 Rattler 1 E1 5b
A dominating groove line in a strenuous old style.
1) 5b, 18m. Climb the groove past a big flake, then climb through a break in the bulge above to a good ledge at the fault-line.
2) 5a, 18m. Follow the groove past a huge, dubious block and continue to the top. The block is the size of a Mini, and has no visible means of attachment, but is still there - feeling lucky?
FA. Mick Nunn, Richard Crewe 17.7.1968 (2 pts aid)
FFA. Brian Snell, W.Lyons

5 Fish Supper . . . . 1★ E3 5c

An exposed second pitch. Start 5m right of *Rattler* below a left-facing corner crack.

1) 5a, 18m. Pass a roof and follow the crack until it is possible to break right and climb a corner. Step left onto a hanging boulder then move up and right to follow a crack to the fault-line.

2) 5c, 20m. Move up left and take a corner to a roof. Go over on jugs and continue to another roof. Pass this then move right to finish up a groove.

FA. Nigel Coe, Tim Dunsby 8.12.1984

6 Sinbad . . . . 2★ E1 5b

A very pleasant outing with lots of variety. Start at a V-groove in the buttress front. The start has the 5b move but the fantastic second pitch feels the harder of the two.

1) 5b, 18m. Thrutch up the groove to a crack (thread). Move left over a roof then right onto the face. Ascend a deep crack to the fault-line.

2) 5a, 20m. Gain the wall above and take a crack to a bulge. Pass this and climb slabs to a small exit-corner finishing rightwards.

FA. Richard Crewe, Kenny Winkworth 11.5.1969

7 Mickey Mouse . . . . Top 50 E3 6a

A wonderful and hugely-impressive route with two completely differing pitches. If the second falls off the top wall they will land in Brittany! Start beneath the big leaning cracks in the side of the huge groove of *Buccaneer*.

1) 5b, 20m. Ascend the cracks in the left wall and thug up to the fault-line, passing a large poised block. Belay on a ledge to the left.

2) 6a, 25m. Climb a curving crack on the left to a niche. Gain the roof above, then move out left with difficulty to reach the sensational wall above (peg). Move up and left to an exit corner as for *Sinbad*.

FA. Brian Snell, Richard Crewe, T.Tanswell 8.2.1975
FFA. Arni Strapcans, Gordon Jenkin 1.1979

8 Buccaneer . . . . Top 50 E2 5b

A truly magnificent climb that ascends the big narrowing groove to a wild finish. It gets an extra star for the beauty of the line, though the climbing is just a touch dirty. Climb the corner crack to a bulge. Shift right into a parallel crack then back left into the main corner. Continue up the corner (peg) to the capping roof - superb large thread and resting place. Drop out and over to a strenuous exit crack.

FA. Richard Crewe, Kenny Winkworth 7.6.1969
FFA. Gordon Jenkin, Richard Harrison 2.1978

9 Cutlass . . . . 1★ E5 6a

A good looking direct line up the intimidating face 8m right of *Buccaneer*. Very bold. Ascend direct to a blind flake in a tiny groove. Push on with commitment to the fault-line and step left to a crack. Trend right above to reach the big roof, pulling over the central part and exiting right.

FA. Crispin Waddy, John Alcock 4.6.1987

10 Koo-koo . . . . 1★ E2 5c

A tough start leads to the big corner.

1) 5c, 20m. Surmount the roof, then follow the corner. Traverse right to a pillar. Climb this to the fault-line and belay on the right.

2) 5a, 18m. Gain a ledge above a bulge. Traverse left around the exposed arete to a groove line which is followed to the top.

FA. Richard Crewe, P.Charman 2.9.1973
FFA. Arni Strapcans, Gordon Jenkin 12.8.1978

Finale Groove - p.387 (25m) →

Marmolata Area - Left

This and the neighbouring Lightning Wall Area are the most popular sections of the Boulder Ruckle. The climbs are of a high quality, mostly solid and accessible but it is a potentially serious location should things not go to plan.

Tides - All routes start from non-tidal boulders below the face but in rough seas the boulders beneath *Marmolata Buttress* may be impassable.

Approach - About 400m along from the lighthouse is the jutting bulk of *Marmolata Buttress*. The path leading to it is 22 fence posts beyond the 2nd stone wall, when walking west from the lighthouse. Make a 40m free-hanging abseil, from stakes, down the face just to the east (left - looking out) - see page 338.

1 Wide Awake in America  **E6 6b**

Two contrasting pitches - a strenuous crack and a superb grey headwall. Start at a short, deep groove 5m left of *Finale Groove*.

1) 6a, 18m. Ascend the groove to a rest on a slab (thread). Make powerful moves through the impending bulge to a jammed flake and climb the hand crack to a belay at the fault-line.

2) 6b, 20m. Step left and climb leftwards up the wall to a small foot-ledge. Move up to the grey headwall and make very hard moves (2 pegs) to a good hold. Easier ground leads to the top.

FA. Pete Oxley, A.Blakely 11.12.1984

2 Boatpusher's Arete.   **E5 6a**

The arete left of *Finale Groove*, has good climbing but with a serious start. Climb the steep arete direct (hard and bold) to easier ground that leads to the fault-line. Pull over, as for *Finale Groove*, for 3m, then move out left to ascend the seaward face of the upper arete.

FA. Pete Oxley, Tim Dunsby 4.11.1984

3 Finale Groove . . . . Top 50 HVS 4c
One of the classics of the area, which follows an awesome line up a tapering groove that is packed with good gear and large holds. A great introduction to the big routes at Swanage. Climb the right-facing corner past a bulge at 15m into a niche. Then climb leftwards past the bulge at the fault-line to ascend the narrowing continuation groove in a very spectacular position.
FA. Gordon Smith, D.Hadlum 12.4.1966

4 'B' Line. . . . . 2 VS 5a
A good outing that takes in some intimidating territory. Start at a rightward slanting flake-crack in the wall right of *Finale Groove*. High in the grade.
1) 4b, 18m. Climb the juggy crack and its continuation to the fault-line. Traverse right to a ledge and belay next to a boulder.
2) 5a, 20m. The second pitch of *Sweet SA*.
FA. D.Boone, M.Talbot, D.Hadlum, P.Grainger 10.4.1966

5 Buzz Light Year . . . . . . 2 HVS 5a
Varied and interesting climbing on solid rock. Pitch 2 is at the top end of the grade. Start 9m to the right of the base of *Finale Groove* at a head-height overhang. *Photo on page 271*.
1) 5a, 18m. Arm up on big holds to get established above the lip of the overhang. Move right to a crack and take this to a small overhang. Step right and then back up left to another small overhang. Climb the short crack in the wall above to a large ledge at the fault-line and belay next to a boulder.
2) 5a, 20m. Step up off the boulder and move up 4m and then right to a depression. Traverse 2m left and move up to a jug in a pocket and a good medium size nut. Climb the fine, sustained wall and small corner directly above to a stable exit.
FA. Pete Finklaire 2000s

6 Sweet SA . . . . . 2 VS 5a
A challenging climb featuring a tough first pitch and a fine upper pitch shared with *'B' Line*. High in the grade.
1) 4c, 20m. Climb the corner past a bulge to a ledge. Continue to the fault-line and belay over to the left next to a boulder.
2) 5a, 20m. Move up and leftwards to below a groove. Climb the grey wall boldly up right and then back left to the groove. Climb this with difficulty past an old peg to the top.
FA. F.Clarke, Al Alvarez 1963

7 All Guns Blazing 1 E3 6a
The highlight is the lovely roof on the first pitch.
1) 6a, 20m. Start as for *Sweet SA* then at 5m traverse right, out of the corner and cross the two metre ceiling to an easier crack (4 threads). Belay at the fault-line.
2) 5c, 20m. Overcome a bulge on the right, then bypass the upper overhang on its right (spike and thread) to a ledge. Finish more easily up the wall above.
FA. Pete Oxley, Crispin Waddy 29.8.1986

8 The Heidelberg Creature 2 VS 4c
An outrageously-steep corner-line that is well protected but hard for the grade. Start on a small ledge below the corner.
Photo on page 269.
1) 4c, 20m. Climb the corner and make a steep pull up left to a ledge below an overhang at 8m. Continue steeply up the corner on good holds to a ledge and belay at the fault-line.
2) 4b, 20m. Pull through the overhang using a finger-crack and move up to a slim corner. Climb the sustained corner to a sloping ledge on the right at its end. Finish carefully.
FA. Tony Willmott, A.Heppenstall 18.9.1966

9 Children of the Sun 2 E2 5b
The wall between the upper sections of *Heidelberg Creature* and *The Tool*.
1) 4c, 20m. The first pitch of *Heidelberg Creature*.
2) 5b, 25m. Traverse right for 9m and move over the overhang onto the wall above. Climb up right to a crack and small overhang (peg). Traverse left 2m and climb a bulge to a ledge and finish up some thin cracks.
FA. Pete Finklaire, Sue Hazel 20.3.2002

10 The Tool 2 E2 5b
A fine, sustained outing with good positions which is now climbed in a single pitch. Start 5m right of *Heidelberg Creature*. Climb steeply up parallel cracks to pass a blocky bulge on the left. Follow the hanging corner above past a large overhang at the fault-line and on up to a small overhang. Step left around an arete and follow a thin crack and shallow groove to the top.
FA. Brain Snell, W.Lyons 6.7.1974. FFA. George Hounsome 9.10.1977

11 The Tool (The Bad Workman Finish)
. . . . E3 5b
Follow *The Tool* to its step left, and then continue up the main corner until stopped by a roof. Place gear and climb boldly out over the left side of the roof to finish as for *The Tool*.
FA. Marti Hallett, Rich White 28.6.2007

12 Bert and Ernie 2 E2 5b
Climb *The Tool* past the fault-line to its small overhang, then traverse diagonally up and right below a slanting overlap into a beautiful crack and bridging corner. *Photo on page 267*.
FA. Chris Weedon, Nathan Murphy 4.6.2011

Portland | Lulworth | Swanage | Winspit | Hedbury and Smokey | Dancing Ledge | Guillemot Ledge | Blackers Hole | Fisherman's Ledge | The Promenade | Cattle Troughs | Boulder Ruckle | Subluminal

Marmolata Area

These routes are on the Marmolata Buttress itself and are all high quality, multi-pitch climbs on solid rock, nevertheless it is a potentially serious location.

Tides - All the routes start from non-tidal boulders below the buttress, but in rough seas the boulders beneath *Tatra* may be sea-washed.

Approach - About 400m along from the lighthouse is the jutting bulk of *Marmolata Buttress*. The path leading to it is 22 fence posts beyond the 2nd stone wall when walking west from the lighthouse. Make a 40m free-hanging abseil, from stakes, down the face just to the east (left - looking out).

Lots of sun · 15 min · Abseil in · Multi-pitch

1 Tatra .... Top 50 VS 5a

The best VS in Boulder Ruckle. Well protected, but at the very upper limit of the grade. Start on a ledge below a large sentry box. *Photo opposite.*

1) 5a, 18m. Climb up until a move right can be made to the base of a crack in the right wall of the sentry box. Climb the crack and pull right to an easing at the right-hand side of the overhang above. Follow the steep crack to a ledge and belay.

2) 4b, 10m. Move right along a foot-ledge to a short vertical crack. Pull up the crack to the break and make a strenuous traverse along this to a ledge and belay just around the arete.

3) 4c, 22m. Climb the large corner above the belay via some wide bridging to a ledge and finish up a short, steep corner.

FA. Barry Annette, P.Kemp pre 1963

2 Marmolata Arete .. 1 E4 6a

Good climbing up the prow, but there are some serious moves.

1) 6a, 18m. Climb just right of the arete then step left and up a hanging groove to a short slab (optional stance as for *Marmolata Buttress*). Continue up the arete to belay on *Tatra*.

2) 6a, 22m. Ascend the arete on the right, past a peg, direct to the top in a superb position.

FA. George Hounsome, Pete Finklaire 31.3.1979. FA. (Direct) Pete Oxley 1986

3 Marmolata Buttress ... 2 E3 5c

A gnarly first pitch leads to fine and varied climbing on the east face of the buttress.

1) 5c, 12m. Start as for the last route then climb a thin crack with difficulty to a large ledge on the seaward face.

2) 5b, 15m. Traverse around the corner to a groove leading to the fault-line. Traverse right again to a second groove which leads onto a ledge. Belay in the corner.

3) 5b, 15m. Step left out onto the wall where a lovely flake system leads to the top.

FA. Gordon Smith, Richard Crewe 2.6.1973
FFA. George Hounsome, Scott Titt 20.11.1977

4 Marmolata Combination 1 E1 5b

The first pitch of this line suffered a major rockfall. It has been re-climbed since and much of the loose rock removed.

1) 5b, 18m. Climb the chimney to a large belay ledge.

2) 5b, 15m. Step left out onto the wall where a lovely flake system leads to the top. This is the third pitch of *Marmolata Buttress*.

Top of *Marmolata Buttress*
40m
A
Top pitches hidden
Area of rockfall
1 2 3 4

Director's Groove - p.390

Carrie Hill moving across the exposed traverse on the second pitch of the Boulder Ruckle classic *Tatra* (VS 5a) - *opposite*.

Lightning Wall Area

This is one of the most popular sections of Swanage, and not just because it is close to the car park. The routes here are mostly excellent, with a number of classics in the HVS to E2 range.

Tides - The routes to the right of *Marmolata Buttress* (looking in) are well shielded from the sea by a substantial boulder beach, which means access is possible in most sea conditions - apart from the far eastern end of the wall which is tidal.

Approach - About 400m along from the lighthouse is the jutting bulk of *Marmolata Buttress*. The path leading to it is 22 fence posts beyond the 2nd stone wall when walking west from the lighthouse. Make a 40m free-hanging abseil, from stakes, down the face just to the east (left - looking out).

1 Director's Groove. . . . .  **HVS 5a**

This rather worrying route starts up a wide groove in the wall just right of the abseil line (looking in).

1) 5a, 25m. Climb the groove, passing a roof on the right, then move left to gain an arete. Traverse diagonally right to belay below a wide crack. Awkward belays.

2) 4c, 15m. Follow the wide crack to the top. Poor gear.

FA. D.Hadlum, P.Grainger 10.4.1966

2 Lightning Wall . . . . Top 50 HVS 5a
An intimidating, but essential tick of the Boulder Ruckle which can be climbed in two pitches. Start below a groove, just left of a deep corner 25m from the base of the abseil. Enter the groove and follow it to the fault-line. Move right and up through a bulge into a short corner (possible belay). Move right onto the wall above the roof and traverse this up rightwards on good holds to the arete. Follow the arete to a niche, old peg, move up and then head right to an easier corner that leads to the top.
Photo on page 13.
FA. George Smith, A.Webster 10.4.1966

3 Elysium . . . . Top 50 E1 5b
A great, technical pitch. Start 5m right of a large corner, beneath a huge roof at the fault-line. Climb a crack to a ledge at the base of a thin crack in the smooth wall below the roof. Climb the thin crack past a peg to the roof, traverse rightwards to below a corner and climb this strenuously to another corner. Move left around the arete to join and finish more easily up *Lightning Wall*.
FA. Richard Crewe, Kenny Winkworth 7.1.1968

4 Brisingamen . . . 1 E5 6b
A eliminate paralleling *Singing Winds*, Start as for *Elysium*. Climb a faint, run-out groove (peg) and the short crack above. Take the bold headwall, trending right up a thin crack, to finish more easily up a corner.
FA. Mike Robertson, Barry Clarke 27.8.1996

5 Singing Winds . . 2 E4 6a
A big wall pitch just right of *Elysium* with some fine, bold face work. Start as for *Elysium*. Climb the initial crack, then move right to a spike. Move up then launch up the blank, shallow groove to the fault-line (peg) - bold. Climb direct to another peg, then move left to a thin crack and the finish of *Brisingamen*.
FA. Martin Crocker, Jim Robertson 24.7.1983

6 Dune Dust 2 E4 6a
A good route that maintains interest throughout both its pitches. The pegs are old but there is good gear available to back them up. Start below an overhung, right-leaning corner.
1) 6a, 25m. Move up the right-leaning corner for 5m, then pull straight up through the bulge to gain a horizontal break. Climb the thin black streak above (2 pegs) to the main fault-line. Move right and up through a bulge to a corner and a stance.
2) 4c, 15m. Climb up and leftwards around an arete to enter and finish up a corner.
FA. Pete Oxley, J.Preston 5.9.1986

7 Thunder Groove . . . . . . 2 HVS 5b
A quality route. Start at a small corner behind the highest boulder.
1) 5b, 25m. Head right for 5m then make a hard move upwards past a pinnacle block to a ledge. The groove above leads, with difficulty, to the fault-line. Place good gear then tackle another groove that gains a large belay ledge on the left.
2) 4c, 15m. Step right and climb the groove past a ledge to reach an exit corner.
FA. Richard Crewe, Kenny Winkworth 16.9.1967
FFA. Pat Littlejohn

8 Gypsy . . . . Top 50 E2 5b
Well-travelled and protectable climbing, sustained but never too desperate. Start below a slim, right-facing corner in the smooth face below the main fault-line.
1) 5b, 16m. Pull up strenuously onto a ledge and move up a corner to an overhang. Climb another overhang and the slim corner to the fault-line and belay.
2) 5b, 22m. Step right and pull over the overhang into an open groove. Follow the groove to an overhang before moving right and climbing to the top.
FA. Richard Crewe, Kenny Winkworth 29.10.1967

40m
7
8
Strongbow - p.392

Lightning Wall Area - Right

The right-hand section of the area is a fine section of cliff that is tidal towards its eastern end.

Tides - The routes up to *The Planet* are non-tidal, to the right the climbs can only be accessed at lowish tides.

Approach - About 400m along from the lighthouse is the jutting bulk of *Marmolata Buttress*. The path leading to it is 22 fence posts beyond the 2nd stone wall when walking west from the lighthouse. Make a 40m free-hanging abseil, from stakes, down the face just to the east (left - looking out).

1 The Adventures of Portland Bill 2 E2 5b

An unusual low-level traverse that provides a long and interesting tour of some of the very best rock and positions on this section of cliff. Well protected and easily combined with the excellent pitch of *White Dwarf* to give a better ending. Start as for *Elysium* (see page 391). *Photo on page 262*.

1) 5b, 25m. Climb the large crack on *Elysium* to a ledge, then move right along a twin horizontal break until a step down gains a ledge and belay.

2) 5b, 17m. Follow the breaks rightwards to a spike belay at the edge of the wall, on *Acapulco*.

3) 5b, 10m. Climb the flake-crack on the right to the fault-line - strenuous - then belay on the right in the fault-line.

4) 4c, 20m. Ascend flakes on the right, then move leftwards steeply to a roof. Cross this and continue up the exit corner.

FA. Pete Oxley, Jon Biddle 9.8.1986

2 Strongbow 2 E1 5b

Similar quality to *Gypsy* (page 291) with some nice steep climbing. Start at a right-facing corner. High in the grade.

1) 5a, 12m. Climb the corner and move left around an arete to a ledge. Trend rightwards to another ledge and belay.

2) 5b, 30m. Climb cracks above, passing the fault-line with conviction and move up to a second roof. Traverse right to a shallow corner (peg) then continue to a bigger corner and finish up it.

FA. Richard Crewe, P.Charman 19.5.1974

3 Vortices 2 E2 5c

A mix of the sustained and strenuous on a strong line makes this a route worth tracking down. Start right of a corner, below a large roof.

1) 5c, 20m. Move up the thin wall to a large hanging flake and pull right into a short corner. Go up to a horizontal break, and traverse rightwards again, until just beyond a vertical crack. Climb the wall on reasonable holds to the fault-line and belay.

2) 5b, 20m. Pull onto the wall above, follow it to a corner, and climb this to the top - the upper section of *Strongbow*.

FA. Pete Finklaire, D.Glover 21.4.1985

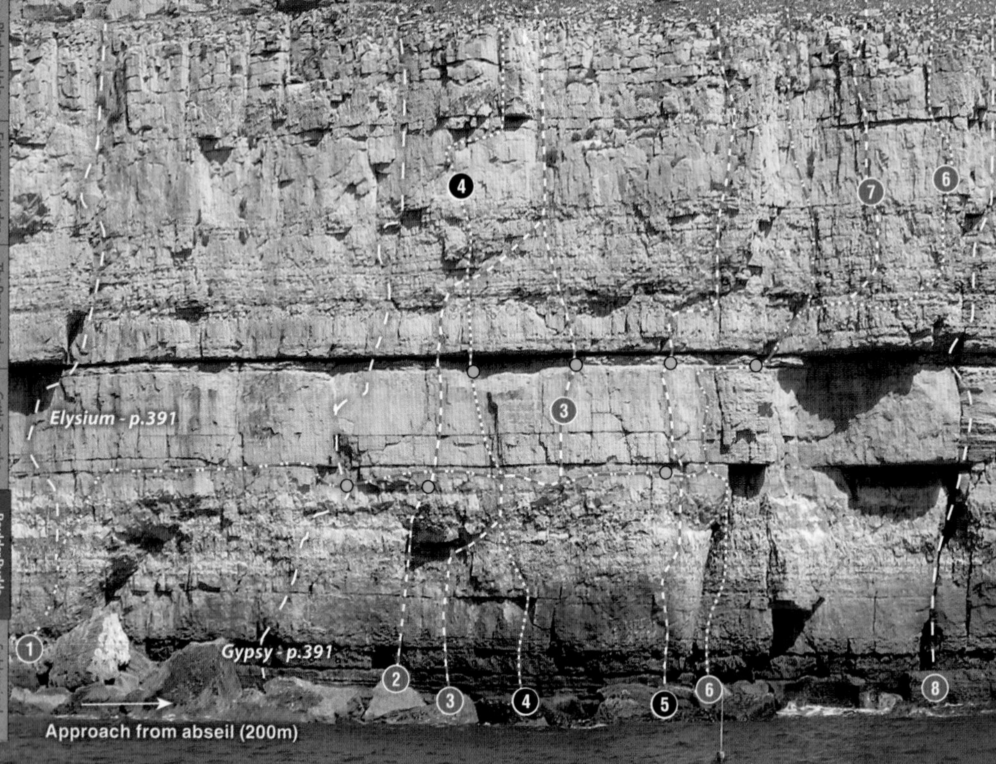

4 The Mace 1 **E5 6b**
Bold and technical on both pitches. Recommended.
1) 6b, 18m. Ascend past a triangular niche - thread - and move leftwards to beneath a shallow groove. Boldly climb up it to the fault-line. Belay on wires and a large cam over the roof.
2) 5c, 20m. Step left and go over the overhang and climb the wall to below a roof. Swing left and climb a bold face prior to moving right into a hanging exit groove.
FA. Crispin Waddy, P.Windall 30.11.1986

5 Acapulco. 2 **E4 6a**
More strenuous than bold but with a committing start. Start 3m left of where the flat ledges drop away.
1) 6a, 18m. Climb the steep buttress just left of an arete to twin spikes. Cracks lead more easily to the fault-line.
2) 5c, 18m. Go rightwards into a curving groove and climb up it to a roof. Cross this to easier ground and finish slightly left.
FA. Crispin Waddy, P.Windall 5.4.1987

6 The Planet 2 **E3 5c**
A great trip - very exposed and a touch run-out on the second pitch. The first pitch has suffered a rockfall but has been re-climbed with no change in grade.
1) 5b, 20m. Climb the corner with ironstone flakes - just left of the rockfall - to the roof. Move left to a crack that leads to the fault-line. Belay on the right.
2) 5c, 25m. Follow flakes on the right and then traverse out right above the roof to ledges. Climb the wall just left of the arete past a spike to a break. Exit up a short groove.
FA. Crispin Waddy, Andy Ford 31.7.1985

7 White Dwarf 1 **E2 5c**
Variation to *The Planet* pitch 2. Climb the centre of the fine wall above the middle section of *The Planet* traverse.
FA. Barry Clarke 18.10.1998

The next routes start from a lower level and need low tide and calm seas to gain access.

8 Ximenes. . . . . Top 50 **E2 5c**
A classic crack-line which is sustained, athletic and protectable all the way. Start 10m right of the big corner below the line.
1) 5c, 18m. Climb the crack and strenuously gain an overhanging corner which leads to the fault-line.
2) 5b, 18m. Pull through the roof above and move up to another one. Step right and over the roof then continue up the right-hand of two grooves. At the top step left to an exit scramble.
FA. Gordon Smith, Richard Crewe 4.9.1971
FFA. Kevin Turner, Nick Buckley 1977

9 Gimcrack . . . . 1 **VS 4b**
One of the more amenable, but difficult-to-access climbs on this section of the Boulder Ruckle. Start at a low-angled section of the cliff that stands proud of the wall.
1) 4a, 17m. Follow the rib for 7m and move left to a corner. Climb the corner to a large ledge below a roof and belay.
2) 4b, 22m. Pull over the overhang and climb a groove to a large ledge. Finish up a corner on the left.

Lots of sun | 15 min | Abseil in | Multi-pitch | Tidal

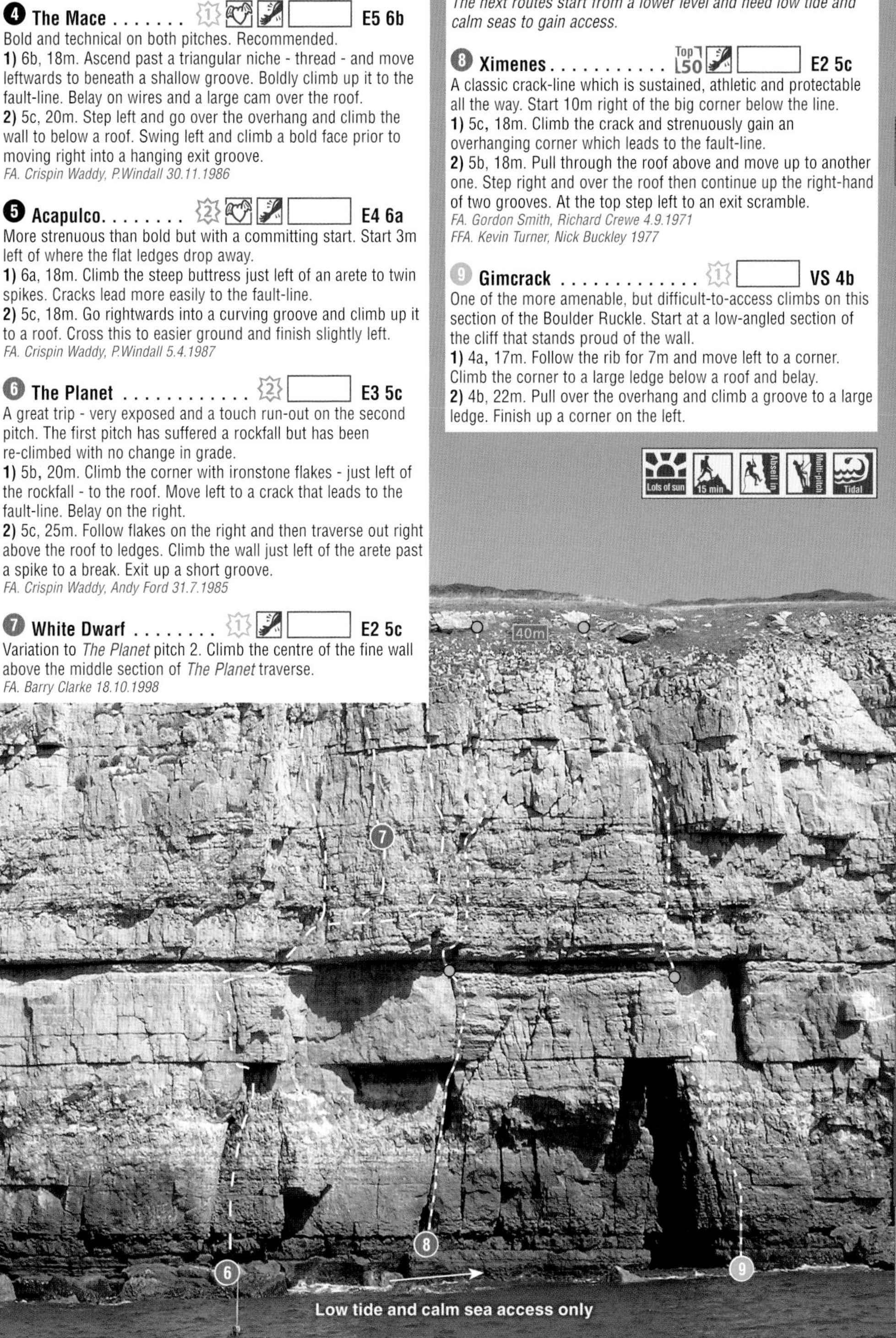

Old Faithful Area

A fantastic section of the Boulder Ruckle which is peppered with some awesome lines that have climbing and atmosphere to match.

Tides - The boulders at the base are non-tidal, but keep away in rough seas, when getting along the crag base becomes difficult.

Approach - Walk west from the lighthouse to 17 fence posts after the first stone wall passed on the coast path. A small path leads straight down to a large tubular Old Faithful abseil stake (with back up). The abseil ends at a large fin-backed boulder. All routes finish at stake belays. The remains of the original Old Faithful stake is still visible, flattened down to grass level.

Restriction (all routes) - No climbing from 1st March to 31st July due to nesting birds.

1 October Lady . . . . 2 stars **E1 5b**

Start at a small corner, 15m left of the huge block sat under the roof. Unusually thuggy climbing.

1) 4c, 15m. Climb the corner to a ledge at the fault-line.

2) 5b, 20m. Climb the crack above then undercut the long roof rightwards to an exposed exit groove (thread). Finish up this.

FA. Dave Gunn, George Hounsome 25.10.1975

2 Ice Queen . . . . 2 stars **E5 6a**

An excellent direct start to *October Lady*, starting 8m further right. Climb the bottom bulging rib with difficulty (2 pegs) to the fault-line. Move slightly right then back left to the exit groove and thread on *October Lady*. Finish up this.

FA. Pete Oxley 29.12.1985

3 Sun King . . . . 1 star **E4 6a**

Start on the left of a massive block in an alcove. Climb direct to a crack (on *Jasper*) then make a hard swing left on the lip of the roof to a peg in a crack. Climb direct past the fault-line to eventually reach a large flake. Finish boldly up the white headwall to a horizontal crack finishing rightwards over a strip roof.

FA. Pete Oxley 29.11.1990

4 Jasper . . . . 1 HVS 4c

Two very different pitches - the first strenuous and the second more balancy and requiring good route finding. Possibly best climbed as a single pitch.
1) 4c, 15m. Climb the right-hand side of the massive block and then move left to ascend a crack to an awkward belay at the fault-line.
2) 4b, 18m. Surmount a bulge and trend rightwards past a ledge and small corner to another smaller ledge. Exit to the left of a small roof at the top.
FA. Richard Crewe, Kenny Winkworth, R.Kent 4.5.1969

5 Via Concordia 1 E2 5b

A direct route on good rock. Start at the right side of the massive block that *Jasper* climbs, 10m west of *Old Faithful*. Climb the crack/chimney to its top. Pull out right and climb another crack to the fault-line. Continue direct through the bulge on good holds, past a horizontal crack and short corner to a ledge on the right. Move up and finish left of small roof, as for *Jasper*.
FA. Pete Finklaire, Sue Hazel, Paul Lloyd 7.9.1997

6 Big Bertha. 1 E2 5c

The first pitch is very gritstone-like, and is good in its own right. Start 2m west of *Old Faithful*.
1) 5b, 15m. Climb the steep wall on jugs past good cam-slots halfway, then follow rounded breaks to a large ledge and belay at the fault-line.
2) 5c, 20m. Climb the crack 1m left of the *Old Faithful* corner, and pull over the roof - hard. Climb straight up to finish, passing the small roof at the top on the right - take care with some doubtful blocks here.
FA. Nigel Coe, Tim Dunsby 9.12.1989

7 Old Faithful . . . . 2 VS 4c

The abseil line is the safest escape, and also a worthy route.
1) 4b, 14m. Climb the crack above the fin-backed boulder to a large fault-line ledge.
2) 4c, 21m. Climb the next crack boldly around a roof and continue to a ledge on the left. Move right into a corner to finish.
FA. R.Kent, Richard Crewe, Kenny Winkworth 4.5.1969

8 Baker's Dozen . . . . 1 VS 4c

A wandering but very worthwhile couple of pitches on good rock with good protection. Start as for *Old Faithful*.
1) 4c, 14m. Move up to a thin crack/groove and climb it with difficulty to the fault-line and belay.
2) 4c, 22m. Move right around the arete and climb a tough crack to a ledge. Traverse back left for 6m and move up to join and finish as for *Old Faithful*.
FA. T.Baker, Richard Crewe 13.9.1975

9 Argo. . . . . 2 HVS 5a

A thin and poorly protected start, but good climbing above, and the top pitch is stunning.
1) 5a, 16m. Climb over a fingery bulge, then move left to the main groove, which leads to a belay at the fault-line.
2) 4c, 22m. Pull left onto the side wall and climb up to a niche. Follow the right-hand crack above to the top.
FA. Richard Crewe, D.Close 6.9.1975

10 The Golden Fleece . . . . 2 HVS 5a

A superb outing. Steep and varied with good gear when you need it. Start 15m right of *Old Faithful*, beyond a large corner, beneath an undercut buttress.
1) 5a, 18m. Climb a steep corner on the right to a ledge on its left. Continue up the tricky wall to a belay on a prow at the fault-line.
2) 5a, 22m. Steep moves gain holds above and right. Pull into a groove and continue on jugs to a ledge from where a corner leads to the top.
FA. Richard Crewe, Scott Titt 2.8.1975

11 Moose's Tooth 2 E3 6a

A good, but much harder way up the buttress. High in the grade.
1) 5b, 18m. Start as for *Golden Fleece*, but break right along a sloping ledge to the arete. Follow this to a belay in the fault-line.
2) 6a, 22m. Pull over a bulge on the left and pass an overhang above - hard. Finish up the left-hand side of the arete above.
FA. Crispin Waddy, C.Mullen 28.2.1986
FFA. Crispin Waddy, Pete Oxley 29.9.1986

Behemoth Area

The left-hand side of this area is a tall and steep section of the cliff that has some striking lines and is home to one of the best HVSs around - *Behemoth* - plus a few other gems worth seeking out. The right-hand side has harder climbs and is less frequented.

Tides - The boulders before the *White Horse* zawn are non-tidal but keep away in rough seas when getting along the crag base becomes difficult. The base of the cliff beyond the zawn is tidal and needs a lowish tide to gain access, or abseil in directly.

Approach - Walk west from the lighthouse to 17 fence posts after the first stone wall passed on the coast path. A small path leads straight down to a large tubular Old Faithful abseil stake (with back up). The abseil ends at a large fin-backed boulder. Cross boulders left (looking out) to the base of the first climbs. All routes finish at stake belays.

Restriction - No climbing from 1st March to 31st July due to nesting birds.

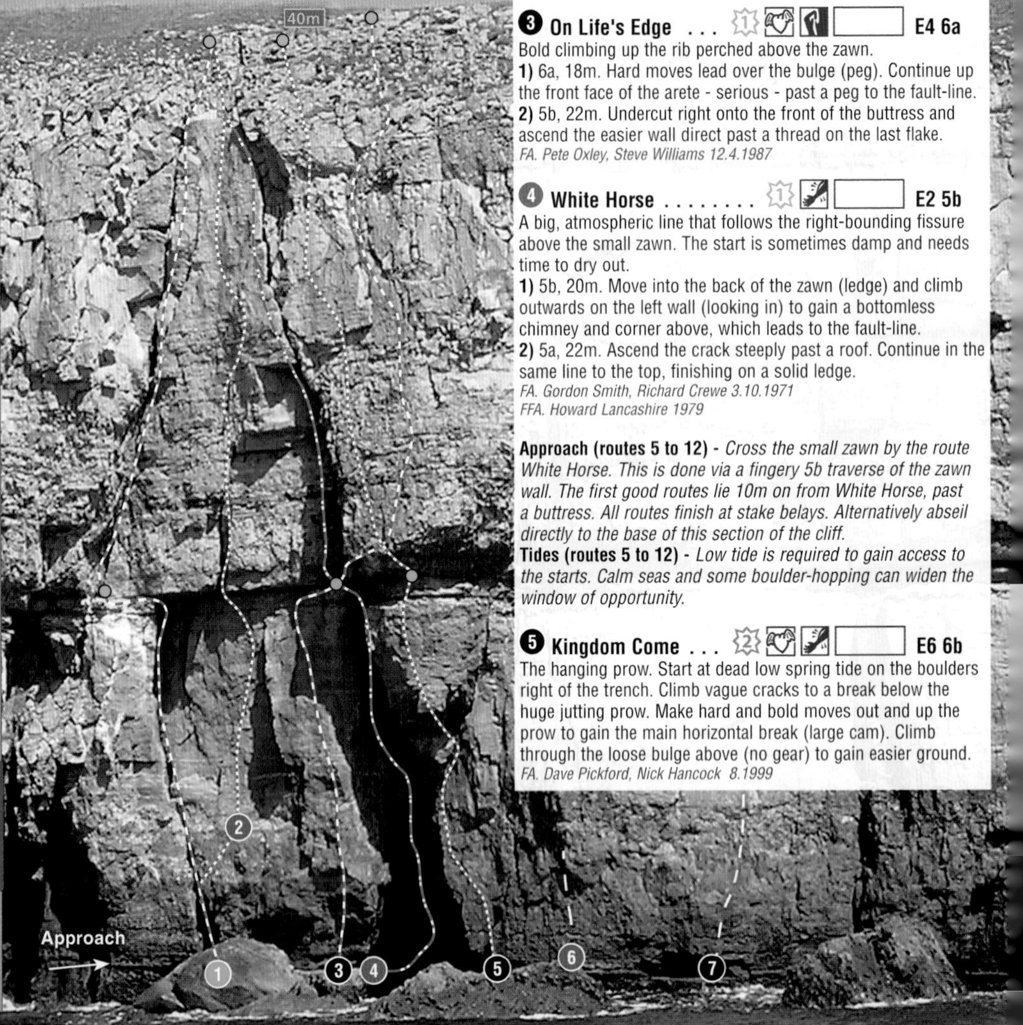

40m

Approach

1 2 3 4 5 6 7

Tides (routes 1 to 4) - *The boulders are non-tidal but access along the base is easier at low tide. Keep away in rough seas.*

1 Behemoth . . . . Top 50 **HVS 5a**
A well protected classic with a sensational top pitch. It follows the steep corner 30m right of *Old Faithful* (looking in).
1) 5a, 18m. Climb the crack and corner to a roof. A tricky move around an arete leads to a belay at the foot of the main corner.
2) 5a, 22m. Ascend the corner past a bulge, then climb the arm-blowing cracks to a rightward exit via a cleaned ledge.
FA. Richard Crewe, Gordon Smith 14.11.1971
FFA. Howard Lancashire, Falco Rech 1.1975

2 Soul Sacrifice . . . . Top 50 **E3 5b**
A brilliant pitch up the centre of the soaring face. It has good gear but is strenuous and sustained. Start up the crack of *Behemoth*, then traverse right to take thin cracks to the fault-line. Fight through the short chimney and cruise up the rib (peg) and white headwall on pockets, to eventually exit onto a ledge.
FA. Martin Crocker, Jim Robertson 2.2.1983

3 On Life's Edge . . . 1 **E4 6a**
Bold climbing up the rib perched above the zawn.
1) 6a, 18m. Hard moves lead over the bulge (peg). Continue up the front face of the arete - serious - past a peg to the fault-line.
2) 5b, 22m. Undercut right onto the front of the buttress and ascend the easier wall direct past a thread on the last flake.
FA. Pete Oxley, Steve Williams 12.4.1987

4 White Horse 1 **E2 5b**
A big, atmospheric line that follows the right-bounding fissure above the small zawn. The start is sometimes damp and needs time to dry out.
1) 5b, 20m. Move into the back of the zawn (ledge) and climb outwards on the left wall (looking in) to gain a bottomless chimney and corner above, which leads to the fault-line.
2) 5a, 22m. Ascend the crack steeply past a roof. Continue in the same line to the top, finishing on a solid ledge.
FA. Gordon Smith, Richard Crewe 3.10.1971
FFA. Howard Lancashire 1979

Approach (routes 5 to 12) - *Cross the small zawn by the route White Horse. This is done via a fingery 5b traverse of the zawn wall. The first good routes lie 10m on from White Horse, past a buttress. All routes finish at stake belays. Alternatively abseil directly to the base of this section of the cliff.*
Tides (routes 5 to 12) - *Low tide is required to gain access to the starts. Calm seas and some boulder-hopping can widen the window of opportunity.*

5 Kingdom Come . . . 2 **E6 6b**
The hanging prow. Start at dead low spring tide on the boulders right of the trench. Climb vague cracks to a break below the huge jutting prow. Make hard and bold moves out and up the prow to gain the main horizontal break (large cam). Climb through the loose bulge above (no gear) to gain easier ground.
FA. Dave Pickford, Nick Hancock 8.1999

6 Dublin Packet .... 2 ☐ HVS 5b
The start of this route needs a low tide and a calm sea.
1) 4c, 18m. Start on a ledge on the left side (looking out) of White Horse Zawn. Drop down on to a part-submerged boulder and fall across on to the right side of zawn. Traverse right to small niche and climb cracks up right then back left to a good belay on fault-line.
2) 5b, 22m. Climb the groove above to easier ground to finish.
FA. Richard Crewe, Gordon Smith, R.Kent 13.11.1971

7 Anger is an Energy. 1 ☐ E5 6b
A bold face climb starting 10m right of the fissure of *White Horse* (looking in).
1) 6b, 12m. Climb the centre of the smooth wall, past a poor peg, to the fault-line.
2) 6a, 18m. Layback around the overhang above then move strenuously leftwards up to a thin roof. Pull over this on good holds then follow the slab above to the top.
FA. Pete Oxley, G.Anstey 4.7.1987

8 Sparky .... 1 ☐ E5 6b
Climb the centre of the broad pillar (left of *Let the Punka Burn*) past a thread on the right to a very committing last move for the fault-line. Finish up *Let the Punka Burn.*
FA. Martin Crocker, John Harwood 1.10.1994

9 Let the Punka Burn.... 1 ☐ E3 6a
A good technical first pitch.
1) 6a, 12m. Climb a thin crack, just right of a slight buttress, to the fault-line and a belay on the left.
2) 5b, 20m. Pull over a roof - tough - and move into a niche in the next roof. Continue direct up an easy crack to the top.
FA. Pete Oxley, Crispin Waddy 31.8.1986

10 Too Precious ... 2 ☐ E6 6b
A superb but serious direct line up the blank face, starting 5m right of *Let the Punka Burn,* with a possible 'desmond' from high up. Climb up easily and place runners on the left in a short crack then step right and take the centre of the face to the fault-line. Pull over on the right at a tiny corner then step back left to finish direct past an alcove to a finishing crack.
FA. Pete Oxley 14.8.1987

The next routes are located in a smooth walled bay 5m further on.

11 Prudence .... 2 ☐ HVS 5b
The obvious line on the left-hand side of the bay.
1) 4c, 14m. Climb the right-hand crack out of a small cave to the fault-line. Belay on the left.
2) 5b, 20m. Pull over the overhang on the right and continue up the crack, passing another bulge rightwards, to an easy finish.
FA. K.Cartwright 26.11.1967

Two routes currently breach the face to the right, but use some bolt protection. It is hoped these will be re-climbed without the bolts to give a pair of hard trad routes. Neither are described here.

12 Ganymede .... 2 ☐ E1 5b
Another good route taking the crack on the right of the bay.
1) 5a, 16m. Follow the crack to the fault-line. Move left then over a bulge to a belay (poor peg plus good nuts).
2) 5b, 16m. Traverse right for 5m and gain the right-hand side of the high roof line. Pass it leftwards - tricky - and take the groove above to the top.
FA. George Hounsome, T.Daniels 13.8.1977

Portland Lulworth Swanage Winspit Hedbury and Smokey Dancing Ledge Guillemot Ledge Blackers Hole Fisherman's Ledge The Promenade Cattle Troughs Boulder Ruckle Subluminal

Airy Legs Area

The furthest east section of the Boulder Ruckle runs into Subluminal and combines the seriousness of The Ruckle with the ease of viewing and reasonable access of Subluminal. The selection of climbs on offer are rarely climbed. Escape is only possible by climbing back out, or Prusiking in emergency.

Tides - The boulders at the base of the cliff are non-tidal but keep away in rough seas.

Approach - All the routes are accessed by abseil. For the bulk of the routes abseil from stakes high on the slope 20m to the west of the protruding ledge at the western end of Subluminal (where *Greasy Chimney* finishes). *The Long Goodbye*, *Seventh Wave* and *Second Sight* can also be reached by a traverse and down-climb from the western end of Subluminal.

Restriction (routes 1 to 4) - *No climbing from 1st March to 31st July due to nesting birds.*

1 In the Heat of the Night . . . 1 star **E1 5c**

Needs low water and a calm sea to start, alternatively start up *Callisto* and traverse left to the wide crack.

1) 5c, 15m. Traverse left and up to the steep wide crack in the bulge above. Climb this with difficulty and a reach to a ledge and belay at the fault-line.

2) 4a, 20m. Climb the corner above and continue to another which leads to the top.

FA. Crispin Waddy, Guy Percival 27.9.1984

2 Callisto . . . . 1 star **HVS 5b**

A direct line that crosses the second pitch of *Insectitude*. Start below and right of a thin leftward slanting crack. Move up leftwards with difficulty to the crack and climb it and the slab above to the fault-line. Pull through the overhang at a crack to the right and climb the groove above to a ledge. Move right and finish up another corner/groove.

FA. Crispin Waddy, Guy Percival 27.9.1984

3 Insectitude . . . . 1 star **VS 4c**

A wandering route with a tough first pitch up a wide crack.

1) 4c, 9m. Pitch 1 of *Airy Legs*.

2) -, 9m. Traverse left under the overhang to a good belay ledge.

3) 4a, 20m. Move up and right on to the wall above the overhang. Climb up to an easing and finish up some flakes.

FA. c.1963

4 Airy Legs . . . . 2 star **VS 4c**

A direct on *Insectitude* and relatively popular. Well protected. *Photo on page 373.*

1) 4c, 9m. Climb the wide crack to a small overhang. Make a long reach to gain good holds and jams. Pull up to the large belay ledge at the fault-line just above.

2) 4a, 20m. Climb the chimney and corner crack above, moving left just below the top to avoid loose ground.

FA. D.Oldroyd, D.Burrin, D.Eastwood 1963. Reclimbed by Kevin Turner and Gordon Jenkin after rockfall in 1984

5 Insecticide . . . . . . 2 star **E2 5b**

Climb the thin crack just left of the larger flake-crack to gain the fault-line. Continue direct to meet and follow the right-trending corner, which is quit on the right to pass a steepening below the top. Poorly protected in its upper half.

FA. Tim Dunsby, Pamela Holt, Nigel Coe, R.Elder 16.11.1991

Belay/abseil stakes high up on slope
A
30m
3
3
Ganymede - p.397
1
2
4
5
6
Low tide access only

6 Nutcracker Exit II . . . . . 2 HVS 4c
A good pitch. Climb the large flake-crack past the fault-line to a ledge on the left. From the ledge move leftwards to flakes and climb these, and the wall to the right, trending rightwards to the top.
FA. B.Snell, K.Knight 30.9.1979.
FA. (Finish as described) A.Davis, S.Arnold 11.9.1988

7 Warriors 1 E1 5b
A hard-won line that is high in the grade. Start from the boulders on the right side of the bay. From a small ledge at 1m, climb a crack to the roof at the fault-line. Traverse left to gain a thin crack. Climb this and the continuation flake line to the top.
FA. Kevin Turner, Nick Buckley 2.1980

8 Intersection. . . . . 1 S
An adventurous and well-positioned climb in a serious setting. Start from the boulders on the right-hand side of the bay.
1) -, 8m. From a small ledge at 1m, climb a crack to the roof at the fault-line, move right to a belay on a ledge.
2) -, 17m. Traverse along the fault-line and climb the right-trending crack and flake to the top. Continuing along the fault-line to Subluminal is **The Nutcracker Traverse, S 4a**.

9 War . . . . 1 HVS 5b
Fierce climbing on an intimidating line puts this route at the upper end of the grade. However, the protection is good.
1) -, 8m. As for *Intersection*. From a small ledge at 1m, climb a crack to the roof at the fault-line, move right to a belay.
2) 5b, 16m. Climb the short wall and overhang-laden corner.
FA. Brian Snell, W.Lyons 7.7.1975

10 The Long Goodbye . . . . 2 HVS 4c
Neat wall climbing with good but spaced gear. From the ledge climb to a smaller one at 3m and then on to the fault-line. Pull onto and climb the wall above the fault-line until moves rightwards and then back left finish at a notch.
FA. Tim Dunsby 8.1984

11 Seventh Wave . . . . 1 VS 5a
From a thread belay on the right-hand ledge, climb up leftwards to the fault-line. Pull over the overhang to below another roof, step left and climb the wall to the top.
FA. Nigel Coe, Frank Farrell 4.8.1984

12 Second Sight. . . . . 1 VS 5a
Follow *Seventh Wave* to below its second roof and then step right and climb the flake-line to the top.
FA. Gordon Jenkin, Frank Farrell 1.7.1984

The Subluminal Cliffs

Ken Palmer placing some gear before the final moves of *Tittsworth* (HVS 5a) - *page 405* - at the popular and friendly section of Swanage's Subluminal cliff.

	No star	1 star	2 star	3 star
Mod to S	6	7	2	1
HS to HVS	10	19	5	1
E1 to E3	6	10	5	1
E4 and up	2	5	3	-

The western section of Subluminal is a very friendly sea cliff, which has a substantial collection of good, lower-grade trad routes in a largely un-intimidating environment. This is a popular destination due to its ease of access, pleasant cliff-top ledges and sunny aspect - a fine place to climb, socialise and relax.
In contrast, just to the east, and directly below the lighthouse, is the Black Zawn with its exceptional set of routes that require both commitment and experience. Just viewing these from the zawn rim above is a dizzying experience.
Bracketing Black Zawn are some large cliffs that compliment the two main areas well. The Lighthouse Cliff has some long single pitch mid-to-high grade lines, whilst the Avernus Area holds a number of rarely-climbed steep and hard trad pitches.

Approach Also see map on page 266

Drive through the centre of Swanage and pick up signs for Durlston Castle and Country Park. Drive to the Country Park car park (fee). Walk west along the tarmac road from the car park to the coast path and walk over to the lighthouse. From the lighthouse a path leads diagonally right (looking out) down the grass slope to cliff-top ledges directly above the western end of Subluminal. All of the areas require an abseil approach, these are described with the individual area information.

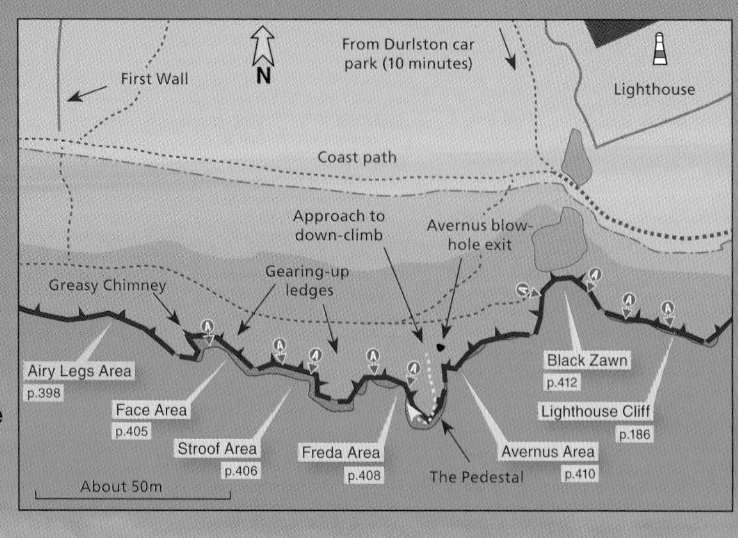

Tides and Conditions

The Face, Stroof, Freda area's, and the Lighthouse Cliff, are above raised ledges, so there are no tidal problems, but do not visit in rough seas as freak waves can break over the ledges. The Avernus Area needs calm seas and preferably lowish tides. The Black Zawn has some lines that are tidal. There are no seepage problems at Subluminal, and all the routes face south. Black Zawn can be damp and slow to dry due to its recessed nature.

The left-hand side of Subluminal has some great short pitches on fantastic rock. Here Olivia and Amy Colson tackle *Face* (S) - *page 405*. Photo: Dave Mason.

Face Area

An excellent section of cliff with superb rock. There is a wide selection of grades and style of climbing of offer varying from bold face lines to some thuggy pump-outs.
Tides - The routes start from a non-tidal ledge well above the sea but keep away in rough seas.
Approach - Abseil down *Suspension* to ledges. All routes finish at stake belays.

1 Via Christina . . . . . 2 stars — **HVS 5a**
A wild route with great moves on big holds up the steep arete. Start just beyond the far end of the high ledges. Climb the steep buttress starting from the left. Watch out for a loose but avoidable block at the top. A better and more comfortable way of starting the route is to scramble or abseil directly to ledges at sea level.
FA. K.Cartwright 1.4.1966

2 Dead Good **E5 6b**
The left wall of the gully, starting from the gully as for *Greasy Chimney*. Move left and up the wall on small holds to a little corner. Reachy moves lead boldly to the top.
FA. Steve Taylor, Mike Robertson 19.4.1992

3 Greasy Chimney . . . . **VDiff**
An atmospheric and slightly exposed start but easy climbing thereafter. Not always as unpleasant as the name implies.

4 Suspension . . . . 1 star — **S 4a**
A great climb with lots of good protection. Climb a short corner then move slightly left and climb easily to the top. Can be a bit guano covered at times.

5 Whynot . . . . 1 star — **HS 4b**
Follow a thin crack and pass a small overhang on its right to gain a ledge. Move up a small ramp and pull over a bulge to easier ground.
FA. G.Foster, J.Ross 13.5.1990

6 Dolphin . . . . VS 4b
A nice pitch up the blank rib with no gear to speak of but with steady climbing.

7 Curving Crack . . . . 1 S 4a
Safe bridging up the steep corner crack eases as height is gained. Take some large nuts.

8 Face. . . . . 1 S 4a
An unlikely looking route at the grade which is well worth doing. Climb the left edge of the wall which is protectable once the first intimidating moves have been negotiated. *Photo on page 403*.

9 Face Central . . . . 1 VS 4c
Poorly-protected but good climbing up the wall past a hole.

10 Face Away . . . . 1 VS 4c
The groove and wall just right of *Face Central*. As with the previous line, the climbing is good but the gear is minimal.

15m
A
13
14 15 16
Balcony - p.406

11 Tittsworth . . . . 1 HVS 5a
Climb up the right-trending flake for a couple of metres and then move left on to the wall. Climb directly to a small corner and finish delicately up it. *Photo on page 401*.
FA. Jim Titt, W.Wheeler 18.4.1976

12 Dead Man Hunt 1 E1 5b
Climb up the right-facing flake to a roof. Pull up steeply left into a groove and finish up it.
FA. Jim Titt 7.5.1976

13 Baboon. . . . . 1 HVS 5b
A fun route which has seen some frustrated attempts over the last few years since the demise of **the** hold on the crux. Climb up the right-facing flake to a roof. Swing right and pull over the roof to gain the corner above with difficulty.
FA. Tony Wilmott 7.1965

14 The Grobbler. 1 E1 5b
A pumpy eliminate up the thin cracks and bulges just right of *Baboon*. Finish as for *Baboon*.
FA. Tony Wilmott 7.1965

15 Transcript Direct . . 1 HVS 5a
Good, physical climbing up the steep corner and narrow chimney/crack. A forceful approach pays dividends but don't forget to place the bomber gear.

16 Paralysis E2 5c

A neat, committing test-piece up a blank wall. Climb the wall to the left of an overhang (on *Balcony*) and finish up the technical wall above.
FA. Tony Wilmott 7.1965

Portland
Lulworth
Swanage
Winspit
Hedbury and Smokey
Dancing Ledge
Guillemot Ledge
Blackers Hole
Fisherman's Ledge
The Promenade
Cattle Troughs
Boulder Ruckle
Subluminal

Stroof Area

One of Swanage's busiest trad areas. The climbs are all steep but mostly have reasonable protection and are on well-travelled and solid rock.

Tides - The routes start from a non-tidal ledge 5m above high tide level, however keep well away in rough seas.

Approach - Abseil direct down the route *High Street*, or, if this is busy, try abseiling down near the line of *Gangway*.

1 Balcony . . . . 2 ☐ **HS 4b**
An enjoyable, well-travelled line that features some difficult, but well-protected climbing. Gain the jutting block by moving right beneath it and then its top (The Balcony). Finish up the small corner and the flake above.

2 Gangway. . . . . 1 ☐ **S 4a**
A decent warm up. Climb some rightward-trending flakes to a rest, then follow the ramp to its end and finish straight up. The start gives the hardest climbing.

3 Joker . . . . ☐ **VS 5a**
Follow the steep groove to an easing, move right and take a thin crack to the top.
FA. A.Blakely 1988

4 Juggler. . . . . . . 1 ☐ **E1 5b**
A nice and varied climb with adequate protection. Climb the roof above a narrowing in the ledge, then go direct up the smooth wall on finger edges. It feels bold to start and again to finish.
FA. S.Evans 1970

5 Stroof. . . . . 2 ☐ **E1 5c**
A route for those who like them short, sharp and well protected. Amble up the lower section and assault the central crack in the white headwall. Brief but excellent.
FA. Tony Wilmott 12.1965

6 Graunchy Grippers E1 5b
Climb direct to an undercut in an overhang. Pull over to a narrow groove and follow it with difficulty to the top. A runner in *Spreadeagle* is often utilised.
FA. Kevin Turner 1977.

7 Spreadeagle . . . . VS 5a
Great gear and superb moves on the upper section make this one a must do. Take a direct line to the roof then pull over into the interesting main groove. The finish is a touch polished.

8 Back Street . . . . VS 4c
Contrasting features define this popular route. Easy climbing leads upwards to a delicate slab, which leads in turn leftwards to an enjoyable roof. Unusual climbing for the area and a bit run out.

9 High Street . . . . Diff
A good route for a first trad lead on solid rock. Good jugs all the way - enjoyable. This is the easiest way out.

10 Station Road . . . . HS 4b
Make fingery moves up the wall and past a crack to a ledge on the right. Finish up thin cracks.
FA. Jim Titt, Frank Farrell 22.5.1976

11 Bypass . . . . S 4b
Engaging, varied and well protected. Climb direct up the rounded rib to a prominent left-facing layback flake.

12 Slip Road . . . . VS 4c
An improbable-looking line for the grade - well protected and thoroughly enjoyable. Climb a short flake in the front of the buttress, then pull over a bulge with some difficulty to gain the corner and finish up it.

13 Republic E2 6a
With a runner in *Slip Road* pull over the bulge move left and go for it up the face of the block.
FA. Scott Titt, Nigel Coe 8.2.1992

Portland
Lulworth
Swanage
Winspit
Hedbury and Smokey
Dancing Ledge
Guillemot Ledge
Blackers Hole
Fisherman's Ledge
The Promenade
Cattle Troughs
Boulder Ruckle
Subluminal

Portland
Lulworth
Swanage
Winspit
Hedbury and Smokey
Dancing Ledge
Guillemot Ledge
Blackers Hole
Fisherman's Ledge
The Promenade
Cattle Troughs
Boulder Ruckle
Subluminal

Freda Area

A popular and easily-accessed section of Subluminal that has some strong lines and sound rock.

Tides - The routes start from a non-tidal ledge. Keep away in rough seas.

Approach - On first acquaintance it is best to abseil down *Grandma's Groove* or *First Corner*. An alternative approach is to down-climb *Pedestal Crack* (Diff). Care is needed when crossing the two gaps in the ledge below the climbs.

1 Thompson's Chimney . . . . . 1 HS 4b
Awkward and exposed moves up the steep chimney directly above the exposed step across a wide gap in the ledge.

2 Straights of Hormuz E3 6a
Boulder to the roof and climb over its centre before reaching right to a good hold on the arete. Finish up the arete.
FA. Pete Oxley, Brian Tilley, Steve Williams 23.8.1987

3 Botany Bay . . . . 1 VS 4c
A fun little route - the crux is low. Charge through the burly bulge before settling into the easier but less-protectable corner above.

4 Battleship Bow . . . . . . 1 HVS 4c
A serious lead up the rib above a gap in the ledge. Nice positions but bold.

5 Double Chockstone . . . 1 HVD
The deep gap in the ledge crossed by the awkward move is capped by a short hanging slab, start below this. Step up onto the short hanging slab and move up into a massive niche. Climb the chimney above via awkward moves past the chockstones to finish in a cliff-top crevasse.

6 Skinhead . . . . HVS 5a
A worthwhile eliminate straight up steep ground, parallel to *Double Chockstone*.
FA. M.Hunt, A.Gilbert 28.8.1977

7 Bird's Nest . . . . S 4a
A good climb that is fairly high in the grade. Take a diagonal line rightwards from the start of *Skinhead*, passing a big ledge, to finish on the arete.

8 Puffin . . . . 1 VS 5a
An intense climb, direct to the ledge on *Bird's Nest*. Finish up the pleasant crack in the wall above.
FA. R.C.White 4.1965

9 The Indirect Route . . . . E1 5b?
Good climbing but poor gear. Assault the lower roof and the more delicate arete above. The start is now harder since the loss of a block on the starting ledge - possibly 6a.
FA. Jim Titt, Scott Titt 14.11.1976

10 First Corner . . . . 2 S 4b
Excellent moves and good gear up the bottomless corner. Keep an eye out for a loose block near to the top of the pitch.

11 Philatus 2 E3 5c
A real cracker of a face climb. Use the diagonal crack to reach the first overlap, move straight through and pass a second overlap on its right to gain a small niche. The final wall gives a fitting finale.
FA. Tony Wilmott 7.1965

12 Poetry in Motion . . 1 E3 6a
A direct line parallel to *Philatus,* but on smaller holds. Staying directly on line maintains the grade. Starting slightly left and moving right in the middle section makes things easier (E2 5c) but still worthwhile.
FA. Pete Oxley 19.2.1984

13 Second Corner. . . . . . . 2 S 4a
A Subluminal classic with masses of atmosphere. Start by the bad step in the ledge. Classy, open climbing up the groove, finishing either left or right. *Photo this page.*

14 Freda . . . . Top 50 VS 5a
An all-time favourite of the area that pleases time after time. Start by the bad step in the ledge, and follow the thin crack past a rusty peg to an easing. The appealing, smooth-looking wall on the right is taken intricately to the top. *Photo this page.*

15 Grandma's Groove . 2 E2 5c
Boldly climb the fingery lower wall to safe, but still hard, moves up the narrow groove.
FA. Tony Wilmott 7.1965

16 Grandpa's Grope . . . . 1 VS 4c
Start up *Pedestal Crack* then step left to a tricky groove.
FA. Tim Dunsby 14.7.1971

17 Pedestal Crack . . . . Diff
This is the eastern descent or escape route taking the chimney corner at the right-hand end of the ledge to the top of The Pedestal, then easy ground. Polished at the base.

The next routes start from The Anvil - a block down at sea level.

18 Pedestal Face . . . . 1 VS 4b
Climb a crack, above The Anvil to the fault-line. Then move leftwards across the face of The Pedestal.

19 Pedestal Chimney . . . . VDiff
Start as for *Pedestal Face* then climb the nondescript corner on the right of The Pedestal.

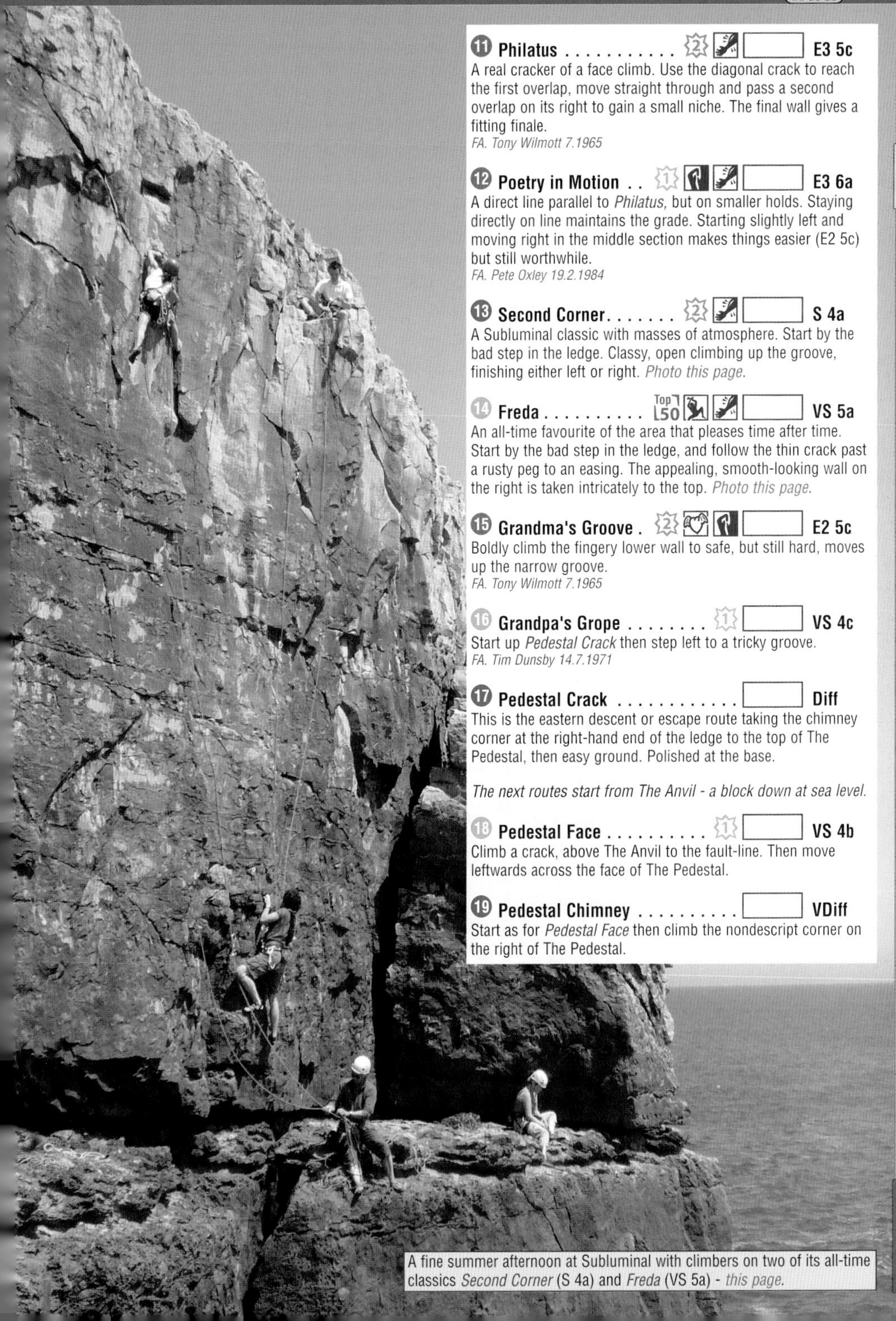

A fine summer afternoon at Subluminal with climbers on two of its all-time classics *Second Corner* (S 4a) and *Freda* (VS 5a) - *this page.*

Avernus Area

A more serious section of cliff than those to its west with a collection of hard, steep pitches that are not always on reliable rock. The unusual adventure of *Avernus* is by far and away the most popular climb hereabouts.

Tides - The access to all of the lines is tidal and requires calm sea conditions.

Approach - Abseil down *Grandma's Groove*, or down-climb *Pedestal Crack* (see previous page). Scramble down to sea level and then traverse left (looking out) at sea level.

1 Styx . . . . **S**

Climb the corner to the fault-line and then its continuation above to reach the top of The Pedestal.

2 Cerberus . . . . **S 4a**

Climb the wall to the fault-line and continue up the corner above to a loose finish.

FA. A.Yeend, D.McFadyen 28.12.1974

3 Strenuosity . . . . **HVS 4c**

Climb the crack to the overhung niche. Move left along the fault-line until a short and loose corner and wall can be climbed to meet the top section of *Cerberus*.

FA. R.Stead (1pt) 28.7.1975

FFA. Pete Finkclaire, George Hounsome 31.3.1979

4 Graduation Day 1 **E2 5c**

A good climb up the left-hand wall of the zawn that requires some bizarre contortions. Start at a corner and ascend flakes to the first roof. Traverse left, then over it, to attain a full body bridge. Climb direct up the chimney to a belay in the rock blow-hole. Takes a while to come into condition.

FA. Scott Titt, Nigel Coe 24.6.1989

5 Avernus . . . . Top 50 **S 4a**

A hugely entertaining and fun outing exiting through the same blow-hole as *Graduation Day*, but at a significantly easier grade. Start near the back of the cave and climb all the way through the chimney/roof to the rock blow-hole belay. Some find a head-torch a big help.

FA. M.Hurn, F.Higgins, D.Partridge 22.8.71

6 The Ferryman Waits **E3 6a**

The non-line opposite *Graduation Day*. Gain the scoop by a rightward hand-traverse from the left-hand crack. A hard, blind semi-mantel leftward out of the scoop onto the black slab leads to a thin crack and then jug pulling to the belay of *Graduation Day*.

FA. Scott Titt c.1996

Portland Lulworth Swanage Winspit Hedbury and Smokey Dancing Ledge Guillemot Ledge Blackers Hole Fisherman's Ledge The Promenade Cattle Troughs Boulder Ruckle Subluminal

7 Crepitus . . . . HVS 4c
Start from the higher ledge east of the zawn. Climb the lower bulge and corner - loose.
FA. George Hounsome, Scott Titt 16.7.1978

8 Rainy Day, Dream Away . . . E2 5c
A double roof stack above the first part of the ledge.
FA. Tim Dunsby, Scott Titt 7.7.1991

9 Chance Encounter E4 6a
Start as for *All the Shakespearoes*. Climb to the lower overhang. Just below the corner, move left via powerful moves into a hanging groove. Continue up the left-hand wall to the top.
FA. Chris Weedon, Matt Cooper 12.6.2010

10 All the Shakespearoes . 1 E3 5c
Start above the next rift in the ledge and follow the steep corner, finishing rightwards to skirt the roofs.
FA. Pete Oxley 11.12.1988

11 The Great Rock 'n' Dole Swindle
. . . . 1 E3 6a
The leaning buttress right of the last route has a hard pull over a roof in to a V-groove.
FA. Pete Oxley 27.11.1988

The next set of routes are much more serious propositions. Drop down to sea-level boulders. **Calm seas only.**

12 Tangerine Dream 1 E1 5b
In the left wall of the bay, climb a crack, overhang and steep groove to the top.
FA. George Hounsome, Kevin Turner 8.4.1978

13 A Subtle Shade of Emptiness
. . . . 2 E5 6b
The hardest route in this area traces a line through the overhung bay, with awkward gear and plenty of arm work. From the back of the bay climb an arete, traverse left then blast straight over a bulge. A shallow groove (thread) leads to the top.
FA. Pete Oxley 11.5.1988

14 Close to the Sun 1 E4 6b
More steep stuff through multiple roofs in the right-hand side of the bay. There are four threads on the route.
FA. Pete Oxley 27.11.1988

Beyond here the boulders disappear and the cliff turns a corner to form the impressive Black Zawn.

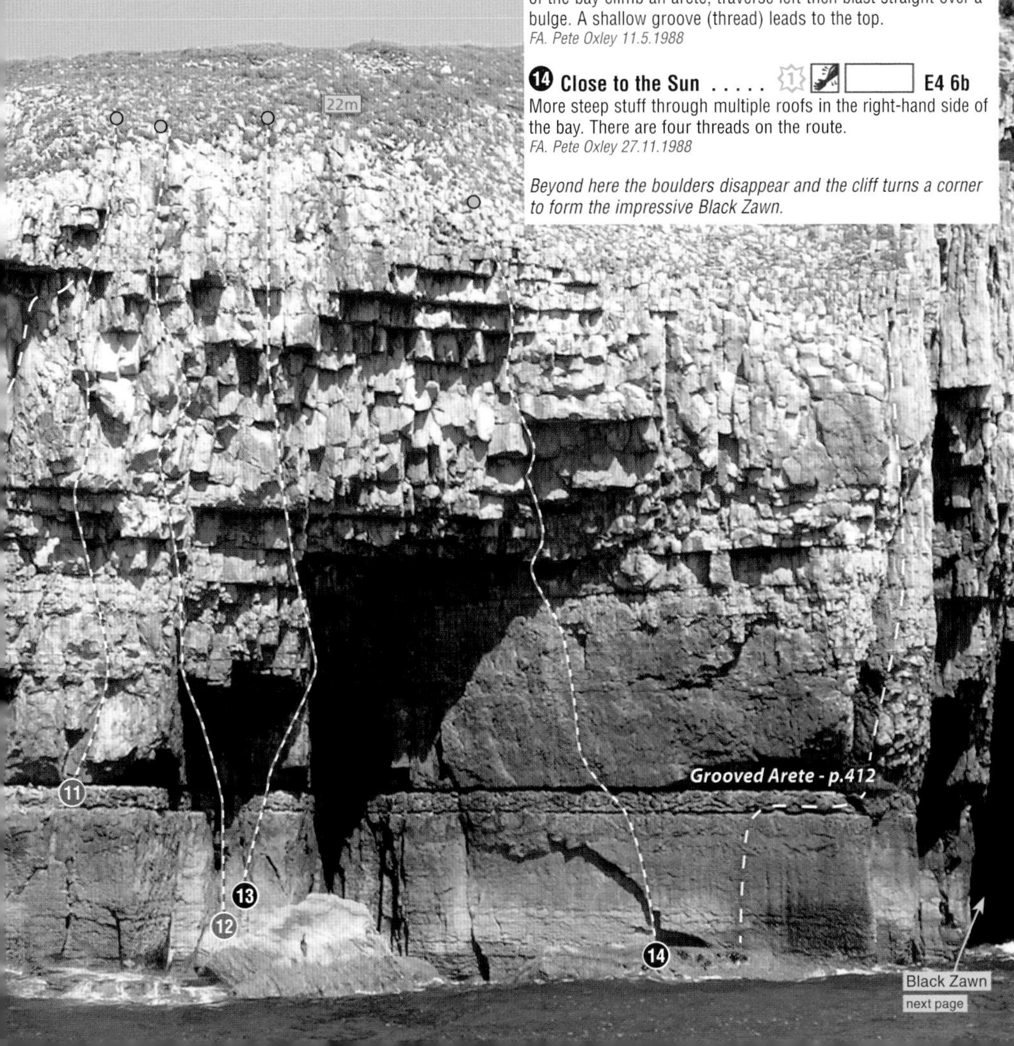

22m

11 12 13 14

Grooved Arete - p.412

Black Zawn
next page

Portland | Lulworth | Swanage | Winspit | Hedbury and Smokey | Dancing Ledge | Guillemot Ledge | Blackers Hole | Fisherman's Ledge | The Promenade | Cattle Troughs | Boulder Ruckle | Subluminal

Black Zawn

Black Zawn is an enclosed and highly atmospheric zawn with big, long routes that require abseil approaches and a degree of commitment significantly higher than the other nearby sections of Subluminal. This is an awesome venue and the classic routes from the likes of Richard Crewe and Pat Littlejohn will leave lasting memories for all who venture in. Black Zawn should be considered a place for experienced parties only.

Approach - The Black Zawn is the section of cliff just to the east of the more popular Subluminal cliffs, below the lighthouse. All the climbs are accessed by abseil. The abseil stakes are on a small ledge above the zawn. It is best to view the wall from the opposite side of the zawn so the line of the abseil can be identified before commit-ting. The abseil leads down the overhanging line of *Astrid* to its hanging stance (place nuts to keep in contact with the crack). Keep the ropes out of the sea so they do not snag in the boulders. For the three lines on the east face abseil from stakes on the slope above. For access to the start of *Grooved Arete* see the approach on page 410.

Tides - *Achelous*, *Io* and *The Last Great Innocent* start from a boulder in the zawn bed, which is covered at mid-to-high tide. The access to the start of *Grooved Arete* is tidal - see page 411. The remaining routes are non-tidal, but keep well away in rough seas.

Conditions - Although there is no seepage problem, the west face is prone to dampness owing to its enclosed nature. Do not enter in rough seas or on damp days when the zawn can become very greasy.

1 Grooved Arete . . . . VS 4b
Start as for *Close to the Sun* (page 411). Climb to a ledge, move right to below the groove in the arete and climb it and the loose rocky slope above.
FA. Richard Crewe, D.Little 29.6.1975

Routes 2 to 6 all start from the same belay (a spike and nuts), 4m above the sea at the base of Astrid. All routes finish at the abseil stake belays.

2 Sweet Sixteen 1 E5 6a
Supersedes the climb **Just Seventeen** up the face left of *The Peccary*. Bold low down with little protection. Traverse left past *The Peccary* and climb the bulging wall direct past a poor peg. Continue up the sustained face (thread) to finish up a thin crack.
FA. Mike Robertson, Barry Clarke 13.8.1996

3 The Peccary 2 E2 5b
A top little route although the best of it, the crack at the bottom, is over all too quickly. Lovely holds, flowing moves, loads of gear and fair at the grade. Traverse left for 4m then follow the thin crack on fine holds to a niche and finish up the wall above.
FA. George Hounsome, Martin Barnicott 31.5.1976

4 Astrid . . . . 2 HVS 5a
Vast amounts of character, good climbing and an exciting abseil approach make this a memorable climb. The groove and crack-line in the centre of the wall gives steady climbing in impressive surroundings. Good gear.
FA. Richard Crewe, S.Garner, Tim Dunsby 11.8.1974

5 Melpomene. . . . . Top 50 E4 5c
Fine climbing which is both steep and pumpy - the E is for Effort on this one. Good gear but beware of rope drag. Climb diago-nally right into *Mars*, above the fault-line. Move up then swing right under a roof, to the arete. Sprint up the leftward-slanting cracks, saving some 'umph' for the top face, staying right of a square-cut groove.
FA. Pat Littlejohn, Chris King 1978

6 Mars . . . . Top 50 E2 5b
Stunning positions, excellent rock and sound protection.
You can't go wrong - or can you? For the best experience, wait until it is in good condition and has had a bit of sun on it.
1) 5b, 5m. Traverse right along the fault-line, or drop down to sea level and back up, to a sloping ledge beneath the roofs.
2) 5b, 20m. Climb the intimidating roofed corner and the stamina draining groove above to the top.
FA. Richard Crewe, Tim Dunsby 11.8.1974

Approach (route 7) - *The next route is approached by abseil from twin stakes, down the east wall of the zawn, to a rock platform in the zawn bed. See Black Zawn East approach opposite. Calm seas and low tide only.*

7 Achelous. 1 E5 6a
Even pumpier than *Melpomene*. Protection is available when needed. Climb a short arete to the fault-line, then a steep rib to a thin crack. Before an overhang is reached, swing left - hard - to a good knob and thread. Follow a thin crack leftwards to join and finish up *Melpomene*.
FA. Pete Oxley 11.12.1988

Two traverses of the zawn have been done, but these are very esoteric and not a patch on the quality of the vertical climbs.

Kayakers rounding the cliffs below the Subluminal lighthouse.

The next two routes are located on the east side of the zawn.
Approach and Tides - *Scramble down left of bushes to a twin abseil point. The abseil gains a platform in the zawn bed at low tide only.*

8 Io. . . . . VS 5a
A pleasant outing up the crack in the East Face. Good gear. Low tide is required. Climb the crack past a rest out left to an overhang. Step right and up the groove to easy ground. Amble to the top.
FA. Gordon Jenkin, Frank Farrell 12.8.1984

Sun and shade · 10 min · Abseil in

9 Last Great Innocent   **E5 6b**
Break out rightwards from *Io* and boulder out the lower arete, at the edge of the zawn, on its left-hand side wall. Then continue more easily to the top. The first ascent was soloed above not-very-deep water at E6 6b, but there is gear.
FA. Mike Robertson (solo) 3.5.1997

Bushes 10m down from the lighthouse

38m

Abseil and gearing-up ledges

25m

Mellow Yellow - p.414

Lighthouse Cliff

The wall that lies directly beneath the lighthouse is hard to see from the land, but has some good routes that are rarely climbed. The climbs are on generally sound rock but care is required when abseiling in, as on first acquaintance it is difficult to spot the best lines of descent to hit the ledges at the bottom.

Approach - The routes are all approached by abseil from various stakes in the grass slope above the cliff.

Tides - The starting ledges are non-tidal but keep away in rough seas.

Lots of sun | 10 min | Abseil in

1 Mellow Yellow. . . . . . . 2 **VS 4c**

A hidden gem. From the left-hand end of the ledge system, climb a tough crack to the fault-line. Step right and follow a pleasant groove to an easy slab. The slab leads up rightwards to finish.

FA. Richard Crewe, Tim Dunsby 18.8.1974

2 Ray of Sunshine 2 **E2 5c**

A highly recommended pitch, on good rock with good gear where it matters. From the ledge climb easily to the fault-line and junction with *Mellow Yellow*. Head rightwards to a steep shallow groove-line - climb this to the top.

FA. Tim Dunsby, Ray Mardon 25.5.1983

Last Great Innocent - p.413

3 Magic Mountain. . . 2 stars E4 6a
From the right-hand end of the abseil ledge, ascend cracks right of a pillar to the fault-line. Climb steeply to an undercut block, then head left on to the upper face to good small holds. Move left and climb fairly direct to finish at an excavated ledge. Take plenty of small and medium wires.
FA. Martin Crocker, D.Light 6.11.1983

4 Magic Mushroom. . . . . 1 star E5 6a
Climb *Magic Mountain* to its undercut block. Where *Magic Mountain* swings left, go diagonally up rightwards until under the roof which is split by a narrow crack. Make a difficult move over the roof and continue to a large sloping ledge and a junction with *Live at the Witch Trials*. Make hard moves directly up the vague groove above to finishing jugs.
FA. Bernard Exley, Sue Hazel 30.7.2006

5 Fraggle Rock. . . . . 2 stars HVS 5a
Adventurous climbing at the upper end of the grade. Start below and left of a jutting overhang at the fault-line. Climb past the corner of the overhang and swing right onto its front face. Ascend the buttress to the top. Take care to avoid rope drag on this pitch.
FA. Nigel Coe, Tim Dunsby 20.5.1984

Approach (routes 6 to 8) - *The next four routes start from a belay ledge, just to the right of a jutting overhang. The ledge can be reached by a scramble rightwards from the lower ledge or directly by abseil.*

6 Live at the Witch Trials. 1 star E2 5b
Move up onto the arete and climb diagonally left to good runners at 5m. Climb up to a flake and then leftwards to a sloping ledge. Continue leftwards and finish up the final groove of *Magic Mountain*.
FA. Crispin Waddy, G.Banks 7.1984

7 Hard Nose the Highway . . . 1 star HVS 5a
Exposed. Follow *Live at the Witch Trials* for 5m to good runners. Climb up and traverse right at a roof line to gain a groove that leads to the top.
FA. Tim Dunsby, Pete Oxley 7.4.1984

8 Harvest Gold. . . . . 1 star HVS 4c
Climb the corner and cracks to its right to an overhang. Pass this on its right-hand side with difficulty and continue to the top.
FA. A. Parker, S.Allen 17.5.1975

9 Yellow Brick Road . . . . 1 star VS 5a
Climb diagonally rightwards to a half-way ledge. Finish direct up the tasty wall using a thin crack.
FA. Tim Dunsby, Pete Oxley 7.4.1984

10 Shakin' Off the Ghosts . . . . HVS 5a
Belay below the wall on the right-hand side (looking in) of a narrow zawn. High in the grade. Climb the wall rightwards to the arete and a small niche. Go left - loose blocks - and climb the steep headwall to finish.
FA. Pete Oxley, Tim Dunsby 27.10.1984

11 Zoe . . . . VS 5a
Climb a slim, left-facing corner and move right to a ledge. Move up to another ledge and then gain a groove on its left. Climb leftwards towards the edge of the wall and finish up a groove. High in the grade.
FA. B.Jefferies, J.Cross 13.9.1975

12 Rout. . . . . HVS 5b
Climb up leftwards with difficulty (a loose flake has fallen off) into a corner. Follow the corner to the top.
FA. Jim Titt, Scott Titt 9.4.1977

Portland | Lulworth | Swanage | Blacknor N | Blacknor C | Blacknor S | Blacknor B | Blacknor FS | Battleship | Battleship BC | Walsend N | Walsend S | Coastguard N | Coastguard S | White Hole | Lighthouse | Cheyne Weare | Cuttings

Portland | Lulworth | Swanage | Blacknor N | Blacknor C | Blacknor S | Blacknor B | Blacknor FS | Battleship | Battleship BC | Wallsend N | Wallsend S | Coastguard | Coastguard S | White Hole | Lighthouse | Cheyne Weare | Cuttings

Portland | Lulworth | Swanage | Blacknor N | Blacknor C | Blacknor S | Blacknor B | Blacknor FS | Battleship | Battleship BC | Wallsend N | Wallsend S | Coastguard N | Coastguard S | White Hole | Lighthouse | Cheyne Weare | Cuttings

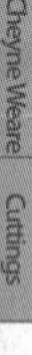

About 10km

Emergencies

Dial 112 and ask for coastguard or other emergency services. Have details of your location and what the incident involves.